Recent Applications of Financial Risk Modelling and Portfolio Management

Tihana Škrinjarić
University of Zagreb, Croatia

Mirjana Čižmešija
University of Zagreb, Croatia

Bryan Christiansen
Global Training Group, Ltd, UK

IGI Global
PUBLISHER of TIMELY KNOWLEDGE

A volume in the Advances in Finance, Accounting, and Economics (AFAE) Book Series

Published in the United States of America by
IGI Global
Business Science Reference (an imprint of IGI Global)
701 E. Chocolate Avenue
Hershey PA, USA 17033
Tel: 717-533-8845
Fax: 717-533-8661
E-mail: cust@igi-global.com
Web site: http://www.igi-global.com

Library of Congress Cataloging-in-Publication Data

Names: Škrinjarić, Tihana, 1989- editor. | Čižmešija, Mirjana, 1967- editor. | Christiansen, Bryan, 1960- editor.
Title: Recent applications of financial risk modelling and portfolio management / Tihana Škrinjarić, Mirjana Čižmešija, and Bryan Christiansen, editors.
Description: Hershey, PA : Information Science Reference, [2021] | Includes bibliographical references and index. | Summary: "This book provides vital research on the use of modern data analysis as well as quantitative methods for developing successful portfolio and risk management techniques. While highlighting topics such as credit scoring, investment strategies, and budgeting, this publication explores diverse models for achieving investment goals as well as improving upon traditional financial modelling methods"-- Provided by publisher.
Identifiers: LCCN 2020004159 (print) | LCCN 2020004160 (ebook) | ISBN 9781799850830 (hardcover) | ISBN 9781799854111 (paperback) | ISBN 9781799850847 (ebook)
Subjects: LCSH: Financial risk management. | Portfolio management.
Classification: LCC HD61 .R426 2021 (print) | LCC HD61 (ebook) | DDC 658.15/5--dc23
LC record available at https://lccn.loc.gov/2020004159
LC ebook record available at https://lccn.loc.gov/2020004160

This book is published in the IGI Global book series Advances in Finance, Accounting, and Economics (AFAE) (ISSN: 2327-5677; eISSN: 2327-5685)

British Cataloguing in Publication Data
A Cataloguing in Publication record for this book is available from the British Library.

For electronic access to this publication, please contact: eresources@igi-global.com.

Advances in Finance, Accounting, and Economics (AFAE) Book Series

Ahmed Driouchi
Al Akhawayn University, Morocco

ISSN:2327-5677
EISSN:2327-5685

Mission

In our changing economic and business environment, it is important to consider the financial changes occurring internationally as well as within individual organizations and business environments. Understanding these changes as well as the factors that influence them is crucial in preparing for our financial future and ensuring economic sustainability and growth.

The **Advances in Finance, Accounting, and Economics (AFAE)** book series aims to publish comprehensive and informative titles in all areas of economics and economic theory, finance, and accounting to assist in advancing the available knowledge and providing for further research development in these dynamic fields.

Coverage

- Evidence-Based Studies
- Ethics in Accounting and Finance
- Taxes
- Labor Economics
- International Economics
- Economics of Agriculture and Biotechnology
- Internet Banking
- Economics of Natural and Environmental Resources
- Auditing
- E-finance

The Advances in Finance, Accounting, and Economics (AFAE) Book Series (ISSN 2327-5677) is published by IGI Global, 701 E. Chocolate Avenue, Hershey, PA 17033-1240, USA, www.igi-global.com. This series is composed of titles available for purchase individually; each title is edited to be contextually exclusive from any other title within the series. For pricing and ordering information please visit http://www.igi-global.com/book-series/advances-finance-accounting-economics/73685. Postmaster: Send all address changes to above address.

Titles in this Series

For a list of additional titles in this series, please visit: http://www.igi-global.com/book-series/advances-finance-accounting-economics/73685

Theory of Shocks and Self-Development Laws of Economic Systems Emerging Research and Opportunities
Olga Ivanovna Pilipenko (The Russian Presidential Academy of National Economy and Public Administration, Russia) Zoya Andreevna Pilipenko (Bank of Russia, Russia) and Andrey Igorevich Pilipenko (The Russian Presidential Academy of National Economy and Public Administration, Russia)
Business Science Reference • ©2021 • 250pp • H/C (ISBN: 9781799843092) • US $165.00

Handbook of Research on Emerging Theories, Models, and Applications of Financial Econometrics
Burcu Adıgüzel Mercangöz (Istanbul University, Turkey)
Business Science Reference • ©2020 • 300pp • H/C (ISBN: 9781799831969) • US $275.00

Circular Economy and Re-Commerce in the Fashion Industry
Archana Shrivastava (Jaypee Business School, JIIT, Noida, India) Geetika Jain (FMS, Amity University, Noida, India) and Justin Paul (University of Puerto Rico, Puerto Rico)
Business Science Reference • ©2020 • 204pp • H/C (ISBN: 9781799827283) • US $195.00

Mapping, Managing, and Crafting Sustainable Business Strategies for the Circular Economy
Susana Serrano Rodrigues (Polytechnic Institute of Leiria, Portugal) Paulo Jorge Almeida (Polytechnic Institute of Leiria, Portugal) and Nuno Miguel Castaheira Almeida (Polytechnic Institute of Leiria, Portugal)
Business Science Reference • ©2020 • 401pp • H/C (ISBN: 9781522598855) • US $195.00

Applied Econometric Analysis Emerging Research and Opportunities
Brian W. Sloboda (University of Phoenix, USA) and Yaya Sissoko (Indiana University of Pennsylvania, USA)
Business Science Reference • ©2020 • 264pp • H/C (ISBN: 9781799810933) • US $195.00

Handbook of Research on Accounting and Financial Studies
Luís Farinha (University of Beira Interior, Portugal) Ana Baltazar Cruz (School of Management, Polytechnic Institute of Castelo Branco, Portugal) and João Renato Sebastião (Polytechnic Institute of Castelo Branco, Portugal)
Business Science Reference • ©2020 • 487pp • H/C (ISBN: 9781799821366) • US $295.00

Emerging Tools and Strategies for Financial Management
Begoña Álvarez-García (Universidade da Coruña, Spain) and José-Pablo Abeal-Vázquez (Universidade da Coruña, Spain)

IGI Global
PUBLISHER of TIMELY KNOWLEDGE

701 East Chocolate Avenue, Hershey, PA 17033, USA
Tel: 717-533-8845 x100 • Fax: 717-533-8661
E-Mail: cust@igi-global.com • www.igi-global.com

Editorial Advisory Board

List of Reviewers

Table of Contents

Detailed Table of Contents

are related, on one hand to field operations (drilling time, delays due to drilling problems, rig failures and materials supply, electric submersible pump [ESP] installations failures with the consequences of losing the well), and on the other hand, the second set of uncertainties are related to costs (operational expenditures-OPEX and capital expenditures-CAPEX, daily drilling rig costs), prices (oil, gas, separation, and water injection preparation), production profiles, and discount factor. All the calculations are probabilistic. The authors are intending to provide a comprehensive solution for assessing the business performance of an oil field development.

Keeping risk behavior and country governance in observation, this study has investigated the trends in financial stability for a sample of 22 commercial banks in Pakistan while controlling the effect of economic growth. Over the period of 2007 to 2016, the authors have applied OLS, FE, and RE regression methods to investigate which risk and governance factors are influencing the stability measures of the banks. It is found that financial stability in overall banks is affected by credit risk, operational risk, country risk, and financial crisis risk while control of corruption is also affecting ZROA in an adverse way.

This chapter tackles the problem of automatic recognition of favorable days for intra-day trading. The problem is modeled as a binary classification problem, and several approaches are tested for solving it. Croatian stock index CROBEX data is used and 22 technical indicators are calculated as predictor variables. Performance of five classifiers is evaluated and compared by using Cohen's kappa as evaluation metric: artificial neural network, support network machine, random forest, k-nearest neighbors, and naïve Bayes classifier. The results give insight to effectiveness of technical analysis in predicting the day favorability for CROBEX index and suggest that technical analysis makes sense and might work for this case.

The Reserve Bank of India suspected a cartel among 15 banks in fixing interest rates on deposits of the savings bank accounts over a period from 2011-12 to 2012-13 and lodged a complaint with the Competition Commission of India. The latter could not find any motive of the banks to collude and hence ruled out the complaint. The authors collected data on the banks' activities and performances on the said periods and examined in this chapter whether the commission was right in ruling out the complaint. The results of the analyses in this work lead to the conclusion that the commission was right in ruling out the complaint, but there are certain limitations and policy prescriptions that cropped out of this work, which should be conveyed to policy makers and researchers.

The given research is devoted to the acute issue of efficiency of valuable assets positioning carried out by commercial banks. The chapter is aimed at examining factors that affect the efficiency of securities placement by commercial banks, as well as an econometric analysis based on the least squares method of the significance of the selected factors and their impact on the efficiency indicator. While researching this issue, the phenomenon of adaptability, which means the higher the price set, is in comparison with the medium price scale, the higher the underpricing at setting with corresponding other equal terms was singled out The methods of critical literature review, statistical analysis, and econometric model creation have been used to justify it. Moreover, the research resulted in model creation, which characterizes the state of a definite commercial bank to be ready for emission of assets by means of initial public offering.

Since the introduction of CAPM in the 1960s, the asset pricing literature has documented hundreds of characteristics that capture the cross-sectional variation in stock returns. Traditionally, multifactor models seek a multidimensional representation of common risks; this approach entails selecting a small number of representative characteristics from a set of candidate characteristics that, together, explain most of the cross-sectional variation in stock returns. Characteristics-based long-short portfolios are partially loaded on the true underlying risk factors and are at best noisy proxies for true latent factors. However, the expansive list of potential characteristics, along with developments in the field of dimensionality reduction, offers us an opportunity to seek better approximations of the unobservable latent risk factors. A recent stream of literature has investigated how to appropriately extract relevant features from the "factor zoo" while incorporating information from the expansive list of factors. This chapter aims to summarize this novel paradigm in factor modeling.

The multidimensional Riesz potential type operators are of interest within mathematical modelling in economics, mathematical physics, and other, both theoretical and applied, disciplines as they play a significant role for analysis on fractal sets. Approaches of operator theory are relevant to researching various equations, which are widespread in financial analysis. In this chapter, integral equations with potential type operators are considered for functions from generalized Hölder spaces, which provide content terminology for formalizing the concept of smoothness, briefly described in the presented chapter. Results on potentials defined on the unit sphere are described for convenience of the analysis. An inverse operator for the Riesz potential with a logarithmic kernel is carried out, and the isomorphisms between generalized Hölder spaces are proven.

Foreword

Modern quantitative research in finance comprises analyses of financial institutions, international financial markets, and their links with real economies. Statistical and econometric methods are steadily developed and applied to describe behavior of economic agents, predict prices of financial instruments, and verify economic hypotheses. Contemporary methods and current datasets are more robust and better suited to specific and current problems analyzed in finance than former methods and older data samples.

A principal objective of this book is to present new results on the well-known problems of financial research such as stock return predictability and portfolio investment. These novel results provide new insights from theory and empirical applications and are tailored to the current state of developments and our knowledge in economics and finance.

Large databases containing hundreds and thousands of observations enable researchers to apply larger statistical models and new methods designed to specify, estimate or calibrate large numbers of parameters. Especially the machine learning algorithms and nonlinear econometric methods are well fitted to analyze big datasets and are currently gaining popularity. A very interesting approach to such an analysis is an evaluation of different classification algorithms to predict stock prices. Certainly, there is a need for predictive methods applied to emerging stock markets and this gap is filled by analyzing the CROBEX stock market index. It is interesting to learn if classification algorithms are successful in predicting this stock market index. The first chapter of the book covers this topic. Some other chapters analyze the predictive ability of financial econometric models in case of equity returns in developed and emerging markets.

The studies discussed above are directly linked to investigations of the efficient market hypothesis. Momentum trading strategies across different asset classes discussed in this book also deal with this topic because momentum trading investors aim to beat the market, to earn excess returns, and to falsify the weak form of the efficient market hypothesis. The same aim to earn excess returns is present in the research on calendar effects where the second-order stochastic dominance approach is taken.

Another important econometric approach to modeling of financial markets is factor analysis. This statistical method is often used to explain the changing prices of financial instruments when many instruments and explanatory variables are available. Researchers describe variability among observed stock returns (or other financial variables) using fewer unobserved factors. One application of this method is presented in this book.

Financial investment requires rational decisions based on full available information regarding past realized and predicted future distributions of asset returns. The expected utility-entropy decision model helps investors select stocks and other instruments for their investment portfolios. An important problem of applying such a model is how the model fits the current stage of capital market development. This problem is analyzed in the book and the appropriate values of expected utility and entropy ratio are determined for the decision-making model. Another approach also discusses portfolio hedging strategies by using a third-degree stochastic dominance approach and data envelopment analysis.

Early analyses of financial linkages and volatility spillovers between were primarily based on the estimated correlations between international stock returns. This book contains an analysis that attempts to investigate such linkages with the help of a global macro-econometric model. This is an important step forward in the studies of financial spillovers because macroeconomic factors are considered as variables affecting the spillover channels. What is more interesting, this investigation covers the sample of Central, Eastern, and South-Eastern European markets. Macroeconomic factors are also used to quantify economic uncertainties and risks in the oil and gas industries, as well as to explain developments in the financial and ICT (information and communication technologies) sectors discussed in chapters of this book.

This volume also touches crucial challenges of institutional finance such as corporate bankruptcies, institutional efficiency, and stability, pricing of mergers and acquisitions.

One of the most important problems in research on private and public firms, including financial institutions, is the prediction of financial distress in these firms. The topic of predicting financial distress is heavily studied because of its significance for investors, creditors, and business counterparties. Bankruptcies of corporations can cause huge costs for the whole economy and specific groups of economic agents. In this book, an early warning signal approach is taken to predict corporate failures.

The efficiency of banking institutions is investigated with the use of data envelopment analysis. Stock prices are also used to position efficiency in commercial banks and to estimate the prices of banks in merger and acquisition transactions in Europe. Another related problem considered in this book is related to financial stability and the performance of banks conditional on country governance and risks. These topics are presented using examples of Pakistan and India. All these studies may help improve the financial stability and competitiveness of banks and provide insight into lowering the monopolistic power of banks in some countries.

Finally, theoretical methods are used in some investigations presented in the book. In the asset pricing, coupon bond duration and convexity are analyzed with a non-calculus approach. The mathematical methodology is applied to discuss Riesz potential with a logarithmic kernel in generalized Hölder spaces.

In my opinion, this book will suit as a remarkable source of information and stimulating knowledge for financial analysts, managers, and academics interested in the analyses of financial markets and financial institutions. Moreover, the macro and microeconomic channels linking financial markets, financial institutions, and a real economy are investigated in this book. These channels are of great interest to macroeconomic policymakers and regulators, too.

Dobromił Serwa
Collegium of Economic Analysis, Warsaw School of Economics, Poland

Preface

Portfolio and risk management faces many challenges today. This is due to the different knowledge needed in order to conduct the total portfolio management. This includes knowledge from the area of finance, economics, but quantitative disciplines as well. The data available today is also increasing at a rapid rate, as well as the different quantitative approaches. This includes many different models and methods for the goals of achieving particular investment goals. Furthermore, many different financial markets face rising uncertainty and risks in the global market. The McKinsey Global Institute (2016) predicts that in the next 20 years the possibilities of making profits on financial markets will decline. In order to facilitate the decision-making process within the portfolio and risk management, a lot of different mathematical and statistical methods and models are being developed almost daily. Categorizations were made over the last couple of decades (see Granger, 1989; Taylor and Allen, 1992; Ho et al., 2002; Wallis, 2011; Jo, 2003; Liu et al., 2012 or Khuman et al., 2014). Financial data characteristics are specific (see Pagan and Scwert, 1990; Amado and Teräsvirta, 2014; Nelson, 1990, 1991; Ruey, 2002, etc.), and thus, they should be modelled adequately.

The last three decades have experienced rapid development of financial markets and computer technology, expansion of the number of financial products, a greater number of available information, and especially tick-by-tick data. Fabozzi, Focardi, and Jonas (2004) have conducted research on American and European institutional investors. Authors have found that in the last couple of years, the profits on financial markets have been mostly caused by quantitative methods expansion. These methods have become more applicable due to greater computational power and greater data availability.

Thus, the goal of this book is to analyze recent achievements in theory and practice of portfolio and risk management, with a focus on quantitative methods. The explosive growth of financial products (their number and variations), different needs, and goals of investors ask for continuous education in order to understand and harvest the benefits within the portfolio management. Investors and other potential parties on financial markets face more and more information that needs to be taken into consideration. In that way, quantitative models and methods can help to collect, group, and process the data. Hubbard (2009) concluded that risk management in practice would be more successful if the quantitative analysis would be enhanced in practice, alongside publicizing specialized mathematical literature.

Since many different approaches of financial modelling are being developed today, a newer publication which includes most recent contributions is needed so that existing practices can be updated to be more tailored to the real state of economics and finance. Thus, this book fills this gap in the existing literature with newer approaches within the area of financial modelling. In that way, the practical applications of those models and methods can be used on a wide range of different assets. This makes this book comprehensive guidance for all parties involved in the portfolio management and financial applications in general. The book focuses on different investment assets, with stocks and bonds having the greatest focus. Furthermore, the banking industry and failure have also experienced an increased interest in the research. That is why several chapters in this book provide the readers with some useful tools in conducting quality research within this area. As stock price evaluation represents a great problem even today (for some examples see Fama and French, 1992, 1993, 1995; Modigliani and Miller, 1958, 1963), several chapters deal with some issues within this area of research.

The target audience of this book includes financial analysts, managers, and academics within the field of financial modelling and portfolio management. New insights from theory and empirical applications can increase the current level of their knowledge. Since the book is focusing on microeconomic and macroeconomic applications and theory, a wide range of potential readers could benefit from this book. Furthermore, both returns and risks on financial markets are in the center of the focus, which makes this book attractive for those who wish to distinguish what makes a market, stock or a bank more profitable than others, but for those who aim at risk mitigation and risk hedging.

As the interest for quantitative methods in finance and economics is rising, alongside greater computational power, with data availability, it is crucial to follow the latest trends and findings in theory and practice. Thus, this book tries to do just that: it compiles most recent findings in theory and practice, i.e. empirical applications within finance and portfolio management in general, alongside bankruptcy prediction (Roje, 2005; Chan-Lau, 2006; Demerjian, 2007), and other relevant fields of finance and financial modelling. Both individual and institutional investors can have benefits from this book. This is especially true for the institutional ones, as risk management is extremely important for financial institutions (Merton, 1993).

ORGANIZATION OF THE BOOK

The book is organized into 18 chapters. A brief description of each of the chapters follows:

Chapter 1 deals with expected utility-entropy decision models within the portfolio selection. An additional contribution of this research is found in testing whether a trade-off exists between the risky action and expected utility, with additional analysis of its dependence on the capital market development. The model was applied to the European Union capital markets so that the results could be relevant for different investors in the longer run.

Chapter 2 observes chosen hedging strategies with options in order to determine the usefulness of such risk hedging instruments. The first three moments of the return distribution are observed: expected return, standard deviation, and coefficient of skewness. The stochastic dominance criteria were applied alongside data envelopment analysis in the empirical part of the research. The chapter shows how the third-degree stochastic dominance criteria can be integrated into the data envelopment modelling.

Chapter 3 applies the second-order stochastic dominance approach in examining calendar anomalies on selected stock markets. Authors have chosen five developed and five developing stock market indices to estimate inefficient and efficient months and weekdays. Additionally, a back-testing procedure was performed out of the sample so that investing strategies could be advised. December returns were found to be efficient in 8 indices, Monday and Friday's returns were inefficient for the majority of indices.

Chapter 4 is focusing on the relationship between the cross-section of equity returns and the various firm-specific variables on a sample of 26 developed countries. The prominent factors which affect the return series were: low beta, book-to-market equity, and momentum analysis. On the other side, the short-term reversal and downside beta are not priced in the cross-section of the return series. Furthermore, other factors that are related to the expected stock returns are momentum, short-term reversals, illiquidity, idiosyncratic volatility, hybrid tail risk, and lower partial moments.

Chapter 5 observed what are the impacts of bank mergers and acquisitions on the bank efficiency, alongside examining how these efficiencies influence the bank shareholder value upon the merger announcements. The methodology applied in this chapter includes the stochastic frontier analysis and event study methodology, with regression analysis. The data sample included large commercial bank mergers and acquisitions from 22 European countries. The main results indicated that stock markets price the operational efficiency of banks when predicting value gains.

Chapter 6 focuses on the rise in the records of the public debt of the most industrialized nations, contrasting these facts to the state in Nigeria. Authors apply the debt overhanging theory, Marilyn's ex-post facto research design, and Creswell's mix method research approaches. Results indicated that a high degree of political rascality among the ruling elite was observed, with a lack of viable ICT oriented public debt management tools.

Chapter 7 focuses on eleven Central, Eastern, and South-Eastern European stock markets in order to examine potential macroeconomic factors that contribute to the dynamics of real equity prices. The main methodology applied consists of a global vector autoregressive methodology so that the potential cross-country linkages and spillovers are accounted for. The results indicated that the main spillovers to the observed countries come from the German stock market.

Chapter 8 presents an economic model that takes into consideration risks and uncertainties in the oil and gas industry. The following field of operations is observed: drilling time, delays due to drilling problems, rig failures, and materials supply, alongside electric submersible pump installations failures and losing the well. In order to solve those problems, the authors provide a comprehensive solution for assessing business performance in the area of oil field development.

Chapter 9 deals with the financial stability of 22 commercial banks in Pakistan keeping the risk behaviour, country governance in observation, and controlling for the effects of economic growth. The panel regressions were estimated via usual panel models. The main results of this chapter include the following. The financial stability of the observed banks is mostly affected b the credit, operational, county, and financial crisis risks.

Chapter 10 mostly deals with the problem of automatic recognition of favourable days for the purposes of the intra-day trading on the stock market. Predictor variables used in the study include twenty-two technical indicators. The main problem which was in the focus of the chapter was a binary classification problem. The performance measurement was made via Cohen's kappa, whereas several classifiers were used: k-nearest neighbours, naive Bayes classifier, artificial neural network, random forest, and support vector machine. The results here indicate that technical analysis makes sense in favour of predicting the day favourability for trading.

Chapter 11 showed how to investigate possible cartel behaviour. Authors observed 15 banks in India, which the Reserve Bank of India suspected a cartel in the period 2011-2013. The results in this chapter showed that the Competition Commission of India was right in ruling out the complaint which the Reserve Bank made.

Chapter 12 examines factors that affect the efficiency of the securities placement in commercial banks via regression analysis. The phenomenon of adaptability (which means the higher the price set is in comparison with the medium price scale the higher the underpaying is) was observed. Authors have created a model that characterizes the state of a commercial bank which will be ready for the emission of new assets via IPOs (initial public offerings).

Chapter 13 investigates the literature on stock characteristics that affect asset pricing. Authors were motivated by the vast amount of literature which deals with multifactor models in determining the relationship between stock characteristics and stock prices. Due to the expansive list of potential characteristics with the development of the field of dimensionality reduction, research can investigate better approximations of the unobservable latent risk factors.

Chapter 14 is more of a theoretical approach within the book, as it investigates integral equations with the potential type of operations for functions from the generalized Hölder spaces. Authors carried out an inverse operator for the Riesz potential with a logarithmic kernel since the multidimensional Riesz potential type operations are of interest within mathematical modelling in economics.

Chapter 15 observes asset price factors as underlying performance drivers, with a special focus on the momentum. Since the factor models are developed as a simplification of the diversification principle within the Markowitz portfolio selection, authors in this chapter aim to popularize the factor models, with the special focus on the momentum effects on stock and bond markets. A description of the methodology and a detailed literature overview are given.

Chapter 16 deals with bonds as a special financial asset of interest. Namely, coupon bond duration and convexity are examined as the primary risk measures for bonds. This chapter fills the gap in the related literature by analysing the duration and convexity without the use of differential calculus, as the observed functions are usually not differentiable. Besides the theoretical findings, the chapter observes these findings on real data.

Chapter 17 focuses on an alternative approach to modelling stock prices. The Grey Models methodology is applied in forecasting the stock prices as a relatively new and unknown tool in portfolio management. Besides the literature overview, the chapter provided an empirical analysis of the benefits of using the Grey Models in price prediction. Results of the analysis indicated that out-of-sample forecasts of stock prices were better for the Grey Models when compared to the usual econometric approaches. Furthermore, the chapter simulated investment strategies based on the estimation results, which is not usually found in the literature.

Chapter 18 is dealing with spectral risk measures, due to them being the most attractive subclass of coherent quantile-based risk measures. The chapter thus reviews the standard spectral risk measures, with a detailed discussion about the topic. A critical approach was made in the research, as authors spotted problems with each of the measures.

Tihana Škrinjarić
University of Zagreb, Croatia

Mirjana Čižmešija
University of Zagreb, Croatia

Bryan Christiansen
Global Training Group, Ltd, UK

REFERENCES

Amado, C., & Teräsvirta, T. (2014). Specification and testing of multiplicative time-varying GARCH models with applications. *Econometric Reviews*, *36*(4), 421–446. doi:10.1080/07474938.2014.977064

Chan-Lau, J. (2006). *Fundamentals-Based Estimation of Default Probabilities - A Survey*. IMF Working Papers 2006(149).

Demerjian, P. R. (2007). *Financial Ratios and Credit Risk: The Selection of Financial Ratio Covenants in Debt Contracts. AAA 2007 Financial Accounting & Reporting Section (FARS)*. Meeting Paper.

Fabozzi, F. J., Focardi, S. M., & Jonas, C. L. (2004) Trends in Quantitative Asset Management in Europe. *Journal of Portfolio Management, 31*(4), 124-132.

Fama, E. F., & French, K. (1992). The cross-section of expected stock returns. *The Journal of Finance*, *47*(2), 427–465. doi:10.1111/j.1540-6261.1992.tb04398.x

Fama, E. F., & French, K. (1993). Common risk factors in the returns on stocks and bonds. *Journal of Financial Economics*, *33*(1), 3–56. doi:10.1016/0304-405X(93)90023-5

Fama, E. F., & French, K. (1995). Multifactor Explanations of Asset Pricing Anomalies. *The Journal of Finance*, *51*(1), 55–84. doi:10.1111/j.1540-6261.1996.tb05202.x

Granger, C. J. (1989). Combining forecasts – twenty years later. *Journal of Forecasting*, *8*(1), 167–173. doi:10.1002/for.3980080303

Ho, S., Xie, M., & Goh, T. (2002). A comparative study of neural network and box-jenkins ARIMA modeling in the time series prediction. *Computers & Industrial Engineering*, *42*(2), 371–375. doi:10.1016/S0360-8352(02)00036-0

Hubbard, D. W. (2009). *The Failure of Risk Management – Why It's Broken and How to Fix It*. John Wiley & Sons.

Jo, T. C. (2003). The effect of virtual term generation on the neural based approaches to time series prediction. In *Proceedings of the IEEE fourth conference on control and automation* (vol. 3, pp. 516-520). Montreal, Canada: IEEE. 10.1109/ICCA.2003.1595075

Khuman, A. S., Yang, Y., & John, R. (2014). A commentary on some of the intrinsic differences between grey systems and fuzzy systems. In *2014 IEEE International Conference on Systems, Man, and Cybernetics (SMC)*. San Diego, CA: IEEE. 10.1109/SMC.2014.6974220

McKinsey Global Institute. (2016). *Diminishing returns: why investors may need to lower their expectations*. McKinsey & Company, Report.

Merton, R. C. (1993). Operation and regulation in financial intermediation: A functional perspective. In P. Englund (Ed.), *Operation and Regulation of Financial Markets*. The Economic Council.

Modigliani, F., & Miller, M. (1958). The Cost of Capital, Corporation Finance and the Theory of Investment. *The American Economic Review*, *48*(3), 261–297.

Modigliani, F., & Miller, M. (1963). Corporate income taxes and the cost of capital: A correction. *The American Economic Review*, *53*(3), 433–443.

Nelson, D. B. (1990). Stationarity and persistence in the GARCH(1,1) model – modelling stock market volatility. *Econometric Theory*, *6*(3), 318–334. doi:10.1017/S0266466600005296

Nelson, D. B. (1991). Conditional Heteroskedasticity in asset returns: A new approach. *Econometrica*, *59*(2), 37–64. doi:10.2307/2938260

Pagan, A. R., & Schwert, G. W. (1990). Alternative models for conditional stock volatility. *Journal of Econometrics*, *45*(1-2), 267–290. doi:10.1016/0304-4076(90)90101-X

Roje, G. (2005). The role of accounting determinants in predicting long term credit ratings. In *28th European accounting association Congress: collected abstracts*. Goteborg, Sweden: BAS Publishing House.

Ruey, S. T. (2002). *Analysis of Financial Time Series*. John Wiley & Sons.

Taylor, M., & Allen, H. (1992). The use of technical analysis in the foreign exchange market. *Journal of International Money and Finance*, *11*(3), 304–314. doi:10.1016/0261-5606(92)90048-3

Wallis, K. F. (2011). Combining forecasts – forty years later. *Applied Financial Economics*, *21*(1-2), 33–41. doi:10.1080/09603107.2011.523179

Acknowledgment

We would like to thank all of those involved in this project: authors, reviewers, and other parties included in the whole process. Without the quality work authors have provided and quality reviews which were made on time, this book would not become reality. Furthermore, we would like to thank especially the Advisory Editorial Board who have contributed to the coherence and quality of the reviews and chapters overall.

We are obliged to give a special thank you to Ms. Jan Travers, Mr. Josh Christ, and other Editors from IGI Global, who were very supportive of the entire project duration.

Editors

Chapter 1
Determining Expected Utility and Entropy Ratio in the Expected Utility-Entropy Decision Model for Stock Selection Depending on Capital Market Development

Branka Marasović
Faculty of Economics, Business, and Tourism, University of Split, Croatia

Tea Kalinić
Faculty of Economics, Business, and Tourism, University of Split, Croatia

Ivana Jerković
Faculty of Economics, Business, and Tourism, University of Split, Croatia

ABSTRACT

Appropriate securities selection is an important step in formation of an investment portfolio. The expected utility-entropy (EU-E) decision-making model is one of the models that can be applied to investment portfolio stock selection. The decision-maker subjective preference is reflected by the expected utility, and the objective uncertainty is measured using Shannon entropy. In this model, the measure of risky action is the weighted linear average of expected utility and entropy using a risk tradeoff factor. This chapter tests whether tradeoff coefficient depends on capital market development. With this aim, EU-E model was applied on European Union (EU) capital markets with different development according to FTSE equity country classification. It tests whether the EU-E model applied to the three different capital markets gives the best stock selection results for the same tradeoff coefficient values, or whether tradeoff coefficient depends on capital market development.

DOI: 10.4018/978-1-7998-5083-0.ch001

INTRODUCTION

An investment portfolio is a set of assets that can hold stocks, bonds, cash and other financial or nonfinancial assets. It also refers to a group of investments that an investor mixes in order to earn a profit while making sure that it reflects the investor's risk tolerance and financial goals. In a context of uncertainty but also great opportunities, investors repeatedly have to select investment assets from a wide range of securities listed on worldwide capital markets.

One of the most important components of investment portfolio management called portfolio selection problem refers to the problem of dividing an investor's wealth amongst a set of available securities. Taking into consideration the stock's market complexity, a high level of knowledge on the part of the financial analyst is required in order to obtain strategies that allow risk minimization and/or maximization of the investor's return, thereby achieving both high and low periods (Pinho & Melo, 2018).

Furthermore, investment portfolio management is not possible without strong quantitative support, which is based on the application of appropriate mathematical models for asset valuation, risk management, portfolio optimization and rebalancing and on the development of new models that will allow investors to make better decisions with better investment results in comparison to previous models.

To this date, many mathematical models have been developed to support the decision-making process when selecting an investment portfolio. Most models aim to find a portfolio that maximizes return for a given rate of risk or a portfolio that minimizes risk for a given rate of return, the so-called efficient portfolio. Depending on the characteristics of securities and investment strategies on the one side and those of the capital market on the other, different risk measures can be applied in these models.

In addition, as there are many securities in the capital markets, in the first step of the model the number of securities is often reduced using the criteria chosen by the decision maker, and only then the optimal portfolio from the selected reduced set of securities is chosen. Such a model is also used and presented in this chapter. In the first step, the best stocks are selected using the normalized EU-E measure of risk and in the second step mean-variance efficient portfolios are formed. On the basis of the presented model, an attempt will be made to determine whether the model has the same characteristics and parameters in the markets at different levels of development.

In line with the Financial Time Stock Exchange (FTSE) classification criteria, national capital markets are divided into four categories: developed markets, advanced emerging markets, secondary emerging markets and frontier markets. Emerging markets and frontier markets, which the Croatian market belongs to, are characterized by high returns but also volatility, strong links with developed markets, low liquidity, reduced capitalization, underdevelopment of financial instruments, political instability, exchange rate volatility, and high transaction costs. Despite the limitations of the emerging and frontier markets, such as e.g. insufficient liquidity, weak regulations, they still represent a challenge and provide opportunities for higher returns as compared to developed markets.

Since stock returns in markets at different levels of development do not have the same characteristics, it is interesting to investigate how the EU-E model for stock selection behaves in different markets.

In the analysis, German, Hungarian and Croatian capital markets were taken as representatives of developed market, advanced emerging market and frontier market respectively. Emerging markets are divided into advanced and secondary emerging markets, but no EU country is classified as the secondary emerging market. It will be tested whether the EU-E model applied to the three different capital markets, previously presented, gives the best stock selection results for the same trade-off coefficient values, or whether trade-off coefficient depends on capital market development. The success of the model will be tested by forming efficient portfolios, in the sense of the mean-variance model, made up of the resulting stock sets and comparing them with the efficient portfolios of the initial set, for each capital market.

The chapter is divided into five parts. The Section 2 is the literature review which provides an overview of the theoretical background of the research on the portfolio selection problem and shows the results of previously conducted research. Section 3 explains the methodology used for the analysis. Section 4 presents the results of empirical analyses on the German capital market, Hungarian capital market and Croatian capital market. Finally, a brief summary and concluding remarks are given in Section 5.

LITERATURE REVIEW

The beginning of modern portfolio management, which is based on strong quantitative support dates back to the middle of the last century when in 1952 Markowitz published his paper *Portfolio Theory* (Markowitz, 1952) which laid the foundations of the modern portfolio theory. It was the first serious attempt to describe the market using a consistent mathematical model. The Markowitz's model is based on two criteria: return and risk as measured by variance, i.e. standard deviation. His idea was to find a balance between risk and return and choose a stock portfolio that results in the highest possible return with the least possible risk. Of course, when taking on more risk, a higher return can be expected.

Thus, his idea was to form a mathematical model for portfolio selection that brings in the highest rate of return, but with a certain given level of risk. Markowitz referred to this portfolio that has the highest rate of return for a given risk rate, i.e. the portfolio that has a minimum risk for a given rate of return, an efficient portfolio. The Markowitz's portfolio optimization model, also known as the MV model (mean-variance model), is highly valued. Markowitz was awarded the Nobel Prize in Economics for his contributions to the development of modern portfolio theory in 1990 (Marasovic, B. 2016).

Since then, researchers have developed many portfolio optimization models that are based on Markowitz's MV model. Modern portfolio theory research follows two main lines: (i) incorporation of alternative risk measures and (ii) inclusion of other criteria in the mathematical formulation of the model (Anagnostopoulos & Mamanis, 2010). Righi and Borenstein (2018) compared eleven risk measures regarding performance of optimal portfolio strategies (Standard Deviation, Value at Risk, Expected Loss, Expected Loss Deviation, Expected Shortfall, Shortfall Deviation Risk, Expected Value at Risk, Deviation Expected Value at Risk, Entropy, Deviation Entropy, Maximum Loss). They considered risk measures from different classes (losses risk measures, deviation risk measures and loss-deviation risk measures). "Results indicate there is no clearly dominant risk measure. Despite this lack of dominance, including deviation terms consistently exhibits advantages regarding performance." (Righi & Borenstein, 2018, p. 105). "Furthermore, contrary to the expectations of the modern portfolio theory, the tests carried out on a number of ðnancial markets have revealed the existence of other indicators, besides return and risk, important in portfolio selection. Considering the importance of variables other than return and risk, the selection of the optimal portfolio becomes a multi-criteria problem which should be solved using the appropriate techniques" (Marasović & Babić, 2010, p. 58). A review of multi-criteria methods applied in portfolio selection and management is well presented in papers by Zopoundis and Doumpos (2002), Marasović and Babić (2010), Aouni, Doumpos, Pérez Gladish and Steuer (2018).

Entropy is one of the alternative risk measures used as an alternative to variance. Entropy was initially implemented in thermodynamics by Clausius (1870). Later, Shannon (1948) showed that the entropy concept can be applied in the fields of science where probabilities must be determined. Since then, entropy has become a major cornerstone of information theory (Deeva, 2017). In addition, as entropy is a measure of uncertainty in information theory, the use of entropy as an alternative risk measure of portfolio selection has developed as well.

Philippatos and Wilson (1975) applied entropy as a risk measure to select optimal portfolios on the New York Stock Exchange (NYSE) over a 14-year period. In their work, they found that portfolios selected on the basis of the expected return and entropy were also MV effective. Philippatos and Gressis (1975) applied the concept of entropy to portfolio selection theory and analyzed MV and ME efficient portfolios. They found that effective portfolios obtained by MV and ME models were equal at normal and lognormal return distributions. The most important conclusion of the paper is the preference of entropy over variance as a measure of risk because the assumption of a normal return distribution is not required.

Furthermore, Usta and Kantar (2011) described an approach in which an entropy measure is added to the mean-variance-skewness model (MVSM) to generate a well-diversified portfolio and present a multi-objective approach based on a mean-variance-skewness-entropy portfolio selection model (MVSEM). They evaluated the performance of the MVSEM in terms of several portfolio performance measures and they demonstrated that the MVSEM performs well out-of-sample relative to the traditional portfolio selection model.

In their papers, Ormos and Zibriczky (2014) and Deeva (2017) compared traditional risk measures such as beta and standard deviation with entropy in asset valuation. Unlike beta, entropy does not require a market portfolio to be defined, nor does it make strict assumptions as the capital asset pricing model (CAPM) model. In the regression analysis, Ormos and Zibriczky (2014) found that entropy has a higher explanatory power for the expected return than the capital asset pricing model.

Most previous researches focused on the case when investors already selected a set of shares and were looking for an optimal portfolio from a given set of shares. However, the first step in practice is that investors actually select a particular set of shares from thousands of listed shares and only then do they form efficient portfolios from the selected set of shares.

The commonly used way is to select a certain set of stocks with the highest expected utility of stock returns of all the stocks in the market. However, this type of selection method does not take the uncertainty of stock returns into account. From previous studies, it can be concluded that entropy, as a measure of uncertainty of returns, can be an important factor for the selection of an appropriate set of stocks in which to invest. For that reason, Yang and Qiu (2005; 2014) mixed entropy and expected utility and they developed a decision-making model under risk, the expected utility-entropy (EU-E) decision-making model. The EU-E model combines the decision-maker's subjective preference and the objective uncertainty of the state of nature. The decision-maker's subjective preference is reflected by the expected utility and the objective uncertainty is measured using Shannon entropy. In this model, the measure of risky action is the weighted linear average of expected utility and entropy using a risk trade-off factor. Yang et al. (2017) applied Yang and Qiu model from 2014 with normalized EU-E measure of risk to stock selection, i.e., selecting the set of stocks with the lowest EU-E measure of risk for trade-off coefficients within certain intervals, and then deriving the efficient portfolios using these sets of stocks in the mean-variance framework proposed by Markowitz. They applied the EU-E model on developed capital markets and showed that the EU-E decision model can be a useful method for stock selection. The results show that efficient portfolios composed of the set of stocks selected using the EU-E model are more efficient than those of the set of stocks selected using only the expected utility criterion. Moreover, the efficient frontiers of portfolios for intermediate values of λ are almost the same as those of portfolios composed from the sample of all stocks. Marasović and Kalinić (2019) investigated if the expected utility - entropy decision model for stock selection gives the same results in emerging capital markets which are characterized by higher expected returns and risk. By using the EU-E decision model for selecting stock on the Croatian capital market they managed to reduce the number of shares by 50% without a major change to the properties of efficient portfolios.

Papers by Yang et al. (2017) and Marasović and Kalinić (2019) encouraged the authors to conduct the following research.

In this chapter, it will be tested whether the trade-off coefficient λ in the EU-E model for stock selection depends on the capital market development. With this aim, the EU-E model was applied on EU capital markets at different levels of development according to the Financial Times Stock Exchange (FTSE) equity country classification.

EXPECTED UTILITY-ENTROPY DECISION ANALYSIS MODEL UNDER RISK AND ITS APPLICATION TO STOCK SELECTION

Risk is an inevitable part of decision making in the fields of economics and it can have different meanings in different disciplines. Consequently, different types of measures of risk have been developed. In order to properly describe the concept of risk measure as used in this chapter, the general decision analysis model is described. The three main parts of a general decision analysis model under risk are: the action space $A=\{a_1,a_2,...,a_m\}$, the state space $\Theta=\{\theta_1,\theta_2,...,\theta_m\}$ and the payoff function $X{:}A\times\Theta\to R$ (Yang & Qiu, 2005). Suppose that the state space element θ_i that corresponds to an action $a_i \in A$ has n_i outcomes $\theta_i=\{\theta_{i1},\theta_{i2},...,\theta_{in_i}\}$. The probability that states θ_{ij} will occur when action a_i is taken is denoted by $p_{ij}=P\{\theta=\theta_{ij}\mid a=a_i\}$, $i\in\{1,2,\ldots,m\}$, $j\in\{1,2,\ldots,n_i\}$ and $\{\theta_{i1},p_{i1};\ldots;\theta_{in_i},p_{in_i}\}$ is the probability distribution of θ_i. The payoff for taking action a_i with the corresponding state θ_i is defined with $x_{ij}=X(a_i,\theta_{ij})$. Suppose that the decision maker's utility function is $u=u(X)$, then the general decision analysis model under risk can be noted by $G=(\Theta,A,u)$.

This decision analysis model is used because it takes into consideration the results of actions which have an impact on the states of nature and that different actions result in different states of nature that may not have the same distribution. The decision analysis model defined this way is a generalized and more realistic case of the classical decision analysis model where the distributive laws of all θ_i are equal, i.e., $n_1=n_2=\ldots=n_m=n$ and $p_{1j}=p_{2j}=\ldots=p_{mj},\forall j\in\{1,2,\ldots,n\}$.

The two main factors that affect the choice of action a decision maker is going to make are uncertainty of the outcomes and expected utility. With higher uncertainty comes higher riskiness and higher expected utility results in less riskiness (Yang & Qiu, 2005). This motivated Yang and Qiu to propose a risk measure that combines both the decision maker's subjective expected utility and the objective uncertainty of the outcomes. Uncertainty of the outcomes is measured using the normalized Shannon entropy. Given a discrete random variable X with probability distribution $(x_1,p_1;\ldots;x_n,p_n)$, the normalized Shannon Information Entropy $NH(X)$ of X is defined as follows:

$$NH(X)=\begin{cases}\left(-\sum_{i=1}^{n}p_i\ln p_i\right)/\ln(n), & n>1\\ 0 & ,n=1\end{cases} \quad (1)$$

In terms of the decision analysis model, for an action $a\in A$ and its corresponding state θ the entropy of θ is in further work denoted by $H_a(\theta)$.

Follows the definition of Yang and Qiu's proposed measure called the normalized EU-E measure of risk (Yang, Zhang & Chen, 2010, p. 220):

Definition 1. Given a general decision analysis model $G=(\Theta,A,u)$, action $a\in A$, state of nature $\theta\in\Theta$. Suppose there exist at least two actions in action space and at least two states in state space respectively, the decision maker's utility function $u(X)$ is mono-increasing. If $\max_{a\in A}\left\{\left|E\left[u\left(X\left(a,\theta\right)\right)\right]\right|\right\}$ is nonzero, the normalized EU-E measure of risk when taking action a is defined as follows:

$$R(a)=\lambda H_a(\theta)-(1-\lambda)E\left[u\left(X\left(a,\theta\right)\right)\right]/\max_{a\in A}\left\{\left|E\left[u\left(X\left(a,\theta\right)\right)\right]\right|\right\}$$

Where $\lambda\in[0,1]$ is a constant, $R(a)$ denotes the risk of action a, $H_a(\theta)$ denotes information entropy of the distribution of its corresponding states; $X(a,\theta)$ denotes the outcome corresponding to state θ when taking action a.

The constant $\lambda\in[0,1]$ used in the previous definition is the trade-off coefficient and it represents the trade-off between decision maker's subjective expected utility and the objective uncertainty of the outcomes. If the decision maker wants the expected utility to have a greater effect on the overall risk measure than entropy, the trade-off coefficient should then be closer to zero and if the decision maker wants the objective unsteadiness of outcomes to have more sway then λ should be closer to 1. Risk $R(a)$ of an action $a\in A$ lays within interval [0,1] and represents a relative measure of how risky an action is. Hence, the closer $R(a)$ is to zero, the less risky an action is. Measure $R(a)$ increases with the increase of entropy and with the loss of expected utility. Similarly, it decreases with the decrease of entropy and the increase of expected utility. This reflects people's common risk attitudes where they are more willing to take an action if the expected gain is bigger and uncertainty is lower. The normalized EU-E measure of risk will be used to rank actions in order to select actions with the lowest risk. The following definition is used (Yang, Zhang & Chen, 2010, p. 221):

Definition 2. For a given general decision analysis model $G=(\Theta,A,u)$, actions $a_1,a_2\in A$, $R(a_1),R(a_2)$ denote normalized EU-E measure of risk of a_1 and a_2 respectively. If $R(a_1)<R(a_2)$, then action a_1 is preferred to action a_2 in the sense of normalized EU-E measure of risk, denoted by $a_1\succ a_2$; if $R(a_1)\le R(a_2)$, then the action a_2 is not superior to a_1, denoted by $a_1\succeq a_2$.

It is easily determined from the definition of the EU-E measure that if two or more actions have the same expected utility, the optimal action, i.e. the one that has the lowest risk, is the one with the lowest normalized entropy. Similarly, if two or more actions have the same entropy, the optimal action is the one with the highest expected utility.

Furthermore, a model for stock selection that uses the described EU-E decision analysis model under risk is given. Suppose that an investor wants to reduce his portfolio of m stocks to a portfolio of k stocks. The process of selecting stocks to be included in the new portfolio is a decision-making problem. It is assumed that the investor prefers the new portfolio to be composed of those stocks that have the lowest risk and in this chapter the risk is determined using the previously described EU-E measure of risk. Let $S=\{S_1,S_2,...,S_m\}$ be the set of stocks aimed to be reduced to a subset $S'\subseteq S,|S'|=k\leq m,\ k,m\in \mathrm{N}$. Let $A=\{a_1,a_2,...,a_m\}$ be the action set where a_i denotes the action of selecting stock S_i, $i\in\{1,2,\ldots,m\}$. For each stock S_i, $i\in\{1,2,\ldots,m\}$ the prices p_{ij}, $j\in\{1,2,\ldots,q+1\}$ for $q+1$ consecutive periods of time need to be collected based on which q returns r_{ij} are calculated using the formula $r_{ij}=\ln\frac{P_{i,j}}{P_{i,j-1}}$, $i\in\{1,2,\ldots,m\}$, $j\in\{1,2,\ldots,q+1\}$. In that way, a return series $\{r_{i1},r_{i2},...,r_{iq}\}$ for each stock S_i is defined. Next, $a=\min_{1\leq i\leq m}\{r_{i1},r_{i2},...,r_{iq}\}$ and $b=\max_{1\leq i\leq m}\{r_{i1},r_{i2},...,r_{iq}\}$ need to be calculated in order to compose an interval $[a,b]$ that is then divided into $n\in N$ subintervals of length Δr as follows:

$$\Delta \boldsymbol{r}=(b-a)/n,\ \boldsymbol{n}\in \mathrm{N}\Rightarrow r_i:=\begin{cases} a & ,i=0 \\ r_{i-1}+\Delta r, i\in\{1,2,...,n-1\} \\ b & ,i=n \end{cases}.$$

n subintervals $[r_0,r_1\rangle,[r_1,r_2\rangle,\ldots,[r_{n-1},r_n\rangle$ are obtained and denoted by $\theta_j=[r_{j-1},r_j\rangle$, $j\in\{1,2,\ldots,n\}$. These intervals define a state space $\Theta=\{\theta_1,\theta_2,...,\theta_n\}$. Moreover, for each stock S_i, $i\in\{1,2,\ldots,m\}$ and each state space element θ_j, $j\in\{1,2,\ldots,m\}$ the relative frequency of the returns of stock S_i that lay in interval θ_j is calculated and denoted by ρ_{ij}, i.e.,

$$(\forall i\in\{1,2,...,m\})(\forall j\in\{1,2,...,n\})\,\rho_{ij}:=v_{ij}/q,$$

where $v_{ij}:=\left|r_{il}\in\{r_{i1},r_{i2},...,r_{iq}\}:r_{il}\in\theta_j\right|$.

Next, the expected return of stock S_i that falls into interval θ_j is calculated and denoted by $\bar{x}_{ij}$ i.e.

$$(\forall i\in\{1,2,...,m\})(\forall j\in\{1,2,...,n\})\,\bar{x}_{ij}:=\frac{\sum_{r_{ij}\in\theta_j}r_{ij}}{v_{ij}}.$$

According to Bernoulli's law of large numbers (LLN), for a large number of observed prices q, ρ_{ij} should be close to p_{ij} where p_{ij} is the probability that the return of stock S_i will fall into the interval θ_j and take an expected return of $\bar{x}_{ij}$.

As previously noted, risk measure for choosing to invest in stock S_i used in this model is defined with

$$R(a_i) = -\lambda \sum_{i=1}^{n} p_{ij} \ln p_{ij} / \ln(n) - (1-\lambda) \sum_{j=1}^{n} \left[u(\bar{x}_{ij}) p_{ij} \right] / \max_{1 \le i \le m} \left\{ \left| \sum_{j=1}^{n} \left[u(\bar{x}_{ij}) p_{ij} \right] \right| \right\} \tag{2}$$

The process of choosing utility function u, as stated by Warren (2019), is a subjective process and the utility function should be selected and parameterized to reflect investor circumstances. Since utility function describes individual behaviour of people there cannot exist one single best function. On the other hand, Starmer (2000) suggests it is not a good practice to simply extract one utility function based on literature without taking into consideration investors' preferences. Therefore, utility function used in this article contains the trade-off coefficient λ. Moreover, Kahneman and Tversky (1979) conducted an experiment that suggested that subjects are more risk aware when nonnegative outcomes occur and show risk seeking if outcomes are changed to losses with equal absolute value. Such a behaviour can be mirrored with the help of utility function being convex in the nonnegative domain and concave otherwise. Based on previously mentioned findings, the utility function chosen to be used in this article is:

$$u(x) = \begin{cases} 1 - e^{-x} & , x \ge 0 \\ -\lambda\left(1 - e^{x}\right), & x < 0 \end{cases}. \tag{3}$$

Its S shape reflects the aforementioned behaviour of risk seeking for negative and risk awareness for positive outcomes, and the exponential type of function is chosen because of its common usage in decision analysis in economics. After the utility function is chosen, it is possible to calculate the risk of investing in each stock S_i based on which selection of k stocks with the lowest risk can be made.

USING THE EU-E MODEL FOR STOCK SELECTION ON DIFFERENTLY DEVELOPED EU CAPITAL MARKETS AND THE ANALYSIS OF THE TRADE-OFF COEFFICIENT

The previously presented EU-E decision model is applied to stock selection on three markets in the European Union, which are at different levels of market development according to the FTSE equity country classification.

FTSE country classification process is designed to be transparent and evidence-driven. Consistent with the Principles for Financial Benchmarks published by the International Organization of Securities Commissions (IOSCO) in 2013, the operation of the country classification process is overseen by FTSE Russell's strong internal governance structure. By classifying countries according to objective criteria and engaging with stock exchanges, regulators and central banks in countries where the market is being considered for potential promotion or demotion, the process provides portfolio managers and asset allocators with a clear view of expected future index evolution. The FTSE Global Equity Index Series (GEIS) was founded in 1987 by the Financial Times and the Institute and Faculty of Actuaries. Over the years, the index was renamed several times and in 2000 its coverage extended to include 90% of global equity markets when 20 more countries from the Barings Emerging Market Index were added. This combination of the Barings index and the previous FTSE World Index was named the All-World Index. At the time of this expansion, the countries from the existing World index were classified into

"Developed" and "Advanced Emerging" markets and the countries from the Barings index were classified as "Secondary Emerging" markets. In 2008, a fourth grouping named "Frontier" markets was formed and was introduced to collect the markets not yet sufficiently evolved to be categorized as Emerging. In March 2018, the FTSE All-World index included 47 countries with a further 29 countries classified as Frontier markets. The classified list of countries is shown in Figure 1. In 2003, the expansion of the GEIS prompted FTSE to start a client consultation which proposed a structured framework for classifying markets consistent with FTSE's philosophy of rules-based, objective indexes. In addition to considering countries per capita income, the proposal set out other guiding principles for market classification. These were: Quality of Market, Materiality, Consistency and Predictability, Cost Limitation, Stability and Market Access. The results of the consultation were published in November 2003 and FTSE moved ahead with implementing this country classification scheme in 2004. (Russell, 2018)

Figure 1. FTSE Country Classification (Source: (Russell, 2019))
**Saudi Arabia reclassification to Secondary Emerging commenced in March 2019 and is to be completed by March 2020.*
***China A Share reclassification to Secondary Emerging commenced in June 2019 and is to be completed by March 2020.*
****Iceland reclassified as Frontier, effective with the annual review of the FTSE Frontier Index Series in September 2019.*
*****Romania to be reclassified as Secondary Emerging effective with the FTSE GEIS semi-annual review in September 2020.*
******Tanzania to be reclassified as Frontier effective with the annual review of the FTSE Frontier Index Series in September 2020.*

Developed	Advanced Emerging	Secondary Emerging	Frontier
Australia	Brazil	Chile	Argentina
Austria	Czech Republic	China**	Bahrain
Belgium/Luxembourg	Greece	Colombia	Bangladesh
Canada	Hungary	Egypt	Botswana
Denmark	Malaysia	India	Bulgaria
Finland	Mexico	Indonesia	Côte d'Ivoire
France	South Africa	Kuwait	Croatia
Germany	Taiwan	Pakistan	Cyprus
Hong Kong	Thailand	Peru	Estonia
Ireland	Turkey	Philippines	Ghana
Israel		Qatar	Iceland***
Italy		Russia	Jordan
Japan		Saudi Arabia*	Kazakhstan
Netherlands		UAE	Kenya
New Zealand			Latvia
Norway			Lithuania
Poland			Malta
Portugal			Mauritius
Singapore			Morocco
South Korea			Nigeria
Spain			Oman
Sweden			Palestine
Switzerland			Republic of North Macedonia
UK			Romania****
USA			Serbia
			Slovak Republic
			Slovenia
			Sri Lanka
			Tunisia
			Vietnam
			*****Tanzania

For each market group, following the FSTE classification, one representative in the European Union was chosen; German stock market was chosen as a representative of developed markets, Hungarian stock market as a representative of emerging markets and Croatian stock market as a representative of frontier markets. Considering that there is no market in the European Union classified as "Secondary Emerging" market, the previously mentioned "Emerging" markets refer to both "Advanced Emerging" and "Secondary Emerging" markets.

In the following paragraphs the EU-E measure of risk is applied. The initial set S consisting of stocks that are components of corresponding country market index in the observed period is formed. In the case of Croatian market, the initial set S consists of 18 stocks that were liquid components of the Croatian market index CROBEX in March 2019. The German initial set S consists of 29 stocks which were liquid components of the German market index DAX and the Hungarian initial set S consists of 12 stocks which were liquid components of the Hungarian market index BUX in May 2019.

In all three cases, the number of components of the market index in the observed period was higher, but as a significant number of daily prices was not available, some of them were not included in the analysis. The elements of these initial sets are presented in Table 1, Table 2 and Table 3, respectively.

Table 1. The components of CROBEX

Variable	Stock Company	Variable	Stock Company
S_1	AD PLASTIK	S_{10}	Ingra
S_2	Adris grupa	S_{11}	Končar, d.d
S_3	Arena hospitality group	S_{12}	Kraš
S_4	Atlantic grupa	S_{13}	MAISTRA
S_5	Atlantska plovidba	S_{14}	Ot-optima telekom
S_6	Đuro Đaković grupa	S_{15}	Podravka
S_7	Dalekovod	S_{16}	Valamar Riviera
S_8	Ericsson Nikola Tesla	S_{17}	Brodogradilište Viktor Lenac
S_9	HT	S_{18}	Zagrebačka banka

Source: (www.zse.hr, *2019)*

Further steps are presented on the example of the German market. The same steps can be applied to the other two markets.

The stocks in the initial set are sorted in ascending order using the EU-E measure. The aim is to maximally reduce the initial set so that the generated subset consisting of stocks with the lowest EU-E risk, is a sufficiently good approximation of the initial set in the sense of mean-variance model. Daily closing prices of DAX stocks over the period from January 2017 to January 2019 are collected. $q+1=503$ closing prices $\{P_{i0}, P_{i1}, \ldots, P_{i503}\}$ for each component stock S_i, $i \in \{1,2,\ldots,29\}$ are obtained.

According to the closing prices $q=502$ returns $\{r_{i1}, r_{i2}, \ldots, r_{i502}\}$ are calculated using the formula:

$$r_{ij} = \ln \frac{P_{ij}}{P_{i,j-1}}, \; i \in \{1,2,\ldots,29\}, j \in \{1,2,\ldots,502\}$$

Table 2. The components of DAX

Variable	Stock Company	Variable	Stock Company
S_1	Adidas	S_{16}	Fresenius Medical Care
S_2	Allianz	S_{17}	Fresenius SE
S_3	BASF	S_{18}	HeidelbergCement
S_4	Bayer	S_{19}	Henkel & Co
S_5	BMW ST	S_{20}	Infineon Technologies
S_6	Beiersdorf AG	S_{21}	Merck
S_7	Continental AG	S_{22}	Muench. Rueckvers.
S_8	Covestro	S_{23}	RWE AG ST
S_9	Daimler	S_{24}	SAP
S_{10}	Deutsche Bank AG	S_{25}	Siemens AG
S_{11}	Deutsche Boerse	S_{26}	ThyssenKrupp
S_{12}	Deutsche Lufthansa	S_{27}	Volkswagen VZO
S_{13}	Deutsche Post	S_{28}	Vonovia
S_{14}	Deutsche Telekom AG	S_{29}	Wirecard
S_{15}	E.ON SE		

Source: (www.boerse-frankfurt.de, *2019)*

Table 3. The components of BUX

Variable	Stock Company	Variable	Stock Company
S_1	ANY	S_7	MOL
S_2	Appeninn	S_8	Magyar Telekom
S_3	CIG Pannonia	S_9	OPUS GLOBAL
S_4	Gedeon Richter	S_{10}	OTP Bank
S_5	Graphisoft Park Se	S_{11}	PannErgy
S_6	KONU	S_{12}	Takarek Mortgage Bank

Source: (www.bse.hu, *2019)*

After finding minimum a= -0.19489 and maximum b=0.106011 of all stock returns, interval [-0.19489, 0.106011]which contains all stock returns is constructed, and then divided into n sub-intervals: [-0.19489, -0.09), [-0.09, -0.08), [-0.08, -0.07),…, [0.08, 0.09), [0.09, 0.10+077) denoted by $\{\theta_1, \theta_2, ..., \theta_{20}\}$. For each interval θ_j, $j\in\{1,2,\ldots,20\}$ and for each stock S_i, $i\in\{1,2,\ldots,29)$ the expected return $\overline{x}_{ij}$ and relative frequency ρ_{ij} are calculated. Bernoulli's LLN theorem allows using ρ_{ij} as an estimation of p_{ij}. Thus, the probability distribution of each sample stock is obtained. Using equations (1), (2) and (3) entropy, the expected utility and EU-E measure of risk for selecting each stock S_i, $i\in\{1,2,\ldots,29\}$ when the value of λ varies from 0 to 1 are calculated. Stocks are ranked in ascending order according to the obtained risk measures of selecting each stock for different values of λ. The results are shown in Table 4. The results for the Croatian and Hungarian market are shown in Table 5 and Table 6 respectively.

Table 4. Shares ranking using EU-E risk measure applied on the German market

		S_i														
λ	Q_i	**1**	**2**	**3**	**4**	**5**	**6**	**7**	**8**	**9**	**10**	**11**	**12**	**13**	**14**	**15**
0		9	8	20	25	18	7	23	24	22	29	4	3	19	14	6
0.05		9	8	20	25	18	7	23	24	22	29	4	3	19	13	6
0.1		9	8	20	25	18	7	23	24	22	29	4	3	19	13	6
0.15	**1**	9	8	20	25	18	7	23	24	22	29	3	4	19	12	6
0.2		9	8	20	25	18	7	23	24	22	29	3	4	19	12	6
0.25		10	8	20	24	18	6	23	25	22	29	3	4	19	12	7
0.3		10	8	20	24	18	6	23	26	22	29	3	4	19	12	7
0.35		10	7	20	25	18	6	23	26	22	29	3	5	19	12	8
0.4		10	7	20	25	18	6	23	26	21	29	3	5	19	12	8
0.45		10	7	20	25	18	5	23	26	21	29	3	6	19	12	9
0.5		11	6	20	25	18	5	23	26	21	29	2	7	19	12	9
0.55	**2**	11	6	20	25	17	5	23	26	21	29	2	8	19	12	9
0.6		11	6	20	25	16	4	23	26	21	29	2	9	19	12	8
0.65		12	5	20	25	16	4	23	27	21	29	2	11	18	10	9
0.7		11	5	19	25	16	2	24	27	20	29	4	12	17	9	10
0.75	**3**	12	5	18	25	15	2	24	27	19	29	4	13	17	7	10
0.8	**4**	12	3	19	25	13	1	24	27	18	29	5	17	16	7	10
0.85	**5**	14	3	18	24	10	1	23	27	17	29	6	20	16	5	12
0.9		16	3	12	23	9	1	21	28	11	29	6	24	13	4	15
0.95	**6**	18	4	12	20	9	1	19	28	11	29	8	25	13	3	15
1		20	4	10	17	8	1	18	26	7	29	13	27	12	3	19
		S_i														
λ	Q_i	**16**	**17**	**18**	**19**	**20**	**21**	**22**	**23**	**24**	**25**	**26**	**27**	**28**	**29**	
0		21	28	26	16	12	15	10	2	11	17	27	13	5	1	
0.05		21	28	26	16	12	15	10	2	11	17	27	14	5	1	
0.1		21	28	26	16	12	15	10	2	11	17	27	14	5	1	
0.15	**1**	21	28	26	16	13	15	10	2	11	17	27	14	5	1	
0.2		21	28	26	16	13	15	10	2	11	17	27	14	5	1	
0.25		21	28	26	16	13	15	9	2	11	17	27	14	5	1	
0.3		21	28	25	16	13	15	9	2	11	17	27	14	5	1	
0.35		21	28	24	16	13	15	9	2	11	17	27	14	4	1	

continued on following page

Table 4. Continued

0.4	2	22	28	24	14	15	13	9	2	11	17	27	16	4	1	
0.45		22	28	24	13	15	14	8	2	11	17	27	16	4	1	
0.5		22	28	24	13	17	14	8	3	10	16	27	15	4	1	
0.55		22	27	24	13	18	14	7	4	10	15	28	16	3	1	
0.6		22	27	24	13	18	14	7	5	10	15	28	17	3	1	
0.65		22	26	24	13	19	14	6	7	8	15	28	17	3	1	
0.7		22	26	23	13	21	14	6	7	8	15	28	18	3	1	
0.75	**3**	22	26	23	11	21	16	6	9	8	14	28	20	3	1	
0.8	**4**	21	26	23	9	22	15	2	11	8	14	28	20	4	6	
0.85	**5**	19	26	22	8	25	13	2	15	7	11	28	21	4	9	
0.9	**6**	19	25	20	7	26	14	2	17	8	10	27	22	5	18	
0.95		16	23	17	6	26	14	2	21	7	10	27	22	5	24	
1		16	21	15	5	25	14	2	23	9	11	24	22	6	28	

Source: (Authors' calculation, 2019)

Table 5. Shares ranking using EU-E risk measure applied on the Croatian market

		S_i																	
λ	Q_i	**1**	**2**	**3**	**4**	**5**	**6**	**7**	**8**	**9**	**10**	**11**	**12**	**13**	**14**	**15**	**16**	**17**	**18**
0	**1**	2	8	13	1	9	18	17	11	7	10	12	14	3	15	6	4	16	5
0.05		2	8	13	1	9	18	17	10	6	11	12	14	3	16	7	4	15	5
0.1	**2**	2	7	13	1	10	18	17	9	5	11	12	14	3	16	6	4	15	8
0.15		2	6	13	1	10	18	17	9	5	11	12	14	3	16	7	4	15	8
0.2		2	6	13	1	11	18	17	9	5	12	10	14	3	16	7	4	15	8
0.25		2	6	13	1	11	18	17	9	4	12	10	14	3	16	7	5	15	8
0.3		1	6	11	2	12	18	17	9	4	14	10	13	3	16	7	5	15	8
0.35		1	6	11	2	13	18	17	9	4	14	10	12	3	16	7	5	15	8
0.4		1	6	11	2	13	18	17	9	3	14	10	12	4	16	7	5	15	8
0.45		1	6	11	2	13	18	17	8	3	14	10	12	4	16	7	5	15	9
0.5	**3**	1	5	11	2	13	18	17	8	3	14	9	12	4	16	7	6	15	10
0.55		1	5	11	3	13	18	17	8	2	14	9	12	4	16	7	6	15	10
0.6		2	4	10	3	13	18	17	8	1	14	9	11	5	16	7	6	15	12
0.65		2	4	10	3	13	18	17	8	1	14	9	11	5	16	7	6	15	12
0.7		2	4	11	3	13	18	17	8	1	14	9	10	6	16	7	5	15	12
0.75		2	3	11	4	13	18	17	9	1	14	8	10	6	16	7	5	15	12
0.8		3	2	11	4	13	18	17	9	1	14	8	10	6	16	7	5	15	12
0.85	**4**	3	2	10	4	13	18	17	11	1	14	7	9	6	16	8	5	15	12
0.9	**5**	3	2	8	5	13	18	17	11	1	14	6	7	9	16	10	4	15	12
0.95	**6**	3	2	7	8	13	18	17	9	1	15	6	4	11	16	10	5	14	12
1		5	2	6	9	14	18	16	8	1	17	4	3	11	15	10	7	13	12

Source: (Authors' calculation 2019)

Table 6. Shares ranking using EU-E risk measure applied on the Hungarian market

		S_i											
λ	Q_i	**1**	**2**	**3**	**4**	**5**	**6**	**7**	**8**	**9**	**10**	**11**	**12**
0		7	5	3	12	9	1	10	11	2	6	4	8
0.05		7	5	3	12	9	1	10	11	2	6	4	8
0.1		7	5	3	12	9	1	10	11	2	6	4	8
0.15	**1**	7	5	3	12	9	1	10	11	2	6	4	8
0.2		7	5	3	12	9	1	10	11	2	6	4	8
0.25		7	5	3	12	9	1	10	11	2	6	4	8
0.3		7	5	3	12	9	1	10	11	2	6	4	8
0.35		7	5	3	12	9	1	10	11	2	6	4	8
0.4		6	5	3	12	9	1	10	11	2	7	4	8
0.45		6	5	3	12	8	1	10	11	2	7	4	9
0.5		6	5	3	12	8	1	10	11	2	7	4	9
0.55	**2**	6	5	3	12	8	1	10	11	2	7	4	9
0.6		5	6	4	12	8	1	10	11	2	7	3	9
0.65		5	6	4	12	8	1	10	11	2	7	3	9
0.7		5	6	4	12	8	1	10	11	2	7	3	9
0.75		4	8	5	12	6	1	11	10	2	7	3	9
0.8	**3**	3	9	5	12	6	1	11	8	2	7	4	10
0.85		3	10	6	12	5	1	11	7	2	8	4	9
0.9	**4**	3	11	7	12	6	1	10	4	2	8	5	9
0.95		2	12	8	11	4	1	9	3	6	7	5	10
1	**5**	1	10	9	4	3	11	7	2	12	6	5	8

Source: (Authors' calculation, 2019)

Furthermore, for different values of λ, fourteen stocks with the lowest EU-E risk are selected and the subsets of the initial set consisting of these stocks are formed. It can be seen from Table 4 that for λ=0, λ=0.05,…, λ=0.35 the subsets are formed of the same stocks. Therefore, for λ∈[0, 0.035] one subset is observed and denoted by

$$Q_1 = \{S_1, S_2, S_6, S_{11}, S_{12}, S_{14}, S_{15}, S_{20}, S_{22}, S_{22}, S_{24}, S_{27}, S_{28}, S_{29}\}.$$

Subsets Q_2, Q_3, Q_4, Q_5, Q_6 are defined in the same way.

First, the EU-E decision model is used to select stocks and then Markowitz's mean-variance model is used to construct an efficient frontier. The efficient frontier consists of a set of all efficient portfolios. In the mean-variance model, every portfolio is described with two criteria: expected return and standard deviation as a measure of risk. Efficient portfolio is a portfolio which has the highest expected return for a given level of risk or the lowest risk for a given level of expected return.

For each subset of stocks $Q_1, Q_2, Q_3, Q_4, Q_5, Q_6$, an efficient frontier that consists of efficient portfolios is plotted and each frontier is compared with the efficient frontier of the initial set *S*. The graphs

Figure 2. The results of comparison of efficient frontiers on the German market. Source: (Authors' calculation, 2019)

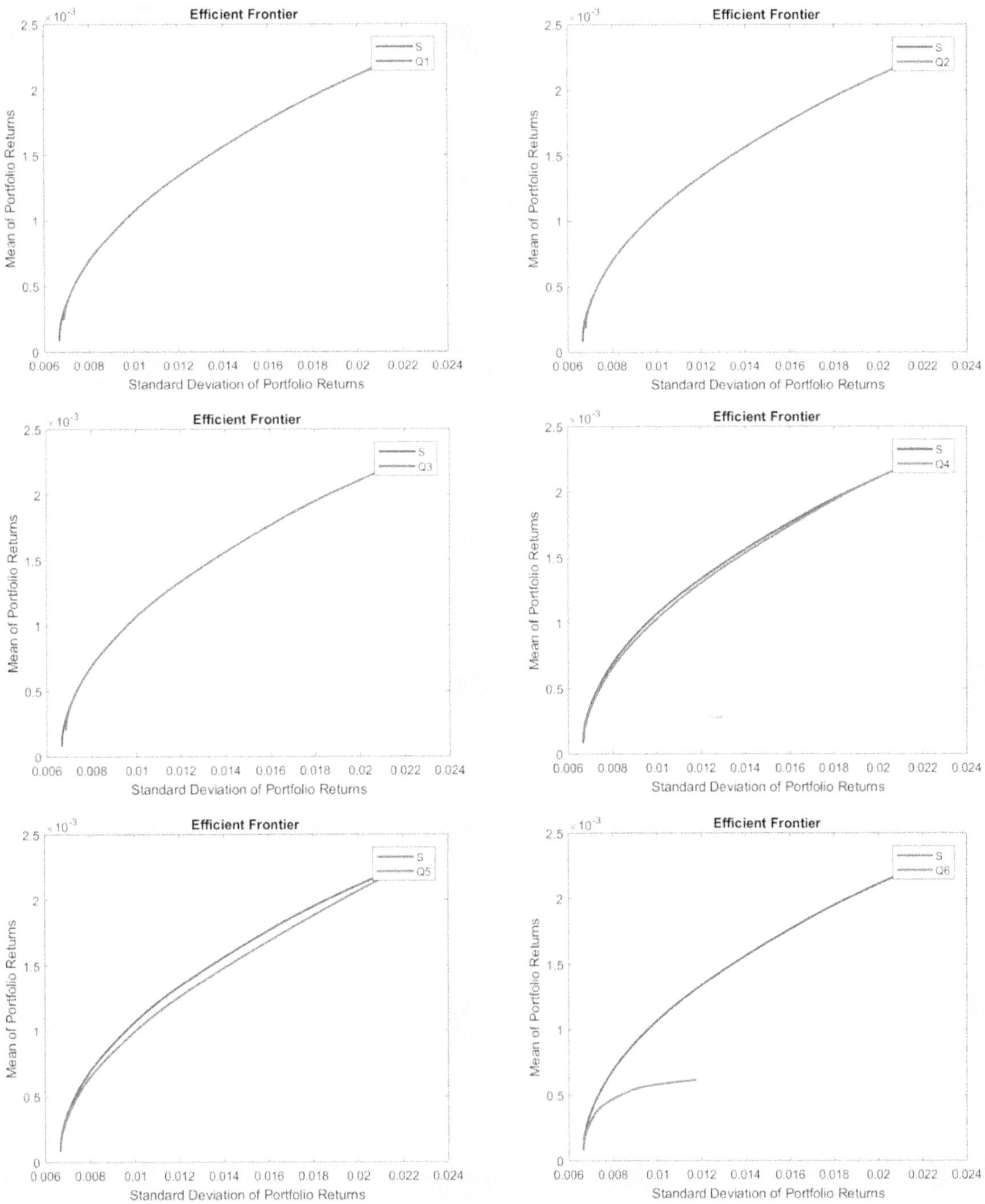

used for comparison are shown in Figure 2. Each graph shows the efficient frontier of portfolios composed of stocks from the corresponding subsets Q_i, $i\in\{1\ldots6\}$ denoted with a red line and the efficient frontier of portfolios composed of stocks from the initial set *S*denoted with a blue line. Comparing the results presented in these six graphs, it can be seen that the efficient frontier of portfolios composed of

Figure 3. The results of comparison of efficient frontiers on the Croatian market. Source: (Authors' calculation, 2019)

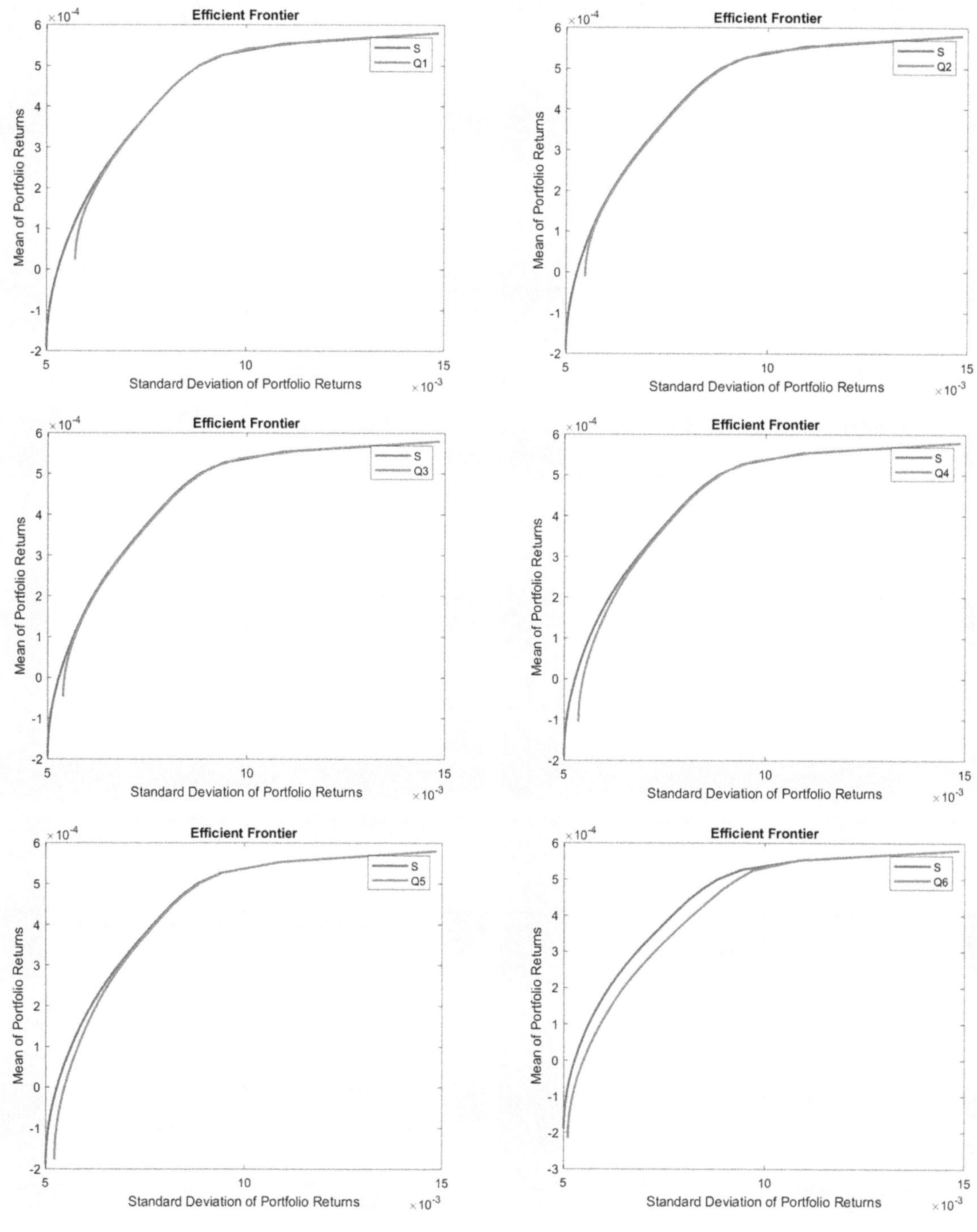

Figure 4. The results of comparison of efficient frontiers on the Hungarian market. Source: (Authors' calculation, 2019)

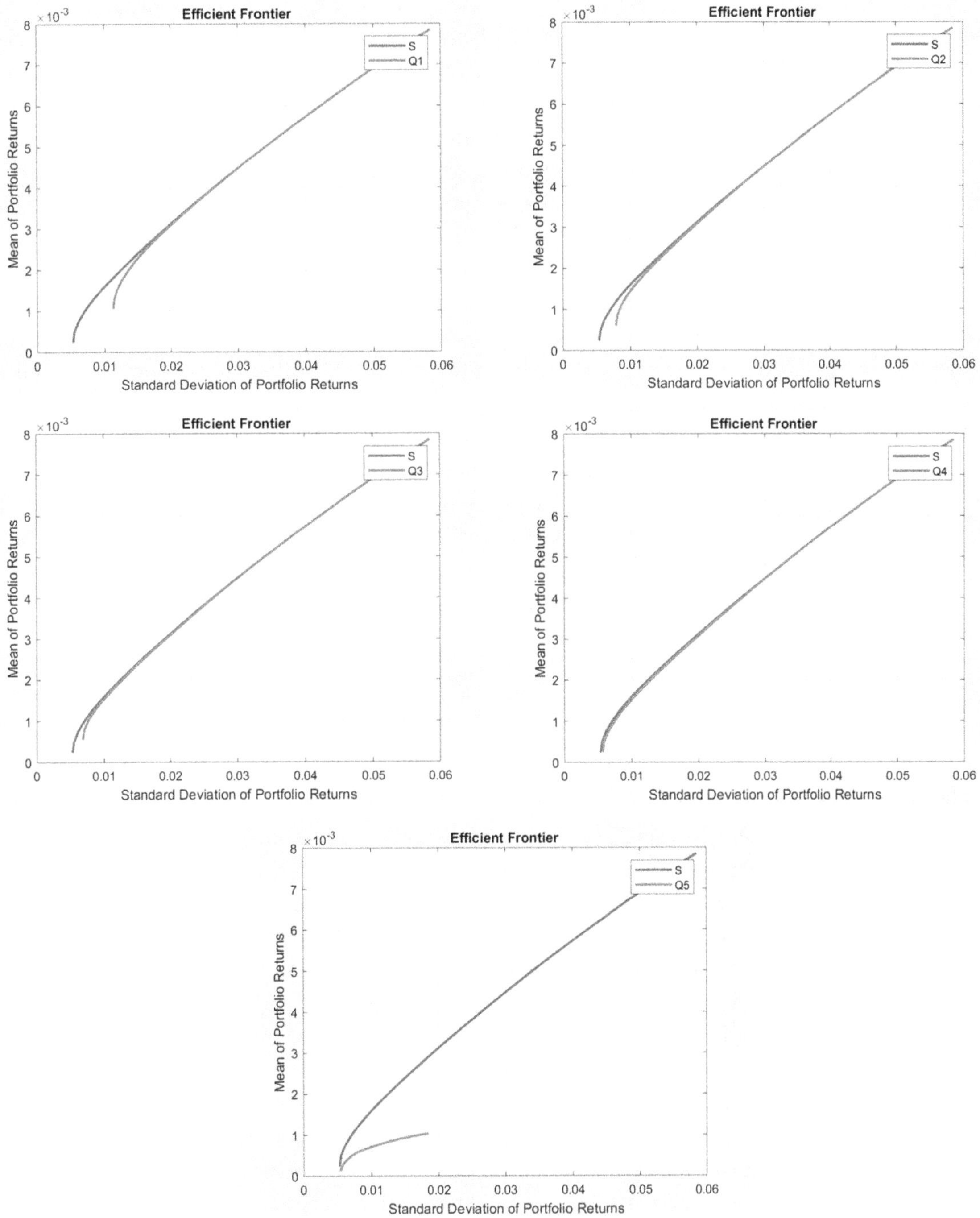

stocks from set Q_2 performs best according to the sample of all stocks. For fixed risk, the expected return of efficient portfolios composed using set Q_2 is nearly the same as expected return of efficient portfolios composed using the initial set. This result suggests that the set Q_2 for $\lambda \in [0.4, 0.7]$ is as an appropriate approximation of the initial set S, meaning the number of stocks can be reduced without major changes in the relation between risk and expected return. The remaining sets are not as good approximation as the aforementioned set for the following reasons. In the case of sets Q_1 and Q_3, the efficient frontier is shorter than the efficient frontier of set Q_2 and particularly shorter than the efficient frontier of the initial set S. This means that the interval of expected return in which the efficient frontier of the specified sets does not extend, while the effective frontier of the initial set is defined, is greater than the one in the case of set Q_2. The difference in the stated intervals is especially notable in the case of set Q_6. This means that for a given rate of expected return at these intervals there is an efficient portfolio of the initial set but it is not possible to construct an efficient portfolio consisting of shares contained in reduced sets. On the other hand, in the case of sets Q_4 and Q_5, the previously observed interval is shorter than in the case of the prominent set Q_2, but these sets are not a good enough approximation as set Q_2 because efficient frontiers of these sets, in a large area, do not match the efficient frontier of the initial set S. This means there is a large number of values of the expected return for which efficient portfolios of reduced sets have a greater risk than the efficient portfolio of the initial set, while in the case of set Q_2 this difference is lower or does not exist.

The process of obtaining the results for the remaining two markets is analogous to the procedure described above. The results obtained are shown in Figure 3 and Figure 4. In the case of Croatian market, the best set for approximation is the set Q_3 for $\lambda \in [0.5, 0.8]$. Whereas in the case of the Hungarian market, the best approximation is obtained for the combination of stocks contained in set Q_4 for $\lambda \in [0.9, 0.95]$.

For all three types of markets, the values of λ corresponding to the sets selected as suitable for approximation are closer to 1 than to 0, thus emphasizing entropy as a variable with a greater proportion in the calculation of risk than the expected utility.

CONCLUSION

In this chapter, the authors presented the application of the EU-E decision model for stock selection on the differently developed EU capital markets. This model has been proven useful in stock selection on all observed capital markets, where the subset made up of 50% of stock included in the initial set which has almost the same efficient frontier as the initial set. The main aim of the chapter was to test whether the EU-E model applied to the three differently developed capital markets gives the best stock selection results for the same trade-off coefficient values or whether the trade-off coefficient depends on the capital market development.

The results have shown that the value λ, which offers the best choice of stocks, varies in different capital markets. The EU-E model, which offers the best choice of stocks in the Hungarian stock market, has the highest trade-off coefficient $\lambda \in [0.9, 0.95]$. In the case of the Croatian market, the best results are for $\lambda \in [0.5, 0.8]$ and in the case of the German market the best results are for $\lambda \in [0.4, 0.7]$.

It can be concluded that for all three types of markets, the values of the λ corresponding to the sets selected as suitable for approximation are closer to 1 than to 0, thus emphasizing entropy as a variable with a greater weight in the calculation of risk than the expected utility. It was expected that λ grows as the development of the market gets lower and because the dispersion of incomes is higher in such markets. However, λ for the Hungarian market is much higher than for the Croatian market, which can be explained by the fact that the stock risk in the Hungarian market, during the observed period, was much higher. Therefore, it is important to include entropy as a risk measurement into this model with a higher trade-off coefficient.

This research, once again, confirms the results obtained in previous scientific papers on similar topics, showing that the EU-E model is very useful in the process of selecting an investment portfolio. Furthermore, this research has shown that entropy is a very important part of the EU-E model, which can be concluded from the entropy weight in the model with the best results. However, based on this research, it cannot be concluded that the expected utility and entropy ratio in the model depends on the development of the capital market. In future research, the authors suggest that a comparison of the results obtained by the EU-E decision model in equally developed capital markets is done.

REFERENCES

Anagnostopoulos, K., & Mamanis, G. (2010). A portfolio optimization model with three objectives and discrete variables. *Computers & Operations Research, 37*(7), 1285–1297. doi:10.1016/j.cor.2009.09.009

Aouni, B., Doumpos, M., Pérez Gladish, B., & Steuer, R. E. (2018). On the increasing importance of multiple criteria decision aid methods for portfolio selection. *The Journal of the Operational Research Society, 69*(5), 1–18. doi:10.1080/01605682.2018.1475118

Borse Frankfurt - historical data of stock trading. (n.d.). Retrieved February 17, 2019, from www.boerse-frankfurt.de

Budapest Stock Exchange - historical data of stock trading. (n.d.). Retrieved February 17, 2019, from www.bse.hu

Clausius, R. (1870). On a mechanical theorem applicable to heat. *The London, Edinburgh and Dublin Philosophical Magazine and Journal of Science, 40*(265), 122–127. doi:10.1080/14786447008640370

Deeva, G. (2017). Comparing entropy and beta as measures of risk in asset pricing. *Acta Universitatis Agriculturae et Silviculturae Mendelianae Brunensis, 65*(6), 1889–1894. doi:10.11118/actaun201765061889

Kahneman, D., & Tversky, A. (1979). Prospect Theory: An Analysis of Decision under Risk. *Econometrica, 47*(2), 263–291. doi:10.2307/1914185

Marasović, B. (2016). Model za rebalans portfelja s uključenim transakcijskim troškovima i donjom polu-apsolutnom devijacijom kao mjerom rizika. *Ekonomska Misao i Praksa, 2*, 515–534.

Marasović, B., & Babić, Z. (2011). Two-step multi-criteria model for selecting optimal portfolio. *International Journal of Production Economics, 134*(1), 58–66. doi:10.1016/j.ijpe.2011.04.026

Marasović, B., & Kalinić, T. (2019). Is the expected utility- entropy decision model for stock selection applicable on emerging capital markets? *Economic and Social Development: Book of Proceedings, 39*, 225–235.

Markowitz, H. M. (1952). Portfolio selection. *The Journal of Finance, 7*, 77–91.

Ormos, M., & Zibriczky, D. (2014). Entropy-Based Financial Asset Pricing. *PLoS One, 9*(12), 1–21. doi:10.1371/journal.pone.0115742 PMID:25545668

Philippatos, G. C., & Gressis, N. (1975). Conditions of Equivalence Among E-V, SSD and E-H Portfolio Selection Criteria: The Case for Uniform, Normal and Lognormal Distributions. *Management Science*, *21*(6), 617–625. doi:10.1287/mnsc.21.6.617

Philippatos, G. C., & Wilson, C. J. (1972). Entropy, market risk, and the selection of efficient portfolios. *Applied Economics*, *4*(3), 209–220. doi:10.1080/00036847200000017

Pinho, C., & Melo, A. (2018). Composition of an Optimal Portfolio in the Capital market – Elton & Gruber Model in Portugal's Capital Market. *Account and Financial Management Journal*, *3*(8), 1678–1685. doi:10.31142/afmj/v3i8.03

Righi, M., & Borenstein, D. (2018). A simulation comparison of risk measures for portfolio optimization. *Finance Research Letters*, *24*, 105–112. doi:10.1016/j.frl.2017.07.013

Russell, F. T. S. E. (2018, March). *FTSE Country Classification Process*. Retrieved February 17, 2019, from https://research.ftserussell.com/products/downloads/FTSE_Country_Classification_Paper.pdf

Russell, F. T. S. E. (2019, September). *FTSE Classification of Equity Markets*. Retrieved December 10, 2019, from https://research.ftserussell.com/products/downloads/FTSE-Country-Classification-Update-2019.pdf

Shannon, C. (1948). A Mathematical Theory of Communication. *The Bell System Technical Journal*, *27*(3), 379–423. doi:10.1002/j.1538-7305.1948.tb01338.x

Starmer, C. (2000). Developments in Non-Expected Utility Theory: The Hunt for a Descriptive Theory of Choice under Risk. *Journal of Economic Literature*, *38*(2), 32–382. doi:10.1257/jel.38.2.332

Usta, I., & Kantar, Y. M. (2011). Mean-Variance-Skewness-Entropy Measures: A Multi-Objective Approach for Portfolio Selection. *Entropy (Basel, Switzerland)*, *13*(1), 117–133. doi:10.3390/e13010117

Warren, G. (2019). Choosing and Using Utility Functions in Forming Portfolios. *Financial Analysts Journal*, *75*(3), 39–69. doi:10.1080/0015198X.2019.1618109

Yang, J., Feng, Y., & Qiu, W. (2017). Stock Selection for Portfolios using Expected Utility-Entropy Decision Model. *Entropy (Basel, Switzerland)*, *19*(10), 508. doi:10.3390/e19100508

Yang, J., & Qiu, W. (2005). A measure of risk and a decision-making model based on expected utility and entropy. *European Journal of Operational Research*, *163*(3), 792–799. doi:10.1016/j.ejor.2004.01.031

Yang, J., & Qiu, W. (2014). Normalized expected utility-entropy measure of risk. *Entropy (Basel, Switzerland)*, *16*(7), 3590–3604. doi:10.3390/e16073590

Yang, J., Zhang, L., & Chen, X. (2010). Normalized expected utility-entropy investment decision model and its application in stock selection. In *Proceedings of the IEEE International Conference on Progress in Informatics and Computing*, (pp. 220–224). Shanghai, China: IEEE. 10.1109/PIC.2010.5687461

Zagreb stock exchange - historical data of stock trading. (n.d.). Retrieved February 17, 2019, from https://www.zse.hr/

Zopounidis, C., & Doumpos, M. (2002). Multi-criteria decision aid in ðnancial decision making: Methodologies and literature review. *Journal of Multi-Criteria Decision Analysis, 11*(4-5), 167–186. doi:10.1002/mcda.333

KEY TERMS AND DEFINITIONS

Efficient Frontier: A set of all efficient portfolios.

Efficient Portfolio: A portfolio that provides the highest expected return for a given level of risk or, equivalently, the lowest risk for a given expected return.

Entropy: Entropy is a measure of randomness. Entropy is used to help model and represent the degree of uncertainty of a random variable. It is used by financial analysts to determine the chances of a specific type of behaviour by a security or market.

Markowitz, H. M.: Harry Max Markowitz (born August 24, 1927) is an American economist, and a recipient of the 1989 John von Neumann Theory Prize and the 1990 Nobel Memorial Prize in Economic Sciences. He is best known for his pioneering work in modern portfolio theory, studying the effects of asset risk, return, correlation and diversification on probable investment portfolio returns.

Portfolio: A set of assets that can hold stocks, bonds, cash and other financial or not financial assets.

Portfolio Selection: A collection of risky assets combined with different weights to provide an acceptable trade-off between return and risk to an investor.

Stock Selection: An active portfolio management technique that focuses on advantageous selection of particular stock rather than on broad asset allocation choices.

Chapter 2
Evaluating the Efficiency of Portfolio-Hedging Strategies by Incorporating Third Degree Stochastic Dominance Criteria and Data Envelopment Analysis

Margareta Gardijan Kedžo
https://orcid.org/0000-0001-5390-057X
Faculty of Economics and Business, University of Zagreb, Croatia

ABSTRACT

The chapter investigates chosen hedging strategies with options as useful risk hedging instruments. Assuming that average investor prefers greater return, is risk-averse, and prefers greater positive skewness, the performance of different hedged and unhedged portfolios is evaluated using stochastic dominance (SD) criteria and data envelopment analysis (DEA). The SD is examined up to the third degree (TSD) using Davidson-Duclos (DD) test. In the DEA, a super efficiency BCC model is used. It is investigated how these two methodologies can be combined and how the TSD criteria can be integrated into DEA in order to simplify the analysis of determining efficient hedging strategies with options.

INTRODUCTION

Portfolio risk management is becoming more important and challenging than ever before. The field of risk management has evolved into a sophisticated and demanding process that requires significant quantitative knowledge and tools, as well as the integration of all new and existing scientific findings. Significant challenges in portfolio management arise when portfolios contain some type of financial derivatives. Derivatives are most commonly used for risk management, but they create an asymmetric return distribution and further complicate portfolio management. The groundbreaking portfolio selection methodology proposed by Markowitz (1952) and Tobin (1958) is based on a comparison of the mean

DOI: 10.4018/978-1-7998-5083-0.ch002

and variance of the portfolio returns. As such, it is applicable only in cases where all return distributions are symmetric two-parameter distributions that can be described with the first two moments (such as the normal distribution), or when the investor's utility function is a quadratic function that describes the investor's utility using the first two moments of the distributions considered. Even though it is a great textbook example, this approach has many limitations (see, for example, Fabozzi et. al. (2012)). Portfolio management research should take into account that, in most cases, investors' utility functions are not known, and that portfolio return distributions must be described with more than just the first two moments. In this chapter, portfolio strategies are analyzed in terms of their efficiency. The starting point in this approach is to describe the investors' preferences which define the efficiency of the strategy. If a particular portfolio strategy generates portfolio returns which are never worse than those generated by other strategies for a group of investors with equal preferences, such strategy is considered efficient. All strategies that generate portfolios that are not bettered by any others constitute a set of efficient strategies.

One approach that allows evaluating the efficiency of investment alternatives using multiple criteria is Data Envelopment Analysis (DEA). This mathematical programming method evaluates the relative efficiency of the estimated units based on their inputs and outputs. The basic assumption in DEA is that inputs have to be minimized and outputs have to be maximized. The variables that define an investor's utility can be used as inputs and outputs, and the application of this methodology makes it possible to evaluate the relative efficiency of a set of portfolio strategies.

Another method that allows efficiency analysis is stochastic dominance (SD). It is particularly useful in cases where only certain assumptions about the decision maker's preferences and their utility functions are known. By comparing the return distributions of mutually exclusive portfolio strategies using the SD criteria, it possible to identify those strategies that never have smaller utility than the alternatives for all investors with the same preferences. In this way, the SD can be applied for the comparison of the return distributions generated by portfolio strategies and, if possible, used to identify those strategies that are efficient for all decision makers whose utility functions share the same general characteristics.

Thus, in this chapter, DEA and SD are used as tools for distinguishing efficient from inefficient portfolio strategies. Moreover, an integration of these two approaches is proposed. This integration aims at overcoming the deficiencies of each method and leads to the simplification of the analysis.

Against this background, this chapter uses the SD and DEA for examining the efficiency of equity portfolios with derivatives. The methods are used on a sample of returns generated by hedging strategies with options which are characterized by asymmetric distributions. The reason for analyzing hedging strategies with options is that options are the most efficient tools in the financial arsenal for successfully managing the risk and volatility that characterize today's financial markets (Lehman & McMillan, 2011). Simplified analysis of strategies with options (see for example Aljinović, Marasović & Šego (2011)) always shows strategies as suitable tools for equity portfolio hedging. However, the textbook strategies are not always simple nor always feasible in practice, so options are justifiably considered risky instruments. Therefore, the first objective of the chapter is to demonstrate the alternative approach to the efficiency analysis of portfolio strategies. The second objective is to reach conclusions on the efficiency of portfolio hedging strategies with options by using suitable approaches and more realistic market constraints.

This introduction has given a brief explanation of the research problem, its aims and the methodology. The second section provides an extensive literature overview of similar research. The third section further discusses the methodology, and the empirical findings can be found in the fourth section. This chapter ends with recommendations for future research and the overall conclusion of the research.

BACKGROUND

Data envelopment analysis is a powerful tool for solving different multi-criteria decision-making problems and is often used in the field of finance. Among other things, it is used for evaluating the efficiency of investment alternatives. Powers & McMullen (2002) were among the first to apply the Charnes, Cooper, Rhodes (CCR) model as a method for assessing stock performance in the US market. Following their methodology, Lopes et al (2008) investigated a multi-period investment strategy based on investing in DEA-efficient stocks in equal shares. Joro & Na (2006) discussed a portfolio performance indicator based on the mean-variance-skewness framework by utilizing DEA, but to the best of the authors' knowledge, no research extended this framework. These investigations were followed with many other innovative applications of DEA models used for trading on different markets, such as those by Edirisinghe & Zhang (2007, 2010), Patari, Leivo & Honkapuro (2012), Lim, Oh & Zhu (2014), Gardijan & Kojić (2012), Škrinjarić (2014), Gardijan & Škrinjarić (2015). One of the first papers that emphasized the necessity of portfolio diversification in DEA framework was by Branda (2013), who proposed diversification-consistent DEA tests which take into account dependencies between the returns of individual assets in a portfolio. Branda (2016) examines DEA models that are also suitable for negative data with the potential for diversification. Given the growing interest in DEA as a tool for efficiency analysis in the area of investment, many future contributions can be expected in this area. Apart from some results, which are presented in more detail in the author's doctoral thesis (Gardijan, 2016), DEA has not been explored in the analysis of options strategies in general, nor in hedging strategies applying options.

The application and significant development of SD theory in the field of finance began with four key papers:

- Hadar & Russell (1969) introduced criteria and proofs for SD,
- Hanoch & Levy (1969) further examined the appropriateness of using the mean and variance as necessary and sufficient criteria for determining the efficiency of risky investments,
- Rothschild & Stiglitz (1970) dealt with the definition of risk, and proposed an SD rule consistent with the concept of expected utility with the intuitive and theoretical understanding of risk, and
- Whitmore (1970) defined the third degree stochastic dominance (TSD).

Since then, significant progress has been made in the development of SD theory, algorithms and necessary conditions that improve the SD calculations. An overview of significant research in the field of SD published up to 1982 is given in Bawa (1982). Guo (2012) provides a literature review of SD rules, tests and their application in risk and portfolio management over the last 40 years.

The comparison of the mean-risk models and the SD criteria in portfolio selection intrigued scientists from the very beginning. There are several papers on this topic that make observations on the theoretical level, such as Bawa (1975), Aharony & Loeb (1977), Gandhi & Saunders (1981), and Ogryczak & Ruszczynski (1999). Empirical applications of the SD have been published in, for example, Burr Porter & Gaumnitz (1972) and Abid, Mroua & Wong (2014) who compared international and domestic diversified portfolios based on the mean-variance (MV) and SD criteria, and in De Giorgi (2005) who performs the portfolio selection model using measures consistent to the second degree stochastic dominance (SSD). In her doctoral thesis, Javanmardi (2013) explores the problem of portfolio selection by applying the SSD for all investors with an aversion to risk. Trifunovic (2005) applies the SD criteria to bond returns and market index data. Lončar & Tepavac (2012) published a professional paper in which they apply the TSD algorithm for equity portfolio selection that helps them to identify 2.8% of shares as efficient.

Efficiency analysis of different portfolio hedging strategies using SD can be found in many papers. For example, Zagst & Kraus (2011) compare an Option Based Portfolio Insurance strategy (OBPI) and a Constant Proportion Portfolio Insurance (CPPI) strategy, while Harrison (1998) examines hedging strategies with futures and options. Abid, Mroua & Wong (2007) analyze single-share portfolio hedging with simple options hedging strategies on the French market using SD criteria and indicators based on the CAPM. Annaert, Van Osselaer & Verstraete (2008) evaluate the performance of OBPI strategy, stop-loss and synthetic put strategy on the US, UK, Japan, Australian and Canadian markets over 30 years and could not determine dominance between hedged and unhedged portfolios. Abid, Mroua & Wong (2007) conclude that hedging strategies, in particular the protective put and the covered call strategy, have better performance than the uncovered stock portfolio and that the in-the-money (ITM) protective put is better than the out-of-the-money (OTM) covered call strategy.

Comparisons of models based on DEA and SD have been examined, for example, by Branda and Kopa (2012, 2014) and Wu & Olson (2008). Branda & Kopa (2012) examine the efficiency of market indices using SD, DEA and mean-variance (MV) criteria, from which they reach different results. Their robustness tests show that Value at Risk (VaR) as a variable has a significant influence in DEA efficiency rating, while in Branda & Kopa (2014) they find that the results of convex SSD-efficiency and the DEA efficiency with the Conditional VaR (CVaR) are the same.

The majority of the papers investigating hedging strategies with options focus on two basic strategies: covered call and protective put. There are several papers which assess covered call in terms of variance alone, such as Bookbinder (1976), Kassouf (1977), Pounds (1978), Grube & Panton (1978), or Yates & Kopprasch (1980) (originally from Lhabitant 2000). They conclude that covered call achieves a higher return and a smaller variance. Bookstaber & Clarke (1984) also conclude that covered call dominates over protective put. Merton, Scholes & Gladstein (1978, 1982) reach the opposite conclusion regarding the covered call strategy. Booth, Tehranian & Trennepohl (1985), Clarke (1987), and Brooks, Levy & Yoder (1987) apply the SD criteria for this problem. Booth, Tehranian & Trennepohl (1985) find the covered call strategy is dominant, based on option price data simulated using the Black and Scholes (BS) formula and holding all positions to maturity between 1963 and 1978. Brooks, Levy & Yoder (1987) do not find evidence of SD up to the third degree for a covered call strategy.

A significant drawback of the research referenced here is that the SD is computed without any statistical tests. By comparing the Sharpe ratio of a covered call, protective put and long stock portfolios with simulated stock and option prices, Lhabitant (2000) finds that protective put is dominated by a long stock and that the MV-dominant strategy is a slightly OTM covered call. He also concludes that options strategies produce systematic biases when evaluated using traditional portfolio performance measures. Dash & Goel (2014) find that the efficiency of a protective put and a covered call as hedging strategies depends on the distribution characteristics of the observed stocks. Castellano & Giacometti (2001) propose comparing covered call and protective put using the GARCH methodology. Bollen (1999), in turn, proposes a Monte Carlo approach that simulates the effect of options strategies in different scenarios. Trennepohl & Dukes (1981) simulate portfolios with long stock and long or short call options of different maturity and conclude that covered call portfolios have smaller variance, improved return and reduced skewness than the buy-and-hold (long stock) strategy and that the superior strategies include OTM options. Isakov and Morard (2001) show that their diversified portfolio hedged with short OTM options is better than the unhedged portfolio and the equally weighted portfolios in terms of the

SD and Treynor ratio with a modified beta coefficient. Hemler & Miller (2015) evaluate covered call, protective put, collar and covered combination using Sharpe, Jensen, Treynor and Sortino ratios and conclude that these portfolios achieve better performance, particularly covered combination and covered call. Finally, Szado & Schneeweis (2012) examine different versions of rolling collar strategy including bid-ask spread by comparing their returns, variances and indices which they defined, and conclude that collar strategy allows risk management, reduces volatility and drawdowns for most underlying assets, and in some cases even increases returns.

Based on the literature overview, both DEA and SD have significant application in portfolio hedging and management. However, there is still a significant vacant space that needs to be filled by considering more hedging strategies, including more real-world constraints, and also using more appropriate methodologies. The need for further research is even more pronounced regarding the integration of DEA and SD in the area of portfolio efficiency, as well as their application in a comprehensive analysis of option hedging strategies.

METHODOLOGY FOR EVALUATING PORTFOLIO HEDGING STRATEGIES

The portfolios are evaluated in terms of their efficiency. Efficiency is a relative property that is assigned to the units under consideration based on specific criteria. Thus, it is crucial to select criteria that are useful in characterizing the efficiency of investments.

Definition of Efficiency of the Investment Alternatives

Efficiency in economic science is generally considered through the relationship between the results achieved and the resources invested. Since not everything is of a productive nature, for which outputs and inputs can be unambiguously identified, efficiency in this research is generally viewed through the relationship of desirable, beneficial properties, whose values should be as large as possible, and undesirable, bad properties whose values should be as small as possible. A unit is considered efficient if it has the same level of desirable properties with fewer undesirable properties, compared to others. Therefore, efficiency is a relative feature that can be attributed to a particular unit based on its comparison with other comparable units with respect to the ratio of desirable and undesirable properties. Efficiency, therefore, is not the cardinal but the ordinal property of the observed unit. The selection of desirable and undesirable properties should stem from the attitudes and the resulting preferences of the decision makers. According to Levy (1973), the efficiency criterion is a rule by which a given set of alternatives (units) can be divided into an efficient and inefficient subset, where for each inefficient alternative there must be a preferred efficient alternative. An efficiency criterion, based on a set of assumptions about the decision makers' preferences, which minimizes the set of efficient options is considered the optimal efficiency criterion (Levy, 1973). The fewer assumptions it applies, the more general it is, but at the same time, it is more useful if it manages to differentiate as few efficient alternatives as possible. With the introduction of new alternatives/ units in the analysis, some efficient units may become inefficient, but inefficient units can't become efficient.

The identification of efficient and inefficient alternatives provides a critical appraisal of the alternatives considered and a basis for decision making. If the decision makers are rational, then they should consider only units that are relatively efficient. Therefore, in determining the efficiency of investment alternatives, it is necessary to use criteria which, based on assumptions about the preferences of the investor as a decision maker, can distinguish investment alternatives that are better than all others. Also, the set of assumptions about investors' preferences should remain as small as possible for the conclusions to have greater application. Based on the assumptions about investors' preferences, we can define efficiency criteria and select models that can rank investment alternatives according to given criteria (based on Wu, Olson, 2008).

Decision Making Under Uncertainty

The most popular definitions of risk, and of a risky and an uncertain situation were given by Knight (1921). Reformulating Knight's definition more precisely, Runde (1998) suggests that, risky situations are those in which a decision maker knows *a priori* or the statistical probabilities of possible outcomes, whereas in uncertain situations it is not possible to determine either *a priori* or the statistical probabilities of outcomes. In real-life situations, including those on the financial markets, the probabilities of outcomes cannot be *a priori* known or statistically estimated, and in those situations decision-makers give subjective estimations of probabilities, thus turning an uncertain situation into a risky situation (Levy, 2016). Therefore, in this paper terms risk and uncertainty are used interchangeably.

Mathematical models aimed at finding the optimal alternative in the presence of uncertainty are based on a set of assumptions about how decision makers make (or should make) their choices. If decision makers are rational, they should choose the efficient alternatives, or, if possible, the optimal one. A model with a small number of assumptions about the preferences of decision makers may fail to provide rational guidance or may not have sufficient strength to differentiate between efficient and inefficient opportunities. On the other hand, using more assumptions creates a stronger and more complicated decision criterion, but also reduces the applicability of the model to a larger group of investors with different preferences.

Suppose all investors are rational and prefer more profitable investments. Let x_{ij} be the return of the i-th investment in the outcome j, and p_{ij} are the corresponding probabilities. In the case where there is only one possible outcome for each alternative such that a set of feasible alternatives $\{(x_i,p_i)\}$ contains pairs $(x_i,1)$, $i\in\{1,\ldots,n\}$, the return on each investment is certain. Any decision maker who prefers more to less will prefer x_k such that $x_k>x_i$, $\forall i\in\{1,\ldots,n\}$. In the case where outcomes are uncertain, applying the criterion of maximum expected return weighted with given probabilities can lead to irrational choices (known as Petrograd paradox). Bernoulli in 1738 and Cramer in 1728 (Cont, 2010, Utility Theory: Historical Perspectives 2) proposed a decision criterion based on maximum expected utility. Specifically, they develop the idea that values of outcomes *per se* are not relevant, but the utility that they bring to the decision maker is. The utility is an indicator of desirability or a degree of satisfaction that decision makers attribute to the possible consequences of decisions and actions and indicates the subjective value that arises from decision makers' preferences (Sikavica et al, 2014). According to the expected utility theory, rational individuals make decisions under uncertainty by maximizing their expected utility, which is a weighted average of the utilities of all outcomes, with the probabilities of their realization as weights. The maximum expected utility criterion assumes that the analytical form of the utility function $U(x)$ is known and can be denoted as

$$\max_i E_i\left[U(x)\right]=\sum_{j=1}^{m}U\left(x_{ij}\right)p\left(x_{ij}\right),\ i\in\{1,\ldots,n\},$$

where index $i\in\{1,\dots,n\}$, $n<\infty$, denotes possible alternatives and $j\in\mathcal{S}=\{1,\dots,m\}$ denotes possible outcomes or states of nature in the following period. It is assumed that $\mathcal{S}$ contains all states of nature that can happen in the future (for example, business cycles or demand levels) and that the set $\mathcal{S}$ is finite ($m<\infty$). Criterion identifies the optimal i-th alternative (investment) whose expected utility is the greatest. Levy (2006) states that the expected utility is the correct criterion for comparing risky alternatives if the preference relation satisfy certain axioms. Experimental studies in behavioral economics have shown that individuals (investors) do not always behave rationally and in accordance with the assumptions of the expected utility theory (Tversky & Kahnemann (1974, 1979); Thaler (1993)). However, expected utility theory is a theoretical framework that allows a formal and analytical approach to the problem of decision making under uncertainty, and as a normative theory it explains how rational individuals should make decisions.

The utility function U has the expected utility property if and only if:

$$U\left(\sum_{i=1}^{n} p_i x_i\right)=\sum_{i=1}^{n} p_i U(x_i).$$

Functions that have the expected utility property (1.2) are called von Neumann-Morgenstern (VNM) functions. If a decision maker's preferences can be expressed by a VNM utility function and if the decision maker chooses the alternative he prefers, then, considering two risky alternatives, he will choose the first risky alternative over the second one if and only if the expected utility of the first risky option is greater (proof in Jehle & Reny (2011)). If the preferences satisfy certain axioms (again, see Jehle & Reny (2011), there must be a continuous, real-valued utility function. Then, if the utility function has the expected utility property, and $f(\bullet)$ is a continuous probability distribution, the expected utility can be expressed as

$$E\big(U(x)\big)=\int_{-\infty}^{+\infty} U(x)f(x)dx,$$

and, if it is continuously differentiable on its domain, $U(x)$ can be written as Taylor series:

$$U(x)=\sum_{n=0}^{N}\frac{U^{(n)}\left[E(x)\right]\cdot\left[x-E(x)\right]^{n}}{n!}+R_{N+1},$$

where $U^{(n)}$ is the n-th derivative of the $U(x)$, and R_{N+1} is the Lagrange remainder (Jurczenko & Maillet, 2006). Even though differentiability is a stronger requirement than continuity, this assumption allows us to use calculus. Under certain assumptions (see Jurczenko and Maillet (2006), from and, it follows:

$$E\big(U(x)\big)\approx\sum_{n=0}^{N}\frac{U^{(n)}\left[E(x)\right]}{n!}\cdot E\left[\left(x-E(x)\right)^{n}\right].$$

Since distribution variance is calculated as $\sigma^2 = E\left\{\left[x - E(x)\right]^2\right\}$, the asymmetry of the distribution is $s^3 = E\left\{\left[x - E(x)\right]^3\right\}$, and the kurtosis is $\kappa^4 = E\left\{\left[x - E(x)\right]^4\right\}$, can be written as

$$E\big(U(x)\big) \approx U\left[E(x)\right] + \frac{U^{(2)}E(x)\sigma^2}{2} + \frac{U^{(3)}E(x)s^3}{3!} + \frac{U^{(4)}E(x)\kappa^4}{4!} + R_5$$

where R_5 is the remainder of the series.

Expression shows expected utility as a function of the moments of the distribution of a risky variable x. It is an important basis for applying the expected utility theory in investment analysis. It is obvious that the expected utility theory, with its axiomatic approach, offers a powerful analytical apparatus. However, it requires the knowledge of the utility function, which is an abstract theoretical idea. Rarely can an individual say what his utility function looks like. Empirical research can estimate utility functions, but in most cases the actual form of the investor's utility function is unknown and only some features of the utility function, derived from preferences, are known. This is why it is necessary to establish portfolio selection criteria based only on available information about preferences and find methodologies that can work with this information.

Stochastic Dominance

Stochastic dominance criteria are selection criteria that can identify efficient alternatives under uncertainty for all decision makers who share the same preferences, or who have utility functions that belong to the same class, without knowing the exact form of the utility functions (Hannoch & Levy, 1969). The flexibility of the approach stems from less rigid assumptions compared to similar methodologies, which makes it applicable to a wide range of problems. The implementation of the SD concept in the field of finance was introduced as early as 1969 (Hadar & Russel (1969), Hanoch & Levy (1969)), but its real-world application started more recently as significant computer development enabled faster computing of SD algorithms. Since 1969, important advances have been made in the theory and application of SD. Citing Zhang (2001), SD theory is now a basic tool used in the field of finance.

Following the expected utility theory (von Neumann & Morgenstern, 1953), several criteria are derived that can identify efficient alternatives which are not dominated by any other option in terms of the expected utility. These alternatives are the optimal choices for all utility functions belonging to the same class. Although the idea of SD and its application was developed within the expected utility theory, SD criteria are not disturbed even when the expected choice theory and value function are introduced, although these two paradigms lead to different final choices (Levy, 2016). The SD approach distinguishes n degrees of dominance, $i \in \{1,\ldots,n\}$, such that SD of degree k also implies the SD of degree $k+1$, $k+2$, $\ldots \leq n$. First degree stochastic dominance (FSD) is the strongest form of domination. It uses the fewest assumptions on decision makers' preferences and implies dominance in all other degrees. Each higher SD degree introduces an additional assumption about the decision makers' preferences, i.e. their utility function, so each additional degree is defined for a more limited class of utility functions. Specifically, the k-th degree SD uses k assumptions about the signs of the first k derivatives of the utility function. Thus, k-degree SD-efficient alternatives are only efficient for utility functions that satisfy these assumptions. Since each higher degree of SD places more constraints on the utility function, the SD of degree k is a stronger form of dominance than the degree of $k+1 \leq n$. Higher degrees of dominance have greater discriminatory power and manage to differentiate more alternatives into an inefficient set, but they are less general. Efficiency analyses under uncertainty most commonly use stochastic dominance criteria of the first degree (FSD), second degree (SSD) and third degree (TSD). If, after applying the TSD criteria, the efficient set is still too large, higher-degree SD criteria may be applied until satisfactory differentiation is obtained. However, the assumptions in each degree of SD must be compatible with the characteristics of the decision makers' utility functions.

In the context of investment analysis, the SD criteria can be used to identify efficient investment options compared to which there are no alternatives that have greater expected utility for a given class of utility functions. The approach also takes into account the whole distribution of the considered risk variable, which is why SD is applicable when the return distributions considered are not normally distributed.

The k-th degree SD criteria can be used to find efficient alternatives for all investors whose preferences toward the first k moments of the distribution of a risk variable (return) are known. These preferences are reflected in the signs of the first k derivatives of their utility functions. This is illustrated by formula . The study of preferences and properties of the utility function was addressed, for example, in Scott & Horvath (1980), who conclude that odd-order derivatives of the utility function should be positive and that those of even-order should be negative, implying a positive preference for higher values of odd-order moments and aversion to higher values of even-order moments. While the assumptions used in the first three degrees of SD criteria have a sound economic basis, for the time being, there is no economic rationale for using the fourth-degree SD rule for the average investor.

Let each risky alternative be described by the distribution of a return X, with values x. For simplicity, the criteria will be presented for continuous distributions which have continuous monotonically increasing distribution functions, but they can also be easily adapted for discrete distributions (Jean, 1984). Let f and g be the probability density functions, and let $F(x)$ and $G(x)$ be their cumulative distributions, which in continuous distributions are given as follows

$$F(x_i) = \int_{-\infty}^{x_i} f(x)dx, \quad G(x_i) = \int_{-\infty}^{x_i} g(x)dx,$$

According to the VNM utility function, which is the starting point for the criteria, the distribution functions are non-decreasing, continuous from the right where $F(-\infty)=0$, and $F(\infty)=1$ (Hanoch & Levy, 1969). The k-th integral of $F(x)$, $k \in \mathbb{N}$, is denoted as $F_k(x)$. If $F_k(0)=0$, $\forall k \in \mathbb{N}$, then from the fundamental theorem of calculus we have:

$$F_k(x) = \underbrace{\int_0^t \cdots \int_0^t}_{k} F(t) \underbrace{dt \cdots dt}_{k}, k \in \mathbb{N}.$$

The notations F and G henceforth also symbolize the risky alternatives characterized by their continuous distributions of return probabilities $f(x)$ and $g(x)$ (and accordingly, the terms *alternative* and *distribution* are used in the same sense). The expected utility of some risky alternative F is given as:

$$E_F\left(U(x)\right)=\int_a^b f(x)\,U(x)dx,\ x\in\left[a,b\right].$$

Expressions (1.7), (1.8) and (1.9) will be used for derivation of the first, second and third degree SD criteria.

First Degree Stochastic Dominance

Let $\mathcal{U}_1$ be a set of utility functions that are monotonically increasing and have a continuous first derivative in a closed interval *I*=[*a*,*b*], $\mathcal{U}_1=\left\{U\,|\,U'(\cdot)\geq 0\right\}$. It is said that F stochastically dominates G for all utility functions $U\left(x\right)\in\mathcal{U}_1$ by FSD, that can be symbolically written as $F\succeq_{FSD}G$ (or FD_1G) if:

$$F(x)\leq G(x),\forall x\ \wedge\ \exists x_0 \text{ such that } F(x_0)<G(x_0)$$

$$\Leftrightarrow$$

$$E_F\left[U(x)\right]\ \geq\ E_G\left[U(x)\right],\forall U\in\mathcal{U}_1,\ \wedge\ \exists U_0\in\mathcal{U}_1 \text{ such that } E_F\left[U_0(x)\right]\ >\ E_G\left[U_0(x)\right]$$

This means that F has expected utility greater than or equal to G if, and only if, its cumulative distribution is less than or equal to G for all *x*∈[*a*,*b*]. This means that the variable *X* in distribution *F* has a smaller or equal probability of realizing values smaller than the threshold *x*∈[*a*,*b*] compared to *G*. FSD exists if and only if relation is satisfied and there are some x_0 and a utility function $U_0\left(x\right)\in\mathcal{U}_1$ such that right-hand side inequalities in are strict.

Following the assumption of a non-decreasing *U*(*x*), FSD is an efficiency criterion applicable for all investors who prefer more profitable investments. Since FSD can be determined just between two non-intersecting distributions (Levy, 2006), this criterion can still leave a large number of efficient options. To further reduce the FSD-efficient set, it is possible to apply higher degree SD criteria.

Second Degree Stochastic Dominance

Second degree stochastic dominance (SSD) criteria serve to identify dominant alternatives for all utility functions that are non-decreasing and have a positive second derivative, that is, for all decision makers who prefer more profitable investments and are risk-averse. So let $\mathcal{U}_2=\left\{U\,|\,U'(x)\geq 0, U''(x)\leq 0\right\}$. *F* dominates *G* by SSD (symbolically $F\succeq_{SSD}G$ or FD_2G) for all $U\in\mathcal{U}_2$ if the following relations are true:

$$F_1(x)\leq G_1(x),\forall x,\ \wedge\ \exists x_0 \text{ such that } F_1(x_0)<G_1(x_0)$$

$$\Leftrightarrow$$

$$E_F\left(U\left(x\right)\right)\geq E_G\left(U\left(x\right)\right),\forall U\in\mathcal{U}_2,\ \wedge\ \exists U_0\in\mathcal{U}_2 \text{ such that } E_F\left(U_0\left(x\right)\right)>E_G\left(U_0\left(x\right)\right).$$

To determine the SSD of F over G, the total area enclosed by the distribution *G*(*x*) must be larger than the area below the distribution *F*(*x*) for every *x*. In other words, *G*(*x*) must have a thicker left tail for every x. However, values of the integrals F_1 and G_1 in need to be checked only at the intersection points, which simplifies the computation (see Levy (2001)). If it is not possible to determine SSD between a set of observed alternatives, higher degrees of SD can be applied by introducing additional assumptions about the characteristics of the decision makers' utility function.

Third Degree Stochastic Dominance

Third degree stochastic dominance (TSD) criteria apply to all investors with utility functions $U \in \mathcal{U}_3$, such that $\mathcal{U}_3 = \{U \mid U'(x) \geq 0, U''(x) \leq 0, U'''(x) \geq 0\}$. According to (1.6), a positive third derivative of the utility function implies a positive preference for a higher value of the third moment of the distribution, i.e., positive skewness. The justification for using this assumption can be found in Friedman & Savage (1948), Scott & Horvath (1980) and Levy (2006). Friedman & Savage (1948) advocate that individuals prefer positive asymmetry based on the fact that they buy lottery and insurances. Lottery increases the variance and positive asymmetry of their wealth, and insurance eliminates variance and negative asymmetry. An empirical study presented in Levy (2006) used cross-section regression to explain the mutual funds returns with distribution moments as independent variables. It concluded that the coefficients of the first three moments are statistically significant, where investors on average seek larger compensation in the case of negative asymmetry. Therefore, they dislike negative asymmetry and prefer positive asymmetry. Furthermore, the assumption that individuals are more willing to take a greater risk at higher levels of wealth requires a decreasing risk premium, which holds for $U'(x) > 0$ only if $U'''(x) > 0$ (Levy, 2006). F stochastically dominates G by TSD for each $\mathcal{U}_3 = \{U \mid U'(\cdot) \geq 0, U''(\cdot) \leq 0, U'''(\cdot) \geq 0\}$, symbolically $F \succeq_{TSD} G$ or FD_3G for the following set of conditions

$$F_2(x) \leq G_2(x), \forall x, \ \wedge \ F_1(b) \leq G_1(b),$$

and

$$\exists x_0 \text{ such that } F_2(x_0) < G_2(x_0) \ \vee \ F_1(b) < G_1(b),$$

where

$$G_2(x_0) - F_2(x_0) = \int_a^x \int_a^z [G(t) - F(t)]\,dtdz \equiv I_3(x).$$

Since $G_2(x)$ and $F_2(x)$ have a quadratic term, it can appear that $F_2(x_2) > G_2(x_2)$ even though $F_2(x_1) \leq G_2(x_1)$ and $F_2(x_3) \leq G_2(x_3)$ for $x_1 < x_2 < x_3$. Therefore, for checking TSD between F and G, it is not enough to check only the points of intersection, as in SSD, but the entire intervals between these points.

To determine any degree of SD, a large number of pairwise comparisons need to be made. This is why computer algorithms for SD first check the necessary conditions for each degree before checking the conditions (1.11 - 1.14), which speeds up the computation (see Levy, 2006). For further reading on stochastic dominance, see Levy (2016).

Davidson Duclos Non-Dominance Test

The stochastic dominance criteria previously presented are defined for population distributions. As empirical data are usually a sample, it is recommended to use statistical tests of SD. The most popular tests for stochastic dominance are Anderson (1996), Kaur, Prakasa Rao & Singh (1994), Davidson & Duclos (2000, 2006, 2013), Barrett & Donald (2003), Linton, Maasoumi &Whang (2003) and Davidson (2009). These tests differ in the formulation of the null hypothesis, the test statistic, the calculation of the p-value and whether they account for the correlated samples (Hodder, Jackwerth & Kolokolova, 2013). Following the literature review of SD statistical tests, this research uses the Davidson-Duclos nondominance test (Davidson & Duclos, 2006) (hereinafter DD test). It is convenient because, in contrast to other SD tests, it uses non-dominance as a null hypothesis, whereby the rejection of the null directly implies dominance. However, if the null hypothesis cannot be rejected, then one cannot simply conclude reverse dominance. To make the testing procedure more convenient, the set of hypotheses can be reformulated following the idea of Bishop (1992) who proposes introducing weaker sub-hypotheses, as will be shown in the text below.

Let there be distributions A and B, with observations $y_i^K \in Y^K$, $i\in\{1,\ldots,N_K\}$, $K=A,B$. Their empirical dominance functions of degree s, for a given threshold $z\in R$, are defined as:

$$\widehat{D}_K^s(z)=\frac{1}{N_K(s-1)!}\sum_{i=1}^{N_K}\left(z-y_i^K\right)_+^{s-1},\quad K=A,B.$$

The t-test statistic of the DD test is calculated as

$$\min_z t_s(z)=\frac{\widehat{D}_A^s(z)-\widehat{D}_B^s(z)}{\sqrt{Var\left(\widehat{D}_A^s(z)\right)+Var\left(\widehat{D}_B^s(z)\right)-2Cov\left(\widehat{D}_A^s(z),\widehat{D}_B^s(z)\right)}}.$$

The thresholds set $\{z\}$ is chosen arbitrarily but it should contain unique values from $Y^A\cup Y^B$ which lie in the joint support of those samples, excluding the top and bottom values because of the test strength (Hodder, Jackwerth & Kolokolova, 2013). Tse & Zhang (2004) suggest that thresholds z should divide middle 98% of the joint support into L equidistant or equiprobable subintervals, $L>2$. The hypotheses of the test can be formulated as follows (Wong, Phoon & Lean, 2008):

$$H_0 \dots D_A^s(z_j) - D_B^s(z_j) = 0, \ \forall z_j,$$
$$H_1 \dots D_A^s(z_j) - D_B^s(z_j) \neq 0, \text{ for some } z_j,$$
$$H_{1A} \dots D_A^s(z_j) \leq D_B^s(z_j), \forall x_j \wedge \exists\left(D_A^s(z_j) < D_B^s(z_j)\right),$$
$$H_{1B} \dots D_A^s(z_j) \geq D_B^s(z_j), \forall z_j \wedge \exists\left(D_A^s(z_j) > D_B^s(z_j)\right),$$
$$j = 1, \dots, k.$$

The null hypothesis assumes that the two distributions are equal and the alternative H_1 assumes that the distributions are not equal but cannot be ranked by a given criterion. Hypothesis H_{1A} assumes the dominance of distribution A over B, while H_{1B} assumes the dominance of distribution B over A. The hypotheses are rejected using the following set of rules:

$$\left|t_s(z_j)\right| < M_{\infty,\alpha}^k, \forall z_j, j = 1, \dots, k \Rightarrow H_0, \tag{1}$$

$$\exists t_s(z_j) > M_{\infty,\alpha}^k \wedge \exists t_s(z_j) < -M_{\infty,\alpha}^k, j = 1, \dots, k \Rightarrow H_1, \tag{2}$$

$$t_s(z_j) < M_{\infty,\alpha}^k, \forall z_j \wedge \exists\left(t(z_j) < -M_{\infty,\alpha}^k\right), j = 1, \dots, k \Rightarrow H_{1A}, \tag{3}$$

$$t_s(z_j) > -M_{\infty,\alpha}^k, \forall z_j \wedge \exists\left(t(z_j) > M_{\infty,\alpha}^k\right), j = 1, \dots, k \Rightarrow H_{1B}, \tag{4}$$

where $M_{\infty,\alpha}^k$ is a critical value of Studentized Maximum Modulus (SMM) distribution (Richmond, 1982). Davidson & Duclos (2013) emphasize that bootstrapping provides greater power of the test for samples that are smaller than 500 observations. Due to the large sample in this research, the standard test approach at α=5% was used and distributions were checked at 100 equally-distributed consecutive values.

Super-Efficiency Data Envelopment Analysis Model

Data envelopment analysis (DEA) is a non-parametric methodology that applies mathematical programming to empirical data on common inputs and outputs of decision-making units (DMUs) to determine their relative efficiency (Lukač & Neralić, 2013). The first DEA models, the CCR model (Charnes, Cooper & Rhodes (1978)), which assumes constant returns to scale (CRS) and the BCC model (Banker, Charnes & Cooper (1984)), which assumes variable returns to scale (VRS), were developed to evaluate the performance of production entities. However, DEA is a general method designed for performance evaluation and benchmarking with best practices (Cook, Tone & Zhu, 2013). A large number of applications of the basic models and the development of new models has shown, and have further enabled, DEA to be a versatile efficiency estimation tool even outside the production setting. The prerequisites for a valid DEA, as for any other analysis, are well-chosen criteria and variables. In DEA, variables are classified into inputs - variables whose values for an efficient solution should be as small as possible, and outputs - variables whose values should be as large as possible.

The advantage of DEA is the evaluation of the relative efficiency of DMUs based on multiple criteria without the use of subjective weights on individual criteria. The formulation of the problem is as follows. Let there be N decision makers DMU_1, DMU_2, …, DMU_N which use the same m inputs to obtain the same s outputs. Let x_{ij} be i-th input, $i \in \{1,\dots,m\}$, and y_{rj} r-th output, $r \in \{1,\dots,s\}$, for some DMU_j, $j \in \{1,\dots,N\}$. It is suggested that the total number of inputs and outputs is not too large relative to the number of DMUs because of the stability of the model. In this analysis, a super-BCC input-oriented model (Cooper, Seiford & Tone, 2006) is used. Input orientation indicates that efficiency is estimated by analyzing the possible reduction of the inputs for a given level of outputs. A super-efficiency model is chosen because it allows the ranking of DMUs by their efficiency score. In this setting, a measure of efficiency of a $DMU_o = DMU_j$, is obtained by solving:

$$\theta^* = \min_{\lambda,\theta} \theta$$

$$\text{s. t. } \theta x_{io} \geq \sum_{j=1,\neq o}^{N} \lambda_j x_{ij} \quad (i = 1,\dots,m)$$

$$y_{ro} \leq \sum_{j=1,\neq o}^{N} \lambda_j y_{rj} \quad (r = 1,\dots,s)$$

$$\sum_{j=1}^{N} \lambda_j = 1,$$

$$\lambda_j \geq 0, \ (j \in \{1,2,\dots,N\}).$$

The DMU with the greatest value of the efficiency score θ^* is considered the most efficient. The other units can be ranked according to their score, from biggest to smallest value. By solving DEA models, interesting results can be obtained, but this research is primarily focused on the efficiency score itself (for additional explanation and model assumptions see, for example, Cooper, Seiford & Tone (2006)).

The Integration of DEA and SD

Data envelopment analysis is a flexible and, unlike stochastic dominance criteria, a computationally less intensive method that allows group comparisons of units. The flexibility of DEA allows incorporating SD efficiency as one of the variables, as well as the assumptions about decision makers' preferences that are in line with the SD criteria. DEA can also be useful in situations where SD criteria (or some other criteria or method) are not strong enough to make sufficient efficiency differentiation between units. Therefore, two DEA models are proposed. Their difference is in the selection of inputs and outputs. One model uses the return distributions' parameters considered in the TSD efficiency model (that is, return, risk and skewness). Those parameters, where we want greater values, are used as outputs and those indicators, where we want smaller values, are used as inputs. The second DEA model includes an additional variable, an SD-indicator reflecting the SD-efficiency, which must be calculated beforehand. The indicator takes the value of the highest degree of SD criterion according to which an estimated unit is in the efficient set. For example, if a unit is in the SSD-efficient set but not in the TSD-efficient set, then it is assigned a value of 2. If the strategy is inefficient according to FSD, then it is assigned a value of 0. This value is used in the DEA model as an output variable because the indicator implies that the unit observed is efficient for a greater number of criteria. The value of the SD-indicator is calculated according to the results of the DD test.

EMPIRICAL ANALYSIS

The empirical part of this research uses SD and DEA models for efficiency estimation of stock portfolio hedging strategies with options, against the buy-and-hold strategy. The efficiency assessment of the strategies is based on the comparisons of the return distributions of portfolios applying these strategies. The analyzed strategies are simulated using market prices of S&P100 stocks from 1996 to 2014 and underlying standard put and call options. To simplify the analysis, shares that had splits were excluded from the analysis in that particular year. The number of stocks used in the analysis varied from 43 to 96 per year of observation. All portfolios contain a long position in a single share, and hedged strategies assume that all initial positions are opened at the same time. The following strategies were simulated:

- buy-and-hold (SP),
- covered call (long stock + 5% OTM short call) (CC),
- protective put (long stock + 5% ITM long put) (PP),
- ratio covered call (long stock + 2 short 5% OTM call + long call with higher strike) (RC), and
- collar (long stock + 5% OTM short call + 5% ITM long put) (CP).

Each simulated strategy assumes holding a long stock position up to one year (thus avoiding capital gains tax) or until the data is available, regardless of the price changes. If necessary, positions in options are rolled every 28 days following the hedging strategy rules, unless the day of the roll is a non-working day (then the previous business day is a rolling day) or if a position cannot be formed on a particular day (then the position is rolled on the next possible date). On rolling days, if necessary and possible, the existing positions in options are closed and new positions are opened with new options that provide a hedge according to the rules of the strategy. If the options with required characteristics are not available on the market, then a deviation from the required characteristics is allowed, but only if it does not harm the hedge. Options with a maturity greater than or equal to the roll period (28 days) are preferred, but in case no options meet the initial requests, positions with shorter maturity are opened. In that case, positions in options are closed before the rolling day which remains fixed as previously determined by the algorithm.

When it is not possible to open all the positions in options in strategies with more than one option (CP and RC strategies), the strategy applies only one option position, which then becomes a simple hedging strategy CC or PP (if possible) for one period. Portfolio returns are calculated at corresponding ask and bid prices for both stocks and options. This incorporates transaction costs that can make a significant difference in the evaluation of strategies.

Descriptive statistics of the portfolio returns obtained for each strategy are shown in Table 1. The Kolmogorov-Smirnov test for normality shows that portfolio returns are not normally distributed at α=5%. This confirms the initial assumption that the assessment of the relative efficiency of hedging strategies with options cannot be obtained by using standard approaches which assume normality. They must be analyzed using models that take into account the non-normal returns and incorporate realistic assumptions such as the investor's aversion to loss described by the prospect theory, and empirically confirmed preference to positive skewness. As previously explained, this will be enabled by using the DD test of SD criteria and the SD-consistent DEA model.

The returns of hedged strategies and the buy-and-hold strategy were compared using the DD test and the dominance functions of the return distributions up to the third degree. The DD test examines

Table 1. Descriptive statistics of returns for simulated portfolio strategies

	CC	PP	RC	CP	S
Average return	-1,31%	-2,14%	-1,21%	-2,40%	-1,34%
Variance	23,65%	4,67%	24,78%	2,36%	32,19%
Semi-variance	31,67%	4,65%	32,68%	2,97%	37,08%
Skewness*	-0,62	0,08	-0,59	-0,43	-0,30
Kurtosis	2,77	3,01	2,75	3,03	2,65
Value-at-Risk (5%)	-10,71%	-5,87%	-10,80%	-5,32%	-11,76%
Expected shortfall (ES)	-12,67%	-6,61%	-12,78%	-5,95%	-13,73%

* standardized skewness of a sample
Source: Author's calculation.

the non-dominance. Therefore, the non-dominance of hedged strategies (CC, PP, RC, and CP) over buy-and-hold was examined at α=5% for FSD, SSD and TSD. The results of the test are presented in Table 2. The first column states the null hypotheses and the second one the degree for which the nulls were tested. The third column shows the outcome of each test and the last column presents the overall conclusion. For example, the first row of Table 2 presents the hypothesis of the stochastic dominance of strategy CC over SP of the first degree (1). The DD test result is that distributions are not the same but they cannot be ranked (which is stated by rule 2 from (1.17)). By testing the first three degrees of SD, we can conclude that CC stochastically dominates SP by the third degree. The last column of Table 2 clearly shows that PP and RC dominate SP even by SSD. But overall, all hedging strategies stochastically dominate the buy-and-hold by TSD and all hedging strategies are TSD-efficient. In other words, these strategies are efficient for all investors who prefer greater returns, are risk averse in terms of volatility and loss and who prefer greater positive skewness.

Accordingly, the results indicate that all investors with preferences consistent to the TSD do not have smaller utility from undertaking hedging strategies compared to holding an unhedged portfolio.

Table 2. DD test results of stochastic dominance of hedging strategies over buy-and-hold

Hypothesis	Degree of SD	Decision	Conclusion
$CC \succcurlyeq SP$	1	the distributions cannot be ranked (rule 2)	$CC \succcurlyeq_{TSD} SP$
	2	the distributions cannot be ranked (rule 2)	
	3	the dominance of *CC* over *SP* (rule 3)	
$PP \succcurlyeq SP$	1	the distributions cannot be ranked (rule 2)	$PP \succcurlyeq_{SSD} SP$
	2	the dominance of *PP* over *SP* (rule 3)	
	3	the dominance of *PP* over *SP* (rule 3)	
$RC \succcurlyeq SP$	1	the distributions cannot be ranked (rule 2)	$RC \succcurlyeq_{SSD} SP$
	2	the dominance of *RC* over *SP* (rule 3)	
	3	the dominance of *RC* over *SP* (rule 3)	
$CP \succcurlyeq SP$	1	the distributions cannot be ranked (rule 2)	$CP \succcurlyeq_{TSD} SP$
	2	the distributions cannot be ranked (rule 2)	
	3	the dominance of *CP* over *SP* (rule 3)	

Source: Author's calculation.

The selection of inputs and outputs in DEA is based on the preference assumptions related to TSD, as follows: (1) investors prefer greater returns, (2) investors have aversion to loss, (3) investors have aversion to downside return variability, and (4) investors have a positive preference for insurance, that is, precaution, implying that they prefer higher values of positive asymmetry of the returns distribution. Based on these assumptions, variables used in DEA models are average return, expected shortfall (*ES*), semi-variance and skewness coefficient. The return and the skewness coefficient, whose values in an efficient solution should be as great as possible, are treated as outputs. Risk measures *ES* and semi-variance are variables whose values should be as small as possible, and they are treated as inputs. The BCC model is formulated for non-negative variables only. Output variables with negative values are translated into positive values by adding a large positive constant. This does not affect the results (Pastor and Ruiz, 2008). For negative values of the input variable ES the absolute values are used instead. The DEA model used pooled yearly data and compared the performance of the strategies by treating each portfolio in each year as a single entity (DMU). Since the purpose of hedging strategies is to decrease the riskiness of a portfolio, the analysis uses an input orientated DEA model which estimates efficiency by observing the possible reduction of inputs for a given level of outputs.

By solving the super-BCC model with 4 variables (return, skewness, absolute ES and semi-variance) on pooled data, efficiency scores were obtained for each portfolio in each year in the period of analysis (5 strategies × 19 years = 95 portfolios). Portfolios are ranked, based on the values of their scores, from largest to smallest.

To discover which strategy is the most efficient, the cumulative number of appearances of each strategy in the rankings list is observed. Figure 1 shows the cumulative number of the occurrences of strategies CC, PP, CP, RC and SP in a rank-ordered set. The x-axis in Figure 1 shows the rank in the rank-ordered set and the y-axis shows the cumulative number of occurrences of each strategy up to that rank.

From Figure 1, it is evident that DEA analysis shows comparable results with the SD analysis which was previously performed, shown in Table 2. The collar strategy (CP) and the protective put (PP) strategy have the greatest number of occurrences in the top of the ordered set. According to Figure 1, these two strategies can be ranked first and second, respectively. Ranking of covered call (CC) and ratio covered call (RC) strategies cannot be uniquely determined. However, the buy-and-hold strategy (SP) is undoubtedly at the bottom, indicating that unprotected portfolio is the least efficient strategy for investors who prefer greater returns, are risk and loss averse and prefer positive skewness. The descriptive statistics (Table 1) show that strategies which have smaller (super) DEA-efficiency score have greater returns, greater variability and smaller asymmetry. Thus, this DEA model estimates that lower returns can be compensated with smaller variance or higher values of skewness, that is, smaller loss in the event of extremely adverse events. The important implication of these results is that input and output variables in DEA analysis were correctly chosen to reflect the preference assumptions of investors consistent with TSD.

The second DEA model (henceforth DEA-SD model) incorporates an SD-indicator as an additional output variable, as previously explained. This approach aims to examine whether new information on

Figure 1. The cumulative occurrences of strategies in the super-BCC ranking list (Source: Author)

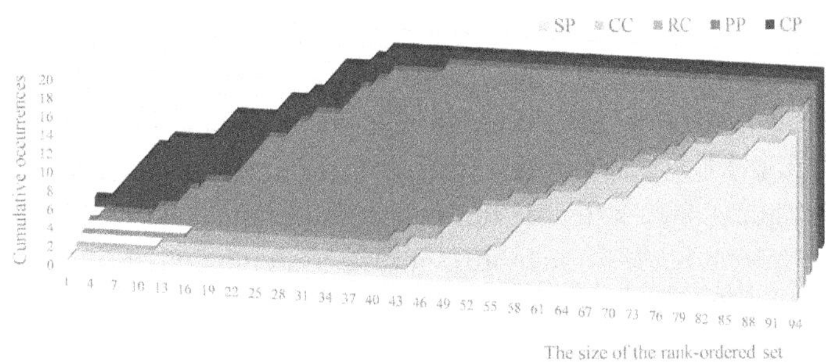

SD will contribute to the first DEA model, and possibly change the main results. Following the results of the DEA-SD model, strategies are ranked according to their efficiency scores. Figure 2 presents the number of cumulative appearances of each strategy in the rank-ordered list. By comparing Figure 1 and Figure 2, the conclusion is that the differences in the results are negligible. The SD variable did not bring significant new information nor change the final result. This result additionally confirms that the first DEA model included a good selection of variables which describe investors' preferences in line with the TSD.

Finally, the results of both the sole DEA model and the integrated DEA-SD model confirmed the findings obtained by sole SD model. All considered hedging strategies with options are more efficient than the buy-and-hold strategy for all investors who prefer greater returns, are risk averse in terms of loss and downside volatility and prefer positive skewness. It can be confirmed now that all models showed that the protective put strategy can be considered the most efficient hedging strategy in this trading algorithm.

Figure 2. The cumulative occurrences of strategies in the ranking list obtained by super-BCC model with an SD indicator (Source: Author).

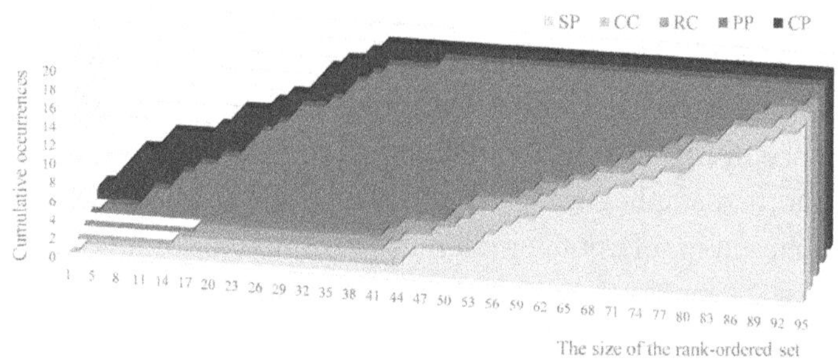

FUTURE RESEARCH DIRECTIONS

The analysis presented opens up numerous possibilities for further research. Firstly, there is the application of the proposed methodology of DEA and SD for evaluating other portfolio strategies, portfolio selection problems and risk management techniques. Secondly, further research should address statistical tests comparing how well the DEA-SD model agrees with TSD. Further research should also consider integrating other DEA models and exploring the vast possibilities of DEA models and their results. In research on option hedging strategies, some more complex strategies and those that are of a more speculative nature could be examined with more sophisticated algorithms. Another significant path of research could be evaluating the effectiveness of hedging strategies with regards to the (expected) characteristics of the return distribution of stocks and portfolios which should be hedged. Such research could produce interesting findings applicable to risk management using options.

CONCLUSION

This chapter has examined using stochastic dominance criteria, data envelopment analysis and their integration, for evaluating the efficiency of portfolio hedging strategies with options. While the concept of stochastic dominance is directly related to the theory of expected utility and incorporates investors' preference for greater return, positive skewness and aversion to loss and downside variability, DEA models must be formed to include variables which reflect decision makers' preferences. Stochastic dominance criteria was shown to be a promising methodology for dealing with this problem, but it is still computationally intensive and there is no commercial software which could make it accessible for wide-scale application. DEA is a computationally less intensive methodology which allows setting of the efficiency model consistent to third degree stochastic dominance. This chapter showed a possible integration of these quantitative methods aimed at improving decision-making by making it more valid and less time-consuming. It was found that the results of a BCC input-oriented model, with return and skewness as output variables, and expected shortfall and semi-variance as input variables, is consistent with the results of the third degree stochastic dominance criteria and reflects the preferences of decision makers who prefer more profitable investments, are risk averse in terms of loss and downside variability and prefer positive skewness. In this way, the DEA approach is directly connected to the expected utility theory. This approach was demonstrated in the efficiency analysis of hedging strategies with options. The returns of simulated covered call, protective put, ratio covered call, collar and buy-and-hold strategies using bid and ask price data for S&P100 stocks over a period of 19 years, were shown to be non-normally distributed and therefore not suitable for traditional and mean-variance-based analysis. The results of the empirical analysis suggested that hedging strategies are more efficient than the buy-and-hold for all investors who prefer higher returns, lower risk and greater positive asymmetry. Moreover, both methodologies recognized protective put as a hedging strategy with superior characteristics compared to others. Since risk management is one important area of portfolio management which receives more and more attention, the aim of the presented research methodology and final results is not to close, but to open new research possibilities that will help decision-making in practice.

ACKNOWLEDGMENT

This research received no specific grant from any funding agency in the public, commercial, or not-for-profit sectors.

This research was partially written during a visiting study at Manchester Business School. The author thanks Manchester Business School for providing the facilities and the resources for the research.

The author also thanks Simon and Caroline Durk of the ōbex project for providing language editing support.

REFERENCES

Abid, F., Mroua, M., & Wong, W.-K. (2007). *The Impact of Option Strategies in Financial Portfolios Performance: Mean-Variance and Stochastic Dominance Approaches*. Retrieved from http://ssrn.com/abstract=982332

Abid, F., Mroua, M., & Wong, W.-K. (2014). International Diversification Versus Domestic Diversification: Mean-Variance Portfolio Optimization and Stochastic Dominance Approaches. *Journal of Risk and Financial Management*, *2014*(2), 45–66. doi:10.3390/jrfm7020045

Aharony, J., & Loeb, M. (1977). Mean-Variance Vs Stochastic Dominance: Some Empirical Findings On Efficient Sets. *Journal of Banking & Finance*, *1*(1), 95–102. doi:10.1016/0378-4266(77)90020-6

Aljinović, Z., Marasović, B., & Šego, B. (2011) Financial Modeling (2nd ed.). Split: Faculty of Economics Split.

Annaert, J., Van Osselaer, S., & Verstraete, B. (2008). Performance Evaluation of Portfolio Insurance Strategies Using Stochastic Dominance Criteria. *Journal of Banking & Finance*, *33*(2), 272–280. doi:10.1016/j.jbankfin.2008.08.002

Bawa, V. S. (1975). Optimal Rules for Ordering Uncertain Prospects. *Journal of Financial Economics*, *2*(1), 95–121. doi:10.1016/0304-405X(75)90025-2

Bawa, V. S. (1982). Stochastic Dominance: A Research Bibliography. *Management Science*, *28*(6), 698–712. doi:10.1287/mnsc.28.6.698

Bishop, J. A., Formby, J. P., & Thistle, P. D. (1969). Convergence of the South and Non-South Income Distributions, 1969-1979. *The American Economic Review*, *82*(1), 262–272.

Bollen, N. P. B. (1999). *Measuring the Benefits of Option Strategies for Portfolio Management, report prepared for Catalyst Institute.* Retrieved from http://www2.owen.vanderbilt.edu/nick.bollen/themes/asx1.pdf

Bookstaber, R., & Clarke, R. (1984, October). Option Portfolio Strategies: Measurement and Evaluation. *The Journal of Business*, *57*(4), 469–492. doi:10.1086/296275

Booth, J. R., Tehranian, A., & Trennepohl, G. L. (1985). Efficiency analysis and option portfolio selection. *Journal of Financial and Quantitative Analysis*, *4*(4), 435–450. doi:10.2307/2330760

Branda, M. (2013). Diversification-consistent data envelopment analysis with general deviation measures. *European Journal of Operational Research*, *226*(3), 626–635. doi:10.1016/j.ejor.2012.11.007

Branda, M. (2016). Mean-value at risk portfolio efficiency: approaches based on data envelopment analysis models with negative data and their empirical behaviour. *A Quarterly Journal of Operations Research, 14*(1), 77-99.

Branda, M., & Kopa, M. (2012). DEA-Risk Efficiency and Stochastic Dominance Efficiency of Stock Indices. *Czech Journal of Economics and Finance*, *62*(2), 106–126.

Branda, M., & Kopa, M. (2013). *From stochastic dominance to DEA-risk models: portfolio efficiency analysis*. International Workshop "Stochastic Programming for Implementation and Advanced Applications" (STOPROG–2012), Neringa, Lithuania.

Branda, M., & Kopa, M. (2014). On relation between DEA-risk models and stochastic dominance efficiency tests. *Central European Journal of Operations Research*, *22*(1), 13–35. doi:10.100710100-012-0283-2

Brooks, R., Levy, H., & Yoder, J. (1987). Using stochastic dominance to evaluate the performance of portfolios with options. *Financial Analysts Journal*, *43*(March/April), 79–82. doi:10.2469/faj.v43.n2.79

Burr Porter, R., & Gaumnitz, J. E. (1972). Stochastic Dominance vs. Mean-Variance Portfolio Analysis: An Empirical Evaluation. *The American Economic Review*, *62*(3), 438–446.

Castellano, R., & Giacometti, R. (2001). Performance of a Hedged Stochastic Portfolio Model in the Presence of Extreme Events. *Computational Economics*, *17*(2/3), 239–252. doi:10.1023/A:1011632311173

Clarke, R. G. (1987). Stochastic dominance properties of option strategies. In F. J. Fabozzi (Ed.), *Advances in Futures and Options Research* (Vol. 2). JAI Press.

Cont, R. (Ed.). (2010). *Encyclopedia of Quantitative Finance*. Wiley. doi:10.1002/9780470061602

Cooper, W. W., Seiford, L. M., & Tone, K. (2006). *Introduction to Data Envelopment Analysis and Its Uses*. Springer.

Dash, M., & Goel, A. (2014). A Comparison of ITM and OTM Protective-Puts and Covered-Calls. *Asian Journal of Finance & Accounting*, *6*(1), 126–137. doi:10.5296/ajfa.v6i1.3945

De Giorgi, E. (2005). Reward-risk portfolio selection and stochastic dominance. *Journal of Banking & Finance*, *29*(4), 895–926. doi:10.1016/j.jbankfin.2004.05.027

Edirisinghe, N. C. P., & Zhang, X. (2007). Generalized DEA model of fundamental analysis and its application to portfolio optimization. *Journal of Banking & Finance*, *31*(11), 3311–3335. doi:10.1016/j.jbankfin.2007.04.008

Edirisinghe, N. C. P., & Zhang, X. (2010). Input/output selection in DEA under expert information, with application to financial markets. *European Journal of Operational Research*, *207*(3), 1669–1678. doi:10.1016/j.ejor.2010.06.027

Fabozzi, F. J., Markowitz, H. M., Kolm, P. N., & Gupta, F. (2012). Mean-Variance Model for Portfolio Selection. In *Encyclopedia of Financial Models*. Retrieved from https://onlinelibrary.wiley.com/doi/full/10.1002/9781118182635.efm0003

Gandhi, D. K., & Saunders, A. (1981). The superiority of stochastic dominance over mean variance efficiency criteria: Some clarifications. *Journal of Business Finance & Accounting*, *8*(1), 51–59. doi:10.1111/j.1468-5957.1981.tb00803.x

Gardijan, M. (2016). *Assessing the relative efficiency of portfolio hedging strategies with options* (Unpublished doctoral dissertation). University of Zagreb, Faculty of Economics and Business.

Gardijan, M., & Kojić, V. (2012). DEA-based investment strategy and its application in the Croatian stock market. *Croatian Operational Research Review*, *3*(1), 203–212.

Gardijan, M., & Škrinjarić, T. (2015). Equity portfolio optimization: A DEA based methodology applied to the Zagreb Stock Exchange. *Croatian Operational Research Review*, *6*(2), 405–417. doi:10.17535/crorr.2015.0031

Guo, Z. (2012). *Two Essays on Stochastic Dominance and One Essay on Correlation Stress Tests* (Doctoral dissertation). University of Konstanz, Faculty of Politics, Law and Economics. Retrieved from http://kops.uni-konstanz.de/handle/123456789/24222

Hadar, J., & Russell, W. (1969). Rules for Ordering Uncertain Prospects. *The American Economic Review*, *59*(1), 25–34.

Hanoch, G., & Levy, H. (1969). The Efficiency Analysis of Choices Involving Risk. *The Review of Economic Studies*, *36*(3), 335–346. doi:10.2307/2296431

Hanoch, G., & Levy, H. (1970). Relative Efficiency of Efficiency Criteria for Portfolio Selection. *Journal of Financial and Quantitative Analysis*, *5*(1), 63–76. doi:10.2307/2979007

Harrison, W. R. (1988). Stochastic dominance analysis of futures and option strategies for hedging feeder cattle. *Agricultural and Resource Economics Review*, *27*(2), 270–280. doi:10.1017/S1068280500006596

Hemler, M. L., & Miller, T. W. (2015). *The Performance of Options-Based Investment Strategies: Evidence for Individual Stocks During 2003–2013*. Mendoza College of Business, University of Notre Dame. Retrieved from https://www.optionseducation.org/referencelibrary/research-articles/page-assets/perf-options-strategies.aspx

Isakov, D., & Morard, B. (2001). Improving Portfolio Performance with Option Strategies: Evidence from Switzerland. *European Financial Management, 7*(1), 73–91. doi:10.1111/1468-036X.00145

Javanmardi, L. (2013). *Portfolio Selection by Second Order Stochastic Dominance based on the Risk Aversion Degree of Investors* (Doctoral dissertation). University of Toronto, Graduate Department of Chemical Engineering and Applied Chemistry.

Jehle, G. A., & Reny, P. J. (2011). *Advanced Microeconomic Theory* (3rd ed.). Pearson Education Limited.

Joro, T., & Na, P. (2006). Portfolio performance evaluation in a mean–variance–skewness framework. *European Journal of Operational Research, 175*(1), 446–461. doi:10.1016/j.ejor.2005.05.006

Jurczenko, E., & Maillet, B. (2006). *Multi-moment Asset Allocation and Pricing Models*. John Wiley & Sons, Ltd.

Kahnemann, D., & Tversky, A. (1979). Prospect Theory: An Analysis of Decision under Risk. *Econometrica, 47*(2), 263–291. doi:10.2307/1914185

Knight, F. (1921). *Risk, Uncertainty, and Profit*. Houghton Mifflin Company.

Lehman, R., & McMillan, L. G. (2011). Options for volatile markets: managing volatility and protecting against catastrophic risk (2nd ed.). Hoboken, NJ: John Wiley & Sons, Inc. doi:10.1002/9781118531518

Levy, H. (1973). Stochastic Dominance, Efficiency Criteria, and Efficient Portfolios: The Multi-Period Case. *The American Economic Review, 63*(5), 986–994.

Levy, H. (2006). *Stochastic dominance: Investment Decision Making under Uncertainty* (2nd ed.). Springer.

Levy, H. (2016). *Stochastic dominance: Investment Decision Making under Uncertainty* (3rd ed.). Springer. doi:10.1007/978-3-319-21708-6

Lhabitant, F.-S. (2000). *Derivatives in portfolio management: Why beating the market is easy*. EDHEC risk and asset management research centre working chapter. Retrieved from https://risk.edhec.edu/publications/derivatives-portfolio-management-why-beating-market-easy

Lim, S., Oh, K. W., & Zhu, J. (2014). Use of DEA cross-efficiency evaluation in portfolio selection: An application to Korean stock market. *European Journal of Operational Research, 236*(1), 361–368. doi:10.1016/j.ejor.2013.12.002

Lončar, S., & Tepavac, E. (2012). Primena algoritma za trećestepenu stohastičku dominaciju u rangiranju investicija. *Škola biznisa, 2012*(2), 119–127.

Lopes, A., Lanzer, E., Lima, M., & da Costa, N. (2008). DEA investment strategy in the Brazilian stock market. *Economic Bulletin, 13*(2), 1–10.

Lukač, Z., & Neralić, L. (2013). *Operational Research*. Element.

Merton, R. C., Scholes, M., & Gladstein, M. L. (1978). The returns and risks of alternative call option portfolio investment strategies. *The Journal of Business*, *51*(2), 183–242. doi:10.1086/295995

Merton, R. C., Scholes, M. S., & Gladstein, M. L. (1982). The Returns and Risks of Alternative Put-Option Portfolio Investment Strategies. *The Journal of Business*, *55*(1), 1–55. doi:10.1086/296153

Ogryczak, W., & Ruszczynski, A. (1999). From stochastic dominance to mean-risk models: Semideviations as risk measures. *European Journal of Operational Research*, *116*(1), 33–50. doi:10.1016/S0377-2217(98)00167-2

Pastor, J. T., & Ruiz, J. L. (2007). Variables with negative values in DEA. In J. Zhu & W. D. Cook (Eds.), *Modeling Data Irregularities and Structural Complexities in Data Envelopment Analysis*. Springer. doi:10.1007/978-0-387-71607-7_4

Patari, E., Leivo, T., & Honkapuro, S. (2012). Enhancement of equity portfolio performance using data envelopment analysis. *European Journal of Operational Research*, *220*(3), 786–797. doi:10.1016/j.ejor.2012.02.006

Powers, J., & McMullen, P. R. (2002). Using data envelopment analysis to select efficient large cap securities. *Journal of Business and Management*, *7*(2), 31–42.

Richmond, J. (1982). A general method for constructing simultaneous confidence intervals. *Journal of the American Statistical Association*, *77*(378), 455–460. doi:10.1080/01621459.1982.10477832

Rothschild, M., & Stiglitz, J. (1970). Increasing Risk I: A Definition. *Journal of Economic Theory*, *2*(3), 225–243. doi:10.1016/0022-0531(70)90038-4

Runde, J. (1998). Clarifying Frank Knight's discussion of the meaning of risk and uncertainty Cambridge. *Journal of Economics*, *22*(5), 539–546.

Scott, R. C., & Horvath, P. A. (1980). On the Direction of Preference for Moments of Higher Order than the Variance. *The Journal of Finance*, *35*(4), 915–919. doi:10.1111/j.1540-6261.1980.tb03509.x

Sikavica, P., Hunjak, T., Begičević Ređep, N., & Hernaus, T. (2014). *Business decision-making*. Zagreb: Školska knjiga.

Škrinjarić, T. (2014). Investment Strategy on the Zagreb Stock Exchange Based on Dynamic DEA. *Croatian Economic Survey*, *16*(1), 129–160. doi:10.15179/ces.16.1.5

Szado, E., & Schneeweis, T. (2012). *Option-Based Risk Management in a Multi-Asset World*. Options Education documents. Retrieved from https://www.optionseducation.org/ referencelibrary/research-articles/page-assets/options-based-risk-mgmt-summary.aspx

Thaler, R. (Ed.). (1993). *Advances in Behavioral Finance* (Vol. 2). Russell Sage Foundation, Princeton University Press.

Trennepohl, G., & Dukes, W. (1981). An Empirical Test of Option Writing and Buying Strategies utilizing In-the-money and Out-of-the-money Contracts. *Journal of Business Finance & Accounting*, *8*(2), 185–202. doi:10.1111/j.1468-5957.1981.tb00813.x

Tse, Y. K., & Zhang, X. (2004). *A Monte Carlo Investigation of Some Tests for Stochastic Dominance.* Institutional Knowledge at Singapore Management University. doi:10.1080/00949650310001593221

Tversky, A., & Kahnemann, D. (1974). Judgment under Uncertainty: Heuristics and Biases. *Science. New Series, 185*(4157), 1124–1131. doi:10.1126cience.185.4157.1124 PMID:17835457

von–Neumann, J., & Morgenstern, O. (1953). *Theory of Games and Economic Behavior.* Princeton University Press.

Whitmore, G. A. (1970). Third-Degree Stochastic Dominance. *The American Economic Review, 60*(3), 457–459.

Wong, W. K., Phoon, K. F., & Lean, H. H. (2008). Stochastic dominance analysis of Asian hedge funds. *Pacific-Basin Finance Journal, 16*(3), 204–223. doi:10.1016/j.pacfin.2007.07.001

Wu, D., & Olson, D. L. (2008). A comparison of stochastic dominance and stochastic DEA for vendor evaluation. *International Journal of Production Research, 46*(8), 2313–2327. doi:10.1080/00207540601039775

Zagst, R., & Kraus, J. (2011). Stochastic dominance of portfolio insurance strategies. *Annals of Operations Research, 185*(1), 75–103. doi:10.100710479-009-0549-9

Zhang, S. (2001). General N-th Degree Stochastic Dominance. *Tsinghua Science and Technology, 6*(1), 93–96.

KEY TERMS AND DEFINITIONS

Data Envelopment Analysis: A method of mathematical programming for an evaluation of the relative efficiency of units under assessment which are characterized with common inputs and outputs.

Efficiency: The ordinal attribute of a unit observed, given efficiency criteria.

Hedging: The risk management procedure aimed at limiting the riskiness of the portfolio.

Investment Alternative: One of the two investment possibilities that may be undertaken.

Options: Financial derivatives which give the right but not the obligation to buy or sell an underlying asset under specified conditions.

Options Hedging Strategies: Portfolio strategies using specific options and their combinations for risk hedging.

Stochastic Dominance: A methodology that provides the criteria for finding efficient alternatives consistent with the expected utility theory.

Chapter 3
Investigation of the Calendar Effect:
Second-Order Stochastic Dominance Approach

Murat Isiker
https://orcid.org/0000-0002-1327-9982
Istanbul Sabahattin Zaim University, Turkey

Umut Ugurlu
https://orcid.org/0000-0002-6183-969X
Bahcesehir University, Turkey

Oktay Tas
https://orcid.org/0000-0002-7570-549X
Istanbul Technical University, Turkey

ABSTRACT

This chapter aims to examine calendar anomaly in selected sample countries by using second-order stochastic dominance (SSD) approach. Day-of-the-week and month-of-the-year effects are analysed for a group of 5 developed and 5 developing country indexes to estimate efficient (inefficient) weekdays and months for the period between 1988 and 2016. Then, back-testing procedure is applied for each sample country to compare performance of index returns for 2017-2019 with the strategy arisen by estimation results. Findings suggest that Monday and Friday returns are inefficient and efficient respectively in all developing countries where different results obtained for developed ones. In monthly analysis, December returns found efficient in 8 indexes including S&P 500. However, October is inefficient for all indexes. Positive January effect seems disappeared in most cases. Back-testing results indicate that in a bearish market condition SSD strategy outperforms index returns in general for daily and monthly comparison.

DOI: 10.4018/978-1-7998-5083-0.ch003

INTRODUCTION

There have been ongoing debates among researchers whether there exists a calendar anomaly on financial markets or not. Many studies in the finance literature focus on showing whether a day in a week, a week in a month or a month in a year, has statistically different and significant returns, in both developed and emerging markets. If a calendar anomaly is detected, researchers assert the absence of the strong form of the Efficient Market Hypothesis (EMH), which means that all publicly or privately available news is not yet reflected in capital markets. In general, calendar anomaly in the literature of finance is described as an unusual and consistent return behaviour of a financial instrument in a specific time frame, which cannot be attributed to all related news about this instrument and the facts of the economic environment. For example, if average of Monday returns of a security is statistically different from the returns of the other trading days in the long-term, it can be concluded that return of this security shows an anomaly in a daily basis. This kind of anomaly contradicts with the EMH. Thus, anomalies attract investors' attention to chase arbitrage opportunity in the markets and researchers' interest to seek possible answers about its causation.

The first important calendar effect which will be discussed in this chapter is the day-of-the-week effect. Pettengil (2003) provides an extensive literature review for the day-of-the-week effect. In this study, the author exemplifies about very early studies starting from the 1930s (See Kelly (1930)). Early studies analyse that day-of-the-week effect reveals a tendency for Mondays that has lower returns than the other trading days in the US stock markets. Moreover, many studies, such as Cross (1973), French (1980), Linn & Lockwood (1988), Lakonishok & Smidt (1988), show evidence that Monday has significant negative returns for different periods. Monday negative effect has been presented not only in the US but also in other developed markets. Jaffe & Westerfield (1985) show that capital markets of Canada and the UK have negative Monday returns while Tuesday returns are the lowest for Japan and Australia. The reason for negative Monday returns is stated in the literature as Monday returns are affected by positive Friday's return (Lim, Mun & Dollery (2010), Tong (2000)).

The second major part of calendar anomaly literature is the month-of-the-year effect which in most studies investigated as the January effect. The first possible explanation for this effect has been that investors sell their stocks during December for tax-loss purposes and repurchase them in January. Secondly, individual investors who receive their year-end bonuses in January are likely to buy shares from stock markets that cause an abnormal rise. The third explanation is portfolio rebalancing strategies by fund managers that cause an abnormal increase in January. Many researchers empirically test this effect. Rossi (2015) provides a literature review study for the January effect (literature about other calendar anomalies can also be found in this study).

This chapter aims to show whether calendar anomaly still exists in stock markets of selected sample countries on a daily and monthly basis. Secondly, if there exists a calendar anomaly, performance comparison analysis will be conducted to determine whether a portfolio strategy suggested by findings that can beat benchmark indexes of each sample country in the back-testing period. Thirdly, it will also be examined whether there is a difference in terms of day-of-the-week and month-of-the-year effects between the developed and emerging countries. For this purpose, we selected five developed and five emerging countries indexes, namely US (S&P500), UK (FTSE100), Japan (Nikkei225), Germany (DAX30), France (CAC40), for developed countries; South Korea (KOSPI), Indonesia (Jakarta Composite), Malaysia (FTSE KLCI), Thailand (Bangkok SET), Turkey (BIST-100), for emerging countries. Closing values of the indexes are obtained from 04.01.1988 to 31.12.2019 from Bloomberg. The estimation period is chosen as 04.01.1988 - 31.12.2016 and the back-testing period is from 01.01.2017 to 31.12.2019. Second-order stochastic dominance (SSD) pairwise efficiency test will be performed in MATLAB, both for day-of-the-week and month-of-the-year effects. Firstly, we will be able to check whether there is a calendar anomaly in the sample indexes or not. Then, according to the stochastic dominance relationship, the trading strategy will be applied for both cases, and it will be compared with the benchmark indexes in the back-testing period. Furthermore, the performance difference related to the calendar effect in the developed and emerging markets will also be evaluated.

The remainder of the paper is structured as follows: Next section, the literature review, will discuss the related calendar effect papers in the literature from both the stochastic dominance and conventional perspectives. Table 10 and 11 in the appendix part shows a summary of the literature review Section 3 will give information about the data and Section 4 about the methodology. Section 5 states the results of our second-order stochastic dominance analysis in addition to the back-testing results of the portfolio performance. The last two sections consist future research ideas and conclusion of the chapter.

LITERATURE REVIEW

Day-of-the-Week Effect

The presence of calendar anomaly among weekdays is investigated in the developed stock markets by many researchers, especially after the 1990s. The findings of these studies indicate different results for the same countries even though a similar research period was used. Chang, Pinegar & Ravichandran (1993) apply a robust check for the Monday effect in 23 countries. Authors find that there exists a calendar anomaly in France, Italy, the Netherlands and Sweden on the negative side; however, it is found as positive for Spain. Researchers fail to reject the existence of the Monday effect for the US market. On the other hand, Tong (2000) asserts that the Monday effect does not exist only in the US; but also in Canada, Germany, France and the UK. Positive Monday effect is also found in Spain and Austria. The research concludes that the negative Monday effect is conditionally partial on Friday's return. Papers published in the new millennia reveal that the Monday effect has disappeared partially or vanished in some capital markets. Steeley (2001) shows that the Monday effect no longer exists in the UK stock market after the 1990s. Kohers, Kohers, Pandey, & Kohers (2004) analyse the existence of daily calendar anomaly between 1980 and 2002 under two sub-periods. Findings of the study suggest that the existence of negative Monday effect between 1980 and 1990 has disappeared after a decade for countries such as the US, the UK, France, Canada, and so on. However, Japan still has an anomaly on Monday rather than Tuesday. Although daily anomaly is not observed in France and the UK in Borges (2009), positive Tuesday returns are detected for Germany where all three models indicate the same result.

Calendar anomaly topic attracts researchers' attention not only in developed markets but in developing ones. Since testing the hypothesis of efficient markets is still one of the most popular issues in financial literature, studies are being conducted to test the level of efficiency of developing markets. Thus, the calendar anomaly is an intriguing topic to test this hypothesis. Since selected sample for developing countries is limited to Indonesia, Malaysia, South Korea, Thailand and Turkey, literature will be discussed only about these countries.

Findings of Chia, Liew, Wafa & Wafa (2006) suggest that daily anomaly exists in Malaysia before and after the 1997 crisis. Positive Wednesday and Friday returns are found significant for the pre-crisis period, where this impact disappears for the post-crisis period. However, negative Monday returns exist for both periods. Another study about the Malaysian stock market conducted by Lim, Mun & Dollery (2010) confirm significant negative Monday returns. However, it is noted that this case is subject to Friday returns. Unlike Chia et al. (2006), Wednesday and Friday are found significant and positive between 2000 and 2006.

Bildik (2004) compares Borsa Istanbul's daily returns with the dataset from 1988 to 2004. Low Monday and high Friday returns are valid for the sample period. However, findings show that different settlement types change daily anomaly. After a two-day settlement policy application, Tuesday and Thursday become low and high return days, respectively. In addition to this study, Cinko & Avci (2009) extend the sample period until 2008 for Borsa Istanbul. Regression model results underline that negative Monday and positive Thursday and Friday effects exist. Benchmark index and value-based portfolio analysis show similar results in this study. Finally, Georgantopoulos & Tsamis (2008) explore significant negative Monday and positive Friday effects during the period between 2000 and 2007 for Borsa Istanbul.

Yakob, Beal & Delpachitra (2005) employ GARCH models to find the presence of daily and monthly calendar anomaly effects for Asia-Pacific stock markets between 2000 and 2005. Study results reveal that Indonesia has negative Monday and positive Friday returns. Similarly, Faisal & Majid (2016) test the existence of weekend effect in the Jakarta Composite Index (JCI) between 2001 and 2014 and conclude that Friday has higher returns while returns of Mondays are the lowest.

Brooks & Persand (2001) show that South Korea has no daily anomaly during the research period between 1989 and 1996. For Malaysia and Thailand, Monday is slightly positive and significant. Tangjitprom (2011) also examine the Thailand stock market. Results for the day-of-the-week effect shows that negative Monday and positive Friday returns are significant for this market. It can be derived from the results that the last three days of the week outperform Monday and Tuesday returns. Lastly, even though abnormal returns are detected, it is concluded that due to transaction cost and tick size issues, it is not possible to get higher returns than the benchmark index.

Two more studies analyse a wide range of developing countries for detection of the day-of-the-week effect. First, Yalcin & Yucel (2006) use return and volatility models for 20 developing countries where 5 of them are also included in this study. According to the results, the lowest and highest returns are Monday and Friday respectively for indexes of Indonesia, Malaysia, Thailand and Turkey. However, Tuesday is the lowest and Wednesday is the highest for South Korea. Second, Basher & Sadorsky (2006) apply five different models in 21 emerging stock markets. Even though there are slight changes in results according to models that are applied, the general picture shows that Mondays cause negative returns for Malaysia, Thailand and Turkey. Additionally, positive returns are observed in Turkey on Thursday and Friday. Indonesia and South Korea stay relatively anomaly free. Indonesia has a positive Tuesday return just in one model.

Month-of-the-Year Effect

The second major literature about calendar anomaly is the month-of-the-year effect. The most popular one among these anomalies is known as "January Effect". The presence of this effect varies for developed countries according to methodologies that are employed, selected sample period and countries. Rozeff & Kinney (1976) is one of the primary studies on the January effect. Authors examine the US market and find evidence that January has relatively higher returns than other months, excluding great depression years. Moller & Zilca (2008) suggest that the January effect still exists in the US market for the period between 1995 and 2004. Besides, findings show that the first part of January has a higher return than the second part. Gu (2003) asserts that after 1988, the January effect shows a decreasing trend in the US market. Findings of Lean, Smyth, & Wong (2007) show contradictions between the US and Asian markets on the direction of the results for the January effect. Patel & Evans (2003) examine seven developed countries under four decades from 1960 until 2000. Findings show that the appearance of the January effect is more obvious in the 1970s for France, Germany, Japan and the US. However, only Germany and Italy show higher significant January returns after the 1990s.

Apart from January, researchers have studied the effect of other months, such as May and December. "May Effect" (i.e. Halloween Effect) is analysed by Maberly & Pierce (2003), Lucey & Zhao (2008). Haggard & Witte (2010) and Bachmann, Tegtmeier, Gebhardt & Steinborn (2019). Maberly & Pierce (2003) posit that returns between May and October are statistically lower than the returns between November and April only in bullish years for the Japanese Market in the 1980s. Lucey & Zhao (2008) also apply May-October and November-April comparison in the US market, where the difference is found not significant. On the other hand, Haggar & Witte (2010) assert that investing in the November-April period, even excluding January, provide significant positive returns in the US market for the 1954-2008 period. Bachmann et al. (2019) study eleven indexes where weak May effect is found.

December effect is documented by different markets such as Japan, Indonesia, Malaysia, Thailand, the UK, and so on. For instance, Keong, Yat & Ling (2010) use the GARCH methodology to test the month-of-the-year effect for 11 Asian countries for 20 years period starting from 1990. December returns are found positive for Indonesia, Malaysia and Thailand. In addition, Faisal & Majid (2016) find that daily average returns of December are significantly higher than the rest of the months' return in JCI. Moreover, Kato & Schallheim (1985) examine the January effect in the Japanese stock market. Test results suggest that January returns are higher than remaining months except for December. In addition, January, June and December average returns are found positive. It is underlined that the difference between these months and others that the bonuses paid by companies to their employees which cause a rise, especially on stocks with small market cap. As a currently published study, Plastun, Sibande, Gupta & Wohar (2020) investigate the historical transformation of January, October and December effects for selected developed markets since their presence. Findings show that the January effect has diminished after the 1960s and totally vanished in the last two decades. Also, the October effect is not the case currently, and only the UK market still has a significant December effect while in Germany, the presence of this effect is weak.

Finally, it would be beneficial to share other studies that analyse monthly calendar anomalies. Yakob, Beal & Delpachitra (2005) find September is negative for Malaysia and South Korea, while November and December are positive for Indonesia. In addition, South Korea shows positive August effect. Tangjitprom (2011) divides his data period into two groups as before and after the Asian crisis to test the existence of a calendar anomaly for the stock market of Thailand by using the GARCH methodology. The researcher finds significantly positive returns for December, and he attributes this difference to the turn-of-the-year effect where positive returns are concentrated at the end of December and at the beginning of January. Chia, Liew, Wafa & Wafa (2006) assert that there is no monthly anomaly in the Malaysian stock market for pre and post-crisis periods where the 1997 Asian Crisis is set as a distinct point. Keong, Yat & Ling (2010) mention a positive abnormal return for April in 10 Asian countries and added that August has downward behaviour for Indonesia. Georgantopoulos & Tsamis (2008) find no monthly effect for Borsa

Istanbul, while Borges (2009) examines 17 European countries by applying three different models. Low September returns are detected for France and Germany. November seems significant and positive for Germany only in the regression model. The UK does not show any anomaly on a monthly basis. Finally, Rossi & Gunardi (2018) examine four developed European markets for the first decade of the 2000s. Bootstrapping procedure and GARCH model detect positive return anomaly for Germany in February while negative anomaly in September. A significant anomaly is not detected for France.

Stochastic Dominance Literature on Calendar Anomaly

As stochastic dominance (SD) strategy will be applied on daily and monthly calendar anomaly issue in this chapter, it will be beneficial to mention previous studies which use this methodology on these topics. As an early study, Wingender & Groff (1989) uses SD methodology for S&P 500 Index with the sample size of 1003 weeks. Findings assert that Monday is dominated by all the other days in different stochastic dominance orders. Also, Friday can only dominate Monday and Tuesday in the third-order. Another important study conducted by Seyhun (1993) investigates January effect in NYSE between 1926 and 1991. The researcher tries to find out whether the January effect can be different according to the firm size. Thus, ten different portfolio indexes created to analyse this statement. According to the findings, the portfolio index consists of the smallest size companies dominate others. Furthermore, January returns are compared with other months' returns. It is found that January dominates other months in different order forms of SD. The study concludes that a positive January effect exists in NYSE, which supports tax-loss selling or window-dressing hypothesis (i.e. the price pressure hypothesis). A sample group of 7 Asian stock markets are tested by Lean, Smyth & Wong (2007) for both daily and monthly aspects. Results show that Monday is dominated by some other weekdays in all countries except Indonesia in different levels of SD. Moreover, the January effect is applicable only for Hong Kong and Singapore. But here January is dominated by July for both countries and by November and December for Singapore only. Findings of this paper show a contradiction between the US and Asian markets on the dominance relationship direction for the January effect.

SD methodology for calendar anomaly effect is used for some developing markets such as Turkey, Greece, Nigeria and Pakistan. Basdas (2011) examines the day-of-the-week effect in Borsa Istanbul and suggests that Friday dominates all trading days except for Wednesday, while Monday is dominated by Wednesday, Thursday and Friday. In addition, Tuesday is dominated by Wednesday and Friday. Athens stock market is analysed by Al-Khazali, Koumanakos & Pyun (2008) for 1985-2004. Results show that Friday dominates other days in the first-order. Also, Tuesday is dominated by other days in the first and higher orders. Monthly results show that January dominates ten other months except for February for the first and higher orders, which proves the existence of seasonality anomaly for stock exchange of Athens. Furthermore, Rashid & Kausar (2019) show that January returns with low and high beta portfolios are found different from other months' returns under SD analysis in Pakistan stock market. Finally, Adinya, Oke & Edeki (2019) assert that March and April dominate other nine months in the Nigerian stock market. Also, November is found as the weakest performing month where this month cannot dominate other months. Finally, the January effect is not found in this study.

DATA

In this paper, closing values of the five developed and five emerging countries' indexes are taken from Bloomberg L.P. (2020) for the time frame of 04.01.1988 to 31.12.2019. The highest volume indexes are taken for the developed countries. For the emerging countries, the countries with the available data from 1988 are selected. The chosen countries, indexes and their Bloomberg codes can be found in Table 1. The frequency of the data is selected as daily and monthly for checking the seasonality effect in these different frequencies. The data from 04.01.1988 to 31.12.2016 is chosen as the analysis period, and the remaining data from 01.01.2017 to 31.12.2019 is left for the back-testing period.

Table 1. Chosen countries and their corresponding indexes with the Bloomberg codes

Country	Index	Bloomberg Code
United States	S&P 500	SPX
United Kingdom	FTSE 100	UKX
Japan	Nikkei 225	NKY
Germany	DAX 30	DAX
France	CAC 40	CAC
South Korea	Korea Composite Stock Price Index	KOSPI
Indonesia	Jakarta Stock Exchange Composite Index	JCI
Malaysia	FTSE Bursa Malaysia KLCI	FBMKLCI
Turkey	Borsa Istanbul 100	XU100
Thailand	Stock Exhange of Thailand SET	SET

Then, the simple daily and monthly returns are calculated for each index. By using the analysis period data, the pairwise second-order stochastic dominance efficiency test is performed using the self-developed MATLAB code for both frequencies and each country. The days or months, which are not second-order stochastically dominated by any other day or month, are called efficient days or months. The remaining ones, which were dominated by any other day or month, are named inefficient days or months. Regarding the requirements of the pairwise SSD efficiency (Hanoch and Levy, 1969), an efficient portfolio should only contain efficient days or months.

Daily and monthly simple average returns are calculated for sample stock markets that can be found in Table 2 and 3, respectively. The number of observation in average daily return calculation for each weekday is 1650, where this number is 29 for average monthly return case. Here, the aim is to see the overall picture of the distribution of the returns. There are some issues here worth underlining. First of all, minimum average daily returns (underlined) are clustered on Mondays except Germany and the US. Interestingly, the average daily return is observed on Fridays in these countries. On the other hand, the maximum average daily returns (shown in italic) are varied for countries. Monday for Germany, Tuesday for the US, the UK and France, Wednesday for South Korea and Indonesia, Thursday for Japan and finally Friday for Malaysia, Thailand and Turkey are the maximum daily average return days. When all countries are grouped into one, Monday has the lowest (-0,028%), and Friday has the highest return (0,087%). Low Monday return effect seems obvious in general. Monday returns are negative in seven countries. On the contrary, returns of Tuesday, Wednesday and Friday are positive in nine countries, and all countries show positive returns on Thursday.

Table 2. Average Daily Return for Sample Countries (1988-2016, in %)

	Mon	Tue	Wed	Thu	Fri	Min	Max
SPX	0.0346	0.0668	0.0406	0.0169	0.0144	*Fri*	*Tue*
UKX	-0.0128	0.0632	-0.0015	0.0254	0.0479	*Mon*	*Tue*
NKY	-0.0515	0.0297	0.0453	0.0505	-0.0281	*Mon*	*Thu*
DAX	0.0587	0.0466	0.0506	0.0304	0.0280	*Fri*	*Mon*
CAC	-0.0430	0.0586	0.0407	0.0580	0.0372	*Mon*	*Tue*
KOSPI	-0.0132	0.0249	0.0752	0.0411	0.0276	*Mon*	*Wed*
JCI	-0.0236	0.0169	0.1315	0.0925	0.1227	*Mon*	*Wed*
FBMKLCI	-0.0829	0.0345	0.0878	0.0264	0.0955	*Mon*	*Fri*
XU100	0.0187	0.0284	0.1726	0.2665	0.2950	*Mon*	*Fri*
SET	-0.1626	-0.0417	0.1177	0.0270	0.2309	*Mon*	*Fri*
Average	**-0.0278**	**0.0328**	**0.0761**	**0.0635**	**0.0871**	***Mon***	***Fri***

Months with the minimum returns are concentrated in August and September, except for the UK and Turkey. In all countries, August returns are negative. September returns are also found negative, except for Turkey. Maximum returns are clustered in December and January for all countries except France, which has the maximum return in April. These results give a preview about the existence of the turn-of-the-year effect, which is not in the interest of this study. In addition, positive returns are observed in April, July and December for all selected countries. All countries have positive returns in January except for the UK, in February except for South Korea and in November except for Thailand. Finally, the average return is highest in December, April and January whilst it is the lowest in August, September and June, respectively.

Table 3. Average Monthly Return for Sample Countries (1988-2016, in %)

	Jan	Feb	Mar	Apr	May	Jun	Jul	Aug	Sep	Oct	Nov	Dec	Min	Max
SPX	0.09	0.30	1.34	1.69	1.11	-0.35	1.06	-1.01	-0.32	1.52	1.38	1.71	***Aug***	***Dec***
UKX	-0.15	0.70	0.15	1.91	-0.02	-1.09	1.35	-0.26	-1.04	1.44	0.76	2.14	***Jun***	***Dec***
NKY	0.05	0.50	0.85	1.40	0.06	-0.71	0.23	-1.71	-1.45	-0.03	1.06	1.64	***Aug***	***Dec***
DAX	0.45	1.39	1.09	2.51	0.84	0.02	1.67	-2.28	-2.57	2.56	2.39	2.80	***Sep***	***Dec***
CAC	0.38	1.82	1.19	2.46	0.00	-1.11	0.79	-1.42	-1.77	2.17	0.98	1.88	***Sep***	***May***
KOSPI	2.79	-1.00	1.67	1.33	-0.11	-1.17	1.86	-1.39	-0.21	1.07	2.36	1.16	***Aug***	***Jan***
JCI	2.65	1.49	2.36	2.06	2.60	1.36	1.29	-1.41	-1.44	-0.09	1.18	7.31	***Sep***	***Dec***
FBMKLCI	0.87	2.70	-0.37	1.56	0.63	-0.03	0.90	-2.85	-0.59	1.95	0.12	4.11	***Aug***	***Dec***
XU100	8.59	2.45	1.73	6.73	-1.47	4.36	3.41	-1.08	4.89	3.90	2.95	8.02	***May***	***Jan***
SET	3.22	1.25	-0.42	2.13	-0.20	1.38	0.65	-1.02	-0.80	1.11	-0.38	3.33	***Aug***	***Dec***
Average	**1.89**	**1.16**	**0.96**	**2.38**	**0.34**	**0.27**	**1.32**	**-1.44**	**-0.53**	**1.56**	**1.28**	**3.41**	***Aug***	***Dec***

Shapiro Wilk test is employed for Normality check of the data. Firstly, daily return data is not normally distributed for all weekdays (p-values are approximately 0 in all cases). This result is expected because of the characteristics of the financial daily return series. Secondly, results vary in monthly case, where normal and non-normal distributions are observed. Since the method applied in this study is non-parametric, it can still be applied under non-normality conditions.

METHODOLOGY

Stochastic Dominance

Stochastic dominance is a sound method in decision theory under uncertainty. It describes that when a particular random prospect, such as a lottery or a stock, is better than another random prospect based on the preferences regarding outcomes which may be expressed in terms of utility values.

Two important types of stochastic dominance are known as the first-order stochastic dominance (FSD) and the second-order stochastic dominance (SSD). SSD is much more usable due to the practical interpretability of the results; however, it has the assumption of the investors to be risk-averse. The definitions of FSD and SSD are as below in (1) and (2).

i) FSD: A is first-order stochastically dominant over B, if;

$F(t)$ £ $G(t)$, for all t with strict inequality for at least one $t \in R$ (1)

where F and G represent the cumulative probability distributions of A and B respectively.

ii) SSD: A is second-order stochastically dominant over B, if;

$$\int_{-\infty}^{x} F(t)\,dt \leq \int_{-\infty}^{x} G(t)\,dt \qquad (2)$$

for all values of x, and there is at least one value of x for which the above inequality is strict, where F and G represent the cumulative probability distributions of A and B respectively.

FSD is a stronger form of stochastic dominance compared to SSD. In terms of portfolio optimization, the results of FSD is valid for all rational investors; however, SSD is only valid for risk-averse investors. While most of the investors are risk-averse, SSD is still applicable as a non-parametric portfolio choice approach. The advantages of SSD is that it does not carry the two shortcomings of MV, finite variance assumption and limitation of the model to only two parameters, mean and variance (Guran et al., 2019).

Pairwise Efficiency for FSD and SSD

A portfolio is pairwise SSD inefficient if there is an asset that second-order stochastically dominates the portfolio. Otherwise, the portfolio is pairwise SSD efficient (Branda and Kopa, 2014). The set of all assets which are not second orderly dominated by other ones is an SSD pairwise efficient set. In this study, we take these assets as the days-of-the-week and the months-of-the-year.

Following Levy (2015); let v_i^t, t= 1,2,…., T denote the ordered returns of the day/month i in ascending order, that is, $v_i^1 \leq v_i^2 \leq \ldots \leq v_i^T$. Then the day/month i dominates the day/month j with respect to the first-order stochastic dominance if and only if;

$v_i^t \geq v_j^t$, t= 1,2, …., T with at least one strict inequality. (3)

Furthermore, day/month j is classified as FSD pairwise inefficient, if there exists a day/month i satisfying (1). Otherwise, day/month j is FSD pairwise efficient. Thus, the algorithm of testing for the FSD pairwise efficiency of the j day/month consists of two steps. Firstly, the returns are ordered in ascending order v_i^t for all i= 1,2, …, N, t= 1,2, …, T. Secondly, it is tried to find some i satisfying (3). If such i exists, then the day/month j is FSD pairwise inefficient. If not, then the day/month *j* is FSD pairwise efficient (Branda and Kopa, 2012).

Testing of SSD pairwise efficiency is performed in a similar way to the previous algorithm, using criterion (4) instead of (3).

$\sum_{t=1}^{s} v_i^t \geq \sum_{t=1}^{s} v_j^t, s = 1, 2, \ldots, T$ with at least one strict inequality. (4)

As it can be easily interpreted from the definitions of pairwise efficiency, the days/months can be grouped in four discrete clusters. Groups A and D contain efficient days/months. On the other hand, groups B and C consist of inefficient days/months.

A: The days/months which dominate at least one day/month and are not dominated by any other day/month
B: The days/months which are dominated by at least one day/month and do not dominate any other day/month
C: The days/months which are dominated by at least one day/month and dominate at least one other day/month
D: The days/months which are not dominated by any other day/month and do not dominate any other day/month

RESULTS

The days and months, which were found efficient according to the pairwise SSD efficiency test can be seen in Tables 4 and 5 for daily and monthly frequencies, respectively. Table 4 shows that in 8 of the ten indexes; Tuesday, Wednesday and Friday are efficient. Thursday is efficient in 6 and Monday is efficient in 3 of the indexes. We observe that Monday is inefficient in all the emerging country indexes in addition to British and French indexes.

Table 4. Pairwise SSD Efficient Days of Each Index

Daily	Mon	Tue	Wed	Thu	Fri
SPX	×	×	×		
UKX		×		×	×
NKY	×	×	×	×	
DAX	×	×	×		×
CAC		×	×	×	×
KOSPI		×	×	×	×
JCI		×	×	×	×
FBMKLCI			×		×
XU100		×			×
SET			×	×	×

Table 5 demonstrates the pairwise SSD efficiency of the months according to the indexes. December is efficient in 8 of the ten indexes. Moreover, April is efficient in 6 country indexes. Additionally, October is dominated by all the other months for all the indexes. Moreover; March, May, August and September are dominated by only one index, which makes them inefficient for most of the indexes. Finally, KOSPI seems different from other indexes since it does not follow a general pattern.

Table 5. Pairwise SSD Efficient Months of Each Index

Monthly	Jan	Feb	Mar	Apr	May	Jun	Jul	Aug	Sep	Oct	Nov	Dec
SPX				×								×
UKX												×
NKY		×		×								×
DAX				×	×						×	×
CAC				×								
KOSPI	×	×	×			×	×	×	×		×	
JCI												×
FBMKLCI												×
XU100	×			×		×	×					×
SET				×								×

In this back-testing part, an SSD investment strategy is developed according to the results in Tables 4 and 5, and it is compared with the benchmark index. In the SSD strategy, the main assumption is that when the index is efficient, it is overbought in this period, and when the index is inefficient, it is oversold in that period. Due to the mean reversion tendency, it is assumed that the oversold period will be followed by an overbought period and an increasing trend. On the other hand, the overbought period will be followed by an oversold period and a decreasing trend. Here, it is also assumed that indexes can be traded as ETFs. Therefore, after an inefficient period of an index, a long position will be opened with all the amount (100 at the starting point) Oppositely, after an efficient month for an index, a whole long position will be closed. If there are consecutive inefficient periods, a long position will be opened after the end of the last inefficient period and it will be held until an efficient period. If there are consecutive efficient periods, a long position will be closed after the end of the last efficient period, and a new long position will not be opened until the end of the inefficient period. We assume short-sale is not allowed and other costs are exempted, which can occur due to transactions such as commission and tax.

As a daily case example from SPX, a long position is opened on Fridays, and it is closed on Wednesdays. Both transactions are done from the closing price. These moves are repeated recursively until the end of the back-testing period. In the same sense, a monthly example from SPX is performed in this way: Long position is opened at the end of March, closed at the end of April, opened at the end of November and closed again at the end of December. These four moves are repeated recursively in the back-testing period for the SPX.

The back-testing results for the daily returns are given in Table 6 for all the indexes. This table shows the result of the 3-years back-testing period. In the index column, the return of the benchmark index is given. In the SSD column, the return of the SSD strategy is shown. In DAX, CAC, JCI and FBMKLCI indexes, SSD strategy outperforms the benchmark. However, for the other indexes, the strategy cannot outperform the benchmark.

Table 6. Back-testing results for the daily returns of the benchmark index and the SSD strategy for 2017-2019

Daily returns	2017-2019	
	Index	SSD
SPX	44.31%	18.09%
UKX	5.59%	-2.61%
NKY	23.76%	12.65%
DAX	15.40%	34.79%
CAC	22.95%	28.88%
KOSPI	7.34%	5.27%
JCI	18.93%	22.25%
FBMKLCI	-3.23%	-0.05%
XU100	46.44%	26.71%
SET	2.39%	-4.71%

To further evaluate the relatively bad performance of SSD strategy, the back-testing performance of the daily returns are evaluated for bearish and bullish market conditions. (Table 7). In this analysis, in 2017, the SSD strategy outperforms the benchmark only in DAX. On the contrary, SSD strategy outperforms the benchmark for all the indexes, but JCI, in the bearish 2018. In 2019, the performance of the SSD strategy and the benchmark are even. In DAX, CAC, JCI, FBMKLCI and XU100; SSD strategy outperforms the benchmark. On the other hand, the benchmark outperforms the SSD strategy for the other indexes.

Table 7. Back-testing results for the daily returns of the benchmark index and the SSD strategy for 2017, 2018 and 2019

Daily returns	2017		2018		2019	
	Index	SSD	Index	SSD	Index	SSD
SPX	19.42%	13.37%	-6.24%	-1.09%	28.88%	5.31%
UKX	7.63%	0.52%	-12.48%	-11.84%	12.10%	9.90%
NKY	19.10%	12.25%	-12.08%	-10.26%	18.20%	11.83%
DAX	12.51%	15.16%	-18.26%	-8.44%	25.48%	27.84%
CAC	9.26%	5.83%	-10.95%	-5.48%	26.37%	28.85%
KOSPI	21.76%	17.49%	-17.28%	-14.37%	6.57%	4.64%
JCI	19.99%	15.80%	-2.54%	-5.55%	1.70%	11.77%
FBMKLCI	9.45%	4.51%	-5.91%	-2.78%	-6.02%	-1.63%
XU100	47.60%	9.43%	-20.86%	-12.12%	25.37%	31.77%
SET	13.66%	9.48%	-10.82%	-7.84%	1.02%	-5.56%

In Table 8, back-testing results for the monthly returns of the indexes for the period 2017-2019 can be found. In this table, monthly returns' performance according to the SSD strategy and the benchmark indexes are compared. Overall, the SSD strategy outperformed the benchmark only for three indexes, namely KOSPI, FBMKLCI and XU100. It must be mentioned that all these indexes are emerging country indexes.

Table 8. Back-testing results for the monthly returns of the benchmark index and the SSD strategy for 2017-2019

Monthly returns	2017-2019	
	Index	SSD
SPX	44.31%	-0.79%
UKX	5.59%	3.84%
NKY	23.76%	0.40%
DAX	15.40%	0.73%
CAC	22.95%	14.70%
KOSPI	7.34%	12.23%
JCI	18.93%	14.45%
FBMKLCI	-3.23%	7.08%
XU100	46.44%	57.76%
SET	2.39%	-0.51%

Table 9. Back-testing results for the monthly returns of the benchmark index and the SSD strategy for 2017, 2018 and 2019

Monthly returns	2017		2018		2019	
	Index	SSD	Index	SSD	Index	SSD
SPX	19.42%	1.90%	-6.24%	-8.93%	28.88%	6.90%
UKX	7.63%	4.93%	-12.48%	-3.61%	12.10%	2.67%
NKY	19.10%	2.11%	-12.08%	-10.40%	18.20%	9.74%
DAX	12.51%	0.04%	-18.26%	-3.89%	25.48%	4.76%
CAC	9.26%	2.83%	-10.95%	6.84%	26.37%	4.41%
KOSPI	21.76%	6.71%	-17.28%	-0.98%	6.57%	6.20%
JCI	19.99%	6.78%	-2.54%	2.28%	1.70%	4.79%
FBMKLCI	9.45%	4.60%	-5.91%	0.64%	-6.02%	1.73%
XU100	47.60%	30.12%	-20.86%	-13.36%	25.37%	39.93%
SET	13.66%	2.74%	-10.82%	-4.54%	1.02%	1.44%

For evaluating the performance of the monthly returns in different years, the performance of the SSD strategy and the benchmark index are compared in the years 2017, 2018 and 2019 (Table 9). In the bullish 2017, benchmark index outperformed the SSD strategy in all the indexes. However, in the bearish 2018, SSD strategy outperformed the benchmark index for all the investigated countries, but the US. In 2019, the SSD strategy outperforms the benchmark index for JCI, FBMKLCI and XU100. The benchmark index performs better than the SSD strategy portfolio for the rest of the indexes in 2019.

CONCLUSION

In this paper, the seasonality effect is investigated in five developed and five emerging countries' stock market indexes. The seasonality effect is analysed from two different aspects: The day-of-the-week and the-month-of-the-year effects. SSD is performed to investigate the difference between the days of the week and months of the year, respectively. After that, an SSD portfolio strategy is proposed, and portfolio management is done according to the results of the pairwise SSD efficiency tests. Then, the SSD strategy returns are compared with the benchmark index returns in the back-testing period. Moreover, the test period is divided into three terms; 2017, 2018 and 2019 and further evaluated to see the results of the SSD portfolio strategy for the upside and downside trending years. There are several points we can conclude from this research.

Firstly; Tuesday, Wednesday and Friday found as the efficient days for 8 of the ten indexes. On the other hand, Monday is efficient only for three indexes; all of them are from the developed country indexes. This result is in line with the literature (Yakob et al, 2005; Yalcin & Yucel, 2006; Cinko & Avci, 2009; Lim, Mun & Dollery, 2010; Basdas, 2011; Tangjitprom, 2011) regarding that the Monday is the worst performing day among the days of the week as well as Friday is the best performing one. The reason for this result is discussed thoroughly in the literature. Moreover, findings suggest that the emerging countries' indexes are much more inefficient and tend to be affected by such seasonality effects.

From the month of the year seasonality point of view, April and December are the efficient months. The December effect is already investigated in the literature (Borges, 2009; Keong et al., 2010; Faisal & Majid, 2016; Plastun et al., 2020) as well as in practice. April effect is an interesting finding of the research, and it shows dissimilarity with (Yakob et al. 2005). Keeping in mind April is efficient in 6 of the ten stock markets, and possible explanation for this effect is the dividend distribution announcements. Regarding that 4 of the six, April efficient stock market indexes are developed ones, explanation of the chapter may be supported easily due to the higher dividend distribution rates of the developed countries' companies. Moreover, the difference of the efficient months in KOSPI, XU100; and the other markets also proposes the idea of the inefficiency of the emerging markets. Another effect may be the "Sell in May" effect or so-called "Halloween effect", which evidences the stronger performance of the stocks from November to April compared to the average of the other months.

Secondly, according to the results, it cannot be concluded that SSD strategy can be used in any situation and in any market. For the day-of-the-week, SSD strategy gives better results only for DAX, CAC, JCI and FBMKLCI, if all the test period from 2017 to 2019 is evaluated. For the-month-of-the-year effect, only KOSPI, FBMKLCI and XU100 perform better with the SSD strategy. The-month-of-the-year results suggest that the SSD strategy may perform better in the much inefficient emerging market indexes than the efficient developed market indexes. Therefore, it may be better to use the SSD portfolio strategy only in the emerging market indexes.

Last but not least, the results are evaluated according to the bullish and bearish time periods of the stock markets. In 2017 and 2019 all the markets, but FBMKLCI in 2019, were bullish. On the other hand, in 2018 all the markets were in a bearish trend. The results differ a lot according to the situation of the markets. The daily SSD strategy outperforms only DAX among the benchmark indexes in 2017. In 2019; DAX, CAC, JCI, FBMKLCI and XU100 are better performing with the SSD portfolio strategy than the benchmark index. It must be mentioned that the SSD strategy outperforms the benchmark very slightly for the DAX and CAC indexes. Moreover, the gain of the JCI index is slightly positive in 2019, whereas there is a loss in the FBMKLCI index. On the other hand, in the bearish 2018, according to the daily results, all the SSD strategy portfolios outperform the benchmark indexes, except JCI. This shows the positive performance of the SSD portfolio strategy in the bad performing periods. We can suggest that the markets become much more inefficient in the bad performing periods and by using SSD, it is possible to detect the seasonality inefficiencies in the markets, which allows the investors to beat the market.

The monthly returns also support this suggestion. In the bullish 2017, all the benchmarks outperform the SSD strategy. In 2019, in four emerging market indexes; namely JCI, FBMKLCI, XU100 and SET; SSD strategy outperforms the benchmark. It must be mentioned that the index returns are below 2% for three of these four indexes in 2019. In the bearish 2018, in all the indexes, but SPX, SSD strategy outperforms the benchmark index. These monthly results support both of the main conclusions. Firstly, inefficient emerging market indexes are better to use according to SSD strategy chosen portfolios. Therefore, the SSD portfolio strategy outperforms the benchmark index more frequently in the emerging market indexes. Secondly and more importantly, in the bearish times, the inefficiencies due to seasonality are much more visible, and it is easier to benefit from the effects of the seasonality at these times. All in all, it may be much more profitable to use SSD in the bearish trends and especially in the emerging market indexes. To conclude, the reason for the relatively successful performance of the emerging market indexes is the possible inefficiency of these markets (See Fama (1970) for the efficient market hypothesis). Furthermore, the reason for the successful performance in the bearish periods may be the nature of SSD, which is valid only for risk-averse investors.

FUTURE RESEARCH DIRECTIONS

There are many opportunities for further research in this area. Firstly, third-order stochastic dominance, as well as higher orders, is an emerging research area. Secondly, the effect of the seasonality on different sectors can be further investigated by using SSD. Thirdly, the rule of thumb is using the simple returns instead of logarithmic returns in the stochastic dominance literature due to the non-parametric nature of the method. However, using the logarithmic returns and evaluating the difference may be another future research topic. Last but not least, getting out of the theoretical borders of the second-order stochastic dominance, i.e. changing the decision method of inefficient and efficient stocks or giving weights to the stocks according to their efficiency level might be substantial research topic.

REFERENCES

Adinya, I., Oke, T., & Edeki, S. O. (2019). Analysis of Month-of-the-year Effect in an Emerging Market via Stochastic Dominance Approach. *Academy of Entrepreneurship Journal*, *25*(2), 1–6.

Al-Khazali, O. M., Koumanakos, E. P., & Pyun, C. S. (2008). Calendar anomaly in the Greek stock market: Stochastic dominance analysis. *International Review of Financial Analysis*, *17*(3), 461–474. doi:10.1016/j.irfa.2007.02.001

Bachmann, C., Tegtmeier, L., Gebhardt, J., & Steinborn, M. (2019). The "sell in May" effect: An empirical investigation of globally listed private equity markets. *Managerial Finance*, *45*(6), 793–808. doi:10.1108/MF-07-2018-0322

Basdas, Ü. (2011). The day-of-the-week effect for Istanbul stock exchange: A stochastic dominance approach. *Journal of Applied Finance & Banking*, *1*(4), 223–238.

Basher, S. A., & Sadorsky, P. (2006). Day-of-the-week effects in emerging stock markets. *Applied Economics Letters*, *13*(10), 621–628. doi:10.1080/13504850600825238

Bildik, R. (2004). *Are calendar anomalies still alive? Evidence from Istanbul Stock Exchange. Evidence from Istanbul Stock Exchange (May 27, 2004)*. Academic Press.

Bloomberg L.P. (2020). *Stock prices of various indexes from 01/04/1988 to 31/12/2019*. Retrieved Jan. 8, 2020 from Bloomberg database.

Borges, M. R. (2009). *Calendar effects in stock markets: critique of previous methodologies and recent evidence in European countries*. Academic Press.

Branda, M., & Kopa, M. (2012). DEA-Risk Efficiency and Stochastic Dominance Efficiency of Stock Indices. *Finance a Uver. Czech Journal of Economics & Finance*, *62*(2).

Branda, M., & Kopa, M. (2014). On relations between DEA-risk models and stochastic dominance efficiency tests. *Central European Journal of Operations Research*, *22*(1), 13–35. doi:10.100710100-012-0283-2

Brooks, C., & Persand, G. (2001). Seasonality in Southeast Asian stock markets: Some new evidence on day-of-the-week effects. *Applied Economics Letters*, *8*(3), 155–158. doi:10.1080/13504850150504504

Chang, E. C., Pinegar, J. M., & Ravichandran, R. (1993). International Evidence on the Robustness of the Day-of-the-Week Effect. *Journal of Financial and Quantitative Analysis*, *28*(4), 497–513. doi:10.2307/2331162

Chia, R. C. J., Liew, V. K. S., & Syed Khalid Wafa, S. A. W. (2006). *Calendar anomalies in the Malaysian stock market (No. 516)*. University Library of Munich.

Cinko, M., & Avci, E. (2009). Examining the day of the week effect in Istanbul Stock Exchange (ISE). *International Business & Economics Research Journal*, *8*(11).

Cross, F. (1973). The behavior of stock prices on Fridays and Mondays. *Financial Analysts Journal*, *29*(6), 67–69. doi:10.2469/faj.v29.n6.67

Faisal, N., & Majid, M. S. A. (2016). Re-examination of calendar anomalies in the Indonesian stock market. *Journal of Applied Economic Sciences*, *11*(8/46), 1714-1723.

Fama, E. F. (1970). Efficient capital markets: A review of theory and empirical work. *The Journal of Finance*, *25*(2), 383–417. doi:10.2307/2325486

French, K. R. (1980). Stock Returns and the Weekend Effect. *Journal of Financial Economics*, *8*(1), 55–69. doi:10.1016/0304-405X(80)90021-5

Georgantopoulos, A. G. G., & Tsamis, A. D. (2008, December). The Istanbul Stock Exchange: Testing the significance of calendar anomalies. In *7th Annual Conference of the Hellenic Finance and Accounting Association* (pp. 12-13). Academic Press.

Gu, A. Y. (2003). The Declining January Effect: Evidence from the U.S. Equity Market. *The Quarterly Review of Economics and Finance*, *43*(2), 395–404. doi:10.1016/S1062-9769(02)00160-6

Guran, C. B., Ugurlu, U., & Tas, O. (2019). Mean-Variance Portfolio Optimization of Energy Stocks Supported with Second Order Stochastic Dominance Efficiency. *Finance a Uver*, *69*(4), 366–383.

Haggard, K. S., & Witte, H. D. (2010). The Halloween effect: Trick or treat? *International Review of Financial Analysis*, *19*(5), 379–387. doi:10.1016/j.irfa.2010.10.001

Hanoch, G., & Levy, H. (1969). The efficiency analysis of choices involving risk. *The Review of Economic Studies*, *36*(3), 335–346. doi:10.2307/2296431

Jaffe, J., & Westerfield, R. (1985). The Week-End Effect in Common Stock Returns: The International Evidence. *The Journal of Finance*, *40*(2), 433–454. doi:10.1111/j.1540-6261.1985.tb04966.x

Kato, K., & Schallheim, J. S. (1985). Seasonal and size anomalies in the Japanese stock market. *Journal of Financial and Quantitative Analysis*, *20*(2), 243–260. doi:10.2307/2330958

Kelly, F. C. (1930). *Why You Win or Lose: The Pshycology of Speculation*. Academic Press.

Keong, L. B., Yat, D. N. C., & Ling, C. H. (2010). Month-of-the-year effects in Asian countries: A 20-year study (1990-2009). *African Journal of Business Management*, *4*(7), 1351–1362.

Kohers, G., Kohers, N., Pandey, V., & Kohers, T. (2004). The Disappearing Day-of-the-Week Effect in the World's Largest Equity Markets. *Applied Economics Letters, 11*(3), 167–171. doi:10.1080/1350485042000203797

Kroll, Y., & Levy, H. (1980). Sampling Errors and Portfolio Efficient Analysis. *Journal of Financial and Quantitative Analysis, 15*(3), 655–688. doi:10.2307/2330403

Lakonishok, J., & Smidt, S. (1988). Are Seaosonal Anomalies Real? A Ninety-year Perspective. *Review of Financial Studies, 1*(4), 403–425. doi:10.1093/rfs/1.4.403

Lean, H. H., Smyth, R., & Wong, W. K. (2007). Revisiting calendar anomalies in Asian stock markets using a stochastic dominance. *Journal of Multinational Financial Management, 17*(2), 125–141. doi:10.1016/j.mulfin.2006.05.003

Levy, H. (2015). *Stochastic dominance: Investment decision making under uncertainty*. Springer.

Lim, S. Y., Mun Ho, C., & Dollery, B. (2010). An empirical analysis of calendar anomalies in the Malaysian stock market. *Applied Financial Economics, 20*(3), 255–264. doi:10.1080/09603100903282648

Linn, S. C., & Lockwood, L. J. (1988). Short-term Stock Price Patterns: NYSE, AMEX, OTC. *Journal of Portfolio Management, 14*(2), 30–34. doi:10.3905/jpm.1988.409139

Lucey, B. M., & Zhao, S. (2008). Halloween or January? Yet another puzzle. *International Review of Financial Analysis, 17*(5), 1055–1069. doi:10.1016/j.irfa.2006.03.003

Maberly, E. D., & Pierce, R. M. (2003). The Halloween effect and Japanese equity prices: Myth or exploitable anomaly. *Asia-Pacific Financial Markets, 10*(4), 319–334. doi:10.100710690-005-4240-0

Moller, N., & Zilca, S. (2008). The evolution of the January Effect. *Journal of Banking & Finance, 32*(3), 447–457. doi:10.1016/j.jbankfin.2007.06.009

Patel, J. B., & Evans, D. A. (2003). Seasonal Stock Return Patterns in the Seven Industrialized Nations. *Journal of Applied Business Research, 19*(3). Advance online publication. doi:10.19030/jabr.v19i3.2177

Pettengil, G. N. (2003). A Survey of the Monday Effect Literature. *Quarterly Journal of Business and Economics, 42*(3/4), 3–27.

Philpot, J., & Peterson, C. A. (2011). A brief history and recent developments in the day-of-the-week effect literature. *Managerial Finance, 37*(9), 808–816. doi:10.1108/03074351111153203

Plastun, A., Sibande, X., Gupta, R., & Wohar, M. E. (2020). Historical evolution of monthly anomalies in international stock markets. *Research in International Business and Finance, 52*, 101127. doi:10.1016/j.ribaf.2019.101127

Rashid, A., & Kausar, S. (2019). Testing the Monthly Calendar Anomaly of Stock Returns in Pakistan: A Stochastic Dominance Approach. *Pakistan Development Review, 58*(1), 83–104. doi:10.30541/v58i1pp.83-104

Rossi, M. (2015). The efficient market hypothesis and calendar anomalies: A literature review. *International Journal of Managerial and Financial Accounting, 7*(3-4), 285–296. doi:10.1504/IJMFA.2015.074905

Rossi, M., & Gunardi, A. (2018). Efficient market hypothesis and stock market anomalies: Empirical evidence in four European countries. *Journal of Applied Business Research*, *34*(1), 183–192. doi:10.19030/jabr.v34i1.10111

Rozeff, M. S., & Kinney, W. R. Jr. (1976). Capital Market Seasonality: The Case of Stock Returns. *Journal of Financial Economics*, *3*(4), 379–402. doi:10.1016/0304-405X(76)90028-3

Seyhun, H. N. (1993, June). Can Omitted Risk Factors Explain the January Effect? A Stochastic Dominance Approach. *Journal of Financial and Quantitative Analysis*, *28*(2), 195–213. doi:10.2307/2331286

Steeley, J. M. (2001). A Note on Information Seasonality and the Disappearence of the Weekend Effect in the UK Stock Market. *Journal of Banking & Finance*, *25*(10), 1941–1956. doi:10.1016/S0378-4266(00)00167-9

Tangjitprom, N. (2011). The calendar anomalies of stock return in Thailand. *Journal of Modern Accounting and Auditing*, *7*(6), 565.

Tong, W. (2000). Intenational Evindence on Weekend Anomalies. *Journal of Financial Research*, *23*(4), 495–522. doi:10.1111/j.1475-6803.2000.tb00757.x

Wingender, J., & Groff, J. E. (1989). On Stochastic Dominance Analysis of Day-of-the-week Return Patterns. *Journal of Financial Research*, *12*(1), 51–55. doi:10.1111/j.1475-6803.1989.tb00100.x

Yakob, N. A., Beal, D., & Delpachitra, S. (2005). Seasonality in the Asia Pacific stock markets. *Journal of Asset Management*, *6*(4), 298–318. doi:10.1057/palgrave.jam.2240183

Yalcin, Y., & Yucel, E. M. (2006). The day-of-the-week effect on stock-market volatility and return: Evidence from emerging markets. *Finance a Uver-Czech Journal of Economics and Finance*, *56*(5-6), 258–279.

KEY TERMS AND DEFINITIONS

Back-Testing: An analysis that assesses the relative performance of a trading strategy using historical financial data in the test period.

Calendar Anomaly: A seasonality effect that is observed mostly in financial markets within a specific time frame.

Day-of-the-Week Effect: A certain trading day in a week that shows distinctive performance either for positive or negative sides during the analysis period.

December Effect: An upward pattern in stock markets due to investors' fiscal year-ending transactions.

Month-of-the-Year Effect: A certain month in a calendar year that exhibits idiosyncratic return behaviour either for positive or negative sides during the analysis period.

Pairwise SSD Efficiency: The set of all assets, which are not second order stochastically dominated by the other ones, is an SSD pairwise efficient set.

Stochastic Dominance: A non-parametric approach that uses cumulative distribution functions to compare and rank return datasets disregarding their realization time.

APPENDIX

Table 10. Literature Review Summary for the Day-of-the-Week Effect

Study	Sample Countries	Sample Period	Methodology	Findings
French (1980)	U.S	1953 - 1977	OLS	· Monday (-)
Jaffe & Westerfield (1985)	Australia, Canada, Japan, U.K, U.S	Different for Each Country - 1983	OLS Using Dummy for Each Weekday	· Monday Canada, U.K & U.S (-), · Tuesday Australia & Japan (-)
Chang et al. (1993)	13 European and 6 Pacific Basin Countries & Canada, Mexico, South Africa and U.S	1985 - 1992	OLS Using Dummy for Monday	· Monday Spain (+), 8 Indices (-)
Tong (2000)	11 European and 8 Asian Countries & Australia, Canada, South Africa and U.S	1980 - 1995 (for most indices)	OLS Using Dummy for Monday	· Monday Austria and Spain (+), 16 Indices (-)
Brooks & Persand (2001)	5 Southeast Asian Countries	1989 - 1996	OLS Using Dummy for Each Weekday	· Monday Malaysia & Thailand (+), · Tuesday Malaysia (-), · Wednesday Taiwan (-), Thursday Malaysia (+)
Steeley (2001)	U.K	1991-1998	OLS Using Dummy for Monday	· No Monday Effect after the 1990s
Bildik (2004)	Turkey	1988 - 1999	OLS Using Dummy for Each Weekday, Kruskal-Wallis	· Tuesday (-), · Thursday (+)
Kohers et al. (2004)	11 Largest Market Cap. MSCI Indices	1980 - 2002	ANOVA and Kruskal-Wallis	· Monday Japan (-) after the 1990s
Yakob et al. (2005)	10 Asia-Pacific Countries	2000 - 2005	GARCH	· Monday Indonesia (-), · Wednesday Indonesia (+), · Thursday China (-), · Friday Taiwan (+)
Basher & Sadorsky (2006)	21 Emerging Countries	1992 - 2003	OLS Using Dummy for Each Weekday	· Monday Malaysia & Thailand (-), · Tuesday Pakistan (-), · Thursday Turkey (+), · Friday Taiwan & Turkey (+)
Yalcin & Yucel (2006)	20 Emerging Countries	1994 (different for some countries) - 2005	GARCH	· Monday Indonesia & Lithuania (-), · Thursday & Friday Russia (+)
Al-Khazali et al. (2008)	Greece	1985 - 2004	Stochastic Dominance	· Friday (+)*
Borges (2009)	17 European Countries	1994 - 2007	OLS Using Dummy for Each Weekday, GARCH	· Friday Effect 4 countries (+), · Tuesday Effect Germany(+), · Monday Effect Greece, Iceland (-)
Cinko & Avci (2009)	Turkey	1988 - 2008	OLS Using Dummy for Each Weekday	· Monday (-) · Thursday & Friday (+)
Lim et al. (2010)	Malaysia	2000 -2006	OLS Using Dummy for Each Weekday, Kruskal-Wallis, Wilcoxon Rank-Sum	· Monday (-) · Wednesday & Friday (+)
Basdas (2011)	Turkey	1988 - 2010	Stochastic Dominance	· Wednesday & Friday (+)*
Tangjitprom (2011)	Thailand	1988 - 2009	OLS and GARCH	· Monday (-) · Friday (+)

*(+) and (-) mean efficient and inefficient for stochastic dominance relation respectively.
Source: Author's Calculation

Table 11. Literature Review Summary for the Month-of-the-Year Effect

Study	Sample Countries	Sample Period	Methodology	Findings
Rozeff & Kinney (1976)	U.S	1904 - 1974	Kruskal-Wallis, Siegel-Tukey & Pairwise Comparison	- January (+), - February & June (-)
Kato & Schallheim (1985)	Japan	1952 - 1980	OLS, Kruskal Wallis	- January (+)
Seyhun (1993)	U.S	1926 - 1991	Stochastic Dominance	- January (+)*
Yakob et al. (2005)	10 Asia-Pacific Countries	2000 - 2005	GARCH	- January Malaysia (+), - April India (-), Indonesia (+), - May India (+), - June Indonesia (+), - September China & Malaysia (-)
Lean et al. (2007)	7 South Asian Countries	1988 - 2002	Stochastic Dominance	- January (-)* Singapore
Al-Khazali et al. (2008)	Greece	1985 - 2004	Stochastic Dominance	- January (+)*
Lucey & Zhao (2008)	U.S	1926 - 2002	OLS Dummy for January	- No significant Halloween Effect
Borges (2009)	17 European Countries	1994 - 2007	OLS Using Dummy for Each Weekday, GARCH	- January 3 Countries (+), - September 6 Countries (-), - November 3 Countries (+)
Haggar & Witte (2010)	U.S	1954 - 2008	OLS Using Dummy	- Halloween Effect (+)
Keong et al. (2010)	11 Asian Countries	1990 - 2009	GARCH	- December Indonesia, Malaysia & Thailand (+)
Tangjitprom (2011)	Thailand	1988 - 2009	OLS and GARCH	- January (-) - December (+)
Rossi & Gunardi (2018)	France, Germany, Italy & Spain	2000 - 2010	OLS, GARCH	- January Spain(+), - May Spain (-), - September Germany(-)

*(+) and (-) mean efficient and inefficient for stochastic dominance relation respectively.
Source: Author's Calculation

Chapter 4
Predicting Equity Returns in Developed Markets

A. Doruk Günaydin
https://orcid.org/0000-0001-5235-6664
Sabanci University, Turkey

ABSTRACT

This chapter examines the relation between various firm-specific variables and the cross-section of equity returns in 26 developed countries. Univariate portfolio analyses using equal-weighted returns show that low beta, book-to-market equity, and momentum analysis are also priced in the cross-section of developed market returns, whereas short-term reversal and downside beta manifest themselves in the opposite direction. Univariate portfolio analysis based on value-weighted returns reveal that the predictive power of book-to-market equity and short-term reversal is driven by small stocks. Multivariate firm-level cross-sectional regression analysis document that momentum, short-term reversal, illiquidity, idiosyncratic volatility, hybrid tail risk, lower partial moment are related to expected stock returns. Overall, the most robust cross-sectional predictor in developed market is found to be return momentum.

INTRODUCTION

According to the capital asset pricing model (CAPM) of Sharpe (1964), Lintner (1965), and Mossin (1966), market beta should be the only variable that explains the cross-section of equity returns. Although this model has huge impact on the academic research on stock return predictability, current literature has found many firm-specific attributes that add additional explanatory power for expected stock returns. Previous literature has discovered so many variables for explaining the cross-sectional variation in equity returns that Cochrane (2011) called researchers to refine the firm-specific variables that provide unique and statistically significant predictive power for equity return since only systematic factors should provide explanatory power.

DOI: 10.4018/978-1-7998-5083-0.ch004

This chapter can be regarded as an answer to this call in the developed market environment to identify the cross-sectional return determinants that are correlated with the systematic factors. Literature documents so many variables as potential return determinants in U.S.; however, the evidence outside of the U.S. is incomplete, and this chapter aims to reinvestigate this U.S. evidence in developed markets.

Although there are some studies on the cross-section of equity returns in developed markets, these studies have restrictions in two dimensions. First, they only examine a limited number of potential expected return determinants. Second, they restrict their analysis in a single country or a small group of countries. The main goal of this chapter is to investigate the relation between a comprehensive set of firm-specific attributes that can affect equity returns for a sample of equities from 26 developed countries. Therefore, the reader will be able to examine the unique information that a firm-specific variable provides compared to other variables and compare these results across all developed countries.

This chapter will examine the potential return determinants which can only be extracted from the empirical return distribution of equity returns. These variables are, the market beta, size and value effects (Fama and French (1993)), return momentum (Jegadeesh and Titman (1993)), short term reversal (Jegadeesh (1990)), illiquidity (Amihud (2002)), idiosyncratic volatility (Ang, Hodrick, Xing and Zhang (2006)), co-skewness (Harvey and Siddique (2000)), tail risk proxies such as value-at-risk, expected shortfall, lower partial moment and hybrid tail covariance risk (Bali, Cakici and Whitelaw (2014)), downside beta (Bawa and Lindenberg (1977)), and lottery demand (Bali, Cakici and Whitelaw (2011)). There are various accounting-based variables that are documented to explain the cross-section of equity returns in U.S.; however, it is not quite practical to compare accounting information across these countries due to the sparsity of accounting data and variations in accounting practices in different countries. Therefore, the set of variables are limited to be the ones that can be extracted from the equity return distribution. The only exception is the book-to-market ratio of equity since book value of equity is easier to calculate and compare across counties.

Several methodologies are utilized to test the hypothesis. First, the author forms decile portfolios based on one of the firm-specific attributes and examines whether equities in the highest firm-specific attribute decile generate significant return than those in the lowest firm-specific attribute decile. In addition to univariate portfolio analysis, bivariate and multivariate analysis are implemented to investigate which firm-specific attributes have the power to explain the cross-section of developed market equity return using data from 26 countries.

LITERATURE

In contrast to the prediction that is put forward by the CAPM, prior literature has documented various anomalies that are shown to predict the cross-section of stock returns. Those studies primarily focus on the U.S market. Banz (1981) show that smaller stocks have higher expected returns even after controlling for market beta; Fama and French (1993) find that stocks with high book-to-market ratios outperforms stocks with low book-to-market ratios; and Jegadeesh and Titman (1993) document that stock returns tend to show return momentum in the intermediate (6-12 month) horizon, however they exhibit short-term reversal in the short-term as shown by Jegadeesh (1990). Asness, Moskowitz and Pedersen (2013) suggest that value and momentum are also correlated with expected returns in developed countries. Moreover, Griffin, Kelly and Nardari (2010) find evidence that short-term reversal is also alive in international context. Another cross-sectional return predictor is stock illiquidity. Amihud (2002) find evidence that illiquid stocks tend to have higher future returns. Amihud et al. (2015) test this conjecture in international context and find similar results. Moreover, Ang et al. (2009) document that there exists a significant negative relation between idiosyncratic volatility and expected equity returns both in U.S. and international markets. Additionally, Harvey and Siddique (2000) show that co-skewness is also negatively related to expected equity returns in U.S. markets.

There has been a huge amount interest in recent years to examine the link between downside risk and expected equity returns. Initially, Ang et al. (2006) find that downside beta is positively related with future stock returns in U.S. This finding has been challenged by subsequent studies. Atilgan et al. (2020) show a contradicting evidence that the relation between downside beta and future stock returns is flat in U.S. Moreover, Atilgan et al. (2018) find evidence that downside beta fails to predict the cross-section of equity returns in international setting.

Stock-specific tail risk is also investigated in the literature. Atilgan et al. (2020) document a significant negative link between stock-specific extreme tail risk and expected equity returns. They calculate stock-specific tail risk using value-at-risk which measures how much the value of an investment declines over a given period with a given probability. For example, if the given time period is one month and the given probability is 1%, then VaR would be an estimation of a decrease in the investment's value that could occur with a 1% probability over the next month. In addition to systematic and idiosyncratic tail risk, hybrid tail risk is also examined in the literature. Bali, Cakici and Whitelaw (2014) show a positive and significant relation between hybrid tail risk and future equity returns. Prior studies document that investors tend to overvalue stocks which exhibit lottery-like characteristics. Bali, Cakici and Whitelaw (2011) use the maximum daily return of a stock in each month to proxy for the lottery-demand and show that there exists a strong negative relation between lottery-demand and expected equity returns in the U.S. All these documented anomalies have been challenged by several recent studies. Hou, Xue and Zhang (2020) argue that most of these anomalies are not robust to construction methodologies and their economic magnitudes are smaller than originally outlined. Additionally, it is worthwhile to mention that all these firm-specific variables are examined in isolation. Put differently, anomalies are investigated separate from each other and analysis are mostly conducted separately for each country. Although some of the potential expected return determinants are analyzed in a single country or group of countries in the prior literature, this chapter aims to provide a unique evidence by investigating them jointly for a sample of equities from 26 developed markets.

METHODOLOGY

Data

The equity return data are obtained from Thomson Reuters Datastream. Daily total return index is used for each stock to calculate the daily returns. This return index is adjusted for distribution events. Monthly stock returns are calculated by compounding daily returns. Following Lee (2011), U.S. dollar denominated returns are used in this study, since using returns denominated in local currency may make the returns incomparable across countries. Different countries have different currency risks and inflation rates, thus using local currencies may affect the results through purchasing power parity. The dataset includes equities from 26 developed countries, namely, Australia, Austria, Belgium, Canada, Denmark, Finland, France, Germany, Greece, Hong Kong, Ireland, Israel, Italy, Japan, Luxembourg, Netherlands, New Zealand,

Norway, Portugal, Singapore, South Korea, Spain, Sweden, Switzerland, the United Kingdom, and the United States. The sample period extends from January 1988 to December 2014.[1] Previous international finance literature such as Bekaert, Harvey and Lundblad (2007), Lee (2011) and Karolyi, Lee and van Dijk (2012) which obtain data from Datastream implement additional screening to eliminate errors in the data. Following their suggestion, stocks are selected only from major exchanges defined as those in which the majority of equites in a given country are traded. Other than Germany, Japan and the US, the remaining countries in the sample have only one major exchange. Depository receipts, real estate investment trusts and preferred stocks are excluded from the sample. All defunct equities are retained in the sample to avoid survivorship bias. Non-trading days are excluded from the data. Following Lee (2011), a day is classified as a non-trading day if more than 90% of equities have zero return on that day. To implement this last screen, daily returns are computed from the daily return index denominated in local currencies since return denominated in U.S. dollar fluctuates daily as exchange rates change daily. As a result of these screens, 5,855,284 firm-months remained in the sample for which monthly returns could be calculated.

The goal of this chapter is to examine the relation between expected equity returns and a comprehensive list of cross-sectional return determinants than can be calculated using return data. First, commonly used control variables in U.S. cross-sectional studies which form the backbone of the popular asset pricing models such as four-factor model of Carhart (1997) are explained. The first of these variables is market beta (*BETA*) as the regression coefficient of daily excess return of an equity on daily excess market return during the past 250 trading days. Specifically, market beta is defined as the ratio of covariance between daily excess stock and market return to the variance of daily market excess return during the prior 250 trading days:

$$BETA_t^{i,k} = \frac{Cov_{t-250,t-1}\left(r^{i,k}, r^{m,k}\right)}{Var_{t-250,t-1}\left(r^{m,k}\right)} \tag{1}$$

where $r^{i,k}$ and $r^{m,k}$ are excess return of stock i and market portfolio in country k during the past year. Datastream value-weighted country index is used as the market portfolio and this index is constructed for each country. When estimating beta, the author imposes the restriction that a minimum of 200 non-missing observation must exist during the prior year for each stock. The risk-free rate is taken as the one-month U.S. T-bill rate obtained from the Federal Reserve database and it is utilized to calculate the excess stock and market returns. Following Fama and French (1992,1993), firm size (*SIZE*) is defined as the logarithm of market capitalization and book-to-market ratio (*BM*) as the ratio of book value of equity at the end of the prior fiscal year to the market value of equity. Firm size (book-to-market ratio) is expected to have a negative (positive) relation with future stock returns. Following Jegadeesh and Titman (1993), momentum (*MOM*) is measured as the 11-month cumulative stock return. One month is skipped before portfolio formation to capture short term reversal (*STR*) effect as shown by Jegadeesh (1990) in U.S. Thus, the one-month lagged stock return is included in the list of firm-specific variables.

Next, the author investigates whether stock illiquidity is priced in the cross-section of equity returns in developed countries. Following Amihud (2002), illiquidity proxy (*ILLIQ*) is calculated as the ratio of absolute daily return to the daily dollar trading volume, averaged in a month for each stock. Idiosyncratic volatility (*IVOL*) is calculated as the standard deviation of the residuals from a regression of excess equity return on the excess market return for each month as in Ang et al. (2006). The author again imposes the restriction that a minimum of 15 daily return observation must exist within the given month when calculating *ILLIQ* and *IVOL*.

Co-skewness (*COSKEW*) is calculated as the regression coefficient of squared market excess return from a regression of equity's excess return on the market's excess return and the squared market excess return during the past 250 trading days. Total skewness (*SKEW*) is also included in the analysis and calculated as the skewness of daily stock return over the past 250 trading days. At least 200 daily non-missing return observation must exist during the prior year to calculate co-skewness and skewness.

Five distinct downside risk metrics are used to investigate downside risk in developed markets. Following Bawa and Lindenberg (1977), the systematic downside risk measure (*DBETA*) is calculated as the slope coefficient of market excess return from a regression of stock's excess return on the days that market's excess return is less than the average market excess return during the prior year. Specifically, downside market beta is defined as the ratio of covariance between daily excess stock and market return to the variance of daily market excess return on the days when the market's excess return is less than the average market excess return during the prior 250 trading days:

$$DBETA_t^{i,k} = \frac{Cov_{t-250,t-1}(r^{i,k}, r^{m,k} \mid r^{m,k} < \mu^{m,k})}{Var_{t-250,t-1}(r^{m,k} \mid r^{m,k} < \mu^{m,k})} \tag{2}$$

where $r^{i,k}$ and $r^{m,k}$ are excess return of stock i and market portfolio in country k and $\mu^{m,k}$ is the average market excess return during the past year.

Following Atilgan et al. (2020), 1% value-at-risk (*VaR*) and expected shortfall (*ES*) are used to capture the link between stock-specific extreme tail risk and expected equity returns. The lower tail of the actual empirical distribution is used for each stock to calculate a non-parametric value-at-risk measure and *VaR* is estimated as the 1st percentile of the daily returns over the past 250 trading days. Expected shortfall (*ES*) is an alternative measure of left-tail risk which is first proposed by Artzner, Delbean, Eber and Heath (1999) and calculated as the average of the observations that are less than or equal to the 1st percentile of the daily returns for each stock during the past 250 trading days. Since the maximum likely loss values for value-at-risk and expected shortfall are negative, these measures are multiplied by -1 so that higher values actually correspond to higher extreme left-tail risk. For stock-specific tail risk, a lower partial moment (*LPM*) measure is calculated as the expected value of the squared negative deviations of daily returns with respect to a reference point during the prior 250 trading days. The reference point is taken as the 10th percentile of the actual return during the prior year. In addition to systematic and idiosyncratic tail risk measures, a hybrid tail risk measure is also included in the analysis. Relying on the measure provided by Bali, Cakici and Whitelaw (2014), hybrid tail covariance risk (*HTCR*) is defined as the co-lower partial moment between extreme daily excess return on a stock and the corresponding daily excess returns of the market portfolio during the days that the stock return is below a reference point during the prior 250 trading days. The reference point is again chosen as the 10th percentile of the daily return distribution. Specifically, *HTCR* is constructed by pinpointing the days during which the stock return is less than its 10th percentile during the prior year and calculating the average of the product of the deviation of daily stock return from its 10th percentile and the deviation of the daily market return from its 10th percentile. A minimum of 200 daily return observation must exist during the prior year to calculate these five downside risk measures. The final firm-specific variable, motivated by Bali, Cakici and Whitelaw (2011) to proxy for the lottery-demand with the maximum daily return of a stock in each month, is shown to have a negative relation with expected equity returns in the U.S. Following this study, *MAX1* and *MAX5* are proxied as the maximum daily stock return and the average of five highest daily stock returns during the given month, respectively.

Discrete univariate portfolio analysis is conducted each month to examine the relation between each firm-specific variable and expected equity returns. Specifically, each month stocks are grouped into 10 decile portfolios based on an ascending order of one firm-specific variable, with each portfolio having the same number of equities. Next, the one-month-ahead returns are compared for the portfolio that includes stocks with the highest values of firm-specific variable and the portfolio that includes stocks with lowest values of firm-specific variables. For example, if the firm-specific variable is firm size, portfolio 10 consists of stocks with the largest market capitalization and portfolio 1 consists of stocks with the lowest market capitalization. The decile portfolios are formed every month from January 1989 to December 2014. The univariate portfolio analysis conducted in this chapter contains all stocks in the sample, in other words, stocks in each decile portfolio may come from numerous countries. As a robustness check, overall developed country sample is divided into two geographic region and the whole analysis is repeated for these two sub-samples. Both equal- and value-weighted one-month-ahead average returns are calculated for each decile to examine whether the return spread between the extreme decile portfolios is statistically significant. (10 minus 1). Additionally, the author also checks whether any significant return differences between decile 10 and decile 1 can be explained by two alternative international asset pricing factors. The first asset pricing model is obtained from Asness and Frazzini (2013) which covers global market, size, value and momentum factors. The second asset pricing model is obtained from Fama and French (2017) which generates global market, size, value, profitability and investment factors.[2] Empirically, monthly return differences between the extreme firm-specific attribute deciles are regressed on the global asset pricing factors from these two models and the intercept terms from these regressions are observed whether they are statistically significant. The alphas from these regressions are denoted as AF alpha and FF alpha, respectively. The numbers in parenthesis are Newey-West (1987) adjusted t-statistics which are calculated using six lags.[3]

One handicap of the portfolio analysis mentioned above is that, sorting stocks into decile portfolios using firm-specific attributes allows researcher to control for only one potential return determinant at a time. Furthermore, just focusing on the return differences between the extreme portfolios neglects the returns in the interim portfolios. Thus, univariate analyses are augmented with univariate and multivariate regressions following Fama and MacBeth (1973). Specifically, one-month-ahead stock excess return is regressed on combinations of firm-specific attributes. These monthly regressions generate time-series regression coefficients on the above-mentioned cross-sectional firm-specific variables.[4] These monthly estimates are averaged and statistical significance tests are performed using Newey-West (1987) standard errors.

EMPIRICAL RESULTS

Descriptive Statistics

Descriptive statistics and correlations for each firm-specific attribute used in this chapter are displayed in Table 1. Time series averages of the cross-sectional statistics are tabulated in Panel A for all firm-specific variables and monthly equity returns (*RET*).[5] The average monthly return of a sample firm in developed markets is 0.5% with a standard deviation of 12.1% and a large kurtosis statistic. The mean value of standard market beta is 0.606, however downside beta has a higher average of 0.673, indicating that stocks are more sensitive to negative market movements. The mean values of logarithm of market value of equity and book-to-market equity ratio are 4.677 and 0.87, respectively. Momentum return has a mean of 6.3% which is higher than the median momentum return of 1.9%. The average sample firm has a monthly idiosyncratic volatility of 2.2%. The average firm exhibits negative co-skewness with a value of -2.345, however positive skewness with a value of 0.295. Value-at-risk has an average of 6.5% indicating that there is only 1% probability that the typical firm in the sample has a return less than -6.5% during the prior year. The maximum value of value-at-risk is 20.6% implying that there exists a sample firm for which the 1st percentile of daily returns during the past year corresponds to -20.6%. The mean value of expected shortfall is 7.8% for a typical firm. By construction, expected shortfall has higher central tendency statistics than value-at-risk has. *LPM* and *HTCR* have mean values of 1.5% and -0.4%, respectively, and they both exhibit highly leptokurtic distributions. The maximum daily return for the average firm has been 5.3% with a maximum of 24%.

Table 1 presents the descriptive statistics and correlation matrix for various monthly firm-specific attributes. RET is the monthly return of each stock. BETA is the market beta calculated using daily excess market returns during the past year. SIZE is the logarithm of market value of equity. BM is the ratio of the book value of equity to the market value of equity. MOM is the 11-month cumulative stock return after skipping one month. ILLIQ is Amihud's illiquidity ratio calculated as the absolute daily return of a stock divided by its daily dollar trading volume averaged over the month. IVOL is idiosyncratic volatility calculated as the standard deviation of error terms calculated from a market model which uses daily returns in each month. COSKEW is co-skewness calculated as the regression coefficient of squared market excess return from a regression of equity's excess return on the market's excess return and the squared market excess return during the past 250 trading days. SKEW is the skewness of daily returns during the past year. VaR is the 1% value-at-risk that corresponds to -1 times the 1st percentile of daily returns in the past year. ES is the 1% expected shortfall and calculated as -1 times the average of the returns below the 1st percentile of daily returns in the past year. LPM is the lower partial moment calculated as the expected value of the squared negative deviations of stock returns from the 10th percentile of daily returns in the past year. HTCR is the hybrid tail risk calculated as the co-lower partial moment between extreme daily stock returns and the corresponding daily market returns conditional on the stock return being below the 10th percentile of daily returns in the past year. DBETA is the downside beta calculated as the slope coefficient of market excess return from a regression of stock's excess return on the days that market's excess return is less than the average market excess return during the prior year. MAX1 is the maximum daily return of each stock in each month. MAX5 is the average of the five highest daily returns of each stock in each month. Table 1a presents the mean, standard deviation, 25th percentile, median, 75th percentile, minimum, maximum, skewness and kurtosis statistics for each variable. Statistics are computed as the time-series averages of the monthly cross-sectional means. Table 1b presents the pooled monthly correlations between the firm-specific attributes.

Table 1b presents the pooled averages of the cross-sectional correlations for all variables. Observe that the correlation between market beta and downside beta is equal to 0.81. Larger firms tend to have lower idiosyncratic volatility, lower stock-specific left-tail risk as proxied by value-at-risk, expected shortfall and lower partial moment, higher hybrid tail risk and lower lottery like characteristics. Idiosyncratic volatility is positively correlated with stock-specific tail risk with correlation coefficients ranging be-

Table 1a. Descriptive Statistics

	Mean	Std Dev	25th	Median	75th	Min	Max	Skew	Kurt
RET	0.005	0.121	-0.056	-0.001	0.056	-0.585	1.898	1.526	22.595
BETA	0.606	0.409	0.316	0.560	0.851	-1.258	2.813	0.566	4.275
SIZE	4.677	2.170	3.224	4.572	6.092	-7.325	12.494	0.106	3.236
BM	0.870	0.699	0.401	0.685	1.111	0.050	5.073	1.982	8.664
MOM	0.063	0.399	-0.192	0.019	0.253	-0.727	1.888	0.908	5.005
ILLIQ	0.006	0.019	0.000	0.000	0.002	0.000	0.221	6.061	47.753
IVOL	0.022	0.014	0.012	0.019	0.028	0.000	0.127	1.593	7.367
COSKEW	-2.345	12.576	-6.357	-1.417	2.570	-130.934	131.878	-0.393	15.667
SKEW	0.295	0.858	0.024	0.267	0.529	-14.834	15.029	0.631	69.630
VaR	0.065	0.030	0.045	0.060	0.079	0.000	0.206	1.044	5.064
ES	0.078	0.033	0.056	0.073	0.094	0.000	0.225	0.963	4.772
LPM	0.015	0.019	0.006	0.010	0.017	0.000	0.381	5.355	62.619
HTCR	-0.004	0.005	-0.006	-0.003	-0.001	-0.051	0.019	-1.266	16.621
DBETA	0.673	0.527	0.326	0.644	0.985	-2.861	4.053	0.268	5.730
MAX1	0.053	0.036	0.027	0.045	0.070	-0.001	0.240	1.446	6.501
MAX5	0.030	0.021	0.016	0.026	0.039	-0.004	0.193	1.676	8.219

Table 1b. Correlation Matrix

	BETA	SIZE	BM	MOM	ILLIQ	IVOL	COSKEW	SKEW	VaR1	ES1	LPM	HTCR	DBETA	MAX1	MAX5	RET
BETA	1.00															
SIZE	0.45	1.00														
BM	-0.05	-0.11	1.00													
MOM	0.03	0.15	0.00	1.00												
ILLIQ	-0.02	-0.05	0.11	-0.01	1.00											
IVOL	0.00	-0.37	0.05	-0.11	0.04	1.00										
COSKEW	0.03	0.06	0.01	-0.03	0.00	-0.07	1.00									
SKEW	-0.07	-0.08	0.01	0.16	0.00	0.06	0.04	1.00								
VaR	0.08	-0.42	0.06	-0.18	0.04	0.70	-0.05	-0.06	1.00							
ES	0.07	-0.41	0.06	-0.17	0.04	0.66	-0.06	-0.12	0.95	1.00						
LPM	-0.06	-0.37	0.05	-0.11	0.05	0.45	-0.02	-0.10	0.77	0.80	1.00					
HTCR	0.21	0.40	-0.05	0.08	-0.04	-0.39	-0.01	-0.04	-0.51	-0.47	-0.51	1.00				
DBETA	0.81	0.32	-0.04	0.03	-0.02	0.05	-0.39	-0.10	0.13	0.13	0.00	0.18	1.00			
MAX1	0.06	-0.27	0.04	-0.09	0.03	0.86	-0.04	0.13	0.61	0.58	0.42	-0.32	0.09	1.00		
MAX5	0.14	-0.19	0.03	-0.07	0.03	0.87	-0.04	0.08	0.60	0.56	0.36	-0.28	0.15	0.89	1.00	
RET	-0.01	0.07	0.00	0.05	0.00	0.03	0.00	0.09	-0.04	-0.04	0.00	0.01	-0.01	0.24	0.36	1.00

tween 0.45 and 0.70, however it is negatively correlated with hybrid tail risk. Idiosyncratic volatility and lottery demand measures have high correlations. Stock-specific tail risk measures are highly correlated with each other with coefficients ranging between 0.77 and 0.95. Nonetheless, hybrid tail risk measures are negatively correlated with stock-specific tail risk measures with coefficients ranging between -0.47 and -0.51. Two lottery demand measures have higher correlations with stock-specific tail risk measures with correlations between 0.36 and 0.61. Lastly, monthly equity returns do not display a high correlation with any of the firm-specific variables.

Univariate Portfolio Analysis

To test the relation between various firm-specific attributes and future stock returns, the author conducts discrete univariate portfolio analyses where portfolios are formed every month by grouping stocks into deciles based on an ascending sort of various firm-specific attributes and observes the future returns of the highest and lowest firm-specific attributes deciles. Specifically, decile portfolios are formed each month from January 1989 to December 2014 by grouping stocks based on various firm-specific attributes where decile 10 contains stocks with the highest firm-specific attribute and decile 1 contains stocks with lowest firm-specific attribute. Next, one-month-ahead equal- and value-weighted returns are computed for each decile portfolio to test whether the extreme deciles generate different future returns. The author also checks whether the return differences between extreme decile portfolios can be explained by famous asset pricing models.

*Table 2 presents return comparisons between equity deciles formed based on various firm-specific variables. The decile portfolios are formed every month. Port1 is the portfolio of stocks with the lowest values of the firm-specific variables and Port10 is the portfolio of stocks with the highest values of the firm-specific variables. The equal-weighted monthly portfolio returns are calculated for each portfolio. The table reports the average value of each firm-specific variable and one-month ahead excess returns for each portfolio. The last three columns show the differences of monthly excess returns and alpha measures between portfolios 10 and 1. AF Alpha is the intercept term from a regression of portfolio returns on the global market, size, value and momentum factors calculated by Asness and Frazzini (2013). FF Alpha is the intercept term from a regression of portfolio returns on the global market, size, value, investment and profitability factors calculated by Fama and French (2017). Firm-specific variables are defined in Table 1. Newey-West (1987) adjusted t-statistics are presented in parentheses. *,** denote statistical significance at the 5% and 1% levels, respectively.*

Table 2 Univariate Portfolio Analysis with Equal-Weighted Returns

BETA	Port1	Port2	Port3	Port4	Port5	Port6	Port7	Port8	Port9	Port10	High-Low	AF Alpha	FF Alpha
Average Value	-0.0040	0.2064	0.3157	0.4131	0.5104	0.6116	0.7229	0.8528	1.0247	1.4063			
Excess Return	0.0049*	0.0037	0.0033	0.0029	0.0025	0.0018	0.0010	0.0007	0.0002	0.0001	-0.0048	-0.0040*	-0.0047*
	(2.15)	(1.46)	(1.16)	(0.97)	(0.77)	(0.55)	(0.29)	(0.20)	(0.06)	(0.01)	(-1.50)	(-2.07)	(-2.04)
SIZE	Port1	Port2	Port3	Port4	Port5	Port6	Port7	Port8	Port9	Port10	High-Low	AF Alpha	FF Alpha
Average Value	0.9853	2.5034	3.2199	3.7866	4.3098	4.8443	5.4220	6.0986	6.9678	8.6324			

continued on following page

Table 2. Continued

Excess Return	0.0049	0.0001	-0.0005	-0.0007	-0.0005	0.0014	0.0028	0.0045	0.0055	0.0058*	0.0009	-0.0004	-0.0018
	(1.42)	(0.04)	(-0.17)	(-0.22)	(-0.16)	(0.43)	(0.90)	(1.51)	(1.88)	(2.14)	(0.39)	(-0.18)	(-0.69)
BM	**Port1**	**Port2**	**Port3**	**Port4**	**Port5**	**Port6**	**Port7**	**Port8**	**Port9**	**Port10**	**High-Low**	**AF Alpha**	**FF Alpha**
Average Value	0.1348	0.2768	0.3743	0.4751	0.5775	0.7098	0.8672	1.0758	1.4269	4.1315			
Excess Return	-0.0037	-0.0005	0.0012	0.0018	0.0025	0.0029	0.0037	0.0036	0.0045	0.0049	0.0086**	0.0059**	0.0062**
	(-0.96)	(-0.14)	(0.34)	(0.57)	(0.81)	(0.91)	(1.20)	(1.15)	(1.41)	(1.39)	(3.47)	(2.85)	(2.70)
MOM	**Port1**	**Port2**	**Port3**	**Port4**	**Port5**	**Port6**	**Port7**	**Port8**	**Port9**	**Port10**	**High-Low**	**AF Alpha**	**FF Alpha**
Average Value	-0.5569	-0.3245	-0.1987	-0.1037	-0.0212	0.0602	0.1495	0.2619	0.4388	1.1622			
Excess Return	-0.0166**	-0.0055	-0.0014	0.0010	0.0026	0.0046	0.0061**	0.0074**	0.0096**	0.0140**	0.0306**	0.0238**	0.0278**
	(-3.25)	(-1.33)	(-0.38)	(0.31)	(0.91)	(1.73)	(2.39)	(2.92)	(3.59)	(3.99)	(8.95)	(8.85)	(8.31)
STR	**Port1**	**Port2**	**Port3**	**Port4**	**Port5**	**Port6**	**Port7**	**Port8**	**Port9**	**Port10**	**High-Low**	**AF Alpha**	**FF Alpha**
Average Value	-0.1882	-0.0948	-0.0569	-0.0311	-0.0107	0.0084	0.0294	0.0568	0.0997	0.2376			
Excess Return	-0.0049	-0.0026	-0.0008	0.0006	0.0016	0.0036	0.0048	0.0062*	0.0063*	0.0069	0.0117**	0.0099**	0.0116**
	(-1.16)	(-0.74)	(-0.25)	(0.21)	(0.62)	(1.38)	(1.81)	(2.26)	(2.06)	(1.72)	(4.79)	(3.28)	(3.50)
ILLIQ	**Port1**	**Port2**	**Port3**	**Port4**	**Port5**	**Port6**	**Port7**	**Port8**	**Port9**	**Port10**	**High-Low**	**AF Alpha**	**FF Alpha**
Average Value	0.0000	0.0000	0.0000	0.0001	0.0002	0.0005	0.0011	0.0027	0.0077	0.1490			
Excess Return	0.0074**	0.0059*	0.0032	0.0019	0.0013	0.0002	-0.0002	-0.0003	0.0003	0.0051	-0.0023	-0.0026	-0.0012
	(2.83)	(2.04)	(1.01)	(0.57)	(0.38)	(0.07)	(-0.07)	(-0.09)	(0.08)	(1.27)	(-0.93)	(-0.97)	(-0.46)
IVOL	**Port1**	**Port2**	**Port3**	**Port4**	**Port5**	**Port6**	**Port7**	**Port8**	**Port9**	**Port10**	**High-Low**	**AF Alpha**	**FF Alpha**
Average Value	0.0049	0.0092	0.0122	0.0148	0.0175	0.0204	0.0238	0.0282	0.0350	0.0533			
Excess Return	0.0022	0.0050*	0.0050*	0.0045	0.0040	0.0032	0.0021	0.0007	-0.0015	-0.0031	-0.0054	-0.0052	-0.0029
	(1.43)	(2.21)	(1.96)	(1.64)	(1.35)	(1.00)	(0.61)	(0.19)	(-0.37)	(-0.61)	(-1.26)	(-1.76)	(-0.92)
COSKEW	**Port1**	**Port2**	**Port3**	**Port4**	**Port5**	**Port6**	**Port7**	**Port8**	**Port9**	**Port10**	**High-Low**	**AF Alpha**	**FF Alpha**
Average Value	-26.313	-10.762	-6.4234	-3.9917	-2.2017	-0.6907	0.7693	2.6136	5.6660	17.9016			
Excess Return	-0.0007	0.0008	0.0008	0.0022	0.0032	0.0042	0.0042	0.0031	0.0024	0.0009	0.0016	0.0024	0.0015
	(-0.17)	(0.24)	(0.22)	(0.68)	(1.04)	(1.45)	(1.48)	(1.11)	(0.83)	(0.27)	(1.15)	(1.84)	(1.47)
SKEW	**Port1**	**Port2**	**Port3**	**Port4**	**Port5**	**Port6**	**Port7**	**Port8**	**Port9**	**Port10**	**High-Low**	**AF Alpha**	**FF Alpha**
Average Value	-0.9382	-0.1433	0.0222	0.1321	0.2233	0.3116	0.4087	0.5315	0.7265	1.6759			
Excess Return	0.0026	0.0037	0.0030	0.0019	0.0013	0.0005	0.0002	0.0005	0.0023	0.0064*	0.0037**	0.0025*	0.0043**

continued on following page

Table 2. Continued

	(1.07)	(1.28)	(0.96)	(0.60)	(0.39)	(0.14)	(0.05)	(0.15)	(0.66)	(2.12)	(3.07)	(2.09)	(3.27)
VaR	**Port1**	**Port2**	**Port3**	**Port4**	**Port5**	**Port6**	**Port7**	**Port8**	**Port9**	**Port10**	**High-Low**	**AF Alpha**	**FF Alpha**
Average Value	0.0227	0.0373	0.0448	0.0511	0.0571	0.0634	0.0706	0.0797	0.0938	0.1274			
Excess Return	0.0043**	0.0058**	0.0050	0.0037	0.0023	0.0016	0.0007	-0.0010	-0.0013	0.0011	-0.0032	-0.0036	-0.0024
	(2.92)	(2.65)	(1.94)	(1.29)	(0.74)	(0.48)	(0.18)	(-0.25)	(-0.29)	(0.20)	(-0.67)	(-1.03)	(-0.61)
ES	**Port1**	**Port2**	**Port3**	**Port4**	**Port5**	**Port6**	**Port7**	**Port8**	**Port9**	**Port10**	**High-Low**	**AF Alpha**	**FF Alpha**
Average Value	0.0313	0.0474	0.0558	0.0629	0.0697	0.0767	0.0845	0.0946	0.1094	0.1459			
Excess Return	0.0045**	0.0051*	0.0038	0.0029	0.0022	0.0011	-0.0002	0.0015	0.0000	0.0014	-0.0032	-0.0036	-0.0025
	(2.81)	(2.22)	(1.44)	(1.02)	(0.70)	(0.33)	(-0.06)	(0.38)	(0.00)	(0.25)	(-0.69)	(-1.04)	(-0.64)
LPM	**Port1**	**Port2**	**Port3**	**Port4**	**Port5**	**Port6**	**Port7**	**Port8**	**Port9**	**Port10**	**High-Low**	**AF Alpha**	**FF Alpha**
Average Value	0.0018	0.0040	0.0056	0.0072	0.0090	0.0110	0.0137	0.0174	0.0241	0.0551			
Excess Return	0.0041**	0.0032	0.0019	0.0013	0.0010	0.0009	0.0012	0.0013	0.0016	0.0059	0.0018	0.0005	0.0013
	(2.36)	(1.27)	(0.67)	(0.44)	(0.30)	(0.26)	(0.35)	(0.34)	(0.40)	(1.30)	(0.50)	(0.17)	(0.42)
HTCR	**Port1**	**Port2**	**Port3**	**Port4**	**Port5**	**Port6**	**Port7**	**Port8**	**Port9**	**Port10**	**High-Low**	**AF Alpha**	**FF Alpha**
Average Value	-0.0136	-0.0078	-0.0059	-0.0046	-0.0037	-0.0028	-0.0019	-0.0009	0.0002	0.0031			
Excess Return	0.0042	-0.0006	-0.0016	-0.0013	-0.0004	0.0010	0.0030	0.0044	0.0053*	0.0070*	0.0028	0.0021	0.0007
	(0.91)	(-0.17)	(-0.47)	(-0.39)	(-0.14)	(0.35)	(1.11)	(1.80)	(2.11)	(2.13)	(1.09)	(0.87)	(0.29)
DBETA	**Port1**	**Port2**	**Port3**	**Port4**	**Port5**	**Port6**	**Port7**	**Port8**	**Port9**	**Port10**	**High-Low**	**AF Alpha**	**FF Alpha**
Average Value	-0.1735	0.1744	0.3251	0.4565	0.5821	0.7071	0.8386	0.9870	1.1811	1.6568			
Excess Return	0.0033	0.0029	0.0033	0.0033	0.0029	0.0027	0.0014	0.0015	0.0009	-0.0013	-0.0046	-0.0042**	-0.0047*
	(1.32)	(1.24)	(1.23)	(1.14)	(0.97)	(0.86)	(0.43)	(0.41)	(0.23)	(-0.27)	(-1.59)	(-2.70)	(-2.31)
MAX1	**Port1**	**Port2**	**Port3**	**Port4**	**Port5**	**Port6**	**Port7**	**Port8**	**Port9**	**Port10**	**High-Low**	**AF Alpha**	**FF Alpha**
Average Value	0.0095	0.0190	0.0269	0.0341	0.0413	0.0492	0.0584	0.0700	0.0867	0.1299			
Excess Return	-0.0003	0.0039	0.0047	0.0044	0.0036	0.0029	0.0019	0.0019	0.0003	-0.0008	-0.0004	-0.0007	0.0012
	(-0.17)	(1.71)	(1.86)	(1.60)	(1.22)	(0.92)	(0.57)	(0.50)	(0.08)	(-0.16)	(-0.13)	(-0.31)	(0.46)
MAX5	**Port1**	**Port2**	**Port3**	**Port4**	**Port5**	**Port6**	**Port7**	**Port8**	**Port9**	**Port10**	**High-Low**	**AF Alpha**	**FF Alpha**
Average Value	0.0058	0.0113	0.0158	0.0198	0.0237	0.0279	0.0329	0.0393	0.0490	0.0753			
Excess Return	-0.0013	0.0034	0.0043	0.0043	0.0038	0.0037	0.0024	0.0020	0.0007	-0.0010	0.0003	0.0001	0.0019
	(-0.69)	(1.52)	(1.72)	(1.61)	(1.33)	(1.19)	(0.74)	(0.56)	(0.18)	(-0.19)	(0.08)	(0.03)	(0.64)

Table 2 presents equal-weighted portfolio returns. Although average excess return is relatively flat across market beta deciles, there exists a sharp drop between portfolio 9 and portfolio 10. The zero-cost strategy which takes a long position in stocks with highest market beta and a short position in stocks with the lowest market beta generates -48 basis points with an insignificant t-statistic of -1.50, the corresponding alpha metrics are negative and significant consistent with the beta anomaly in U.S. markets. (Frazzini and Pedersen (2014)). Size anomaly does not manifest itself across decile portfolios in developed markets since the average excess return is flat across the decile portfolios. The average excess return of the *BM*-sorted decile portfolios increases almost monotonically from -0.37% per month for the low *BM*-decile to 0.49% per month to high *BM*-decile. The average monthly return difference between decile 10 and decile 1 is 0.86% with a t-statistic of 3.47. The abnormal returns of this extreme decile portfolio are also statistically significant. Although size anomaly strongly predicts the expected returns in U.S. markets, it is not correlated with expected returns in other developed countries. Contrary, book-to-market anomaly is alive both in U.S. and in other countries. The momentum anomaly is also significant in developed markets with winner stocks during the past year having a higher one-month-ahead return of 3.06% (with a t-statistic of 8.95) compared to loser stocks. This return difference cannot be explained by the well-known two asset pricing models. The results paint a similar picture for short-term-reversal. Stocks with higher past month returns continue to have higher one-month-ahead returns than those with lower past month returns. The monthly return to zero-cost portfolio based on *STR* is 1.17% with a t-statistic of 4.79 and statistically significant alphas ranging between 0.99% and 1.16%. In other words, the short-term reversal anomaly documented in U.S. manifests itself as short-term momentum into the developed market setting. Contrary to the U.S. evidence that illiquidity is correlated with future stock returns, the average excess return is almost flat across illiquidity deciles in developed countries. The significant negative link between idiosyncratic volatility and future returns documented in U.S. is not a common phenomenon in developed markets either. The returns decrease from 0.22% for the lowest *IVOL* portfolio to -0.31% for the highest *IVOL* portfolio. The return and alphas to the zero-cost strategy ranges between -0.54% and -0.29%, however they are not statistically distinguishable from zero. The insignificant relation with future returns also exists for co-skewness. However, stocks with higher total skewness tend to have higher expected returns than those with lower total skewness. The average monthly return difference between the extreme deciles is 0.37% with a t-statistic of 3.07. The alphas are statistically significant as well with t-statistics ranging between 2.09 and 3.27. For value-at-risk and expected shortfall, the average returns decrease as one moves from the decile 1 to decile 10, however the returns and alphas to the zero-cost strategy are not statistically distinguishable from zero. Contrary to the U.S studies, similar insignificant relations with future returns also exist for lower partial moment and hybrid tail risk. Equities with higher *LPM* (*HTCR*) earn higher one-month-ahead returns than those with lower *LPM* (*HTCR*), however the return and abnormal return difference between the extreme deciles are not statistically significant. The zero-cost strategy based on downside beta earns a negative AF (FF) alpha of -0.42% (-0.47%) with a t-statistic of -2.7 (-2.31). The last two firm-specific variables proxy for the lottery demand in equity markets. For both *MAX1* and *MAX5*, the relation between lottery demand and expected returns is flat. One should also note that this relation is inverse U-shaped rather than uniform since the returns increase from decile 1 to decile 3 and then begin decreasing from decile 4 to decile 10. This evidence also contradicts with the U.S. studies which find a significantly negative relation between lottery demand and expected returns.

The equal-weighted portfolio returns show that some anomalies such as low beta, book-to-market equity and momentum anomalies are in line with the findings in U.S. studies, however some anomalies such as short-term reversal and downside beta manifests themselves in the opposite direction in developed countries. The other remaining anomalies does not have any significant relation with expected returns. Some of these contradictory evidences may be due to small stocks since equal-weighted portfolio analysis assign equal weights to all stocks in the sample. To examine whether this is the case, the same analyses are repeated using value-weighted returns in Table 3.

The low beta anomaly that was documented in alphas based on the portfolio results using equal-weighted returns does not manifest itself for value-weighted returns. The reason for this lack of significance is that the average return for lowest decile is not very high for value-weighted returns. The return and alpha difference between extreme portfolios are between 2 and 17 basis points with t-statistics between 0.08 and 1.03. Similarly, firm size does not have any significant effect on the cross-section of developed markets stock returns. Contrary to the results based on equal-weighted returns, book-to-market equity turns out be insignificant for value-weighted returns. This insignificant relation stems from relatively high average return for the lowest decile portfolio. On the other hand, return momentum continue to be a robust predictor of expected equity returns. The zero-cost strategy that takes a long position in winner stocks and a short position in loser stocks have one-month-ahead value-weighted return of 2.07% with a t-statistic of 4.21, and a positive AF (FF) alpha of 0.88% (1.52%) with a t-statistic of 3.28 (2.68). The average return across momentum return deciles are almost uniform and monotonically increasing as one moves from decile 1 to decile 10. The short-term reversal anomaly that renders itself as short-term momentum for equal-weighted returns is not detected for value-weighted returns. The average month excess and abnormal return differences between extreme portfolios are all statistically insignificant.

*Table 3 presents return comparisons between equity deciles formed based on various firm-specific variables. The decile portfolios are formed every month. Port1 is the portfolio of stocks with the lowest values of the firm-specific variables and Port10 is the portfolio of stocks with the highest values of the firm-specific variables. The equal-weighted monthly portfolio returns are calculated for each portfolio. The table reports the average value of each firm-specific variable and one-month ahead excess returns for each portfolio. The last three columns show the differences of monthly excess returns and alpha measures between portfolios 10 and 1. AF Alpha is the intercept term from a regression of portfolio returns on the global market, size, value and momentum factors calculated by Asness and Frazzini (2013). FF Alpha is the intercept term from a regression of portfolio returns on the global market, size, value, investment and profitability factors calculated by Fama and French (2017). Firm-specific variables are defined in Table 1. Newey-West (1987) adjusted t-statistics are presented in parentheses. *,** denote statistical significance at the 5% and 1% levels, respectively.*

Table 3. Univariate Portfolio Analysis with Value-Weighted Returns

BETA	Port1	Port2	Port3	Port4	Port5	Port6	Port7	Port8	Port9	Port10	High-Low	AF Alpha	FF Alpha
Average Value	-0.0040	0.2064	0.3157	0.4131	0.5104	0.6116	0.7229	0.8528	1.0247	1.4063			
Excess Return	0.0036	0.0039	0.0051**	0.0050**	0.0056**	0.0052**	0.0041	0.0050	0.0040	0.0039	0.0002	0.0013	0.0017
	(1.94)	(1.72)	(2.77)	(2.57)	(2.98)	(2.61)	(1.78)	(1.94)	(1.37)	(0.99)	(0.08)	(0.76)	(1.03)
SIZE	Port1	Port2	Port3	Port4	Port5	Port6	Port7	Port8	Port9	Port10	High-Low	AF Alpha	FF Alpha
Average Value	0.9853	2.5034	3.2199	3.7866	4.3098	4.8443	5.4220	6.0986	6.9678	8.6324			

continued on following page

Table 3. Continued

Excess Return	0.0032	0.0000	-0.0006	-0.0007	-0.0004	0.0014	0.0028	0.0045	0.0054	0.0047	0.0015	0.0013	0.0009
	(0.90)	(0.01)	(-0.18)	(-0.23)	(-0.14)	(0.45)	(0.93)	(1.53)	(1.89)	(1.77)	(0.69)	(0.59)	(0.40)
BM	**Port1**	**Port2**	**Port3**	**Port4**	**Port5**	**Port6**	**Port7**	**Port8**	**Port9**	**Port10**	**High-Low**	**AF Alpha**	**FF Alpha**
Average Value	0.1348	0.2768	0.3743	0.4751	0.5775	0.7098	0.8672	1.0758	1.4269	4.1315			
Excess Return	0.0043	0.0042	0.0043	0.0048	0.0044	0.0046	0.0058*	0.0059	0.0068*	0.0065	0.0022	-0.0034	-0.0013
	(1.44)	(1.52)	(1.55)	(1.77)	(1.48)	(1.56)	(1.97)	(1.91)	(1.98)	(1.71)	(0.71)	(-1.47)	(-0.57)
MOM	**Port1**	**Port2**	**Port3**	**Port4**	**Port5**	**Port6**	**Port7**	**Port8**	**Port9**	**Port10**	**High-Low**	**AF Alpha**	**FF Alpha**
Average Value	-0.5569	-0.3245	-0.1987	-0.1037	-0.0212	0.0602	0.1495	0.2619	0.4388	1.1622			
Excess Return	-0.0094	-0.0035	-0.0007	0.0010	0.0020	0.0034	0.0051*	0.0060**	0.0079**	0.0113**	0.0207**	0.0088**	0.0152**
	(-1.65)	(-0.75)	(-0.17)	(0.30)	(0.68)	(1.33)	(2.08)	(2.49)	(2.88)	(3.15)	(4.21)	(3.28)	(2.68)
STR	**Port1**	**Port2**	**Port3**	**Port4**	**Port5**	**Port6**	**Port7**	**Port8**	**Port9**	**Port10**	**High-Low**	**AF Alpha**	**FF Alpha**
Average Value	-0.1882	-0.0948	-0.0569	-0.0311	-0.0107	0.0084	0.0294	0.0568	0.0997	0.2376			
Excess Return	0.0039	0.0047	0.0046	0.0053*	0.0045	0.0058**	0.0048	0.0051	0.0042	0.0043	0.0004	0.0001	0.0008
	(0.94)	(1.42)	(1.47)	(1.99)	(1.79)	(2.40)	(1.89)	(1.88)	(1.53)	(1.26)	(0.14)	(0.02)	(0.20)
ILLIQ	**Port1**	**Port2**	**Port3**	**Port4**	**Port5**	**Port6**	**Port7**	**Port8**	**Port9**	**Port10**	**High-Low**	**AF Alpha**	**FF Alpha**
Average Value	0.0000	0.0000	0.0000	0.0001	0.0002	0.0005	0.0011	0.0027	0.0077	0.1490			
Excess Return	0.0060**	0.0050	0.0044	0.0025	0.0017	0.0019	0.0010	0.0007	0.0004	0.0014	-0.0046*	-0.0060**	-0.0055**
	(2.34)	(1.65)	(1.40)	(0.81)	(0.58)	(0.63)	(0.35)	(0.26)	(0.12)	(0.38)	(-1.98)	(-2.73)	(-2.94)
IVOL	**Port1**	**Port2**	**Port3**	**Port4**	**Port5**	**Port6**	**Port7**	**Port8**	**Port9**	**Port10**	**High-Low**	**AF Alpha**	**FF Alpha**
Average Value	0.0049	0.0092	0.0122	0.0148	0.0175	0.0204	0.0238	0.0282	0.0350	0.0533			
Excess Return	0.0050**	0.0055**	0.0052*	0.0045	0.0042	0.0042	0.0044	0.0049	0.0025	-0.0059	-0.0108**	-0.0090**	-0.0049
	(2.34)	(2.44)	(2.07)	(1.64)	(1.39)	(1.26)	(1.25)	(1.23)	(0.54)	(-1.08)	(-2.59)	(-2.82)	(-1.42)
COSKEW	**Port1**	**Port2**	**Port3**	**Port4**	**Port5**	**Port6**	**Port7**	**Port8**	**Port9**	**Port10**	**High-Low**	**AF Alpha**	**FF Alpha**
Average Value	-26.313	-10.762	-6.4234	-3.9917	-2.2017	-0.6907	0.7693	2.6136	5.6660	17.9016			
Excess Return	0.0058	0.0042	0.0032	0.0057*	0.0038	0.0048	0.0056*	0.0045	0.0046	0.0043	-0.0015	0.0026	0.0005
	(1.66)	(1.36)	(1.15)	(2.03)	(1.43)	(1.78)	(2.09)	(1.68)	(1.65)	(1.39)	(-0.85)	(1.38)	(0.26)
SKEW	**Port1**	**Port2**	**Port3**	**Port4**	**Port5**	**Port6**	**Port7**	**Port8**	**Port9**	**Port10**	**High-Low**	**AF Alpha**	**FF Alpha**
Average Value	-0.9382	-0.1433	0.0222	0.1321	0.2233	0.3116	0.4087	0.5315	0.7265	1.6759			
Excess Return	0.0054*	0.0062**	0.0052	0.0040	0.0041	0.0038	0.0041	0.0034	0.0037	0.0064**	0.0010	0.0009	0.0007

continued on following page

Table 3. Continued

	(2.03)	(2.36)	(1.84)	(1.44)	(1.37)	(1.29)	(1.32)	(1.21)	(1.33)	(2.35)	(0.54)	(0.47)	(0.45)
VaR	**Port1**	**Port2**	**Port3**	**Port4**	**Port5**	**Port6**	**Port7**	**Port8**	**Port9**	**Port10**	**High-Low**	**AF Alpha**	**FF Alpha**
Average Value	0.0227	0.0373	0.0448	0.0511	0.0571	0.0634	0.0706	0.0797	0.0938	0.1274			
Excess Return	0.0057**	0.0058**	0.0048	0.0043	0.0027	0.0043	0.0038	0.0052	0.0046	-0.0030	-0.0087	-0.0072*	-0.0047
	(3.28)	(2.59)	(1.82)	(1.45)	(0.79)	(1.16)	(0.88)	(1.14)	(0.93)	(-0.54)	(-1.80)	(-2.14)	(-1.38)
ES	**Port1**	**Port2**	**Port3**	**Port4**	**Port5**	**Port6**	**Port7**	**Port8**	**Port9**	**Port10**	**High-Low**	**AF Alpha**	**FF Alpha**
Average Value	0.0313	0.0474	0.0558	0.0629	0.0697	0.0767	0.0845	0.0946	0.1094	0.1459			
Excess Return	0.0058**	0.0048*	0.0049	0.0036	0.0039	0.0046	0.0051	0.0053	0.0052	-0.0026	-0.0083	-0.0074	-0.0046
	(3.29)	(2.02)	(1.84)	(1.20)	(1.23)	(1.30)	(1.28)	(1.21)	(1.09)	(-0.46)	(-1.81)	(-1.79)	(-1.27)
LPM	**Port1**	**Port2**	**Port3**	**Port4**	**Port5**	**Port6**	**Port7**	**Port8**	**Port9**	**Port10**	**High-Low**	**AF Alpha**	**FF Alpha**
Average Value	0.0018	0.0040	0.0056	0.0072	0.0090	0.0110	0.0137	0.0174	0.0241	0.0551			
Excess Return	0.0053**	0.0046	0.0045	0.0042	0.0046	0.0048	0.0065	0.0051	0.0065	0.0010	-0.0043	-0.0046	-0.0032
	(2.68)	(1.89)	(1.63)	(1.40)	(1.41)	(1.35)	(1.75)	(1.21)	(1.53)	(0.20)	(-1.13)	(-1.19)	(-0.95)
HTCR	**Port1**	**Port2**	**Port3**	**Port4**	**Port5**	**Port6**	**Port7**	**Port8**	**Port9**	**Port10**	**High-Low**	**AF Alpha**	**FF Alpha**
Average Value	-0.0136	-0.0078	-0.0059	-0.0046	-0.0037	-0.0028	-0.0019	-0.0009	0.0002	0.0031			
Excess Return	-0.0027	0.0027	0.0017	0.0031	0.0046	0.0035	0.0030	0.0056*	0.0049*	0.0055	0.0083**	0.0078**	0.0076**
	(-0.56)	(0.63)	(0.45)	(0.89)	(1.34)	(1.17)	(1.03)	(2.23)	(2.20)	(1.86)	(2.56)	(2.48)	(2.37)
DBETA	**Port1**	**Port2**	**Port3**	**Port4**	**Port5**	**Port6**	**Port7**	**Port8**	**Port9**	**Port10**	**High-Low**	**AF Alpha**	**FF Alpha**
Average Value	-0.1735	0.1744	0.3251	0.4565	0.5821	0.7071	0.8386	0.9870	1.1811	1.6568			
Excess Return	0.0009	0.0044**	0.0044**	0.0052**	0.0049*	0.0049*	0.0042	0.0044	0.0045	0.0041	0.0033	0.0050*	0.0063**
	(0.34)	(2.52)	(2.46)	(2.71)	(2.31)	(2.17)	(1.67)	(1.61)	(1.44)	(1.01)	(1.03)	(2.22)	(2.58)
MAX1	**Port1**	**Port2**	**Port3**	**Port4**	**Port5**	**Port6**	**Port7**	**Port8**	**Port9**	**Port10**	**High-Low**	**AF Alpha**	**FF Alpha**
Average Value	0.0095	0.0190	0.0269	0.0341	0.0413	0.0492	0.0584	0.0700	0.0867	0.1299			
Excess Return	0.0045**	0.0053**	0.0057**	0.0055*	0.0040	0.0037	0.0049	0.0051	0.0046	0.0028	-0.0016	-0.0002	0.0021
	(2.63)	(2.76)	(2.59)	(2.25)	(1.47)	(1.17)	(1.43)	(1.29)	(1.10)	(0.62)	(-0.43)	(-0.07)	(0.75)
MAX5	**Port1**	**Port2**	**Port3**	**Port4**	**Port5**	**Port6**	**Port7**	**Port8**	**Port9**	**Port10**	**High-Low**	**AF Alpha**	**FF Alpha**
Average Value	0.0058	0.0113	0.0158	0.0198	0.0237	0.0279	0.0329	0.0393	0.0490	0.0753			
Excess Return	0.0047**	0.0054**	0.0053**	0.0058**	0.0049	0.0045	0.0041	0.0044	0.0043	0.0026	-0.0021	-0.0014	0.0016
	(2.73)	(2.87)	(2.51)	(2.54)	(1.87)	(1.56)	(1.25)	(1.14)	(0.98)	(0.55)	(-0.50)	(-0.47)	(0.53)

Table 2 shows that illiquidity is not priced in the cross-section of developed markets stock returns for equal-weighted returns. For value-weighted returns, the results paint a different picture. The zero-cost portfolio that buys low liquid stocks and sells high liquid stocks earns -0.46% per month with a t-statistic of -1.98. The corresponding AF and FF alphas are -0.6% and -0.55% with t-statistics of -2.73 and -2.94. The insignificant relation documented between idiosyncratic volatility and expected stock returns for equal-weighted returns resurrects for value-weighted returns. The zero-cost strategy earns -1.08% with a t-statistic of -2.59 and both alphas are significantly negative. This evidence for value-weighted returns is similar to those found in U.S. stocks. The excess return and abnormal return difference between the highest and lowest co-skewness deciles were not statistically distinguishable from zero and they continue to be insignificant for value-weighted returns. Total skewness had positive relation with expected stock returns in Table 2, however this relation turns out to be insignificant for return and alphas differences between extreme deciles when value-weighted returns are used.

Equal-weighted portfolio returns for stock-specific left-tail risk metrics documents that the relation between left-tail risk and expected return is flat across the decile portfolios. Nonetheless, the results are quite different for value-weighted returns. The return to zero-cost strategy is -87 basis points for value-at-risk and -83 basis points for expected shortfall, with t-statistics of -1.80 and -1.81, respectively. This marginally significant zero-cost strategy renders itself in alphas. For *VaR* sorted portfolios, the associated AF alpha is statistically negative with a t-statistic of -2.14 whereas the FF alpha is insignificant. For *ES* sorted portfolios, the associated AF alpha is marginally statistically negative with a t-statistic of -1.79. The insignificant relation documented between lower partial moment and expected stock returns for equal-weighted returns continue to be insignificant for value-weighted returns. For the hybrid tail risk, the picture is very different from Table 2. The results point out to a strong indication of a positive relation between hybrid tail risk and expected stock returns in developed countries when value-weighted returns are used. Although the excess returns across the downside beta deciles are almost flat, the associated alphas are 50 (AF) and 63 (FF) basis points, with t-statistics of 2.22 (AF) and 2.58 (FF). Finally, there appears to be no relation between lottery demand and future stock returns even when value-weighted returns are used. This lack of significance contradicts the lottery-demand evidence documented in U.S markets.

To summarize, the analysis based on value-weighted returns shows that despite momentum return anomaly is independent of the weighting scheme, book-to-market equity, short-term reversal and skewness vanish when smaller stocks are given less weight. The strategies based on illiquidity, idiosyncratic volatility, value-at-risk, expected shortfall and hybrid tail risk becomes significant for value-weighted returns. One should note that although the sign of illiquidity contradicts with that of documented in U.S. studies, signs of idiosyncratic volatility, value-at-risk, expected shortfall and hybrid tail risk are in line with U.S. evidences.

Firm-Level Cross-Sectional Regressions

To examine the unique information that each firm-specific variable incorporates about future stock returns, the author runs monthly firm-level Fama and Macbeth (1973) regressions of future equity return on numerous firm-specific variables. Table 4 reports the time-series averages of these regressions as in Fama and Macbeth (1973) as well as the Newey-West (1987) adjusted t-statistics in parenthesis. Note that the firm-specific tail risk variables are included in the regression specification one at a time since they are highly correlated.

Table 4. Fama-MacBeth Cross-Sectional Regressions

	(1)	(2)	(3)	(4)	(5)	(6)	(7)	(8)	(9)	(10)	(11)	(12)	(13)	(14)	(15)
BETA	-0.0035	-0.0056	-0.0053	-0.0041	-0.0041	-0.0029	-0.0031	-0.0033	-0.0029	-0.0037	-0.0037	-0.0030	-0.0030	-0.0030	-0.0022
	(-1.50)	(-1.83)	(-1.69)	(-1.44)	(-1.45)	(-1.15)	(-1.23)	(-1.30)	(-1.09)	(-1.46)	(-1.41)	(-1.12)	(-1.24)	(-1.18)	(-0.85)
SIZE		0.0009*	0.0014**	0.0007	0.0007	0.0002	0.0001	0.0000	0.0000	0.0002	0.0002	0.0003	0.0001	0.0002	0.0002
		(2.08)	(3.00)	(1.69)	(1.70)	(0.60)	(0.36)	(0.07)	(0.09)	(0.60)	(0.84)	(1.07)	(0.33)	(0.56)	(0.70)
BM			0.0001	0.0001	0.0001	0.0001	0.0001	0.0001	0.0001	0.0000	0.0000	0.0000	0.0000	0.0000	0.0000
			(1.41)	(0.79)	(0.68)	(0.61)	(0.54)	(0.43)	(0.44)	(0.28)	(0.28)	(0.34)	(0.19)	(0.19)	(0.26)
MOM				0.0146**	0.0146**	0.0148**	0.0151**	0.0152**	0.0152**	0.0156**	0.0155**	0.0149**	0.0153**	0.0151**	0.0146**
				(7.78)	(7.52)	(7.88)	(8.06)	(8.24)	(8.31)	(9.11)	(8.88)	(8.34)	(9.08)	(8.84)	(8.27)
ILLIQ					0.0372**	0.0413**	0.0399**	0.0398**	0.0396**	0.0351**	0.0358**	0.0255*	0.0339**	0.0343**	0.0247*
					(2.84)	(3.18)	(3.06)	(3.07)	(3.07)	(2.73)	(2.66)	(2.08)	(2.60)	(2.50)	(1.96)
IVOL						-0.1943**	-0.1915**	-0.1759**	-0.1751**	-0.2228**	-0.2431**	-0.2194**	-0.2684**	-0.2845**	-0.2518**
						(-2.95)	(-3.02)	(-2.74)	(-2.74)	(-4.54)	(-4.78)	(-3.62)	(-5.38)	(-5.55)	(-4.21)
COSKEW							0.0000	0.0000	0.0000	0.0000	0.0000	0.0000	0.0000	0.0000	0.0000
							(0.47)	(0.49)	(0.60)	(0.51)	(0.54)	(0.38)	(0.36)	(0.41)	(0.21)
SKEW							-0.0012**	-0.0012**	-0.0012**	-0.0009	-0.0006	-0.0004	-0.0010*	-0.0007	-0.0005
							(-2.62)	(-2.65)	(-2.62)	(-1.70)	(-1.03)	(-0.85)	(-1.97)	(-1.26)	(-1.21)
HTCR								0.3028	0.2994	0.3627	0.4029	0.6884**	0.3439	0.3726	0.6299**
								(1.49)	(1.48)	(1.53)	(1.74)	(2.66)	(1.53)	(1.71)	(2.57)
DBETA									-0.0004	-0.0007	-0.0009	-0.0015	-0.0009	-0.0011	-0.0016
									(-0.38)	(-0.73)	(-0.92)	(-1.41)	(-0.95)	(-1.12)	(-1.56)
VaR										0.0497			0.0592		
										(1.25)			(1.50)		
ES											0.0660			0.0713*	
											(1.89)			(2.08)	
LPM												0.2889**			0.2777**
												(4.60)			(4.62)
STR													0.0154**	0.0150**	0.0144**
													(3.25)	(3.17)	(3.10)
Intercept	0.0038	0.0005	-0.0020	-0.0004	-0.0004	0.0055*	0.0064**	0.0072**	0.0071**	0.0050*	0.0035	0.0052**	0.0055**	0.0041	0.0060**
	(1.49)	(0.16)	(-0.55)	(-0.12)	(-0.12)	(2.19)	(2.60)	(3.26)	(3.28)	(2.15)	(1.46)	(2.41)	(2.41)	(1.72)	(2.87)
Avg R^2	0.0151	0.0236	0.0269	0.0386	0.0392	0.0507	0.0534	0.0567	0.0577	0.0627	0.0629	0.0614	0.0684	0.0687	0.0672

Table 4 shows that market beta is not priced in the cross-section of developed market equity returns. Although firm size has a slope coefficient of 0.0014 with a t-statistics of 3 in regression specification three, its significance vanishes when all variables are controlled for. Similar results are observed for book-to-market equity since the coefficients of this variable are statistically insignificant for all specifications. Consistent with the univariate portfolio analyses, the results in Table 4 document a strong positive cross-sectional relation between momentum and expected equity returns even after controlling for other effects. The coefficients of this variable ranges between 0.0146 and 0.0156 with t-statistics between 7.52 and 9.11. Contrary to the result in portfolio analysis, the relation between illiquidity and stock returns is significantly positive. Similar to the result in Ang et al. (2006), the average coefficient on idiosyncratic volatility is negative and statistically significant with coefficients ranging between -0.2845 and -0.1751. The results show that total skewness, co-skewness, downside beta, value at risk and hybrid tail risk have no robust explanatory power for expected equity returns. On the other hand, the regressions detect a positive relation between expected shortfall and future stock returns. Moreover, contrary to the U.S. findings, the results indicate a significantly positive relation between lower partial moment and expected equity returns. Lastly, the one-month-lagged return exhibits a significantly positive relation with future stock returns consistent with the portfolio analysis. Note that short-term reversal phenomenon documented in U.S. equities becomes short-term momentum in developed market setting.

*Table 4 presents results from cross-sectional regressions of one-month ahead equity returns on various firm-specific variables. Reported coefficients are time-series averages from monthly Fama-MacBeth (1973) regressions and the associated t-statistics are reported using the Newey-West (1987) procedure. Average R-squared statistics for each regression are presented in the last row. Firm-specific variables are defined in Table 1. *, ** denote statistical significance at the 5% and 1% levels, respectively.*

Regional Analysis

Since all developed countries are pooled together, it is possible that some cross-sectional return predictors that do affect future stock returns may lose their predictive power in previous analysis. The reason is that the predictive power of variable may be washed out unless that variable is a common predictor in most countries. Thus, the overall developed market sample are divided into two regions and value-weighted univariate analysis is repeated. The same analysis is again repeated after U.S. equities are excluded from the sample. First, Austria, Belgium, Denmark, Finland, France, Germany, Greece, Ireland, Israel, Italy, Luxembourg, Netherlands, Norway, Portugal, Spain, Sweden, Switzerland and United Kingdom are grouped under Europe. Second, Australia, Hong Kong, Japan, New Zealand, Singapore and South Korea are grouped under Asia.

In the analysis, all stocks in each region are grouped into 10 decile portfolios based on an ascending order of the firm-specific variables that are used earlier analysis and the one-month-ahead value-weighted returns are calculated for each decile portfolio. Next, the excess return difference between decile 10 and decile 1 is computed for each firm-specific variable. Table 5 reports the returns and alphas to zero-cost strategy that buys stocks in highest decile portfolio and sells stocks in the lowest decile portfolio for each firm-specific cross-sectional return predictor. Table 3 shows that return momentum, illiquidity and hybrid tail risk anomalies are significant in the overall sample of developed countries. By looking at the results for Europe and Asia separately, it is possible to see that specific regions drive the results in the overall developed market sample. Size anomaly is positively related to the future stock returns in Europe, whereas it is negatively related to the ones in Asia. Book-to-market affect is more pronounced for equities in Asian countries. The momentum effect is a robust predictor of expected equity returns in all sub-samples with statistically significant extreme portfolio differences of 2.36% and 2.21% for Europe and Asia, respectively, and 2.11% when U.S. is excluded from the sample. Illiquidity is negatively associated with future stocks only for European countries. The significant negative relation between idiosyncratic volatility and expected returns documented in Table 3 is also true for individual regions. Table 3 also showed that hybrid tail risk adduced similar evidences to those documented in U.S. studies. This strong relation is driven by European equities. The zero-cost strategy based on *HTCR* earns 75 basis points with a t-statistic 2.7 in Europe. Note that anomalies such as momentum, idiosyncratic volatility, value-at-risk, expected shortfall and hybrid tail risk continue to be priced in the cross-section of equity returns even when U.S. equities are excluded from the sample.

Table 5 presents the value-weighted returns and alphas to the zero-cost portfolio that have a long position (short position) in stocks in the decile with the highest (lowest) values of various firm-specific

Table 5. Regional Analysis

	Europe			Asia			Developed Excl. USA		
	Ret	AF	FF	Ret	AF	FF	Ret	AF	FF
BETA	-0.0003	0.0002	0.0007	-0.0068**	-0.0064**	-0.0068**	-0.0040	-0.0038**	-0.0033*
	(-0.08)	(0.10)	(0.39)	(-2.34)	(-2.82)	(-2.43)	(-1.30)	(-2.79)	(-2.29)
SIZE	0.0100**	0.0078**	0.0074**	-0.0084**	-0.0091**	-0.0084*	-0.0008	-0.0023	-0.0032
	(5.82)	(5.58)	(4.95)	(-2.53)	(-2.54)	(-2.30)	(-0.35)	(-0.98)	(-1.41)
BM	-0.0001	-0.0046	-0.0029	0.0073	0.0048	0.0049	0.0048	0.0005	0.0016
	(-0.04)	(-1.79)	(-1.05)	(1.82)	(1.32)	(1.24)	(1.46)	(0.16)	(0.53)
MOM	0.0236**	0.0137**	0.0171**	0.0221**	0.0148**	0.0205**	0.0211**	0.0103**	0.0160**
	(4.72)	(3.61)	(3.11)	(4.12)	(3.36)	(3.49)	(3.81)	(2.75)	(2.69)
STR	0.0009	0.0005	0.0015	0.0004	0.0011	0.0012	0.0017	0.0019	0.0028
	(0.29)	(0.15)	(0.36)	(0.08)	(0.20)	(0.23)	(0.47)	(0.47)	(0.66)
ILLIQ	-0.0063**	-0.0052**	-0.0066**	0.0040	0.0033	0.0047	-0.0041	-0.0035	-0.0020
	(-3.07)	(-2.67)	(-3.25)	(1.18)	(0.97)	(1.53)	(-1.92)	(-1.50)	(-1.11)
IVOL	-0.0095*	-0.0098**	-0.0086**	-0.0089*	-0.0079	-0.0091*	-0.0151**	-0.0145**	-0.0144**
	(-2.03)	(-2.85)	(-2.51)	(-2.04)	(-1.83)	(-2.22)	(-3.35)	(-4.02)	(-3.80)
COSKEW	-0.0011	0.0014	0.0012	-0.0032	-0.0015	-0.0026	-0.0014	0.0015	-0.0001
	(-0.61)	(0.64)	(0.53)	(-1.15)	(-0.50)	(-1.05)	(-0.79)	(0.75)	(-0.05)
SKEW	0.0055*	0.0062**	0.0046	-0.0043*	-0.0050**	-0.0048**	0.0016	0.0021	0.0014
	(2.22)	(2.41)	(1.89)	(-1.96)	(-2.33)	(-2.39)	(0.73)	(0.91)	(0.77)
VaR	-0.0082	-0.0074	-0.0052	-0.0107	-0.0120*	-0.0140**	-0.0090	-0.0092*	-0.0085*
	(-1.59)	(-1.93)	(-1.47)	(-1.70)	(-2.00)	(-2.47)	(-1.73)	(-2.16)	(-2.10)
ES	-0.0079	-0.0078*	-0.0050	-0.0081	-0.0093	-0.0110	-0.0114*	-0.0113**	-0.0105**
	(-1.72)	(-2.08)	(-1.55)	(-1.27)	(-1.45)	(-1.77)	(-2.26)	(-2.48)	(-2.53)
LPM	-0.0085*	-0.0098**	-0.0079*	-0.0006	-0.0021	-0.0026	-0.0064	-0.0087*	-0.0078*
	(-2.28)	(-2.70)	(-2.22)	(-0.12)	(-0.41)	(-0.60)	(-1.54)	(-2.18)	(-2.26)
HTCR	0.0075**	0.0059	0.0049	0.0032	0.0029	0.0047	0.0078*	0.0073*	0.0077*
	(2.70)	(1.99)	(1.79)	(0.88)	(0.82)	(1.24)	(2.29)	(2.20)	(2.16)
DBeta	0.0027	0.0034	0.0026	-0.0036	-0.0042	-0.0033	-0.0012	-0.0008	-0.0007
	(0.74)	(1.15)	(0.85)	(-1.21)	(-1.76)	(-1.28)	(-0.35)	(-0.33)	(-0.29)
MAX1	-0.0016	0.0002	0.0011	-0.0013	-0.0012	-0.0021	-0.0028	-0.0009	-0.0010
	(-0.41)	(0.06)	(0.37)	(-0.28)	(-0.28)	(-0.49)	(-0.60)	(-0.25)	(-0.28)
MAX5	-0.0027	-0.0016	0.0001	-0.0036	-0.0046	-0.0053	-0.0045	-0.0036	-0.0038
	(-0.63)	(-0.47)	(0.03)	(-0.69)	(-1.01)	(-1.23)	(-0.96)	(-1.00)	(-1.10)

*variables in three different geographic regions. AF Alpha is the intercept term from a regression of portfolio returns on the global market, size, value and momentum factors calculated by Asness and Frazzini (2013). FF Alpha is the intercept term from a regression of portfolio returns on the global market, size, value, investment and profitability factors calculated by Fama and French (2017). Firm-specific variables are defined in Table 1. Newey-West (1987) adjusted t-statistics are presented in parentheses. *, ** denote statistical significance at the 5% and 1% levels, respectively.*

CONCLUSION

This chapter examines the predictive power of numerous firm-specific variables on the cross-section of equity returns in developed market setting. Although many studies investigated these variables in U.S. environment, the evidence from developed markets other than U.S. is still incomplete. Univariate, bivariate and multivariate analyses are implemented to study which firm-specific attributes are related to the cross-section of developed market equity returns using data from 26 countries and more than 5.8 million monthly observations. Univariate portfolio analysis using equal-weighted return reveal that low beta, book-to-market equity and momentum anomalies are in line with the U.S. studies. On the other hand, short-term reversal and downside beta manifests themselves in the opposite direction in developed markets compared to U.S. Furthermore, value-weighted portfolio analysis document that the predictive power of book-to-market equity and short-term reversal is driven by penny stocks. Firm level cross sectional regressions reveal that momentum, illiquidity, idiosyncratic volatility, hybrid tail risk, lower partial moment and short-term reversal exhibit significant relation with future stock returns.

The findings highlight the importance of investigating well-documented cross-sectional return predictors in different markets. The overall results raise a challenge for scholars and professionals to examine why some cross-sectional determinants behave differently in different regions or even in some specific countries. Further research is needed to comprehend the real economic dynamics behind different results between U.S. and the rest of the developing countries.

REFERENCES

Amihud, Y. (2002). Illiquidity and stock returns: Cross-section and time series effects. *Journal of Financial Markets*, *5*(1), 31–56. doi:10.1016/S1386-4181(01)00024-6

Amihud, Y., Hameed, A., Kang, W., & Zhang, H. (2015). The illiquidity premium: International evidence. *Journal of Financial Economics*, *117*(2), 350–368. doi:10.1016/j.jfineco.2015.04.005

Ang, A., Chen, J., & Xing, Y. (2006). Downside risk. *Review of Financial Studies*, *19*(4), 1191–1239. doi:10.1093/rfs/hhj035

Ang, A., Hodrick, R. J., Xing, Y., & Zhang, X. (2006). The cross-section of volatility and expected returns. *The Journal of Finance*, *61*(1), 259–299. doi:10.1111/j.1540-6261.2006.00836.x

Ang, A., Hodrick, R. J., Xing, Y., & Zhang, X. (2009). High idiosyncratic volatility and low returns: International and further U.S. evidence. *Journal of Financial Economics*, *91*(1), 1–23. doi:10.1016/j.jfineco.2007.12.005

Artzner, P., Delbaen, F., Eber, J., & Heath, D. (1999). Coherent measures of risk. *Mathematical Finance*, *9*(3), 203–228. doi:10.1111/1467-9965.00068

Asness, C. S., & Frazzini, A. (2013). The devil in HML's details. *Journal of Portfolio Management*, *39*(4), 49–68. doi:10.3905/jpm.2013.39.4.049

Asness, C. S., Moskowitz, T. J., & Pedersen, L. H. (2013). Value and Momentum Everywhere. *The Journal of Finance*, *68*(3), 929–985. doi:10.1111/jofi.12021

Atilgan, Y., Bali, T. G., Demirtas, K. O., & Gunaydin, A. D. (2018). Downside Beta and Equity Returns around the World. *Journal of Portfolio Management*, *135*(3), 725–753.

Atilgan, Y., Bali, T. G., Demirtas, K. O., & Gunaydin, A. D. (2020). Left-tail momentum: Underreaction to bad news, costly arbitrage and equity returns. *Journal of Financial Economics*, *135*(3), 725–753. doi:10.1016/j.jfineco.2019.07.006

Atilgan, Y., Demirtas, K. O., & Gunaydin, A. D. (2020). Downside beta and the cross section of equity returns: A decade later. *European Financial Management*, *26*(2), 316–347. doi:10.1111/eufm.12258

Bali, T. G., Cakici, N., & Whitelaw, R. F. (2011). Maxing out: Stocks as lotteries and the cross-section of expected returns. *Journal of Financial Economics*, *99*(2), 427–446. doi:10.1016/j.jfineco.2010.08.014

Bali, T. G., Cakici, N., & Whitelaw, R. F. (2014). Hybrid tail risk and expected stock returns: When does the tail wag the dog? *Review of Asset Pricing Studies*, *4*(2), 206–246. doi:10.1093/rapstu/rau006

Banz, R. W. (1981). The relationship between return and market value of common stocks. *Journal of Financial Economics*, *9*(1), 3–18. doi:10.1016/0304-405X(81)90018-0

Bawa, V. S., & Lindenberg, E. B. (1977). Capital market equilibrium in a mean-lower partial moment framework. *Journal of Financial Economics*, *5*(2), 189–200. doi:10.1016/0304-405X(77)90017-4

Bekaert, G., Harvey, C. R., & Lundblad, C. (2007). Liquidity and expected returns: Lessons from emerging markets. *Review of Financial Studies*, *20*(6), 1783–1831. doi:10.1093/rfs/hhm030

Carhart, M. M. (1997). On persistence in mutual fund performance. *The Journal of Finance*, *52*(1), 57–82. doi:10.1111/j.1540-6261.1997.tb03808.x

Cochrane, J. H. (2011). Presidential address: Discount rates. *The Journal of Finance*, *66*(4), 1047–1108. doi:10.1111/j.1540-6261.2011.01671.x

Fama, E. F., & French, K. R. (1992). The cross-section of expected stock returns. *The Journal of Finance*, *47*(2), 427–465. doi:10.1111/j.1540-6261.1992.tb04398.x

Fama, E. F., & French, K. R. (1993). Common risk factors in the returns on stocks and bonds. *Journal of Financial Economics*, *33*(1), 3–56. doi:10.1016/0304-405X(93)90023-5

Fama, E. F., & French, K. R. (2017). International tests of a five-factor asset pricing model. *Journal of Financial Economics*, *123*(3), 441–463. doi:10.1016/j.jfineco.2016.11.004

Fama, E. F., & MacBeth, J. D. (1973). Risk, return and equilibrium: Empirical tests. *Journal of Political Economy*, *81*(3), 607–636. doi:10.1086/260061

Frazzini, A., & Pedersen, L. H. (2014). Betting against beta. *Journal of Financial Economics, 111*(1), 1–25. doi:10.1016/j.jfineco.2013.10.005

Griffen, J. M., Kelly, P. J., & Nardari, F. (2010). Do Market Efficiency Measures Yield Correct Inferences? A Comparison of Developed and Emerging Markets. *Review of Financial Studies, 23*(8), 3225–3277. doi:10.1093/rfs/hhq044

Harvey, C. R., & Siddique, A. (2000). Conditional skewness in asset pricing tests. *The Journal of Finance, 55*(3), 1263–1295. doi:10.1111/0022-1082.00247

Hou, K., Xue, C., & Zhang, L. (2020). Replicating Anomalies. *Review of Financial Studies, 33*(5), 2019–2133. doi:10.1093/rfs/hhy131

Jegadeesh, N. (1990). Evidence of predictable behavior of security returns. *The Journal of Finance, 45*(3), 881–898. doi:10.1111/j.1540-6261.1990.tb05110.x

Jegadeesh, N., & Titman, S. (1993). Returns to buying winners and selling losers: Implications for stock market efficiency. *The Journal of Finance, 48*(1), 65–91. doi:10.1111/j.1540-6261.1993.tb04702.x

Karolyi, G. A., Lee, K., & van Dijk, M. A. (2012). Understanding commonality in liquidity around the world. *Journal of Financial Economics, 105*(1), 82–112. doi:10.1016/j.jfineco.2011.12.008

Lee, K. (2011). The world price of liquidity risk. *Journal of Financial Economics, 99*(1), 136–161. doi:10.1016/j.jfineco.2010.08.003

Lintner, J. (1965). The valuation of risk assets and the selection of risky investments in stock portfolios and capital budgets. *The Review of Economics and Statistics, 47*(1), 13–37. doi:10.2307/1924119

Mossin, J. (1966). Equilibrium in a capital asset market. *Econometrica, 34*(4), 768–783. doi:10.2307/1910098

Newey, W. K., & West, K. D. (1987). A simple, positive semi-definite, heteroskedasticity and autocorrelation consistent covariance matrix. *Econometrica, 55*(3), 703–708. doi:10.2307/1913610

Sharpe, W. F. (1964). Capital asset prices: A theory of market equilibrium under conditions of risk. *The Journal of Finance, 19*(3), 425–442.

KEY TERMS AND DEFINITIONS

Descriptive Statistics: A summary statistics that describes the basic aspects of the data.

Downside Risk: A measure of risk that the realized return of the portfolio or individual asset is less than the expected return.

Equal-Weighted Return: A type of weighting methodology to calculate portfolio return that gives the same weight to each asset in the portfolio.

Portfolio: A collection of financial assets such as stocks, bonds, currencies, and cash.

Regression: A statistical process for determining the relation between one dependent variable and various other variables (also known as independent variables).

Tail Risk: A measure of portfolio or individual asset risk which is three standard deviations higher than the risk of the normal distribution.

Value-Weighted Return: A type of weighting methodology to calculate portfolio return that gives a weight to an asset in the portfolio based on the asset's market value.

ENDNOTES

1 Sample periods starts in 1990 for Greece and Portugal, 1992 for Luxembourg and 1993 for Israel.

2 These global factors are obtained from AQR Capital Management (https://www.aqr.com/library/data-sets) and Kenneth French (http://mba.tuck.dartmouth.edu/pages/faculty/ken.french/data_library.html).

3 Results are robust to using alternative lags.

4 One year of past trading data is necessary to estimate some of the firm-specific variables. Thus, the first available month to run these cross-sectional regressions is January 1989.

5 Instead of *STR*, *RET* is included in the table since, *STR* is calculated as the lagged value of monthly equity returns.

Chapter 5
Market Pricing of Bank M&As and Efficiency in Europe

Sailesh Tanna
https://orcid.org/0000-0002-2243-3857
Coventry University, UK

Hodian Urio
Mount Meru University, Arusha, Tanzania

Ibrahim Yousef
https://orcid.org/0000-0001-5042-0685
University of Petra, Jordan

ABSTRACT

This study investigates the impact of bank mergers and acquisitions (M&As) on bank efficiency and how such efficiencies are expected to influence bank shareholder value upon merger announcements. It employs stochastic frontier analysis and event study methods along with regression analysis to account for the influences of pre-merger and post-merger efficiencies of bidders and targets in assessing their impact on bidder abnormal returns. Using data for a sample of large commercial bank M&As from 22 European countries, the authors find that bank bidders achieve short-term shareholder value gains from merger announcements, and this could be associated with the perceived efficiencies of bidders and targets. More generally, the evidence supports the view that bank profit efficiency has a positive influence on bidder returns from merger announcements, and therefore markets do take into account the importance of efficiency in value creation. This suggests that stock markets price operational efficiency of banks in predicting value gains from European Bank M&As.

DOI: 10.4018/978-1-7998-5083-0.ch005

INTRODUCTION

'Under the semi-strong efficient market hypothesis, stock prices react positively (negatively) to public events and announcements that informed market participants expect will increase (decrease) long-run firm value. However, realized long-run outcomes need not be consistent with short-run market reactions' (Gayle Delong and Robert DeYoung, 2007).

According to the well-known Efficient Market Hypothesis (EMH), a firm's stock price reflects all available information. As such, investor can predict that the market would take into account the firm's record of efficiency in evaluating its impact on shareholder value following an event. This paper investigates whether a bank's efficiency is assimilated into its stock price when it seeks to acquire, or merge with, another bank. More precisely, consistent with EMH, the authors investigate whether the pre-merger and post-merger efficiency of bank targets and bidders at the time of merger announcement are reflected in the bidder's stock price abnormal returns.

The analysis that a firm's stock price reaction from merger announcements reflects its pre-merger and/or post-merger efficiency is based on two assumptions that are common in the finance literature. The first, grounded in the semi-strong EMH, posits that information not publicly available is perceived by the market. As implied by the above quote from DeLong and DeYoung (2007), it is likely that market participants, some of them with insider information, may influence the firm's stock price through trading. This possibility culminates in markets being able to predict a firm's future performance, one indicator of which is efficiency. The second assumption is that the stock price reflects future earnings performance of the firm, which again may be predicted by its record of efficiency.

We develop several hypotheses relating the impact of bidder and target efficiencies to bidder shareholder value and conduct our empirical analysis using accounting and financial data for a sample of 56 large commercial bank mergers that took place in 22 European countries between 2010 and 2017. Efficiency is estimated using stochastic frontier analysis (SFA), while event study methodology is employed to calculate shareholder returns upon merger announcements. To determine whether efficiency has significant impact on announcement period shareholder returns, we perform numerous cross-sectional and panel regressions relating bidder cumulative abnormal returns (CARs) to various proxies for the efficiency variables while controlling for a number of bank specific, deal specific and environmental factors. We contribute to the literature by combining different methodologies and multiple datasets to study the impact of efficiency on shareholder value. In doing so, we build upon a few previous studies (e.g. Chronopoulos *et al.*, 2010, 2013; Kohers *et al.*, 2000; Aggarwal *et al.*, 2006) which use similar but slightly differentiated methodologies. Importantly, we test several distinct hypotheses and provide recent evidence relating to Europe.

The main finding of this paper is that bank bidders achieve short-term shareholder value gains from merger announcements and this could be associated with the perceived efficiencies of bidders and targets. For example, evidence is found that both pre- and post-merger profit efficiency has a positive effect on shareholder value, whereas target cost efficiency is negatively associated with value creation of bidders. On balance, the results of this study are supportive of the view that bank mergers in Europe are value-creating for the bidding firms and this could be attributed to perceived efficiency gains from mergers (De Young *et al.*, 2009; Urio and Tanna, 2012). If market reaction to bank merger announcements reflects the perceived efficiency of bidder and targets, investors may be able to use such information in predicting short-term performance gains.

RELATED LITERATURE

Many studies have investigated the efficiency of European banks engaged in M&As (Vander Vennet, 1996, 2002; Resti, 1998; Huizinga *et al.*, 2001; Beccali and Frantz, 2009). Although efficiency has been the main focus of investigation associated with bank M&As (Amel *et al.*, 2004), there are also numerous European studies which have examined value creation from bank merger announcements (Cybo-Ottone and Murgia, 2000; Beitel *et al.*, 2004; Campa and Hernando, 2004, 2006; Nnadi and Tanna, 2013). However, studies linking these two indicators of performance (efficiency and value creation) are limited. Another strand of research investigates the risk implications of M&As, which we do not consider in this paper.[1]

A previous European study that sought to examine whether the market takes into account efficiency when reacting to merger announcements is that of Chronopoulos *et al.* (2010), which investigates bank mergers that took place in the period 1997-2003. In their study, 30 European bank mergers are combined with 70 American bank mergers to examine whether the market integrates post-merger bank efficiency in stock prices. The European sub-sample includes only banks from countries in the former EU-15 countries plus Norway and Switzerland. Chronopoulos *et al.* (2010) find that, overall, European bank mergers earned significant cumulative abnormal returns while US mergers made near zero or negative returns. The study also reports that the bidders experienced improvement in post-merger efficiency, while cost efficiency declined. Another study by Chronopoulos *et al.* (2013) investigates whether stock markets price changes in operating efficiency as a result of bank mergers, and if the premiums paid by the acquiring banks reflect these changes. Using a sample of mergers from both US and Europe during the period of 1997 to 2003, they reveal a significant association between announcement-period abnormal returns and the post-merger profit efficiency changes.

In addition to Chronopoulos *et al.* (2010, 2013), which use both US and European bank data, two prior US studies using frontier methods of estimating efficiency have investigated the market's incorporation of bank efficiency in the stock price upon merger announcement. The first one is Kohers *et al.* (2000) who investigate a sample of 94 mergers involving bank holding companies (BHCs). In order to compare the efficiencies of the merged banks with those of its peers, the study engages as its peers all the BHCs which were not involved in mergers in the years analyzed. Upon estimation of efficiency, Kohers *et al.* (2000) find that merged banks are more profit efficient than their peers pre-merger, but they are less cost efficient than their peers in that period. The study tests the relative efficiency hypothesis that suggests that upon taking over a less efficient bank a bidder will make changes that can improve the efficiency of the target and therefore the combined firm upon merger. Also tested, is the low efficiency hypothesis which proposes that where the targets' pre-merger efficiencies are less than either the bidders' or those of their peers, target efficiency will improve post-merger. The results of the study support both the relative and low efficiency hypotheses. Furthermore, the study finds evidence that the greatest wealth effects accrue to the bidder's shareholders when a bidder takes over a relatively less efficient bank, allowing the former to implement a broad range of changes that generate efficiency improvements in the combined BHC. Kohers *et al.* (2000) also test whether efficiency has any influence on the market's valuation of bank mergers. This is done by regressing the bidders' cumulative abnormal returns on efficiency among other control variables. They find evidence that efficiency has an effect on how the market evaluates bank mergers. One indication of this is that the bidder banks' cumulative abnormal returns are negatively associated with targets' cost as well as profit efficiency, but positively correlated with the difference in peer and target efficiency.

The next US study is Aggarwal *et al.* (2006) who analyze 271 large bank mergers that took place in the period 1986-2001 to find out whether there is an association between profit efficiency and cumulative abnormal returns. They find that before mergers, targets are more profit efficient than the bidders but in the three years before the merger, bidders gained more targets in terms of profit efficiency. Post-merger efficiency was also found to have improved over the pre-merger performance. Their regression results using CARs show that the market expects that bidder shareholders of highly efficient banks stand a good chance of benefitting from the merger. Market expectations are similar in those cases where there is considerable difference between the bidder's and the target's profit efficiency. In addition, the findings suggest also that the market will react positively for bidder shareholders upon merger announcement when the merged bank is likely to improve its profit efficiency post-merger. Lastly, the study finds that the market expects bidder banks with prior acquisition experience to generate greater gains for their shareholders

We build upon the above studies to provide recent evidence from European bank mergers, thereby adding to previous European evidence reported by Chronopoulos *et al.* (2010, 2013). Apart from differences in the composition of sample and the time-period investigated, our study uses stochastic frontier analysis (SFA) for estimating efficiency, whereas Chronopoulos *et al.* (2010, 2013) use data envelopment analysis (DEA). Importantly, our study uses multivariate regressions to examine the influence of efficiency on bidder returns to merger announcements.

Hypotheses

In developing our hypotheses, we draw insights from the aforementioned European and US studies, and consider the influence of bidder and target cost and profit efficiencies, the difference between bidder and target efficiencies, and the efficiencies of relevant peers in the market. From the above synthesis of the literature, we propose the following main hypotheses:

Hypothesis H1: Bidder efficiency has a positive effect on bidder shareholder returns (CARs)
Hypothesis H2: Target efficiency has a negative effect on bidder shareholder returns

In addition to these two main hypotheses, we consider two other distinct variants to account for differences in the bidder and target efficiencies, as follows:

Hypothesis H3: All efficiencies involving the deduction of target efficiency from either bidder or peer efficiency have a positive effect on bidder shareholder returns.

Hypothesis H4: Both efficiencies involving the deduction of the average of bidder and target efficiencies from peer efficiency have a positive effect on bidder shareholder returns.

The latter two hypotheses are novel and distinct, derived by taking account of the efficiencies of peers not involved in M&As. The main purpose behind accounting for the influence of peer efficiency in the computation of bidder shareholder value (in addition to bidder and target efficiencies) is to ensure that the efficiency is assessed relative to that of competitors in the market.

These hypotheses, by implication, relate shareholder returns to either cost or profit efficiency, pre-merger or post-merger, and therefore can only be tested by performing CAR regressions after event study results and efficiency proxies are derived. In testing the hypotheses, we incorporate a number of control variables in the CAR regressions in addition to the efficiency proxies. In particular, following De Long and De Young (2007), we allow for learning effects by accounting for *serial* acquirers; and following Aggarwal *et al.* (2006), we also control for market *concentration* in the target's market. As in Aggarwal *et al.* (2006), we examine both bidder efficiency and target efficiency, as well as variants such as bidder efficiency less target efficiency, and peer efficiency less the average of bidder and target efficiency, to account for competitor influences. As with Kohers *et al.* (2000), we analyze both cost and profit efficiency, although Aggarwal *et al.* (2006) examine only profit efficiency.

METHODOLOGY

Using event study methodology, bidder cumulative abnormal returns (CARs) are obtained around the announcement date using a market model and a two-day event period following Aggarwal *et al.* (2006). The CARs are then regressed on the pre- or post-merger cost or profit efficiencies, together with a number of control variables as discussed below.

1. Event Study

The study follows Brown and Warner's (1985) methodology to calculate bidder abnormal returns around the announcement date. Abnormal returns are calculated by subtracting the actual returns during the event window from expected returns. Specifically, for bidder i in period t, the abnormal return is calculated as follows:

$$AR_{i,t} = r_{i,t} - E\left(r_{i,t}\right) \tag{1}$$

where $AR_{i,t}$ is the abnormal return for bidder stock i at time t; $r_{i,t}$ the actual return of the stock i at time t; and $E(r_{i,t})$ is the expected return of the stock i at time t

The expected returns are derived using the market model, which expresses the relation between expected and market returns as follows:

$$E\left(r_{i,t}\right) = \alpha + \beta r_{m,t} + \varepsilon_{i,t}\left(t = -110,\ldots..,-11\right) \tag{2}$$

where $r_{m,t}$ is the market return (determined using a benchmark local market index) at time t; and $\varepsilon_{i,t}$ is the random error term.

The parameters of equation (2) are estimated using bidders' daily stock price data, converted into returns using log differences, for 100 days over the period from 110 days to 11 days prior to deal announcement date. The average abnormal returns (AARs) and cumulative average abnormal returns (CARs) are then calculated according to the formula:

$$AARs = \frac{1}{N}\sum_{i=1}^{N}\widehat{AR}_{i,t} \tag{3}$$

$$CARs\left(T_1,T_2\right)=\frac{1}{N}\sum_{t=T_1}^{T_2}\widehat{AR}_{i,t} \quad (4)$$

where $\widehat{AR}_{i,t}$ is the calculated abnormal return for each stock i at time t; N constitutes the number of deals in the sample, and T_1 and T_2 reflect the start and end dates of the event window around the announcement date. In principle, for the calculation of CARs, we can allow for windows of up to 5 days before and after announcement date but entertain shorter windows of only 2 days for regression purposes.

2. CAR Regression Model

Since our purpose in this paper is to investigate whether the market takes into account the banks' bidder/target efficiency upon merger announcement, CARs regressions are performed on a number of efficiency and control variables cited in the literature as having an influence on the market's reaction to bank merger announcements and stock price performance. The basic regression model is of the form:

$$CAR_i=\alpha+\beta_i EFF_i+\beta_2 RSIZE_i+\beta_3 CROSS_i+\beta_4 CASH_i+\beta_5 SERIAL_i+\beta_6 DIVPAY_{it}+\beta_7 CONC_{it}+\varepsilon_i \quad (5)$$

where: CAR_i is the 2-day cumulative abnormal return; EFF_i is bank efficiency or bank efficiency difference as discussed below; $RSIZE_i$ is the relative size of target to bidder bank measured in total assets; $CROSS_i$ is a dummy variable, taking value 1 for cross-border merger and 0 for domestic; $CASH_i$ denotes method of payment, taking value 1 if the deal is paid for in cash only, 0 otherwise (i.e. if payment is in stock or mixture of cash and stock); $SERIAL_i$ is 1 for the bidder that has been involved in previous mergers, 0 otherwise; $DIVPAY_{it}$ is dividend payout; $CONC_{it}$ is bank concentration in the target's country; i stands for bank, while t stands for time.

While above regression model is estimated using OLS, due to the inclusion of some time-dependent explanatory factors (e.g. dividend payout and bank concentration), the data-set for estimation is an unbalanced panel (i.e. cross-sectional with some time-dependent data).

3. Efficiency Estimation

The CARs regression equation (5) comprises the efficiency variable, representing either cost or profit efficiency, which is computed using stochastic frontier analysis. We use the Batesse and Coelli (1995) method, which estimates efficiency in a single-step while simultaneously controlling for cross-country differences. Focusing on cost efficiency for expositional convenience, the model can be expressed as:

$$\ln C_{i,t}= C(y_{i,t}, w_{i,t}; \beta) + \mu c_{i,t}+ \varepsilon c_{i,t}, \; i=1,2,...,N; \; t=1,2,...,T \quad (6)$$

where: $C_{i,t}$ stands for Total Costs of bank i at time t; $y_{i,t}$ represents a vector of outputs; $y_{i,t}$ is a vector of input price values of a suitable functional form; β is a vector of unknown scalar parameters to be estimated; $\varepsilon c_{i,t}$'s are random errors, assumed to be i.i.d. and have $N(0, \sigma_V^2)$; $\mu c_{i,t}$'s are non-negative inefficiency effects in the model assumed to be independent but not identically distributed, so that $\mu c_{i,t}$ was obtained by truncation at zero of the $N(m_{i,t}, \sigma_u^2)$ distribution where the mean is defined as:

$$m_{i,t} = z_{i,t}\delta \tag{7}$$

with $z_{i,t}$ representing a vector of observable explanatory variables that influence the inefficiency of bank i at time t; and δ stands for a vector of coefficients that were estimated. Following Batesse and Coelli (1995), the parameters of equations (6) and (7) are estimated in a one-step procedure using maximum likelihood.

With regard to profit efficiency, the model specification is the same except that the dependent variable is Profit before Tax (PBT), replacing Total Costs (C), and the inefficiency term is negative ($-\mu c_{i,t}$), so that the profit frontier model is specified in the same way as the cost frontier above with same outputs and input prices.[2]

Using the above frontier estimation method, we need to compute four pre-merger efficiency proxies for both cost and profit efficiency to facilitate testing of the above hypotheses H1-H4. These are: (i) pre-merger bidder efficiency, (ii) pre-merger target efficiency, (iii) the net effect of the bidder-target efficiency i.e., bidder efficiency less target efficiency pre-merger, and (iv) pre-merger *peer* efficiency less average combined efficiency of the merging firms (i.e. bidder efficiency + target efficiency/2), subject to non-merged peers identified on the basis of the bidder and target size.

Apart from these pre-merger efficiency proxies, we need to compute post-merger cost and profit efficiency measures for a sub-sample of mergers for which financial data are available for both the year prior to merger and all of the three years after merger, making it possible to estimate post-merger efficiency for each of the three post-merger years after announcement. In addition, the average post-merger cost and profit efficiencies over the three years after the mergers are considered.

DATA

Relevant data on commercial bank mergers that took place between 2010 and 2017 were obtained from the *Thomson One Banker* M&A Database. Bank M&As included in the sample had to meet the following criteria:

(i) The M&A deals were announced between 1st January, 2010 and 31st December, 2017 and both the bidder and target were commercial banks headquartered in one of the European countries (which include the former EU-15 countries, Sweden, Norway, Switzerland, Turkey, Croatia and the Former Yugoslavia Republic of Macedonia).

(ii) Merger is defined as occurring when the bidder acquires more than 50% holding of equity, which may be all at once or at the instance this threshold is reached following previous acquisitions in the target.

  (ii) The bidder was listed on a stock exchange, but not necessarily so for the target.

  (iii) Only bidders and targets whose income statement and balance sheet data were available for at least one year before the merger were selected.

Starting with an original list of 102 deals, the sample was reduced to 56 after eliminating banks that failed to meet one or more of the above criteria. A similar list was selected for non-merged peers banks, from an initial list of 112 that were identified on the basis of bidder and target size.

Daily stock price data for the bidder banks (from 110 days prior to deal announcement date and up to 5 days after) to calculate event study returns (equations 1-4) were obtained from Thompson Reuter's *Datastream*. The *Thomson One Banker* and Bureau van Dijk's *Bankscope* databases provided the annual financial statement data for the variables in the CAR regressions (equation 5) and for the selected inputs and outputs of all banks (merged and non-merged peers) to determine efficiency scores for up to three years pre-merger (equation 6). Finally, annual data for the variables used in the mean (in)efficiency regression (equation 7) are obtained from the databases of the IMF and World Bank. Thus, combining data from different sources, we computed event study returns, obtained pre-merger and, where possible, post-merger cost and profit efficiencies for the relevant categories mentioned above, and finally performed CAR regressions to test the hypotheses.

EMPIRICAL RESULTS

1. Event Study Results

Table 1 shows the event study results showing values for AARs and CARs over a 10-day window (i.e. 5 days before and 5 days after announcement day). The results indicate that AARs increase steadily before announcement date, peaking up on the day of announcement, and declining thereafter. Intuitively, due to leakage of information, it is reasonable to expect that ARs will increase steadily before announcement day. Correspondingly, as Figure 1 shows, the CARs accumulate steadily up to one day after announce-

Table 1. Abnormal Returns (AARs and CARs)

Days from Announcement	AARs %	t	p-value	CARs%	t	p-value
-5D	0.180%	0.630	0.529	0.180%	0.630	0.529
-4D	0.200%	0.900	0.368	0.380%	1.510	0.130
-3D	0.340%	1.210	0.226	0.720%	2.030	0.042*
-2D	1.120%	4.800	0.000***	1.840%	4.090	0.000***
-1D	1.380%	7.500	0.000***	3.220%	5.430	0.000***
0D	1.709%	5.070	0.000***	4.929%	9.310	0.000***
1D	1.065%	4.276	0.000****	5.994%	7.500	0.000***
2D	-0.981%	4.561	0.000***	5.013%	6.090	0.000***
3D	-1.198%	4.717	0.000***	3.815%	5.950	0.000***
4D	-1.140%	2.748	0.008***	2.675%	3.510	0.000***
5D	-0.310%	1.330	0.184	2.365%	2.510	0.012**

Note: AARs are average abnormal returns and CARs are cumulative average abnormal returns, expressed in percentages. CARs are accumulated values of AARs starting from day 5 before (-5D) announcement day (0D). So, for example, CAR (-5, +5) = 2.365%, CAR (0, +1) = 5.994 – 3.220 = 2.774%, and so on. The symbols *, **, *** denote statistical significance at the 10%, 5% and 1% level, respectively.

ment and decline thereafter. Importantly, the CARs are statistically significant for several days before and after the announcement date. These results suggest that bidder shareholders gain from merger announcements, which may reflect the market's confidence in the future profitability of the merged entities.

Figure 1. Cumulative Abnormal Returns (CARs)

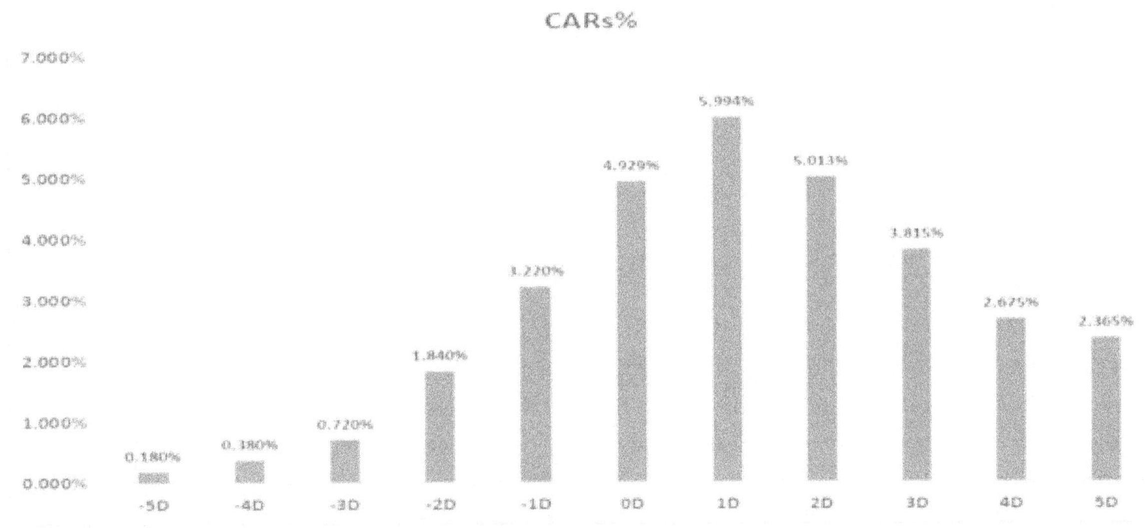

2. Efficiency Analysis

Bank level inputs and outputs for the cost and profit functions were selected using the intermediation approach suggested by Sealey and Lindley (1977), the outputs being loans (*y1*), other earning assets (*y2*), and non-interest income (*y3*); while inputs are the cost of loanable funds (*w1*), the cost of physical capital (*w2*), and the cost of labour (*w3*). To ensure linear homogeneity, the input prices and the dependent variables were normalized by the third input price, *w3*.

Using a translog approximation for the functional form in equation (6), the resulting (cost) frontier model is:

$$\ln\frac{TC}{w3} = \beta_0 + \beta_1 \ln(y1) + \beta_2 \ln(y2) + \beta_3 \ln(y3) + \beta_4 \ln\left(\frac{w1}{w3}\right) + \beta_5 \ln\left(\frac{w2}{w3}\right) + \beta_6 \frac{1}{2}(\ln(y1))^2$$

$$+\beta_7 \ln(y1)\ln(y2) + \beta_8 \ln(y1)\ln(y3) + \beta_9 \frac{1}{2}(\ln(y2))^2 + \beta_{10} \ln(y2)\ln(y3) + \beta_{11} \frac{1}{2}(\ln(y3))^2$$

$$+\beta_{12} \frac{1}{2}\left(\ln\left(\frac{w1}{w3}\right)\right)^2 + \beta_{13} \ln(y1)\ln\left(\frac{w1}{w3}\right) + \beta_{14} \ln(y2)\ln\left(\frac{w1}{w3}\right) + \beta_{15} \ln(y3)\ln\left(\frac{w1}{w3}\right) + \beta_{16} \frac{1}{2}\left(\ln\left(\frac{w2}{w3}\right)\right)^2$$

$$+\beta_{17}\ln(y1)\ln\left(\frac{w2}{w3}\right)+\beta_{18}\ln(y2)\ln\left(\frac{w2}{w3}\right)+\beta_{19}\ln(y3)\ln\left(\frac{w2}{w3}\right)+\beta_{20}\ln\left(\frac{w1}{w3}\right)\ln\left(\frac{w2}{w3}\right)+\beta_{21}\ln(e)$$

$$+\beta_{22}\frac{1}{2}(\ln(e))^2+\beta_{23}\ln(e)\ln(y1)+\beta_{24}\ln(e)\ln(y2)+\beta_{25}\ln(e)\ln(y3)+\beta_{26}\ln(e)\ln\left(\frac{w1}{w3}\right)$$

$$+\beta_{27}\ln(e)\ln\left(\frac{w2}{w3}\right)+\beta_{28}t+\beta_{29}t^2+\beta_{30}\ln(y1)t+\beta_{31}\ln(y2)t+\beta_{32}\ln(y3)t+\beta_{33}\ln\left(\frac{w1}{w3}\right)t$$

$$+\beta_{34}\ln\left(\frac{w2}{w3}\right)t+\beta_{35}\ln(e)t+\ln(\mu c)+\ln(\varepsilon c).$$

A time trend was included to allow for technological changes over time. Consistent with other studies the trend contains both t and t^2 terms since the translog function is a second order approximation. To control for differences in bank capitalization, equity (e) was considered as a fixed input in line with Berger and Mester (1997).

While estimating a global frontier, we account for differences in bank-specific risk and country-specific economic factors, by specifying m_{it} in equation (7) as:

$$m_{it}=\delta_0+\delta_1 EQTA+\delta_2 LONDEP+\delta_3 CONCT+\delta_4 INFL+\delta_5 GDPRT+\delta_6 MACGDP+\delta_7 CLAIMS+\delta_8 CAPRQ$$

where *EQTA* is abbreviation for the equity to total assets ratio, to control for differences in capital strength; *LONDEP* is firm loans to deposits ratio, used to show how much of funding is due to borrowing and not equity; *CONCT* is market concentration as measured by the proportion of total assets of the largest three banks to total bank assets in a country; *INFL* is annual rate of inflation; *GDPRT* is GDP growth rate; *MACGDP* stands for size of a country's stock market as measured by total value of quoted shares (stock market capitalization) divided by GDP; *CLAIMS* represents how active a country's banking sector is as measured by total banks' claims to the private sector; and *CAPRQ* is Basel II bank capital adequacy requirements for a country. *EQTA* and *LONDEP* were calculated from the banks' financial statements, *INFL* and *GDPRT* were obtained from the International Monetary Fund World Economic Outlook (2018), and *CONCT*, *MACGDP*, *CLAIMS* and *CAPRQ* were obtained from an updated version of the World Bank's Financial Structure database originally constructed by Beck *et al.* (2000).

Bank efficiency is estimated as CE_{kt}=exp(uc_i) for cost and as PEF_{kt}=exp(-uc_i) for (alternative) profit efficiency. The value of CE_{kt} ranges from one to infinity, while that of PEF_{kt} ranges from zero to one. In order for the results to be comparable, a cost efficiency index was determined from the expression, $CEF_{kt}=1/CE_{kt}$. This made it possible for efficiency scores to range from zero to one in both cases, with a value closer to one implying higher efficiency.

The pre-merger efficiencies of bidder and target banks reveal that targets are more cost efficient than bidders on average, although the yearly differences in efficiency are not statistically significant.[3] There is a decline in efficiency for several years after 2011 for both the bidders and the targets before it rises again towards the end of the period. For four of the seven years, targets are found to be more cost efficient than bidders, while for three of those years, bidders are more efficient. The average cost efficiency for bidders is at 70.19%, implying that those banks waste 29.81% of their resources to produce the same services offered by the best practice bank, whereas with the average cost efficiency for the targets at 71.39%, the wasted resources amount to 28.61%. While the differences are not statistically significant, they are consistent with those reported by studies that find bidding banks are less cost efficient than targets (Resti, 1998; Huizinga *et al.*, 2001).

The pre-merger profit efficiency scores for the bidders reveal that bidders generate only 55.27% of the profits made by the best practice bank operating under similar conditions, while targets generate only 51.71%. Thus, on average, bidders are more profit efficient than targets but again the differences are not statistically significant. These results reveal support for the view that efficient banks target less efficient ones and are consistent with those reported by other studies (Beitel *et al.*, 2004).

Other pre-merger indicators of efficiency were calculated, including the difference between bidders and targets average efficiencies and those of peers relative to the combined average of the bidders and targets discussed above. These results indicate that, while bidders are less cost efficient and more profit efficient than targets, the peers are generally more efficient than both bidders and targets.

Finally, in an attempt to determine whether efficiency of the combined entity improves after merger, we also calculated post-merger cost and profit efficiencies and compared them with the average pre-merger efficiencies of the combined entities for the first, second and third years after merger. The mean differences indicate that, on average, cost efficiency tended to improve marginally in the post-merger period but profit efficiency did not. However, tests of mean differences revealed insignificant results for both cost and profit efficiency. Overall, the results are not inconsistent with the view that banks engage in takeovers to improve their performance through better management (Nnadi and Tanna, 2014).

3. Impact of Bank Efficiency on Shareholder Value

In the CAR regression results summarized in this section, we consider as the dependent variable the 2-day CARs, the first covering the day before and the day of merger announcement, CAR(-1, 0), and the second covering the day of announcement and the next day, CAR(0, +1), where 0 is the deal announcement date. This follows the approach of Aggarwal *et al.* (2006) and Kohers *et al.* (2000). In practice, given the range of event study results as presented in Table 1, longer CAR window lengths can be entertained as dependent variables in the regressions. Restricting the dependent variable to be 2-days windows, (-1, 0) and (0, +1), allows for a symmetrical structure which serves as a consistency check without biasing the effects with additional noise that might creep in when choosing lengthier CAR windows.

Our focus in this section is on testing the hypotheses H1-H4 using the CAR regression model specified in equation (5). However, given the fact that we investigate the impact of both pre-merger and post-merger efficiency, while distinguishing between cost and profit efficiency, as well as among variants reflecting efficiency differences among bidders, targets and peers, on CARs represented by two different windows, (-1,0) and (0, +1), the empirical analysis would involve conducting numerous regressions reflecting different permutations of CARs with efficiency proxies as explanatory variables in the regressions. It is therefore sensible to focus on providing a selection of results or an overall summary of significant effects rather than present a host of numerical estimates. The discussion below focusses on the results for pre-merger and post-merger efficiency in turn.

3.1 Bidder CARs and Pre-Merger Efficiency

Table 2 presents the estimated coefficients of CAR regressions conducted with various proxies for pre-merger cost and profit efficiencies[4], where the dependent variable is CAR(-1,0).

Table 2. CAR Regressions with dependent variable CAR (-1, 0)

Variable	(1)	(2)	(3)	(4)	(5)	(6)	(7)	(8)	(9)	(10)
R^2	0.433	0.420	0.442	0.429	0.459	0.414	0.471	0.431	0.454	0.430
Adj. R^2	0.109	0.089	0.124	0.103	0.150	0.080	0.169	0.106	0.141	0.104
S.E. of reg.	1.090	1.102	1.081	1.094	1.065	1.108	1.053	1.092	1.070	1.093
F-statistic	1.337	1.268	1.388	1.315	1.487	1.238	1.558	1.325	1.452	1.320
p-value	0.221	0.262	0.193	0.234	0.149	0.283	0.122	0.228	0.163	0.231
Const	-0.466	0.759	1.29	1.199	4.602**	1.1610**	1.382*	1.836	1.497**	1.738*
	-2.373	-0.833	-0.818	-0.755	-1.163	-0.453	-0.762	-1.029	-0.713	-0.928
RSIZE	0.165	0.041	0.173	0.033	0.094	0.071	0.053	0.156	-0.022	0.154
	-0.331	-0.372	-0.415	-0.383	-0.363	-0.357	-0.369	-0.385	-0.333	-0.38
CROSS	-0.65**	-0.634**	-0.53**	-0.64**	-0.49**	-0.53**	-0.392	-0.66**	-0.34	-0.68**
	-0.24	-0.248	-0.235	-0.275	-0.212	-0.219	-0.233	-0.272	-0.288	-0.305
CASH	0.420*	0.411*	0.447**	0.383*	0.361**	0.407**	0.365**	0.420**	0.417**	0.405**
	-0.235	-0.221	-0.188	-0.216	-0.162	-0.185	-0.152	-0.186	-0.17	-0.18
SERIAL	-0.827*	-0.954	-0.864	-0.93	-0.829	-0.874	-0.839	-0.936	-0.84	-0.937
	-0.488	-0.647	-0.675	-0.636	-0.674	-0.689	-0.682	-0.65	-0.693	-0.653
DIVPAY	0.012*	0.012*	0.009*	0.012**	0.008*	0.008	0.007	0.007	0.006	0.008
	-0.006	-0.006	-0.005	-0.006	-0.005	-0.006	-0.005	-0.006	-0.005	-0.005
CONCT	-0.033	-0.817	-0.576	-0.548	-0.847	-0.877	-0.83	-0.721	-1.005	-0.648
	-1.171	-0.766	-0.912	-0.781	-0.962	-1.256	-0.9	-0.749	-0.802	-0.69
BIDCOSEFF	0.019									
	-0.022									
BIDPFTEFF		0.013**								
		-0.004								
BIDTGTCOSEFF			0.022							
			-0.015							
BIDTGTPFTEFF				0.0149*						
				-0.008						
TGTCOSEFF					-0.044**					
					-0.013					
TGTPFTEFF						0.007				

continued on following page

Table 2. Continued

Variable	(1)	(2)	(3)	(4)	(5)	(6)	(7)	(8)	(9)	(10)
						-0.017				
PRTGTCOSEFF							0.048**			
							-0.01			
PRTGTPFTEFF								-0.011		
								-0.011		
PRBDTGTCOSEFF									0.052**	
									-0.02	
PRBDTGTPFTEFF										-0.011
										-0.011

Notes: BIDCOSEFF = pre-merger bidder cost efficiency; BIDPFTEFF = pre-merger bidder profit efficiency; BIDTGTCOSEFF = bidder cost efficiency less target cost efficiency pre-merger; BIDTGT-PFTEFF = bidder profit efficiency less target profit efficiency pre-merger; TGTCOSEFF = pre-merger target cost efficiency; TGTPFTEFF = pre-merger target profit efficiency; PRTGTCOSEFF = peer cost efficiency less target cost efficiency pre-merger; PRTGTPFTEFF = peer profit efficiency less target profit efficiency pre-merger; PRBDTGTCOSEFF = peer cost efficiency less the average of bidder and target cost efficiency pre-merger; PRTGTPFTEFF = peer profit efficiency less the average of bidder and target profit efficiency pre-merger; RSIZE = relative size of target to bidder in total assets; CROSS = 1 when merger is cross-border and 0 when it is domestic; CASH = 1 when deal payment is made in cash and 0 when it is stock or combination of cash and stock; SERIAL = 1 when a bidder has been involved in another acquisition in the past three years and 0 otherwise; DIVPAY = dividend payout ratio calculated as dividend divided by net income; CONCT = concentration calculated as assets of the three largest banks in a market divided by total assets of all banks in that market. The symbols * and ** denote statistical significance at the 10% and 5%, respectively.

The results in columns (1) and (2) reveal that while pre-merger bidder cost efficiency does not have a statistically significant effect on bidder shareholder value, the influence of bidder profit efficiency is positive and statistically significant at the 5% level. Thus, hypothesis H1 is supported for pre-merger profit efficiency, but not for cost efficiency. This result is plausible since, from the efficiency scores discussed in the previous section, bidders are found to be more profit efficient (relative to targets) while the reverse is the case for cost efficiency. Aggarwal *et al.* (2006) also find that bidder profit efficiency is positively associated with CARs, and that the relationship is statistically significant. The results in column (3) and (4) also confirm that, relative to targets (i.e. after netting out target cost or profit efficiency from that of bidder), the effect of bidder cost efficiency is insignificant, while that of profit efficiency is statistically significant (albeit at 10% level). Thus, hypothesis H3 is also supported for bidder profit efficiency (net of target) but not for bidder cost efficiency. In column (5), the results show that target cost efficiency has a negative and statistically significant influence on bidder CAR, but this is not the case for target profit efficiency (column 6) where the effect is insignificant. Thus, hypothesis H2 is supported for cost efficiency but not for profit efficiency. The next four columns (6)-(10) consider the influence of bidder and target efficiencies relative to that of peers, consistent with testing of hypotheses

Table 3. CAR Regressions with dependent variable CAR (0, +1)

Variable	(1)	(2)	(3)	(4)	(5)	(6)	(7)	(8)	(9)	(10)
R^2	0.411	0.499	0.491	0.487	0.504	0.490	0.503	0.493	0.485	0.498
Adj. R^2	0.074	0.213	0.201	0.194	0.220	0.199	0.219	0.204	0.190	0.212
S.E. of reg.	1.696	1.563	1.576	1.582	1.557	1.577	1.558	1.573	1.586	1.565
F-statistic	1.220	1.746	1.690	1.661	1.776	1.684	1.769	1.704	1.647	1.739
p-value	0.295	0.073*	0.085*	0.092*	0.067*	0.087*	0.068*	0.082*	0.096*	0.074*
Const	1.702	-2.191	-0.845	-0.902	2.452	-1.522	-0.775	-0.273	-0.723	-0.287
	-2.465	-1.612	-0.972	-1.074	-2.265	-0.910	-0.936	-1.038	-0.861	-0.928
RSIZE	-0.521	0.162	0.305	0.198	0.249	0.229	0.209	0.322	0.198	0.345
	-0.476	-0.406	-0.508	-0.417	-0.424	-0.357	-0.408	-0.405	-0.361	-0.444
CROSS	0.502	0.749	0.935	0.853	0.974	0.986	1.060	0.796	0.975	0.738
	-0.930	-0.708	-0.655	-0.693	-0.686	-0.700	-0.746	-0.650	-0.797	-0.639
CASH	0.625**	0.879**	0.919**	0.871**	0.839**	0.859**	0.849**	0.898**	0.897**	0.878**
	-0.159	-0.322	-0.388	-0.361	-0.347	-0.376	-0.353	-0.340	-0.365	-0.336
SERIAL	-0.712	-1.012*	-0.801	-0.847	-0.767	-0.853	-0.779	-0.885	-0.789	-0.910
	-0.511	-0.582	-0.483	-0.531	-0.500	-0.510	-0.501	-0.640	-0.489	-0.659
DIVPAY	0.005	0.013	0.008	0.011	0.008	0.006	0.007	0.006	0.007	0.007
	-0.006	-0.011	-0.007	-0.011	-0.006	-0.007	-0.006	-0.006	-0.005	-0.006
CONCT	-0.177	0.178	0.530	0.542	0.285	-0.103	0.319	0.410	0.345	0.507
	-2.092	-1.150	-1.331	-1.249	-1.216	-1.662	-1.209	-1.173	-1.081	-1.206
BIDCOSEFF	-0.021									
	-0.023									
BIDPFTEFF		0.029								
		-0.020								
BIDTGTCOSEFF			0.018							
			-0.029							
BIDTGTPFTEFF				0.011						
				-0.018						
TGTCOSEFF					-0.044					
					-0.035					
TGTPFTEFF						0.022				
						-0.026				
PRTGTCOSEFF							0.042			
							-0.038			
PRTGTPFTEFF								-0.012		
								-0.019		
PRBDTGTCOSEFF									0.015	
									-0.042	
PRBDTGTPFTEFF										-0.016
										-0.022

Note: The variables are as defined in the notes to Table 2. The symbols * and ** denote statistical significance at the 10% and 5%, respectively.

H3 and H4. The results show that the effect of cost efficiency is statistically significant (columns 7 and 9) while that of profit efficiency is not (columns 8 and 10). Thus, hypothesis H3 and H4 are supported when considering the influence of cost efficiency relative to peer or target cost efficiency, or as the difference between peer cost efficiency and the average of bidder plus target cost efficiency, and the consequent effect on bidder CAR is positive and statistically significant. This finding is consistent with the results reported by Kohers *et al.* (2000). The result can be associated with the view that European banks pursue cost-cutting strategies in anticipation of mergers while seeking to enhance their efficiency (Hagendorff and Keasey, 2009).

As for the impact on bidder shareholder value represented by CAR (0,+1), the results presented in Table 3 show that none of the pre-merger efficiency proxies are statistically significant. In this case, there is no support for any of the hypotheses H1-H4, irrespective of whether we consider cost or profit efficiency. What the results suggest, therefore, is the sensitivity of the findings, particularly with regard to the impact of the efficiency proxies, which may differ depending on the length or dates of the window considered for CAR as the dependent variable.

As for the effects of the control variables, the results of Tables 2 and 3 reveal that cash payment deals have a significant influence with a consistently positive effect on bidder returns. The positive effect follows from the signaling effect of cash payment deals, conveying that bidders are confident about the target valuation as targets generally prefer cash payments. The effects of the other control variables are not robustly significant. For example, cross-border deals have a consistently negative and mostly significant impact on bidder returns in Table 2, although its effect is not significant in Table 3. It is plausible that this effect is negative on bidder returns, as cross-border deals carry a higher degree of risk reflecting the challenges of integrating with overseas operations (Tanna and Yousef, 2019). Other control variables which show some degree of statistical significance, though very limited, are dividend payments and serial bidders. The influences of relative size and market concentration on bidder returns are insignificant.

To summarize the overall effects of pre-merger efficiency on bidder shareholder value, it is shown there is some degree of support for hypotheses H1-H4, although this depends on which efficiency proxy and event window is considered in the CAR regressions. In the case of CAR (0, +1) as the dependent variable, the results indicate that bidder profit (but not cost) efficiency influences bidder returns positively. Whereas it is target cost (but not profit) efficiency that impacts on bidder returns negatively. Pre-merger cost efficiency factors are significant on bidder returns when we consider their efficiencies relative to targets or peers. In the case of CAR (0,+1), there is no evidence to suggest that efficiency matters for bidder shareholder value.

3.2 Bidder CARs and Post-Merger Efficiency

To get an overall picture of the impact of post-merger efficiencies on bidder returns, Table 4 summarizes the outcome of CAR regressions accounting for the influences of post-merger efficiency proxies used as explanatory variables in the regressions. The reason we depict the outcome of CAR regressions in this way is because, owing to variations in sample size, some of the coefficient estimates are sensitive both in terms of magnitude and statistical significance as we performed 18 CAR regressions in total. It should be noted that, unlike the case with pre-merger efficiency, the impact of post-merger efficiency is based on estimations of a restricted and varying sample of bank merger deals for which financial data were actually available for both the years prior to merger and up to three years after merger announcement. This possibility excluded any deals that were completed within three years of announcement date (thereby excluding deals beyond 2014) or where post-merger target data did not exist.

The influence of both cost and profit efficiency post-merger is represented for each of the three years after announcement, and for the average of the three years where possible. For each of the three years, the effect of post-merger efficiency is represented relative to pre-merger efficiency, i.e. as the difference between pre-merger and post-merger efficiency of the combined bank (bidder and target). As individual peer and target bank efficiencies are not relevant in this analysis, hypotheses H2 - H4 are not examined in the context of post-merger efficiency.

Table 4. Summary of results for effects of post-merger efficiency on shareholder value

Variables	Frequency of statistically significant results			
	CAR(-1, 0)		CAR(0, +1)	
	5% level	10% level	5% level	10% level
POSTCOS1EFF	0	0	0	0
POSTCOS2EFF	0	0	0	0
POSTCOS3EFF	0	0	0	0
POSTPFT1EFF	0	0	1(+)	0
POSTPFT2EFF	1(+)	0	0	0
POSPFT3EFF	0	0	1(-)	0
POSTCOSAVGEFF	1(-)	0	0	0
POSTPFTAVGEFF	1(+)	0	1(-)	0
SUB-TOTAL	**3**	**0**	**3**	**0**
RSIZE	2(+)	0	0	0
CROSS	1(+)	2(+1, -1)	7(+)	0
CASH	0	0	1(+)	0
SERIAL	7(-)	0	2(-)	0
DIVPAY	0	2(+)	0	0
CONCT	5(-)	1(-)	1(+)	3(+)
SUB-TOTAL	**15**	**5**	**11**	**3**
F-STATISTIC	0	0	0	**1**
TOTAL	**18**	**5**	**14**	**4**

Notes: The table counts the number of estimated coefficients that are statistically significant at the 5% and 10% levels from the estimates of 18 CAR regressions conducted with various proxies of post-merger efficiency on bidder CARs. With the efficiency proxies, which are entered only once in each regression, the frequency is either 1 (statistical significance) or 0 (insignificant). The positive or negative sign in brackets where statistically significant indicates the directional effect of the efficiency proxy on the dependent variable. All explanatory variables are related to post-merger efficiency, measured relative to pre-merger efficiency. No peer or target bank efficiencies are involved in this analysis. The control variables are the same as defined in Table 2-3. POSTCOS1EFF = difference between pre-merger cost efficiency and post-merger cost efficiency for the first year; POSTCOS2EFF = difference between pre-merger cost efficiency and post-merger cost efficiency for the second year; POSTCOS3EFF = difference between pre-merger cost efficiency and post-merger cost efficiency for the third year; POSTPFT1EFF = difference between pre-merger profit efficiency and post-merger profit efficiency for the first year; POSTPFT2EFF = difference between pre-merger profit efficiency and post-merger profit efficiency for the second year; POSTPFT3EFF = difference between pre-merger profit efficiency and post-merger profit efficiency for the third year; POSTCOSAVGEFF = average cost efficiency for the three years after merger; POSTPFTAVGEFF = average profit efficiency for the three years after merger.

The frequencies in Table 4 reveal the number of times the estimates of the relevant explanatory and control variables - among the estimates from 18 CAR regressions performed - showed statistical significance at the 5 or 10 per cent level.[5] In cases where the impact of the explanatory variable is statistically significant, the sign in parentheses indicates whether it has a positive (+) or negative (-) effect on bidder returns, represented by the dependent variables CAR (-1, 0) and CAR (0, +1).

The results indicate that the market's perception of future profit efficiency influences bidder returns, in both sets of CAR regressions, although its impact is mixed, being positive in some cases and negative in other cases. In particular, depending on the window that captures bidder returns, the impact of profit efficiency is statistically significant at the 5% level in each of the three post-merger years, with the effect being positive in the first two years but negative in the third year. The impact of average profit efficiency over the three years post-merger is also statistically significant, but is negative in the CAR (0, +1) regression whereas positive in the CAR (0, +1) regression. In contrast, the influence of cost efficiency is not significant, except in the case of the average post-merger efficiency in CAR (-1, 0) regression, where its effect on bidder returns is negative.

As for the control variables, the results are inconsistent with those of pre-merger efficiencies, at least in the impact of cash payment deals, which is not robustly significant. By and large, the results of both sets of CAR regressions suggest that cross-border mergers and serial bidders have a statistically significant impact on bidder returns, with the effect of former being positive while that of the latter negative. The other control variables with statistically significant impact are market concentration, dividend payouts and relative size, albeit with mixed effects on bidder returns. One could say that there are marked differences in the effects of the control variables compared to the results in Tables 2 and 3, and we attribute these anomalous findings to differences in sample size.

Overall, the summary of results presented in Table 4 suggest that the influence of post-merger profit efficiency is more significant on bidder returns than that of post-merger cost efficiency. These results therefore indicate support for hypotheses H1, but more in the case of profit efficiency.

CONCLUSION

This study has investigated stock market reaction to bank M&As with a focus on evaluating the significance of cost and profit efficiencies of merging banks in predicting shareholder value gains from merger announcement. We incorporate a unique blend of estimation techniques, combining event study to derive announcement period abnormal returns, stochastic frontier analysis to derive cost and profit efficiencies of bidders, targets and peers, and CAR regressions to assess the impact of these efficiency measures on bidder shareholder value. The underlying basis for our investigation is grounded in the semi-strong form of the EMH, which posits that information not publicly available is perceived by the market and culminates in the markets being able to predict a firm's future performance, as reflected in its efficiency indicators. Building upon a limited number of previous studies for European and US bank mergers, we contribute to the literature by testing several distinct hypotheses and providing new evidence for European bank mergers.

Using accounting and financial data for a sample of 56 large commercial bank mergers that took place in 22 European countries between 2010 and 2017, we find that bidders achieve short-term value creation from merger announcements and our analysis suggest that this could potentially be associated with market's perception of the efficiency of the bidders and targets. In particular, pre- and post-merger profit efficiency of bidders and pre-merger cost efficiency of targets could have an important influence on bidder returns upon merger announcements, whereas bidder cost efficiency relative to targets or peer banks may also be an important consideration.

The main policy implication that flows from our analysis is that, if market reaction to merger announcements reflects such efficiency gains, then investors and regulators should account for the perceived efficiency-induced gains on bidder shareholder value from banking sector consolidations. Evidence that pre-merger and post-merger bank efficiency has an influence on bidder returns, and that the market takes into account such efficiency factors, underscores the importance of perceived efficiency as a predictive indicator and suggests that stock markets price the relative efficiency of banks in pricing market value gains from European Bank M&As. Further research could account for different event study windows to represent bidder returns, incorporate a longer time dimension to facilitate using a larger sample and panel data for CAR regressions, and control for country level differences in the regulatbexkory and market-related factors.

REFERENCES

Aggarwal, R., Akhigbe, A., & McNulty, J. E. (2006). Are differences between acquiring bank profit efficiency priced in financial markets? *Journal of Financial Services Research*, *30*(3), 265–286. doi:10.100710693-006-0419-4

Amel, D., Barnes, C., Panetta, F., & Salleo, C. (2004). Consolidation and efficiency in the financial sector: A review of the international evidence. *Journal of Banking & Finance*, *28*(10), 2493–2519. doi:10.1016/j.jbankfin.2003.10.013

Battese, G. E., & Coelli, T. J. (1995). A Model for technical inefficiency effects in a stochastic frontier production function for panel data. *Empirical Economics*, *20*(2), 325–332. doi:10.1007/BF01205442

Beccalli, E., & Frantz, P. (2009). M&A Operations and performance in banking. *Journal of Financial Services Research*, *36*(2-3), 203–226. doi:10.100710693-008-0051-6

Beck, T., Demirgüç-Kunt, A., & Levine, R. (2000). A New Database on Financial Development and Structure. *The World Bank Economic Review*, *14*(3), 597–605. doi:10.1093/wber/14.3.597

Beitel, P., Schiereck, D., & Wahrenburg, M. (2004). Explaining M&As Success in European Banks. *European Financial Management*, *10*(1), 109–139. doi:10.1111/j.1468-036X.2004.00242.x

Berger, A. N., Demsetz, R. S., & Strahan, P. E. (1999). The consolidation of the financial services industry: Causes, consequences, and implications for the future. *Journal of Banking & Finance*, *23*(2–4), 135–194. doi:10.1016/S0378-4266(98)00125-3

Berger, A. N., & Mester, L. J. (1997). Inside the Black Box: What explains the differences in the efficiencies of financial institutions? *Journal of Banking & Finance*, *21*(7), 895–947. doi:10.1016/S0378-4266(97)00010-1

Brown, S. J., & Warner, J. B. (1980). Measuring security price performance. *Journal of Financial Economics*, *8*(3), 205–258. doi:10.1016/0304-405X(80)90002-1

Campa, J. M., & Hernando, I. (2004). Shareholder value creation in European M&As. *European Financial Management*, *10*(1), 47–81. doi:10.1111/j.1468-036X.2004.00240.x

Campa, J. M., & Hernando, I. (2006). M&A performance in the European financial industry. *Journal of Banking & Finance*, *30*(12), 3367–3392. doi:10.1016/j.jbankfin.2006.06.006

Chronopoulos, D. K., Girardone, C., & Nankervis, J. C. (2010). Post-merger bank efficiency and stock market reaction: the case of the US versus Europe. In F. Fiordelisi, P. Molyneux, & D. Previati (Eds.), *New Issues in Financial Institutions Management* (pp. 122–138). Palgrave Macmillan. doi:10.1057/9780230299153_8

Chronopoulos, D. K., Girardone, C., & Nankervis, J. C. (2013). How do stock markets in the US and Europe price efficiency gains from bank M&As? *Journal of Financial Services Research*, *43*(3), 243–263. doi:10.100710693-012-0132-4

Cybo-Ottone, A., & Murgia, M. (2000). Mergers and shareholder wealth in European banking. *Journal of Banking & Finance*, *24*(6), 831–859. doi:10.1016/S0378-4266(99)00109-0

DeLong, G. L., & DeYoung, R. (2007). Learning by observing: Information spillovers in the execution and valuation of commercial bank M&As. *The Journal of Finance*, *62*(1), 181–216. doi:10.1111/j.1540-6261.2007.01205.x

DeYoung, R., Evanoff, D. D., & Molyneux, P. (2009). Mergers and Acquisitions of Financial Institutions: A Review of the Post-2000 Literature. *Journal of Financial Services Research*, *36*(2-3), 87–110. doi:10.100710693-009-0066-7

Hagendorff, J., & Keasey, K. (2009). Post-merger strategy and performance: Evidence from the US and European banking industries. *Accounting and Finance*, *49*(4), 725–751. doi:10.1111/j.1467-629X.2009.00306.x

Huizinga, H. P., Nelissen, J. H. M., & Vander Vennet, R. (2001). *Efficiency effects of bank mergers and acquisitions in Europe*. Working Paper No. 106, Ghent University, Belgium.

Kohers, T., Huang, M., & Kohers, N. (2000). Market perceptions of efficiency in bank holding company mergers: The roles of the DEA and SFA models in capturing merger potential. *Review of Financial Economics*, *9*(2), 101–120. doi:10.1016/S1058-3300(00)00019-7

Nnadi, M. A., & Tanna, S. (2013). Analysis of Cross-border and Domestic Mega-M&As of European Commercial Banks. *Managerial Finance*, *39*(9), 848–862. doi:10.1108/MF-01-2010-0006

Nnadi, M. A., & Tanna, S. (2014). Post Acquisitions Profitability of Banks: A Comparison of Domestic and Cross Border Acquisitions in the European Union, *Global. Business and Economic Review*, *16*(3), 310–331.

Pasiouras, F., Tanna, S., & Zopounidis, C. (2009). The impact of regulations on banks' cost and profit efficiency: Cross-country evidence. *International Review of Financial Analysis*, *18*(5), 294–302. doi:10.1016/j.irfa.2009.07.003

Resti, A. (1998). Can Mergers Foster Efficiency? The Italian Case. *Journal of Economics and Business*, *50*(2), 157–169. doi:10.1016/S0148-6195(97)00075-1

Sealey, C. Jr, & Lindley, J. T. (1977). Inputs, outputs and a theory of production and cost at depository financial institutions. *The Journal of Finance*, *32*(4), 1251–1266. doi:10.1111/j.1540-6261.1977.tb03324.x

Tanna, S., & Yousef, I. (2019). Mergers and acquisitions: Implications for Acquirers market risk. *Managerial Finance*, *45*(4), 545–562. doi:10.1108/MF-09-2018-0446

Urio, H., & Tanna, S. (2012). Consolidation and Performance in the EU Banking Industry: A Survey. In M. Fethi, C. Gaganis, F. Pasiouras, & C. Zopounidis (Eds.), *Financial Services: Efficiency and Risk Management* (pp. 1–40). Nova Science Publishers.

Vander Vennet, R. (1996). The effect of mergers and acquisition on the efficiency and profitability of EC credit institutions. *Journal of Banking & Finance*, *20*(9), 1531–1558. doi:10.1016/S0378-4266(96)00014-3

Vander Vennet, R. (2002). Cost and profit efficiency of financial conglomerates and universal banks in Europe. *Journal of Money, Credit and Banking*, *34*(1), 254–282. doi:10.1353/mcb.2002.0036

KEY TERMS AND DEFINITIONS

Abnormal Returns: Returns in excess of those predicted by the market.
Bidder: A company (bank) that intends to acquire, or merge with, another company.
CAR Regressions: Regressions with cumulative abnormal returns as dependent variable.
Event Study: A methodology for computing abnormal returns of a stock.
Peer: A company (bank) not involved in a merger or acquisition transaction.
Post-Merger Efficiency: Efficiency of bidder or target after merger.
Pre-Merger Efficiency: Efficiency of bidder or target before merger.
Stochastic Frontier Analysis: A parametric method of estimating a frontier.
Target: A company (bank) that intends to merge with, or be acquired, by another company.

ENDNOTES

1 See, e.g., Tanna and Yousef (2019), and references therein, for further details.

2 In this sense, we estimate the alternative profit efficiency, due to its advantages over the standard profit efficiency approach. For banks in the sample that reported losses (negative profits), PBT, the dependent variable, was transformed to be just positive using an adjustment factor, as suggested by Pasiouras *et al.* (2009) among others.

3 For space reasons, we do not report the frontier efficiency results.

4 The notes underneath Table 2 define all the explanatory variables including the different measures of efficiency used.

5 For the efficiency proxies, which are entered only once in each regression, the frequency is either 1 (statistical significance), or 0 (effect is insignificant). Furthermore, as the efficiency estimates that are statistically significant are either at the 5% or 10% level, the frequency of 1 applies to one the columns, 5% or 10%, not both.

Chapter 6
Public Debt, Cloud Computing Technology, and Leadership Crisis in the 21st Century:
The Role of ICT in Nigeria's Finance Sector

Christian Ugwueze Amu
https://orcid.org/0000-0003-2350-7093
Federal University of Technology, Owerri, Nigeria

Nathaniel Chinedum Nwezeaku
Federal University of Technology, Owerri, Nigeria

Linus Eze Akujuobi
https://orcid.org/0000-0002-7162-1299
Federal University of Technology, Owerri, Nigeria

Benedict Anayochukwu Ozurunba
https://orcid.org/0000-0002-3521-088X
Federal University of Technology, Owerri, Nigeria

Sharon Nanyongo Njie
https://orcid.org/0000-0001-9222-6231
Southern University and A&M College, USA

Ikedinachi Ayodele Power Wogu
https://orcid.org/0000-0001-9050-8817
Rhema University Nigeria, Aba, Nigeria

Sanjay Misra
https://orcid.org/0000-0002-3556-9331
Covenant University, Ota, Nigeria

ABSTRACT

Recent literature on the economies of developed and developing nations identify a rise in the records of public debts which most industrialized nations continue to acquire for the purpose of sustaining their economies. Consequently, Nigeria, in 2017, recorded alarming public debts of N19.16trn, representing 10.37% ratio of debt-to-GDP. These figures, scholars infer, explain the disturbing degree of decay inherent in major government infrastructures. Adopting the 'debt overhanging theory', Marilyn's ex-post facto research design, and Creswell's mix-method research approaches, the authors interrogate arguments

DOI: 10.4018/978-1-7998-5083-0.ch006

posited for or against public debt management with a view to proffering ICT and cloud technology as panacea for curbing the alarming rise in the cases of public debt crisis and the leadership crisis raging in the countries under review. A high degree of political rascality among the ruling elite and the lacking of viable ICT-oriented public debt management tools among African polities were observed. A re-orientation of the ruling class with ICT techniques was recommended.

INTRODUCTION

Background of the Study

Contemporary literature on the public debt of nations (Mba, Yuni, and Oburota, 2013; Streeck, 2013; Holtfrerich, Feld, Heun, Illing, Kirchgässner, Kocka, Schularick, Streeck, Wagschal, Walter, and Von Weizsäcker, 2016; Yared. 2019 & Bin, 2020) now abounds which indicates how adversely the phenomenon of public debt has affect established democratic capitalist economies since the beginning of the 1970s. Consequently, most scholars wondered why prosperous and developed nations of the world continued to amass so many public debts to themselves, especially between (1970–2000) (Cecchetti, Mohanty, & Zampolli, 2010 and Sineviciene, & Vasiliauskaite, 2012). The scenarios and consequences arising from haven amassed so many public debts had led to instances where the nations affected become vulnerable to most of the sudden changes taking place in world financial institutions. Changes that put these nations at great risks in areas like the general decline in political participation, growing tax resistance, rising inequality, week economic growth, and rising unemployment. The initial period of fiscal consolidation in the 1990s did not help matters as the records of public debt in the affected nations rose to 'dangerous', unimaginable, and unprecedented heights. The problem is that it has been yet forecasted to continue

Figure 1. Projection of government debt-to-GDP ratio until 2060

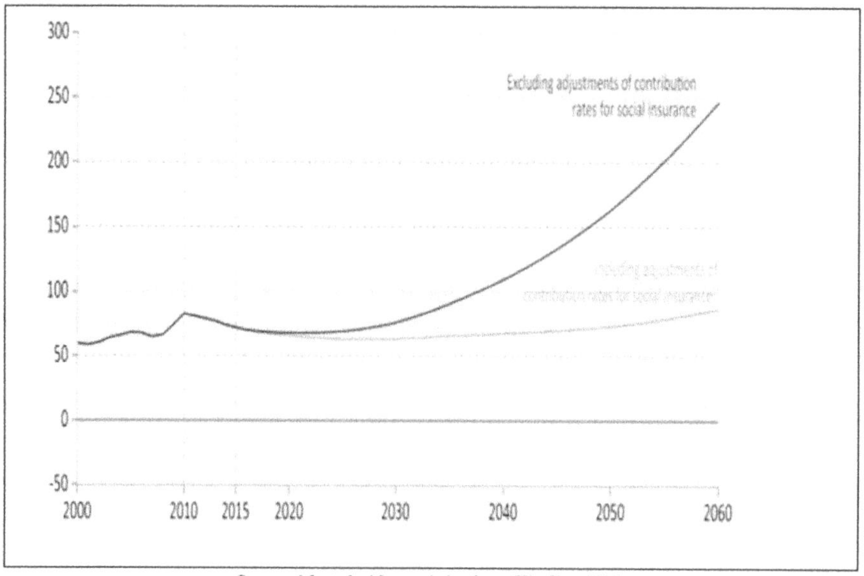

Source: Adopted with permission from (Werding, 2014)

rising for the next four decades (Streeck, 2013 and Yared, 2019), as a result of the great recession that has been forecasted to followed that period.

Efforts made by the affected countries to consolidate and salvage their economies seem only to lead to a further decline in the degree of expenditures that states had initially budgeted to make. Ultimately, these scenarios lead to a depletion in the number of state-owned businesses. There is also the problem of the extensive retrenchment of workers. In the light of the foregoing issues, the urgent need to critically interrogate and to seek out ways of addressing the lackadaisical and reckless attitudes which political office holders manifest without much reservations, which itself, plunge their nations into an economic and political leadership crisis, necessitates the timely conduct and writing of this article.

Statement of the Problem

Contemporary literature on rising public debts alludes to the fact that there is an upward trajectory on the amount of public debt crisis that great hegemonies like the United States of America, Great Britain, and Germany continue to experience since the middle of the 1970s. It has thus been argued that this current trend would continue to increase significantly over the next coming decades (Yared, 2019 & Werding, 2014). Other scholars infer that this current trend of rising public debt is a function of a secular expansion of government spending on specific projects and programs in essential areas like Medicaid, Medicare, Social Security, and the likes, without a proportional increase in income tax revenue of the said countries (Blahous, 2013). The truth, however, is that where there is no one to hold leaders accountable for the choices they make regarding the money they spend, how they spend it, or on what they spend it on, there would always be the tendency to overspend and continue to spend for the fun of it or the good feeling associated with spending. While these trends have been observed to become a global trend, the under listed specific issues prompted the writing this paper:

i. Various political dispensations and governments' in Nigeria have in the past decades, displayed an attitude portrayed as reckless and selfish with regards to the external borrowing of funds, in the guise of providing optimal service to their electorates. This mindless borrowing and spending spree has impoverished and indebted their economy and its citizens.
ii. The lack of requisite ICT techniques and tools for financial management has made it impossible for policymakers to provide appropriate guides and policy direction for government.
iii. There is an adverse socioeconomic and political development implication on the part of citizens who are forced to grapple with high degrees of tax cuts proposed as measures to aid in stabilizing the battered economy. Hence the rising cases of leadership crisis experienced amongst developed and developing economies.

Research Questions

The nature of the problems identified above led to the main research question which simply enquires: What are the nexus between public debt, ICT techniques, and leadership crisis in 21st-century polities? This notwithstanding, the following specific research questions will suffice:

i. Why have different political dispensations/governments in the world, in Africa and in Nigeria in particular - within the last 5 decades - continued with the reckless behavior of borrowing from funding agencies which have further plunged them into untold socioeconomic and leadership crisis?
ii. What roles could the use of ICT tools and techniques play in aiding the formulations and implementation of viable and effective policies which would serve as necessary guides and checks against the reckless behavior of government' personnel who continues in mindless borrowing?
iii. What degrees of socioeconomic and political development implications could the reckless attitude of increased borrowing have on the affected countries under review?

Research Objectives

In the light of the foregoing research questions, this study is largely poised to identify the nexus that exists between public debts, ICT tools/techniques, and leadership crisis in polities and in Nigeria particularly. However, the following specific research objectives direct the conduct of the research:

i. To identify those factors that continue to influence the reckless attitude among political leaders in government to resort to amassing more foreign debts as the only viable way for salvaging their country's economy.
ii. The study would via ICT tools/techniques and platforms, provide viable directions and guidelines for formulating practical policies that should guide political leaders on matters concerning effective public debt management, which invariably would lead to economic recovery and thus, curb leadership crisis.
iii. The authors of this article would strive to identify the current degree of impact which rising public debt continues to exert on the socioeconomic and political development strides of developing and developed polities.

The Methodology of the Research

While drawing insights from (Reinhart, Reinhart, and Rogoff, 2012) 'Debt Overhang Theory', the research questions and objectives raised for the study, necessitates that the authors adopt (Marilyn, 2013 and Wogu, Elegbeleye, Uwaoma, Chukwuedo, Edogiawere, Aguziendu, & Misra, 2020) *Ex-post facto research,* design method. This method is favored because it facilitates and justifies the use of previously analyzed data, surveys reports, experimental and analytic studies that may have been previously undertaken on the subject matter of this research (Public Debt). The authors also adopt Creswell's mix-method approach (Creswell, 2003) which often allows for the combined or separate use of either qualitative or quantitative research designs for gathering qualitative data, the kind often gathered from either Focused Group Discussions (FGD) or structured interview sessions. The methods proposed for adoption here are believed would increase the chances of attaining the objectives highlighted above.

Justifications / Relevance of the Research

Accepted that literature abounds on the subject of public debt management, it is clear that most of all the ideas provided towards addressing the problem of public debt management have not made any headway since even rising hegemonies continue to record rising public debt-to-GDP ratios which invariably continues to plunge them into more and more public debts which invariably leads to the rapid loss of jobs and a harsh toll on the socioeconomic status of citizens in the polity. The need, therefore, arise to urgently identify ways in which the adoption of ICT tools, techniques and applications would aid finding lasting solutions that should help in addressing the attitude and inclination to continue borrowing recklessly from international granting/lending institutions, especially when such actions only lead to further indebtedness.

LITERATURE REVIEW AND THEORETICAL FRAMEWORK

Main Causes of Public Debt

Governments' debt is that accumulated financial obligation which is owed to major financial institutions through the issuance of treasury bonds, treasury bills, borrowings, and such other similar instruments (Amadeo, 2019). In a nutshell, the term public or government debt is often used to refer to the total sum of accrued borrowings that governments' used to finance past deficits (Suman, 2018). Other studies (Holtfrerich, *et al*, 2016; Amadeo, 2019 & Amadeo, 2019) revealed that states often borrow when they are faced with certain specific scenarios: (1) when they desire to meet budget deficits, (2) when the need arises to meet special expenses arising from extraordinary situations like wars and natural disasters, (3) when there is need to urgently finance huge development projects.

Six Major Forms of Public Debt

While various forms of public deb exist, this research reviewed 6 of the most prominent forms of public debt. They include: (1) Funded or Unfunded Debts, (2) Short-term, Mid-term and Long-term Debts, (Amadeo, 2019 and Umana, 2018). (3) Redeemable and Irredeemable Debt, (4) Compulsory and Voluntary Debt, (5) Productive and Unproductive Debt (Amadeo, 2019). (6) Internal and External Debts (Umana, 2018). For want of space, only three forms of public debt are discussed here.

Public Debt Among Rising Hegemonies

When large sums of money are borrowed from a country that is external to her (A foreign country) it is assumed that external debt has been created. A country that largely depends on borrowed funds from other nations to run her economy owes her all to the foreign country that lends. Where the debtor nations are discovered not to have enough reserves of foreign exchange from previous trade or business, they will have no other choice but to export their goods to the creditor nation. They do this by first generating sufficient exportable surplus, which itself is a function of curtailing their domestic consumption (Amadeo, 2019 and Economic Discussion, 2016).

Countries, where these external debts, exist tend to drastically reduce the level of consumption of its citizens since the scenario calls for a net reduction of the resources available in the nations of those owing. This is because it is perceived as the only way to meet the demands of their consumption. This scenario was the case in the 1990s for countries like Mexico, Brazil, and Poland (Please see (UNITFFD 2019:119) for details of diagrams and charts) who faced severe economic hardship as a result of the large amounts of public debts they had encored over a period of time (Amadeo, 2019).

In all, the level of debt encored by these countries continued to hit new heights globally. Studies and records arising from The Institute of International Finance (IIF) reveal that by the end of March 2018, global debt stocks had reached $247.2 trillion, having risen by nearly $25 trillion from a year earlier, and up from $168 trillion at the onset of the financial crisis (IIF, 2018 and UNITFFD, 2019). The data in (https://developmentfinance.un.org/print/maintaining-debt-sustainability-and-improving-debt-sustainability-assessments [page 2]) reveals that public and private debt records have risen astronomically to historical heights for most developing and developed nations and economies of the world. Studies by (IIF, 2018 and UNITFFD, 2019) revealed that public debt records of developing countries have risen by as much as 15%. The study by (UNITFFD, 2019), as exemplified in the data contained in (https://developmentfinance.un.org/print/maintaining-debt-sustainability-and-improving-debt-sustainability-assessments [page 2) further elucidates this fact.

Contemporary literature on the public debt of nations (Amadeo, 2019; IIF, 2018 and IMF, 2001) revealed that the inability for government to formulate and sustain viable financial and fiscal policies is largely at the root of these new debt surprises that have continued to spring up since the past five years. There is, however, fresh research in cloud technology which it believed might just be that technical tool that could address the public debt management crisis problem amongst states.

Functions of Government Debt

Generally, government debts are known to perform three main functions: (1), they perform stabilizing functions (2) they perform bridging functions and (3) they perform the function of sharing the burden of the economy (Gandenberger, 1980).

Stabilizing function: Government in this regard, assume the responsibility of taking actions that would stabilize the economy, especially in times of crisis. In such situations, governments' must seek not to balance their budgets but to find ways of making fiscal policies to contribute to balancing the economic growth. They do so by actually take in more debts to prevent the economy from going under (Gandenberger, 1980 and Lindholm, 1950).

Bridging Function: This function of government focuses largely on the need to smooth the tax policies which governments resort to during the times of necessary adjustments made to cushion the effects of the debts borrowed. Only at such times could the atmosphere of trust be established amongst entrepreneurs who must plan and calculate in advance the most viable investments to embark on (Walter, and Von Weizsäcker, 2016).

Burden sharing functions: In this kind of debt, the government is expected to share or distribute the debt in certain proportions amongst taxpayers of different dispensations, irrespective of the fiscal year. In a nutshell, this function, in the opinion of Lorenz Von Stein: 'it's all about identifying equitable sharing formulas for distributing the burden between taxpayers of different generations'. He further observed that 'a government without government debt is either doing too little for its future or is either asking too much from its present' (Stein, 1871).

The Origin of Nigeria's External Debt

The history of Nigeria's foreign debts can be traced back to 1958 when Nigeria took a loan of $28 million from the World Bank to embark on railroad construction and other development projects. Records (Umana, 2018) also revealed that successive governments in Nigeria embarked on the borrowing of other huge loans with which to finance more development and reconstruction projects necessitated by the just concluded civil war which drastically affected the lives and the economy of its citizens. The study by Kubiat Umana puts it thus:

...in 1964, Nigeria took a loan of US$13.1 million from the Paris Club of Creditor Nations for the building of the Niger Dam. Nigeria went to the International Capital Market (ICM) in 1978 for the much talked "jumbo loan" of $1 billion, and this changed the structure of Nigeria's debt from mainly concessional loans to loans with harsher repayments terms (Umana, 2018).

Consequent to the new trend of borrowing by successive administrations, by 2002, the total debt stock of Nigeria had risen to a whopping $39.9 billion due largely to the crash in the oil prices, penalties paid on rising interests' deficits. As a result of this huge debt situation, Nigeria was forced to experience a decay in infrastructure mostly in the education, health, and socioeconomic sector (Umana, 2018; Okoye, 2000 & FSDH, 2017). By March 2017, data gathered from the Debt Management Office (DMO) revealed that Nigeria's total debt stock had risen to an alarming N19.16trn, which represents an increase of 10.37% from the records of debts recorded in December of 2016, the figures then stood at N17.36trn (FSDH, 2017). A breakdown of the debt stock revealed that "external debts accounted for 22.08% (N4.23trn), while domestic debt stock accounted for 77.92% (N14.93trn)". These studies (Umana, 2018; Okoye, 2000 and FSDH, 2017) generally indicated that the rise in the total debts recorded in the past five years as a function of the need to supplement governments declining revenue and the urgent need for funding decaying infrastructures of the major sectors of the economy. Just recently, the Burahi led government of the APC government through the senate of the Federal Republic of Nigeria, on the 26th day of March 2020, approved yet another whooping borrowing of $22.7billion, supposed to be for capital projects necessitated by the COVID-19 outbreak in Nigeria (The Guardian, 26th March, 2020).

The Political Economy of Public Debt

The rising trend of borrowing among developing economies of OECD countries, have since increased the number of economic actors, government officials, international donor institutions & agencies and a majority of the citizenry in different polities, who have placed a demand on their countries, with a view to understanding their spending patterns and processes, and more importantly, with a view to instituting more transparent policies in government for the purpose of easily identifying 'who gets what, when they get it and how they hope to get it" (Alesina & Perotti,1995; Khagram, Fung, & De Renzio, 2013; Battaglini, Salvatore, & Thomas 2018). These actions, most scholars now believe, are some of the most important actions governments' must now take if they desire to avert the looming danger of public debt crisis which has been predicted to hit both OECD and Non-OECD countries in no distant future.

Where 21st-century polities are able to willingly adopt the open budget policy method, it is believed that they would become more disposed to providing answers to vivid questions such as the once highlighted by (Khagram, Fung, & De Renzio, 2013) in their research: "How and why do improvements in fiscal transparency and participation come about? How are they sustained over time? When and how do increased fiscal transparency and participation lead to improved government responsiveness and accountability"? A general survey of countries where a rigors analysis and efforts have been made towards identifying the causes and consequences of implementing fiscal transparency in governments' monetary issues is currently very slim and not too impressive.

CURRENT TRENDS IN AI AND CLOUD COMPUTING RESEARCH

Studies (Bryant, 2014 and Hawking, Tegmark, Russell & Wilczek, 2014) reveal that today's computers have gone beyond possessing intelligence for ordinary computing as seen in calculators, etc, to machines that now possess the capability for becoming conscious (intentionality) (Wogu, Katende, Elegbeleye, Roland-Otaru, Apeh, Ifeanyi-Reuben, & Misra, 2020). They have today become super-intelligent machines with the capacity to cultivate and maintain a mind of their own (Wogu, Katende, Elegbeleye, Roland-Otaru, Apeh, Ifeanyi-Reuben, & Misra, 2020). Consequent on these new trends of innovations and development in AI technology, there is now a predominance of automated systems that can successfully drive cares, recognize individual faces, play and defeat world-class chess players and even successfully trade on the stock markets (Wogu, Misra, Assibong, Ogiri, Maskeliunas, and Damasevicius, 2018). There is no gainsaying the fact that the advent of AI technology has simplified the work of man to a large extent, especially in whatever field where AI is adopted and implemented.

Recent advancements in the information and communications technology have proven that ICT and advances in AI research and technology have gone beyond having a profound impact on the lives of man, indeed, it has revolutionized the way business and governments' operate (Wogu, Misra, Assibong, Ogiri, Maskeliunas, and Damasevicius, 2018; Wogu, Sanjay Assibong, Adewumi Maskeliunas, & Damasevicius, 2018; Assibong, Wogu, Sholarin, Misra Damasevičius and Sharma, 2020; Wogu, Misra, Assibong, Olu-Owolabi, Maskeliunas, R. and Damasevicius, 2019). Of the most outstanding developments which have taken place in the 21st century, Cloud computing and technology holds one of the biggest promise (PDM Practice, 2019).

ICT for Public Debt Management: A Historical Overview

The attempt to apply ICT to Public Debt Management (PDM) started in the 1980s in the after mart of the Mexican debt crisis. It had been realized that the appropriate analysis of the debt situation was seriously being hampered by a lack of an accurate and timely analysis of the debt situation that hovered around affected countries. Such an analysis would have been utilized by the Paris Club Institution for facilitating the business of borrowing and debt accuracy analysis. The lacking of such platforms motivated countries to begin to look for ways to develop what was then referred to as Computer Based Debt Management Systems (CBDMS). This initial move was enhanced by the contribution of multilateral donors and the contributions of local but specialized IT, staff. This corroborative effort led to the first produced IT application for public debt management (PDM). These first systems were designed to run on the mainframe and small computer of that time (PDM Practice, 2019). With the lunch of the IBM computer by the middle of 1981, many of these systems were running on microcomputers. It was during this period that the commonwealth secretariat and UNCTAD made moves to design their own debt recording and management systems in 1983 and in 1985. Several private companies and banks also embarked on this project. It is, however, important to note that the systems designed during these periods had very limited successes.

With the emergence of Pocket Computers (PCs) came some advantages and disadvantages. While PC's were discovered to be platforms that could run almost on anything, it proved a platform that could not be used for what was then referred to as a mission-critical application. Debt management systems as it were, require a more rigorous computing structure that the PC could not provide. There was need therefore to design better platforms that would ensure that regular backups were made and that IT staff were readily available to provide needed support, unlike the PC hard drives that ended up in the debt manager's desk, making it only possible to take backups occasionally.

Thirty years down the line, the IT needs for debt management had grown enormously. Developing countries had made the business of debt management one of their main say. Some of the software applications that emerged during this era of debt management include:

i. Links to Integrated Financial Management Systems (IFMIS);
ii. Electronic platforms for the trading of government securities;
iii. Central Depository Systems (CDS);

While many of the systems, like the once listed above are privately owned, there were concerns amongst coordinating institutions about the issue of subjectivity and the quality of data, operations, and service provided at each point in time.

The Emergence of Cloud Computing

Of all the technology used in the 21st century, cloud computing has been identified as one of the technology with the potential to revolutionize the world. It is the result of a convergence between Information Technology (IT) and Communications Technology (CT). It is a system that allows for the storage of data and the retrieval of the same via central servers on the internet (PDM Practice, 2019). It could be public or private.

Advantages of Cloud Technology

Where cloud computing is fully deployed by Debt Management Offices, such office would no longer have to worry about applying the latest software to their applications as this is undertaken by the developers themselves. The analysis of data and the various applications would become possible to access from any part of the world. Other specific advantages of cloud technology include:

i. It provides standardization in terms of software applications and databases
ii. It aids the production and integration of aggregate data by individual states
iii. It makes for a real-time and appropriate recording of debt data possible for analysis anytime anywhere (PDM Practice, 2019).

While this system is very efficient, it, however, comes with its own security issues such as loss of data and unauthorized access. There are, however, certain ways of addressing these risks.

Matters Arising from the Implementation of Could Computing in Public Sector Finance

Several works and articles on the implementation of cloud computing in the public sector attest to the fact that, while the technology behind cloud computing is largely and technically easy to manipulate and implement, the part that seems to create any kind of difficulty or that makes the manipulation and full implementation of cloud computing look very hard and difficult to manipulate, is the human factor.

This is largely manifested in the various politics and policy platforms that affected nations are forced to grapple with.

For instance, a study conducted by (Williams, 2012 and Sallehudin, Razak, Ismail, Md-Fadzil, & Baker, 2018) indicates that man by nature is often preoccupied with the politics of migrating from the old and analog ways of doing things to the new and computerized ways of processing information and data. Thus, the government and men of this age tend to present a rather complicated and complex scenario about the processes involved and necessary for migrating to the full use of cloud computing platforms and systems for virtually every other human endeavor in the public sector. Indeed, it is feared that cloud computing amongst other things, will drastically affect the ways people work and do things. More importantly, it is believed that the full implementation of could computing systems in the public sector will eliminate most computer-based jobs as it were, since the services of IA systems and machines would now be required to offer more efficient and reliable services. No doubt, the implementation, and institution of such structures will drastically reduce the high degree of corruption and misappropriation of funds that has been a major factor influencing the rise in public debt (Sallehudin, Nurhizam, Abu-Bakar, Baker, Yahya, Md-Fadzil, 2019). It is for this reason that the authors of this paper opine that the human economic implications of fully migrating and implementing to the use of cloud computing platforms for the public sector, should be given very serious considerations and not be taken lightly (Werding, 2014).

MEASURES OF TACKLING THE 21ST CENTURY PUBLIC DEBT CRISIS ISSUES

Amides wide publicity of global debt levels, government debts continue to hit disturbing records and has been projected to continue in the next few decades (Werding, 2014). Reports from the Institute of International Finance (IIF) revealed that global debt stock, by March 2018 had reached an alarming height of 274.2 trillion. The same records indicated that it had risen by 25 trillion in the previous year (UNITFFD, 2018). Developing countries have since 2010, also recorded a growing level of public debts which had gone beyond the total value of their obligations and had now relatively affected the gross domestic product (GDP) of these countries. These same records indicate that over the past five years, the public debt of developing countries had risen by 15% GDP, thus growing from 36% in 2013 to 51% in 2018. In all, Public debt had averagely risen to 46% of GDP in 2018 and is feared would continue to rise (Blahous, 2013).

Tackling Public Debt Crisis Management via ICT

With a view to finding measures for tackling public debts, individuals are beginning to resort to the use of information technology to help in monitoring their spending and financial future. This is because such AI-powered digital tools have been identified to have the capacity to provide clearer views of every aspect of an individual nation's financial situation. These platforms can thus help states take back full control of their spending habits. These platforms are made possible by Artificial Intelligence systems which technologies today utilized in financial institutions like banks and insurance companies where your credit card and debit card details are always made available at the disposal of the individual managing the said account. These platforms thus making it possible for individuals to view at a glance and on one platform, all the valuable information about their financial transactions in real-time. There are such other systems that track your spending while keeping a lid on the credit scores, thus notifying you of possible negative consequences of a transaction on your account. These systems also come with security features that calls your attention to suspicious activities on your account or where any process or data is bridged by other unauthorized persons who may interfere with the account (Information Age, 2018).

Advanced System for Effectively Managing Public Debts

Today, digital tools abound in virtually every financial sector, have been recognized by finance institutions and industries. Via the use of cloud and AI technology, various institutions like the Commonwealth Meridian Debt Management System, FinTech Systems and the Scottish Trust Deed, which have all specialized in helping countries seeking outfits that would provide services with timely and improved accuracy with the records of government debts and all other necessary analyses for commonwealth states (Information Age, 2018 and Patricia Scotland, 2019). The bottom line here is that where countries lack viable systems necessary for holding government officials accountable for the choices made regarding state finance, it becomes impossible and difficult for electorates to easily keep track on what government officials spend, where they spend it, and how often they spend state resources, (Information Age, 2018).

CONCLUSION

The crisis situation and burden of public debt which Nigeria and other sub-Saharan African Countries (SSAC) currently faces have largely been attributed to the country's inability to use borrowed funds productively. Some studies (Umana, 2018; Okoye, 2000 and FSDH, 2017) argue that most of these countries identified to be facing debt crises, are those whose government officials and politicians, instead of financing domestic and capital investments that would later yield revenue for repaying the borrowed debts, had high jacked such funds and stash them away in foreign banks accounts abroad, a situation technically referred to as 'capital flight'. Put simply, scholars like (Umana, 2018; Okoye, 2000 and FSDH, 2017) identified the following as some of the crucial factors that are responsible for the debt burden and economic crisis which Nigeria currently suffers from:

i. The total abuse of official power and corruption by those in office.
ii. Weak government control and a lack of viable ICT tools for practical policy implementation structures.
iii. A high degree of political rascality in matters of finance and spending among the ruling elites.

Summary of Findings

i. Regarding the 1st research objectives, the authors discovered that political leaders of this dispensation have little or no regard for good governance since their self-interests and ego often take over their will to serve their nation as credible political officeholders.
ii. Regarding the 2nd research objectives, the authors noted that the lack of viable ICT tools and platforms for debt management, the rising presence of week government institutions, already existing high debt rates on borrowed loans, poor debt management practices, poor lending, and inefficient loan utilization practices and the pressure to deliver from a politically rascal elite sect of 21st cen-

tury, are largely at the crux of why there is a dearth of viable policies that should curb the menace of rising public debts in developed and in developing nations.

iii. On the 3rd objective, the authors observed that majority of the public debts borrowed from finance institutions were not utilized for the purpose for which such loans were taken. Consequently, ensuring high-interest rates for servicing such loans usually results in economic hardship on the taxpayers who are forced to service such debts.

Recommendation

Given the findings made above, the authors deem the following recommendations necessary for urgent adoption and implementation:

i. Stated that the problem of rising public debt cries in most countries is a factor of poor leadership, the authors recommend that requisite training, certification, and experience on monetary and economic matters becomes an obligatory condition for qualifying to run for office. Persons without this basic knowledge and experience in finance and economic matters must not be allowed to run for office.

ii. Indebted nations must as a matter of necessity, begin the full adoption, implementation, and use of AI and Could computing technology-based public debt financial management systems (PDFMS) since these platforms have been proven to have the capacity to largely address the public debt management crisis issues.

iii. Countries with a high ratio of public debt-to-GDP should necessarily formulate and implement humane policies that would do the following: lower interest rates; moderately increase tax revenues; reasonably cut spending rates and shift federal spending where possible.

iv. Developed and established economies of the world, should as a matter of necessity, strongly consider writing off certain public debts/debt cancellations owed it by most developing countries of the world. This move is already being practiced by certain donor nations, especially to coastal nations that are always prone to natural disasters which continues to have a crippling effect on the concerned economies.

This paper recognizes that 'public debts' when properly and effectively utilized, has capacity for boosting economies and for stimulating the growth and political development of the borrowing nation. However, the authors note that the place of an informed and dedicated elite group of leaders and the urgent adoption and utilization of AI/ICT based technologies for public debt management purposes and efficient monitoring of the flow of spending rates, is a factor that cannot be overemphasized, that is, where appropriate debt management and the eradication of leadership crisis becomes the sole and ultimate objective of the affected nations.

REFERENCES

Alberto Alesina & Roberto Perotti. (1995). *The Political Economy of Budget Deficits* (Vol. 42). Staff Papers - International Monetary Fund.

Amadeo, K. (2019). *Public debt with its pros and cons, How to tell when it's too high. An online publication of the balance*. Retrieved from the balance online on October 20th, 2019. https://www.thebalance.com/what-is-the-public-debt-3306294

Assibong, P. A., Wogu, I. A. P., Sholarin, M. A., Misra, S., Damasevičius, R., & Sharma, N. (2020). The politics of artificial intelligence behavior and human rights violation issues in the 2016 US Presidential Elections: An appraisal. In Data Management, Analytics, and Innovation. Advances in Intelligent Systems and Computing, (vol 1016). Springer. DOI doi:10.1007/978-981-13-9364-8_22

Battaglini, M., Nunnari, S., & Palfrey, T. R. (2018). *The Political Economy of Public Debt: A Laboratory Study. CEPR Discussion Papers 13097*. C.E.P.R. Discussion Papers.

Bin, D. (2020). The politics of public debt: Financialization, class, and democracy in neoliberal brazil. Studies in Critical Social Science. Brill. doi:10.1163/9789004408722

Blahous, C. P. (2013). *Why we have federal deficits: The policy decisions that created them*. Research paper, Mercatus Center, George Mason University. https://www.mercatus.org/ publication/why-we-have-federal-deficits-policydecisions-created-them

Bryant, M. (2014). 'Artificial intelligence could kill us all'. Meet the man who takes that risk seriously. *The Next Web (TNW)*. https://thenextweb.com/insider/2014/03/08/ai-could-kill-all-meet-mantakes-risk-seriously/#.tnw_hVchaHqU

Cecchetti, S. G., Mohanty, M. S., & Zampolli, F. (2010). *The future of public debt: Prospects and implications* (BIS Working Papers No. 300). Basel: Bank for International Settlements.

Creswell, J. W. (2003). *Research design: Qualitative and quantitative approaches*. SAGE.

Discussion, E. (2016). *Public debt: Meaning, objectives, and problems. Question and answer forum. An online publication of economic discussion*. https://www.economicsdiscussion.net/debt-2/public-debt-meaning-objectives-and-problems/12812

FSDH. (2017). *Nigerian public debt – A comparative analysis. A publication of Proshare Intelligent Investing online*. Retrieved on the 21st of October, 2019. From: https://www.proshareng.com/news/NIGERIA%20ECONOMY/Nigerian-Public-Debt-%E2%80%93-A-Comparative-Analysis-/35222

Gandenberger, O. (1980). Öffentliche Verschuldung II. Theoretische Grundlagen. In W. Albers & ... (Eds.), *Handwörterbuch der Wirtschaftswissenschaft* (pp. 480–504). G. Fischer.

Hawking, S., Tegmark, M., Russell, S., & Wilczek, F. (2014). Transcending complacency on super-intelligent machines. *Hoffpost*.

Holtfrerich, C., Feld, L. P., Heun, H., Illing, G., Kirchgässner, G., Kocka, J., Schularick, M., Streeck, W., Wagschal, U., Walter, S., & Von Weizsäcker, C. C. (2016). Government Debt: Causes, effects and limits. German National Academy of Sciences Leopoldina. Union der deutschen Akademien der Wissenschaften e. V.

IMF. (2001). *Guidelines for public debt management. An online publication of The International Monetary Fund (IMF)*. Retrieved on the 25th of October, 2019 from: https://www.imf.org/external/np/mae/pdebt/2000/eng/index.htm

Information Age. (2018). *How digital technology is helping consumers tackle rising debt. An online publication of information age online*. Retrieved from https://www.information-age.com/digital-technology-rising-consumer-debt-123472498/

Institute of International Finance (IIF). (2018). *Global debt monitor database, July 2018. IFF estimates of global debt stock are based on household, nonfinancial sector, corporate financial, and public sector debt for 72 countries*. IIF.

Khagram, S., Fung, A., & De Renzio, P. (Eds.). (2013). *Open Budgets: The Political Economy of Transparency, Participation*. https://www.brookings.edu/book/open-budgets-the-political-economy-of-transparency-participation-and-accountability/

Lindholm, R. W. (1950). *Public finance and fiscal policy: An analysis of government spending, revenue, and debt*. Pitman.

Marilyn, K. (2013). *Ex-post facto research: Dissertation and scholarly research, Recipes for success*. Dissertation Success LLC. http://www.dissertationrecipes.com/wp-content/uploads/2011/04/Ex-Post-Facto-research.pdf

Mba, P. N., Yuni, D. N., & Oburota, C. S. (2013). Analysis of domestic debt: Implication for economic growth in Nigeria. *Global Journal of Social Sciences*, *12*, 1-9. https://researchcyber.com/major-causes-nigerian-debt-burden-crisis/

Okoye, E. I. (2000). The Nigerian debt problem: Causes consequences and policy options. African Banking and Finance Review, 1.

Practice, P. D. M. (2019). *Cloud technology for effective public debt management: Are we there yet? A publication of PDM Practice*. Retrieved from http://pdmpractice.org/ict-technologies-for-effective-public-debt-management-are-we-there-yet/

Reinhart, C. M., Reinhart, V. R., & Rogoff, K. S. (2012). Public debt overhangs: Advanced-economy episodes since 1800. *The Journal of Economic Perspectives*, *26*(3), 69–86. doi:10.1257/jep.26.3.69

Sallehudin, H., Nurhizam Satar, M. S., Abu-Bakar, N. A., Baker, R., Yahya, F., & Md-Fadzil, A. F. (2019). Modeling the Enterprise Architecture Implementation in the Public Sector using HOT-Fit Framework. *International Journal of Advanced Computer Science and Applications*, *10*(8), 2019.

Sallehudin, H., Razak, R. C., Ismail, M., Md-Fadzil, A. F., & Baker, R. (2018). *Cloud Computing Implementation in the Public Sector: Factors and Impact*. Asia-Pacific Journal of Information Technology and Multimedia.

Scotland, P. (2019). *Blog: The world must not sleep-walk into another debt crisis. The Commonwealth. A presentation by the Commonwealth Secretary-General. An online publication of Commonwealth News Room*. Retrieved from https://thecommonwealth.org/blog/blog-world-must-not-sleep-walk-another-debt-crisis

Sineviciene, L., & Vasiliauskaite, A. (2012). Fiscal policy interaction with private Investment: The case of the Baltic States. *The Engineering Economist*, *23*(2), 233–241.

Stein, L. (1871). *Lehrbuch der Finanzwissen- schaft* (2nd ed.). Brockhaus. Von Stein.

Streeck, W. (2013). *The politics of public debt: Neoliberalism, capitalist development, and the restructuring of the state*. MPIfG Discussion Paper, No. 13/7, Max Planck Institute for the Study of Societies (MPIfG). Retrieved from http://www.publicseminar.org/2014/02/the-politics-of-public-debt/

The Guardian News Paper. (2020). *Uproar as Senate approves Buhari's $22.7b loan request*. The Guardian Online News: https://guardian.ng/news/uproar-as-senate-approves-buharis-22-7b-loan-request/

Umana, K. (2018). *Major causes of the Nigerian debt burden and crisis. Business and economics online.* Retrieved on the 21st of October, from https://researchcyber.com/major-causes-nigerian-debt-burden-crisis/

United Nations Inter-agency Task Force on Financing for Development (UNITFFD). (2019). *Financing for Sustainable Development Report 2019*. Available from https://developmentfinance.un.org/fsdr2019

United Nations Inter-agency Task Force on Financing for Development (UNITFFD). (2018). *Financing For Sustainable Development Report 2018*. UNITFFD.

Werding, M. (2014). *Demographischer Wandel und öffentliche Finanzen. Langfrist-Projektion 2014-2060 unter besonderer Berücksichtigung des Rentenreform-Pakets der Bundesregierung*. Arbeitspapier 01/2014. Wiesbaden: Sachverständigenrat zur Begutachtung der gesamtwirtschaftlichen Entwicklung.

Williams, B. (2012). *The Economics of Cloud Computing: An Overview For Decision Makers*. https://www.ciscopress.com/articles/printerfriendly/1925617

Wogu, I. A., Elegbeleye, A., Uwaoma, K. U., Chukwuedo, C. N., Edogiawere, M., Aguziendu, C., & Misra, S. (2020). The politics of domestic violence laws against women and the dignity of womanhood: An appraisal of human factor issues in emerging polities. In S. Misra & A. Adewumi (Eds.), *Handbook of Research on the Role of Human Factors in IT Project Management* (pp. 221–242). IGI Global. doi:10.4018/978-1-7998-1279-1.ch015

Wogu, I. A., Katende, J. O., Elegbeleye, A., Roland-Otaru, C. O., Apeh, H. A., Ifeanyi-Reuben, N. J., & Misra, S. (2020). Artificial intelligence, other minds, and human factor development: The fate of man in the world of machines. In S. Misra & A. Adewumi (Eds.), *Handbook of Research on the Role of Human Factors in IT Project Management* (pp. 205–220). IGI Global. doi:10.4018/978-1-7998-1279-1.ch014

Wogu, I. A. P., Misra, S., Assibong, P. A., Ogiri, S. O., Maskeliunas, R., & Damasevicius, R. (2018). Super-intelligent machine operations in 21st-century manufacturing industries: A boost or doom to political and human development? In *Towards Extensible and Adaptable Methods in Computing*. Academic Press.

Wogu, I. A. P., Misra, S., Assibong, P. A., Olu-Owolabi, E. F., Maskeliunas, R., & Damasevicius, R. (2019). Artificial intelligence, smart classrooms, and online education in the 21st century: Implications for human development. *Journal of Case on Information Technology*, *21*(3). https://www.igi-global.com/article/artificial-intelligence-smart-classrooms-and-online-education-in-21st-century/227679?camid=4v1

Wogu, I. A. P., Sanjay Misra, J., Assibong, P. A., Adewumi, A., Maskeliunas, R., & Damasevicius, R. (2018). A critical review of the politics of artificial intelligent machines, alienation, and the existential risk threat to America's labor force. In *Computational Science and Its Applications*. Springer. https://rdcu.be/5XTm https://link.springer.com/chapter/10.1007/978-3-319-95171-3_18

Yared. P. (2019). Rising Government Debt: Causes and Solutions for a Decades-Old Trend. *Journal of Economic Perspectives, 33*(2), 115–140.

KEY TERMS AND DEFINITIONS

Artificial Intelligence: AI is the field of study that is dedicated to understanding the ability which computer programs or machines have that gives them the capacity to think and learn. Simply put, it is the field of study which tries to make computers "smart".

Cloud Computing: This is the term largely used to designate the practice of using networks of remote servers hosted on the Internet to store, manage, and process data, rather than a local server or a personal computer.

Governments Debt: This is the kind of debt is the accumulated financial obligation which is owed to major financial institutions through the issuance of treasury bonds,

ICT: The acronym ICT is here used to refer to information communication technology.

Public Debt: The term public debt here refers to the sum or amount of money which a country owes to lenders outside of itself. It is here also referred to as national debt.

Chapter 7
Financial Linkages and Shock Spillovers in the Countries of Central, Eastern, and South-Eastern Europe:
Evidence From a Global Macroeconometric Model

Saša Jakšić
https://orcid.org/0000-0003-4681-4280
Faculty of Economics and Business, University of Zagreb, Croatia

ABSTRACT

At the start of the third decade of the 21st century, the countries of Central, Eastern, and South-Eastern Europe (CESEE) are still lagging behind 'old' EU Member States in regards to various macroeconomic and social indicators. This is particularly evident when considering the development of the financial sector, especially the non-banking part. This chapter focuses on the stock markets of eleven CESEE countries and analyzes potential macroeconomic factors that contribute to explaining the dynamics of real equity prices. To account for cross-country linkages and potential spillovers, global vector autoregressive (GVAR) methodology is applied. The estimated impact elasticities enabled the pinpointing of CESEE countries with stronger linkages to foreign stock markets. Generalized impulse response functions indicated the existence of statistically significant spillovers, the strongest spillovers coming from the German stock market. The empirical results also showed spillovers from CESEE countries' stock markets, bond markets, as well as from real shocks.

DOI: 10.4018/978-1-7998-5083-0.ch007

INTRODUCTION

The fall of the Berlin wall symbolically marked the end of the planned economy systems prevailing in the countries of Central, Eastern and South-Eastern Europe (CESEE) and the beginning of the transition of these countries towards market-oriented economies. Fast forward thirty years later, the transition towards market economies has not gone so smooth and the CESEE countries are still below average EU28 per capita income level (Borosak et al, 2019).

There are many reasons why the CESEE countries' growth is below potential. First, the privatization of state-owned companies was not as successful as it could have been, and in most countries, even after thirty years, it is still not completed! Second, the slow and inefficient justice system (International Monetary Fund, 2017) hinders tackling corruption. Third, lack of commitment towards implementing the necessary structural reforms, along with insufficient investments in infrastructure, education and innovation are standing on the way of achieving higher growth rates (European Commission, 2018).

On the upside, trade integration has been relatively successful particularly with mature economies of Western Europe (Bussière et al, 2005). However, intra-regional trade flows between the CESEE countries are still below full potential, especially regarding their geographical proximity.

The lagging behind advanced economies is particularly evident concerning the financial sector. This does not come as a surprise, as the notion of a capital market and allocation of funds towards profitable projects and initiatives is in complete contrast to a planned economy setting. Consequently, due to the less developed financial sector and weak integration of capital markets, firms and households have limited access to financial services necessary for investment financing, thus limiting economic growth potential.

The focus of this chapter is on the CESEE countries' stock markets. In particular, this chapter analyses eleven CESEE countries. Namely, it centers on EU New Member States (NMS) that joined the EU in the last two decades: eight countries from the 2004 enlargement wave (Czech Republic, Poland, Hungary, Estonia, Latvia, Lithuania, Slovenia and Slovakia), and countries that joined the EU afterwards – Romania and Bulgaria (2007) and Croatia (2013). Therefore, the empirical analysis performed in this chapter does not include Turkey, Russia, Ukraine, Moldova, Belarus and non-EU Balkan states (Albania, Bosnia and Herzegovina, Kosovo, North Macedonia, Montenegro and Serbia). Although the list of countries is narrowed, still the analyzed countries are quite heterogeneous and the 'symptoms' listed above do not equally apply (and to an exact extent) to every country. The heterogeneity especially became apparent in the aftermath of the 2008 economic and financial crisis, as countries were not equally affected. While some economies remained almost unaffected, in some countries (Croatia), the recession lasted for six years.

As it is very unlikely that these differences are just due to unfortunate turn of events, this chapter analyses what are the key determinants of the dynamics of the CESEE countries' stock markets? Along the lines, other interesting questions emerge. Is the role of domestic and foreign factors equally important in all CESEE countries? Does the relative importance of domestic and foreign factors change over time? Considering the setting, the answers to these questions would provide an insight to the potential vulnerabilities and exposures of CESEE countries' stock markets.

In assessing the determinants of the dynamics of the CESEE countries' stock markets there are two prevailing approaches: time series models which base the analysis around individual country models (for instance: Jakšić, 2009; Hsing, 2011) and panel models (Şükrüoğlu & Nalin, 2014) which usually treat the countries in a panel as independent units and neglect possible spillovers. Therefore, the prevailing approaches fail to address the interactions between the countries which are likely to be important in an increasingly globalized setting. For that reason, this chapter aims at filling the gap by providing a setting that allows for modelling interaction for such a large number of countries and variables.

The rest of this chapter is organized in the following manner. After a brief literature review, the main drawbacks of the prevailing approaches to modeling the stock markets dynamics using macroeconomic variables are presented. Fundamentals of the GVAR methodology as an appropriate approach for modeling interactions in a multi-country setting are explained. Then follow the results of the empirical analysis along with recommendations for future research and a conclusion.

Background

Financial and macroeconomic indicators are closely related. Empirical research provides evidence that stock market developments boost economic growth (Carp, 2012). Nevertheless, their connection is not direct and is established through numerous channels. A convenient way to establish a link between the stock market and macroeconomic variables was proposed by Chen, Roll & Ross (1986), henceforth CRR model. The CRR model is a factor model stemming from the arbitrage pricing theory (APT) context. Chen et al. (1986) found that US stock market returns are explained by the following factors: the spread between long and short interest rates, expected and unexpected inflation, industrial production, and the spread between high- and low- grade bonds. Building upon their conclusions, several papers employed a similar setup augmented with an additional set of variables that reflect specific country settings.

Most empirical work for the CESEE countries employed CRR style setup or an adapted version of the basic model postulated as factor models or, more frequently, as Vector Autoregressive (VAR) models. Other approaches will also be mentioned in the remainder of the section.

For Croatia, Cota et al. (2008), Jakšić (2008) and Jakšić (2009) applied VAR methodology using macroeconomic variables such as industrial production, interest rates, consumer price index, money supply and exchange rate. Additionally, Cota et al. (2008) using the present value model (PVM) which links stock prices and the future discount rate of expected cash flows, found that the international economic activity does not have a significant influence on the Croatian stock market in the long run.

Employing two-pass regression procedure Mateev & Videv (2008) found that in explaining fluctuations of Bulgarian stock market, trade deficit, unexpected inflation and country risk premium play an important role.

Using VAR methodology, Pilinkus & Boguslauskas (2009) found that macroeconomic variables are significant determinants for stock market prices in Lithuania. Among the set of macroeconomic variables the authors employed gross domestic product, harmonised consumer price index, the narrow money supply, unemployment rate, short-term interest rates and exchange rate. Similarly, using Granger causality tests, Pilinkus (2009) found that gross external debt, gross domestic product deflator, the producer price index, index of capital goods, import volumes, residential building permits, the retail trade index, change in industrial production prices, nondurable consumer goods, foreign direct investment, the manufacturing index, general government revenue and net exports can be employed to forecast stock market prices in Lithuania.

For Romania, Králik (2012) and Dumitrescu & Horobet (2009) also applied VAR methodology. Králik (2012) investigated the relationship between local and global macroeconomic factors and stock market indices in Romania. As a proxy for local macroeconomic factors the industrial production index, the wholesale price index, the consumer price index and the nominal exchange rate, the official interest rate, the interbank interest rate and money supply were selected, while the oil price, gold price, short-term

3-Month Treasury bill's rate and long-term 10-year Treasury bond proxy for the global macroeconomic factors. Dumitrescu & Horobet (2009) analyze the relationship between stock prices and exchange rates.

All aforementioned research was performed for the individual CESEE country. There are also a few empirical research performed for a group of CESEE countries. For instance, Samitas & Kenourgios (2007) applied VAR methodology and found that "new" European stock markets (Poland, Czech Republic, Slovakia and Hungary) are not perfectly integrated with foreign financial markets, while domestic economic activity and the German factor are more influential on these stock markets than the American global factor. Furthermore, the authors found that CESEE countries' stock markets are influenced by a range of global and local factors such as the domestic industrial production the domestic interest rate, the US interest rate, the US industrial production and German economic activity.

Pilinkus (2010) employed VAR methodology to investigate the relationship between the Baltic States (Lithuania, Estonia and Latvia) stock prices and ten macroeconomic variables: gross domestic product, unemployment, foreign direct investment, public debt, trade balance, money supply, harmonized index of consumer prices, short-term interest rates, exports and imports.

Prats & Sandoval (2016) perform Granger causality test to analyze the connection between the stock market and the economic growth in Bulgaria, Slovakia, Hungary, Poland, Czech Republic and Romania.

Barbić & Čondić-Jurkić (2011) test for informational inefficiencies on stock markets of Croatia, Czech Republic, Hungary, Poland and Slovenia using VAR methodology. The authors employed the following variables: inflation rate, broad money supply, money market interest rate and foreign currency reserves.

Horobet & Dumitrescu (2009) employed VAR methodology to investigate the link between stock markets and macroeconomic variables (gross domestic product, consumer price index, money supply, interest rates and real exchange rates) in Czech Republic, Hungary, Poland and Romania

Kulhanek (2012) also applied VAR methodology to explore causal linkages among stock prices, output and money supply development in the CESEE countries (Czech Republic, Hungary, Poland, and the Slovak Republic).

However, even though these papers covered multiple countries, each country is analyzed separately. In other words, there is no interaction between the countries and the potential spillovers remain out of reach when using this methodology.

Besides VAR methodology, another approach for examining the impacts of macroeconomic variables on the stock markets of CESEE countries was based on GARCH type models. Hsing (2011) applied EGARCH model and found that the Croatian stock market index is positively associated with real GDP, the M1/GDP ratio, the German stock market index and the euro area government bond yield and is negatively influenced by the ratio of the government deficit to GDP, the domestic real interest rate, the HRK/USD exchange rate and the expected inflation rate. Using the same methodology and more or less the same set of variables, the same author also performed analysis for Bulgaria, Poland, Hungary, Czech Republic, Lithuania, Estonia and the Slovak Republic in subsequent research. Although this approach prospectively models time-varying (non-constant) volatility, the author does not report GARCH model diagnostics or the variance equation. Notwithstanding, univariate GARCH model does not account for shock spillovers, nor the volatility spillovers that could be modeled in the context of the multivariate GARCH (MGARCH models). As the individual equations do not model feedback between the variables, this approach also gives rise to the endogeneity problem, which is solved in the VAR models. Furthermore, it also neglects possible cointegration.

Therefore, the nexus between the CESEE countries stock markets and the macroeconomic variables are usually analyzed based on individual country models, without any interaction between the countries whatsoever. In some instances, the impact of foreign shocks is captured by an index/proxy variable or as a two-country model setup which both neglect second- and third-round spillover effects (Feldkircher & Huber, 2016).

Some papers employ panel methodology to relate, among others, CESEE countries' stock markets and macroeconomic variables (Radman Peša & Festić, 2014; Barbić & Čondić Jurkić, 2017; Şükrüoğlu & Nalin, 2014). Combining countries into a panel is tempting, as it enables joint modeling of multiple countries. However, this approach has an important caveat: *the countries that compose the panel are often treated as independent units and cross-country spillovers are ignored* (Bussière et al., 2012).

All analyzed countries are small open economies (SOE) and, as such, they are highly exposed to shocks to foreign activity and commodity prices. Ultimately, countries are connected through numerous channels of interaction. For that reason, separate modeling of individual countries would neglect interdependencies and spillover effects that occur due to cross-country interactions (trade in goods and services, financial assets, movement of labor and capital). Obviously, in a globalized setting, for the model to be well defined, one has to take into account interactions. Particularly, the recent research showed that the financial spillovers and spillbacks have both increased in magnitude in the aftermath of the 2008 global financial and economic crisis (Agenor & Pereira da Silva, 2018).

The question is how to model interaction for such a large number of countries and variables? For instance, an unrestricted one country VAR (2) model with five endogenous variables would require estimation of 55 parameters. For that reason, joint modeling of such large scale system is not feasible using conventional models due to the proliferation of parameters as the dimension of the models grows. Therefore, the question is: how to connect countries for modelling their interactions with a constraint that the approach has to be feasible?

SOLUTIONS AND RECOMMENDATIONS

Inclusion of a large number of countries and/or variables leads to an increase in the model dimensions. Various approaches can be applied to decrease the dimensionality of the parameter space, either through parameter shrinkage or data shrinkage (Chudik & Pesaran, 2011). Feldkircher et al. (2020) distinguish three main approaches to modelling interactions across countries and variables: panel, global, and factor augmented vector autoregressive models.

As an appropriate framework for modelling high-dimensional systems in a theoretically coherent and statistically consistent manner, a Global Vector Autoregressive (GVAR) methodology was employed (Pesaran et al. 2004; Pesaran et al. 2006; Pesaran et al. 2007; Dees et al. 2007). The GVAR approach resolves the dimensionality problem by decomposing the underlying large dimensional VAR models into a subset of conditional models, which are linked together through cross-sectional averages. In doing so, the approach actually combines various techniques: time series, panel data and factor analysis.

The GVAR approach is performed in two steps. In the first step, small scale country-specific models are estimated as conditional on other countries. Individual country-specific models (referred to as VARX* models) include domestic variables and foreign specific variables defined as weighted cross-section averages of endogenous variables of other countries which are treated as weakly exogenous (long-run forcing). In the second step, VARX* models are stacked and solved simultaneously as one large global

VAR model. GVAR allows for interdependencies across individual variables within a given country and/or across countries since lags of all variables enter individual equations and the reduced form errors are allowed to be cross-sectionally dependent. The approach has an extensively vast area of application (see Chudik & Pesaran (2016) for a comprehensive overview of the GVAR approach and its empirical applications).

In a globalized setting, the transmission of shocks is rapid, deeming yearly or quarterly data as inappropriate. Therefore, monthly data were employed in the paper spanning from January 2000 to September 2019, yielding a total of 237 observations. The dataset included 11 CESEE countries: Bulgaria, Croatia, Czech Republic, Estonia, Hungary, Latvia, Lithuania, Poland, Romania, Slovenia and Slovakia. Additionally, Germany was also included in the model as the main trading partner of the analyzed countries and the country through which global shocks are transmitted.

The selection of variables follows the theoretical framework set up in Chen et al. (1986). The employed empirical model includes five endogenous variables: real equity prices (q_{it}), as a central variable of the model, real output (y_{it}), prices (p_{it}), the real effective exchange rate (e_{it}) and risk premium (rp_{it}). Endogenous variables are defined as:

$$y_{it} = \ln\left(\frac{GDP_{it}}{HICP_{it}}\right),\ p_{it} = \ln\left(HICP_{it}\right),\ q_{it} = \ln\left(\frac{EQ_{it}}{HICP_{it}}\right),\ e_{it} = \ln\left(E_{it}\right) \tag{1}$$

where GDP_{it} is the nominal Gross Domestic Product, $HICP_{it}$ is the harmonized index of consumer prices, EQ_{it} is the nominal equity price index, E_{it} is the real effective exchange rate index, for country i during the period t. i=1,…,11 denotes CESEE countries and i=0 indicates Germany as the reference country.

Risk premium is calculated as the difference between the long-term government bond yield for a CESEE country ($ltgby_{it}$) and the long-term government bond yield for Germany ($ltgby_{0t}$) is defined as

$$rp_{it} = ltgby_{it} - ltgby_{0t}\,. \tag{2}$$

Additionally, the log of oil prices ($poil_t = ln(OIL_t)$) was included in the individual country models as a global variable along with foreign specific variables (q^*_{it}, y^*_{it}, p^*_{it}, e^*_{it} and rp^*_{it}) to proxy for unobserved common factors. Therefore, one of the main benefits of the GVAR model is that it relies solely on observables yet is able to capture the impact of the unobserved common factors.

Unit root test were performed to assess the stationarity of the analyzed variables (Table 3 and Table 4 for the domestic variables, Table 5 and Table 6 for the foreign-specific variables and table 7 for the global variable, in Appendix 2). In addition to the usual Augmented Dickey-Fuller (ADF) test (Dickey & Fuller, 1981), a unit root test based on weighted symmetric (WS) estimation of ADF type regressions was also performed (Park & Fuller, 1995). Results of all test unambiguously point to the conclusion that all analyzed variables (domestic, global and foreign specific) are integrated of order 1, i.e. $I(1)$. A complete overview of the employed variables is presented in Table 1. In-depth details on data sources and data preparation procedures are in Appendix 1. Foreign specific variables were defined using the weight matrix (Table 8 in Appendix 2). The results of the empirical analysis were obtained using GVAR Toolbox 2.0 (Smith & Galesi, 2014).

Table 1. Composition of endogenous and foreign specific variables in the individual country models of the GVAR model

Variables	Number of countries	
Endogenous		
Real equity prices (*q*)	12	
Real output (*y*)	12	
Real effective exchange rate (*e*)	11	Excluding: Bulgaria
Prices (*p*)	12	
Risk premium (*rp*)	10	Excluding: Germany and Estonia
Oil prices (*poil*)	1	Germany
Exogenous		
Real equity prices (*q**)	11	Excluding: Germany
Real GDP (*y**)	12	
Real effective exchange rate (*e**)	11	Excluding: Germany
Prices (*p**)	11	Excluding: Germany
Risk premium (*rp**)	12	
Oil prices (*poil*)	11	Excluding: Germany

Individual VARX* models were estimated according to techniques developed by Harbo et al. (1998) and Pesaran et al. (2000). Lag orders for the endogenous variables, p_i, foreign specific and global variables, q_i, were selected according to Akaike information criterion (AIC) and were not allowed to be greater than 4 for the endogenous variables, and 2 for global and foreign specific variables. After that, the corresponding cointegrating VARX* models were estimated and the rank of their cointegrating space was selected using trace statistics due to its better small sample performance compared to maximum eigenvalue statistics, which is also less robust to departures from normal errors (Cheung and Lai, 1993). However, the final choice of lag orders and the rank of cointegrating space were set following the results of diagnostics tests. Appropriate vector error correction model had a restricted trend and unrestricted intercept. Individual county models were then estimated subject to reduced rank restrictions and the corresponding error correcting terms were derived.

The main requirement for the validity of the GVAR approach is the dynamic stability of the model. First of all, the eigenvalues of the estimated global model should be on or inside the unit circle. Analyzed GVAR model has 232 eigenvalues. 47 eigenvalues lie on the unit circle, indicating that some shocks have permanent effects on the levels of endogenous variables. Remaining 185 eigenvalues have moduli less than unity. 56 of the eigenvalues are complex, indicating that impulse responses will have a cyclical pattern. Therefore, the main requirement for the model validity is fulfilled.

An additional possible factor that could lead to the model instability is the residual serial correlation, Table 9 in Appendix 2. The results of the residual serial correlation test (Godfrey 1978a, 1978b) for the estimated country-specific residuals based on *F*-test statistics indicate that, at the 5% significance level, serial correlation is rejected for the majority of equations.

Another important prerequisite of the GVAR approach is that the 'idiosyncratic' shocks of individual county models should be cross-sectionally 'weakly correlated'. Conditioning the country-specific models on weakly exogenous foreign specific variables, the degree of correlation of the remaining shocks across regions should be modest. If this is true, then the weak exogeneity of the foreign variables is ensured. A simple inspection of the extent to which the foreign specific variables have been effective in reducing the cross-section correlation of the variables in the GVAR model is provided by the average pairwise cross-section correlations for the levels and those of the associated residuals over the selected estimation period. For every country and each variable, the pairwise correlation of that country with each of the remaining countries was calculated and then averaged across countries (Table 10 in Appendix 2). The correlations of the residuals from the VARX* models are very small and do not depend on the choice of the variable or country. This indicates that the GVAR model has been successful in capturing common unobserved effects determining CESEE countries' stock market dynamics and ensures that the model tracks the comovements between the variables themselves and not between their trends (spurious correlation).

Additionally, F-tests for weak exogeneity of foreign specific variables were performed (Harbo et al., 1998; Johansen, 1992). The test results (Table 11 in Appendix 2) indicate that at the 5% level weak exogeneity assumptions were rejected in only four out of 68 conducted tests.

As the diagnostics of the estimated GVAR model are satisfying, the solution of the global model can be applied for studying the dynamics of the CESEE countries' stock markets. In this chapter, the most important analytical outputs are contemporaneous effects of foreign specific variables on their domestic counterparts, generalized impulse response functions (GIRF) and generalized forecasting error variance decomposition (GFEVD).

Contemporaneous effects of foreign specific variables on their domestic counterparts are interpreted as impact elasticities between domestic variables in one country and the corresponding foreign specific variables. They reveal (in)existence of linkages between the CESEE countries' stock markets depending on the size and statistical (in)significance of the estimated coefficients. Table 2 depicts the contemporaneous effects of foreign variables on their domestic counterparts along with robust t-ratios computed using the Newey–West heteroscedasticity and autocorrelation consistent variance estimator.

Table 2. Contemporaneous effect of foreign specific variables on their domestic counterparts (Impact elasticities) – real equity prices and risk premium

Country	Real equity prices	Risk premium	Country	Real equity prices	Risk premium
Estonia	0.96 (8.13)		Bulgaria	0.72 (7.66)	0.47 (4.75)
Hungary	0.91 (11.23)	0.73 (5.19)	Croatia	0.70 (5.65)	0.44 (3.67)
Poland	0.81 (11.07)	0.65 (5.76)	Latvia	0.53 (5.22)	0.39 (2.50)
Czech R.	0.76 (5.95)	0.68 (7.67)	Slovenia	0.47 (5.02)	0.55 (3.16)
Lithuania	0.76 (5.25)	0.60 (3.08)	Slovak R.	0.16 (1.97)	0.49 (4.54)
Romania	0.73 (4.58)	0.67 (3.07)			

Note: Newey–West robust t-ratios are given in parentheses.

All elasticities are statistically significant and positive, as expected. The interpretation of the elasticities is straightforward. For instance, a 1% increase in foreign real equity prices in a given month leads to an increase of 0.96% in real equity prices in Estonia within the same month. High elasticities indicate strong comovements between the CESEE countries' stock market and foreign stock markets. Incidentally,

Figure 1. Generalized impulse responses of selected one standard error shocks, effects on real equity prices: a) shock in German real equity prices; b) shock in Czech Republic real equity prices; c) shock in Slovak Republic real equity prices

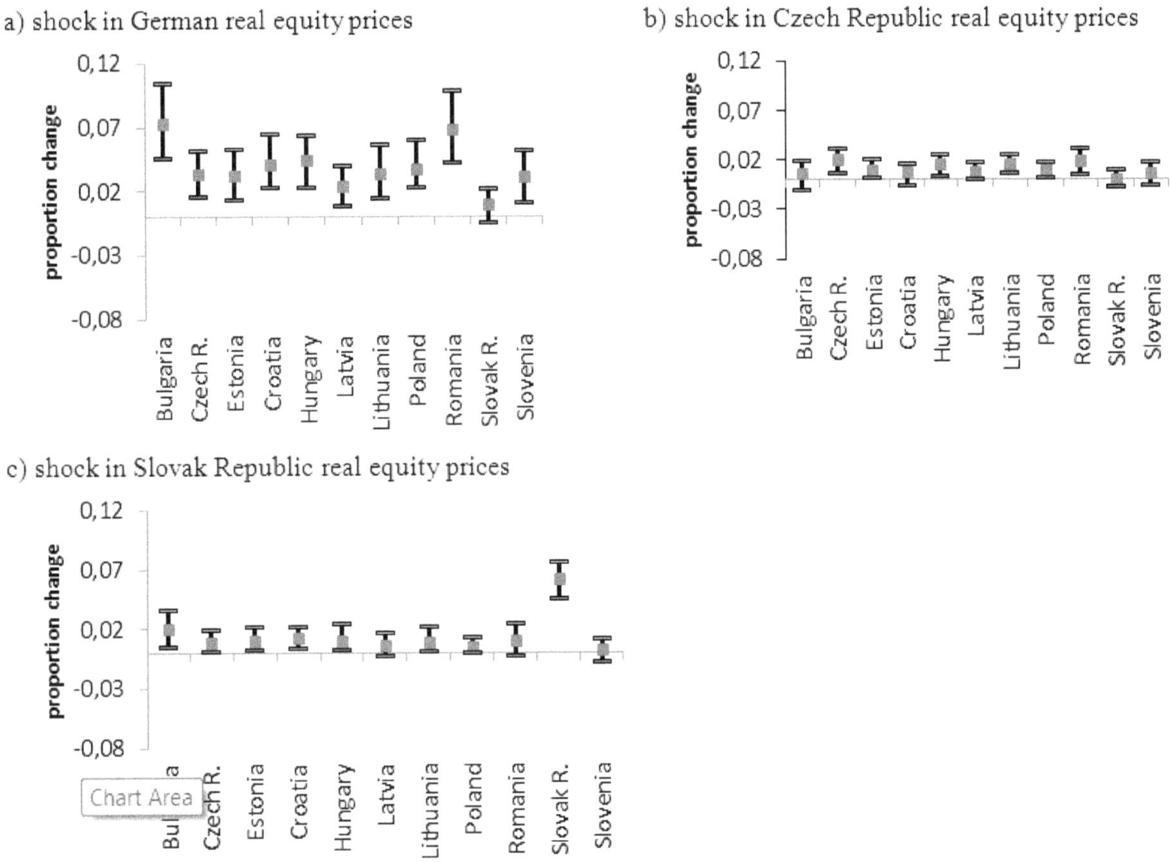

these countries also have higher impact elasticities regarding the risk premium, indicating that these countries also have closer ties to foreign bond markets. On the contrary, low elasticities are estimated for the Slovak Republic, Slovenia and Latvia indicating that in these countries real equity prices are not much affected by changes in foreign real equity prices. It is also interesting to note that impact elasticities are larger for real equity prices indicating a stronger reaction of stock markets compared to bond markets.

These results are in line with findings of Allen et al. (2010) indicating that stock markets of the Czech Republic, Hungary and Poland have stronger linkages and are more sensitive to shocks from other markets. Similarly, Lee & Stewart (2010) found evidence of interdependence among the stock markets in Estonia and Lithuania as well as spillovers from foreign markets especially the German DAX index to these stock markets. On the other hand, the Slovakian stock market seems to be more self-directed and independent of events occurring on the stock markets of other countries.

An indispensable tool for the analysis of dynamic systems, such as GVAR, is the impulse response function (IRF). IRF provides information on the potential reaction of the analyzed variables system to shocks. To avoid variable ordering problems, generalized impulse response functions (GIRF) are usually applied in the GVAR framework. GIRF indicates how the effects of variable-specific shocks on the future states of all the variables in the dynamic model, develop in time.

Figure 2. Generalized impulse responses of one standard error shocks in real output and risk premium, effects on real equity prices: a) shock in Czech Republic real output; b) shock in Romanian risk premium; c) shock in Poland's risk premium

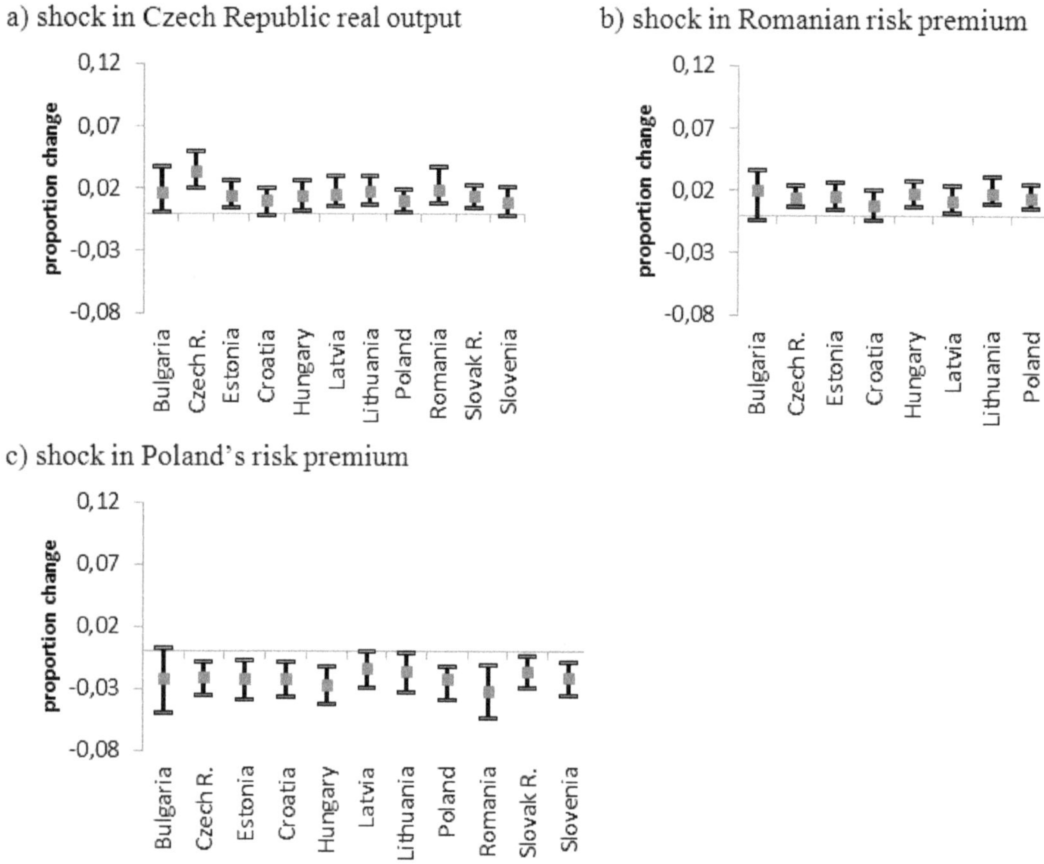

Figure 1 and Figure 2 show the effect of selected shocks on CESEE countries' stock markets after one year. All figures depict bootstrap median estimates along with 90 percent bootstrap confidence bands. For easier comparison of the size of the effects, graphs are scaled so that they have the same minimum and maximum.

Generalized impulse response functions of the analyzed GVAR model unambiguously indicate statistically significant spillovers on the CESEE countries' stock markets. However, the size varies across countries and variables. Panel a) of Figure 1 indicates that a one standard error shock in real equity prices in Germany (equivalent to an increase in German real equity prices by 2.1%) has positive and statistically significant spillovers in all of the CESEE countries' stock markets except for the Slovak Republic which is not surprising as the impact elasticities also indicated its stock market is self-directed. Largest spillovers, around 7% monthly increase in real equity prices, are recorded in Romania and Bulgaria.

Panel b) of Figure 1 depicts a one standard error shock in real equity prices in the Czech Republic which is equivalent to an increase of real equity prices in the Czech Republic by 2.29%. This shock also has spillovers on some of the countries' stock markets. However, these spillovers are smaller in comparison to spillovers occurring from the German stock market. Besides the Slovak Republic, the spillovers from the Czech Republic are not statistically significant in Bulgaria, Croatia and Slovenia.

Even though impact elasticities suggested Slovak stock market is self-directed, there are statistically significant spillovers coming from its stock market. Panel c) of Figure 1 depicts a one standard error shock in real equity prices in the Slovak Republic which is equivalent to an increase of real equity prices in the Slovak Republic by 2.55%.

Panel a) of figure 2 indicates that spillovers to CESEE countries' stock markets also occur from the real market. An increase in real output in the Czech Republic by 1.47% has statistically significant spillovers, i.e. lead to an increase in real equity prices.

There are also spillovers from the bond markets. An increase in Romania's risk premium by 6.3 basis points increases CESEE countries' real equity prices (panel b) of Figure 2). On the other hand, an increase in Poland's risk premium by 7.4 basis points decreases CESEE countries' real equity prices (panel c) of Figure 2). Therefore, an increase in risk premium for a country that is perceived as riskier (according to Fitch, Romania's credit rating is BBB-) leads to a capital flight from debt markets to equity markets, while an increase in risk premium for a country that is perceived as less risky riskier (according to Fitch, Poland's credit rating is A-) directs the capital in the opposite direction.

The GIRF's of statistically non-significant shocks were not reported (but are available upon request). For instance, shocks to oil prices were not statistically significant, suggesting that CESEE countries' stock markets are not sensitive to global political shocks. This was made evident in the 2008 global crisis that was transmitted only through real shocks.

Furthermore, in spite of the importance of German economy for CESEE countries, it appears that real shocks (real output and prices) occurring in the German economy do not have a statistically significant impact on CESEE countries' stock markets.

Other shocks, like country-specific shocks in real output, were also mostly not statistically significant, with exception of few, usually neighboring countries.

Generalized forecasting error variance decomposition (GFEVD) estimates the proportion of the variance of the h-step ahead forecast errors of each variable that is explained by conditioning on contemporaneous and future values of the generalized shocks of the system. GFEVD is not sensitive to the ordering of the variables in the country-specific models and represents the relative contributions of the shocks to reducing the mean square error of forecasts of individual endogenous variables at a given horizon h. The assessment of the relative importance of various factors on CESEE countries' real equity prices on impact and after 40 months is illustrated in Figures 3 - 6.

Figure 3. Share of the forecast error variance of real equity prices explained by the countries' real equity prices

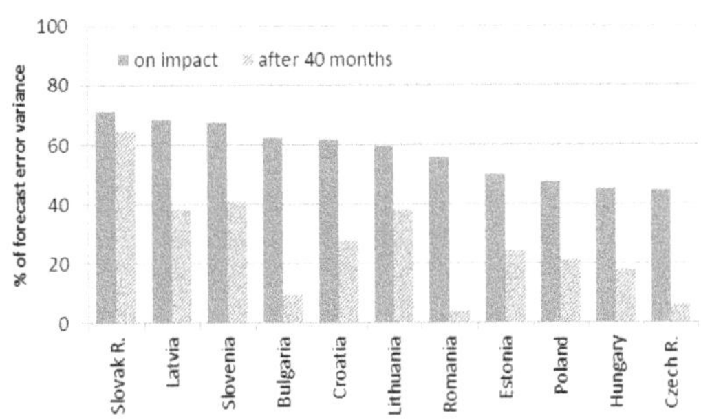

As usual, forecast error variance of real equity prices is, on impact, mostly explained by its dynamics (Figure 3) and the share is in the range from 71.2% (Slovak Republic) to 44.5% (Czech Republic). However, after 40 months the patterns diverge considerably. In the Slovak Republic, the share only slightly dropped to 64.6%. In Slovenia, Latvia and Lithuania the share dropped to around 40%, while in Bulgaria, the Czech Republic and Romania the share is below 10%.

Figure 4. Share of the forecast error variance of real equity prices explained by the domestic factors

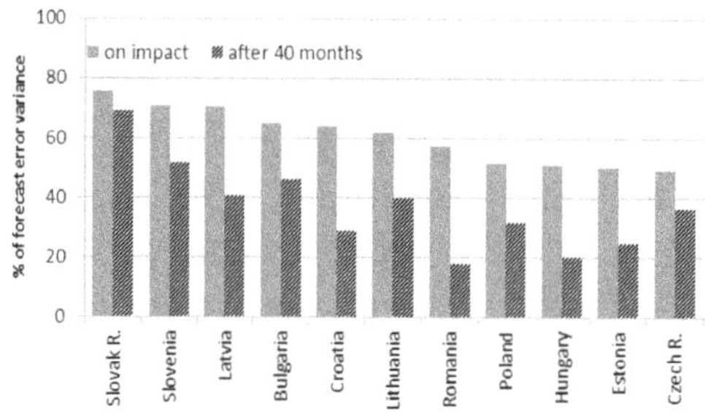

When looking at the share of domestic factors (Figure 4), they explain the most of the forecast error variance of real equity prices on impact. Again, after 40 months, domestic factors are main factors in explaining the dynamics of real equity prices in the Slovak Republic and Slovenia. On the other hand, in Croatia, Estonia, Hungary and Romania foreign factors explain more than 70% of the forecast error variance of real equity prices.

Figure 5. Share of the forecast error variance of real equity prices explained by the German economy

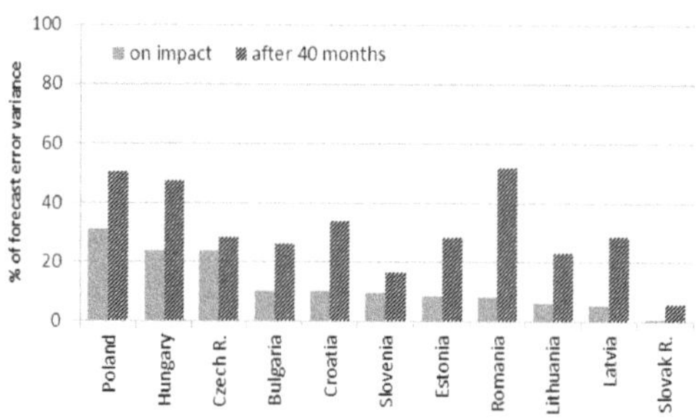

The share of German variables in explaining the forecast error variance of real equity prices is illustrated in Figure 5. On impact, the German variables play the most important role in Poland (31%), in six countries the share is below 10%, while in the Slovak Republic the share is negligible, below 1%. The relative importance of German variables (Figure 5) tends to increase over time. After 40 months German variables explain most of the forecast error variance of real equity prices in Romania and Poland. However, in the Slovak Republic, the share remains low (5.8%).

Figure 6. Share of the forecast error variance of real equity prices explained by the real output

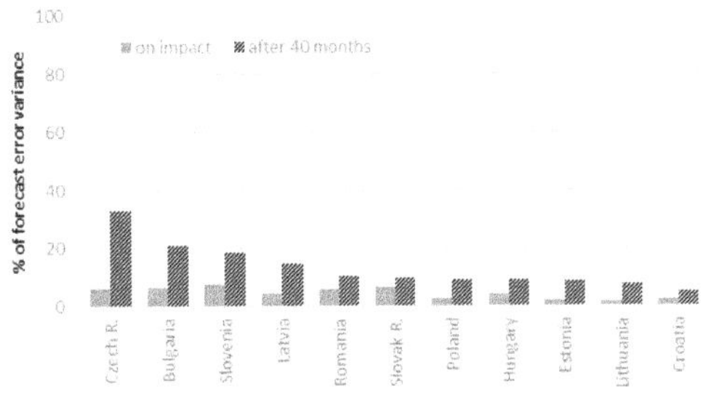

Figure 6 shows the share of the forecast error variance of real equity prices explained by the real output, both domestic and foreign. On impact, the share is below 10% in all CESEE countries. Over time, the share increases. The share is highest in Czech Republic (32.9%), Bulgaria (21.1) and Slovenia (18.4%), which means that the stock markets in these countries keep a closer track of the economic activity. In most countries foreign economic activity plays a substantially larger role, witnessing once again that the analyzed countries are small open economies and justifies once again the application of the GVAR approach in the context of this chapter.

FUTURE RESEARCH DIRECTIONS

GVAR approach is very flexible and offers many potential extensions, creating considerable possibilities for further research. One of the possibilities is the specific choice of weights for defining foreign-specific variables. In other words, as opposed to trade weights employed in this paper, one can apply financial weights or combine the application of specific weights to certain groups of variables. For instance, trade weights for real variables, and financial weights for financial variables.

Another possible extension of the model is the inclusion of the German economy as a dominant unit instead of including it as a reference country. Including Germany as a dominant unit would relax the need for global variables, like oil prices, to enter as a domestic variable in the reference country.

One limitation of the GVAR approach is that it does not allow for missing data, like, for instance unbalanced panel data model. Hence, if only one observation for a variable is missing one has to choose between data interpolation/extrapolation and exclusion of the variable for the specific country. As variable exclusion is basically throwing away of potentially valuable data, basic interpolation/extrapolation methods and regression models were applied in this chapter (Appendix 1).

The chapter is dealing with a multi-country model with a large number of variables. Therefore, it does not come as a surprise that some minor data issues were encountered. Namely, data on risk premium were not available for a certain time span (Appendix 1). As risk premium turned out to be an important factor in explaining stock market dynamics, the missing data were estimated using regression models. Future research should put more effort into methods for estimating missing data. First of all, GARCH type models ought to be applied for estimation of volatility that is likely to be important for estimating risk premium. Second, additional determinants that affect country risk should also be considered.

CONCLUSION

This chapter analyses the impact of financial and real shocks on the stock markets of selected CESEE countries using GVAR approach. GVAR methodology is employed as an appropriate setting for modeling cross-country linkages and spillovers of the financial and the real shocks. Furthermore, the setting of a GVAR approach provides a practical solution to the dimensionality problem inherent to the large multi-country models with a large number of variables. In a globalized setting, the transmission of shocks is rapid, deeming yearly or quarterly data as inappropriate. This was reflected in the choice of monthly dataset for the empirical analysis.

Many interesting conclusions emerged from the performed empirical analysis. The estimated impact elasticities enabled the pinpointing of CESEE countries with stronger linkages to foreign stock markets (Estonia, Hungary, Poland and the Czech Republic) and the countries with weaker linkages (the Slovak Republic, Slovenia and Latvia). It also turned out that countries with stronger linkages to foreign stock markets also have closer ties with foreign bond markets.

Furthermore, generalized impulse response functions indicated the existence of statistically significant spillovers, the strongest spillovers coming from the German stock market. The empirical results also showed spillovers from CESEE countries' stock markets, bond markets as well as from real shocks. An interesting finding was that an increase in the risk premium for a country that is perceived as riskier leads to a capital flight from debt markets to equity markets, while an increase in the risk premium for a country that is perceived as less risky riskier directs the capital in the opposite direction.

Generalized forecasting error variance decomposition pointed out the differences in the importance of domestic and foreign factors in explaining the CESEE countries' stock markets dynamics. In the long-run, stock markets dynamics are predominantly driven by foreign factors in Croatia, Estonia, Hungary and Romania while the opposite holds for the Slovak Republic and Slovenia. Among the foreign factors, German economy plays an important role.

Overall, the results of the empirical analysis point to pronounced heterogeneity of the CESEE countries stock markets dynamics. Furthermore, in the past, the lack of financial integration acted as an unintentional buffer from global shocks and financial crisis transmission. However, the effects of crisis still spillover to CESEE countries through real shocks as a consequence of higher trade integration.

In the future, progress in financial integration is expected, as previous research (Syllignakis & Kouretas, 2010) found that linkages between the CESEE and foreign stock markets have risen after the EU accession, even though the 2008 financial crisis has slowed down the integration process. Hence, with further financial integration, the CESEE countries will become more vulnerable to foreign shocks and larger spillovers are expected. Therefore, the exposure to foreign shocks will be more pronounced in the future which is a fact that policymakers have to take into account. These findings also provide valuable insights for the policymakers as they should be aware that the spillover effects are established not only through German economy

REFERENCES

Agenor, P. R., & Pereira da Silva, L. (2018). Financial Spillovers, Spillbacks, and the Scope for International Macroprudential Policy Coordination. Policy Paper N° 97, Bank of International Settlements.

Allen, D. E., Powell, R. J., & Golab, A. (2010). *Volatility and correlations for stock markets in the emerging economies of Central and Eastern Europe: Implications for European investors*. Available at SSRN 1611472.

Barbić, T., & Čondić-Jurkić, I. (2011). Relationship between macroeconomic fundamentals and stock market indices in selected CEE countries. *Economic Review (Kansas City, Mo.)*, *62*(3-4), 113–133.

Barbić, T., & Čondić-Jurkić, I. (2017). Do fiscal variables affect stock market returns in EU countries? *Economic Review (Kansas City, Mo.)*, *68*(3), 253–266.

Borosak, B., Bykova, A., Heger, N., Muck, B., Schwarzhappel, M., Vasaros, G., & Zenz, D. (2019). wiiw Handbook of Statistics 2019: Central, East and Southeast Europe. The Vienna Institute for International Economic Studies, wiiw.

Bussière, M., Chudik, A., & Sestieri, G. (2012). *Modelling global trade flows: results from a GVAR model*. Globalization and Monetary Policy Institute Working Paper 119, Federal Reserve Bank of Dallas.

Bussière, M., Fidrmuc, J., & Schnatz, B. (2005). *Trade Integration of Central and Eastern European Countries: Lessons from a Gravity Model*. ECB Working Paper No. 545.

Carp, L. (2012). Can Stock Market Development Boost Economic Growth? Empirical Evidence from Emerging Markets in Central and Eastern Europe. *Procedia Economics and Finance*, *3*, 438–444. doi:10.1016/S2212-5671(12)00177-3

Chen, N., Roll, R., & Ross, S. (1986). Economic Forces and the Stock Market. *The Journal of Business*, *59*(3), 383–403. doi:10.1086/296344

Cheung, Y., & Lai, K. S. (1993). Finite-sample sizes of Johansen's likelihood ratio tests for cointegration. *Oxford Bulletin of Economics and Statistics*, *55*(3), 315–328. doi:10.1111/j.1468-0084.1993.mp55003003.x

Chow, G. C., & Lin, A. L. (1971). Best linear unbiased interpolation, distribution, and extrapolation of time series by related series. *The Review of Economics and Statistics*, *53*(4), 372–375. doi:10.2307/1928739

Chudik, A., & Pesaran, M. H. (2011). Infinite-dimensional VARs and factor models. *Journal of Econometrics*, *163*(1), 4–22. doi:10.1016/j.jeconom.2010.11.002

Chudik, A., & Pesaran, M. H. (2016). Theory and Practice of GVAR Modelling. *Journal of Economic Surveys*, *30*(1), 165–197. doi:10.1111/joes.12095

Cota, B., Erjavec, N., & Arnerić, J. (2008). The Impact of Macroeconomic Variables on Croatian Stock Market. In *An Enterprise Odyssey. International Conference Proceedings* (pp. 70). University of Zagreb, Faculty of Economics and Business.

Dees, S., di Mauro, F., Pesaran, M. H., & Smith, L. V. (2007). Exploring the International Linkages of the Euro Area: A Global VAR Analysis. *Journal of Applied Econometrics*, *22*(1), 1–38. doi:10.1002/jae.932

Dickey, D., & Fuller, W. (1981). Likelihood Ratio Statistics for Autoregressive Time Series with a Unit Root. *Econometrica*, *49*(4), 1057–1072. doi:10.2307/1912517

Dumitrescu, S., & Horobet, A. (2009). *On the Causal Relationship between Stock Prices and Exchange Rates: Evidence from Romania*. Available at SSRN 1341703.

European Commission. (2018). *European Financial Stability and Integration Review 2018*. Directorate-General for Financial Stability.

Feldkircher, M., & Huber, F. (2016). The international transmission of US shocks-Evidence from Bayesian global vector autoregressions. *European Economic Review*, *81*, 167–188. doi:10.1016/j.euroecorev.2015.01.009

Feldkircher, M., Huber, F., & Pfarrhofer, M. (2020). Factor Augmented Vector Autoregressions, Panel VARs, and Global VARs. In P. Fuleky (Ed.), *Macroeconomic Forecasting in the Era of Big Data. Advanced Studies in Theoretical and Applied Econometrics* (Vol. 52). Springer. doi:10.1007/978-3-030-31150-6_3

Godfrey, L. G. (1978a). Testing Against General Autoregressive and Moving Average Error Models When the Regressors Include Lagged Dependent Variables. *Econometrica*, *46*(6), 1293–1302. doi:10.2307/1913829

Godfrey, L. G. (1978b). Testing for Higher Order Serial Correlation in Regression Equations When the Regressors Include Lagged Dependent Variables. *Econometrica*, *46*, 1303–1310.

Harbo, I., Johansen, S., Nielsen, B., & Rahbek, A. (1998). Asymptotic inference on cointegrating rank in partial systems. *Journal of Business & Economic Statistics*, *16*(4), 388–399.

Horobet, A., & Dumitrescu, S. (2009). On the causal relationships between monetary, financial and real macroeconomic variables: Evidence from Central and Eastern Europe. *Economic Computation and Economic Cybernetics Studies and Research*, *43*(3), 1–17.

Hsing, Y. (2011). Macroeconomic Variables and the Stock Market: The Case of Croatia. *Economic Research Journal*, *24*(4), 41–50. doi:10.1080/1331677X.2011.11517479

International Monetary Fund. (2017). Regional Economic Outlook, Europe: Europe Hitting Its Stride. World Economic and Financial Surveys. Washington, DC: International Monetary Fund.

Jakšić, S. (2008). Impact of Monetary Aggregate M4 and Interest Rates on CROBEX Index. *Proceedings of the Faculty of Economics and Business in Zagreb*, *6*(1), 131–139.

Jakšić, S. (2009). *Analysis of Influence of Selected Macroeconomic Variables on CROBEX* (Unpublished master's thesis). Faculty of Economics and Business, University of Zagreb.

Johansen, S. (1992). Cointegration in partial systems and the efficiency of single-equation analysis. *Journal of Econometrics*, *52*(3), 231–254. doi:10.1016/0304-4076(92)90019-N

Králik, L. I. (2012). *Macroeconomic Variables and Stock Market Evolution*. Romanian Statistical Review.

Kulhanek, L. (2012). The Relationship between stock markets and gross domestic product in the Central and Eastern Europe. In *Proceedings of the 7th International Conference On Currency, Banking And International Finance - How Does Central And Eastern Europe Cope Up With The Global Financial Crisis?* (*vol. 1*). University of Economics in Bratislava.

Lee, J., & Stewart, G. (2010). Asymmetric volatility and volatility spillovers in Baltic and Nordic stock markets. *European Journal of Economics Finance and Administrative Sciences*, 25.

Mateev, M., & Videv, A. (2008). Multifactor asset pricing model and stock market in transition: New empirical tests. *Eastern Economic Journal, 34*(2), 223–237. doi:10.1057/palgrave.eej.9050031

Park, H. J., & Fuller, W. A. (1995). Alternative Estimators and Unit Root Tests for the Autoregressive Process. *Journal of Time Series Analysis, 16*(4), 415–429. doi:10.1111/j.1467-9892.1995.tb00243.x

Pesaran, M., Shin, Y., & Smith, R. (2000). Structural analysis of vector error correction models with exogenous I(1) variables. *Journal of Econometrics, 97*(2), 293–343. doi:10.1016/S0304-4076(99)00073-1

Pesaran, M. H., Schuermann, T., & Treutler, B. J. (2007). Global Business Cycles and Credit Risk. In M. Carey & R. StultzUniversity of Chicago Press (Eds.), *The risks of financial institutions*. doi:10.7208/chicago/9780226092980.003.0010

Pesaran, M. H., Schuermann, T., Treutler, B. J., & Weiner, S. M. (2006). Macroeconomic Dynamics and Credit Risk: A Global Perspective. *Journal of Money, Credit and Banking, 38*(5), 1211–1262. doi:10.1353/mcb.2006.0074

Pesaran, M. H., Schuermann, T., & Weiner, S. M. (2004). Modeling regional interdependencies using a global error-correcting macroeconometric model. *Journal of Business & Economic Statistics, 22*(2), 129–162. doi:10.1198/073500104000000019

Pilinkus, D. (2009). Stock market and macroeconomic variables: evidences from Lithuania. *Ekonomika ir vadyba, 14*, 884-891.

Pilinkus, D. (2010). Macroeconomic indicators and their impact on stock market performance in the short and long run: The case of the baltic states. *Technological and Economic Development of Economy, 16*(2), 291–304. doi:10.3846/tede.2010.19

Pilinkus, D., & Boguslauskas, V. (2009). The Short-Run Relationship between Stock Market Prices and Macroeconomic Variables in Lithuania: An Application of the Impulse Response Function. *Economics of Engineering Decisions, 65*(5).

Prats, M. A., & Sandoval, B. (2016). *Stock Market and Economic Growth in Eastern Europe. Economics Discussion Papers, No 2016-35.* Kiel Institute for the World Economy.

Radman Peša, A., & Festić, M. (2014). Panel regression of stock market indices dynamics in south-eastern European economies. *Economic Research Journal, 27*(1), 673–688.

Samitas, A., & Kenourgios, D. (2007). Macroeconomic factors' influence on'new'European countries' stock returns: The case of four transition economies. *International Journal of Financial Services Management, 2*(1/2), 34–49. doi:10.1504/IJFSM.2007.011670

Smith, L. V., & Galesi, A. (2014). *GVAR Toolbox 2.0.* Retrieved from https://sites.google.com/site/gvarmodelling/gvar-toolbox

Şükrüoğlu, D., & Nalin, H. T. (2014). The Macroeconomic Determinants of Stock Market Development in Selected European Countries: Dynamic Panel Data Analysis. *International Journal of Economics and Finance, 6*(3), 64–71. doi:10.5539/ijef.v6n3p64

Syllignakis, M. N., & Kouretas, G. P. (2010). German, US and Central and Eastern European stock market integration. *Open Economies Review*, *21*(4), 607–628. doi:10.100711079-009-9109-9

KEY TERMS AND DEFINITIONS

Foreign-Specific Variables: Weighted cross-section averages of endogenous variables of other countries.

Generalised Forecasting Error Variance Decomposition (GFEVD): Estimates the proportion of the variance of the h-step ahead forecast errors of each variable that is explained by conditioning on contemporaneous and future values of the generalized shocks of the system.

Generalised Impulse Response Functions (GIRF): Indicates how the effects of variable-specific shocks on the future states of all the variables in the dynamic model, develop in time.

Impact Elasticities: Contemporaneous effects of foreign specific variables on their domestic counterparts.

Pairwise Cross-Section Correlations: The pairwise correlation of a country with each of the remaining countries calculated for every country and for each variable and then averaged across countries.

VARX* Models: Individual country-specific models that include domestic variables, global variables and foreign specific variables.

Weak Exogeneity Tests: *F*-tests for weak exogeneity of foreign specific variables.

Weight Matrix: In a multi-country setting, a matrix defined on the basis of bilateral relations (trade or financial flows between the countries).

APPENDIX 1

Data Sources and Data Preparation Procedures

A1. Real equity prices

Data on equity price indices (measured in national currencies) are obtained from the national stock exchanges websites. Bulgarian stock market index (SOFIX) was introduced in October 2000. Therefore, to compensate for the missing data backward extrapolation for the period from January 2000 to September 2000 was performed. The stock market indices employed in the paper are:

- SOFIX (Bulgarian stock exchange)
- CROBEX (Zagreb Stock Exchange)
- DAX (Frankfurt Stock Exchange)
- OMX Riga (Riga Stock Exchange)
- BUX (Budapest Stock Exchange)
- PX (Prague Stock Exchange)
- SBITOP (Ljubljana Stock Exchange)
- WIG (Warsaw Stock Exchange)
- BET (Bucharest Stock Exchange)
- SAX (Bratislava Stock Exchange)
- OMX Tallinn (Tallinn Stock Exchange)
- OMX Vilnius (Vilnius Stock Exchange)

A2. Real output

The data source for all countries was Eurostat. Quarterly data series on gross domestic product at market prices in million euros was seasonally adjusted using TRAMO/SEATS procedure within JDemetra+ software. Quarterly GDP series was disaggregated to monthly frequency using Chow-Lin (1971) procedure. In the process of temporal disaggregation, seasonally adjusted series on industrial production indices (2015=100) was employed as a high frequency indicator.

A3. Real effective exchange rates

Real effective exchange rate index (deflator: consumer price index - 42 trading partners - industrial countries), 2010=100, was obtained from Eurostat.

A4. Harmonized index of consumer prices

The data source for all countries was Eurostat. Harmonized index of consumer prices (2015=100) was also applied to obtain real GDP and real equity prices series

A5. Risk premium

Data on long-term government bond yield (in percentage) were obtained from European Central Bank (ECB). Unavailable data were estimated using the regression models. The data were estimated for: Czech Republic, Hungary, Latvia, Lithuania, Poland and Slovakia (2000), Slovenia (2000-2002M2), Bulgaria (2000-2002), Croatia (2000-2005M11) and Romania (2000-2005M3),

A6: Oil prices

For oil prices monthly averages of Europe Brent Spot Price FOB (Dollars per Barrel) were obtained. Data source is Thomson Reuters.

A7. Trade weight matrix

Data for all countries were obtained from Direction of Trade Statistics database (DOTS) of the International Monetary Fund (IMF). Trade weights were calculated based on average trade flows for the period from 2010 to 2018. Data on exports of goods (Free on board – FOB) in US$ and data on imports of goods (Cost, Insurance, Freight – CIF) in US$ were applied.

APPENDIX 2

Table 3. Results of the unit root tests for the domestic variables (Germany and Central and Eastern European countries)

Variable	Test statistic	Critical value	Czech R.	Germany	Hungary	Poland	Slovak R.	Slovenia
y (with trend)	ADF	-3.45	-2.18	-1.85	-1.79	-2.78	-0.62	-1.02
y (with trend)	WS	-3.24	-1.27	-1.70	-1.34	-2.97	-1.07	-1.14
y (no trend)	ADF	-2.89	-1.98	0.31	-1.79	-1.09	-1.82	0.52
y (no trend)	WS	-2.55	1.19	0.24	-1.29	-0.08	0.91	0.24
Dy	ADF	-2.89	-6.49	-8.10	-9.88	-9.75	-8.61	-10.23
Dy	WS	-2.55	-6.57	-8.01	-10.00	-9.85	-8.49	-10.32
e (with trend)	ADF	-3.45	-2.12	-2.28	-2.68	-3.52	-0.77	-3.43
e (with trend)	WS	-3.24	-1.49	-2.42	-1.78	-3.41	-0.82	-3.59
e (no trend)	ADF	-2.89	-2.52	-1.97	-3.02	-3.47	-1.89	-2.76
e (no trend)	WS	-2.55	0.00	-2.24	-1.44	-3.42	0.76	-2.84
De	ADF	-2.89	-8.73	-9.41	-9.79	-10.19	-6.92	-9.38
De	WS	-2.55	-8.70	-9.04	-9.90	-10.11	-7.06	-9.21
p (with trend)	ADF	-3.45	-1.98	-2.66	-1.45	-1.17	-1.78	-3.62
p (with trend)	WS	-3.24	-1.92	-2.82	0.37	-0.40	0.65	1.71
p (no trend)	ADF	-2.89	-1.29	-0.71	-3.51	-2.36	-3.42	-5.83
p (no trend)	WS	-2.55	1.90	1.97	3.10	2.44	3.57	3.56
Dp	ADF	-2.89	-8.27	-8.73	-6.82	-9.27	-10.13	-10.91
Dp	WS	-2.55	-8.40	-8.83	-6.77	-8.95	-9.30	-10.88
q (with trend)	ADF	-3.45	-1.76	-3.15	-2.22	-2.46	-2.02	-2.07
q (with trend)	WS	-3.24	-2.04	-1.69	-2.39	-2.64	-1.47	-1.89
q (no trend)	ADF	-2.89	-1.80	-1.26	-1.59	-1.70	-2.18	-2.03
q (no trend)	WS	-2.55	-1.97	-1.47	-1.81	-1.78	-1.22	-1.90
Dq	ADF	-2.89	-7.54	-11.06	-7.86	-5.90	-5.68	-6.20
Dq	WS	-2.55	-7.62	-11.08	-7.92	-6.04	-5.81	-6.20
rp (with trend)	ADF	-3.45	-2.59		-2.38	-2.49	-2.44	-2.12
rp (with trend)	WS	-3.24	-2.51		-2.61	-1.99	-2.35	-2.12
rp (no trend)	ADF	-2.89	-2.43		-2.40	-2.62	-2.36	-2.11
rp (no trend)	WS	-2.55	-2.47		-2.62	-1.79	-1.80	-1.80
Drp	ADF	-2.89	-10.83		-11.69	-8.30	-10.20	-10.07
Drp	WS	-2.55	-10.95		-11.81	-8.41	-10.31	-10.19

Note: prefix D denotes first differences.

Table 4. Results of the unit root tests for the domestic variables (Baltic countries and Southeastern European countries)

Variable	Test statistic	Critical value	Bulgaria	Estonia	Croatia	Latvia	Lithuania	Romania
y (with trend)	ADF	-3.45	-1.97	-1.77	-2.25	-1.77	-2.04	-2.71
y (with trend)	WS	-3.24	-2.06	-1.17	-0.45	-1.55	-0.93	-1.07
y (no trend)	ADF	-2.89	-0.68	-1.75	-2.94	-1.54	-2.27	-0.67
y (no trend)	WS	-2.55	1.84	1.71	1.29	0.25	1.68	-0.98
Dy	ADF	-2.89	-10.63	-9.58	-5.70	-4.77	-5.08	-7.78
Dy	WS	-2.55	-10.73	-9.69	-5.89	-4.75	-5.07	-7.71
e (with trend)	ADF	-3.45		-2.39	-2.50	-2.28	-3.46	-1.59
e (with trend)	WS	-3.24		-2.61	-1.57	-2.27	-3.44	-1.57
e (no trend)	ADF	-2.89		-0.83	-2.78	-1.08	-1.35	-2.00
e (no trend)	WS	-2.55		0.73	-1.07	-1.28	-0.17	-0.86
De	ADF	-2.89		-9.40	-9.45	-9.99	-9.82	-8.11
De	WS	-2.55		-8.77	-9.53	-10.07	-9.11	-7.89
p (with trend)	ADF	-3.45	-0.99	-1.30	-1.37	-0.83	-1.29	-5.72
p (with trend)	WS	-3.24	-0.21	-1.46	-0.65	-1.24	-1.23	1.20
p (no trend)	ADF	-2.89	-3.44	-1.42	-2.41	-1.47	-0.19	-5.96
p (no trend)	WS	-2.55	1.41	1.58	1.95	0.34	0.95	2.05
Dp	ADF	-2.89	-6.65	-7.30	-8.37	-4.92	-4.95	-3.22
Dp	WS	-2.55	-6.74	-7.41	-8.41	-5.06	-5.00	-1.97
q (with trend)	ADF	-3.45	-1.89	-1.77	-2.24	-2.00	-1.80	-2.28
q (with trend)	WS	-3.24	-1.86	-1.95	-1.97	-1.75	-2.01	-2.30
q (no trend)	ADF	-2.89	-1.98	-1.41	-2.27	-1.90	-1.59	-2.27
q (no trend)	WS	-2.55	-1.75	-0.61	-1.94	-0.91	-1.00	-1.63
Dq	ADF	-2.89	-6.38	-6.27	-5.06	-10.07	-8.27	-6.11
Dq	WS	-2.55	-6.51	-6.41	-5.15	-10.04	-8.38	-6.10
rp (with trend)	ADF	-3.45	-2.50		-2.39	-1.89	-3.24	-2.47
rp (with trend)	WS	-3.24	-2.65		-2.54	-2.15	-3.34	-2.62
rp (no trend)	ADF	-2.89	-2.47		-2.41	-1.87	-3.22	-2.39
rp (no trend)	WS	-2.55	-2.53		-2.63	-2.10	-3.22	-2.59
Drp	ADF	-2.89	-7.69		-7.33	-9.17	-7.28	-6.65
Drp	WS	-2.55	-7.82		-7.45	-9.28	-7.40	-6.80

Note: prefix D denotes first differences.

Table 5. Results of the unit root tests for the foreign specific variables (Germany and Central and Eastern European countries)

Variable	Test statistic	Critical value	Czech R.	Germany	Hungary	Poland	Slovak R.	Slovenia
y* (with trend)	ADF	-3.45	-2.63	-2.10	-2.32	-2.34	-2.28	-2.15
y* (with trend)	WS	-3.24	-2.83	-2.17	-2.48	-2.54	-2.24	-2.22
y* (no trend)	ADF	-2.89	-0.53	-1.12	-0.37	-0.52	-1.00	-0.91
y* (no trend)	WS	-2.55	0.50	0.44	0.35	0.83	0.69	0.63
Dy*	ADF	-2.89	-7.80	-7.70	-7.34	-7.63	-6.72	-7.28
Dy*	WS	-2.55	-7.89	-7.81	-7.45	-7.74	-6.83	-7.39
e* (with trend)	ADF	-3.45	-1.81	-2.18	-1.67	-1.88	-2.15	-1.94
e* (with trend)	WS	-3.24	-1.68	-1.65	-1.50	-1.64	-1.72	-1.47
e* (no trend)	ADF	-2.89	-2.10	-2.41	-2.04	-2.22	-2.42	-2.34
e* (no trend)	WS	-2.55	-1.17	-0.63	-0.79	-1.06	-1.04	-0.95
De*	ADF	-2.89	-7.90	-9.72	-11.25	-10.06	-10.43	-10.95
De*	WS	-2.55	-7.79	-9.75	-11.36	-10.00	-10.53	-11.02
p* (with trend)	ADF	-3.45	-1.79	-1.98	-2.62	-1.66	-1.69	-1.61
p* (with trend)	WS	-3.24	0.01	1.05	0.93	-0.57	-0.15	0.21
p* (no trend)	ADF	-2.89	-3.10	-4.21	-4.27	-2.53	-2.96	-3.40
p* (no trend)	WS	-2.55	2.62	3.39	2.66	2.47	2.28	2.48
Dp*	ADF	-2.89	-7.78	-6.04	-5.65	-8.24	-7.30	-7.58
Dp*	WS	-2.55	-7.86	-6.02	-5.66	-8.39	-7.41	-7.67
q* (with trend)	ADF	-3.45	-2.66	-2.07	-2.46	-2.87	-2.71	-2.66
q* (with trend)	WS	-3.24	-2.40	-2.31	-2.50	-2.54	-2.80	-2.77
q* (no trend)	ADF	-2.89	-1.23	-1.93	-1.44	-1.41	-1.70	-1.60
q* (no trend)	WS	-2.55	-1.54	-1.83	-1.65	-1.72	-1.93	-1.80
Dq*	ADF	-2.89	-7.69	-5.49	-7.44	-7.59	-7.20	-7.30
Dq*	WS	-2.55	-7.81	-5.63	-7.57	-7.70	-7.32	-7.43
rp* (with trend)	ADF	-3.45	-2.44	-2.56	-2.52	-2.48	-2.73	-2.77
rp* (with trend)	WS	-3.24	-2.22	-2.38	-2.29	-2.52	-2.65	-2.79
rp* (no trend)	ADF	-2.89	-2.47	-2.62	-2.59	-2.51	-2.75	-2.77
rp* (no trend)	WS	-2.55	-1.93	-2.30	-2.17	-2.48	-2.65	-2.82
Drp*	ADF	-2.89	-9.42	-9.50	-7.17	-6.76	-10.11	-6.53
Drp*	WS	-2.55	-9.53	-9.61	-7.30	-6.89	-10.22	-6.66

Note: prefix D denotes first differences.

Table 6. Results of the unit root tests for the foreign specific variables (Baltic countries and Southeastern European countries)

Variable	Test statistic	Critical value	Bulgaria	Estonia	Croatia	Latvia	Lithuania	Romania
y* (with trend)	ADF	-3.45	-2.27	-2.08	-1.79	-2.09	-2.31	-2.22
y* (with trend)	WS	-3.24	-2.03	-1.87	-2.06	-1.57	-2.31	-2.30
y* (no trend)	ADF	-2.89	-0.22	-1.32	-0.32	-1.67	-1.12	-0.70
y* (no trend)	WS	-2.55	-0.37	0.74	0.43	1.61	0.43	0.85
Dy*	ADF	-2.89	-7.91	-5.09	-7.55	-7.37	-6.13	-7.97
Dy*	WS	-2.55	-8.01	-5.16	-7.66	-7.48	-6.22	-8.08
e* (with trend)	ADF	-3.45	-1.73	-2.37	-2.05	-2.39	-2.30	-2.16
e* (with trend)	WS	-3.24	-1.28	-2.53	-1.84	-2.18	-2.43	-1.83
e* (no trend)	ADF	-2.89	-2.22	-1.56	-2.29	-1.74	-1.94	-2.40
e* (no trend)	WS	-2.55	-0.69	-0.91	-1.44	0.10	-1.39	-1.52
De*	ADF	-2.89	-10.68	-10.65	-10.64	-8.72	-10.56	-10.56
De*	WS	-2.55	-10.79	-10.71	-10.69	-8.84	-10.65	-10.64
p* (with trend)	ADF	-3.45	-4.29	-0.66	-2.33	-0.96	-0.69	-1.31
p* (with trend)	WS	-3.24	1.64	-1.08	0.82	-1.36	-0.74	-0.14
p* (no trend)	ADF	-2.89	-5.69	-1.48	-4.25	-1.11	-2.10	-3.11
p* (no trend)	WS	-2.55	2.34	1.70	2.69	1.83	2.10	2.33
Dp*	ADF	-2.89	-3.88	-7.99	-7.64	-8.13	-7.12	-7.68
Dp*	WS	-2.55	-3.32	-8.11	-7.56	-8.24	-7.19	-7.81
q* (with trend)	ADF	-3.45	-2.61	-2.58	-2.24	-2.52	-2.42	-2.62
q* (with trend)	WS	-3.24	-2.79	-2.81	-2.48	-2.76	-2.65	-2.57
q* (no trend)	ADF	-2.89	-1.71	-1.66	-1.82	-1.72	-1.56	-1.52
q* (no trend)	WS	-2.55	-1.80	-1.40	-1.95	-1.49	-1.39	-1.78
Dq*	ADF	-2.89	-7.25	-6.14	-6.78	-6.41	-6.52	-7.21
Dq*	WS	-2.55	-7.37	-6.27	-6.90	-6.53	-6.63	-7.34
rp* (with trend)	ADF	-3.45	-2.67	-2.24	-2.24	-3.16	-2.07	-2.68
rp* (with trend)	WS	-3.24	-2.68	-2.37	-2.21	-3.17	-2.13	-2.71
rp* (no trend)	ADF	-2.89	-2.68	-2.24	-2.24	-3.15	-2.09	-2.69
rp* (no trend)	WS	-2.55	-2.68	-2.26	-1.97	-3.02	-2.01	-2.62
Drp*	ADF	-2.89	-5.61	-7.66	-10.13	-7.15	-8.58	-10.05
Drp*	WS	-2.55	-5.76	-7.78	-10.24	-7.26	-8.70	-10.16

Note: prefix D denotes first differences.

Table 7. Results of the unit root tests for the global variable

Variable	Test statistic	Critical value	Statistic
poil (with trend)	ADF	-3.45	-2.00
poil (with trend)	WS	-3.24	-2.15
poil (no trend)	ADF	-2.89	-1.98
poil (no trend)	WS	-2.55	-1.61
Dpoil	ADF	-2.89	-7.70
Dpoil	WS	-2.55	-7.81

Note: prefix D denotes first differences.

Table 8. Weight matrix

Country	Bulgaria	Czech R.	Estonia	Croatia	Germany	Hungary	Latvia	Lithuania	Poland	Romania	Slovak R.	Slovenia
Bulgaria	0	0.007	0.004	0.016	0.020	0.014	0.004	0.006	0.008	0.081	0.008	0.015
Czech R.	0.063	0	0.030	0.055	0.267	0.087	0.029	0.037	0.127	0.065	0.283	0.069
Estonia	0.002	0.002	0	0.001	0.008	0.002	0.205	0.122	0.008	0.002	0.002	0.002
Croatia	0.011	0.004	0.001	0	0.013	0.023	0.001	0.002	0.004	0.006	0.006	0.152
Germany	0.421	0.607	0.260	0.384	0	0.546	0.201	0.279	0.659	0.506	0.378	0.471
Hungary	0.085	0.052	0.024	0.136	0.147	0	0.015	0.020	0.054	0.172	0.126	0.105
Latvia	0.003	0.002	0.286	0.001	0.008	0.002	0	0.244	0.011	0.001	0.003	0.002
Lithuania	0.007	0.005	0.222	0.004	0.015	0.004	0.366	0	0.026	0.003	0.003	0.005
Poland	0.087	0.140	0.145	0.063	0.325	0.096	0.156	0.264	0	0.098	0.136	0.080
Romania	0.262	0.022	0.009	0.026	0.076	0.091	0.004	0.008	0.029	0	0.033	0.033
Slovak R.	0.035	0.148	0.013	0.039	0.088	0.111	0.015	0.012	0.063	0.050	0	0.067
Slovenia	0.024	0.010	0.004	0.275	0.033	0.025	0.004	0.006	0.010	0.016	0.021	0

Data Source: authors calculation based on data from Direction of Trade Statistics database (DOTS) of the International Monetary Fund (IMF)

Table 9. F-Statistics for tests of residual serial correlation for county-specific VARX models*

Country	p_i	q_i		Real output	Real effective exchange rate	Prices	Real equity prices	Risk premium	Oil prices
Bulgaria	2	2	F(4,211)	0.772		0.545	1.270	2.221	
Czech R.	3	2	F(4,205)	1.658	1.151	3.452*	2.469*	1.119	
Estonia	2	2	F(4,211)	6.849*	0.291	1.238	0.031		
Croatia	2	2	F(4,210)	0.495	1.897	0.338	1.341	1.699	
Germany	3	1	F(4,215)	0.965	1.275	2.484	2.036		0.509
Hungary	2	2	F(4,210)	1.224	0.658	1.323	0.939	0.980	
Latvia	3	1	F(4,212)	4.454*	2.249	4.216*	1.241	0.781	
Lithuania	2	2	F(4,211)	11.541*	7.675*	1.255	1.248	2.391	
Poland	3	2	F(4,205)	0.989	0.188	0.638	1.887	2.007	
Romania	4	2	F(4,199)	2.705*	1.877	0.936	0.244	2.755*	
Slovak R.	4	2	F(4,201)	0.497	2.545*	1.968	2.789*	0.356	
Slovenia	4	2	F(4,199)	2.095	2.448	2.171	0.556	1.758	

Note: * indicates the test statistic is statistically significant at 5% level.

Table 10. Average Pairwise Cross-Section Correlations: Variable levels and VECMX residuals*

Country	Real output		Real effective exchange rate		Prices		Real equity prices		Risk premium	
	Levels	VECMX* residuals	Levels	VECMX* residuals	Levels	VECMX* residuals	Levels	VECMX* residuals	Levels	VECMX* residuals
Bulgaria	0.716	0.052	0.825	0.025			0.970	0.009	0.596	0.040
Czech R.	0.711	0.102	0.821	-0.020	0.633	-0.019	0.975	0.077	0.469	-0.042
Estonia	0.728	0.071	0.836	0.010	0.554	0.003	0.981	0.020		
Croatia	0.622	0.072	0.726	0.048	0.566	-0.008	0.985	0.049	0.545	0.010
Germany	0.326	-0.119	0.685	-0.079	0.073	0.030	0.971	-0.137		
Hungary	0.738	0.075	0.242	-0.059	0.517	-0.067	0.985	0.132	0.507	-0.130
Latvia	0.666	-0.021	0.798	-0.037	0.478	0.025	0.975	0.060	0.520	0.013
Lithuania	0.764	0.075	0.836	0.023	0.522	0.023	0.964	-0.014	0.576	-0.048
Poland	0.716	0.028	0.800	-0.063	0.111	-0.070	0.978	0.121	0.444	-0.099
Romania	0.784	0.070	0.757	-0.012	0.522	-0.013	0.954	0.089	0.537	-0.021
Slovak R.	0.659	0.021	0.784	-0.013	0.609	0.021	0.968	0.076	0.527	-0.035
Slovenia	0.580	0.041	0.799	-0.033	0.501	0.042	0.975	0.005	0.374	-0.018

Table 11. Results of weak exogeneity tests of the foreign specific variables

Country		Real output	Real effective exchange rate	Prices	Real equity prices	Risk premium	Oil prices
Bulgaria	F(1,210)	0.2498	0.1007	0.2818	1.7862	0.1174	1.8650
Czech R.	F(1,220)	0.0061	0.0287	2.5948	3.4797	0.0422	1.9818
Estonia	F(1,210)	2.4165	0.6994	0.0020	0.0092	0.5210	0.0193
Croatia	F(1,220)	3.6818	0.8240	0.7085	4.0606	0.1962	0.8614
Germany	F(1,224)	0.0941				0.1888	
Hungary	F(1,220)	0.1500	5.5424*	1.1059	2.6203	0.2581	0.0267
Latvia	F(3,218)	0.1135	2.3540	1.2291	0.8040	1.7783	0.4306
Lithuania	F(4,217)	0.5526	0.5614	1.9240	2.5077*	1.2593	0.4211
Poland	F(1,220)	0.5326	0.0500	3.4826	0.5122	0.0008	1.1585
Romania	F(2,219)	0.6700	1.4151	0.7652	1.4861	0.7009	1.1003
Slovak R.	F(3,218)	3.807*	6.047*	0.949	1.180	2.395	1.715
Slovenia	F(2,219)	2.0528	2.3362	1.9303	1.4949	0.7271	0.6500

Note: * indicates the test statistic is statistically significant at 5% level.

Chapter 8
Quantifying Economic Uncertainties and Risks in the Oil and Gas Industry

Sorin Alexandru Gheorghiu
https://orcid.org/0000-0002-9811-3841
Kuwait Oil Company, Ahmadi, Kuwait

Cătălin Popescu
https://orcid.org/0000-0002-8921-8123
Petroleum-Gas University of Ploiesti, Romania

ABSTRACT

The present economic model is intended to provide an example of how to take into consideration risks and uncertainties in the case of a field that is developed with water injection. The risks and uncertainties are related, on one hand to field operations (drilling time, delays due to drilling problems, rig failures and materials supply, electric submersible pump [ESP] installations failures with the consequences of losing the well), and on the other hand, the second set of uncertainties are related to costs (operational expenditures-OPEX and capital expenditures-CAPEX, daily drilling rig costs), prices (oil, gas, separation, and water injection preparation), production profiles, and discount factor. All the calculations are probabilistic. The authors are intending to provide a comprehensive solution for assessing the business performance of an oil field development.

INTRODUCTION

Assessing the risks and uncertainties are the main challenges in the today professional and non-professional activities. Risk management of any risk type requires the use of various tools and techniques, which could be specific to every single field. Related to the oil and gas field, these tools and techniques allow the identification and analysis of risks as part of the evaluation of investments made in both the upstream and downstream sector.

DOI: 10.4018/978-1-7998-5083-0.ch008

The two terms, *risk* and *uncertainty* are implying ranges and probabilities. The economic model that the authors constructed and described in this chapter is based on probabilistic methods. The authors are intending to provide a practical solution for evaluating, from the economic point of view, the profitability of a field development by using the probabilistic approach.

The mathematical model is based on the well-known *Discounted Cash Flow* method, where some of the input parameters are defined as distributions of probabilities. The whole model was built in Excel and the probabilistic engine used was Oracle Crystal Ball.

The risks and uncertainties taken into account are related to drilling, well completion, production rates and possibility to lose the well due operation failures. It is obvious there are many other risks that eventually can be taken into account, but the authors refrain to the above-mentioned ones. The outputs of the model are economic performance indicators: *Pay Out Time*, *Internal Rate of Return*, *Profit-Investment Ratio*, *Cumulated Net Cash Flow*, *Total Taxes*, *Profit Tax* and *Number of Profitable Years*.

The field development scenario is considering a real oil field, where the field name, wells' names and specific field data were changed to keep the confidentiality of the data, required by the oil company. The useful information is that the oil field is situated in the northern edge of Eastern Arabia. The production and injection profiles were created by using the ECLIPSE™ (mark of Schlumberger) simulator and the data were exported to Excel by using the Eclipse Office package (mark of Schlumberger).

On the other hand, there is some other software, for instance the CASPAR (Computer Aided Simulation for Project Appraisal and Review) program that can be applied in risk analysis and modelling.

Basically, the main objective of the chapter is to build a probabilistic Discounted Cash Flow model to evaluate the economic performance of an oil field developed with producer and injector well embedding uncertainties and risks related to oil field operations (drilling, production and wells interventions). As results the final user will get:

- the economic performance parameters as a range instead of a unique solution;
- the main influencers from the input parameters and their magnitude to economic performance indicators.

These outputs will help the user in the short, medium and long term decisions related to company's evolution and performance.

LITERATURE REVIEW

In the current context of development of our society it is needed the utilization of the advanced techniques and technologies for forecasting the future of a business. Due to the fact that the results of a business are influenced in one way or another by a lot of parameters (controllable and uncontrollable), a deterministic approach is not sufficient. The petroleum industry is a good example of an industry that is characterized by high investments and high uncertainty (Kvalevåg, 2009). In this regard, the topics of investments and investment behavior of the companies are analysed in detail, starting with the so-called traditional theory of investment and continuing with the approach that introduced the analogy with the theory of options in financial markets (Dixit & Pindyck, 1994).

At the same time, the oil and gas domain contains since from the beginning phases of the upstream sector, the parameters that include uncertainties regarding different critical variables, such as: quality of oil, reservoir characteristics or operational costs (Suslick et al., 2009). On the other hand, there are parameters, like oil prices, that generate different signals, depending on values or trends, as is stated in what follows: *the oil and gas sector in developed countries responds more strongly to oil price changes than in emerging markets* or *oil price rises have a greater impact than oil price drops* (Ramos & Veiga, 2011). The approach related to the probabilistic cost and time it integrates very well with probabilistic estimations that are used in the reserve estimating and oil price forecasting (Akins et al., 2005).

Monte Carlo simulation is the most widely used technique for dealing with uncertainty related to various aspects of a system, in relation to the expected performance (Rubinstein & Kroese, 2016). Additionally, the Monte Carlo simulation is mainly used as a method to translate the uncertainties related to the input data of the models, built in uncertainties related to the expected results, in order to calculate the probability of the distribution of the predicted performance (Samawi, 2017).

The Monte Carlo simulation method is increasingly used in business, for the analysis of stochastic problems or in risk conditions, when the same direction of action can have several consequences whose probabilities can be estimated (Fishman, 2013). Another contribution in using Monte Carlo method, but this time in oil industry, states that the approach established by the Monte Carlo simulation for estimating hydrocarbon reserves can be extended in order to generate the basis for a comprehensive planning, assessment and control system useful for the oil companies management (Higgins, 1993). On the other hand, a useful contribution refers to the proposal of an improved methodology for probabilistic quantification of hydrocarbon reserves estimates based on decline-curve analysis, which generates better probabilistic reserves estimation, but also responds, like the present chapter, to highlighting the effect created on economic risk analysis (Cheng et al., 2010). Another research paper, based on the application of real options theory and Monte Carlo simulation, mentions the development of a model that incorporates both uncertainties related to oil prices and investment costs, as well as exchange rate and investment environment uncertainties in order to evaluate the value of oil overseas investment projects related to different type of oil fields and to different tax systems (Zhu et al., 2015).

Monte Carlo simulation is performed using simulation tools. There are simulation tools that are added to spreadsheets, being general and powerful, and can simulate any model that can be created in a spreadsheet. They allow for different types of probability distributions and adjust for correlated variables and are generally used for quantitative risk analysis, such as cost risk analysis, because cost estimates are usually expressed in a spreadsheet. In general, the spreadsheet used is Microsoft Excel and there are at least two popular tools that can simulate under Excel: @Risk, an add-in for Microsoft Excel and MS Project, and Crystal Ball, an add-in for Microsoft Excel, respectively (Charnes, 2012; Brandimarte, 2014).

Recent research and complex analyzes carried out in the last period of time have resorted to Monte Carlo simulation in which two models have been associated, which aimed on the one hand, the estimation of original gas in place, and on the other hand, estimated ultimate recovery, in order to produce a more accurate probability distribution for the recovery factor, a parameter that is considered essential in improving economic efficiency and for increasing the profitability of the oil companies (Richardson & Yu, 2018). Khadem et al. used Monte Carlo simulation and conduct a numerical analysis, through RiskyProject Professional™ software, for identification and quantification of the risks manifested in managing oil and gas projects that are carried out in Oman (Khadem et al., 2018).

At the same time, the oil and gas industry is considering the assertion of several categories of risks and all these risks have to be assessed continuously (Al-Thani & Merna, 2005). Therefore, a better approach is the probabilistic approach in order to evaluate correctly the performance in the case of a business coming from the upstream petroleum sector (Gheorghiu et al., 2008). Upstream petroleum projects have long time horizons covering more than 20-30 years, depending on many factors such as: reservoir characteristics, production rates, technology level, economic issues etc. (Kvalevåg, 2009). In the case of projects with long durations, the key issue is related to the discount rate in order to establish if the project is profitable or not (Dalen et al., 2008).

In the oil and gas sector, economic assessments have uncertainties related to costs, technology and oil prices, but also in establishing the probabilities regarding the identification and generation of economically viable reservoirs (Suslick et al., 2009). In another research study, based on data collected in 2017 in Iran, for a gas injection project, was carry out an assessment for the risk factors that led to a list of top-ten factors, which must be considered essential in the risks analyses made by oil companies (Hatefi, 2018).

Over time, various probabilistic models for the economic evaluation of oil and gas projects have been created. It is worth mentioning an article that introduces in this sense the concept of value at risk (VaR; through VaR can be estimated the probability of the net present value - NPV- exceeding a certain threshold value) but in which, also, was make a useful comparison of the influences of different risk factors on the project's NPV (Cheng, Wang, Liu, M. *et al.*, 2019). There are points of view that consider the value of the project through the Net Present Value (NPV). These approaches are integrated in different types of simulators, such as PSS IV simulator, a simulator for CO2-enhanced oil recovery that propose, in making investment decisions for projects characterized by uncertainties, to use limited foresight and Real Options Analysis (Welkenhuysen et al., 2017).

Also, another important issue, specific to the oil and gas industry is linked to a particular analysis tool, called *Sensitivity Analysis*. This method is focusing on the key factors that could influence, more or less, the profitability of projects. This type of analysis delivers to the decision makers a better image of the key factors in the projects (Kvalevåg, 2009). Often these key factors are interrelated and estimation of future correlation of them could be a challenge in projects valuation (Brealey et al., 2006). Related to this issue, sensitivity analysis, a good example of a simple probabilistic model refers to the costs of synthetic crude oil produced from Canadian oil sands and to which the sensitivity analysis shows that, before 2035, the most influential parameters are the learning parameter (in the case of in-situ bitumen) and the depletion parameter (in the case of mined bitumen) (Mejean & Hope, 2013).

The oil and gas industry remain a vital, complex and dynamic sector for the world economy, even though at present there are obvious concerns about identifying unconventional resources that will replace oil, especially in different situations and for certain purposes. In this sense, the specific companies intend to analyze in detail each situation that gives them a very good image on the development opportunities. Therefore, using appropriate means (economic models, simulations etc.), the most detailed business models are built in order to verify the level of performance generated by each proposed scenario. In fact, the business model aims to create a desired result by combining, in different ways, input factors (Veit et al., 2014).

A general business model for the oil and gas industry appeared in 1990, based on the idea of maximizing production in the hypothesis of a steadily growing demand for oil (Stevens, 2016). Nowadays this approach is considered outdated and lacking in consistency and utility. At the moment, there is a necessity to identify and promote new business models in the oil industry. A particular approach is focused on state companies in the oil industry (Tanţău & Khorshidi, 2016), by presenting and analyzing the business models in two of the main oil producers Iran and Iraq (countries with a huge potential in terms of crude oil and gas reserves and production, as well).

On the other hand, the business models used in the oil and gas industry have to integrate strategies that include other useful approaches such as the share price model, that explains the need to analyze how investments in long-term assets are made, in order to that, the oil companies, can make the transition from losses to profit in the future (Jianu & Jianu, 2018). Another explanation regarding the opportunity to carry out this complex research is given by one of the observations published, this year, in an article regarding the impact generated by the low price of a barrel of crude oil in these last weeks. In this regard, in the case of lower prices for the oil, it is more profitable to use petroleum products than generate energy by using renewable (alternative) sources (Zhang & Lis, 2020).

In relation to the dramatic evolution of the constant decrease of the price of a barrel of crude oil, by reaching, in this period (year 2020), of some historical minimums, we can call to various scientific studies and specialized researches that seek to provide solutions that overcome the challenges and generate the success in uncertain times. Thus, it is mentioned on the one hand, the need to transform business models and on the other hand, the focus on flexibility for management for both upside (from *under-investment*) and downside (from *macro concerns*) risks (Dickson et al., 2019).

At the same time, the type of property is also analyzed by estimating the efficiency differences between private and state-owned companies, which are part of the oil industry sector (Al-Obaidan & Scully, 1991).

Although there are important differences in organization, functioning and management, it is vital to identify for each company the implemented business model. In principle, a business model describes the logical mode of operation, but also includes the way by which each company is able to generate profit (Rack, 2017).

Another important contribution to the main subject it refers to SME's critical role in providing technologies and services to deliver special support in operations of oil industry (Yusuf et al, 2014). The area itself is wide and requires a huge effort and support in terms of resources, infrastructure, logistics etc. In the same way, could be mentioned another approach which can be declared valid for each business models as long as the financial situation reports includes revenues flows and cost structures (Glomsrød & Osmundsen, 2005).

On the other hand, a significant aspect of the performance operation mode of the companies from the oil industry refers to the administrative design of the organization. In this sense, the well-known *Norwegian Model* explains the separation of the commercial type area from the aspects of economic policy and regulation of functioning within the oil sector (Thurber et al., 2011).

THE ECONOMIC MODEL

The authors are acting in the economic environment and are dealing constantly with challenges evaluating the performance of different businesses. Currently, the E&P companies are exploring more and more the uncertainty parameters while building static and dynamic models to explore development solutions for their oil and gas fields. This is possible because the computational power and existing software are allowing it. Under these circumstances, the economic evaluations also must incorporate uncertainties, risks and move from deterministic calculations to probabilistic calculations, and also, from a single answer to a range of probabilities for the same answer, as well.

The authors decided to construct a complex economic model containing many input variables characterized by different ranges and different distributions types, then explain it in details, so who is interested, can get a clear understanding how to construct probabilistic economic model.

This section is containing the step by step explanation about how to construct such model in Excel and the results of a probabilistic run using Oracle Crystal Ball.

Therefore, in what follows will be detailed the economic model with all the inputs and step-by-step calculations. It was simulated a possible solution for developing an oil field with 29 producing wells and 18 water injection wells with a forecast of 12 years. The simulation was carried on in ECLIPSE™ simulator.

The simulation model is based on a real case, designed and adapted for academic purposes.

In Figure 1 it can be observed the field performance. The rates are expressed in thousands (stbo/d or Mscf/d).

Figure 1. Field Performance

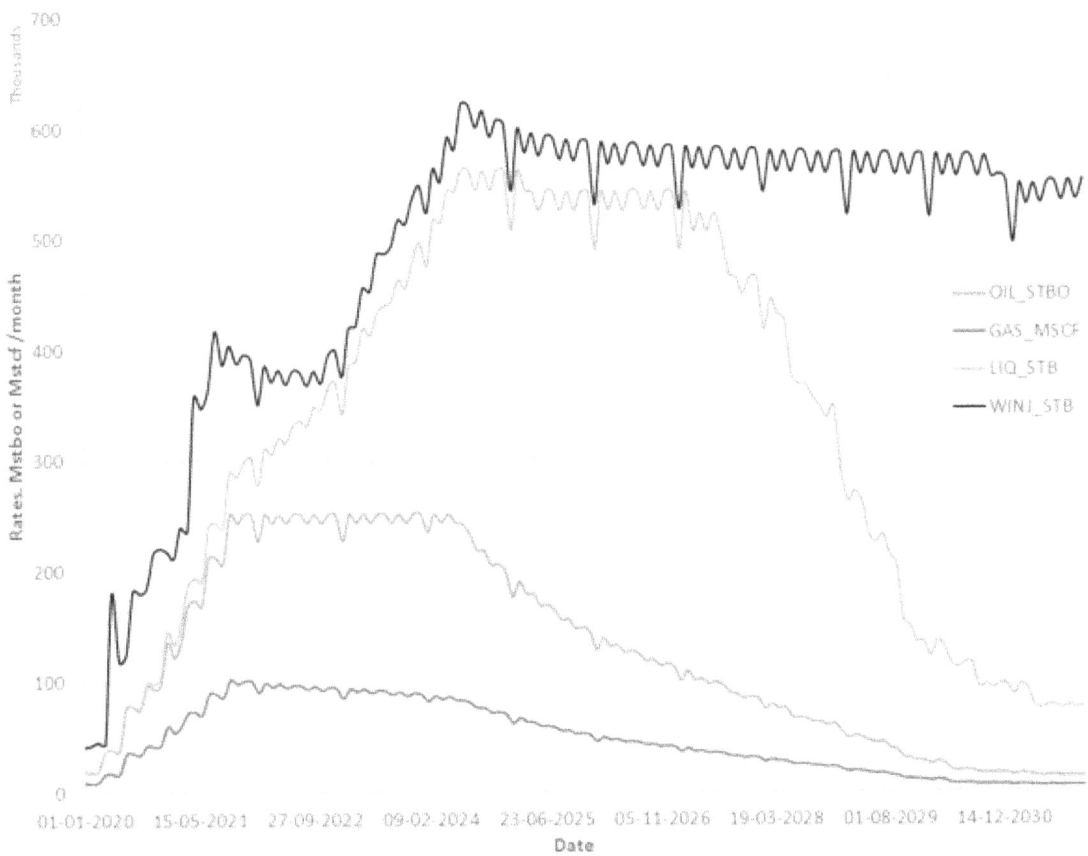

The economic model developed by the authors, it is based on the very well-known *Discounted Cash Flow*, adapted to consider the uncertainties and risks enumerated in the introductory section of this chapter and to run probabilistic calculations.

Depending on number of introduced variables, the model can be from the less complex to the very complex. Complexity is important but it is coming with a price; the increased resources to be utilized in terms of computing power, time, design, implement and debug large and complex models. On the other hand, a very complex model, with many variables, does not necessarily helps to understand which are the main variables that are influencing the output parameters.

In this case, the model was kept to a relative medium to low complexity. The focus was to develop a model that can be easily explained, document and understood, and as a result, would be utilized as starting platform for other economic models.

Other aspects that authors would like to highlight are:

- this is a generic economic model, where the tax calculation formulas differ from country to country, system to system;
- costs and prices are indicative and realistic, but should be treated as examples;
- the selected distributions of all variables were selected based on authors experience and should be treated as examples. They can be easily changed in other circumstances;
- CAPEX and OPEX can be much further detailed than are detailed at a much further extent. In any case, these two parameters, OPEX and CAPEX, are subject to the specific case that is analyzed. Authors intended to implement some realistic numbers based on their exposure to oil and gas industry.

The following tables are presenting the assumptions and input variables and the forecast variables, as well. Some of the forecast variables are embedded in Table 1, for practical reasons.

Table 1. Table with Input Variables and associated Distribution Settings

Various Parameters	Value / Start Value	Unit	Distribution Settings			
			Min.	Most Likely	Max.	Distribution Type
General Settings						
Start date	01-01-2020					
End date	01-01-2032					
WCT triggering ESP (WCT)	50%		45%		60%	Uniform
Equipment's price increase (EI)	6%	per annum	5%		10%	Uniform
Costs and Selling Prices						
Oil price (OP)	60	USD/stbo	30		90	Uniform
Gas price (GP)	2	USD/Mscf	1.5		4	Uniform
Liquid separation cost (ULSC)	0.556	USD/stb	0.243		0.745	Uniform
Water injected cost (UWIC)	0.7949	USD/stb	0.64		1.28	Uniform
Yearly prices increase (YPI)	3%	USD	2%		5%	Uniform
Field cost (OPEX) (FOPEX)	500,000	USD/mnth	400,000		600,000	Uniform
Drilling Related Data						
Drilling time	42	days	30	42	55	Triangular
Daily rig cost	40,000	USD/day	35,000	40,000	55,000	Triangular
Drilling delays related to (Risks)						
Drilling Rig Failures	0	days	0		5	Uniform
Materials Delays	0	days	0		5	Uniform
Drilling Problems	0	days	0		4	Uniform

continued on following page

Table 1. Continued

Various Parameters	Value / Start Value	Unit	Distribution Settings			
			Min.	Most Likely	Max.	Distribution Type
Total days	48					Forecast param
Well cost (CAPEX) (TWC)	1,680,000	USD				Forecast param
Well depreciation time (WDT)	12	months	8		16	Uniform
Production (Risk)						
Rates uncertainty	1		0.85	1	1.3	Triangular
ESP (Electro-Submersible Pumps)						
ESP Cost	550,000	USD	450,000		650,000	Uniform
Installation frequency	12	months	10		16	Uniform
ESP depreciation time (1/2 ESP lifespan)	6	months				
Installation cost per day	15,000	USD/day	10,000		20,000	Uniform
Installation days	1	day	1		3	Uniform
Installation cost	15,000					Forecast param
Total ESP cost (CAPEX)	565,000	USD				Forecast param
Taxes						
Royalty (ROYT)	15%					
Ad-Valorem (ADVT)	2%					
Production tax (PRDT)	4.60%					
Depletion tax (DEPT)	10%					
Taxation (TAX)	16%					
Investments						
Surface facilities (CAPEX) (SFC)	100,000,000	USD				
Depreciation of Surface Facilities (DSFT)	48	months				
Discount Factor (DFA)	3%	annual	2%		7%	Uniform
Discount Factor Monthly (DFM)	0.00246627	monthly				

The following paragraphs will explain some of the contents of the Table 1.

- *Start date* and *End date* are representing the time frame of the field production forecast;
- *WCT triggering ESPs* is the water cut (WCT) value that the well will require installation of an artificial lift system; in the present case, the ESP (electro-submersible pump);
- *Equipment's price inflation* represents the estimated yearly price increase for any needed equipment (drilling and completion materials);
- *Field Cost* it is an estimated cost to run the field. It is containing all the cash (personnel, utilities, cars, etc) and some of production related costs. The separation and injection costs are calculated separately. This is estimated and can be subject of sensitivity analysis;

- *Yearly prices increase* refers to selling prices and costs increases on yearly base;
- *Drilling time* and *Drilling rig cost* are also taking care of materials and costs of any materials (casing, tubing, etc), operations (cementing and cement bond test), logs and tests needed for a well. The values are subject of sensitivity analysis;
- *Drilling delays related to (Risks)* contains some of the drilling associated risks, defined as time, and converted in money;
- *Well cost* – final cost of a well ready to run
- *Well depreciation time* – represent the time that well cost is recovered;
- *Rates uncertainty* is a variable that is containing the risk of getting a certain field production. All the rates (oil, water, liquid, gas and water injection) are adjusted simultaneously with this variable. It is a way to model the uncertainties related to reservoir properties, chances of success of a well, probability to obtain the estimated flow rate, etc.;
- *ESP installation frequency* has two objectives: to replace the pump periodically and to take in consideration any failures that can lead to lose the well during intervention. It is assumed that there are pump failures periodically and pump must be replaced. Another parameter that is considered is the risk to lose the well due to accidents while well is intervened. This variable is in another table.
- *Taxes* – all the taxes are generic taxes and they are depending from country to country, as pet the law and decrees specific to any country, moment in time, etc. They can be further break down in smaller components. The ones in this model are taxes applied in general. Percentages are subject of change, too.
- *Surface facility (CAPEX)* – represents the cost of all surface facilities (gathering centers, tanks, pipes, buildings, infrastructure, etc.) needed to run the field. It is a rough estimation that depends on the size of the field, field production, etc. It is considered as an upfront investment prior development of the field. It can be used as uncertainty variable, too.
- *Discount factor* – future value of money

Table 2 is showing the results for the forecast variables; given as an example.

Table 2. Table with Forecast Variables

Economic Indicators			
Pay Out Time - POT	69	months	Forecast parameter
Internal Rate of Return - IRR	10%	%/year	Forecast parameter
Business Length	11	years	Forecast parameter
SUM_DCF	77	mil. USD	Forecast parameter
Profit-Investment Ratio - PI	1.147		Forecast parameter
Total Taxes	364	mil. USD	Forecast parameter
Total Profit Tax	80	mil. USD	Forecast parameter
Total CAPEX	261	mil. USD	Forecast parameter
Total OPEX	178	mil. USD	Forecast parameter

Table 3 is showing the percentiles for the main input variables, with emphasis to the P50 values, according to the defined distributions (see the next pages due to the huge amount of data).

The following paragraphs will be explained some of the contents of the Table 2.

- *Pay Out Time – POT* represents the time (number of months or years) when the business is becoming profitable.
- *Internal Rate of Return – IRR* represents the discount factor that, at the end of forecast timeframe the Net Present Value (NPV) is zero. This parameter is showing the profitability of a business.
- *SUM_DCF* (*Cumulative of Discounted Cash Flow*) and represents the profit generated by the business at a given time that can be end of the forecast timeframe or any moment in time.
- *Business Length* represents the number of years until the business become unprofitable. It corresponds to the previous year when yearly NCF (*Net Cash Flow*) become negative. Although the forecast is performed for 12 years, some combinations can lead to negative NCF close to the end of the forecast timeframe. In this case it becomes irrelevant to continue a business that becomes unprofitable. The IRR also becomes irrelevant. And must be evaluated only for the beginning until the end of business.
- *Profit-Investment Ratio – PI* represents another indicator of the profitability of a business. I can be explained in other words "how many dollars (or other currency) is generating one invested dollar (or other currency)?". A profitable business must have a PI higher than unity (1). In the case of PI lower than unity, the business is losing money instead of generating money and must be discarded.
- *Total Taxes* and *Total Profit Tax* represent the taxes that are collected by the state where the business is conducted.

Then next section contains the mathematical model that *Discounted Cash Flow (DCF)* method is based on. The DCF method is organized as a table where each column represents an input parameter or a calculated variable as a function of time. Each of the following variables detailed below represent a column in the table. The column-based calculation is very advantageous because can be implemented in MS Excel or other similar worksheet-based software.

Column 1: Date

Date is starting from 01-01-2020 and it is ending at 01-12-2031, every month. All the monthly rates as inputs corresponding to a given month is referenced at 1st of the month; thus, any calculations corresponding to a month is referenced at 1st of the month. Any calculation implying years, are referenced at 1st January of the corresponding year. The NPV (*Net Present Value*) needed to calculate IRR on yearly basis is assigned to 1st of January. Example NPV of 2022 is assigned at 01-01-2022.

Column 2: Month

This column represents the number of months starting from start date (01-01-2020) and start with 1.

Column 3: Year

For each line of the table it is calculated the number of years passed from the start date. The counting starts at 0; thus 2020 represents year 0.

Column 4: Coefficient of yearly price increase of equipment (YPIE)

$$YPIE = \left(1 + EI\right)^{year} \tag{1}$$

where: *EI* represents *Equipment's price increase (EI)* from Table 1, section *General Settings;year* represents variable from Column 3.

Table 3. Table with percentile for the main input variables

Percentile	WCT trig. Inst. of ESPs	Equipment price inflation	Oil price	Gas price	Liquid sep. price	Injected water	Yearly prices increase	Field Cost (OPEX)	Drilling time	Daily rig cost	Drilling Rig Failures	Materials Delays	Drilling Problems	Well depreciation	Rates uncertainty	ESP Cost	Installation cost per day	Installation days	Discount Factor
		per annum	USD / stbo	USD/ Mstcf	USD/ stb	USD/ stb	USD/ UNIT	Th USD/ month	days	Th USD/ day	days	days	days	months		Th USD	Th USD/ day	day	
P100	45%	5%	30	1.5	0.24	0.64	2%	400	30	35	0	0.0	0	8.0	0.85	450	10	1.0	2%
P90	47%	6%	36	1.75	0.29	0.70	2%	420	35	38	1	0.5	0.4	8.8	0.93	470	11	1.2	3%
P80	48%	6%	42	2.00	0.33	0.76	3%	440	38	39	1	1.0	0.8	9.6	0.97	490	12	1.4	3%
P70	50%	7%	48	2.25	0.38	0.83	3%	460	39	41	2	1.5	1.2	10.4	0.99	510	13	1.6	4%
P60	51%	7%	54	2.50	0.43	0.89	3%	480	41	42	2	2.0	1.6	11.2	1.02	530	14	1.8	4%
P50	**53%**	**8%**	**60**	**2.75**	**0.48**	**0.96**	**4%**	**500**	**42**	**43**	**3**	**2.5**	**2**	**12.0**	**1.04**	**550**	**15**	**2.0**	**5%**
P40	54%	8%	66	3.00	0.52	1.02	4%	520	44	44	3	3.0	2.4	12.8	1.07	570	16	2.2	5%
P30	56%	9%	72	3.25	0.57	1.09	4%	540	45	45	4	3.5	2.8	13.6	1.10	590	17	2.4	6%
P20	57%	9%	78	3.5	0.62	1.15	4%	560	47	47	4	4.0	3.2	14.4	1.14	610	18	2.6	6%
P10	59%	10%	84	3.75	0.67	1.22	5%	580	49	50	5	4.5	3.6	15.2	1.18	630	19	2.8	7%
P0	60%	10%	90	4.00	0.72	1.28	5%	600	55	55	5	5.0	4	16.0	1.30	650	20	3.0	7%

Column 5: Coefficient of yearly prices and costs increase (YPCI)

$$YPCI = \left(1 + YPI\right)^{year} \tag{2}$$

where: *YPI* represents *Yearly prices increase (YPI)* from Table 1, section *Costs and Selling Prices;* and *year* represents variable from Column 3.

Column 6: Oil

This column represents the sold monthly oil production. It is expressed in stbo/month.

Column 7: Gas

This column represents the monthly gas production for sale. It is assumed that all produced gas is sold and nothing is kept for internal consumption. This can be modified and it can be discounted a fraction or the production to be used for internal consumption. This can be done if proves profitable to construct a power plant where gas is converted in electricity. It is expressed in Mscf/month.

Column 8: Liquid

This column represents the monthly produced liquid. It is expressed in stb/month.

Column 9: Water Injected

This column represents the monthly injected water. It is expressed in stb/month.

Column 10: Liquid Separation Cost, LSC

$$LSC = Q_{liq} \bullet ULSP \bullet YPCI \tag{3}$$

where: Q_{liq} is monthly liquid produced;
ULSP is *Liquid separation cost (ULSC)* from Table 1, section *Costs and Selling Prices;*
YPCI is column 5.

Column 11: Water Injection Cost, WIC

$$WIC = Q_{wi} \bullet UWIC \bullet YPCI \tag{4}$$

where: Q_{wi} is monthly injected water;
UWIC is *Water injected cost (UWIC)* from Table 1, section *Costs and Selling Prices;*
YPCI is column 5.

Column 12: Surface Facility CAPEX

Represents *Surface facilities (CAPEX) (SFC)* from Table 1, section *Investments.*
This value is assigned to line that virtually corresponds to month zero or, in other words, to the previous month before start date and must be *negative*. In our case should be assigned to virtual date 01-12-2019. This date should not be added as date.

Column 13: Wells CAPEX

The wells are not drilled all at once. They are drilled in sequence in order to meet the field oil production target. Form the simulation results it is identified the start of the well, and subsequently is calculated the drilling date by subtracting the total number of drilling days. Corresponding to this date, it is calculated the cost of the well, adjusted in time.

$$WELL\_CAPEX = TWC \bullet YPIE \quad (5)$$

where: *TWC* is *Well cost (CAPEX) (TWC)* from Table 1, section *Drilling Related Data;* and *YPIE* represents the content of column 4.

The WELL_CAPEX is advisable to be calculated into a separate worksheet. This is to maintain a certain structure and housekeeping of the project. Finally, the CAPEX of all 28 producer and 18 injector wells will be summed together. Similarly, as was done for in the case of *Surface Facility CAPEX* (column 12), this sum will be assigned to a date prior one month to the start date.

Column 14: ESP CAPEX

The electro-submersible pumps (ESP) require a special handling which is challenging in Excel. For this calculation, is utilized a separate worksheet.

Each well, if is producing, from the moment when well's water cut reaches the *WCT triggering ESP (WCT)*, from Table 1, section *General Settings*, it will require installation of a new ESP with the periodicity defined at *Installation frequency* from Table 1, section *ESP* until the end of production of the well. The total ESP cost must be adjusted with *Coefficient of yearly price increase of equipment (YPIE)* calculated with formula 1, in column 4. The calculation formula for each installation is similar with the formula 5.

$$ESP\_CAPEX = TESPC \bullet YPIE \quad (6)$$

where: *TESPC* is *Total ESP cost (CAPEX)* from Table 1, section *ESP*; and *YPIE* represents the content of column 4.

The authors added as associated risk to lose the well due to total fatal failures of interventions. Generally, the wells are intervened for the following:

- water / high GOR shutoffs with surgical closure of perforations or total closure and re-perforations of newly designated intervals;
- adding new perforations to existing ones;
- stimulations (acidizing, fracturing, acid-frac etc);
- reparation of damaged casing;
- tubing cleaning and scales or paraffin removal;
- others.

First two operations are automated in the ECLIPSE simulator and are difficult to trace. Obtaining the closure or opening of a connection triggered by internal events of ECLIPSE is very challenging. Such changes are reported in the PRT file, but it is a tedious work to get the date when such events are occurring.

Stimulations can be triggered only manually, but it requires many runs and a deep study and understanding what is exactly happening in the simulation.

Repairing of a damaged casing and tubing cleaning are the kind of operations that are difficult to account to. They can be added if there is a properly monitoring of such type of operation throughout history of the field or similar fields.

In order to account to fatal failures of the wells, the authors consider that there is a probability to fail after a number of operations. The distribution is uniform defined from 0 to maximum number of installations. From the moment of failure onward, the well's production is discarded.

The total ESP CAPEX is calculated as sum of all the valid ESP installations for each well individually. The total ESP CAPEX that is accounted in column 14 is calculated as sum of all ESP CAPEX from all the wells and the result with sign changed (from positive to negative) will be assigned to a date prior with one month from the start date.

Comment valid for both columns 13 and 14: Normally these CAPEXs (WELL and ESP) should be assigned at the respective dates. The model has this option and it easy to change from defining all the CAPEXEs at the beginning or whenever the wells are drilled and ESP are to be installed. The decision to move it at the month zero (one month before start date) is to be able to properly calculate the *Internal Rate of Return*.

Column 15: Total CAPEX, CAPT

Total CAPEX is the sum of values in columns 13, 14 and 15. This value is assigned to month 0, as the rest of the CAPEXs are assigned.

Column 16: Net Income, NINC

$$NINC = (OIL \cdot OP + GAS \cdot GP) \cdot YPCI \tag{7}$$

where: *OIL* is the content of column 6;

GAS is the content of column 7;

OP and *GP* are the oil and respectively gas prices, *Oil price (OP)* and *Gas price (GP)* from Table 1, section *Costs and Selling Prices*;

YPCI is the content of column 5.

Column 17: Royalty, ROY

$$ROY = NINC \cdot ROYT \tag{8}$$

where: *NINC* is the Net Income, calculated in column 16, with formula 7;

ROYT is the *Royalty (ROYT)* line from Table 1, section *Taxes*

Column 18: Ad-Valorem Tax, ADV

$$ADV = NINC \cdot ADVT \tag{9}$$

where: *NINC* is the Net Income, calculated in column 16, with formula 7;
ADVT is the *Ad-Valorem (ADVT)* from Table 1, section *Taxes.*

Column 19: Production Tax, PRD

$$PRD = NINC \cdot PRDT \tag{10}$$

where: *NINC* is the Net Income, calculated in column 16, with formula 7;
PRDT is the *Production Tax (PRDT)* from Table 1, section *Taxes.*

Column 20: Field Operation Cost, FOPC

$$FOPC = FOPEX \cdot YPCI \tag{11}$$

where: *FOPEX* is *Field cost (OPEX) (FOPEX)* from Table 1, section *Costs and Selling Prices*;
YPCI represents the content of column 5, calculated with formula 2.

Column 21: OPEX

$$OPEX = FOPC + LSC + WIC \tag{12}$$

where: *FOPC* is the content of column 20, calculated with formula 11;
LSC is the content of column 10, calculated with formula 3;
WIC is the content of column 11, calculated with formula 4.

Column 22: Total Expenses, TEXP

$$TEXP = OPEX + ROY + ADV + PRD \tag{13}$$

where: *OPEX* is the content of column 20, calculated with formula 12;
ROY is the content of column 17, calculated with formula 8;
ADV is the content of column 18, calculated with formula 9;
PRD is the content of column 19, calculated with formula 10.

Column 23: Net Income Before Tax, NIBT

$$NIBT = NINC - TEXP \quad (14)$$

where: *NINC* is the content of column 16, calculated with formula 7;
TEXP is the content of column 22, calculated with formula 13.

Column 24: Depletion Tax, DEP

$$DEP = NIBT \cdot DEPT \quad (15)$$

where: *NIBT* is the content of column 23, calculated with formula 14;
DEPT is *Depletion tax (DEPT)* line from Table 1, section *Taxes*.

Depreciation / Return of Investment (ROI)

There are two distinct methods to calculate depreciation (ROI): straight line and accelerated. Straight line depreciation is calculated by dividing the CAPEX to number of months or years and each unit of time (month or year), resulting the depreciation value.

The accelerated method consists in higher depreciation values at the beginning and they are progressively reduced towards the end of depreciation timeframe. One method is known as the SYD (Sum of the Year Digits), and the depreciation in the current model the authors were utilizing this method. In economic calculations it is recommended to utilize the accelerated depreciation methods. They are helping the business at the beginning by reducing the taxes to be paid.

Excel has built-in the Sum of the Year Digits method which is called SYD.

Column 25: Surface Facility Depreciation, DEPRSF

The SYD function must be feed with:

- CAPEX;
- the desired number of months or years for depreciation;
- residual value.

Number of months, in this case, was defined at *Depreciation of Surface Facilities (DSFT)* from Table 1, section *Investment*.

Residual Value was set to 0. There is no plan to sell the surface facilities at depreciation end.

Column 26: Wells' depreciation, DEPRW

The calculation of wells' depletion should be performed into a separate worksheet.

The workflow is, as follows:

- it is identified the first month of production or injection;

- from that index onward until the end of the number of months (years) of depreciation it is calculated the depreciation with SYD function;
- in the same way are calculated depreciations for all the wells;
- for each month (year) are summed together all the depreciations;
- column 26 is populated with sums of depreciations.

The Excel SYD function must be fed with the following:

- CAPEX – is the CAPEX (value of the well) – see column 13 comments;
- number of months is pointing *Well depreciation time (WDT)* from Table 1, section *Drilling Related Data*;
- residual value set to zero.

Column 27: ESPs' Depreciation, DEPRESP

The procedure is similar with the one corresponding to *Wells' Depreciation*, with the amendment that instead of being performed only once, it is performed as many times as the ESPs are installed and the well is not suffering a fatal failure and is lost. Like for the case of *Wells' Depreciation*, the calculations are executed into a separate worksheet.

The workflow is, as follows:

- there are identified the first months when an ESPs are installed successfully;
- from that index onward until the end of the number of months of depreciation it is calculated the depreciation with SYD function and subsequently for all valid ESP installations;
- in the same way are calculated ESPs depreciations for all the wells;
- for each month (year) are summed together all the depreciations;
- column 27 is populated with sums of depreciations.

The Excel SYD function must be fed with the following:

- CAPEX – is the CAPEX (value of the ESP) – see column 14 comments;
- number of months is pointing *ESP depreciation time (1/2 ESP lifespan)* from Table 1, section *ESP*;
- residual value set to zero.

Column 28: Total Depreciation, DEPRT

$$DEPRT = DEPRSF + DEPRW + DEPRESP \quad (16)$$

where: *DEPRSF* is the content of column 25;
DEPRW is the content of column 26;
DEPRESP is the content of column 27.

Column 29: Taxable Income, TINC

$$TINC = NIBT - DEP - DEPRT \tag{17}$$

where *NIBT* – is the content of column 23, calculated with formula 14,
DEP is the content of column 24, calculated with formula 15;
DEPRT is the content column 28, calculated with formula 16.

Column 30: TAXES

$$TAXES = \begin{cases} TINC \bullet TAX, & TINC > 0 \\ 0 & TINC \leq 0 \end{cases} \tag{18}$$

where: *TINC* is the content of column 29, calculated with formula 17;
TAX is *Taxation (TAX)* from Table 1, section *Taxes*

Column 31: Net Income After Tax, NIAT

$$NIAT = TINC - TAXES \tag{19}$$

where: *TINC* is the content of column 29, calculated with formula 17;
TAXES is the content of column 30, calculated with formula 18.

Column 32: Net Cash Flow, NCF

$$NCF = NIAT - CAPT \tag{20}$$

where: *NIAT* is the content of column 31, calculated with formula 19;
CAPT is the content of column 15.

Column 33: Cumulative of Net Cash Flow, SUM_NCF

On the line corresponding to month zero, it is assigned the value of *Total CAPEX*, from column 15.

$$SUM\_NCF_i = SUM\_NCF_{i-1} + NCF_i \tag{21}$$

where: *NCF* is the content of column 32, calculated with formula 20;
index *i* correspond to month and has value from 1 to last month in the array.

Column 34: Discount factor, DISCF

$$DISCF = (1 + DFM)^{(1-MNT)} \tag{22}$$

while

$$DFM = (1 + DFA)^{1/12} - 1 \tag{23}$$

where: *DFM* is the *Discount Factor Monthly (DFM)* from Table 1, section *Investments* and it is calculated with formula 23;

DFA is the *Discount Factor Annual (DFA)* from Table 1, section *Investments*;

MNT is the month, content of column 2.

Column 35: Discounted Cash Flow, DCF

$$DCF = NCF \bullet DISCF \tag{24}$$

where: *NCF* is the content of column 33, calculated with formula 20;

DISCF is the content of column 34, calculated with formula 22.

Column 36: Cumulative of Discounted Cash Flow, SUM_DCF

The algorithm is very similar with the one used for calculating *Cumulative of Net Cash Flow* in column 33. On the line corresponding to month zero, it is assigned the value of *Total CAPEX*, from column 15.

$$SUM\_DCF_i = SUM\_DCF_{i-1} + DCF_i \tag{25}$$

where: *DCF* is the content of column 35, calculated with formula 24;

index *i* correspond to month and has value from 1 to last month in the array.

Column 37: Yearly Net Cash Flow, YNCF

The Yearly Net Cash Flow is used for calculating the IRR. It is calculated by summing the NCF values corresponding to months January to December of the same year and it is assigned to 1st of January every year.

Forecast variables – Discussions and how to calculate them

Pay Out Time

The Pay Out Time (POT) represents the number of the months or years counted from the beginning which are negative *Discounted Cash Flow* plus one.

Internal Rate of Return, IRR

The calculation of IRR may be inaccurate if there are several consecutive negative NCF values, then NCF turns positive, and close to the end of the evaluation time NCF is turning again negative. To avoid a case like this is what should be done: transform Table 4 into Table 5. The IRR is calculated by using the Excel built in function.

Table 4. Initial Yearly Net Cash Flow

Index	Year	Date	Yearly NCF mil USD
1	2019	01-01-2019	-260.885
2	2020	01-01-2020	-34.104
3	2021	01-01-2021	34.451
4	2022	01-01-2022	83.974
5	2023	01-01-2023	82.310
6	2024	01-01-2024	82.295
7	2025	01-01-2025	60.409
8	2026	01-01-2026	39.423
9	2027	01-01-2027	23.432
10	2028	01-01-2028	11.785
11	2029	01-01-2029	3.119
12	2030	01-01-2030	-5.049
13	2031	01-01-2031	-4.438

Table 5. The modified table with yearly NCF suitable to properly evaluate IRR

Old Index	New Index	Yearly NCF mil USD
2	1	-294.989
3	2	34.451
4	3	83.974
5	4	82.310
6	5	82.295
7	6	60.409
8	7	39.423
9	8	23.432
10	9	11.785
11	10	3.119

Table 5, based on table 4, must have first lines with negative NCF summed in one line and from first negative NCF after a line with positive NCF should be discarded.

Business Length

By business length, expressed in years, represents number of years, counted from the beginning until first encountered year with negative yearly NCF.

Profit Investment Ratio

The profit investment ratio is calculated as the ratio of profit (Cumulative of Discounted Cash Flow) and total CAPEX (as absolute value) plus 1.

$$PI = \frac{SUM\_DCF_i}{CAPT} + 1 \tag{26}$$

where: SUM_DCF_i is the cumulative of *Discounted Cash Flow* at the end of business;
CAPT is the total CAPEX.

Total Taxes

The Total Taxes are the sum of all the taxes Royalty, Ad-Valorem Tax, Production Tax and Depletion Tax. These are the values corresponding to columns: 17, 18, 19 and 24.

Total Profit Taxes

It represents the sum of all the elements from column 30.

Total CAPEX

The Total CAPEX is important in order to understand how much money are spent to develop the field.

Total OPEX

The Total OPEX is important in order to understand how much money are spent to run the field.

RESULTS

There were defined 77 assumptions (variables) and 12 forecast variables and the forecast variables are tabbed with highlighting of the most likely value (P50). The number of Monte Carlo performed trials were 10,000 runs to maintain a reasonable run time, less than 10 minutes, on a high-end mobile workstation. The following tables contain the results obtained in the simulation.

Table 6. Run information

Run preferences:	Number of trials run	10,000
	Confidence level	95.00%
Run statistics:	Total running time (sec)	393.65
	Trials/second (average)	25
	Random numbers per sec	1,905
Crystal Ball data:	Assumptions	77
	Decision variables	0
	Forecasts	12

Table 7 Result of the run

Percentiles	Pay Out Time (POT)	Internal Rate of Return	Business Length	Profit at end of the business (SUM_ DCF)	Profit-Investment Ratio (PI)	Total Taxes	Total Taxes on Profit	Total Well Cost	Total ESP Cost	Total CAPEX	Total OPEX	Total Drilling Days
	months		years	mil USD		mil USD	mil USD	mil USD	thousand USD	mil USD	mil USD	
P100	34	-96%	3	-386	0.332	50	6	1.249	462	185	130	33
P90	47	-27%	8	-213	0.566	180	25	1.739	500	223	166	42
P80	52	-16%	8	-153	0.686	216	35	1.857	520	230	176	44
P70	58	-5%	9	-94	0.807	252	46	1.951	540	235	184	46
P60	66	1%	9	-38	0.923	288	58	2.034	560	239	191	48
P50	**87**	**7%**	**9**	**19**	**1.038**	**323**	**70**	**2.113**	**581**	**244**	**197**	**49**
P40	145	12%	10	76	1.155	358	82	2.198	601	248	204	51
P30	145	18%	10	132	1.272	391	94	2.287	621	253	212	52
P20	145	23%	10	191	1.393	428	106	2.400	641	259	221	54
P10	145	30%	11	263	1.547	471	122	2.569	660	267	233	57
P0	145	57%	12	579	2.277	653	185	3.331	703	309	293	66

In a first table (Table 6) are presented the simulation run information.

The next table, table 7, synthesizes the results of the run for the twelve forecast variables for all deciles, with emphasize on P50 results.

The results of the run for the twelve forecast variables can be observed in table 7.

Table 8 is containing the most likely values (P50 case) for the 12 forecast variables.

One of the advantages of having a probabilistic model to evaluate a, in this case, a business case, is that there can be obtained two parameters *Contribution to Variation* and *Rank Correlation.*

Table 8 The most likely values (P50 case) for the 12 forecast variables

No	Forecast Variable	Value	Unit
1	Pay Out Time (POT)	87	months
2	Internal Rate of Return	7%	
3	Business Length	9	years
4	Discounted profit at end of the business (SUM_DCF)	19	mil USD
5	Profit-Investment Ratio (PI)	1.038	
6	Total Taxes	323	mil USD
7	Total Taxes on Profit	70	mil USD
8	Total Well Cost	2,113	mil USD
9	Total ESP Cost	581	thousands USD
10	Total CAPEX	244	mil USD
11	Total OPEX	197	mil USD
12	Total Drilling Days	49.3	days

Contribution to Variance

It is a parameter that records the contribution to variation of R^2 of one forecast variable that is given by each of the input variables (assumptions). The values are between 0 and 1. Values closed to 1 means that the respective input variable has a higher influence in changing the forecast parameter; or, in other words, the forecast parameter is sensitive to variation of input parameters. The values close to 0 means no impact.

Table 9. Results of the main influencing parameters

Assumptions	Contribution to Variance	Rank Correlation
Sensitivity: Pay Out Time		
Oil price	88.26%	-0.888
Rates uncertainty	6.15%	-0.234
Drilling time	1.42%	0.113
Sensitivity: Internal Rate of Return		
Oil price	89.03%	0.942
Rates uncertainty	6.06%	0.246
Drilling time	1.21%	-0.11
Sensitivity: Business Length		
Oil price	78.69%	0.737
WCT triggering installation of ESPs	5.79%	0.2
Injected water	4.28%	-0.172
Rates uncertainty	1.71%	0.109

continued on following page

Table 9. Continued

Assumptions	Contribution to Variance	Rank Correlation
Sensitivity: Profit at end of the business (SUM_DCF)		
Oil price	88.46%	0.938
Rates uncertainty	5.87%	0.242
Drilling time	1.11%	-0.105
Sensitivity: Profit-Investment Ratio (PI)		
Oil price	88.38%	0.938
Rates uncertainty	5.82%	0.241
Drilling time	1.17%	-0.108
Sensitivity: Total Taxes		
Oil price	91.16%	0.948
Rates uncertainty	6.76%	0.258
Sensitivity: Total Taxes on Profit		
Oil price	91.27%	0.953
Rates uncertainty	6.16%	0.248
Yearly prices increase	0.48%	0.069
Sensitivity: Total Well Cost		
Drilling time	48.71%	0.687
Daily rig cost	40.67%	0.627
Drilling Rig Failures	3.86%	0.193
Materials Delays	3.51%	0.184
Drilling Problems	2.36%	0.151
Sensitivity: Total ESP Cost		
ESP Cost	96.09%	0.985
Installation days	2.28%	0.152
Sensitivity: Total CAPEX		
Drilling time	37.10%	0.603
Daily rig cost	30.28%	0.545
ESP Cost	6.46%	0.252
Drilling Rig Failures	2.90%	0.169
Materials Delays	2.73%	0.164
Sensitivity: Total OPEX		
Injected water	48.22%	0.675
Field Cost (OPEX)	15.26%	0.379
Yearly prices increase	14.88%	0.375
Rates uncertainty	14.33%	0.368
Liquid separation price	6.38%	0.245

continued on following page

Table 9. Continued

Assumptions	Contribution to Variance	Rank Correlation
Sensitivity: Total Drilling Days		
Drilling time	83.07%	0.907
Drilling Rig Failures	6.42%	0.252
Materials Delays	5.97%	0.243
Drilling Problems	3.68%	0.191

Rank Correlation

Table 10. Most influencing Input Variables to forecast parameters

No	Sensitivity Parameter	Assumption Input variable	Contribution To Variance	Rank Correlation
1	Pay Out Time (POT)	Oil price	88.26%	-0.888
2	Internal Rate of Return	Oil price	89.03%	0.942
3	Business Length	Oil price	78.69%	0.737
4	Profit at end of the business (SUM_DCF)	Oil price	88.46%	0.938
5	Profit-Investment Ratio (PI)	Oil price	88.38%	0.938
6	Total Taxes	Oil price	91.16%	0.948
7	Total Taxes on Profit	Oil price	91.27%	0.953
8	Total Well Cost	Drilling time	48.71%	0.687
		Daily rig cost	40.67%	0.627
9	Total ESP Cost	ESP Cost	96.09%	0.985
10	Total CAPEX	Drilling time	37.10%	0.603
		Daily rig cost	30.28%	0.545
		ESP Cost	6.46%	0.252
11	Total OPEX	Injected water	48.22%	0.675
		Field Cost (OPEX)	15.26%	0.379
		Yearly prices increase	14.88%	0.375
		Rates uncertainty	14.33%	0.368
12	Total Drilling Days	Drilling time	83.07%	0.907

The *Rank Correlation* is a parameter that is indicating how the variation of one input variable is influencing the variation of a forecast parameter. *Rank Correlation* has values between -1 and 1.

The values close to 0 means that there is no correlation between the input variable and forecast parameters.

Values close to 1, it means that the variations of input parameters are having same impact to forecast parameters. Example: if the input parameters have high variation (as increase) same kind of high variations (as increase) can be observed in forecast parameter. It's like a direct proportionality variation.

If values are close to -1, it means that the variations of input parameters are having opposite impact to forecast parameters. Example: if the input parameters have high variation (as increase) same kind of high variations (as decrease) can be observed in forecast parameter. It's like an inverse proportionality variation.

Table 9 is showing them main influencing input variables to each forecast parameter.

Table 10 is containing top influencing input variables for each forecast parameter.

DISCUSSION

In table 8 are presented the P50 results of the Crystal Ball run. The P50 case is generally considered the *most likely* case; a case that has good chances to happen.

As it was stated in other sections of this chapter, the main goal is to design and implement one economic model to verify the profitability of the development for an oil field using a probabilistic method. This main goal was achieved and the rest of the analysis will be centered to discuss the message given by the numbers associated to the P50 case.

The pay out time is a little above 7 (seven) years which is a slightly long time under the current circumstances in the oil industry. Now-a-days seven years represent a long time to pay off the initial investment, considering the highly dynamic economic world.

On the other hand, an internal rate of return of 7% is higher than any current interest given by any major bank.

The most likely value of the business length is nine (9) years which basically shows that only the last two years of the business are on profit.

The future value of the money at the end of the business is low; nineteen (19) million dollars. Considering the kind of the business that is evaluated here, it represents a small amount. This is backed-up by the low profit investment ratio of 1.038. On other words, it means that each dollar invested is generating supplementary 3.8 cents, which is a very marginal value.

The Taxes (Royalty, Ad-valorem, Depletion and Production tax) represent a respectable value of 323 million USD spanned over nine years. Profit taxes are also seventy (70) million dollars along the nine years of the business.

Regarding the main influencing parameters, the oil price is the highest influencer for the economic parameters. Well cost and CAPEX are mainly influenced proportionally by drilling time and drilling rig cost.

OPEX is manly influenced, in a high proportion, by the water injection cost, total field cost, yearly price increases and uncertainty related to field performance.

These kind of probabilistic economic models are very useful because:

- are providing ranges for the forecast variables instead of single values;
- are flexible in adopting different distributions for the input variables;
- can easily be modified in terms of formulas (adapted to different fiscal models);
- are providing very fast answers

- are very helpful in terms of future strategic decision for the company.

Strictly referring to the current P50% results, the main observation that can be stated is that under the current conditions, the business is risky and marginally profitable, if some measures are not taken that, potentially, can reduce the risks and also to increase the profitability of the business. The following measures can be stated:

- reducing costs without jeopardize the quality of the processes involved
- optimize the learning curve of the drilling process by
    - making sure that materials are always available and having enough stocks to mitigate unexpected situations;
    - reduce the drilling time;
- revise the long term and strategic decisions for the company by
    - considering expansions to other fields and / or joint ventures;
    - involvement in partnerships with a refinery;
    - considering involvement in commercialization of refined products (fuel stations, lubricants, consumer gas, gas distribution networks etc.).

CONCLUSION

The chapter *Quantifying Economic Uncertainties and Risks in Oil and Gas Industry* has provided an insight of how can be performed an economic (business) analysis based on an adapted *Discounted Cash Flow* method by moving to probabilistic calculations.

The whole model's equations and workflow are clearly explained and documented. The distributions and distributions' parameters of the input variables are also clearly documented, as well. The whole chapter itself is designed to be clear enough to be replicated if needed by any petroleum engineer or economist with medium to advanced knowledge.

The authors provided a comprehensive explanation of how to construct such kind of probabilistic models. This model can be adapted to other solution or can be used as is in performing an economic analysis just by changing the input data.

The research consisted in identifying main risks and uncertainties related to oil field development, quantifying them and encode them into a Discounted Cash Flow probabilistic method. The risks and uncertainties were related to:

- Operations
    - Drilling: drilling down-time, delays due to lack of materials;
    - ESP installation;
    - Work over failures.
- Subsurface
    - Possibility to have a dry well or lose the well;
    - Capacity of the well to produce the forecast production.
- Economics
    - Price escalations for materials;

- Price variations (for sold products);
- Installation of artificial lift systems.

As a final product, the two authors created a probabilistic model for the *Discounted Cash Flow* method to assess the economic performance of an oil field developed using water injection.

This model is using results from an Eclipse simulation model (or other sources) and it is easy to modify and adapt to different cases. It is not restricted to one particular case or a particular set of results.

Excel combined with Oracle Crystal Ball engine is providing to the user the needed answers related to understand the economic performance of the field, the main influencers, as well as, an input to mid and long-term company decision strategy.

In fact, the model was designed and implemented in Microsoft Excel using the probabilistic engine by Oracle Crystal Ball considering seventy-seven (77) input parameters and twelve (12) forecast parameters.

FUTURE RESEARCH DIRECTIONS

It is crystal clear that, nowadays, a deterministic evaluation of a business case is no longer an option. The computational power and existing software are good enough to explore areas of uncertainties that were unachievable or a dream not longer than a decade ago.

The current model, with 77 input variables (assumptions) and 12 forecast parameters, running Monte Carlo 10,000 trials, had a runtime of 400 s (~ 7 min). As a future development of this probabilistic economic model, the authors are almost completed the following developments:

- explore options with more input variables (assumptions);
- apply this method to larger fields (larger number of wells);
- add an option of sharing the asset among several stake holders (owners);
- build an interface that feeds the ECLIPSE simulation results directly into the economic model.

REFERENCES

Akins, W. M., Abell, M. P., & Diggins, E. M. (2005, January 1). Enhancing Drilling Risk & Performance Management Through the Use of Probabilistic Time & Cost Estimating. *Society of Petroleum Engineers, SPE/IADC Drilling Conference*. 10.2118/92340-MS

Al-Obaidan, A. M., & Scully, G. W. (1991). Efficiency differences between private and state-owned enterprises in the international petroleum industry. *Applied Economics*, *23*(2), 237–246. doi:10.1080/00036849200000122

Al-Thani, F. F. J., & Merna, T. (2005, January 1). *Risk and Uncertainty Modeling in the Oil and Gas Industry*. Society of Petroleum Engineers, SPE Middle East Oil and Gas Show and Conference. doi:10.2118/93129-MS

Brandimarte, P. (2014). *Handbook in Monte Carlo Simulation. Applications in Financial Engineering, Risk Management and Economics*. John Wiley & Sons, Inc.

Brealey, R., Myers, S., & Allen, F. (2006). *Corporate Finance* (8th ed.). McGraw-Hill Irwin.

Charnes, J. (2012). *Financial Modeling with Crystal Ball and Excel*. John Wiley & Sons, Inc. doi:10.1002/9781119203216

Cheng, C., Wang, Z., Liu, M., & Ren, X.-H. (2019). Risk measurement of international oil and gas projects based on the Value at Risk method. *Petroleum Science*, *16*(1), 199–216. doi:10.100712182-018-0279-1

Cheng, Y., Wang, Y., McVay, D., & Lee, W. J. (2010, April 1). Practical Application of a Probabilistic Approach to Estimate Reserves Using Production Decline Data. *Society of Petroleum Engineers. SPE Economics & Management*, *2*(01), 2010. doi:10.2118/95974-PA

Dalen, D.M., Hoel, M., & Strøm, S. (2008). Kalkulasjonsrenten på lang sikt i en usikker verden. *Samfunnsøkonomen*, 8.

Dickson, D., Slaughter, A. & Mittal, A. (2019, Apr. 23). Succeeding amid uncertainty: A preview of the years ahead. *Deloitte Insights, Collection Decoding the O&G downturn*, 1-6.

Dixit, A. K., & Pindyck, R. S. (1994). Investment under uncertainty. Princeton University Press. doi:10.1515/9781400830176

Fishman, G. (2013). Monte Carlo: Concepts, Algorithms and Applications. Springer Science & Business Media.

Gheorghiu, S., Popescu, C., & Gheorghiu, V. M. (2008). The utilization of Monte Carlo Simulation Method in the oil industry. *Bulletin of the Petroleum-Gas University from Ploiesti, Economics Science Series*, *40*(5C), 1-9.

Glomsrød, S., & Osmundsen, P. P. (Eds.). (2005). *Petroleum industry regulation within stable states. Recent economic analysis of incentives in petroleum production and wealth management. Ashgate Studies in Environmental and Natural Resource Economics 2005*. Ashgate Publishers.

Hatefi, M. A. (2018). Assessment of Risk Factors of a Completed Oil and Gas Project, with the Use of a Hybrid EVM-SAW Method. *Journal of Energy Management and Technology*, *2*(1), 42–53.

Higgins, J. G. (1993). Planning for risk and uncertainty in oil exploration. *Long Range Planning*, *26*(1), 111–122. doi:10.1016/0024-6301(93)90239-C

Jianu, I., & Jianu, I. (2018). The Share Price and Investment: Current Footprints for Future Oil and Gas Industry Performance. *Energies*, *11*(2), 448. doi:10.3390/en11020448

Khadem, M. M. R. K., Piya, S., & Shamsuzzoha, A. (2018). Quantitative risk management in gas injection project: A case study from Oman oil and gas industry. *Journal of Industrial Engineering International*, *14*(3), 637–654. doi:10.100740092-017-0237-3

Kvalevåg, T. (2009, May). *How do discounted cash flow analysis and real options differ as basis for decision making about oil and gas field developments?* (Master thesis). Copenhagen Business School.

Mejean, A., & Hope, C. (2013). Supplying synthetic crude oil from Canadian oil sands: A comparative study of the costs and CO_2 emissions of mining and in situ recovery. *Energy Policy*, *60*, 27–40. doi:10.1016/j.enpol.2013.05.003

Rack, V. (2017, June). *Business model innovation in the oil and gas supply industry* (Master thesis). Nord University.

Ramos, S. B., & Veiga, H. (2011). Risk factors in oil and gas industry returns: International evidence. *Energy Economics*, *33*(3), 525–542. doi:10.1016/j.eneco.2010.10.005

Richardson, J., & Yu, W. (2018). Calculation of estimated ultimate recovery and recovery factors of shale-gas wells using a probabilistic model of original gas in place, *Society of Petroleum Engineers. SPE Reservoir Evaluation & Engineering*, *21*(03), 638–653. Advance online publication. doi:10.2118/189461-PA

Rubinstein, R. Y., & Kroese, D. P. (2016). *Simulation and the Monte Carlo Method* (3rd ed.). John Wiley & Sons, Inc. doi:10.1002/9781118631980

Samawi, H. M. (2017). Improving the Efficiency of the Monte-Carlo Methods Using Ranked Simulated Approach. In Monte-Carlo Simulation-Based Statistical Modeling. Springer Nature Singapore Pte Ltd.

Stevens, P. (2016, May). International Oil Companies: The Death of the Old Business Model. In *The Royal Institute of International Affairs*. London: Chatham House. Retrieved October 25, 2016 from https://www.chathamhouse.org/sites/files/chathamhouse/publications/research/2016-05-05-international-oil-companies-stevens.pdf

Suslick, S. B., Schiozer, D., & Rodriguez, M. R. (2009). Uncertainty and Risk Analysis in Petroleum Exploration and Production. *TERRÆ*, *6*(1), 30–41.

Tanţău, A. D., & Khorshidi, M. (2016). New business models for state companies in the oil industry, *Management & Marketing. Challenges for the Knowledge Society*, *11*(3), 484–497. doi:10.1515/mmcks-2016-0011

Thurber, M., Hults, D., & Heller, P. (2011). Exporting the "Norwegian Model": The effect of administrative design on oil sector performance. *Energy Policy*, *39*(9), 5366–5378. doi:10.1016/j.enpol.2011.05.027

Veit, D., Clemons, E., Benlian, A., Buxmann, P., Hess, T., Kundisch, D., & Spann, M. (2014). Business Models – An Information Systems Research Agenda. *Business & Information Systems Engineering*. Retrieved February 10, 2015 from http://www.wiwi.uniaugsburg.de/de/bwl/veit/lehre/downloads/bm_bise_paper.pdf

Welkenhuysen, K., Rupert, J., Compernolle, T., Ramirez, A., Swennen, R., & Piessens, K. (2017). Considering economic and geological uncertainty in the simulation of realistic investment decisions for CO2-EOR projects in the North Sea. *Applied Energy*, *185*(part 1), 745–761. doi:10.1016/j.apenergy.2016.10.105

Yusuf, Y., Gunasekaran, Y., Musa, A., Dauda, A., Nagham, M., El-Berishy, M., & Cang, S. (2014). A relational study of supply chain agility, competitiveness and business performance in the oil and gas industry. *International Journal of Production Economics*, *147*, 531–543. doi:10.1016/j.ijpe.2012.10.009

Zhang, Z., & Lis, M. (2020). Modeling Green Energy Development Based on Sustainable Economic Growth in China. *Sustainability*, *12*(4), 1368. doi:10.3390u12041368

Zhu, L., Zhang, Z., & Fan, Y. (2015). Overseas oil investment projects under uncertainty: How to make informed decisions? *Journal of Policy Modeling*, *37*(5), 742–762. doi:10.1016/j.jpolmod.2015.08.001

KEY TERMS AND DEFINITIONS

Discounted Cash Flow: Method used to estimate the value of an investment based on its future cash flows.

Economic Model: Set of mathematical equations to describe a theory that is used for quantifying the effects of something on an economy or a company.

Field Development: Exploiting the potential to benefit from the reservoir performance.

Internal Rate of Return (IRR): Discount rate that makes the net present value (NPV) of all cash flows from a project equal to zero.

Net Cash Flow (NCF): Amount of money produced or lost during a period of time by calculating the difference between cash inflows from outflows.

Optimization: The action of making *the best* or most effective use of a situation or resource.

Oracle Crystal Ball: Application used for the risk measurement that is based mainly on the Monte Carlo simulation approach.

Profitability Index (PI): Index that represents the relationship between the costs and benefits of a project.

Reservoir Simulation: The process of mimicking the behavior of fluid flow in a petroleum reservoir system.

Risk: Situation involving exposure to danger and/or loss.

Uncertainty: State of limited knowledge where it is impossible to describe the existing state, a future outcome etc.

Water Injection: Water injected into the oil field in order to increase pressure and stimulate production.

Chapter 9
Risk Behavior, Country Governance, and Bank Stability in Pakistan

Hafiz Waqas Kamran
Iqra University, Pakistan

Abdelnaser Omran
Bright Star University, Libya

ABSTRACT

Keeping risk behavior and country governance in observation, this study has investigated the trends in financial stability for a sample of 22 commercial banks in Pakistan while controlling the effect of economic growth. Over the period of 2007 to 2016, the authors have applied OLS, FE, and RE regression methods to investigate which risk and governance factors are influencing the stability measures of the banks. It is found that financial stability in overall banks is affected by credit risk, operational risk, country risk, and financial crisis risk while control of corruption is also affecting ZROA in an adverse way.

1. INTRODUCTION

From the context of financial markets, banking firms are playing their significant role through provision of credit and cash flows facility. However, since global financial crisis (GFC) of 2007-2009, question of financial stability (FS) for the banks is under the focus of policy makers, researchers, and financial analysts (Acharya & Richardson, 2009; Allen & Gale, 2004). The issue of FS is significantly identified in both developed and emerging economies in recent literature through series of determinants. However, various risk factors as core determinants of FS in both conventional and Islamic banks are under observation. Both types of these banking system are facing various risk factors, affecting their stability. It means that risk and FS are highly associated to each other. The most significant risk factors in banking system are known under the title of liquidity and credit risk, indicating their adverse influence on the banks as specified by(Hassan, Khan, & Paltrinieri, 2019). They further believe that liquidity and credit

DOI: 10.4018/978-1-7998-5083-0.ch009

risk are negatively associated to each other and during the time of financial crisis, both risk factors has affected FS of banks.

In addition, financial institutions are vulnerable towards the operational failures which are in the form of procedural and operational lapses (Allen & Saunders, 2004). Banking system fragility is also affected by operational risk (Barakat & Hussainey, 2013). The reason is that operational hazards reflects the reputational risk for financial firms like banks(Eckert & Gatzert, 2017). The factors of market and country risk are also under significant attention of the reserachers. Increasing volatility in the interest rate is a well-known measure for the market risk (Jorion, 2000). Central banks also use the interest rate to analyze the stability in the economy(Di Giorgio & Rotondi, 2008). At international level, GFC is a well-known category of risk faced by the banks, hampering FS in various financial systems (Avgouleas & Cullen, 2014; Diamond & Kashyap, 2016; Johnson, 2011).

It is believed that the factor of country governance, bank performance and stability measures have their significant association to each other (Ho, Lin, & Tsai, 2016). The objective of this research is to investigate the risk behaviors and country governance as determinants of FS of banks in Pakistan. For a detailed analysis, we have divided overall empirical results into four major categories. The first step is to examine the impact of risk and country governance on two stability measures (ZROA, ZROE). The second phase is to analyze the risk and governance indicators for examining the stability trends in public sector banks. For the third case, only private banks were selected to analyze the impact of risk and governance on their stability profile. In analyzing these relationships, we controlled the effect of bank size (measured through total assets) and overall domestic economic growth (GDP growth rate) due to their consistent and significant effect on FS as specified in previous literature. Furthermore, panel models are applied through robust technique while controlling the issue of biasness in the coefficients. The rest of the paper is structured as follows. Section two defines the literature context of the study. Section three shows the description of the variables. Section four explains methodological context. Section five covers empirical findings and comprehensive discussion. Last section deals with conclusions of the study.

2. LITERATURE REVIEW

Risk behavior and bank stability are closely associated to each other. Literature context has significantly addressed the issue of banking sector fragility and performance under the situation of various risk factors. However, one of the key issue as found in the existing literature is to examine the trends in the banking sector stability through set of the risk factors. The reason is that literature is missing with compiling both bank related, regional economic, and international risk factors in a one setting to examine their effect on the stability of the banks specifically in the developing economies. For example, Shen, Chen, Kao, and Yeh (2009)primarily focuses on the liquidity risk (LR) for twelve advance economies during 1994 to 2006 through two-stage least square (2SLS) regression estimate. They have found that LR is an endogenous indicator for the performance of banking sector in the targeted economies under market bases-financial system. However, in the presence of bank-based financial system, behavior of LR for banking sector performance is insignificant. Such findings has provided a limited context for the generalization as most of the developing economies are missing with either market based or bank-based financial system.

Research work conducted by Hassan et al. (2019)provide a comprehensive assessment for both conventional and Islamic banking as observed through liquidity, credit, and stability measures. It is observed that both Islamic and conventional banks are negatively associated to liquidity and credit risk while explaining their stability. The reason is that lower liquidity position and higher credit in the form of more non-performing loans are more vulnerable to the stability of the banks.

Additionally, during the time of GFC, negative and significant association presents between LR and stability. This is due to fact that international risk factors like GFC have created more financial issues to the banking sector both in developed and emerging economies. They further claim that Islamic banks are more efficient in managing liquidity and credit risk due to strong risk management compliance. However, their study is missing with the implication of advance panel modelling. Ghenimi, Chaibi, and Omri (2017) contribute in the literature through exploring the behavior of liquidity and credit risk for the banking system in MENA region. Authors claim that both liquidity and risk factors are influencing on the bank's stability. Their study provides more understanding of the risk behavior and stability for the bank managers and credit officers. However, both risk factors along with their interaction effect contributes to the banking sector stability.

Besides, liquidity and credit risk, operational risk (OR) is assumed as among the core issues for the banks because of its management and evaluation(Daryakin & Andriashina, 2015). McNulty and Akhigbe (2017) highlight that good internal control system in banks reveal strong performance whereas higher legal expenses are the indication of poor internal control. However, banks with the week internal control tend to face higher operational cost, more fraudulent activities, and less stability in financial terms. In addition, country risk in the form of volatility in the exchange rate also influences on bank's stability. In this regards, research work by Eichengreen (1998) considers both exchange rate and FS for empirical investigation. Authors claim that main threat to the banking system comes from "inside" in the form of domestic monetary policies. The reason is that higher fluctuation in the local currency causes more volatility in the earnings of the banks, hence lower FS. Nevertheless, his study is missing with the more regional implications due to limited empirical contribution. Meanwhile, literature work also supports the insignificant impact of exchange rate risk on the stability measures and banking sector performance. For instance, Taiwo and Adesola (2013) have found insignificant impact of exchange rate fluctuation on financial measures of stability and the bank performance. The behavior of international risk factors like GFC on stability of the banks is also examined in series of empirical studies. In this regard, research work by Fredriksson and Moro (2014) observe the European banks,Middle east, Africa and Southeast Asian regions by Olson and Zoubi (2017), and 30 other regional economies byAshraf, Rizwan, and L'Huillier (2016). These authors justify their argument that GFC has adversely affected the stability of the banks because of mismanagement in liquidity, credit, and operational risk factors. Additionally, business governance is reflected through quality. In this regard,Sayyar, Basiruddin, Elhabib, and Abdul Rasid (2015) specify that audit fee and rotation of audit firms in the business are core indicators of audit quality (AQ). It is observed that AQmeasures are significantly associated to performance and stability measures like ROA and Tobin's Q. However, one of the significant gap in their study is whether the AQ is a good sign for better stability is yet to be explored.

Besides, country governance is an important mechanism to affect the banking sector performance. For instance, Ho et al. (2016) have investigated the role of country governance for the banking sector performance in 39 countries across the globe during 1996-2007. Authors found that privatized banks are tend to outperform non-privatized banks. However, this effect is greater in developing economies, comparatively to the developed states. It is further observed that country governance causing an increase in the privatization effect for developing states. Those countries with good governance mechanism can lower the effect of political intervention. Additionally, for developed economies, country-level governance

(CLG) causing a low effect of privatization due to very little space of improvement. Based on the above discussion, authors observe the following literature gap which needs to be addressed:

- The behavior of the risk factors like liquidity, credit, and operational for the banking sector stability is significantly missing in the developing economies like Pakistan.
- The trends in market risk like exchange rate needs to examine for the stability measures for both public and private sector banks
- Country governance measures are found to be more vulnerable for stability in banks, but no evidence is found for the economies like Pakistan.
- To examine the trends in stability, there is a need to control the effect of macroeconomic dynamics like economic growth and bank's growth too.

Based on the above, points, this study examines the trends in the stability of the banking firms of Pakistan as observed through a range of risk factors and governance measures.

3. DATA SAMPLE AND METHODOLOGY

This study has empirically investigated the effect of risk and country governance factors on FS of banking firms of Pakistan. To achieve this objective, we have collected secondary data from official publications of State Bank of Pakistan (SBP) for 22 commercial banks during 2007 to 2016 with annual observations. The reason to select 22 banks is due to the availability of the data over the study period for both public and private banks. The selected sample portion of 22 banks represents 73.33 percent from total 30 commercial banks as defined by SBP. For econometric analysis, this study has applied the approach of panel regression models under the tile of robust OLS, fixed effect, and random effect, similar to numerous other studies in the field of risk behavior and banking sector stability(Beck, De Jonghe, & Schepens, 2013; Beck, Demirgüç-Kunt, & Merrouche, 2010; Hesse & Cihak, 2007; Yeyati & Micco, 2007). Various benefits for using such panel models are presented in the literature like controlling the time-invariant characteristics through fixed effect (Gujarati, 2009; Hsiao, 1985), assuming variation across the entities to be random under random effect model (Barr, Levy, Scheepers, & Tily, 2013), and consideration of error terms through robust OLS regression (Damodar, 2004; Kiefer, Vogelsang, & Bunzel, 2000; Lucchetti, 2019; Wager, Keller, Lacey, & Jonides, 2005). For better understanding of the variables, operational definitions are provided first.

After describing the variables, followings equations are developed and empirically tested.

$$Y_{it} = \beta 1X_{it} + \beta 2X_{it} + \beta 3X_{it......} + \beta nX_{it} + a_i + u_{it} \quad (1)$$

$$\begin{aligned}\text{ZROA} = \alpha + \beta_1 LR_1 + \beta_2 CR_2 + \beta_3 OR_3 + \beta_4 MR_4 + \beta_5 CTR_5 + \beta_6 FCR_6 + \beta_7 CAR_7 + \beta_8 AQ_8 \\ + \beta_9 CLG1_9 + \beta_{10} CLG2_{10} + \beta_{11} CLG3_{11} + \beta_{12} CLG4_{12} + \beta_{13} SOB_{13} + \beta_{14} GDP_{14} + \varepsilon\end{aligned} \quad (2)$$

Table 1. Definitions of the Variables

Variable	Operational Definition	Formula	Literature Source	Data source
Dependent Variables				
Z-score for ROA: ZROA	Measures the ratio of return on assets plus equation to total assets in percentage, divided by deviation in return on assets	$ZROA = \frac{ROA + (Equity / Total\_Assets)}{\sigma ROA}$	(Lee & Hsieh, 2014)	Authors calculation, data from State Bank of Pakistan (SBP)
Z-Score for ROE:ZROE	Measures the ratio of return on assets plus equation to total assets in percentage, divided by deviation in return on assets	$ZROE = \frac{ROE + (Equity / Total\_Assets)}{\sigma ROE}$	(Lee & Hsieh, 2014)	
Independent Variables				
Liquidity risk: LR	Measures the ratio of liquid assets to total assets.	$LR = \frac{Liquid\_Assets}{Total\_Assets}$	Lakshan and Wijekoon (2017)	
Credit risk: CR	Ratio of non-performing loans to gross loans	$CR = \frac{Non\_perfor\,ming\_Loans}{Gross\_Loans}$	Makri, Tsagkanos, and Bellas (2014)	
Operational risk: OR	Covers operating cost to income ratio	$OR = \frac{annaul\_Operating\_Exp}{Operating\_Income}$	Almazari (2013)	
Market risk: MR	Real interest rate in the economy	Real interest rate in the economy.	Taylor and Wieland (2016)	
Country risk: CTR	Considers the annual exchange rate in the country	Annual real effective exchange rate in USD.	Belloumi (2010)	World bank Group through world development indicator
Financial crisis risk: FCR	Financial crisis risk measure through dummy variable equal to 1 if period is 2007-2012, otherwise zero.	0,1	Tong, Singh, and Li (2018)	
Capital adequacy ratio: CAR	Capital adequacy ratio measure through	$CAR = \frac{Total\_Equity}{Total\_Assets}$	Mathuva (2009)	Authors calculation, data from State Bank of Pakistan (SBP)
Audit Quality:AQ	Audit quality as measured through annual remuneration paid to auditors	Annual payment for audit and inspection to auditors.	Sayyar et al. (2015)	Financial statements of selected banks
Control of corruption:CLG1	Indicates the way public power is used for the personal gains, capturing both petty and gran from of corruption, with "capture of state by elites and private interests"	Through standard normal distribution, ranging from -2.5 to 2.5 approximately.	Ho et al. (2016)	World bank group through world development indicator

continued on following page

Table 1. Continued

Variable	Operational Definition	Formula	Literature Source	Data source
Regulatory Quality:CLG2	Indicates the efficiency of the government to define and implement sound polices and regulations that permit and promote private sector development	Through standard normal distribution, ranging from -2.5 to 2.5 approximately.	Ho et al. (2016)	World bank group through world development indicator
Voice and Accountability: CLG3	Measures the extent to which citizen of the country are able to participate in selecting their government through freedom of expression.	Through standard normal distribution, ranging from -2.5 (weak) to 2.5 (strong) approximately.	Ho et al. (2016)	World bank group through world development indicator
CLG4: Government effectiveness	Measures the quality of public service, civil service and degree of independence from political pressure. The quality of formulation and implementation of polices.	Through standard normal distribution, ranging from -2.5 to 2.5 approximately.	Ho et al. (2016)	World bank group through world development indicator
Size of Bank: SOB	Size of a bank (SOB) expresses the total assets of the bank at a given time (Subramaniam et al., 2009). In various studies, bank size is used as a key determinant of persistent earnings.	It is measured through log of total assets.		Financial statement of banks
Gross Domestic Product: GDP	The factor of gross domestic product (GDP) is explained as production of goods and services in a country over time. GDP is considered as a macroeconomic factor, which has significantly affected the banking sector (Duraj & Moci, 2015).	It is measured through log of gross domestic product (GDP)		World bank group through world development indicator

Considering the above equation 1 in general format, where Y refers to the stability measures of the banks with time *t* and entity as *i*. a_i refers to the unknown intercept for each of the entity *i*, over *t*, X represents each of the explanatory variables with coefficients β1, β2, β3 and up to β*n* for selected sample. Whereas, u_{it} is showing the error term of the model. Modifying the equation 2 into more specific format, relationship between the explanatory and outcome variable is examined through simple OLS method as reflected by Equation 2. Whereas, Equation 3 presents the association between bank stability through ZROA, risk behavior and governance indicators under fixed effect.

$$\text{ZROA} = \partial + \beta_1 LR_1 + \beta_2 CR_2 + \beta_3 OR_3 + \beta_4 MR_4 + \beta_5 CTR_5 + \beta_6 FCR_6 + \beta_7 CAR_7 + \beta_8 AQ_8 + \beta_9 CLG1_9 + \beta_{10} CLG1_{10} + \beta_{11} CLG1_{11} + \beta_{12} CLG1_{12} + \beta_{13} SOB_{13} + \beta_{14} GDP_{14} + \partial_2 Bnk2_{2it} + \partial_{22} Bank22_{22it} + \varepsilon \quad (3)$$

After fixed effect, regression Equation 4 presents the random effect, considering Y for the stability, b for coefficients of X_{it} variables measured for entities i and time t. In addition, U_{it} observes the within-entity error, and ε_{it} for between-entity error.

$$Y_{it} = bX_{it} + \partial + U_{it} + \varepsilon_{it}. \tag{4}$$

Converting the above general equation of random effect into more specific format, Equation 5 indicates the relationship between risk behavior, bank stability through ZROA and governance measures.

$$\text{ZROA} = \partial + \beta_1 LR_1 + \beta_2 CR_2 + \beta_3 OR_3 + \beta_4 MR_4 + \beta_5 CTR_5 + \beta_6 FCR_6 + \beta_7 CAR_7 + \beta_8 AQ_8 + \beta_9 CLG1_9 + \beta_{10} CLG2_{10} + \beta_{11} CLG3_{11} + \beta_{12} CLG4_{12} + \beta_{13} SOB_{13} + \beta_{14} GDP_{14} + \partial_2 Bnk2_{2it} + \partial_{22} Bank22_{22it} + U_i + W_{ij} \tag{5}$$

Now above all equations are reconsidered for the second measure of FS through risk behavior and governance indicators with the controlling effect of bank size and GDP for commercial banks of Pakistan.

$$\text{ZROE} = \partial + \beta_1 LR_1 + \beta_2 CR_2 + \beta_3 OR_3 + \beta_4 MR_4 + \beta_5 CTR_5 + \beta_6 FCR_6 + \beta_7 CAR_7 + \beta_8 AQ_8 + \beta_9 CLG1_9 + \beta_{10} CLG2_{10} + \beta_{11} CLG3_{11} + \beta_{12} CLG4_{12} + \beta_{13} SOB_{13} + \beta_{14} GDP_{14} + \varepsilon \tag{6}$$

$$\text{ZROE} = \partial + \beta_1 LR_1 + \beta_2 CR_2 + \beta_3 OR_3 + \beta_4 MR_4 + \beta_5 CTR_5 + \beta_6 FCR_6 + \beta_7 CAR_7 + \beta_8 AQ_8 + \beta_9 CLG1_9 + \beta_{10} CLG2_{10} + \beta_{11} CLG3_{11} + \beta_{12} CLG4_{12} + \beta_{13} SOB_{13} + \beta_{14} GDP_{14} + \partial_2 Bnk2_{2it} + \partial_{22} Bank22_{22it} + \varepsilon \tag{7}$$

$$\text{ZROE} = \partial + \beta_1 LR_1 + \beta_2 CR_2 + \beta_3 OR_3 + \beta_4 MR_4 + \beta_5 CTR_5 + \beta_6 FCR_6 + \beta_7 CAR_7 + \beta_8 AQ_8 + \beta_9 CLG1_9 + \beta_{10} CLG2_{10} + \beta_{11} CLG3_{11} + \beta_{12} CLG4_{12} + \beta_{13} SOB_{13} + \beta_{14} GDP_{14} + \partial_2 Bnk2_{2it} + \partial_{22} Bank22_{22it} + U_i + W_{ij} \tag{8}$$

4. RESULTS AND DISCUSSION

Research findings for the first proxy of FS through ZROA are presented under Table 2. Through LR, effect on ZROA is significantly negative in pooled regression, while insignificant under random effect and fixed effect. It means that for a pooled effect of liquidity, ZROA is facing negative and significant influence in overall banking industry of Pakistan. Excessive liquidity is not suitable for FS through ZROA. Through CR, significantly negative influence is observed under all three regression models, indicating that lower asset quality like higher NPLs in banks is not suitable for the bank's stability.Similar findings are presented in the research work of (Fu, Lin, & Molyneux, 2014; Soedarmono et al., 2011). Additionally, an adverse impact of CR on FS-ROA implies that higher NPLs is among the critical reasons for the uneven financial situation in commercial banks of Pakistan. The increasing value of NPLs in the country is among the significant issues which need serious attention.

Likewise, OR reflects significant and negative influence on ZROA under all regression models.It explains that there is an issue of higher operational cost and weak internal control system in the commercial banks, which in return, affects the banking sector stability. This fact is consistent with (Mathuva, 2009; Petria, Capraru, & Ihnatov, 2015). In recent years, banking industry of Pakistan has faced lower earnings over its assets, and among several, increasing operational cost is one of them. However, the effect of MR is found to be insignificant in all three cases. The factor of CTR reflects significantly negative influence on ZROA, meaning that exchange rate fluctuation is creating financial shocks for the banks in Pakistan. This issue reflects the failure of various policies defined by the local government and SBP for exchange rate stability. Gradual depreciation of a domestic currency in Pakistan highlights that more attention is required to overcome financial calamity in commercial banks as experienced through instability in the exchange rates.In addition, it is observed that financial crisis during last decade has adversely affected the banking industry and parallel impact is observed for commercial banks in Pakistan. FCR has its significant and negative impact on ZROA which means that lower stability is experienced.This effect isfollowed by the results of (Ghosh, 2017; Lindblom, Olsson, & Willesson, 2011).Meanwhile, CAR has its insignificant influence on ZROA in all cases, except in random effect.

Although adequate capital ratio provides a secure environment for the banks, but excessive level of such amount is not beneficial for banking sector stability. Besides, AQ is found to be significant and negative determinant of ZROA under pooled regression model, but insignificant for both fixed and random effect. This negative effect implies that more payment to the auditors is not advantageous for the banks, hence leading towards instability. For country-governance indicators, effect of CLG1 is significantly negative in all cases.It means that weak governance structure and low control over corruption in Pakistan has adversely affected the banking sector stability It shows that lower control of corruption in the country has its adverse effect on bank's stability, creating serious issues for the key role players in overall financial market. While rest of country governance measures reflect insignificant impact on ZROA. Finally, the comparison of the regression model is conducted for the better understanding which model is more appropriate for the generalization of the findings. The comparison between the fixed and random effect through Hausman Test indicates that random effect is more appropriate. The next comparison between random and pooled regression is conducted where, significant chi-square value of B.P multiplier test implies that random effect is more appropriate. The reason to provide the findings for all three panel models is that it may expand the future implication as different researchers would apply different panel regression models in their upcoming studies.

Table 3 shows regression findings for ZROE. Under OLS, LR, credit and OR are found to be significant determinants of FS. These results are justified with the previous findings by (Fu, Lin, & Molyneux, 2014; Soedarmono et al., 2011; Mathuva, 2009; Petria, Capraru, & Ihnatov, 2015)This would employ that banks in Pakistan are adversely affected by the liquidity issues, higher non-performing loans, and more operational cost. These risk factors are causing adverse impact on the banks stability when it is measured through ZROE. Whereas, MR, CTR, and FCR are found to be insignificant indicators for ZROE, meaning that no impact on the second indicator of FS in the local market of Pakistan. In addition, AQ under OLS is significantly and negatively affecting the ZROE, means that more payment to the auditors is weakening the stability measure in the banking sector of Pakistan. However, governance indicators are found to be insignificant for stability. From control variables, SOB has its significant and positive impact on ZROE.For Fixed effect, CR, OR, CTR, and FCR are found to be significantly & negatively

Table 2. Regression Results for overall banks

	(1)OLS Regression	(2)Random Effect	(3)Fixed Effect
VARIABLES	ZROA	ZROA	ZROA
LR	-0.130***	0.0279	0.0174
	(0.0370)	(0.0290)	(0.0294)
CR1	-0.109***	-0.0447**	-0.0491***
	(0.0194)	(0.0186)	(0.0180)
OR1	-0.0525***	-0.0384***	-0.0433***
	(0.0120)	(0.0128)	(0.0124)
MR	0.0637	0.0480	0.0513*
	(0.0534)	(0.0293)	(0.0306)
CTR	-0.271**	-0.258***	-0.265***
	(0.120)	(0.0694)	(0.0726)
FCR	-2.817*	-2.695***	-2.691***
	(1.654)	(0.928)	(0.970)
CAR1	-0.0280	-0.0381*	-0.0230
	(0.0187)	(0.0201)	(0.0191)
AQ	-1.812***	-0.245	-0.497
	(0.301)	(0.307)	(0.304)
CLG1	-13.29*	-13.46***	-12.84***
	(6.821)	(3.800)	(3.953)
CLG2	0.482	1.775	1.638
	(2.449)	(1.577)	(1.647)
CLG3	0.495	1.652	0.515
	(3.997)	(2.130)	(2.161)
CLG4	8.088	8.105**	7.136*
	(6.167)	(3.692)	(3.806)
SOB	3.867***	0.689	2.680***
	(0.295)	(0.971)	(0.574)
GDP	19.93*	25.86***	22.74***
	(10.52)	(6.377)	(6.505)
Constant	-215.6**	-266.7***	-246.9***
	(107.3)	(63.50)	(65.75)
Observations	192	192	192
R-squared	0.683	0.286	.652
Number of bankid	22	22	22
Breusch and Pagan Lagrangian multiplier test for random effects Estimated results: chibar2(01) = 211.74, Prob > chibar2 = 0.0000			

Robust standard errors in parentheses, *** p<0.01, ** p<0.05, * p<0.1

Table 3. Regression Results for overall banks

	(1)OLS Regression	(2)FEM	(3)REM
VARIABLES	Model 1: ZROE	Model 2: ZROE	Model 3: ZROE
LR	-0.169***	0.0218	0.0193
	(0.0540)	(0.0271)	(0.0274)
CR1	-0.161***	-0.0532***	-0.0544***
	(0.0293)	(0.0173)	(0.0172)
OR1	-0.0416**	-0.0370***	-0.0394***
	(0.0190)	(0.0120)	(0.0119)
MR	0.0465	0.0389	0.0402
	(0.0804)	(0.0273)	(0.0279)
CTR	-0.224	-0.219***	-0.223***
	(0.191)	(0.0647)	(0.0660)
FCR	-2.191	-2.159**	-2.152**
	(2.560)	(0.865)	(0.883)
CAR1	-0.0456	-0.0365*	-0.0284
	(0.0363)	(0.0188)	(0.0183)
AQ	-2.225***	-0.268	-0.365
	(0.492)	(0.287)	(0.288)
CLG1	-11.01	-11.17***	-10.80***
	(10.36)	(3.543)	(3.606)
CLG2	-0.389	1.628	1.565
	(4.306)	(1.470)	(1.500)
CLG3	2.025	2.181	1.575
	(5.615)	(1.986)	(1.994)
CLG4	7.346	6.211*	5.652
	(9.898)	(3.442)	(3.487)
SORC	0.321	0.0479	0.0685
	(0.256)	(0.116)	(0.117)
SOB	4.608***	1.417	2.478***
	(0.508)	(0.905)	(0.730)
GDP	16.24	23.14***	21.45***
	(16.87)	(5.946)	(5.987)
Constant	-181.5	-244.7***	-234.1***
	(171.7)	(59.21)	(60.10)
Observations	192	192	192
R-squared	0.591	0.375	
Number of bankid	22	22	22
Hausman (1978) specification test Chi-square test value 65.55*** P-value 0.000			

Standard errors in parentheses, *** p<0.01, ** p<0.05, * p<0.1

Table 4. Regression Results for public sector banks

	(1)ZROE	(2)ZROE	(3)ZROE
VARIABLES	OLS	FEM	REM
LR	-0.0343	0.0287	-0.0343
	(0.0708)	(0.0906)	(0.0708)
CR	-0.0296	0.0107	-0.0296
	(0.0242)	(0.0378)	(0.0242)
OR	-0.0476**	-0.0552**	-0.0476***
	(0.0180)	(0.0198)	(0.0180)
MR	0.0898	0.0807	0.0898
	(0.0586)	(0.0591)	(0.0586)
CTR	-0.343**	-0.316**	-0.343**
	(0.139)	(0.141)	(0.139)
FCR	-4.114**	-3.663*	-4.114**
	(1.857)	(1.903)	(1.857)
CAR	0.0561	0.0180	0.0561
	(0.0436)	(0.113)	(0.0436)
AQ	-0.554	-0.245	-0.554*
	(0.334)	(0.435)	(0.334)
CLG1	-18.67**	-14.94*	-18.67**
	(7.542)	(8.225)	(7.542)
CLG2	-1.246	-1.286	-1.246
	(2.991)	(3.155)	(2.991)
CLG3	5.721	2.813	5.721
	(4.126)	(4.487)	(4.126)
CLG4	17.53**	12.01	17.53**
	(7.477)	(8.080)	(7.477)
SOB	2.086***	5.169	2.086***
	(0.299)	(4.009)	(0.299)
GDP	24.64*	18.37	24.64**
	(12.30)	(15.02)	(12.30)
Constant	-256.3*	-218.9	-256.3**
	(125.8)	(141.3)	(125.8)
Observations	39	39	39
R-squared	0.833	0.629	
Number of bankid	5	5	5
Hausman (1978) specification test Chi-square test value 3.766 P-value .993			
Breusch and Pagan Lagrangian multiplier test for random effects Estimated results: chibar2(01) = 2.59 Prob > chibar2 = 0.1251			

Standard errors in parentheses, *** p<0.01, ** p<0.05, * p<0.1

Table 5. Regression Results for public sector banks

	(1)ZROA	(2)ZROA	(3)ZROA
VARIABLES	OLS	FEM	REM
LR	-0.0524	0.0103	-0.0524
	(0.0649)	(0.0806)	(0.0649)
CR	-0.0109	0.0412	-0.0109
	(0.0222)	(0.0337)	(0.0222)
OR	-0.0539***	-0.0601***	-0.0539***
	(0.0165)	(0.0177)	(0.0165)
MR	0.123**	0.115**	0.123**
	(0.0537)	(0.0526)	(0.0537)
CTR	-0.407***	-0.376***	-0.407***
	(0.127)	(0.126)	(0.127)
FCR	-4.661**	-4.138**	-4.661***
	(1.702)	(1.694)	(1.702)
CAR	0.0837**	0.105	0.0837**
	(0.0400)	(0.101)	(0.0400)
AQ	-0.715**	-0.436	-0.715**
	(0.306)	(0.387)	(0.306)
CLG1	-22.20***	-17.83**	-22.20***
	(6.914)	(7.323)	(6.914)
CLG2	-1.424	-1.775	-1.424
	(2.742)	(2.810)	(2.742)
CLG3	5.620	2.363	5.620
	(3.783)	(3.995)	(3.783)
CLG4	22.67***	16.95**	22.67***
	(6.855)	(7.194)	(6.855)
SOB	1.922***	6.979*	1.922***
	(0.274)	(3.570)	(0.274)
GDP	27.81**	17.69	27.81**
	(11.27)	(13.37)	(11.27)
Constant	-283.5**	-220.1*	-283.5**
	(115.3)	(125.8)	(115.3)
Observations	39	39	39
R-squared	0.833	0.702	.531
Number of bankid	5	5	5

Hausman (1978) specification test
Coef.
Chi-square test value 5.252
P-value .982
Breusch and Pagan Lagrangian multiplier test for random effects Estimated results:
chibar2(01) = 3.01
Prob > chibar2 = 0.1145

Standard errors in parentheses, *** p<0.01, ** p<0.05, * p<0.1

affecting ZROE.While CAR has also implied its adverse influence on FS in commercial banks. CLG1 explains that control of corruption has its adverse influence on stability of the banks, whereas CLG4 shows its positive impact on stability as measured through ZROE. For random effect, credit, operational and country risk factors are significantly and negatively affecting ZROE. Similar is found through FCR and CLG1 for overall sample of 22 banks. Besides, significant value of chi-square under HM test provides favor for the fixed effect coefficients.

For public sector banks, Table 4 has provided overall findings. It is believed that key determinants of ZROE are OR, CTR and FCR, indicating their significant and negative influence. From governance factors, CLG1 shows its negative influence while CLG4 has its positive impact on bank's stability. For fixed effect, key determinants of ZROE are OR, CTR, and financial crisis risk. It is believed that financial crisis during the time of 2007 to 2009 has adversely affected the financial sector of Pakistan. Meanwhile, increasing corruption is a major threat to the economy and financial system as well. However, other indicators of country governance have shown their insignificant relationship with ZROE. Under random effect findings, key determinants are OR, CTR, FCR and AQ, having their adverse influence on ZROE. Meanwhile, CLG1 shows is negative influence while CLG4 demonstrates its positive impact for the stability measure. For public sector banks, both Hausman and Breusch and Pagan test are applied with their final suggestion for the random effect.

Table 5 presents regression findings for ZROA for public sector banks. Under all three models, operational risk indicates significantly negative influence on ZROA. While market risk observes as positively and significantly affecting the ZROA. It means that public sector banks are more vulnerable towards operational risk. For CTR, all models present significant and negative influence, means that more country risk is putting adverse effect on ZROA for public banks. this fact is also justified with the earlier results of (Ghosh, 2017; Lindblom, Olsson, & Willesson, 2011).Through FCR, all models presents significant and negative influence for FS, proving the fact that public sector banks are adversely affected by FCR during last decade. For CAR, OLS and REM are presenting significant and positive coefficients. It means that excessive capital ratio in public sector banks is positively affecting stability measure. Through AQ, both OLS and REM presents their significant and negative results for ZROA. As discussed earlier, control of corruption is a major issue in the economy of Pakistan, hence adversely impacting on the stability of public sector banks under all models. Whereas, CLG4 is positively and significantly associated to ZROA. Findings of B.P test favors for the random effect which means that its coefficients are more suitable for the decision making.

Table 6 shows the findings for private sector banks. Under all panel models, CR is significantly and negatively affecting ZROE. While OR and CTR are negatively influencing on the stability through fixed and random effect methods. The factor of FCR indicates its adverse influence on the stability of private sector under both FE and RE. It means that not only public sector but private banks are also affected by international risk factor. For governance, none of the coefficient is found to be significant, means that stability in private banks is not influenced by country governance issues.

For ZROA of private banks, Table 7 shows regression results. It indicates that CR and OR is significantly and negatively affecting ZROA for private banks under all three models of the study. while CLG1 shows its adverse impact on ZROA under both fixed and random effect. This would justify the argument that like public sector, private banks are also exposed to credit, and OR factors. This effect further claims that there is a significant need to control the higher NPLs and more operational cost in the private banks too which in return would provide better stability outcome. Meanwhile, the overall

Table 6. Regression Results for private sector banks

	(1)ZROE	(2)ZROE	(3)ZROE
VARIABLES	OLS	FEM	REM
LR	-0.196***	0.00951	0.00935
	(0.0635)	(0.0300)	(0.0305)
CR	-0.210***	-0.0787***	-0.0812***
	(0.0463)	(0.0207)	(0.0210)
OR	-0.0131	-0.0274*	-0.0336**
	(0.0230)	(0.0158)	(0.0155)
MR	0.0592	0.0310	0.0347
	(0.0935)	(0.0310)	(0.0318)
CTR	-0.188	-0.194***	-0.202***
	(0.223)	(0.0738)	(0.0757)
FCR	-1.696	-1.758*	-1.783*
	(2.995)	(0.987)	(1.014)
CAR	0.0170	-0.0336*	-0.0252
	(0.0443)	(0.0197)	(0.0198)
AQ	-2.744***	-0.251	-0.532
	(0.676)	(0.451)	(0.450)
CLG1	-9.148	-9.951**	-9.773**
	(12.08)	(4.026)	(4.132)
CLG2	0.960	2.133	2.278
	(5.105)	(1.714)	(1.759)
CLG3	-0.583	1.648	0.695
	(6.539)	(2.285)	(2.306)
CLG4	-0.642	4.201	3.317
	(11.55)	(3.904)	(3.989)
SOB	6.155***	1.222	2.595***
	(0.728)	(1.030)	(0.891)
GDP	16.80	23.18***	21.75***
	(19.69)	(6.716)	(6.856)
Constant	-204.5	-245.5***	-238.8***
	(200.2)	(67.15)	(68.85)
Observations	153	153	153
R-squared	0.619	0.365	.459
Number of bankid	17	17	17

Hausman (1978) specification test
Coef.
Chi-square test value 15.844
P-value .323
Breusch and Pagan Lagrangian multiplier test for random effects Estimated results:
chibar2(01) = 353.44
Prob > chibar2 = 0.0000

Standard errors in parentheses
*** p<0.01, ** p<0.05, * p<0.1

Table 7. Regression Results for private sector banks

	(1)	(2)	(3)
VARIABLES	**ZROA OLS regression**	**ZROA Random effect**	**ZROA Fixed effect**
LR	-0.134***	0.0105	0.0161
	(0.0406)	(0.0330)	(0.0324)
CR	-0.129***	-0.0763***	-0.0719***
	(0.0296)	(0.0228)	(0.0224)
OR	-0.0328**	-0.0410***	-0.0288*
	(0.0147)	(0.0158)	(0.0171)
MR	0.0592	0.0416	0.0332
	(0.0597)	(0.0353)	(0.0335)
CTR	-0.232	-0.241***	-0.225***
	(0.143)	(0.0842)	(0.0798)
FCR	-2.394	-2.362**	-2.299**
	(1.913)	(1.129)	(1.068)
CAR	0.0148	-0.0177	-0.0373*
	(0.0283)	(0.0211)	(0.0213)
AQ	-2.231***	-0.673	-0.00556
	(0.432)	(0.465)	(0.488)
CLG1	-11.21	-11.45**	-11.80***
	(7.717)	(4.589)	(4.357)
CLG2	1.807	2.435	2.125
	(3.260)	(1.952)	(1.855)
CLG3	-1.609	-0.867	1.122
	(4.177)	(2.514)	(2.472)
CLG4	0.997	3.609	5.519
	(7.379)	(4.407)	(4.225)
SOB	5.087***	3.178***	0.276
	(0.465)	(0.733)	(1.115)
GDP	19.48	22.07***	25.01***
	(12.57)	(7.562)	(7.268)
Constant	-224.9*	-244.8***	-258.6***
	(127.9)	(76.32)	(72.68)
Observations	153	153	153
R-squared	0.725		0.265
Number of bankid	17	17	17

Hausman (1978) specification test
Chi-square test value 13.811
P-value .464
Breusch and Pagan Lagrangian multiplier test for random effects Estimated results
chibar2(01) = 163.86
Prob > chibar2 = 0.0000

Standard errors in parentheses, *** p<0.01, ** p<0.05, * p<0.1

findings under present research are not only applicable to the banking sector of Pakistan but also on the regional economies.

5. CONCLUSION

This study has empirically investigated the risk behavior and country governancefor financial stability of banking firms in Pakistan. Overall 22 commercial banks from financial sector are selected over 2007 to 2016. Both risk factors and country governance measures are applied to examine the stability response. For overall banks, credit, operational, country level and financial crisis risk are significantly and negatively influencing on banking sector stability (ZROA). From governance factors, CLG1 indicates its adverse influence on banks. For ZROE, only CR and OR are found to be significant determinants under all three regression models. While CTR has shown a significant and negative effect on ZROE under both fixed and random effect. These results confirms that overall banks in Pakistan are vulnerable towards banking sector risk and corruption issue in the economy. In addition, specifically for the public sector, OR, CTR, FCR, and CLG1 are found to be significant determinants of ZROE. In case of ZROA, public sector banks are exposed towards OR, MR, CTR, and FCR. While CLG1 and CL4 are also found to be significant causesfor financial instability. For private banks, CR again represents its adverse and significant influence on ZROE under three regression models, but insignificant for country governance measures. For ZROA, effect of CR and OR is found to be negatively significant, while CTR represents adverse influence under both fixed and random effect models. Additionally, control of corruption specifies its adverse influence on stability of the banks. In addition, our empirical facts show various important points for the policy implications specifically in banking sector of Pakistan and generally for the other regional economies. Firstly, significant attention is required to control the adverse effect of various risk factors on FS with more cautions. For example, it is found that liquidity, credit and operational risk are creating more instability in the banks, so risk management framework should be upgraded accordingly. furthermore, policy makers like credit officers, and various officials working in the RM department of banks should immediately consider the lending policies of their respective banks to control all three type of risk factors (liquidity, credit and operational). For the improvement in FS, there is a need to reconsider the risk measures and their impact on financial stability both in public and private sector banks. In this regard, redesigning the loan facility, control over operational risk, improving the quality of audit facility, and governance measures at macroeconomic level need reasonable attention. Besides, present study has several limitations. Firstly, study sample is based on the 22 banks from overall banking sector. Secondly, present research is missing with the implication of some advanced panel models like GMM. Thirdly, cross sectional comparison for the banking sector of other regional economies is also missing. Future studies are highly suggested to target these limitations for better generalization and literature significance.

REFERENCES

Acharya, V. V., & Richardson, M. P. (2009). *Restoring financial stability: how to repair a failed system* (Vol. 542). John Wiley & Sons. doi:10.1002/9781118258163

Allen, F., & Gale, D. (2004). Competition and financial stability. *Journal of Money, Credit and Banking, 36*(3), 453–480. doi:10.1353/mcb.2004.0038

Allen, L., & Saunders, A. (2004). Incorporating systemic influences into risk measurements: A survey of the literature. *Journal of Financial Services Research, 26*(2), 161–191. doi:10.1023/B:FINA.0000037545.38154.8a

Almazari, A. A. (2013). Capital Adequacy, Cost Income Ratio and the Performance of Saudi Banks. *International Journal of Academic Research in Accounting. Finance and Management Sciences, 3*(4), 284–293.

Ashraf, D., Rizwan, M. S., & L'Huillier, B. (2016). A net stable funding ratio for Islamic banks and its impact on financial stability: An international investigation. *Journal of Financial Stability, 25*, 47–57. doi:10.1016/j.jfs.2016.06.010

Avgouleas, E., & Cullen, J. (2014). Excessive Leverage and Bankers' Pay: Governance and Financial Stability Costs of a Symbiotic Relationship. *The Columbia Journal of European Law, 21*(1), 7–46.

Barakat, A., & Hussainey, K. (2013). Bank governance, regulation, supervision, and risk reporting: Evidence from operational risk disclosures in European banks. *International Review of Financial Analysis, 30*, 254–273. doi:10.1016/j.irfa.2013.07.002

Barr, D. J., Levy, R., Scheepers, C., & Tily, H. J. (2013). Random effects structure for confirmatory hypothesis testing: Keep it maximal. *Journal of Memory and Language, 68*(3), 255–278. doi:10.1016/j.jml.2012.11.001 PMID:24403724

Beck, T., De Jonghe, O., & Schepens, G. (2013). Bank competition and stability: Cross-country heterogeneity. *Journal of Financial Intermediation, 22*(2), 218–244. doi:10.1016/j.jfi.2012.07.001

Beck, T., Demirgüç-Kunt, A., & Merrouche, O. (2010). Islamic vs. conventional banking: Business model, efficiency and stability. *Journal of Banking & Finance, 37*(2), 433–447. doi:10.1016/j.jbankfin.2012.09.016

Belloumi, M. (2010). The relationship between tourism receipts, real effective exchange rate and economic growth in Tunisia. *International Journal of Tourism Research, 12*(5), 550–560.

Damodar, N. (2004). *Basic econometrics*: The Mc-Graw Hill. Retrieved from: http://eprints.stiperdharmawacana.ac.id/180/1/Basic%20Econometrics%20-%20Gujarati.pdf

Daryakin, A., & Andriashina, S. (2015). Problems of Evaluation and Management of Operational Risks in Banks. *Procedia Economics and Finance, 24*, 156–165. doi:10.1016/S2212-5671(15)00637-1

Di Giorgio, G., & Rotondi, Z. (2008). *Monetary Policy*. Financial Stability and Interest Rate Rules.

Diamond, D. W., & Kashyap, A. K. (2016). *Liquidity requirements, liquidity choice, and financial stability* (Vol. 2). Handbook of macroeconomics. Elsevier. doi:10.3386/w22053

Eckert, C., & Gatzert, N. (2017). Modeling operational risk incorporating reputation risk: An integrated analysis for financial firms. *Insurance, Mathematics & Economics, 72*, 122–137. doi:10.1016/j.insmatheco.2016.11.005

Eichengreen, B. (1998). Exchange rate stability and financial stability. *Open Economies Review*, *9*(1), 569–608. doi:10.1023/A:1008373022226

Fredriksson, A., & Moro, A. (2014). Bank–SMEs relationships and banks' risk-adjusted profitability. *Journal of Banking & Finance*, *41*, 67–77. doi:10.1016/j.jbankfin.2013.12.026

Ghenimi, A., Chaibi, H., & Omri, M. A. B. (2017). The effects of liquidity risk and credit risk on bank stability: Evidence from the MENA region. *Borsa Istanbul Review*, *17*(4), 238–248. doi:10.1016/j.bir.2017.05.002

Gujarati, D. N. (2009). *Basic econometrics*. Tata McGraw-Hill Education. Retrieved from: http://eprints.stiperdharmawacana.ac.id/180/1/Basic%20Econometrics%20-%20Gujarati.pdf

Hassan, M. K., Khan, A., & Paltrinieri, A. (2019). Liquidity risk, credit risk and stability in Islamic and conventional banks. *Research in International Business and Finance*, *48*, 17–31. doi:10.1016/j.ribaf.2018.10.006

Hesse, H., & Cihak, M. (2007). *Cooperative banks and financial stability*. International Monetary Fund. IMF working paper: WP/07/2.

Ho, P.-H., Lin, C.-Y., & Tsai, W.-C. (2016). Effect of country governance on bank privatization performance. *International Review of Economics & Finance*, *43*, 3–18. doi:10.1016/j.iref.2015.10.028

Hsiao, C. (1985). Benefits and limitations of panel data. *Econometric Reviews*, *4*(1), 121–174. doi:10.1080/07474938508800078

Johnson, P. (2011). The financial stability of sustainable organisations. *Journal of Business & Economics Research*, *9*(10), 1–65.

Jorion, P. (2000). *Value at risk*. Retrieved from: http://bear.warrington.ufl.edu/aitsahlia/Financial_Risk_Management.pdf

Kiefer, N. M., Vogelsang, T. J., & Bunzel, H. (2000). Simple robust testing of regression hypotheses. *Econometrica*, *68*(3), 695–714. doi:10.1111/1468-0262.00128

Lakshan, A. I., & Wijekoon, W. (2017). The use of financial ratios in predicting corporate failure in Sri Lanka. *GSTF Journal on Business Review*, *2*(4), 37–43.

Lee, C.-C., & Hsieh, M.-F. (2014). Bank reforms, foreign ownership, and financial stability. *Journal of International Money and Finance*, *40*, 204–224. doi:10.1016/j.jimonfin.2013.09.001

Lucchetti, R.J. (2019). *Basic Econometrics*. Academic Press.

Makri, V., Tsagkanos, A., & Bellas, A. (2014). Determinants of non-performing loans: The case of Eurozone. *Panoeconomicus*, *61*(2), 193–206. doi:10.2298/PAN1402193M

Mathuva, D. (2009). Capital adequacy, cost income ratio and the performance of commercial banks: The Kenyan scenario. *The International Journal of Applied Economics and Finance*, *3*(2), 35–47. doi:10.3923/ijaef.2009.35.47

McNulty, J. E., & Akhigbe, A. (2017). What do a bank's legal expenses reveal about its internal controls and operational risk? *Journal of Financial Stability*, *30*, 181–191. doi:10.1016/j.jfs.2016.10.001

Olson, D., & Zoubi, T. (2017). Convergence in bank performance for commercial and Islamic banks during and after the Global Financial Crisis. *The Quarterly Review of Economics and Finance*, *65*, 71–87. doi:10.1016/j.qref.2016.06.013

Sayyar, H., Basiruddin, R., Elhabib, M., & Abdul Rasid, S. (2015). The impact of audit quality on firm performance: Evidence from Malaysia. *Journal of Advanced Review on Scientific Research*, *10*(1), 1–19.

Shen, C.-H., Chen, Y.-K., Kao, L.-F., & Yeh, C.-Y. (2009). *Bank liquidity risk and performance*. Paper presented at the 17th Conference on the theories and practices of securities and financial markets, Hsi-Tze Bay, Kaohsiung, Taiwan.

Taiwo, O., & Adesola, O. A. (2013). Exchange rate volatility and bank performance in Nigeria. *Asian Economic and Financial Review*, *3*(2), 178.

Taylor, J. B., & Wieland, V. (2016). Finding the equilibrium real interest rate in a fog of policy deviations. *Business Economics (Cleveland, Ohio)*, *51*(3), 147–154. doi:10.105711369-016-0001-5

Tong, T., Singh, T., & Li, B. (2018). Country-level macro-corporate governance and the outward foreign direct investment: Evidence from China. *International Journal of Social Economics*, *45*(1), 107–123. doi:10.1108/IJSE-09-2016-0243

Wager, T. D., Keller, M. C., Lacey, S. C., & Jonides, J. (2005). Increased sensitivity in neuroimaging analyses using robust regression. *NeuroImage*, *26*(1), 99–113. doi:10.1016/j.neuroimage.2005.01.011 PMID:15862210

Yeyati, E. L., & Micco, A. (2007). Concentration and foreign penetration in Latin American banking sectors: Impact on competition and risk. *Journal of Banking & Finance*, *31*(6), 1633–1647. doi:10.1016/j.jbankfin.2006.11.003

Chapter 10
Evaluation of Alternative Approaches in Classification Algorithms for Prediction of Stock Market Index:
Case of Crobex

Silvija Vlah Jerić
https://orcid.org/0000-0003-4738-6337
Faculty of Economics and Business, University of Zagreb, Croatia

ABSTRACT

This chapter tackles the problem of automatic recognition of favorable days for intra-day trading. The problem is modeled as a binary classification problem, and several approaches are tested for solving it. Croatian stock index CROBEX data is used and 22 technical indicators are calculated as predictor variables. Performance of five classifiers is evaluated and compared by using Cohen's kappa as evaluation metric: artificial neural network, support network machine, random forest, k-nearest neighbors, and naïve Bayes classifier. The results give insight to effectiveness of technical analysis in predicting the day favorability for CROBEX index and suggest that technical analysis makes sense and might work for this case.

INTRODUCTION

Stock market index is often used to describe the aggregate movements in a market as it represents a measurement of value of a section of the stock market and reflects the level of the free float value. Since its changes involve a stochastic component, it is very difficult to predict and forecasting stock market index value has always been one of the hottest topics in research. One of the ways of analyzing stock movement is technical analysis which consists of using past market information to predict the direction of prices.

DOI: 10.4018/978-1-7998-5083-0.ch010

The problem of automatic recognition of favorable days for intra-day trading can be modeled as a binary classification problem. Day trading consists in buying and selling financial instruments within the same trading day and favorable for intra-day trading means that the increase between the opening price and the closing price of the same day is large enough for obtaining a profit by buying at the opening price and selling at the closing price. Thereby "large enough" is defined by selecting a certain threshold. The underlying classification problem consists of attribution of one of two labels to daily records according to values of a selection of technical indicators. The class that is assigned to each daily record is 1 if the subsequent day is favorable for intra-day trading and 0 otherwise. The problem is to discover the relation between the selected indicators at a certain day and the market situation at the following day that would determine the class of day that is observed, according to technical analysis (Lo & Hasanhodzic, 2010). The objective, as in any classification problem, is to achieve the highest accuracy possible when comparing the prediction with the real class.

The goal of this chapter is to evaluate and compare different classification algorithms on automatic recognition of favorable days for intra-day trading. Classification problems has been intensively studied and there are many classification algorithms available today (Bruni & Bianchi, 2015; Hastie, Tibshirani, & Friedman, 2001). Different families of algorithms are tested: neural network, support vector machine, random forest, as well as *k*-nearest neighbors and naïve Bayes classifier as more typical classifiers. The idea is to test different families of algorithms but to give more attention to algorithms which are used more rarely than typical statistical methods which are still considered to be "mainstream" although is a lot of research in alternative approaches nowadays too. The algorithms will be applied to Croatian stock index CROBEX and it is the first attempt of such kind to the best of authors' knowledge and should fill some gap in this area of research observed in literature (Šego & Škrinjarić, 2018). The results will give insight to effectiveness of technical analysis in predicting the index value, as well to observe the accuracy of different classification methods.

Background

There are many research efforts in the literature on different topics regarding stock market prediction. Some of them address regression problems by trying to predict stock market prices, while others treat them as classification problems, for example, by trying to predict the direction of changes in prices. Besides classical statistical approaches, there are many examples of using machine learning algorithms in stock market prediction problems, most often neural networks. One of the first efforts was by Kimoto, Asakawa, Yoda and Takeoka (1990) for predicting the index of Tokyo stock market by neural networks. Mizuno, Kosaka, Yajima and Komoda (1998) also used neural networks to predict the trade of stocks in Tokyo stock market. Also, Bayes classifiers (Shin & Kil, 1998; Tsaih, Hsu, & Lai, 1998; Pop, 2006) and SVM (Ince & Trafalis, 2007; Moreira, Jorge, Soares, & Sousa, 2006) have been used by researches for financial market prediction. Kara and Boyacioglu (2011) discussed stock price index movement using two models based on neural networks and support vector machine. Qi and Zhang (2008) investigated the best model of time series using neural network. Zemke (1999) compared neural network, *k*-nearest neighbor, naïve Bayesian classifier, and genetic algorithm, developing classification rules for their prediction accuracies on stock exchange index data. Qian and Rasheed (2007) investigated the predictability of the Dow Jones Industrial Average index using neural network, decision tree, and *k*-nearest neighbor.

In this chapter five algorithms are compared in terms of performance in predicting Croatian stock index CROBEX. Since the idea was to test different families of methods, as mentioned before, the following approaches are used: neural networks, support vector machines, random forest, k-nearest neighbors and naïve Bayes classifier. This research should fill some gap in this area of research pointed out for example by Šego and Škrinjarić (2018). The work by Šego and Škrinjarić (2018) summarizes the results of most quantitative research Zagreb Stock Exchange since its foundation until today and systematizes existing relevant stock market research in Croatia. According to them, there is much more room for incorporating atypical methodology for stock market research and this is the motivation for this chapter too.

To get an insight into the Croatian Stock market situation, it should be mentioned that the Zagreb Stock Exchange is the only securities market in Croatia. The first and most relevant Zagreb Stock Exchange equity index is CROBEX. CROBEX, whose base date is July 1st, 1997 and base value 1000, is constituted of 25 shares, weighted by free-float market capitalization with maximum share weight of 10%. CROBEX is perceived as an indicator of Croatian Stock market prices movement. This research uses the CROBEX data for the last ten years, more precisely from the beginning of year 2010 until the end of year 2019. Figure 1 shows CROBEX closing values in the chosen time interval.

Figure 1. CROBEX closing values – historical data
Source: The Zagreb Stock Exchange (ZSE)

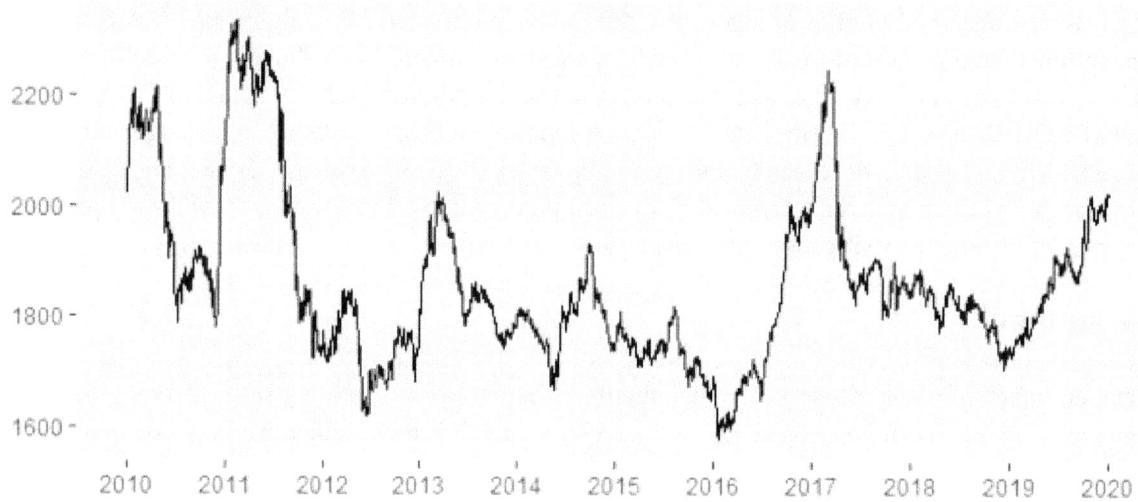

As each data record refers to a single trading day, there are 2492 records (observations) for the selected time period. The indicators used are chosen following Bruni (2016). The values of parameters used in calculations are chosen as values commonly used as default by traders and authors of research papers in the area of intraday trading, although there are ways to determine better values for the parameters for specific cases. There are a total of 22 indicators calculated for each data record as described below.

- **Momentum:** It shows the direction of movement in index value by remaining positive while an uptrend is sustained or negative while a downtrend is sustained. The momentum $M_t(n)$ of the current time period t is computed as the difference between the current closing price c_t and the closing price of n days ago c_{t-n}. Momentum can take any real value, either positive (denoting that the index is increasing) or negative (denoting that the index is increasing). In this research $M_t(5)$ is used and labeled as **MOM**.

- **EMA:** An exponential moving average (EMA) applies weighting factors which decrease exponentially in the past, but never reach zero. $EMA_t(n)$ is computed using the current closing price c_t and the EMA of the previous day as

$$EMA_t(n) = \left(\frac{2}{n+1}\right)c_t + \left(1 - \frac{2}{n+1}\right)EMA_{t-1}(n).$$

EMA can take any real positive value and has the same range of the price of the asset. In this research $EMA_t(12)$ and $EMA_t(26)$ are used and labeled as **EMA12** and **EMA26**, respectively.

- **Moving Average Convergence/Divergence:** This is an oscillator that should reveal changes in the strength, direction, momentum, and duration of a change in a stock's price. In this research it is calculated as the difference between two moving averages, one over a shorter period n and one over a longer period m, denoted as $MACD_t(n,m)$ and also subtracting from that a third moving average of the $MACD_t(n,m)$ itself over a period s, called "signal line" $SL(s)$, so the formula is

$$MACD_t(n,m,s) = EMA_t(n) - EMA_t(m) - SL(s).$$

MACD can take any real value, either positive (the index is increasing) or negative (the index is decreasing). In this research $MACD_t(12, 26, 9)$ is used and labeled **MACD**.

- **Return On Investment:** It is one way of considering profits in relation to capital invested. In this research $ROI(n)$ is calculated as the ration between average return over the last n days and the current closing value. It can take any real value, either positive (denotes income) or negative (denotes loss). On the data in this chapter ROI(10), ROI(20) and ROI(30) are calculated and labeled as **ROI10**, **ROI20** and **ROI30** respectively.
- **Relative Strength Index:** A momentum oscillator that measures speed and change of price movements of a security

$$RSI_t(n) = 100 - \frac{100}{1 + RS_t(n)},$$

where $RS_t(n)$ is the relative strength calculated as average of the last n upward changes divided by the average of the last n downward changes in price. RSI oscillates between 0 (close to this value when the upward changes are near to 0) and 100 (close to this value when the downward changes are near to 0). In this research $RSI_t(10)$, $RSI_t(14)$ and $RSI_t(30)$ are used and labeled **RSI10**, **RSI14** and **RSI30**, respectively.

- **Stochastic Relative Strength Index:** This indicator attempts to predict price turning points is calculated as

$$SRSI_t(n) = \frac{RSI_t(n) - \min\{RSI_t, RSI_{t-1}, \dots, RSI_{t-n+1}\}}{\max\{RSI_t, RSI_{t-1}, \dots, RSI_{t-n+1}\} - \min\{RSI_t, RSI_{t-1}, \dots, RSI_{t-n+1}\}}$$

and rages between 0 and 1. In this research $SRSI_t(10)$, $SRSI_t(14)$ and $SRSI_t(30)$ are used and labeled **SRSI10**, **SRSI14** and **SRSI30**, respectively.

- **Average True Range**: As a measure of the degree of price volatility is the exponential moving average of the True Range

$$TR_t = \max\{max_t, c_{t-1}\} - \min\{min_t, c_{t-1}\},$$

where $\max_t$ and $\min_t$ are the maximum and the minimum closing price at t respectively. In this research $ATR_t(14)$ is used and labeled **ATR**.

- **Average Directional Index:** It indicates only trend strength and is computed using the positive directional indicator, the negative directional indicator and ATR. Average directional index ranges between 0 and 100 and its values below 20 indicate trend weakness, and values above 40 indicate trend strength. In this chapter, average directional index is calculated over the last 14 periods i.e. $ADX_t(14)$ is used and labeled as **ADX**.
- **Williams %R:** It is an oscillator that analyzes whether a stock or commodity market is trading near the high or the low, or somewhere in between of its recent trading range. It is calculated using the current closing price c_t as well as the maximum and the minimum closing prices at a certain days as

$$\%R_t(n) = -100 \frac{\max\{max_t, max_{t-1}, \dots, max_{t-n+1}\} - c_t}{\max\{max_t, max_{t-1}, \dots, max_{t-n+1}\} - \min\{min_t, min_{t-1}, \dots, min_{t-n+1}\}}$$

and ranges between -100 (the close was the lowest low of the past n days) and 0 (the close was the highest high of the past n days). In this work, $\%R_t(14)$ is used and labeled **WPR**.

- **Commodity Channel Index**: This indicator is an oscillator originally developed by Lambert (1980) to identify commodity cycles. The assumption is that commodities (and other instruments) move in cycles in a sense that highs and lows occur in regular intervals. Its values are high when prices are far above their average and low when prices are far below their average so it can be used to identify overbought and oversold items. Also, it can be used to identify new trend. For example, surges above 100 reflect strong price action that can signal the start of an uptrend. It measures an asset value's deviation from its average and it is calculated by computing the simple average over the last n periods of the typical price and its standard deviation as

$$CCI_t(n) = \frac{TP_t - average\{TP_t, TP_{t-1}, \ldots, TP_{t-n+1}\}}{0.015 stdev\{TP_t, TP_{t-1}, \ldots, TP_{t-n+1}\}},$$

where typical price is calculated as

$$TP_t = \frac{max_t + min_t + c_t}{3}.$$

The values fluctuate around zero and in this research $CCI_t(20)$ is used and labeled **CCI**.

- **Ultimate Oscillator**: This indicator uses buying or selling "pressure", represented by where the daily closing price falls within the daily true range. It is calculated as

$$UO_t(n, m, s) = 100\frac{4AVG_t(n) + 2AVG_t(m) + AVG_t(s)}{7},$$

where

$$AVG_t(n) = \frac{BP_t + BP_{t-1} + BP_{t-n+1}}{TR_t + TR_{t-1} + TR_{t-n+1}}$$

is the total buying pressure over the past n days and

$$BP_t = c_t - \min\{min_t, c_{t-1}\}$$

is the buying pressure. It ranges between 0 and 100. In this chapter $UO_t(7, 14, 28)$ is used and labeled **UO**.

Due to the indicators calculation, 39 data records are lost because some of the indicators cannot be calculated for the first 39 records. Hence, the total number of data records which are used in the following experiments is 2453. Summary statistics for the data are given in Table 1.

As mentioned before, the class that is assigned to each daily record is 1 if the subsequent day is favorable for intra-day trading and 0 otherwise. If the increase between the opening price and the closing price of the same day is larger than than 0.3%, it is considered large enough for obtaining a profit by buying at the opening price and selling at the closing price. In that case the day is marked as favorable and labeled "YES" in the data. Otherwise, the day is marked as unfavorable and labeled "NO" in the data. The categorical variable indicating class in the data is labeled with **CLSS**. It should be noted that

Table 1. Data summary statistics

	Min	Max	Mean	St.dev.
OPEN	1577.13	2334.96	1857.26	154.23
HIGH	1590.29	2338.31	1864.13	155.53
LOW	1570.05	2323.92	1849.14	152.73
CLOSE	1576.47	2333.76	1857.18	154.14
MOM	-237.10	179.18	0.20	29.48
EMA12	1594.33	2307.58	1856.90	151.84
EMA26	1601.54	2295.04	1856.44	148.07
MACD	-5.00	3.47	0.01	0.95
ROI10	$-8.02\cdot10^{-6}$	$4.82\cdot10^{-6}$	$-3.68\cdot10^{-10}$	$1.20\cdot10^{-6}$
ROI20	$-4.57\cdot10^{-6}$	$3.20\cdot10^{-6}$	$-8.50\cdot10^{-10}$	$9.23\cdot10^{-7}$
ROI30	$-4.33\cdot10^{-6}$	$2.42\cdot10^{-6}$	$-2.66\cdot10^{-9}$	$7.97\cdot10^{-7}$
RSI10	7.77	84.03	49.58	15.96
RSI14	11.34	79.68	49.57	13.91
RSI30	17.66	72.56	49.58	10.24
STOCHRSI10	0.00	1.00	0.49	0.38
STOCHRSI14	0.00	1.00	0.49	0.38
STOCHRSI30	0.00	1.00	0.49	0.39
ATR	8.41	73.39	19.15	8.46
ADX	6.54	78.11	26.54	13.21
WPR	0.00	1.00	0.49	0.30
CCI	-294.16	392.65	-0.28	115.07
UO	30.77	70.00	52.00	5.42

this computation of the class causes the loss of the last data record, so the data set now contains 2452 records. There are 657 favorable days and 1795 unfavorable days, according to the previous definition. Thus, the data is imbalanced since there are significantly more unfavorable days than the favorable ones. Table 2 shows summary statistics for the data grouped by class.

To visually examine how the predictors (indicators) influence the class (favorability of a given day), the predictors are converted to range between 0 and 1. The predictors are grouped by class to observe the degree of mean shift amongst the groups which should be an indicator that a given variable will have a significant role to help predict the class. This shift can be observed in Figure 2 which presents the box plots for all of the variables.

Since the box plots do not seem to reveal much for this data, the density curves are examined. The density curves are expected to be significantly different for the two classes if the variable is important. Taking a look at the density curves for this data, it seems that WPR and RSI30 will likely be significant predictors of day favorability and the corresponding density curves for the two variables are given in Figure 3. However, it may not be beneficial to conclude which variables are not important because sometimes variables with uninteresting pattern can help explain some aspects of the outcome that may not be visually important. In this research, feature selection will not be performed in advance. Instead,

Table 2. Data summary statistics by class

	Favourable day (YES)				**Unfavourable day (NO)**			
	Min	**Max**	**Mean**	**St.dev.**	**Min**	**Max**	**Mean**	**St.dev.**
OPEN	1593.14	2330.01	1879.24	165.30	1577.13	2334.96	1849.22	149.21
HIGH	1594.03	2337.02	1887.35	166.89	1590.29	2338.31	1855.63	150.31
LOW	1579.77	2323.92	1870.79	163.94	1570.05	2323.75	1841.22	147.67
CLOSE	1585.73	2330.19	1879.71	165.17	1576.47	2333.76	1848.94	149.10
MOM	-213.43	158.00	-1.41	32.76	-237.10	179.18	0.78	28.17
EMA12	1599.89	2307.30	1880.98	164.15	1594.33	2307.58	1848.09	146.14
EMA26	1605.59	2294.83	1881.11	160.59	1601.54	2295.04	1847.41	142.19
MACD	-4.94	3.44	-0.02	1.01	-5.00	3.47	0.03	0.93
ROI10	$-7.89 \cdot 10^{-6}$	$4.10 \cdot 10^{-6}$	$-9.48 \cdot 10^{-8}$	$1.33 \cdot 10^{-6}$	$-8.02 \cdot 10^{-6}$	$4.82 \cdot 10^{-6}$	$3.42 \cdot 10^{-8}$	$1.14E \cdot 10^{-6}$
ROI20	$-4.57 \cdot 10^{-6}$	$3.20 \cdot 10^{-6}$	$-4.99 \cdot 10^{-8}$	$1.00 \cdot 10^{-6}$	$-4.50 \cdot 10^{-6}$	$3.04 \cdot 10^{-6}$	$1.71 \cdot 10^{-8}$	$8.93 \cdot 10^{-7}$
ROI30	$-4.33 \cdot 10^{-6}$	$2.30 \cdot 10^{-6}$	$-2.40 \cdot 10^{-8}$	$8.48 \cdot 10^{-7}$	$-4.25 \cdot 10^{-6}$	$2.42 \cdot 10^{-6}$	$5.13 \cdot 10^{-9}$	$7.78 \cdot 10^{-7}$
RSI10	9.04	84.03	49.04	16.45	7.77	81.80	49.78	15.78
RSI14	11.50	79.68	49.13	14.35	11.34	77.51	49.73	13.74
RSI30	19.35	72.56	49.45	10.60	17.66	70.87	49.63	10.11
STOCHRSI10	0.00	1.00	0.49	0.38	0.00	1.00	0.49	0.38
STOCHRSI14	0.00	1.00	0.48	0.38	0.00	1.00	0.49	0.38
STOCHRSI30	0.00	1.00	0.48	0.39	0.00	1.00	0.49	0.38
ATR	8.41	69.07	20.39	8.93	9.08	73.39	18.70	8.23
ADX	7.28	75.11	26.29	13.79	6.54	78.11	26.63	12.99
WPR	0.00	1.00	0.51	0.30	0.00	1.00	0.48	0.31
CCI	-292.15	264.84	-5.12	114.69	-294.16	392.65	1.49	115.20
UO	30.77	67.10	51.81	5.33	31.84	70.00	52.07	5.46

the classification algorithms will be allowed to learn the relationship between the variables their own way since the dataset is not too large and there is always a chance to neglect the predictors which do not seem to be worth including in the model.

SELECTED CLASSICATION ALGORITHMS

Different approaches are tested in solving the day trading problem with CROBEX. Since the idea was to try different families of classification algorithms, the following approaches are tested: Neural Network (NN), Support Vector Machine (SVM), Random Forest (RF), *k*-Nearest Neighbors (KNN) and Naïve Bayes classifier (NB).

For all of the approaches, the models are cross-validated and their hyper parameters are tuned for optimal model performance. Namely, when choosing models, it is common practice to separate the available data into two portions, training and test data, where the training data is used to estimate any parameters

Figure 2. Box plots

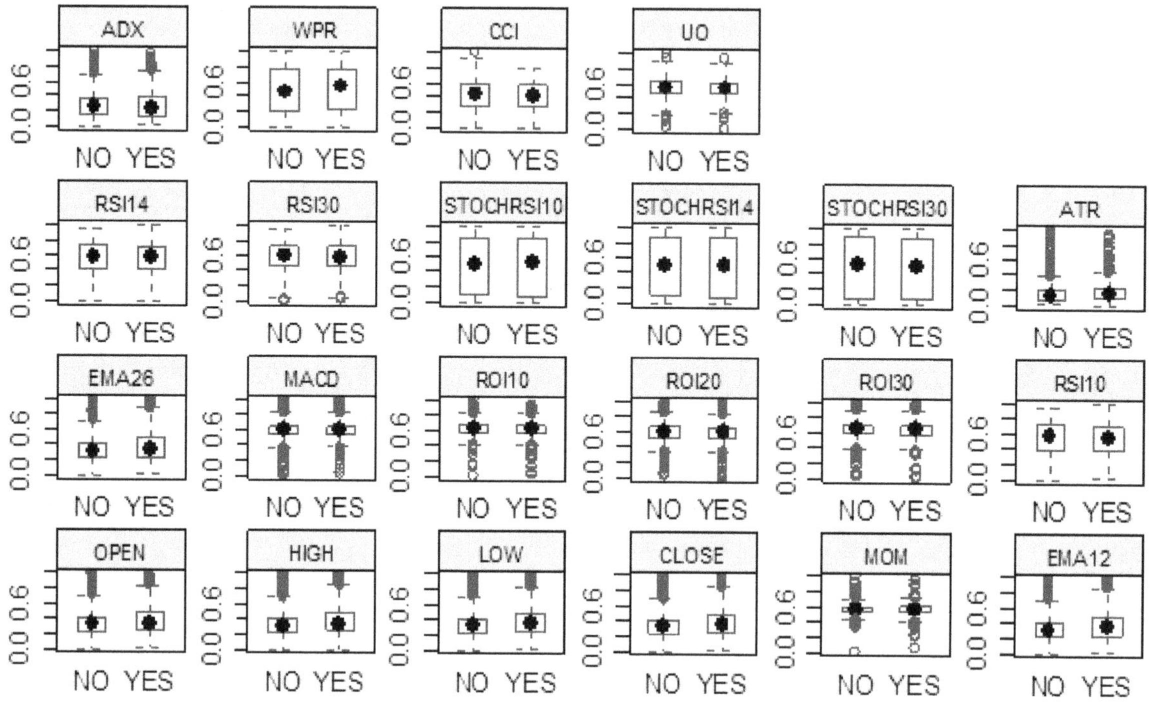

Figure 3. Density plots

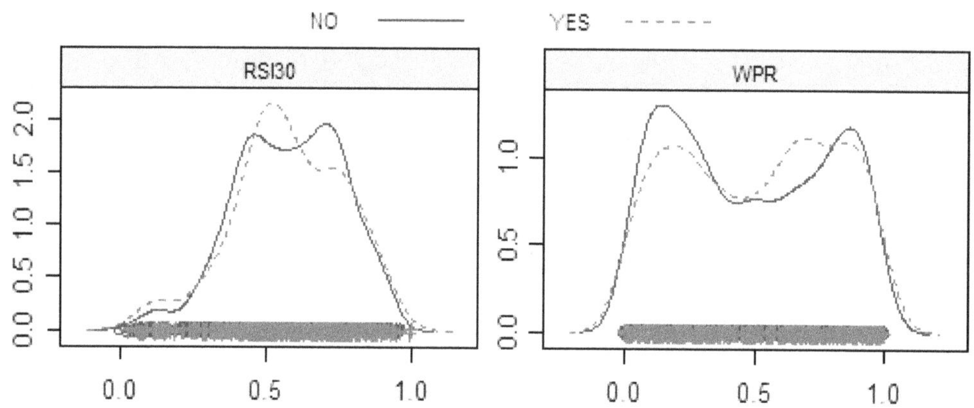

of a forecasting method and the test data is used to evaluate its accuracy. This is typically repeated more than once and is known as cross-validation: resampling procedure used to evaluate machine learning models on a limited data sample i.e. used for estimating the performance of a machine learning model on unseen data. Thus, cross-validation combines (averages) measures of fitness in prediction to derive a more accurate estimate of model prediction performance (Seni & Elder, 2010).

There are many types of cross-validation and data splitting for cross validation in this research is performed with rolling forecasting origin technique that moves the training and test sets in time (Hyndman & Athanasopoulos, 2020). The three parameters for this type of splitting are: the initial number of consecutive values in each training set sample, the number of consecutive values in test set sample and a logical that determines whether the training set always start at the first sample and the training set size will vary over data splits or the first point of training set will also move in time. For CROBEX data the number of consecutive values in each training set sample is set at 350, the number of consecutive values in test set sample is set at 85, which also the number of resamples to skip to thin the total amount to 36. Therefore 36 resamples are used for evaluating the effect of model tuning parameters on performance and choosing the optimal model across these parameters. This also allows estimation and comparison of models performances from resamples. It should be mentioned that during the cross-validation, the data were preprocessed and transformed to [0, 1] interval of normalized values.

Although the most common metric for evaluation of classification methods is accuracy, for the CROBEX data, Cohen's kappa (Cohen, 1960) is used as evaluation metric because it behaves better with imbalanced data. Namely, accuracy is a good choice of evaluation for classification problems which are well balanced and not skewed. It is calculated as the proportion of true results (true positives and true negatives) among the total number of cases examined. However, for imbalanced data, accuracy is not a suitable measure of classification performance since it can lead to simply choosing the same class all the time for the model to be accurate, which is actually of no value at all. That means that for imbalanced classification, a high accuracy (or low error) is achievable by a no skill model that only predicts the majority class. On the other hand, Cohen's kappa statistic is a measure that can handle imbalanced class problems. It basically tells how much better a chosen classifier is performing over the performance of a classifier that simply guesses at random according to the frequency of each class. The problem with Cohen's kappa is that it is harder to interpret than simple accuracy.

The main ideas of each of the approaches are described in the following text, while the results of the computation experiments are given in the section afterwards.

Neural Network

An artificial neural network or simply neural network in this context is a computational model that is inspired by the way biological neural networks in the human brain process information. The basic unit of computation in a neural network is the neuron, often called a node or unit. It receives input from some other nodes or from an external source and computes an output. Each input has an associated weight, which is assigned on the basis of its relative importance to other inputs. The node applies an activation function to the weighted sum of its inputs. There are several activation functions that can be used. The literature on neural networks in quite comprehensive, see i.e. Ripley (2007), Haykin (1999), Bishop (1995).

The first and simplest type of artificial neural network devised was the feedforward neural network. It contains multiple nodes arranged in layers. Nodes from adjacent layers have connections or edges between them. All these connections have weights associated with them. A feedforward neural network can consist of three types of nodes: input nodes, hidden nodes and output nodes. In a feedforward network, the information moves only in one direction, forward, from the input nodes, through the hidden nodes (if any) and to the output nodes, without forming a cycle. A neural network with one or more hidden layers is called multi-layer perceptron. On the other side, a neural network may be without any hidden layers in which case it is called single layer perceptron. The process by which a multi-layer perceptron learns is called the backpropagation algorithm where the output values are compared with the correct answer to compute the value of some predefined error-function and the weights are adjusted accordingly.

In this research the feed-forward neural networks with a single hidden layer is fitted, after being tuned by varying the number of hidden units and weight decay. The activation function is logistic. The amount of granularity in the tuning parameter grid is set to 10 i.e. the number of levels for tuning parameters is 10.

Support Vector Machine

The main goal of the support vector machine algorithm is to find a hyperplane in an N-dimensional space (N being the number of features) that distinctly classifies the data points. Maximizing the margin distance i.e. the distance between data points of both classes, provides some reinforcement so that future data points can be classified with more confidence. Support vectors are data points that are closer to the hyperplane and influence the position and orientation of the hyperplane. Support vector machines are looking to maximize the margin between the data points and the hyperplane. Support vector machine uses so called kernel to implicitly map their inputs into high-dimensional feature spaces which allows efficiently performing a non-linear classification. More on SVM methodology can be found, for example, in work by James (2013), Kuhn and Johnson (2013), Hastie, Tibshirani and Friedman (2001).

The CROBEX data are processed by support vector machine with radial basis function (RBF) kernel which is tuned over the cost parameter and the RBF kernel parameter sigma. The cost parameter controls the trade-off between errors of the SVM on training data and margin maximization. The number of levels for tuning parameters is 20.

Random Forest

Random forests are an ensemble learning method for classification, regression and other tasks that operate by constructing a multitude of decision trees and outputting the class that is the mode of the classes (in case of classification) of the individual trees (Ho, 1998; Breiman, 2001). Basically, the main concept behind random forest is the wisdom of crowds. It uses bagging and feature randomness when building each individual tree to try to create an uncorrelated forest of trees whose prediction by committee is more accurate than that of any individual tree. More on random forests can be found for example, in Izenman (2008) and Hastie (2001).

In this chapter, random forest is tuned by varying the number of randomly selected predictors i.e. the number of variables randomly sampled as candidates at each split. The number of levels for tuning parameters is 20.

K-Nearest Neighbors

The method of k-nearest neighbors makes mild structural assumptions and its predictions are often accurate but sometimes also unstable, as stated by Hastie, Tibshirani and Friedman (2001). The KNN algorithm assumes that similar things are near to each other. More precisely, an object is classified by a plurality vote of its neighbors, with the object being assigned to the class most common among its k nearest neighbors. The best choice of k depends upon the data and in this research it is tuned by trying 20 different values. More on this can be read in Hall (2008).

Naïve Bayes Classifier

A naïve Bayes classifier is a probabilistic machine learning model that's used for classification task (Murty & Devi, 2011; Russel, 2010). It is based on the Bayes theorem. The assumption made is that the predictors are independent which is mostly violated in practice. However, by making this assumption the calculation can be simplified such that the posterior probability is simply the product of the probability distribution for each individual variable conditioned on the response category. This is the main disadvantage of NB classifier, but on the other hand, it has advantages such as being is simple, fast, performing well with small amounts of training data and scaling well to large data sets. One additional issue to be aware of is that NB classifier can run into a problem when new data includes a feature value that never occurs for one or more levels of a response class which will always force the posterior probability to be zero for that class. A solution to this problem involves using the Laplace smoother which adds a small number to each of the counts in the frequencies for each feature, which ensures that each feature has a nonzero probability of occurring for each class.

On CROBEX data, NB classifier is tuned for Laplace correction – parameter that allows usage of a kernel density estimate for continuous variables versus a Gaussian density estimate, distribution type – parameter that allows adjusting the bandwidth of the kernel density (larger numbers mean more flexible density estimate) and bandwidth adjustment, which allows incorporating the Laplace smoother.

SOLUTIONS AND RECOMMENDATIONS

All the analysis was conducted using R (R Core Team, 2019) and the core for performing the experiments by tuning each of the selected algorithms and comparing their performance was caret package (Kuhn, 2020). The R packages for running the selected algorithms were: nnet (Venables & Ripley, 2002) for neural network, kernlab (Karatzoglou, Smola, Hornik, & Zeileis, 2004) for support vector machine, randomForest (Liaw & Wiener, 2002) for random forest, class (Venables & Ripley, 2002) for *k*-nearest neighbors and naivebayes (Majka, 2019) for naïve Bayes classifier. For calculations of technical indicators, packages TTR (Ulrich, 2019) and quantmod (Ryan & Ulrich, 2019) were used.

To evaluate the performance of the selected classification algorithms, they are collectively evaluated on resamples (the same resampling sets are used for all models.) Therefore, the differences between models are characterized by their resampling distributions. Since models were fit on the same versions of the training data, it makes sense to make inferences on the differences between models. In this way the within-resample correlation that may exist is reduced. After the differences between models were computed, a simple *t*-test to evaluate the null hypothesis that there is no difference between models is used. The summary of the results is given in Table 3.

Table 3. Summary of model performances on resamples (Kappa value, the bigger – the better)

	Min	1st Qu.	Median	Mean	3rd Qu.	Max
NN	-0.13793	-0.02525	0.02588	0.04924	0.12586	0.34000
SVM	-0.09873	-0.00219	0.04743	0.06069	0.13758	0.29787
RF	-0.14000	0.00000	0.04957	0.04594	0.09771	0.28000
KNN	-0.15000	-0.03327	0.00000	0.03397	0.09040	0.33210
NB	-0.26227	-0.03878	0.01392	0.00974	0.07083	0.25424

The results reveal that the best mean Kappa value was obtained by SVM, while the worst mean Kappa value was with NB. When looking at the median Kappa values, the best one was obtained by RF, while the worst was by KNN. However, median Kappa for SVM is very close to median Kappa for RF and has less negative values which mean that the classification was very bad. Thus, it seems that SVM was of slightly better performance than RF for the CROBEX data.

To get a better insight into differences between different methods, resampling distributions can be visualized. Figure 4 shows box-whisker plots for resampling summary of model performance based on Kappa values.

Figure 4. Box plots for summary of model performance measured by Kappa

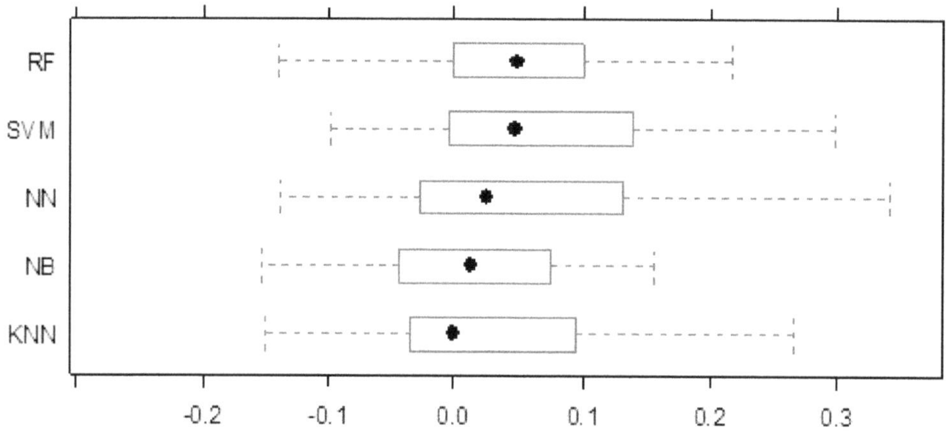

As expected by looking at the box-whisker plots, the null hypothesis that there is no difference between models could not be rejected after performing *t*-test. However, we observe that there is a greater variability for example for SVM than for RF, the two classifiers with the highest median Kappa that were already commented before.

Table 4. Confusion matrices obtained by different classifiers

	ACTUAL															
	NN			SVM			RF			KNN			NB			
PREDICTION		**NO**	**YES**		**NO**	**YES**		**NO**	**YES**		**NO**	**YES**		**NO**	**YES**	
	NO	54.5	19	**NO**	56.1	19.4	**NO**	59.5	21.4	**NO**	63.7	23	**NO**	43.1	15.9	
	YES	18.5	8	**YES**	16.9	7.5	**YES**	13.6	5.5	**YES**	9.4	3.9	**YES**	30	11.1	
	Sens.		0.25			0.23			0.19			0.13			0.41	
	Spec.		0.30			0.28			0.20			0.14			0.41	
	Acc.		0.62			0.64			0.65			0.68			0.54	

To observe more details on the results obtained by different classifiers, the confusion matrices for each of the classifiers, as well as the associated sensitivity, specificity and accuracy are presented in Table 4. Looking at those results, it can be seen that if a model that predicts the favorable days better is preferred, NB may be considered, given its high sensitivity. Although accuracy is not a good measure of classifiers' performance for imbalanced data, its values are given because of its popularity due to its easy interpretability.

Figure 5 shows importance plots obtained from running SVM and RF methods. The plots look quite different which is partially also due to differences in obtaining these values by caret package for the two methods. However, for example, both methods show the high importance for ATR.

Figure 5. Importance plots obtained from SVM and RF resamples results

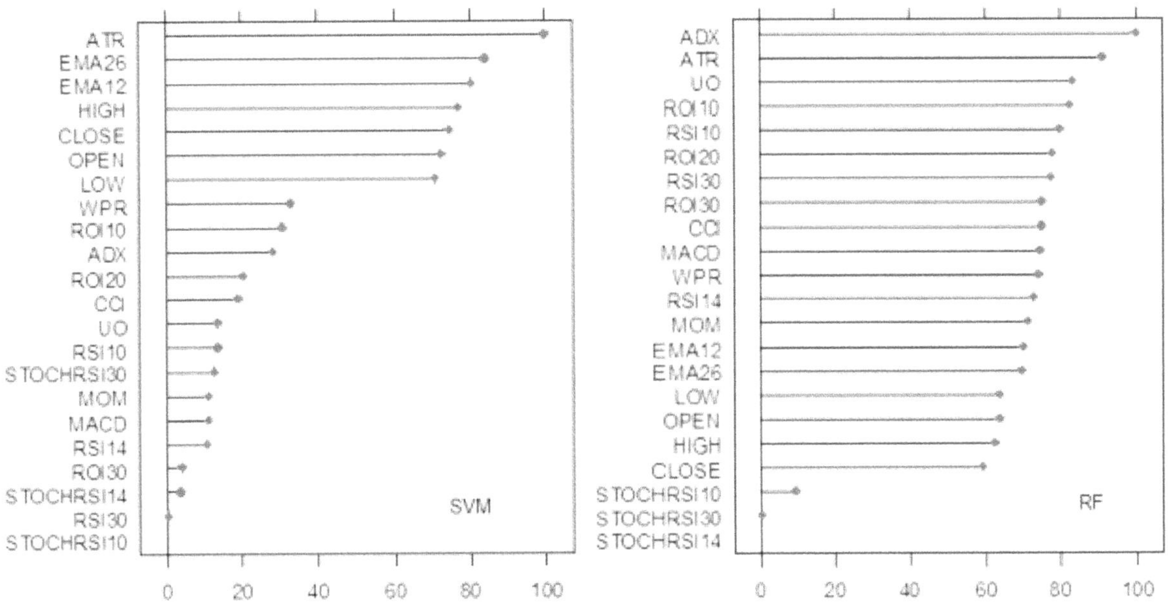

CONCLUSION AND FUTURE RESEARCH DIRECTIONS

In summary, this chapter evaluated and compared different classification algorithms on automatic recognition of favorable days for intra-day trading. Evaluations of neural network, support vector machine, random forest, *k*-nearest neighbors and naïve Bayes classifier showed little difference in performance on resamples according to Cohen's kappa. However, support vector machines and random forest seem to be most promising. When looking at the mean accuracy values, they range between 0.62 and 0.68 for all methods, which is acceptable, except for the naïve Bayes which is by far the worst. Regarding accuracy, one should keep in mind its bad representativeness of the imbalanced classification performance. Future research directions lie in trying many possible different approaches.

This chapter adds to a growing corpus of research efforts on stock market prediction. In addition, it should fill some gap in this area of research for Croatian market which is observed in literature. The results give insight to effectiveness of technical analysis in predicting the day favorability for CROBEX index and the obtained performance measures are not bad and implicate that technical analysis makes sense and might work. In this chapter, the various classification algorithms were tested on resamples. However, in future, though the best model was selected in this research for each classification method based on resamples and model tuning, what remains now is to confirm this by using each model to make predictions on new data, the data that has not been used in tuning the algorithms.

These findings also provide a good starting point for discussion and further research which would add interpretability to the classification models. One possibility for this could be searching for a rule set from random forest model that would increase scalability and comprehensibility while preserving satisfactory level of accuracy. Random forest seems to be promising when looking at its performance which was analyzed in this chapter. Nevertheless, a possible limitation of RF is that it generates a forest consisting of many trees and rules, thus it is viewed as a black box model. However, a very appealing possibility with random forest is the fact that it can be used for extracting rules which can allow an easy interpretation of such a model – i.e. obtaining a set of rules that are easy to understand. There are papers in the literature that demonstrate that for other datasets which gives idea for this direction of future work. Namely, once the RF is built, some type of algorithm can be used to search for a rule set such that it reduces the number of rules dramatically, which signiðcantly improves comprehensibility of the underlying model built by RF. For example, Mashayekhi and Gras (2015) proposed such methods that are evaluated on 22 data sets and their experimental results show that the proposed methods outperform one of the state-of-the-art methods in terms of scalability and comprehensibility while preserving the same level of accuracy.

In conclusion, this chapter enables readers to get a glance at how using different approaches with classifiers and technical analysis might work as an investment decision making tool. Thus, it can be beneficiary to both academics and practitioners. In future, investors might especially be interested what set of rules for investment would be extracted from the underlying RF classifier.

REFERENCES

Bishop, C. M. (1995). *Neural Networks for Pattern Recognition*. Oxford University Press.

Breiman, L. (2001). Random Forests. *Machine Learning*, *45*(1), 5–32. doi:10.1023/A:1010933404324

Bruni, R. (2017). Stock Market Index Data and indicators for Day Trading as a Binary Classification problem. *Data in Brief*, *10*, 569–575. doi:10.1016/j.dib.2016.12.044 PMID:28070548

Bruni, R., & Bianchi, G. (2015). Effective Classification using Binarization and Statistical Analysis. *IEEE Transactions on Knowledge and Data Engineering*, *27*, 2349–2361. doi:10.1109/TKDE.2015.2416727

Cohen, J. (1960). A coefficient of agreement for nominal scales. *Educational and Psychological Measurement*, *20*(1), 37–46. doi:10.1177/001316446002000104

Hall, P., Park, B. U., & Samworth, R. J. (2008). Choice of neighbor order in nearest-neighbor classification. *Annals of Statistics*, *36*(5), 2135–2152. doi:10.1214/07-AOS537

Hastie, T., Tibshirani, R., & Friedman, J. (2001). *The Elements of Statistical Learning: Data Mining, Inference, and Prediction*. Springer. doi:10.1007/978-0-387-21606-5

Haykin, S. (1999). *Neural Networks: A Comprehensive Foundation*. Prentice Hall.

Ho, T. K. (1998). The Random Subspace Method for Constructing Decision Forests. *IEEE Transactions on Pattern Analysis and Machine Intelligence*, *20*(8), 832–844. doi:10.1109/34.709601

Hyndman, R. J., & Athanasopoulos, G. (2018). Forecasting: principles and practice (2nd ed.). OTexts.

Ince, H., & Trafalis, T. B. (2007). Kernel principal component analysis and support vector machines for stock price prediction. *IIE Transactions*, *39*(6), 629–637. doi:10.1080/07408170600897486

Izenman, A. J. (2008). *Modern multivariate statistical techniques: Regression, classification, and manifold learning*. Springer. doi:10.1007/978-0-387-78189-1

James, G., Witten, D., Hastie, T., & Tibshirani, R. (2013). *An Introduction to Statistical Learning: with Applications in R*. Springer. doi:10.1007/978-1-4614-7138-7

Kara, Y., Boyacioglu, M. A., & Baykan, O. K. (2011). Predicting direction of stock Price index movement using artificial neural networks and support vector machines: The sample of the Istanbul stock exchange. *Expert Systems with Applications*, *38*(5), 5311–5319. doi:10.1016/j.eswa.2010.10.027

Karatzoglou, A., Smola, A., Hornik, K., & Zeileis, A. (2004). kernlab - An S4 Package for Kernel Methods in R. *Journal of Statistical Software*, *11*(9), 1–20. doi:10.18637/jss.v011.i09

Kimoto, K., Asakawa, K., Yoda, M., & Takeoka, M. (1990). Stock market prediction system with modular neural network. *Proceedings of the International Joint Conference on Neural Networks*. 10.1109/IJCNN.1990.137535

Kuhn, M. (2020). *caret: Classification and Regression Training. R package version 6.0-85*. https://CRAN.R-project.org/package=caret

Kuhn, M., & Johnson, K. (2013). *Applied predictive modeling*. Springer. doi:10.1007/978-1-4614-6849-3

Lambert, D. (1980). *Commodity Channel Index: Tool for Trading Cyclic Trends. Commodities Magazine*.

Liaw, A., & Wiener, M. (2002). Classification and Regression by randomForest. *R News*, *2*(3), 18–22.

Lo, A. W., & Hasanhodzic, J. (2010). *The Evolution of Technical Analysis: Financial Prediction from Babylonian Tablets to Bloomberg Terminals*. Bloomberg Press.

Majka, M. (2019). *_naivebayes: High Performance Implementation of the Naive Bayes Algorithm in R_. R package version 0.9.6*. https://CRAN.R-project.org/package=naivebayes

Mashayekhi, M., & Gras, R. (2015). Rule Extraction from Random Forest: the RF+HC Methods. In Advances in Artificial Intelligence. Canadian AI 2015. Lecture Notes in Computer Science, (vol. 9091). Springer.

Mizuno, H., Kosaka, M., Yajima, H., & Komoda, N. (1998). Application of Neural Network to Technical Analysis of Stock Market Prediction. *Studies in Informatics and Control*, *7*(3), 111–120.

Moreira, J. M., Jorge, A. M., Soares, C., & Sousa, D. J. F. (2006). Improving SVM-Linear predictions using CART for example selection. In *Proceedings of the 16th International Conference on Foundations of Intelligent Systems*. Springer-Verlag. 10.1007/11875604_70

Murty, M. N., & Devi, V. S. (2011). *Pattern Recognition: An Algorithmic Approach*. Springer-Verlag. doi:10.1007/978-0-85729-495-1

Pop, I. (2006). An approach of the Naive Bayes classifier for the document classification. *General Mathematics*, *14*(4), 135–138.

Qi, M., & Zhang, G. P. (2008). Trend time series modeling and forecasting with neural networks. *IEEE Transactions on Neural Networks*, *19*(5), 808–816. doi:10.1109/TNN.2007.912308 PMID:18467210

Qian, B., & Rasheed, K. (2007). Stock market prediction with multiple classifiers. *Applied Intelligence*, *26*(1), 25–33. doi:10.100710489-006-0001-7

R Core Team. (2019). *R: A language and environment for statistical computing*. R Foundation for Statistical Computing. URL https://www.R-project.org/

Ripley, B. D. (2007). *Pattern Recognition and Neural Networks*. Cambridge University Press.

Russell, S. J. (2010). *Artificial intelligence: a modern approach*. Prentice Hall.

Ryan, J. A., & Ulrich, J. M. (2019). *quantmod: Quantitative Financial Modelling Framework. R package version 0.4-15*. https://CRAN.R-project.org/package=quantmod

Šego, B., & Škrinjarić, T. (2018). Kvantitativna istraživanja Zagrebačke burze - pregled istraživanja od osnutka do 2018. Godine. *Ekonomski Pregled*, *69*(6), 655–743. doi:10.32910/ep.69.6.3

Seni, G., & Elder, J. (2010). Ensemble Methods in Data Mining: Improving Accuracy Through Combining Predictions. *Synthesis Lectures on Data Mining and Knowledge Discovery*, *2*(1), 1–126. doi:10.2200/S00240ED1V01Y200912DMK002

Shin, F. B., & Kil, D. H. (1998). Classification Cramer–Rao bounds on stock price prediction. *Journal of Forecasting*, *17*(5-6), 389–399. doi:10.1002/(SICI)1099-131X(1998090)17:5/6<389::AID-FOR703>3.0.CO;2-N

The Zagreb Stock Exchange Website. (n.d.). Available from: www.zse.hr

Tsaih, R., Hsu, Y., & Lai, C. C. (1998). Forecasting S&P 500 stock index futures with a hybrid AI system. *Decision Support Systems*, *23*(2), 161–174. doi:10.1016/S0167-9236(98)00028-1

Ulrich, J. (2019). *TTR: Technical Trading Rules. R package version 0.23-6*. https://CRAN.R-project.org/package=TTR

Venables, W. N., & Ripley, B. D. (2002). *Modern Applied Statistics with S* (4th ed.). Springer. doi:10.1007/978-0-387-21706-2

Zemke, S. (1999). Nonlinear index prediction. *Physica A*, *269*(1), 177–183. doi:10.1016/S0378-4371(99)00091-6

KEY TERMS AND DEFINITIONS

Artificial Neural Network: A computational model that is inspired by the way biological neural networks in the human brain process information.

Binary Classification: The task of classifying the elements of a given set into two groups.

CROBEX: Croatian stock index.

Day Trading: Buying and selling financial instruments within the same trading day.

Favorable for Intra-Day Trading: The increase between the opening price and the closing price of the same day is large enough for obtaining a profit by buying at the opening price and selling at the closing price.

K-Nearest Neighbors: Classification method in which an object is classified by a plurality vote of its neighbors, with the object being assigned to the class most common among its *k* nearest neighbors.

Naïve Bayes Classifier: A probabilistic machine learning model used for classification problems based on the Bayes theorem.

Random Forest: Ensemble learning method for classification, regression and other tasks that operates by constructing a multitude of decision trees.

Support Vector Machine: A computational model that finds a hyperplane in an N-dimensional space that distinctly classifies the data points.

Technical Analysis: The problem to discover the relation between the selected indicators at a certain day and the market situation at the following day that would determine the class of day that is observed, according to technical analysis.

Chapter 11
Connection Between Bank Competition and Bank Performance in India in Light of the Reserve Bank of India's Complaint

Rituparna Das
https://orcid.org/0000-0002-6877-9343
Adamas University, Kolkata, India

Gargi Guha Niyogi
Bhawanipur Gujarat Education Society College, University of Calcutta, India

ABSTRACT

The Reserve Bank of India suspected a cartel among 15 banks in fixing interest rates on deposits of the savings bank accounts over a period from 2011-12 to 2012-13 and lodged a complaint with the Competition Commission of India. The latter could not find any motive of the banks to collude and hence ruled out the complaint. The authors collected data on the banks' activities and performances on the said periods and examined in this chapter whether the commission was right in ruling out the complaint. The results of the analyses in this work lead to the conclusion that the commission was right in ruling out the complaint, but there are certain limitations and policy prescriptions that cropped out of this work, which should be conveyed to policy makers and researchers.

DOI: 10.4018/978-1-7998-5083-0.ch011

NEED FOR THE RESEARCH ON THE CONNECTION BETWEEN BANK COMPETITION AND BANK PERFORMANCE

In the Budget 2020 the Government of India proposed to infuse INR 70000 crore in addition to already infused 3.5 crore capital to the public sector undertaking (PSU) banks in India after the recovery of over 4 trillion INR of bad loans in the last 4 years through Insolvency and Bankruptcy code (IBC). The overall bad loans of Indian scheduled commercial banks peaked reportedly to 10.36 trillion as of March 2018. This decision came against the backdrop of slowdown of economic growth and chronic non-performing loan or asset (NPA) problems facing the PSU banks. The slowdown of economic growth costs India the downgrade of sovereign rating from stable to negative assigned by Moody's. The banking system plays a major role in financing economic growth as lender to the business. Performances of the banks in playing this role need to be backed by adequate strength in the form of a strong capital to asset ratio. But being rivals of each other in the same industry, they need to strive to keep up performance in order to compete well with each other. In Moody's sovereign rating methodology, capital to asset ratio is an indicator of the strength of the banking system to face an event risk like loan default. The PSU banks are either lacking that health or need to maintain more than the prescribed capital adequacy ratio in order to take risk in lending as suspected by the academia. So is the need for capital infusion by the Union Government. There is a room to suspect presence of collusion in lieu of competition if all of them are suffering from bad health. This can be deemed as the price of a banking crisis and the consequent output loss that could occur in absence of capital infusion. The infusion is to be financed by the recapitalization bonds that the government would issue to some banks against the excess deposits generated out of demonetization and those banks later can sell these bonds in the market for raising further resources. The performance of a bank may be measured by the indicators like return on equity, i.e. net income by shareholder's equity. A part of net income may be provisioned toward credit risk capital in the case of inadequacy of capital. The inadequacy of capital reflects on the government's decision to infuse capital. This also reflects the PSU banks' susceptibility to event risk in terms of Moody's. Researchers take it to be an indicator of the banks' capital cushion size to manage expected or unexpected losses and excessively low levels of this ratio points to potential defaults and can be a forerunner of a banking crisis. Thus, it is clear that the PSU banks are not performing well. So, the PSU banks' individual credit ratings may be affected adversely. The individual bank credit ratings need to be indicative of individual strength of banks, after the effect of government or other guarantees has been taken into account. Credit rating is a rule of thumb indicator of banks' condition and likely to influence their future capital requirement. So, there is a need to investigate into the connection between bank performance and their competition against the backdrop of downgrade of sovereign rating. India's effort to seek changes in international financial governance through BRICS is in the process of shaping global economic policies and promoting financial stability which should have influenced positively the performances of the banks, but is thwarted by the geopolitical factors like political interferences (Shi, 2004; Sengupta and Vardhan, 2019) and bureaucracy in the BRICS (Indrakanti and Sridevi, 2019).

CHAPTER SUMMARY

In 2015 the Indian regulator Reserve Bank of India suspected fifteen banks including the largest public sector player State Bank of India and the largest private sector player ICICI Bank to have colluded in matter of deposit pricing and lodged a complaint with the Competition Commission of India. The latter rejected the complaint after an investigation on the basis that there is no operational motivation found that can suggest a possibility of collusion. Against this backdrop, authors initiated an inquiry into whether the Commission was right in ruling out the RBI's complaint, i.e. whether performances of the said banks motivate them to collude. With this view in the end, they measured conjectural variation as measure of competition and calculated its correlation with the return on equity as performance indicator of the banks. The correlation is found very low. In order to examine the validity of this result the change in efficiency of the banks over the years from 2011-12 to 2012-13 through constant return input-oriented data envelopment analysis have been examined and measured the correlation between such changes and conjectural variation have been measured. The results corroborate the decision of the Commission to rule out any motivation to cartel or collude because the above correlations are found to be weak. 'Cartel' means making price or output decisions by one firm in collusion with another or others.

THE DETAILED BACKGROUND

On the day marking the third anniversary of demonetisation, global ratings agency Moody's cut its outlook for India's sovereign rating to "negative" from "stable", citing the ongoing economic slowdown, financial stress among rural households, weak job creation, and the liquidity crunch in non-banking financial companies, as reported by the Business Standard on 9 November 2019. Sovereign rating implies the credibility of a country as a borrower from international institutions like IMF or as a bond issuer in the foreign markets. Sovereign rating can also be called an indicator of sovereign risk or credit default probability. In general, a credit rating is used by sovereign wealth funds, pension funds and other investors to gauge the credit worthiness of India thus having a big impact on the country's borrowing costs. The three most popular sovereign ratings firms include Standard & Poor's Sovereign Ratings, Moody's Investor Services Sovereign Ratings, Fitch Ratings. Sovereign Ratings as per media reports India's continued low per capita income and economy-wide chronic non-performing-asset disease are prominent factors contributing toward India's being awarded medium rating by these agencies. This is however not a problem because a poor performer is not supposed to receive a high grade. The issue is elsewhere - there are countries with relatively weaker macroeconomic fundamentals (e.g. Italy has higher non-performing loan to total gross loan ratio than has India) but are awarded higher grades of rating than is India by Fitch and Moody's despite the fact that their provisions are falling fast while India's provisions are rising fast. Authors seek to resolve the above puzzle through a study on the connection between bank competition and bank performance.

INTRODUCTION

Sovereign rating is an assessment of the creditworthiness or sovereign risk of a sovereign entity in matter of honoring its financial obligations primarily toward foreign lenders and investors. There are three major CRAs who rate the sovereigns: Standard and Poor's, Moody's and Fitch. As reflected by the reports of these agencies sovereign rating of a country depends on broadly three categories of criteria: (I) macroeconomic fundamentals including the fundamentals of government sector and foreign sector,

(II) administrative and regulatory fundamentals and (III) banking and financial sectors' fundamentals. The performance of the banking sector belongs to category III.

The contribution of saving bank interest rate (SBIR) as a cost of fund toward determining the performance of a bank is known to all. In January 2015 the Reserve Bank of India (RBI) suspected that either coordination is happening among banks in pricing of savings bank deposits from 2011 onward (Times of India, 2018). The RBI observed that the Indian banking sector has an oligopolistic structure where 55% of total deposits are held by a countable number of the public sector banks. As a result, there is little incentive for price competition among these banks. The RBI sought an investigation into the above suspected cartelization in January 2015. The conducts of 12 PSU banks and 3 new generation private sector banks – (i) State Bank of India (SBI), (ii) State Bank of Bikaner and Jaipur (SBBJ), (iii) State Bank of Hyderabad (SBH), (iv) State Bank of Patiala (SBP), (v) State Bank of Travancore (SBT), (vi) State Bank of Mysore (SBM), (vii) Bank of Baroda, (viii) Bank of India, (ix) Canara Bank, (x) Central Bank of India, (xi) Punjab National Bank, (xii) United Bank of India, (xiii) Axis Bank, (xiv) HDFC Bank and (xv) ICICI Bank, were examined by the Competition Commission of India (CCI). The CCI investigation ruled out the possibility of cartelization (Competition Commission of India, 2018a).

DEFINITIONS

Bank Competition-It is the competition in the functioning of the banking system. It relates to the efficiency, quality and innovation of the production of financial services. A poor bank competition endangers financial stability. The definition of competition is available in any standard text book of undergraduate Microeconomics.

Bank Performance – It is the adoption of a set of indicators which are indicative of the bank's current status and the extent of its ability to achieve the desired objectives. There are different key indicators of bank performance like customer profitability, revenue per employee, risk-adjusted net interest margin, return on equity, credit quality etc. The indicators are part and parcel of ration analysis.

Bank Efficiency – It is a measure of bank's ability to turn resources into revenue. The degree to which a bank is able to leverage its fixed costs also affects its efficiency. Again efficiency measures are available from ratio analysis.

OBJECTIVES

- To obtain a measure of competition or collusion following non-structural approach.
- To explore whether there is any link between competition among the aforesaid 15 banks and their performances.
- To estimate the connection between the return on equity and conjectural variation.

LITERATURE SURVEY

Léon(2014) distinguished between structural and non-structural approaches in measuring banking competition. The former is based on economic theory of market structure while the latter is based on observations on behaviours of firms. The work however provided a comprehensive account of the literature on different measures of competition classified in terms of the schools of economic thought.

Carlton and Perloff (2000) put forth a precise summary of how to measure collusion in oligopoly. They narrated the discussion of price competition in an oligopolistic structure in Cournot, Bertrand and Stackleberg. The measure of collusion is conjectural variation, i.e. whether change in price by a firm causes the change in price by another firm. More positive the conjectural variation, more is the collusion and vice versa.

Before measuring performance of a bank, it is necessary to define the nature of outputs generated by a bank and the nature of concerned inputs. Colwell and Davis (1992) is a review of literature on various approaches to measuring outputs and inputs of a bank. This work concludes that there is no unique measurement thereof and each approach is open to some or other criticism. For analysis purpose authors need data on inputs and outputs measured in terms of these approaches. Authors found the production approach is the most compatible with the available data, but after a bit modification. As per production approach deposit is an output. Authors like to treat deposits as raw materials in matter of generating investments and advances.

In Singh (2007), we find that performance of banks is implied by the following all indicators: (a) Indicators of Efficiency:

(i) Return on Assets (ROA)
(ii) Return on Equity (ROE)
(iii) Cost to Income Ratio
(iv) Non performing loan (NPL) to Asset Ratio
    (b) Indicator of Quality of Assets: Ratio of NPL to Loans
    (c) Indicator of Financial Strength: Capital Adequacy Ratio

In the above work there is a table for comparison of India with other SAARC members between 2000 and 2005, Korea, USA, Japan, Canada and UK. Inside the SAARC India is the lowest but outside the SAARC India is the highest in that ratio.

Krish (2018) observed that India's nonperforming assets net of provisions to capital is increasing steadily when compared to Italy, South Africa, USA, UK, Korea, China and Brazil between 2010 and 2017 in terms of panel data. Again, in terms of cross section data in 2017 capital adequacy ratios of only Bangladesh and Russia are below India among SAARC, Latin America, USA, UK, Europe and BRICS.

If performance reflects on returns on assets and equity and continuously decreasing returns signal instability Parida and Padhi (2018) is a noteworthy contribution. This work reviewed the existing literature of the findings on positive as well as negative relations between competition and stability.

There is no work till date on the link between banks' operating performances and competition in India. However, Arrawatia et al. (2015) is a work on the link between bank efficiency and bank competition. In the work the efficiency measure indicates whether a bank uses the minimum quantity of inputs to produce a given quantity of outputs or maximizes the output quantity, given a certain quantity of inputs. When price data for the inputs and/or outputs are available, one can also estimate cost and/or profit efficiency measures. Cost efficiency is the product of technical efficiency and allocative efficiency. The later refers to the ability of a bank to use the optimum mix of inputs, given their respective prices. Consequently, cost efficiency shows the ability of a bank to provide services without wasting resources as a result of technical or allocative inefficiency.

Zhao et al. (2018) has taken bond spread, stock returns and risk-taking indicators as alternative measures of bank performance. This work aimed to explore the causality from change in sovereign rating to bank performance (i) directly and (ii) indirectly through change in bank rating.

Sharma (2018) measured the connection between banks' market performances and bank efficiency. This work has conducted an extensive literature survey on the data envelope analysis (DEA) of measuring efficiency of the banks.

METHODOLOGY

The entire study is based mostly on the secondary data collected from different websites, journals, newspaper & Books on Research Methodology. To find out and execute this whole research study the work is divided into the following three parts. Authors plan

(a) To obtain a measure of competition or collusion following non-structural approach through calculation of conjectural variation in prices over 2011-12 and 2012-13

(b) To collect cross section data of the annual stock return of the Indian banks for 2011-12 and 2012-13 and to estimate the connection between the return on equityas a performance indicator on the one hand and conjectural variation on the other. Among other key indicators, Return on equity has been chosen since it measures the company's return in a format that is easily comparable with other institutions.

(c) To collect data on (i) capital, reserves and surplus and (ii) wages as percentage of total expenses, i.e. share of labour in total cost as inputs on the one hand and (iii) investments and (iv) advances as outputs in a bit modification of the production approach narrated in Colwell and Davis (1992) for the purpose of running the constant return to scale (RTS) input oriented DEA using DEA software developed by Joe Zhu (2019) after ensuring $n \geq \{x*y, 3(x+y)\}$ in line with Sharma (2018), where n is the number of decision making units (DMUs) or here banks, x is the number of inputs and y is the number of outputs, with a view to validate or invalidate the results of (b) above through measures of efficiency of the banks in matter of minimizing the volume of inputs assuming at least constant return to scale if increasing return to scale is a distant hope.

SAMPLING AND REPORTING DATA

There are 12 public sector banks and 22 private-sector banks in India. Other banks include small finance banks, regional rural banks, private sector banks, payments banks and local area banks as of April 1, 2019. The information on SBIRs is to be distilled out of the annual data on the profile of banks provided by the RBI for measuring conjectural variation. This data is available till 2012-13. Therefore, the data are collected for 2011-12 and 2012-13. In those relevant years amalgamation of banks did not happen. Therefore, 27 Public Sector banks were in existence. Approximately 30% of public and private sector banks have been selected using Convenience method of sampling.

There are two parts in reporting data. Part I is for the purpose of exploring cartelization and Part II is for the purpose of measuring performance and its correlation with cartelization if any.

The data on interest rate charged on loan is not available. The data on interest income is available. Interest income can increase if the total advances increase at the same rate of interest. Net interest margin (NIM) is a better measure because it neutralizes the effect of increase in advances and also focuses on net interest, other things remaining unchanged. It contains information on both the rates earned as well as paid.

The expression for measure of NIM may be constructed as follows. Let us suppose in a particular maturity bucket the volume of rate-sensitive asset is A, the volume of rate-sensitive liability is B, the interest rate earned from asset is r_1 and interest rate charged on liability is r_2. Here $A - B = b$, such that $A = B+b$. So NIM equals $r_1A - r_2B = r_1(B+b) - r_2B = (r_1-r_2)B - (r_1-r_2)b$. If b is a negligible amount, NIM = $(r_1-r_2)B$. If there are 'n' number of maturity buckets the cumulative NIM across buckets is $\sum_{i=1}^{n}(r_{1i} - r_{2i})B_i$. This is to be interpreted as follows - at any given level of B, the net interest is the interest rate on loan vis-à-vis the interest rate on deposit.

Data on own NIM of every bank is provided in the annual profile of banks by the RBI. Out of the 15 banks suspected by the RBI to have colluded, facing every one bank, the average NIM of other 14 banks can play the role of proxy for others' SBIRS.

It is an accepted fact that Net Non-Performing Asset (NNPA) goes up during economic downswing and vice versa. So, the negative Net Non-Performing Asset (NNPA) could play the role of proxy of Gross Domestic Product. The theoretical reasoning is that higher the NNPA, the lower is the Gross Domestic Product and so less is the demand for loan.

The Net Interest Margin (NIM) data are given in Table 1.

Table 1. Net Interest Margin (NIM) Data for Estimation of Conjectural Variation

	Financial Year	2012-13	2011-12	2012-13	2011-12
Serial No.	**Name of the Bank**	**NIM**	**NIM**	**Others' NIM**	**Others' NIM**
1	SBI	3.06	3.38	2.72	2.79
2	SBBJ	3.24	3.28	2.71	2.79
3	SBH	3.08	2.99	2.72	2.82
4	SBM	2.88	2.82	2.74	2.83
5	SBP	2.37	2.6	2.77	2.84
6	SBT	2.27	2.42	2.78	2.86
7	BOB	2.28	2.56	2.78	5.62
8	BOI	2.16	2.26	5.06	8.69
9	Canara Bank	2.00	2.17	5.07	8.70
10	Central Bank of India	2.30	2.35	5.36	9.30
11	PNB	3.17	3.21	4.99	8.55
12	UBI	2.30	2.73	5.05	8.64
13	Axis Bank	3.09	3.04	4.99	8.56
14	HDFC Bank	4.28	4.19	4.91	8.20
15	ICICI Bank	2.70	2.40	3.90	5.94

Source: A Profile of Banks, Reserve Bank of India

ANALYSIS AND RESULTS

(a) Based on the data on the NIMs of aforesaid 15 banks for 2012-13 and 2011-12 in Table 1, the authors calculated the conjecture variations in Table 2.

Table 2. Estimation of Conjectural Variation

	Financial Year	*2012-13 (i)*	*2011-12 (ii)*	*i/ii*
Serial No.	*Name of the Bank*	*Change in NIM*	*Change in Others NIM*	*Conjectural Variation*
1	SBI	-0.32	-0.06	4.98
2	SBBJ	-0.04	-0.08	0.47
3	SBH	0.09	-0.09	-0.96
4	SBM	0.06	-0.09	-0.66
5	SBP	-0.23	-0.07	3.25
6	SBT	-0.15	-0.08	1.96
7	BOB	-0.28	-2.85	0.10
8	BOI	-0.10	-3.63	0.03
9	Canara Bank	-0.17	-3.63	0.05
10	Central Bank of India	-0.05	-3.94	0.01
11	PNB	-0.04	-3.56	0.01
12	UBI	-0.43	-3.59	0.12
13	Axis Bank	0.05	-3.57	-0.01
14	HDFC Bank	0.09	-3.30	-0.03
15	ICICI Bank	0.30	-2.04	-0.15

(b) Next the authors will investigate the correlation(i) between conjectural variation and bank performance and (ii) between conjectural variation and bank efficiency. In Table 3 the data on conjectural variation and return on equity as a measure of bank stock performance and their correlation coefficient is given.

(c) With a view to validating or invalidating the result of (b) the authors plans to conduct CRS input-oriented DEA using the DEA software of Jhu (2019). In Table 4 and Table 5, the aforesaid 3 inputs and 2 outputs of aforesaid 15 banks are given for 2011-12 and 2012-13 are given.

The change in efficiency measures and the types of RTS, and the correlation between the change in efficiency and conjectural variation of the banks from 2012-13 to 2011-12 are given in Table 6.

(a) Table 2 reflects that except the private sector banks, SBH and SBM, all of other 9 banks in consideration have a tendency to collude the strength of which varies from bank to bank, i.e. the strongest tendency belongs to the SBI. (b) Table 3 reflects that there is 27% correlation between return on equity

Table 3. Correlation between Return on Equity and Conjectural Variation

Serial No.	Bank	ROE	Conjectural Variation
1	SBI	15.43	0.437794
2	SBBJ	16.36	0.054077
3	SBH	17.70	-0.12101
4	SBM	10.00	-0.08077
5	SBP	13.17	0.313458
6	SBT	14.94	0.203735
7	Bank of Baroda	15.07	0.382416
8	Bank of India	12.25	0.135536
9	Canara Bank	12.08	0.231096
10	Central Bank of India	7.31	0.067625
11	Punjab National Bank	15.70	0.054077
12	United Bank of India	6.84	0.382416
13	Axis Bank	18.53	-0.06734
14	HDFC Bank	20.34	-0.12101
15	ICICI Bank	13.10	-0.39983
	Correlation Coefficient	-0.271194	

Table 4. Input-Output Table 2011-12

	Inputs			Outputs	
Bank	Capital, reserves and surplus	Deposit	Wage Ratio	Investment	Advances
SBI	839512	10436474	19.01	3121976	8675789
SBBJ	41649	615721	15.18	166695	492443
SBH	64977	987319	12.77	292418	770523
SBM	39885	501863	13.68	147327	398353
SBP	47810	794166	11.74	220429	629345
SBT	38662	714698	12.68	224376	553460
Bank of Baroda	274769	3848711	12.18	832094	2873773
Bank of India	209618	3182160	12.22	867536	2488333
Canara Bank	226900	32070537	10.68	1020574	2824898
Central Bank of India	124515	1961733	14.14	592433	1475129
Punjab National Bank	278154	3795885	15.71	1227030	2937748
United Bank of India	55797	891163	12.98	290588	630433
Axis Bank	228085	2201043	10.41	931921	1697595
HDFC Bank	299247	2467064	14.01	974829	1954200
ICICI Bank	604052	2555000	11.47	1595600	25372777

Table 5. Input-Output Table 2012-13

Bank	Inputs			Outputs	
	Capital, reserves and surplus	Deposit	Wage Ratio	Investment	Advances
SBI	988837	12027396	17.57	3509273	10456166
SBBJ	47641	721162	15.17	201459	575350
SBH	76317	1133243	13.31	339680	898565
SBM	43325	569690	12.24	167746	449326
SBP	53419	886721	11.02	239567	737998
SBT	43650	846237	11.15	272255	674836
Bank of Baroda	319694	4738833	11.57	1213937	3281858
Bank of India	239182	3818396	11.09	946134	2893675
Canara Bank	248778	3558560	10.38	1211328	2421766
Central Bank of India	153129	2260383	14.21	726038	1719358
Punjab National Bank	46041	706415	11.34	225425	514308
United Bank of India	58837	1006515	11.28	334634	689087
Axis Bank	331079	2626136	9.73	1137375	1969660
HDFC Bank	362141	2962470	13.01	1116136	2397206
ICICI Bank	667060	2926136	11.4	1713936	2902494

Table 6. Correlation between Change in Efficiency and Conjectural Variation

DMU (Bank) Name	2011-12		2012-13		Change in Efficiency	Conjectural Variation
	Efficiency	RTS	Efficiency	RTS		
SBI	1.00000	Constant	1.00000	Constant	0.00000	0.43779
SBBJ	0.79274	Increasing	0.95387	Increasing	0.16113	0.054077
SBH	0.89548	Increasing	0.95463	Increasing	0.05916	-0.12101
SBM	0.79816	Increasing	0.93246	Increasing	0.13430	-0.08077
SBP	0.87102	Increasing	1.00000	Constant	0.12898	0.31345
SBT	1.00000	Constant	1.00000	Constant	0.00000	0.20373
Bank of Baroda	0.74671	Increasing	0.93329	Increasing	0.18658	0.38241
Bank of India	0.95402	Increasing	1.00000	Constant	0.04598	0.13553
Canara Bank	1.00000	Constant	1.00000	Constant	0.00000	0.23109
Central Bank of India	1.00000	Constant	0.98858	Decreasing	-0.01142	0.06762
Punjab National Bank	1.00000	Constant	0.93255	Increasing	-0.06745	0.05407
United Bank of India	0.99071	Decreasing	1.00000	Constant	0.00929	0.38241
Axis Bank	1.00000	Constant	1.00000	Constant	0.00000	-0.06734
HDFC Bank	0.87777	Increasing	0.93923	Decreasing	0.06146	-0.12101
ICICI Bank	1.00000	Constant	1.00000	Constant	0.00000	-0.3998
					Correlation	0.12840

and conjectural variation. (c) Table 6 reflects that there is 13% correlation between change in bank efficiency and conjectural variation. Punjab National Bank and Central Bank of India suffered from loss of efficiency and the latter also suffered from downgrade of return to scale from constant to decreasing but their conjectural variations are very low.

SCOPE OF FURTHER RESEARCH

In Table 6, Bank of India's and HDFC Bank's efficiencies increased over time but return to scale downgraded. This means if the return to scale remained unchanged their efficiency could have further increased. So there is scope for research on the policies pertaining loan, deposit and employment pertaining to operational aspects of these banks.

LIMITATION AND POLICY PRESCRIPTION

The limitation of this paper is that the work could have extended beyond 2013 upto the present but the RBI did not publish 'A Profile of Banks' after 2013. Some of the banks like State Bank of Hyderabad, State Bank of Travancore ceased to exist after 2017.

The policy prescription is that the banks should publish in their Annual Reports the return to scale achieved in their operations such that a signal regarding efficient use of scarce resources goes to the policy makers and researchers. This would motivate further research on production functions followed by banks as a service sector and how to ensure more efficient utilization of resources.

CONCLUSION

In 2015 the Indian regulator Reserve Bank of India suspected fifteen banks including the largest public sector player State Bank of India and the largest private sector player ICICI Bank to have colluded in matter of deposit pricing and lodged a complaint with the Competition Commission of India. The latter rejected the complaint after an investigation on the basis that there is no operational motivation found that can suggest a possibility of collusion. Against this backdrop the authors initiated an inquiry into whether the Commission was right in ruling out the RBI's complaint, i.e. whether performances of the said banks motivate them to collude. With this view in the end, they measured conjectural variation as measure of competition and calculated its correlation with the return on equity as performance indicator of the banks. The correlation is found very low. In order to examine the validity of this result the authors examined the change in efficiency of the banks over the years from 2011-12 to 2012-13through constant return input oriented data envelopment analysis and measured the correlation between such changes and conjectural variation. The results corroborate the decision of the Commission to rule out any motivation to cartel or collude because the above correlations are found to be weak.

FULL NAMES OF BANKS

SBI: State Bank of India

SBBJ: State Bank of Bikaner and Jaipur

SBH: State Bank of Hyderbad
SBM: State Bank of Mysore
SBP: State Bank of Patala
SBT: State Bank of Trivancore
BOB: Bank of Baroda
BOI: Bank of India
PNB: Punjab National Bank
UBI: United Bank of India

REFERENCES

Arrawatia, R., Mishra, A., & Dawar, A. (2015). Bank Competition and Efficiency: Empirical Evidence from Indian Market. *International Journal on Law and Management*, *57*(3), 217–231. doi:10.1108/IJLMA-03-2014-0029

Colwell, R., & Davis, E. (1992). Output and Productivity in Banking. *The Scandinavian Journal of Economics*, *94*, S111–S129. doi:10.2307/3440252

Competition Commission of India. (2018a). *Suo Motu Case No. 01 of 2015*. Retrieved from https://www.cci.gov.in/sites/default/files/Suo-%20Moto%2001-2015.pdf

Indrakanti, N., & Sridevi, V. (2019). Non performing Loans in BRICS Countries. *International Journal of Recent Technology and Engineering*, *8*(3S3), 625-630.

Krish, P. (2018). *Indian banks have very low capital compared to other countries*. Retrieved from https://www.moneycontrol.com/news/business/indian-banks-have-very-low-capital-compared-to-other-countries-3150211.html

Léon, F. (2014). *Measuring competition in banking: A critical review of methods*. Clermont University Working Paper. Retrieved from https://ideas.repec.org/p/cdi/wpaper/1577.html

Paridha, T., & Padhi, D. (2018). Does Bank Competition Affect Financial Stability in Banking Sector: Some Empirical Evidence from India. Competition Commission of India Working Paper. Retrieved from https://www.cci.gov.in/sites/default/files/whats_newdocument/3.%20Does%20Bank%20Competition%20Affect%20Financial%20Stability%20in%20Banking%20Sector.pdf

Sengupta, R., & Vardhan, H. (2019). *How Banking Crisis is impeding India's Economy*. Retrieved from https://www.ideasforindia.in/topics/money-finance/how-banking-crisis-is-impeding-india-s-economy.html

Sharma, D. (2018). Stock Market Performance and Efficiency of Banks in a Developing Economy: Evidence from the Indian Banking Sector. *IIM Kozhikode Society & Management Review*, *7*(2), 1–16.

Shih, V. (2004). Dealing with Non-Performing Loans: Political Constraints and Financial Policies in China. *The China Quarterly*, *180*(180), 922–944. doi:10.1017/S0305741004000682

Singh, P. (2007). *Global Competitiveness of Indian Banks: A study of select banking indicators, issues of concern and opportunities*. Retrieved from http://dspace.iimk.ac.in/handle/2259/48

Times of India. (2018). *No cartelisation among banks in fixing savings bank rates, says CCI*. Retrieved from https://timesofindia.indiatimes.com/business/india-business/no-cartelisation-among-banks-in-fixing-savings-bank-rates-says-cci/articleshow/63897976.cms

Zhao, S., Moeira, F., & Wang, T. (2018). *The Relationship among Sovereign Ratings, Bank Ratings and Bank Performances, Evidence from European Commercial Banks*. University of Edinburgh Business School Working Paper. Retrieved from www.efmaefm.org/0EFMAMEETINGS/.../2018.../EFMA2018_0265_fullpaper.pdf

Zhu, J. (2019). *DEA Frontier Free Version*. http://www.deafrontier.net/deafree.html

KEY TERMS AND DEFINITIONS

CRS: Constant return to scale; this means if employment of inputs increases by k times of the initial level the volume of output will increase by k times of the initial size.

NIM: Net interest margin; it is the difference between interest earnings from assets and interest expenses on liabilities.

NPA: Nonperforming asset; it means an asset in the balance sheet that has become unable to generate any further income, e.g. a defaulted loan.

PSU: Public sector undertaking; this acronym applies to the nationalized companies in India like major banks, insurance companies and several manufacturing companies where majority stakes are with the central government.

Quality of Loan: It means repayment capacity combined in absence of any moral hazard on part of the borrower.

Chapter 12
Estimation of Securities Positioning Efficiency in Commercial Banks

Natalia Frolova
https://orcid.org/0000-0002-3438-2962
National Research University Higher School of Economics, Russia

Evgeniy Frolov
National Research University Higher School of Economics, Russia

ABSTRACT

The given research is devoted to the acute issue of efficiency of valuable assets positioning carried out by commercial banks. The chapter is aimed at examining factors that affect the efficiency of securities placement by commercial banks, as well as an econometric analysis based on the least squares method of the significance of the selected factors and their impact on the efficiency indicator. While researching this issue, the phenomenon of adaptability, which means the higher the price set, is in comparison with the medium price scale, the higher the underpricing at setting with corresponding other equal terms was singled out The methods of critical literature review, statistical analysis, and econometric model creation have been used to justify it. Moreover, the research resulted in model creation, which characterizes the state of a definite commercial bank to be ready for emission of assets by means of initial public offering.

INTRODUCTION

In the modern banking system of Russia, the issue of equity of commercial banks is of great interest to the regulator. It is particularly acute to analyze the efficiency of securities placement by commercial banks as it has been regulated by The Central Bank of Russia by withdrawing several dozens of commercial banks licenses. This has negatively influenced the system and put pressure in terms of non-compliance with the standard of capital adequacy. In this regard, the issue of increasing capitalization is the most relevant for banks, as well as ways to increase the size of their own funds. Being aware of

DOI: 10.4018/978-1-7998-5083-0.ch012

potential advantages of the method of public offering of shares on the stock market, many organizations prefer to use this method. However, in the process of entering the exchange, banks and companies are not always able to achieve the desired level of borrowed funds. One of the main reasons for underuse of funds during a public offering of securities is the underestimation of shares, which indicates the amount of money that the bank could have attracted, but did not managed to.

Various financial and banking issues have been under the thorough world scholars' observation and deep analysis though the efficiency of share placement and initial public offering indicators have not been careful researched so far. Moreover the special features of Russian financial market are poorly addressed for this reason the problem needs to be explained in the context of modern financial analysis, with the emphasis on capital structure issues and empirical research.

Based on the information mentioned above, the development of a model for analyzing the readiness of a commercial bank to issue securities is one of the most important stages of a successful placement of shares. It is likely that it is possible to borrow a similar model used in Western countries that follows the Basel III standard, but it will need transformation to correspond to Russian reality.

The main objective of the current research is to identify factors influencing the effectiveness of public offerings through underestimation of shares based on the data obtained due to the evidence about the placements already made.

To achieve this goal, the following tasks were identified:

1. To describe the existing methods of increasing the capitalization of commercial banks;
2. To analyze the pricing of securities and identify an indicator characterizing the effectiveness of the public offering;
3. To conduct an econometric analysis of the degree and direction of influence of the formed set of factors on the effectiveness of public offering;

The main purpose of the study is to analyze the degree of readiness of commercial banks to issue securities.

To achieve this goal, the following tasks were formed:

In preliminary research for the study, a number of hypotheses, that will be tested in the given research paper, was formed. Firstly, it is assumed that there is a positive correlation between the return on equity of the organization and the effectiveness of the IPO. Secondly, the impact of underwriter's country on the effectiveness of the IPO is really significant.

CAPITALIZATION INCREASE

The capitalization of commercial banks is one of the challenges in the list of priorities of the modern banking system. In most cases, the main way to expand equity is the process of placing securities on the stock market. However, in the process of entering the exchange, the bank may encounter some difficulties that will subsequently affect the outcome of the transaction and the success of the increase in capitalization in general. For this reason the issue of estimation of securities positioning is particularly acute.

In the modern financial world, there are certain ways to increase the capitalization of commercial banks. It is important for each bank to choose the most suitable strategy, taking into account all key points, paying special attention to both positive and negative ones.

The most frequently used methods of capitalization by commercial banks are the following:

1. The use of its own profit to increase capital.

Reinvesting a bank's profit in its own capital is the main way to increase it. However, the profit margin correlates with the size of the bank and its activities, as well as with the efficiency of the credit institution upon the whole. As for established banks with high profits, this method is the most cost-effective due to the lack of organizational costs. It should be noted that the capital gain via such profit does not allow to lose control over the activities of the entire bank (Geddes, 2008).

The use of its own profit to increase the capital of a commercial bank has been an exceptional way for a time being. In addition, for some conservatively-minded banks it is still the only way to increase equity. However, it is logical that the volumes of this resource are limited and are not able to provide a significant increase in capital over a relatively short period of time. Many authors in their studies note that using bank's own profit as the only strategy to increase capital is unacceptable and inefficient. This method must be combined with others (Gnezdilov et al, 2018).

Bearing in mind the information given above, it is possible to highlight certain advantages and disadvantages of this method.

The list of advantages includes: the absence of organizational costs, there is no threat of losing control of the bank. Moreover, it can be an incentive to increase the profitability of the bank to increase the size of its own funds.

Among the negative issues can be identified: the increase in capital is slow, and the size of the profit may depend on external factors which the bank management is not able to handle.

2. *Revaluation of the funds.* The increase in the market value of real estate and fixed assets is a good source of capital increase for banks that have made investments in property with a rising price. However it is worth noting that this method cannot be used by all commercial banks. Moreover the value of the assets that the bank has invested in can be very volatile, especially in modern unstable situation. Thus, it is possible to receive not capital gains, but the opposite it can lead to capital outflow (Zhiharev,2011).
3. U*sing dividends strategy*. Making changes to the amount of dividends paid may be a flexible strategy for increasing equity.

The high volume of dividends on shares, of course, attracts many investors to make investments in the bank, but simultaneously it reduces the amount of profit, which affects the increase in equity upon the whole. Moreover, the growth of active operations generating the bank's revenue slows down, as well as the overall risk level increases. Subsequently, this may lead to a decrease in loyalty to the bank, and therefore shareholders will seek to reinvest their funds in other assets and sell risky shares, which, in turn, will reduce the bank's total capital.

Most contemporary authors who have conducted research on the topics closely related to the capitalization of commercial banks usually offer two methods for increasing their own funds through dividends. The first and perhaps the most trivial way is to reduce premium payments to holders of ordinary shares. The second method (Ivaskovskaya, 2007) involves providing shareholders with the opportunity to reinvest the amounts paid by the bank into the purchase of an additional volume of shares through a special program called the Dividends Reinvestment Plan (DRIP).

The dividend reinvestment program seems to be an effective strategy for both banks and shareholders. Investors are interested in reinvestment of payments due to the ability to buy shares omitting the exchange commission and broker's service. Moreover, shares in such cases may be sold with a discount compared to the average market price.

It should be noted that the program itself is also beneficial for the bank to attract equity due to low organizational costs of increasing capitalization. According to research papers mentioned above, when using DRIP, a bank can sell ordinary shares only among a restricted circle of shareholders, which eliminates the need to register for a new prospective emission, and therefore reduces costs.

However, despite the advantages mentioned above, this method has its drawbacks. Some investors will be reluctant to such programs, because during its implementation they will not be able to participate in the purchase of new shares. Moreover, dividends under DRIP can be realized at the time of raising the share price, which is disadvantageous for the shareholders themselves, since if they fall, it will be possible to buy a larger volume of securities at the same cost.

4. *Use of subordinated debt. Capital debt obligations issuing.* The previous three methods of raising capital assumed the use of internal resources, while this method refers to external sources. The strategy implies issuing debt securities, opening special deposit accounts and attracting long-term loans. Such bank liabilities are called subordinated and are characterized by fixed periods of paying back the amount that was raised. It also involves low interest rate on such types of loans, and sometimes even their absence.

It should be noted that in case of bank bankruptcy the paying back of such assets occurs once all creditors' claims are satisfied.

One of the main positive aspects of this method of increasing equity is that there are no interest payments on debt in taxable income. Most banks use subordinated loans. Moreover, when the term of the contract comes to an end and there is a need to pay the debt, refinancing is often used, which implies covering an old loan by registering a new one. This tool allows the bank, which is experiencing the need for additional significant amount of funds to maintain fixed capital at the required level.

Another advantage of this method is the ability to increase such a financial indicator as profit per share. Perhaps this is the case when the funds raised bring income that exceeds the interest paid on them. Moreover, when using this method, there is no reduction in the owners' control over the certain stakes in the bank (Kosarenko, 2011)

Undoubtedly, along with the pros this method has some drawbacks. Firstly, the investment risks of bank creditors are increased. Secondly, the financial indicator, which implies the ratio of one's own and borrowed funds, suffers. Thirdly, although a subordinated loan increases the bank's equity as a whole, it does not increase the basic capital, which can undermine the credibility of the bank. Fourthly, there are costs associated with organizing and placing a new issue of debt securities.

It is worth noting that despite the mentioned disadvantages, many banks still use this tool.

5. *State participation in the capitalization of a commercial bank.* This method involves the state payment some funds to help banks in the form of direct injections or tax relief. Considering the fact that almost all credit organizations in Russia are non-governmental this method is possible for those banks where the state a major stake holder. In Russia, such banks are Sberbank, VTB, Gazprombank and others. An undisputable positive aspect of this method is that a significant amount of funds is

attracted at no cost for the bank. Though it is worth mentioning that this method is not applicable for all commercial banks in this country (Lukashov, Mogin, 2008).

6. *Sale of certain assets, rental of fixed assets.* The research results confirm that it is possible to increase capitalization through the sale of assets and rental of fixed assets. However, there is some risk that the market price of assets at some point may exceed their value. In this case, selling them is extremely unprofitable and the bank may resort to a bonus emission instrument. This means the process of compensating for the difference between the book value and market cost through the creation of revaluation reserves for assets and their subsequent use in the form of additional free placement of shares between the bank's shareholders. Bonus issue increases the capital of a credit institution, but does not reduce the owner's control over it and does not change the value of already issued shares.
7. *Mergers and acquisitions.* This mechanism of increasing capitalization implies the unification of credit organizations into a single bank with common capital. According to some researchers, the banking system of Russia requires the consolidation of commercial banks to confront current economic difficulties and stimulate sustainable economic growth (Lvutin, Fetzer, 2007).

The given method has some advantages over the others. When several banks merge, it becomes possible to enter a new geographic market within a short period of time, while still imposing control over the income and expenses of the core business of a credit institution. Another advantage is the ability to quickly start in a new industry. This method is more profitable while creating a new organization, as in case of failure at conducting business in the new industry after the merger, the bank can sell the previously connected structure and cover part of the losses. Moreover, it becomes possible to use the assets and liabilities of the absorbed organization. By way of illustrating there is the use of qualified personnel or a ready-made customer base. One of the advantages of a merger is a way to avoid another takeover or increase some financial indicators.

However using this method, the bank may encounter some of its disadvantages. When two banks merge, the positive effect does not appear immediately. According to a study by E. Supronovich (2015) at the first stages, the total profit of the combined banks may turn out to be much appealing than the combined profit of these banks when working separately. Moreover when merging banks, the organization of a corporate governance system is exposed to a number of problems. The former owners have to put up with the status of minority shareholders, which may contradict the current mentality of absolute power when making decisions. It consequently may lead to some problems in the decision-making process or management centralization. Moreover, this strategy is not suitable for all banks with regards to combining their types of business. On the one hand it is possible to make the mortgage departments, lending to small and medium-sized businesses and some others work collaboratively. On the other hand no one can predict how some key customers and borrowers who were considered "premium" by one of the merged banks will behave.

8. *Attracting foreign investments.* Attracting a foreign strategic investor funds is very tempting due to the fact that not only a significant amount of finance is attracted, but also foreign partnerships are established. Such investors may be large foreign companies or various private equity funds.

However, this method has an apparent drawback in the form of limitations. Sellers and buyers often do not find a compromise in terms of the amount of funds received. In other words, shareholders, as a rule, overestimate their requirements too much, so investors refuse to deal. It should be remembered that for foreign investors, a change in corporate governance is very important, which in turn cannot coincide with the bank's management mindset. For example, for some Russian credit institutions, maintaining sole control will be much more important than attracting financial injections.

9. *The use of bank shareholders' private funds*. This method is very attractive for the bank upon the whole, but it becomes difficult to convince shareholders that it is necessary to reinvest their funds in a commercial bank at times. This can be done by reviewing the activities of the bank and explaining in this case the ownership structure will not be changed. In long run the development of the bank's activities will be stimulated, which will consequently increase every shareholder's dividends. This method is often carried out via an increase in the number of already existing shareholders' shares.
10. *Placement of shares by limited private subscription*. This method of capital gain implies a procedure for issuing a limited block of shares established in accordance with Russian law, which is proposed to be bought by a limited, thoroughly selected number of investors. Keeping in mind that the stock exchange is not involved it means that there are some advantages.

The group of investors who is allowed to purchase shares by private subscription mostly consist of the current shareholders or their affiliates and organizations, or some of the institutional investors of a commercial bank. It should be noted that when using this method of capitalization, there is no need to draw up an issue prospectus, and a credit institution does not need to reveal information about itself.

11. *Issue of shares by an initial public offering (IPOs)*. The issue of shares by a commercial bank and their subsequent placement on the stock market is the most attractive way to increase capitalization.

The main advantages of this approach compared to the previously considered ones are equity growth strategies. In fact while entering the securities market the bank can attract a significant amount of funds from a large number of investors. However, such funds do not need any service assistance in contrast to subordinated credit, for instance. Moreover, the securities are sold at a fair price and at the same time the transparency of the bank's activities is enhanced, as this is one of the primary conditions for public offering.

It is worth mentioning that IPO has its drawbacks. One of the most unpleasant, namely for the owners, will be a decrease in their shares in the total volume of shares, as their number will increase. Another important disadvantage of this method is the exorbitant costs of organizing and conducting the placement process itself. In this case, after the start of the IPO, the credit institution must support the market for offered shares in order to prevent the outflow of shareholders. In addition there may be inconsistencies in the corporate governance system used by the bank and potential share buyers' requirements which may become a barrier to successful IPO.

THE CURRENT METHODS OF SECURITY POSITIONING

According to Draho (2004)the term Initial public offering (IPO) refers to the process of the first public offering of an organization's shares on the stock exchange, during which its securities are potentially offered to a large circle of investors who can purchase them (Micheeva, 2017). Under realization of this method of placement, the company's securities can be sold again which increases their liquidity and market share price.

The process of IPO traditionally is known to include the issuing firm, the underwriter(s), and the investors where they play various roles and accomplish certain functions within the IPO. The firm tries to avoid fluctuations, while the investors' want to set the competitive price and obtain the best offer and the underwriters are middlemen who work in the interest of both the issuing firm as well as the investors (Jenkinson and Ljungqvist, 2001).

The analysis of a commercial bank level of readiness for initial public offering (IPO) is the most critical criterion of securities emission's success in general. When preparing to IPO, the banks mostly pay attention only to formal and necessary features, such as an arrangement legal form, compliance with the requirement to trading admission on the financial platform. However, the investment attractiveness of a particular commercial bank is not virtually taken into account, which subsequently affects the underestimation of the IPO. Analysis of the research results shows that the initial public offering of shares does not increase capitalization during every issue. According to Kim (Kim, 2005), only 79% of issuers from 38 countries managed to increase their equity capital during the IPO, while approximately 3570 of commercial banks did not receive the necessary amount of money or suffered losses associated with the organization of securities placement. According to the statistics mentioned above, it sounds reasonable to develop a model of readiness of a commercial bank to issue shares. Undoubtedly, many authors have already worked in this field, but the overwhelming majority of the presented theoretical models is not suitable for the modern Russian banking system and requires some modifications. When developing such a model, it is necessary to take into account the fact that the success of the initial public offering largely depends on the investors' interest in a particular bank. In other words, the investors' personal interest should be associated with the maximum level of capitalization of the credit institution.

Capitalization of the commercial banks is one of the main problems of Russian banking system after the adoption of Basel III standard. Noncompliance with capital requirements has been one of the most common reasons for the revocation of licenses by the Bank of Russia in recent years. According to numerous studies, the best way to increase the capitalization of the bank is the initial public offering. In the contemporary world it is common practice for it, while determining the price of a share placement in the initial public offering, is to be carried out with the help of a book of bids. Russian commercial banks follow the same system. According to this method, the underwriter seeks to know the maximum price at which investors are willing to purchase the Bank's shares through the preparation of applications, while the investors themselves are not interested in disclosing information about their demand, as this will increase the future price of securities placement. Though, this method has a significant drawback in the form of undervalued shares, as the issuer and the underwriter seek to increase the placement price, as the investors make every effort to reduce it. Thus, there is an asymmetry of information.

It should be noted that if the investor himself is mostly interested in the company, he will need to successfully increase the capitalization of the company for its further growth and maximize its profits. Moreover, the investors' interest is not reflected only in the size of the assets of a commercial bank. In order for the issue of shares to be successful, it is necessary to analyze many indicators of the company that may be of interest to potential buyers.

INITIAL PUBLIC OFFERING SPECIFICITY IN RUSSIA

For the last few years, the topic of primary public offering has been very relevant for the Russian banking sector and is of great theoretical and practical interest. For a complete understanding of the studied topic it is necessary to analyze the normative legal acts.

The Russian law classifies primary and secondary placements into one category - public offerings of securities. In particular, the Federal Law dated 22.04.1996 N°39-FZ "On the securities market" discloses these concepts:

- «placement of issue-grade securities - alienation of securities to the first hand owners by civil transactions;
- initial public offering of securities - placement of securities by open subscription, including placement on trading stock exchanges.»

In academic literature one finds a variety of significant works devoted to the study of IPO. The authors analyze the advantages and disadvantages of primary public offering as a source of capitalization for organizations of various sectors of the economy; explore the problems arising in the process of placement, phenomena and issues; prove their existence; explain the reasons for their appearance; as well as offer possible ways to solve them and improve the efficiency of IPO.

According to K. Hanley (Hanley, 1993) the partial adjustment phenomenon is a direct relationship between the average level of prices of the placed shares when compared to the medium price range and underestimation of the initial public offering. In other words, the higher the closing price of a particular bank's shares, the more undervalued the shares were in preparation for the issue. This phenomenon is visible in every Russian IPO to some extent, due to the fact that according to the rules of the Moscow exchange companies are allowed to use only the method of book bids for share pricing. At the same time, the underwriter does not have full information about the investors' intentions. When he receives information from investors that the shares are actually of high quality, he raises the offer price to such a level as to reward investors for the disclosed information, that means, he only partially adapts the offering price corresponding to the demand generated in the book of bids (Benveniste, Spindt, 1989).

Moreover, Bybel N. (Bybel et al, 2009) in the second part of their work says that the most important factor influencing the result and efficiency of public offering of ordinary bank shares is the pricing process.

Five years prior to that, Cliff and Denise (Cliff & Denis, 2004) proposed and tested a hypothesis that the reason of underestimation of the IPO is to compensate the high-quality underwriter for the quality of research coverage following the IPO. However, even earlier in the study, Harley (Harley, 1994) said that a wide price corridor, as a rule, signaled to investors about the uncertainty of the company's estimates. Thus, greater uncertainty on the part of underwriters increases underestimation.

In the review of modern economic literature, there may be a dual impression of the root of the problem. On the one hand, the success of an IPO in Russia is estimated by many researchers through this indicator: the lower the underestimation of shares, the higher the success rate of the placement. On the other hand, the main objective of the issuer is to maximize his capital, with a fixed volume of shares. For this reason, the commercial bank is more interested in the value of the issued securities being at or above the upper limit of the price range set by the underwriter. This conclusion is drawn by M. Tolstel in his study "the level of readiness of a commercial bank for an IPO" (Tolstel, 2011), where the analysis of a commercial bank on a foreign model is carried out, followed by a check on the placement of shares by VTB Bank. However, when analyzing this model, it becomes clear that it cannot be used in modern Russian situation, taking into account the adoption of the standard by Basil III.

Numerous studies of different authors attempt to single out the key criterion for a successful issuer's bank. In her work "The efficiency of pricing of Russian IPO" Ivashkovskaya (2008) states that one of the important factors to improve the results of IPO pricing is the volume of placement. This is explained by the fact that investors are willing to pay a higher price at a large stake, due to the formation of greater influence of such an investor presented in the board of shareholders of the bank. Moreover, the favorable conditions of the stock market at the eve of the IPO allow the issuer to receive additional income during the IPO, without affecting the amount of underestimation.

IPO MODEL ANALYSIS

The best way to achieve the main goal of the study is to analyze the data using certain methods. The first approach is to study the literature, scientific journals and information related to the initial public offering, as well as the results of the capitalization of some banks. These measures are aimed at identifying the criteria necessary to build an econometric model. Moreover, it will allow to build a scenario of the practical part of the work. An analysis of previous studies on this topic should identify the factors that lead either to the success or failure of the entire emission. Provided the data source is not time series, the use of autoregressive models will not be in demand. After checking the identified factors with the help of econometrics, it is planned to use a comparative analysis of the successful initial public offering of a commercial bank with an emphasis on these criteria. This stage of work will be performed to set the intervals or values of the indicators necessary for the successful issue of securities. For comparative analysis empirical information was collected using the total number of conducted public offerings by Russian banks and companies over the period 2007-2017. Selected time interval has been chosen due to the fact that time period up to 2007 has already been thoroughly studied from the point of view of Russian IPOs. In addition, it was in 2007 that the first full-fledged public offerings of shares of Russian banks were made. Moreover, this amount of observations will be enough to build an accurate regression.

It is worth mentioning that while in the theoretical part of this work, research papers by foreign and domestic authors were considered, the purpose of the empirical part is to analyze the phenomenon of underestimation. Most of papers reviewed assess the undervaluation of IPOs in terms of information asymmetry theory. The scholars suppose that here is a probability of partial adaptation while filling out the order book. However, their research also resulted in the assumption and identification of other factors that influence the undervaluation of placed shares, which is to be improved.

Taking into account all mentioned above, it was decided to use the model firstly proposed by Hanley in 1993, with a modification for the purpose of the given research (Stoughton, N. M., Zechner, 1998).

In order to conduct an econometric survey of all the factors affecting the level of underestimation of IPO, linear regression was used which was based on the least squares method. The model, taken as a basis, was used by Ivashkovskaya (2008) and modernized with the help of augmented variables responsible for the profitability of capital and for the underwriter's country of origin (Carter et al, 1998).

The final model of the current research is depicted bellow, given below. In this model, i - means the value of the underestimation of the placement in the dependent variable UNi.

$$UN_i = \beta_0 + \beta_1 PRI_i + \beta_2 WPR_i + \beta_3 RTS15_i + \beta_4 Log(CAP_i) + \beta_5 REPU_i + \beta_6 COUNTR_i + \varepsilon_i \quad (1)$$

The remaining variables are explained below:

- **PRIi** (Price Range Index) - the index of the change in the price of the i-th placement, which implies a percentage change in the placement price compared to the middle of the price range;
- **WPRi** - width of the price range of the i-th placement;
- **RTS15i** - percentage change in the RTS index for 15 working sessions until the i-th placement;
- **CAPi** - The size of the organization's capitalization at the time of entering the IPO; the regressor was added to the model due to the fact that some investors trust companies with a large volume of capitalization more and require a lower risk premium, which reduces underestimation;
- **REPUi** - return on equity at the time of placement. This variable was added to test the effect of bank ROE on IPO efficiency. The impact of return on equity on the effectiveness of an IPO is indirect and is demonstrated through the degree to which the organization is prepared for public offering (Tinic,1998);
- **COUNTRi** - binary regressor responsible for the country of the main underwriter; assumes a value of 1 if one or both of the bidders is a Russian company and a value of 0 if he is foreign.

It is to be noted that various researchers tried to have the Hanley's model improved in different ways and the given one is not a genuine. It was modernized for the purpose and scope of this work, with some of the regressors that were used in the framework of research by other authors, removed.

For complete immersion in the study, more detailed descriptions of the regressors will be given below, with formulae for their calculation and data sources for sampling.

1. **UN** - underestimation of IPO - The difference between the closing price of the first trading day and the placement price. It is calculated by the formula:

$$UN = \frac{(P1 - P0)}{P0} \quad (2)$$

P_0 – price of the initial positioning;
P_1 – closing of trades' price.

2. **PRI** – Price Range Index is the change in the price of positioning. It is calculated as the difference between the placement price and the average me of the price range. The formula is below

$$PRI = \frac{(P0 - Pe)}{Pe}, \quad (3)$$

$$Pe = \frac{Ph + Pl}{2}, \quad (4)$$

where
Ph – is the highest level of price range;
Pl – is the lowest level of price range

3. **WPR** - Width of the Price Range, which reflects the degree of confidence of the underwriter in the upcoming placement of securities. The higher the value of this indicator, the greater is the uncertainty of the organizer, which may subsequently affect the underestimation of shares. Below is the formula for calculating the regressor:

$$WPR = \frac{(Ph - Pl)}{Pe} \quad (5)$$

4. **RTS15** – (Rate of Trade Session) is an increase in the RTS index for 15 working trading sessions until the start of the public offering of the organization. It characterizes the position of the Russian stock market before the transaction. An increase in the index may reduce underestimation during placement. It is calculated according to the formula below:

$$RTS15 = \frac{RTS_t - RTS_{t-15}}{RTS_{t-15}}, \quad (6)$$

where
RTS_t – initial Rate of Trade Session;
RTS_{t-15} – 15 working sessions in advance of Rate of Trade Session.

Some other regressors have already been described above; there is no need to calculate their value, since their value can be found in open sources, such as PREQVECA and Bigcapital (Welch, 1992). Data on the size of capitalization at the time of placement, the trade organizer and other regressors were taken from these platforms. To calculate the indicators according to the above mentioned formulae, the Finam resource was used.

In this regard, a sample was formed using the above formulae with the data taken from the sources mentioned. Evaluation of the influence of factors on the underestimation of public offering was carried out using linear regression calculated by the least squares method. The data sample was compiled from 2007 to 2017. Such a large time period is explained by the extremely infrequent access of banks to the stock exchange; in general, 16 IPOs and SPOs were conducted during this period. It is worth noting that both primary and secondary public offerings were included in the sample, since the main factor affecting the value of shares in both cases is the interest in the company of investors, therefore, the developed model is suitable for both types of placements.

Thus, the analysis included the companies and banks conducting the placement in the period from 2007 to 2017. The data sample did not account for those companies which official IPO information is not available. Bank regression (Regression 1) was estimated based on 16 observations, bank and company regression (Regression 2) was based on 97 observations. The indicated number of freedom degrees is quite small even in a mixed sample, however, it represents all the information currently available. Moreover, with the subsequent placement of the organization on the stock market, this sample can be expanded, which is of interest for further research in this area.

An Econometric Study

An econometric study began with an analysis of the generated data. One of the main points at this stage is the elimination of outliers and data errors to obtain reliable results in the construction of the regression. Analysis of histograms for a sample of banks (Sample 1) is presented in Figure 1.

Figure 1. Sample 1

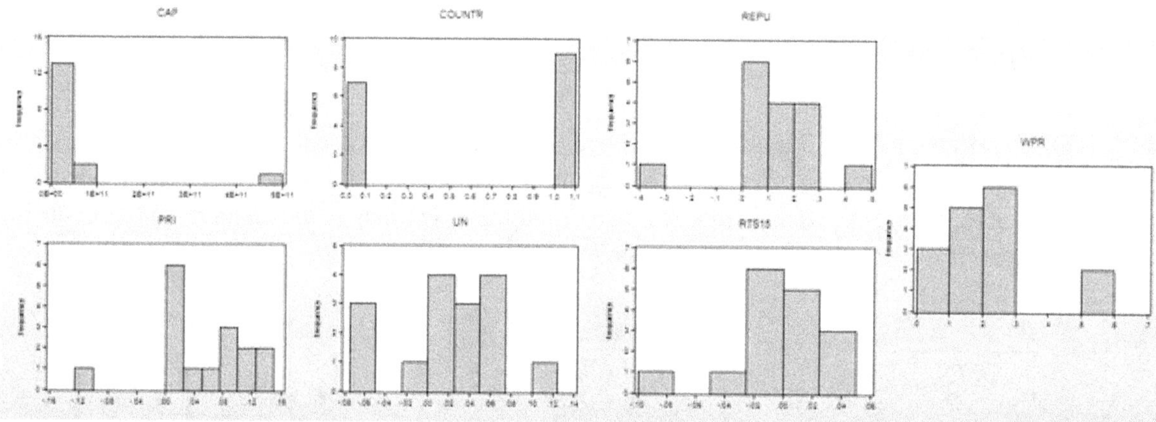

According to the given graphs, there are no errors and outliers in Sample 1, which is explained by a small number of degrees of freedom. The next point of checking the data sample is descriptive statistics of the data obtained. A detailed analysis of it is presented in Table 1.

Table 1. Descriptive Statistics

	CAP	Countr	Repu	PRI	UN	RTS15	WPR
Mean	4.11E+10	0.562500	0.113131	0.048173	0.017892	0.000924	0.208773
Median	2.94E+09	1.000000	0.140000	0.039890	0.022345	0.003689	0.185415
Maximum	4.74E+11	1.000000	0.450000	0.141030	0.105660	0.041858	0.590909
Minimum	1.75E+08	0.000000	-0.350000	-0.107140	-0.061290	-0.075900	0.000000
Std. Dev.	1.17E+11	0.512348	0.172691	0.064272	0.049602	0.030865	0.155650
Skewness	3.430068	-0.251976	-0.760376	-0.534196	-0.217676	-0.827667	1.112936
Kurtosis	13.19482	1.063492	4.840427	3.201866	2.225422	3.329597	3.902140
Jarque-Bera	100.6639	2.669354	3.799905	0.788140	0.526335	1.899179	3.845575
Probability	0.000000	0.263243	0.149576	0.674307	0.768613	0.386900	0.146199
Sum	6.57E+11	9.000000	1.810100	0.770773	0.286277	0.014782	3.340365
Sum Sq. Dev.	2.06E+23	3.937500	0.447331	0.061963	0.036906	0.014290	0.363404
Observations	16	16	16	16	16	16	16

Source- Authors

According to descriptive statistics on the bank public offerings' sample, the average underestimation in the period from 2007 to 2017 was 0.018 (1.8%), and its maximum size was 10.6%. Moreover, the average rate of return on equity was 11.3%, and the minimum value of this ratio was -35%. It is worth noting that the average width of the price range in the process of public offerings for the analyzed period is 0.2. It is also essential that the maximum percentage growth of the RTS index over 15 working sessions in Sample 1 is 4.2%.

Another important point in the analysis of the presented sample is the creation of a correlation matrix. It is necessary to check the relationship between variables, if in any case it is necessary to change the model. The correlation matrix for the banking sample is presented in Table 2.

Table 2. Correlation Matrix for Sample 1

	CAP	Countr	Repu	PRI	UN	RTS15	WPR
CAP	1.000000	0.186843	0.010356	-0.578563	-0.011401	0.101802	0.523826
Countr	0.186843	1.000000	0.001898	-0.401396	-0.220809	0.196509	-0.115050
Repu	0.010356	0.001898	1.000000	-0.409239	0.188521	0.390981	-0.601800
PRI	-0.578563	-0.401396	-0.409239	1.000000	0.247698	-0.428879	0.209030
UN	-0.011401	-0.220809	0.188521	0.247698	1.000000	0.077148	-0.007846
RTS15	-0.101802	0.196509	0.390981	-0.428879	0.077148	1.000000	-0.211768
WPR	0.523826	-0.115050	-0.601800	0.209030	-0.007846	-0.211768	1.000000

Source- Authors

According to the given Table 2, the dependence between the variables does not exceed the critical value of 0.8, therefore, there are no problem with multicollinearity in this sample.

Checking the generated data is to be proceeded directly to the construction of the regression. However, to compare the quality of the constructed regressions, it is necessary to verify a mixed sample of banks and companies. Histograms for analyzing data for errors and outliers are presented in Figure 2.

As it is seen in the Figure 2, the generated sample has several emissions in the level of capitalization at the time of placement, as well as in the values of the coefficient of return on capital. To eliminate them, it is necessary to introduce a restriction: REPU> -7 and CAP <4739640000000. As a result of the removal of emissions, the number of observations was reduced to 95.

The given Table 3 provides descriptive statistics of a mixed sample of data on banks and companies for the time period from 2007 to 2017.

Based on the descriptive statistics given, main conclusions are logical to be made:

- The average underestimation rate for companies and banks for the period from 2007 to 2017 amounted to 4.2%. Moreover, the maximum size of underestimation is approximately 46%.
- The largest rate of return on equity for the analyzed period is 99%. However, its average value in the sample is 12.7%.
- The strongest decline in the RTS index over 15 working sessions for the analyzed period was 44.7%. Moreover, on average, this index has increased by 0.7%

Figure 2. Sample 2

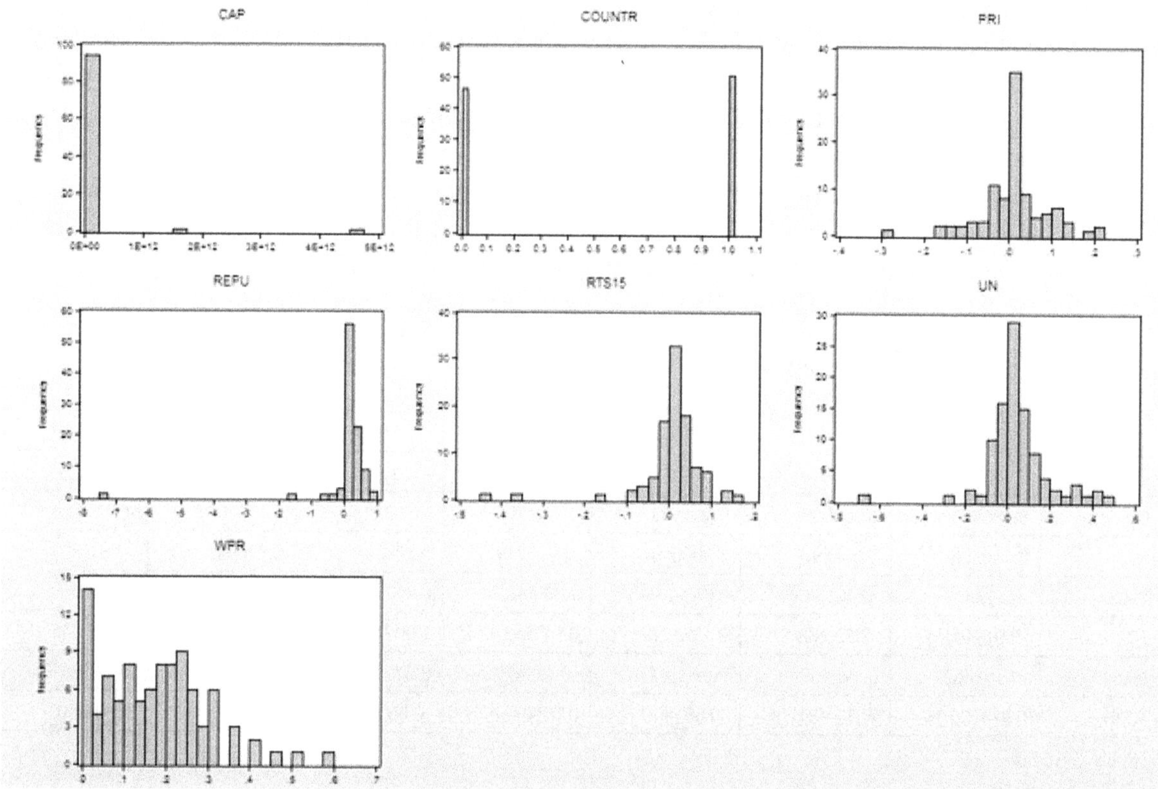

Table 3. Descriptive analysis of mixed Sample

	CAP	Countr	Repu	PRI	UN	RTS15	WPR
Mean	6.92E+10	0.520833	0.127818	0.09326	0.042885	0.007116	0.169369
Median	1.44E+09	1.000000	0.210000	0.004376	0.025585	0.016162	0.168193
Maximum	4.74E+12	1.000000	0.994800	0.217390	0.458330	0.154262	0.590909
Minimum	2291000.	0.000000	-7.450000	-0.280000	-0.666667	-0.446920	0.000000
Std. Dev.	5.06E+11	0.502188	0.840995	0.076007	0.145949	0.074863	0.120501
Skewness	8.574501	-0.083406	-7.824260	-0.216993	-0.421071	-3.586705	0.583031
Kurtosis	78.02836	1.006957	70.42740	5.162509	8.837663	21.69427	3.427567
Jarque-Bera	23693.37	16.00019	19165.32	19.45916	139.1501	1603.734	6.170055
Probability	0.000000	0.000335	0.000000	0.000059	0.000000	0.000000	0.045729
Sum	6.65E+12	50.00000	12.27050	0.895314	4.116935	0.683157	16.25940
Sum Sq. Dev.	2.43E+25	23.95833	67.19084	0.548820	2.023615	0.532420	1.379455
Observations	96	96	96	96	96	96	96

Source- Authors

- The number of placements with participation of Russian underwriters exceeds the number of placements organized by foreign investment banks.

The analysis of the relationship between the variables is the final point in accomplishing building the regression. Taking into account the delimitations of the current research of the data obtained it is recommended to use the correlation matrix which is representatives in terms of those variables correlation. The mixed-sample correlation matrix is shown in Table 4.

Table 4. 2nd Sample correlation matrix

	CAP	**Countr**	**PRI**	**Repu**	**RTS15**	**UN**	**WPR**
CAP	1.000000	-0.139990	0.013909	0.019829	0.190936	-0.063283	-0.125636
Countr	-0.139990	1.000000	0.046889	0.078655	-0.045615	-0.146620	0.008962
PRI	0.013909	0.046889	1.000000	0.082277	0.115237	0.068714	0.183543
Repu	0.019829	0.078655	0.082277	1.000000	-0.012823	0.091779	-0.042062
RTS15	0.190936	-0.045615	0.115237	-0.012823	1.000000	0.047593	0.091398
UN	-0.063283	-0.146620	0.068714	0.091398	0.047593	1.000000	0.136182
WPR	-0.125636	0.008962	0.183543	-0.042062	0.091398	0.136182	1.000000

Source- Authors

Analyzing Table 4, it may be concluded that there are no problems in the sample with multicollinearity, since the degree of dependence between the regressors does not exceed a critical value of 0.8.

After checking both data samples for possible errors and problems, it is necessary to deal with regressions. To begin with, a regression was built on a bank data sample. The result is shown in Table 5.

Moreover, it is necessary to compare the formed regression in the banking sample with the regression in mixed data. The result of building Regression 2 is shown in Table 6.

Before interpreting the results, it is necessary to check them using the White's test. The results are shown in Table 7.

According to the White test result, heteroskedasticity is absent at a significance level of 5%, since Prob. F> 0.05. In this regard usage of White's amendments for the second regression is not required.

It is empirical to compare two constructed regressions to identify the most accurate. Firstly, both of them are significant only at the level of 10%. Secondly, R^2 adjusted is larger in the second regression, however, this is not a good indicator of the efficiency of the study. The most accurate reflection of the accuracy of post-mortem regression is the sum of the squared residuals. With a decrease in this indicator, the effectiveness of the regression increases. When comparing two regressions given above, it is to be concluded that the sum of the squares of the residuals is smaller for the second regression constructed from the mixed sample. Thus, the results of the research will be interpreted according to the second sample with regards to all the factors mentioned above: a small number of observations, the inability to conduct tests, a large value of the sum of the residual squares.

Despite the fact that Sample 2 is more accurate, it is still applicable at only a 10% significance level. One of the reasons for this may be the presence of a large number of insignificant factors. For this test, various model specifications were considered to test the stability of the coefficients with a different set

Table 5. Sample 1 regression

Variable	Coefficient	Std.Error	t-Statistic	Prob.
C	-0.445049	0.122438	-3.634891	0.0054
PRI	0.579440	0.199744	2.900909	0.0176
WPR	-0.144247	0.094908	-1.519859	0.1629
RTS15	0.692558	0.373767	1.852913	0.0969
LOG(CAP)	0.020903	0.005779	3.617099	0.0056
REPU	0.031010	0.081765	0.379259	0.7133
COUNTR	-0.000257	0.020975	-0.012267	0.9905
R-squared	0.675182	Mean dependent var		0.017892
Adjusted R-squared	0.458637	S.D. dependent var		0.049602
S.E. of regression	0.036496	Akaike info criterion		-3.483583
Sum squared resid	0.011988	Schwarz criterion		-3.145575
Log likelihood	34.868866	Hannan-Quinn criterion		-3.466274
F-statistic	3.117976	Durbin-Watson stat		1.055751
Prob(F-statistic)	0.061410			

Dependent variable: UN
Method: Least Squares
Sample: 1 16
Included observations: 16

Source- Authors via EViews 10

Table 6. Sample 2 regression

Variable	Coefficient	Std.Error	t-Statistic	Prob.
C	0.371406	0.211103	1.759370	0.0820
PRI	0.165771	0.199125	0.832496	0.4074
WPR	0.103749	0.128399	0.808017	0.4213
RTS15	3.02E-05	3.96E-05	0.763584	0.4472
LOG(CAP)	-0.017464	0.009076	-1.924197	0.0576
REPU	0.057950	0.048553	1.193549	0.2359
COUNTR	-0.067251	0.033113	-2.030957	0.0453
R-squared	0.686175	Mean dependent var		0.043492
Adjusted R-squared	0.552326	S.D. dependent var		0.146575
S.E. of regression	0.036421	Akaike info criterion		-0.978020
Sum squared resid	0.005092	Schwarz criterion		-0.789839
Log likelihood	34.45594	Hannan-Quinn criterion		-0.901981
F-statistic	3.742215	Durbin-Watson stat		1.884299
Prob(F-statistic)	0.090571			

Dependent variable: UN
Method: Least Squares
Sample: 1 97 IF REPU>-7 AND CAP<4739640000000
Included observations: 95

Source- Authors via EViews 10

Table 7. White's test for regression 2

F-statistic	**1.207763**	**Prob. F(26,68)**	**0.2638**
Obs*R-squared	0.371406	Prob. Chi-Square(26)	0.2672
Scaled explained SS	0.165771	Prob. Chi-Square(26)	0.0000
Heteroskedasticity Test: White Null Hypothesis: Homoskedasticity			

Source- Authors via EViews 10

of available regressors. In this regard, the original model was transformed: the WPR regressor characterizing the width of the price range, as well as the PRI regressor characterizing the price change index were removed from it. Regression based on the final model is shown in a Table 8.

Table 8. Modernized model of regression

Variable	**Coefficient**	**Std.Error**	**t-Statistic**	**Prob.**
C	0.345891	0.207111	1.670073	0.0984
RTS15	4.70E-05	3.64E-05	1.290699	0.2001
LOG(CAP)	-0.016524	0.008940	-1.848432	0.0678
REPU	0.046986	0.047549	0.988147	0.3257
COUNTR	-0.062836	0.032804	-1.915497	0.0586
R-squared	0.613166	Mean dependent var		0.043492
Adjusted R-squared	0.509307	S.D. dependent var		0.146575
S.E. of regression	0.142794	Akaike info criterion		-1.003638
Sum squared resid	0.003509	Schwarz criterion		-0.869224
Log likelihood	52.67282	Hannan-Quinn criterion		-0.949325
F-statistic	3.261101	Durbin-Watson stat		1.819916
Prob(F-statistic)	0.048695			
Dependent variable: UN Method: Least Squares Sample: 1 97 IF REPU>-7 AND CAP<4739640000000 Included observations: 95				

Source- Authors via EViews 10

Once comparing Table 8 with Table 6, it becomes obvious that the regression according to the updated model (Regression 3) is more accurate, since the sum of the squares of the residuals in it is less. In other words, the interpretation of the results should take place in Sample 3, but after the White test for heteroskedasticity. The result of this correlation is shown in Table 9.

The analysis of Table 9 proves that there is no heteroskedasticity residues in regression 3. Thus, the results of the study can be interpreted based on Table 8.

Moreover, according to the results of the constructed regression it is obvious that at a 5% significance level its predicted strength is 61. Consequently, several conclusions can be made:

Table 9. White's test for regression 3

F-statistic	0.458469	Prob. F(13,81)	0.9412
Obs*R-squared	6.511138	Prob. Chi-Square(13)	0.9256
Scaled explained SS	22.91942	Prob. Chi-Square(13)	0.0427
Heteroskedasticity Test: White Null Hypothesis: Homoskedasticity			

Source- Authors via EViews 10

- The regressor characterizing the level of capitalization is significant at the level of 7%. Based on this, with an increase in the size of the organization's capitalization at the time of the start of public offering by 1%, underestimation of shares will decrease by an average of 1.6% under other similar conditions.
- The regressor characterizing the country of the underwriter is significant at a 7% significance level. In this regard, when the Russian organization is the underwriter of the public offering, underestimation decreases on average by 0.063 under other similar conditions.
- The regressor characterizing the change in the RTS index over the past 15 working sessions and the regressor responsible for the return on equity of the company were insignificant.

Thus, the hypothesis of a positive relationship between the level of profitability of the bank's capital and the level of underestimation has not been confirmed. At the same time, the second hypothesis about the influence of the host country of the main underwriter was confirmed as a result of the study.

Based on the data about regression obtained, an underestimation forecast for public offering can be made. In the given research the results of an econometric analysis will be verified by Sberbank. To carry out the forecast, current performance indicators will be taken and inserted into the regression. As a result of the forecast, underestimation of the shares will be revealed if the placement of securities occurs on the same day as the taking of indicators. Thus, the values of the regressors for PJSC Sberbank are presented below:

- RTS15 = 0,033968;
- CAP = 75600000000;
- REPU = 0.2427;
- COUNT = 0.

According to the regression, the predicted underestimation is 0.002687. This result was obtained by supplementing the sample with another observation with the value of Sberbank regressors. Moreover the Forecast feature integrated in EViews 10 was used.

SOLUTIONS AND RECOMMENDATIONS

As it has been mentioned, the process of initial public offering is one of the most effective ways to increase the Bank's equity capital. However, this goal can be achieved only in case of successful issue of shares. Based on this, the main result of the study should be a set of factors responsible for the success of the

IPO. Having this list, commercial banks will be able to prepare for the process of placement of securities better, followed by the achievement of the required level of capitalization. Moreover, the identification of factors responsible for the success of the issue will help improve the IPO pricing process by reducing the amount of underestimation. It is planned to develop a model to verify the degree of readiness of a commercial Bank for initial public offering. This model will be based on previously identified factors responsible for the success of the issue.

It should be noted that in the process of research the presence of qualitative factors that fundamentally affect the success of the placement of shares has been found. This proof will help explain the phenomenon when two large commercial banks, which are at the top of Russia's rating according to the portfolio of assets, conduct initial public offering with different amounts of capital raised.

The paper has analyzed such methods of increasing the equity capital of a commercial bank as the issue of securities through initial public offering. Moreover, the study thoroughly examined the process of initial public offering of shares on the stock market as a way to increase the banks ' equity capital in detail. It has been highlighted that pricing of the offering is the most important factor affecting the efficiency of the IPO. In Russia, this process is carried out by the book of bids. When considering the existing approaches, models and theories to assess the effectiveness of IPO pricing, it has been found that the most acute problem in the framework of IPO pricing, which requires the most attention, is the problem of undervaluation of shares (IPO Underpricing), which is the excess of the closing price of the first day of trading over the offering price.

The analysis of the IPO pricing efficiency of Russian banks for the period 2007-2018 was also carried out. As a result of the analysis, it was found that due to the use of the book of bids method as the only pricing mechanism of IPO in Russia, there is a phenomenon of partial adjustment, which increases the underestimation of shares and reduces the efficiency of the IPO. It should be noted that the main problem of inefficiency of primary public offering is the lack of investors' interest in a particular commercial bank, which implies the presence of a number of factors that potential buyers pay attention to. To confirm this assumption, a regression model based on the above period was used. According to the econometric study, qualitative non-price indicators have been identified, which have a strong impact on the success of the placement of securities. Despite the relevance of this problem, there is a relatively small number of modern studies aimed at analyzing the success of the IPO of commercial banks in Russia. Summarizing the changing nature of the country's banking system, it is necessary to develop new models to assess the readiness of commercial banks to issue shares in the conditions of increasing compliance with the requirements of the Bank of Russia.

Though the main goal of an IPO is to raise money for a business it facilitates easier acquisition deals (share conversions). Moreover, IPOs can give a company a lower cost of capital for both equity and debt. Consequently it adds to company image contributing to its profits in the long run.

As for the opposite factors, which include the expensiveness of IPO and exposure of internal documents such as financial, accounting, fiscal etc., they have also been listed among the findings of the research.

CONCLUSION

The research including both theoretical literature review and econometrics the pricing of securities and various methods of raising capital were analyzed. The efficiency of the public offering and its Russian origin's impact and unique implementations have been given evidence to which justify the forwarded hypotheses.

As a result of the given research the following conclusions were drawn:

Firstly, one of the most effective ways to increase the capitalization of a commercial bank is to publicly place its shares. The biggest advantage of this method is the significant amount of attracted funds and the possibility of further obtaining funds from investors. In this regard, the given study was limited to an analysis of factors affecting the efficiency of placement of securities by banks in the IPO process.

Secondly, the most frequently used criterion for assessing the effectiveness of public offering in many sources of scientific literature is the underestimation of stocks. This interest is caused by the relationship of this indicator with the amount of capital that the organization could have attracted, but failed because of the low price of placement of its own shares. For this reason, the study was aimed at analyzing factors affecting the underestimation of shares in a public offering of a bank.

Thirdly, underestimation of shares has always existed, with the exception of cases of revaluation. This pattern is associated with the emergence of the phenomenon of partial adaptation, due to which there is also an underestimation. However, the underestimation of shares may be reduced.

Fourthly, in an econometric study of factors that presumably affect the volume of underestimation of shares in a public offering, the least squares method revealed insignificant indicators: Index of changes in the placement price, width of the price range, growth of the RTS index 15 working sessions before the placement and return on equity. In this regard, the hypothesis of a positive relationship between ROE and underestimation of shares has not been confirmed. At the same time, the size of the organization's capitalization at the time the placement begins, as well as the country of the main underwriter, is influencing the underestimation of shares. Thus, the hypothesis about the influence of the origin of the investment bank on the placement efficiency was confirmed.

Thus, the conclusions drawn in this study allow us to make some recommendations to banks that intend to use such an instrument for increasing equity as public offering. When entering the organization's stock exchange, it is necessary to focus on the country of the organizer of the auction, as well as on the level of its capitalization in order to target the size of the subsequent underestimation of securities. If the company's securities are already traded on the stock market, the organization must predict the most favorable capitalization at the time the additional public offering begins to minimize subsequent underestimation of the shares.

ACKNOWLEDGMENT

The authors express special thanks to the Senior Teacher of the NRU Higher School of Economics Suchkova Ekaterina for valuable guidelines and contribution to the given research.

REFERENCES

Aggarwal, R., Prabhal, N. R., & Puri, M. (2002). Institutional allocation in initial public offerings: Empirical evidence. *The Journal of Finance, 57*(3). https://www.nber.org/papers/w9070.pdf

Baker, M., & Wurgler, J. (2007). Investor sentiment in the stock market. *Journal of Economic Perspectives, 21*(2). https://pubs.aeaweb.org/doi/pdfplus/10.1257/jep.21.2.129

Baron, D. (1982). A Model of the Demand for Investment Banking Advising and Distribution Services for New Issues. *The Journal of Finance*, *37*(4), 955–976. doi:10.1111/j.1540-6261.1982.tb03591.x

Benveniste, L. M., & Paul, A. S. (1989). How investment bankers determine the offer price and allocation of new issues. *Journal of Financial Economics*, *24*(2), 343–361. doi:10.1016/0304-405X(89)90051-2

Bybel, N., Rutledge, G. P., & Worley, M. (2009). *Capital Raising Strategies*. Bybel Rutledge LLP.

Cliff, T. M., & Denis, J. D. (2004). Do Initial Public Offering Firms Purchase Analyst Coverage with Underpricing? *The Journal of Finance*, *LIX*(6), 2871–2901. doi:10.1111/j.1540-6261.2004.00719.x

Federal Law of 22 April 1996 No. 39-FZ "On the securities market". (n.d.). Available at https://www.cbr.ru/Content/Document/File/36165/39-FZ.pdf

Geddes, R. (2008). *IPO and subsequent placement of shares*. Olympus - Business.

Gnezdilov, I., Levin, M., & Tolmacheva, O. (2018). Problems and prospects for the placement of shares of Russian enterprises through IPO. In *Russian regions in the focus of change: Collection of reports from special events*. http://elar.urfu.ru/bitstream/10995/68202/1/978-5-8295-0582-0_2018-88.pdf

Hanley, K. (1993). Underpricing of Initial Public Offerings and the Partial Adjustment Phenomenon. *Journal of Financial Economics*, *34*(2), 231–250. doi:10.1016/0304-405X(93)90019-8

Hanley, K., & Wilhelm, W. (1994). Evidence on the Strategic Allocation of Initial Public Offerings. *Journal of Financial Economics*, 37.

Ivashkovskaya, I., & Kharlamov, L. (2007). Pricing efficiency of Russian IPOs. *Corporate Finance*, *3*(3). Available at URL: https://cyberleninka.ru/article/v/effektivnost-tsenoobrazovaniya-rossiyskih-ipo

Ivashkovskaya, I. V. (2008). Pricing Efficiency Of Russian IPO. *The Journal Corporate Finance*.

Jenkinson, T., & Ljungqvist, A. (2001). *Going public – The theory and evidence on how companies raise equity finance* (2nd ed.). Oxford University Press.

Kosarenko, N. (2011). The securities market in Russia: a training manual. Flint.

Ljungqvist, A. (2006). IPO Underpricing. In Handbook of Corporate Finance: Empirical Corporate Finance. Academic Press.

Lukashov, A., & Mogin, A. (2008). *IPO from I to O. A Handbook for CFOs and Investment Analysts*. Alpina Publisher.

Lvutin, P.P., & Fetzer, O. (2007) Initial public offerings: a review of studies. *Journal of Corporate Finance*, 1.

Mikheeva, N. (2017). Advantages and disadvantages of some methods of increasing capital of commercial banks. *Bulletin of OSU*, *13*(119).

Mozgaleva, T. (2007). IPO process of Russian banks. *Finance and Credit*.

Pereverzev, N. (2016). Methodology for assessing the effectiveness of IPO. *Financial Director*, 2.

Qian, J., & Philip, S. (2007). How do laws and institutions shape financial Contracts? The case of bank loans. *The Journal of Finance*, 62.

Rock, K. (1986). Why new issues are underpriced. *Journal of Financial Economics*, 15.

Tinic, S. (1988). Anatomy of initial public offerings of common stock. *The Journal of Finance*, *43*(4), 789–822. doi:10.1111/j.1540-6261.1988.tb02606.x

Tolstel, M. S. (2008). *Factors influencing the development of IPO of commercial banks in Russia.* Academic Press.

Tolstel, M. S. (2011). *Commercial Bank readiness for IPO: A new approach to valuation*. Academic Press.

Welch, I. (1992). Sequential sales, learning, and cascades. *The Journal of Finance, 47*(2). Available at URL: http://citeseerx.ist.psu.edu/viewdoc/download?doi=10.1.1.24.340&rep=rep1&type=pdf

Zhikharev, K. (2011). Ways to increase the capitalization of the banking system of the country. *Economics of Megacities and Regions, 3*(43).

Chapter 13
Reevaluating Factor Models:
Feature Extraction of the Factor Zoo

Usama Ali Khan
University of Massachusetts, Boston, USA

Josephine M. Namayanja
University of Massachusetts, Boston, USA

ABSTRACT

Since the introduction of CAPM in the 1960s, the asset pricing literature has documented hundreds of characteristics that capture the cross-sectional variation in stock returns. Traditionally, multifactor models seek a multidimensional representation of common risks; this approach entails selecting a small number of representative characteristics from a set of candidate characteristics that, together, explain most of the cross-sectional variation in stock returns. Characteristics-based long-short portfolios are partially loaded on the true underlying risk factors and are at best noisy proxies for true latent factors. However, the expansive list of potential characteristics, along with developments in the field of dimensionality reduction, offers us an opportunity to seek better approximations of the unobservable latent risk factors. A recent stream of literature has investigated how to appropriately extract relevant features from the "factor zoo" while incorporating information from the expansive list of factors. This chapter aims to summarize this novel paradigm in factor modeling.

INTRODUCTION

The essence of asset pricing boils down to one central question: Why do different assets earn different returns? Much of the investment literature produced over the last four decades has been dedicated to addressing this question. The risk-return tradeoff applied by investors and academics alike has proven to be a good starting point to understanding this issue. Synonymous to the English phrase "there is no such thing as a free lunch", this fundamental assumption has been extensively explored and is widely accepted in investment circles. In order to make higher returns, investors must take risky positions and

DOI: 10.4018/978-1-7998-5083-0.ch013

to avoid risky investments, they must settle for lower expected returns. However, measuring risk is an extremely challenging problem empirically and is still very much an issue of debate in asset pricing.

Measuring Common Risk

A simple measure of risk is the volatility in the assets returns because it signals uncertain future returns. Consider a simplistic assumption that assets with more volatile returns are riskier and investors would rather have positions in less volatile assets than highly volatile ones (for a given level of average returns). This is to say that investors would only accept higher volatility in returns if the average returns were higher. Another important assumption is that investors can choose to invest from a variety of correlated assets and can hold diversified portfolios. These two assumptions combined are key to how we measure risk.

It is important at this point to establish what is meant by risk and what type of risks are interesting. The risks in an investment can be divided into two broad classes: idiosyncratic risk and systematic risk. This distinction is important when allowing for diversification because, idiosyncratic or unsystematic risk is the risk faced by a firm and can be managed through effective diversification. For example, an investor can choose to invest in fossil fuels and renewables and hence have a position in the energy sector. Moreover, such diversification could be across industries and asset classes. In a market where the market participants are well diversified, the idiosyncratic risk should not bother the investors much, and hence, will not be priced.

Systematic risk, however, is faced by the overall market and all market participants are exposed to such risks. As a result, the systematic risk is priced (i.e. the investors demand compensation for this risk because they are unable to diversify this risk). This is the risk that factor models are concerned about: the undiversifiable risk that affects the overall market. This chapter focuses on this (priced) systematic risk and its approximation using factor models.

A good approach proposed by Cochrane (2001) is the Stochastic Discount Factor (SDF) approach, which sums up the problem of measuring common risk effectively. This states that there exists a Stochastic Discount Factor (SDF) that explains the cross-sectional return differential in equity returns.

SDF elegantly sums up asset pricing in two equations:

$$P_t = E\left(m_{t+1}x_{t+1}\right) \tag{1}$$

$$m_{t+1} = f\left(data, parameters\right) \tag{2}$$

where P_t is the price at time t, m_{t+1} is the stochastic discount factor, and x_{t+1} is the payoff at period t+1.

The SDF at can be estimated as a general function of data and estimated parameters. Traditionally, linear multifactor models have been used to approximate the SDF, where factors are approximated using characteristic sorted stock portfolios. Additionally, modern deep learning models have introduced less restrictive approaches that can accommodate higher dimensional inputs and incorporate flexible functional forms. Recent literature in asset pricing has proposed theoretically motivated deep learning models to approximate the SDF and show promising results in the form of consistent SDF functional forms and a many-fold increase in prediction accuracy. It is clear that these models are doing a much better job at capturing the expected returns and possibly would shape directions for future research in the field. However, these deep learning estimations result in complex functional forms of the SDF and are out of scope of this chapter. This chapter focuses on dimensionality reduction approaches to approximate latent factors that capture the common risk (the SDF) effectively.

Factor models have been widely used to measure risk and are especially helpful in evaluating performance of diversified portfolios. These models can be traced back to a single market factor in the 1960's, where the riskiness of an asset is its sensitivity to the market portfolio. The most recent and widely used is a multifactor model with four additional risk factors in addition to the market factor (Fama & French, 2015). However, recent studies have documented several other cross-sectional predictors of stock returns or potential risk factors. This phenomenon has been dubbed as the infamous "factor zoo" (Cochrane, 2011). A good approximation of the SDF should incorporate most if not all of these so-called factors. The factor zoo makes this approach challenging and there is limited theoretical guidance as to which characteristics to base the SDF estimation on. Feature extraction techniques developed in machine learning not only offers a viable solution to the problem but also offers an opportunity for better approximation of the true factors. Instead of having to choose a small set of factors among a much larger list, there are methods to extract meaningful information from all such predictors.

This chapter seeks to propose dimensionality reduction (feature extraction) as viable methodologies to address the factor zoo. The goal of this chapter is to give the readers a perspective on factor models and an understanding of the factor zoo problem. This discussion is crucial in order to fully appreciate the promise that this approach entails. The chapter is organized as follows:

In the first section, this chapter discusses the evolution of factor models starting from the Modern Portfolio Theory (MPT) of Markowitz (1952) to the Capital Asset Pricing Model (CAPM) of Sharpe (1964), Lintner (1965), and Black (1972). This discussion is important when discussing factor models since the CAPM can be considered as a single factor model and the multifactor models are created by adding more risk factors to this model. A key consideration for the market model is its theoretical motivation, which is discussed briefly in the background section. This would help give perspective on why anomalies were considered as deviations from the CAPM. The anomalies led to the introduction of multifactor models by Fama and French (1993), in an effort to accommodate a more flexible multi-dimensional representation of common risks. The multifactor models draw their theoretical motivation from the Arbitrage Pricing Theory (APT) of Ross (1976). The CAPM can be presented as a special case of the APT and hence can be included in a multifactor setting. This provided Fama and French (1993) with a solid theoretical motivation in support of their multifactor models.

The second part of this chapter makes a case for feature extraction methodologies as an opportunity to incorporate a wider range of factors in our estimation of true risk factors. The important point to get across to the readers in this section is how feature extraction provides better estimates of true risk factors. Firstly, we demonstrate why it is appropriate to use feature extraction for latent feature extraction when dealing with noisy signals using an intuitive example. Moreover, this section presents empirical results from a small experiment demonstrating superior model fits of extracted features compared to the baseline Fama and French 5-factor models, with anomaly portfolio returns as the dependent variable. Finally, this section outlines some notable studies in the recent literature that utilize dimensionality reductions methodologies and summarizes their findings.

The third section concludes the chapter and outlines a general future direction for factor models.

BACKGROUND

In the beginning, there was chaos. Practitioners thought that one only needed to be clever to earn high returns. Then came the CAPM. Every clever strategy to deliver high average returns ended up delivering high market betas as well. Then anomalies erupted, and there was chaos again. (Cochrane, 2011)

The market model, also known as the Capital Asset Pricing Model (CAPM), was derived from appealing theories like optimal portfolio and the efficient market hypothesis. However, the anomaly literature pointed toward deficiencies in the theory. The multifactor models were introduced to reconcile to the growing anomaly literature in the 1980's with the market model (Fama & French, 1993). These multifactor models included characteristic sorted portfolios or anomaly portfolios as additional factors in the market model regression. This section briefly summarizes the historical evolution of factor models, which is important to provide the readers with a background of the discussion and to provide a perspective for the problem being discussed.

Optimal Portfolio and Efficient Markets

Markowitz (1952) introduced the concept of a mean-variance efficient "optimal portfolio", based on the simplistic assumption that investors consider high average returns "desirable" and high variance "undesirable". In his paper titled "Portfolio Selection", Markowitz shows how risk averse investors can construct portfolios to maximize expected returns for a given level of portfolio variance. An equally weighted portfolio of N correlated assets would have portfolio returns equal to the average returns of the underlying assets; however, the standard deviation of portfolio returns would be lower than the average standard deviation of the underlying securities. This can be demonstrated by a simple Monte Carlo experiment.

Given a set of random series, we can show that different combinations of these series' yield many possible different risk-to-reward ratios. It can be shown that there exists an optimal choice that maximizes the Sharpe ratio of expected returns.

Figure 1, Panel A shows the effects of diversification using five zero mean, randomly generated series. Random weights are assigned to each series to make a portfolio, such that the sum of the weights add up to one. With expected returns on x-axis and volatility on y-axis, each point plots the returns and volatility for every randomly generated portfolio (i.e. every set of weights). This exercise repeated over all these points yields a concave function and hence has an optimal solution. Therefore, it is possible to make an optimal portfolio such that the return to standard deviation ratio is maximized (i.e. for a given level of volatility, investors can maximize the returns to their portfolio).

Figure 1. Panel A shows the Monte Carlo simulation for 5 randomly generated series with average on y-axis and volatility on x-axis. Panel B shows the Monte Carlo simulation for Fama and French 5-factors as portfolios.

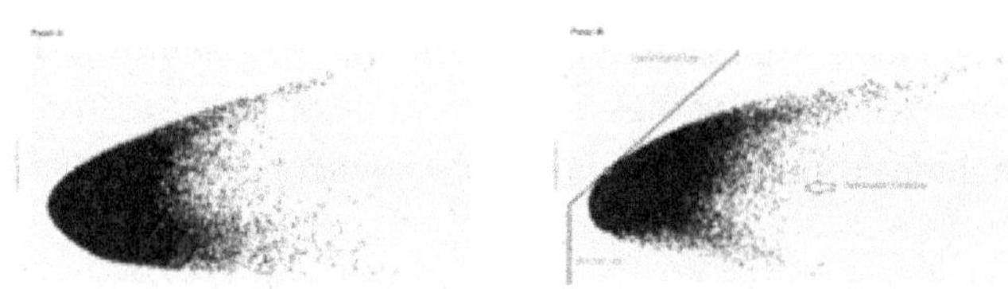

Markowitz's optimal portfolio was extended by Sharpe (1964), Lintner (1965), and Black (1972), resulting in the widely used Capital Asset Pricing Model (CAPM). The central prediction of CAPM is that in an efficient market, the market portfolio is the optimal portfolio. In presence of a positive risk-free rate, each investor will have a utility maximizing portfolio that is a combination of the risk-free portfolio and the optimal portfolio of risky assets. If investors have homogeneous beliefs, they have the same linear efficient set called the Capital Market Line (CML). Panel B of Figure 1 shows that a combination of the mean-variance efficient portfolio can be combined with the risk-free rate to result in this linear set. Any point that is below the CML should not be acceptable to investors (with homogenous beliefs).

The CAPM provided a theoretically motivated model to determine the relative riskiness of assets. According to the CAPM, the riskiness of an asset can be determined by its relative riskiness to the market portfolio. This relative riskiness is measured by running a linear regression of excess returns (returns in excess of the risk-free rate) of the asset to the market excess returns. The coefficient in this regression is the market beta, the measure of how risky a security is compared to the market. The CAPM concludes that one market portfolio is sufficient to explain the whole cross-section of stock returns (i.e. to explain the differences in returns across securities). This portfolio selection paradigm still dominates much of how we think about risk and return and, has evolved into a multifactor approach.

The general form of CAPM is presented as the following:

$$R_i = R_f + \beta_M \left(R_M - R_f \right), \text{ for all i } =1,2,\dots,\text{n} \tag{3}$$

where, R_M is the expected rate of return on the market portfolio, R_i is the return on security i, β_M is the market beta of security i, R_M–R_f is the market risk premium, R_f is the risk-free rate.

Size, Value, and the Multi-Factor Model

Soon after the CAPM was introduced, researchers documented patterns in the equity markets that were not explained by the market factor. These deviations from the CAPM came to be known as market anomalies and suggested further inquiry. For example, Banz (1981) documented that smaller firms have higher CAPM risk adjusted return than larger firms. A portfolio with a long position in smallest firms and a short position in the largest firms would have positive CAPM alphas on average. This "size effect" was not captured by the market beta of the firms, and hence, Banz (1981) concluded that the CAPM was mis-specified.

The size effect was among the first "anomalies" documented in the 1980's. Some other prominent anomalies that followed were the "value effect" (Stattman, 1980; Rosenberg, Reid, & Lanstein, 1985), the "leverage effect" (Bhandari, 1988), and the Earning to Price Ratio effect (Ball, 1978) among others. These so-called anomalies contradicted one of the central predictions of CAPM because these effects should have been captured by the market beta if the CAPM specification were true. Moreover, many of these anomalies could generate a positive CAPM alpha in a long-short portfolio.

In order to reconcile these anomalies with a risk-based explanation, Fama and French (1992, 1993) suggested that risk is multidimensional, and risk factors could be approximated by characteristic-sorted long-short portfolios. This interpretation is still predominant in multifactor models and the approach presented in this chapter is consistent with this interpretation.

Fama and French (1993) proposed a 3-factor model to accommodate a multidimensional representation of common risk. Fama and French included a decile based long-short portfolio sorted on size, and another one sorted on book-to-market ratio as the two additional factors. They show that including size and value portfolios as factors subsumed most of the prominent anomalies at the time.

If assets are priced rationally, our results suggest that stock risks are multidimensional. One dimension of risk is proxied by size, ME. Another dimension of risk is proxied by BE/ME, the ratio of the book value of common equity to its market risk. (Fama and French, 1992)

The theoretical motivation for the additional two factors was derived from the Arbitrage Pricing Theory (APT) of Ross (1976). The APT, unlike CAPM, does not assume perfectly efficient markets, and is flexible in incorporating multiple factors.

The general form of APT can be written as:

$$R_i = R_f + \beta_1 f_1 + \beta_2 f_2 + \beta_3 f_3 + \ldots + \beta_k f_k \text{, for all i} = 1,2,\ldots,n \tag{4}$$

Where f_k is the kth factor, and β_k is relative loading of the factor.

The CAPM can be viewed as a single factor model in the APT since the latter does not specify which factors should be used. However, like the CAPM, the APT assumes that a factor model can be used to describe the correlation between risk and return. The APT suggests that asset returns are linearly related to multiple variables that capture systematic risk. The central idea in the APT is that there exists no arbitrage opportunity among well-diversified portfolios and if such an opportunity arises, it is exploited away by rational investors (arbitrageurs). The CAPM adjusted differential in security returns when sorted on characteristics like size and value should not exist in the APT framework unless these portfolios load on systematic risk. If these anomaly portfolios proxy some underlying common risk, then the arbitrageurs are unable to exploit these portfolios and demand compensation for these positions. This would explain the CAPM adjusted differential on the anomaly portfolios.

Fama and French (1993) suggest that the size and value portfolios have partial exposure to unobserved state variables that affect the risk premiums in equity markets. Along with the market portfolio and the risk-free rate, these two factors span the linear efficient set. An important consideration here is that the size and value effects are not factors themselves but have partial loadings on the underlying systematic variable (as posed by Fama and French, 1993). This interpretation is very important for understanding the key arguments of this chapter.

Fama and French 3-Factor Model can be written as:

$$R_i = R_f + \beta_M \left(R_M - R_f \right) + \beta_{SMB} SMB + \beta_{HML} HML, \text{ for all i} = 1,2,\ldots,n \tag{5}$$

Where, β_{SMB} is the size beta, β_{HML} is the value beta, *SMB* is the small-minus-big portfolio, while *HML* is the high-minus-low portfolio.

Characteristic- Sparse Factor Estimation

Despite the multidimensional approach of Fama and French (1993), more anomalies were introduced in the following literature and are being introduced to date. The 3-factor model did not explain much of these new effects. Recently, Fama and French (2015) proposed a 5-factor model with two additional factors, namely an investment factor and a profitability factor. This incorporated the gross profitability premium (Novy-Marx, 2013) and the investment premium (Aharoni, Grundy, & Zheng, 2013). The interpretation for these factors is the same in that these additional four factors are noisy signals for underlying systematic risks. In addition to these five factors, researchers also incorporate a momentum factor based on the momentum effect first documented by Jegadeesh and Titman (1993).

However, in addition to the factors mentioned above, hundreds of new "factors" that explain asset returns have been proposed in the literature. Green et al. (2013) count 330 such stock- level predictive signals. Harvey et al. (2016) study 316 signals, which include 213 firm level characteristics, and 113 common factors to describe stock return behavior. They note that this is only a subset of those studied in the literature.

These predictive signals can be broadly classified as firm specific signals and common risk factors. The firm specific signals, also referred to as firm characteristics, provide information on the financial health of a firm. Since these characteristics are firm specific, they do not necessarily result in return co-movement and are diversifiable.

On the other hand, common risks are affecting the whole cross-section of returns and result in return covariance. Although these factors are approximated using characteristics sorted portfolios, they approximate a common risk factor that eventually results in observed co-movements in returns. This co-movement is the anomaly that Fama and French (1993) seek to address with their multifactor approach. For example, if size is a firm level characteristic that predicts the financial health of a firm, why do stocks in the same size bucket move together? This co-movement of returns is what is typically referred to as a factor structure. These factor structures are indicative of common underlying risk for a set of stocks. It is important to note that the predictive characteristics and characteristics based covariances are not necessarily mutually exclusive.

A key takeaway from this section is that a predictive signal for stock returns does not necessarily constitute a factor. There are various strains of asset pricing literature that deal with factors identification and distinguishing between characteristics and covariances. For the purpose of this chapter, characteristic based portfolios are assumed to have partial loadings on the systematic factor and not a firm-level predictor variable.

A characteristic-sparse factor model (For example, Fama and French 5-factor model) takes into account only a subset of the factors discovered in the literature. In addition, as Fama and French (1992) suggest, these factors can be interpreted as partially loading on the true systematic factors and are at best weak approximations of true underlying factors. Given the large number of potential factors in the literature, emphasizing on only a few of these partially loaded portfolios might not be the optimal solution. Moreover, unlike the market factor in the CAPM, the additional factors in the Fama and French 5-factor model do not have any meaningful interpretation beyond the APT and eventually the law of one price. Therefore, a factor model that relies on most if not all potential factors can lead to a better estimation of the underlying risk compared to a characteristic sparse model.

The next section provides an alternative to the characteristic-sparse representation of the common risk. The methodologies discussed incorporate a larger set of potential factors to approximate the true underlying systematic risk factors.

REEVALUATING FACTOR MODELS

We are going to have to repeat Fama and French's anomaly digestion, but with many more dimensions. We have a lot of questions to answer. First, which characteristics really provide independent information about average returns? Which are subsumed by others? Second, does each new anomaly variable also correspond to a new factor formed on those same anomalies? Third, how many of these new factors are really important? Can we again account for N independent dimensions of expected returns with K < N factor exposures? Can we account for accruals return strategies by betas on some other factor, as with sales growth? (Cochrane, 2011)

To address this "multidimensional challenge" of Cochrane (2011), machine learning offers a variety of dimensionality reduction techniques. One potential solution to the factor zoo is feature selection. Feature selection, as the name suggests, incorporates selecting most informative features from a given set of features and filtering out redundant ones, based on a certain selection criterion. Fama and French (2015) 5-factor model is one example of important features selected manually over the past two decades. Alternatively, one could simply identify groups of factors that are correlated with each other, and then select one feature from each group that explains most of the expected returns. Kogan and Tian (2015) conduct a similar factor mining exercise to select appropriate features. There are other studies that explore more sophisticated dynamic feature selection techniques (DeMiguel et al., 2017; Freyberger et al., 2017; Feng et al., 2017). However, despite an initial consideration of more characteristics, information loss is inevitable when relying on a small subset. Financial data is notorious for noise and the noise to signal ratio in these characteristic sorted portfolios is very high.

On the other hand, feature extraction extracts new features from the initial features that are meant to be informative and non-redundant. These techniques are especially effective in estimating the underlying latent structure in the data in presence of noise. Hence, feature extraction is well suited to the factor zoo since the observed "factors" are interpreted as noisy signals for the underlying latent state variables (Fama & French, 1992; 1993; 2015). Feature extraction remedies the noise concern given a large enough feature space and observations. Additionally, feature selection applied to the factor zoo would lead to a characteristic-sparse model and could potentially lead to spurious overfitting (i.e. fitting the noise instead of the true signal).

Recent literature has explored a wide range of feature extraction methods for factor mining (Kelly et al., 2018; Kozak et. al, 2018). The following subsections are organized as follows. First subsection uses a simple example to provide the readers with a general intuition for feature extraction and its possible benefits in presence of noisy signals. The next sub-section demonstrates the main idea using a simple PCA applied to characteristics sorted portfolios. The third section briefly discusses the modern literature and two major approaches to the factor zoo problem.

A Case for Feature Extraction

In this section, the authors demonstrate with a simple visual example why feature extraction is an appropriate methodology for the factor zoo problem.

Figure 2. An object moving through a 3-dimensional space, captured by 3 cameras at different positions

Figure 2 shows a 3-dimensional space with three cameras focused on a single point. The cameras capture moving objects (the school bus) in the 3-dimensional space. For simplicity, let us assume that the output from each camera is a vector. The direction of the vector points to the direction of the moving object and the length of the vector determines the speed of the object. These three output vectors are the three features under consideration.

In the base case scenario where the cameras A, B, and C are fixed in their positions, it is possible to reconstruct the vector output from camera A and B given the output of camera C and vice versa, The vector output from each camera would be a simple linear transformation of the vector output from either of the two other cameras. In this case, output from one camera should be enough to provide us with the information we need (i.e. the speed and direction of the moving object). An appropriate method would be to "select" any one of the three features.

In a more nuanced scenario, let us add noise to the vector outputs. Assume that each of the cameras oscillate at random time periods and random frequencies. The noise to signal ratio in this case would depend on the wavelength of the oscillation (i.e. higher wavelengths would make it harder to determine the direction and speed of the moving object). With this added noise, the vector output from one camera is not enough to give us the information to get the true velocity of the object. Moreover, since the noise is random, it is not possible to reconstruct the output vectors from other cameras, given the output from one camera. The best approximation for the true velocity of the object should utilize information from all three cameras. There are two key takeaways from this example. Firstly, the random noise in the three features is uncorrelated since it is random; however, the common component in the three features is approximately the true velocity of the object. Secondly, the more cameras there are, the better the approximation. This is especially true for high noise to signal ratios.

The later scenario is more suited to the factor zoo problem. The SDF is synonymous to the object moving through space with time and it is represented by k true systematic factors. The characteristics based long-short portfolios have partial loadings on the true systematic factors, but they also have added noise with high noise to signal ratios. A feature extraction technique that captures the common components given a list of factors would provide a good approximation for the true underlying latent factors. These approximations would get better as the list of factors grows (more cameras to capture the moving object).

There could be many potential ways of extracting the feature from a given set of anomaly returns. Many feature extraction algorithms are applied in the literature for tackling this problem. In addition, studies have altered dimensionality reduction methods to incorporate asset pricing theory. The next section uses a simple Principal Component Analysis (PCA) to demonstrate the benefits of using extracted features (principal components) compared to the characteristic-sparse Fama and French 5-factor model. This is to verify the key point of this chapter and is a crucial prerequisite to the discussion of more advanced techniques used in the literature.

Principal Component Analysis

The Principal Component Analysis (PCA) is the most common feature extraction technique that is widely applied. PCA is used to reduce a large number of possibly correlated variables into a small number of uncorrelated variables such that the first principal component (PC) captures most of the variance in the data; the second PC captures most of the remaining variance and so on. Hence, PCA is geared to represent a higher dimensional data in lower dimensions such that maximum possible variance is captured by the low dimensional representation.

More formally, PCA takes the N-dimensional feature set and finds M orthogonal directions in which the data have the most variance. Where N is the number of features in the original feature set and M is its lower dimensional representation. PCA reduces the dimensions of a given feature set by orthogonally transforming the data into a set of principal components such that the first principal component has the most variance, the second principal component has the second most variance and so on. The first few principal components capture the most variance and are treated as the "extracted" features in PCA.

If the goal were simply to explain the maximum variation in characteristics managed portfolios, a Principal Component Analysis (PCA) would do a better job compared to the Fama and French multifactor model. This is demonstrated with a simple experiment. The first five Principal Components (PC) of 50 long-short anomaly portfolio daily returns used by Kozak et al., 2020, along with the market factor, can explain the anomaly portfolio returns better than the Fama, French, and Cahart 6-factor model.

Following Kozak et al. (2020), the characteristic portfolios are orthogonalized to the market returns to take care of any correlation with the market factor, which is the level factor. The first 5 PC's of the orthogonalized characteristics managed portfolios are used. The resulting model is a 6-PC-factor model with the 5 PC's and one market factor included in the regressions. Then we run 50-pooled regressions with the characteristics managed portfolios as the dependent variables and, 5 PC's and market excess returns as independent variables. For comparison, our baseline model is the Fama, French and Cahart 6-factor model, which includes the momentum factor in addition to the five factors in the Fama and French 5-factor model.

Figure 3 reports the regression R-Squares from the pooled regressions. The 6-PC-factor model outperforms the Fama, French, and Cahart 6-factor model in terms of the model fit (i.e. the portfolio return variation is better captured by the extracted features as compared to the characteristic-sparse model). An important trend to note here is that the PC model captures substantial variation among most of the characteristic portfolios. This suggests that there is substantial commonality among these portfolios and indicates the existence of an underlying latent structure. The characteristics sparse model, however, does not do as well in explaining the portfolio returns.

These results, however, are only to demonstrate that extracted features can be used to explain portfolio returns and not to make inferences regarding the stock return behavior.

Figure 3. Shows the regression R-Squares where each characteristic managed portfolio is regressed on the 5 PC + Market Factor, as well as the Fama, French and Cahart 6-Factor Model

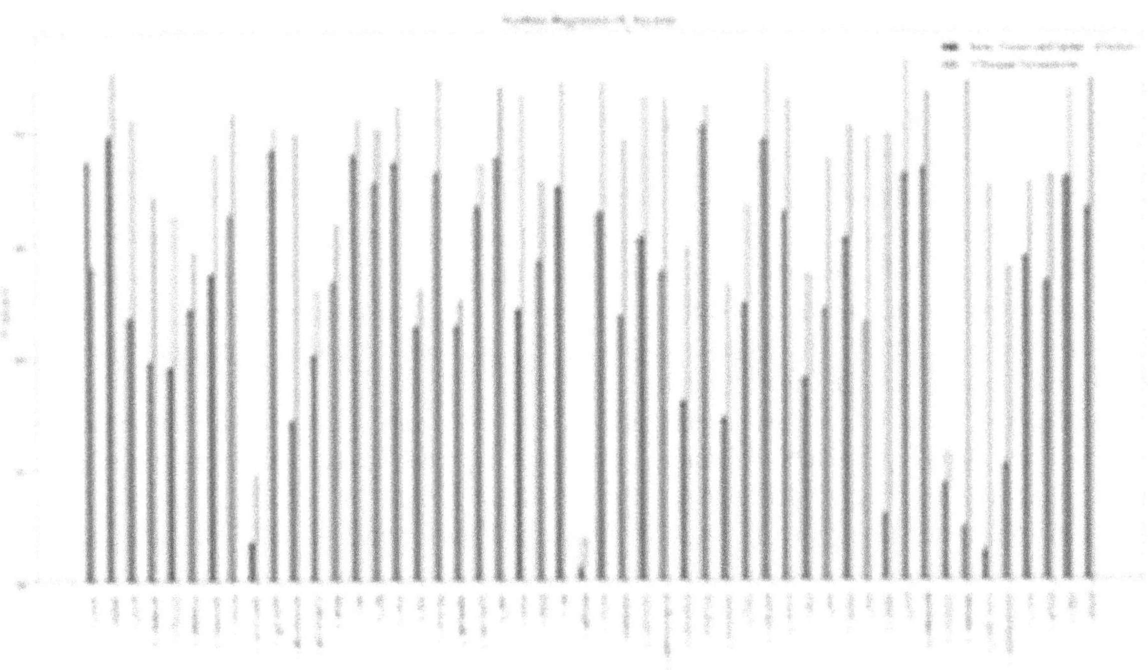

The issue demands more scrutiny given the incomplete theory and elusive empirical evidence. However, recent studies published in notable peer reviewed journals in Finance explore the issue with more scrutiny. The next section provides a brief review of these papers and speaks to the promise of this avenue in future research.

The asset pricing literature models stock returns performance either as latent factor models or as a function of characteristics. Then there is literature that seeks to estimate the latent factors themselves as a function of characteristics (Fama & French, 1993; 2015). To say that it is a large literature is an understatement and it is a challenge to summarize given the empirical puzzles (or theoretical gaps). Feature extraction of characteristics sorted portfolios is related to all three strands of the literature and a discussion of all three approaches is important to establish the contribution of this paradigm in asset pricing research. This section seeks to summarize the literature briefly and discuss the implications of feature extraction of characteristics sorted portfolios for future research.

ADRESSING THE FACTOR ZOO

As a response to the expansive list of predictive characteristics, recent literature attempts to model stock returns as a function of many characteristics at once. The literature can be divided into two broad categories and this relates to the famous characteristic versus covariance debate (Daniel and Titman, 1997; 1998).

Firstly, there are studies that focus on characteristics side of the isle and consider the characteristics (e.g. size and value) to be firm level predictive signals. This approach is beneficial because this allows inclusion of most firm level characteristics and can be considered a somewhat brute-force solution to the factor zoo problem. In addition, sophisticated machine learning predictive models can be used to fully exploit this high dimensional data. Lewellen (2015) studies the predictive power of 15 characteristics in an OLS regression. Freyberger et al. (2017) consider a larger number of characteristics and more sophisticated LASSO models. The most promising study that has explored this prediction problem across a larger list of characteristics and various model specifications is Gu et al. (2018). They explore a variety of machine learning algorithms for predicting returns with more than 900 firm level signals (including characteristics, macro variables and their interactions). They report higher out-of-sample R-Squares compared to benchmarks and show that non-linear prediction models like neural networks and decision trees perform better than their counterparts show. These studies take an approach of purely forecasting returns and do not seek to develop an asset pricing model. The drawback to this approach is limited theoretical guidance into the latent structure of the SDF.

On the other hand, there are the papers that tilt toward the covariance side of the debate and seek to explore latent factor representation of common risk. This approach has been extensively explored since the Arbitrage Pricing Theory (APT) of Ross (1976). Fama and French (1993; 2015), for instance, interpret characteristics sorted long-short portfolios as approximations for unobservable common risk factors. This is a theoretically elegant approach, with a well-established no-arbitrage equilibrium condition and a risk-based explanation. However, the existence of a large number of latent risk factors are not plausible and hence not consistent with the factor zoo if we consider each characteristic to approximate a unique risk. With the assumption that the characteristic-sorted portfolios have an underlying low-dimensional latent structure, feature extraction tools are well suited to marrying this approach with the growing list of factors. In other words, we can apply feature extraction on the factor zoo only under the assumption that there are a small number of underlying risk factors that explain much of the cross section of stock returns.

A third stream of literature seeks to combine the two approaches outlined above. Chen et. al., 2019 use a hybrid approach using a novel deep learning model. Their model considers both the systematic factors as well as firm level characteristics. This study by far has the most impressive results and allows for no-arbitrage conditions and time series behavior of systematic factors. They show that the SDF is more stable and has better out-of-sample prediction compared to previous models. Although these results are potentially paradigm shifting and the readers are highly recommended to explore these models, we limit our focus to the dimensionality reduction side of the problem for the purpose of this chapter.

Empirical Results

Recent studies find that once the latent factors are accounted for, the characteristics-sorted long-short portfolios have little to no predictive power (Kelly et. al., 2019). This is an important finding since it substantiates the claim that the factor zoo is a manifestation of an underlying low dimensional factor structure. Kozak et al. (2018, 2020) demonstrate that a small number of principal components of anomaly portfolios are able to account for the alphas of these anomalies. This is an important result since ideally the alphas should be zero in the APT. The principal components are designed to maximize the factor variance. Huang et al. (2018) propose a reduced rank approach designed to reduce the dimensions of the factor zoo to explain the cross section of returns. This is more in line with theory and a five-factor version of this approach outperforms the equivalent Fama and French 5- factor model for pricing target portfolios.

Over the last half-decade, a variety of techniques has been explored to address the factor zoo. This section discusses two prominent dimensionality reduction approaches proposed in the literature and their empirical performance. One approach is a PCA inspired approach, which allows for time-varying loadings while the other is a deep learning inspired autoencoder. These two approaches are selected for discussion because they provide an interesting contrast of linear and non-linear methods available to cater to this problem.

Instrumented Principal Component Analysis

Kelly et al. (2019) propose a novel Instrumented Principal Component Analysis (IPCA), which allows for latent factors as well as time-varying loadings. Their IPCA technique is flexible to accommodate characteristics effects in the characteristic managed portfolios. If the main driver of the characteristic/ return relation is a common risk, then the IPCA identifies the corresponding risk factor. Whereas, if there exists no such factor, IPCA infers it as a characteristic effect and allocates it to the anomaly intercept. This ensures that the latent structure extracted with IPCA is truly the common risk. The authors show that this IPCA model outperforms the Fama, French and Cahart 6-factor model in explaining the cross-section of stock returns. In addition, this method outperforms PCA in explaining test portfolios that are different from the characteristic portfolios used to estimate the latent factors: suggesting that it captures the true systematic risk better. The main findings of this study show that most of the so-called anomaly characteristics have predictive power for stock returns because of time-varying exposures to underlying unobservable factors.

Figure 4. Alpha of characteristics managed portfolios, the left and middle panel shows the alphas for unconditional models. The right panel reports time series averages of conditional alphas in the 5 factor IPCA model. (Kelly et. al., 2019)

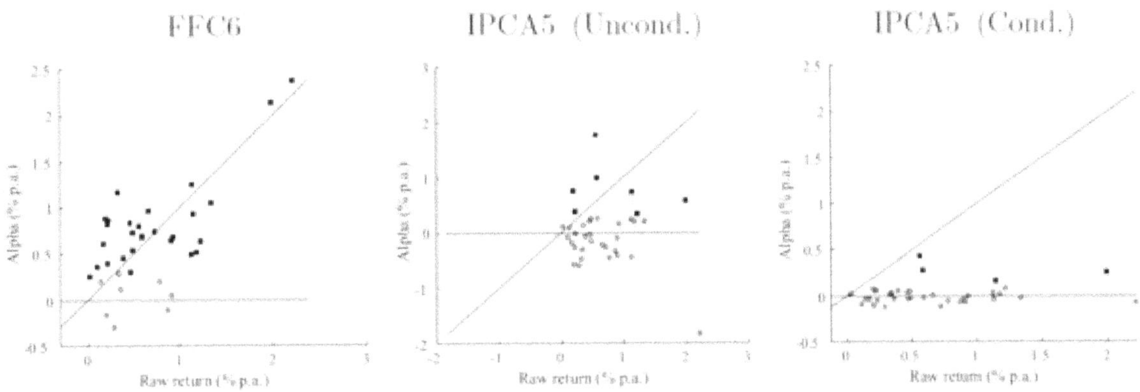

Figure 4 (Figure 1 in the original paper) shows the performance of the conditional IPCA model compared to Fama, French and Cahart 6-factor models. The so-called anomaly-return alphas see a significant reduction in anomaly portfolio alphas. This is a very important result, which suggests that the so-called factor zoo can be explained by time-varying exposure to real unobservable factors. This common latent structure is also evident in the higher regression R-squares of the first 5 principal components, presented in Figure 3.

Deep Learning Autoencoder

The IPCA approach described in the above section has very important implications for the so-called factor zoo. However, this model is restrictive because it imposes a linear mapping of the characteristic anomaly returns to the latent factors. There is no theoretical guidance to such a restriction in dimensionality reduction. An autoencoder is well suited to non-linear dimensionality reduction. Gu et. al. (2019) use an autoencoder to model the latent factors as nonlinear functions of the characteristic assets. Their model is sophisticated as it models the conditional exposures as well as imposes a no-arbitrage condition. While the model architecture is out of scope of this chapter, the main results of this study shows the promise of this technique when applied to the factor zoo problem.

Figure 5. Out-of-Sample total R-Squares (Kelly et. al., 2020).

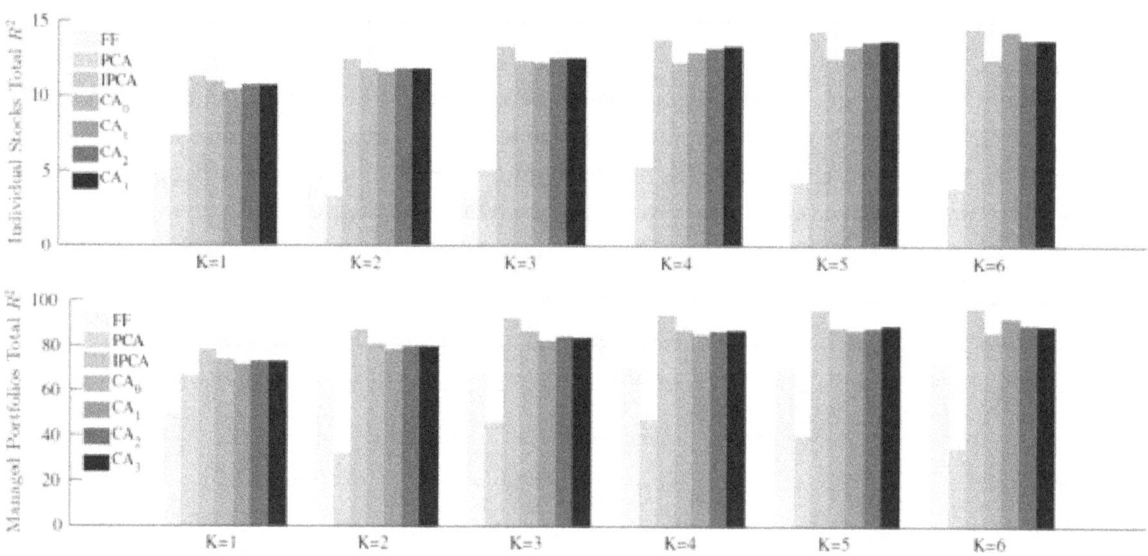

Figure 5 shows the out-of-sample total R-squares for individual stock as well as managed portfolios. The CA stands for various specifications of the Conditional Autoencoder and K is the number of latent factors. The IPCA outperforms all model candidates for out-of-sample R-Squares. However, for out-of-sample predictive performance, the autoencoder performs better compared to all other models. This suggests that incorporating non-linearities can aid in better generalizations. The results for out-of-sample predictive performance are given in Figure 6.

Figure 6. Out-of-Sample predictive R-Squares (Kelly et. al., 2020).

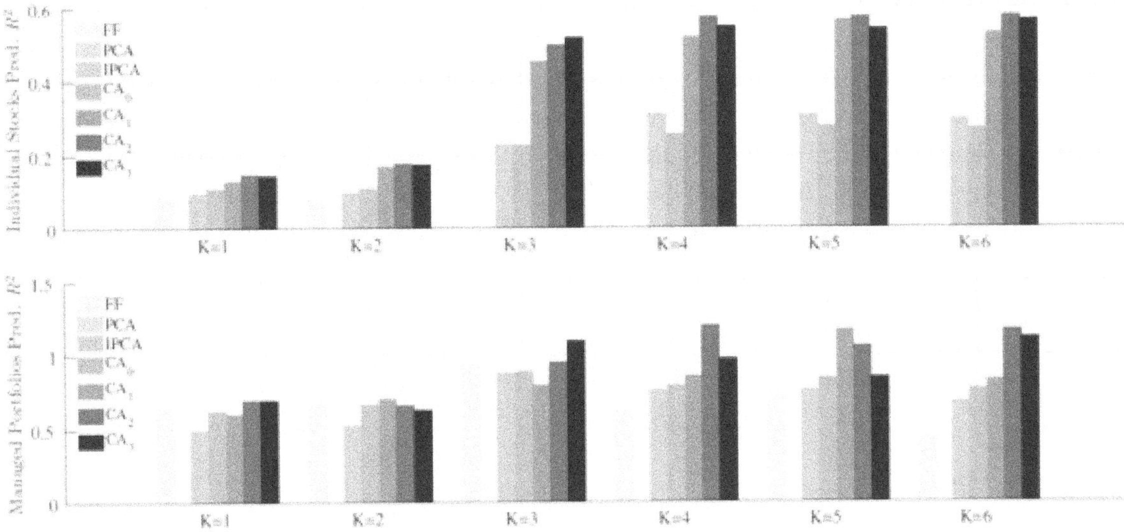

CONCLUSION AND RECOMMENDATIONS

In the last decade, the view that characteristics based long-short portfolio returns are "anomalous" has been challenged. We now contend that these portfolio returns are actually manifestations of an underlying factor structure that approximates the true Stochastic Discount Factor (SDF). This chapter seeks to summarize, explain, and present evidence to support this view. Modern feature extraction tools applied to the factor zoo provide us with very good approximation of the true latent factors. This approach has the theoretical elegance of APT inspired factor models and incorporates much of the factor zoo.

This chapter starts with a background of factor models starting as early as the CAPM and discusses the anomalies that necessitated a multifactor representation of the SDF. Then we discuss the factor zoo problem and the challenges that the expansive list of potential factors poses. Finally, this chapter seeks to propose feature extraction as an appropriate methodology to have a multifactor model that incorporates the factor zoo. A discussion on characteristics-sparse models and their challenges is necessary to make a case for feature extraction as a viable technique to address these issues.

Recent literature presents evidence of substantial commonality in the characteristic portfolio returns, and shows that once this commonality is extracted, there is little to no predictive power left in the characteristics portfolio. This empirical fact alone is suggestive that these portfolio returns are not anomalous and has important implications for discussion surrounding risk and market sentiment. However, this discussion evades the scope of this chapter. The authors seek to present this empirical pattern in data along with a discussion to provide readers with a perspective.

The literature in such dimensionality reduction methodologies is in its early stages and recent developments in machine learning offers many other viable methodologies to explore the issue. For example, most of the approaches introduced in the field seek a latent representation, which is linearly related to the expected returns. This is consistent with the prior literature on factor modelling and the resulting approaches use linear or non-linear dimensionality reduction approaches. However, this approach is restrictive even while using non-linear mapping functions like the conditional autoencoder example discussed in the chapter, because these models impose a limiting functional form on the SDF.

From a pure prediction standpoint, studies have documented that nonlinear prediction algorithms perform well in modelling stock returns using firm level characteristics as well as macroeconomic states (including characteristic portfolios). Using a deep learning model not as a dimensionality reduction tool (autoencoder) but as a predictive model increases the prediction accuracy many-fold, both in, in-sample and out-of-sample (Gu et al.,2018; Chen et. al., 2019). Additionally, it makes more sense theoretically not to restrict the functional specification of the SDF. The higher out-of-sample prediction accuracy suggests that the models are estimating robust risk prices and the SDF estimates are extremely consistent over time. Although the literature is new, the results in these studies are potentially paradigm shifting in risk modelling and is definitely something that would improve and gain more consensus in the risk modelling literature in the future.

REFERENCES

Aharoni, G., Grundy, B., & Zeng, Q. (2013). Stock returns and the Miller Modigliani valuation formula: Revisiting the Fama French analysis. *Journal of Financial Economics*, *110*(2), 347–357. doi:10.1016/j.jfineco.2013.08.003

Ball, R. (1978). Anomalies in relationships between securities' yields and yield-surrogates. *Journal of Financial Economics*, *6*(2-3), 103–126. doi:10.1016/0304-405X(78)90026-0

Banz, R. W. (1981). The relationship between return and market value of common stocks. *Journal of Financial Economics*, *9*(1), 3–18. doi:10.1016/0304-405X(81)90018-0

Bhandari, L. C. (1988). Debt/equity ratio and expected common stock returns: Empirical evidence. *The Journal of Finance*, *43*(2), 507–528. doi:10.1111/j.1540-6261.1988.tb03952.x

Black, F. (1972). Capital market equilibrium with restricted borrowing. *The Journal of Business*, *45*(3), 444–455. doi:10.1086/295472

Chen, L., Pelger, M., & Zhu, J. (2019). *Deep learning in asset pricing*. Available at SSRN 3350138

Cochrane, J. H. (2011). Presidential address: Discount rates. *The Journal of Finance*, *66*(4), 1047–1108. doi:10.1111/j.1540-6261.2011.01671.x

Cox, J. C., & Ross, S. A. (1976). The valuation of options for alternative stochastic processes. *Journal of Financial Economics*, *3*(1-2), 145–166. doi:10.1016/0304-405X(76)90023-4

Daniel, K., Grinblatt, M., Titman, S., & Wermers, R. (1997). Measuring mutual fund performance with characteristic-based benchmarks. *The Journal of Finance*, *52*(3), 1035–1058. doi:10.1111/j.1540-6261.1997.tb02724.x

Daniel, K., & Titman, S. (1998). Characteristics or covariances. *Journal of Portfolio Management*, *24*(4), 24–33. doi:10.3905/jpm.1998.24

DeMiguel, V., Martin Utrera, A., Nogales, F. J., & Uppal, R. (2017). *A portfolio perspective on the multitude of firm characteristics*. Academic Press.

Fama, E. F., & French, K. R. (1992). The cross-section of expected stock returns. *The Journal of Finance, 47*(2), 427-465.

Fama, E. F., & French, K. R. (1993). *Common risk factors in the returns on stocks and bonds*. Academic Press.

Fama, E. F., & French, K. R. (2015). A five-factor asset pricing model. *Journal of Financial Economics, 116*(1), 1–22. doi:10.1016/j.jfineco.2014.10.010

Feng, G., Giglio, S., & Xiu, D. (2017). *Taming the factor zoo.* Chicago Booth research paper, (17-04).

Freyberger, J., Neuhierl, A., & Weber, M. (2017). Dissecting characteristics nonparametrically (No. w23227). National Bureau of Economic Research.

Green, J., Hand, J. R., & Zhang, X. F. (2017). The characteristics that provide independent information about average us monthly stock returns. *Review of Financial Studies*, *30*(12), 4389–4436. doi:10.1093/rfs/hhx019

Gu, S., Kelly, B., & Xiu, D. (2018). Empirical asset pricing via machine learning (No. w25398). National Bureau of Economic Research.

Gu, S., Kelly, B. T., & Xiu, D. (2019). *Autoencoder asset pricing models.* Available at SSRN. doi:10.2139srn.3335536

Harvey, C. R., Liu, Y., & Zhu, H. (2016). … and the Cross-Section of Expected Returns. *Review of Financial Studies*, *29*(1), 5–68. doi:10.1093/rfs/hhv059

Jegadeesh, N., & Titman, S. (1993). Returns to buying winners and selling losers: Implications for stock market efficiency. *The Journal of Finance*, *48*(1), 65–91. doi:10.1111/j.1540-6261.1993.tb04702.x

Kelly, B. T., Pruitt, S., & Su, Y. (2019). Characteristics are covariances: A unified model of risk and return. *Journal of Financial Economics*, *134*(3), 501–524. doi:10.1016/j.jfineco.2019.05.001

Kogan, L., & Tian, M. H. (2015). *Firm characteristics and empirical factor models: A model-mining experiment*. FRB International Finance Discussion Paper.

Kozak, S., Nagel, S., & Santosh, S. (2018). Interpreting factor models. *The Journal of Finance*, *73*(3), 1183–1223. doi:10.1111/jofi.12612

Kozak, S., Nagel, S., & Santosh, S. (2020). Shrinking the cross-section. *Journal of Financial Economics*, *135*(2), 271–292. doi:10.1016/j.jfineco.2019.06.008

Lewellen, J., Nagel, S., & Shanken, J. (2010). A skeptical appraisal of asset pricing tests. *Journal of Financial Economics*, *96*(2), 175–194. doi:10.1016/j.jfineco.2009.09.001

Lintner, J. (1965). Security prices, risk, and maximal gains from diversification. *The Journal of Finance*, *20*(4), 587–615.

Markowitz, H. (1952). Portfolio Selection. *Journal of Finance*, 77-91.

Novy-Marx, R. (2013). The other side of value: The gross profitability premium. *Journal of Financial Economics*, *108*(1), 1–28. doi:10.1016/j.jfineco.2013.01.003

Rosenberg, B., Reid, K., & Lanstein, R. (1985). Efficient Capital Markets: II. *Persuasive Evidence of Market Inefficiency*, *11*(3), 9–16.

Sharpe, W. F. (1964). Capital asset prices: A theory of market equilibrium under conditions of risk. *The Journal of Finance*, *19*(3), 425–442.

Stattman, D. (1980). Book values and stock returns. *The Chicago MBA: A Journal of Selected Papers*, *4*(1), 25-45.

KEY TERMS AND DEFINITIONS:

Arbitrage Pricing Theory: Arbitrage pricing theory is a general theory in finance that suggests that, expected returns on any asset can be modelled as a linear function of some underlying risk factors.

Autoencoder: An autoencoder is a type of artificial neural network that is used to encode the data in lower dimensional representations.

Capital Asset Pricing Model: The capital asset pricing model models the expected returns on financial assets as a linear function of the market returns.

Deep Learning: Deep learning is a subfield of machine learning that uses artificial neural networks to predict, classify, and generate data.

Dimensionality Reduction: Dimensionality reduction is the process of reducing the number of random variables under consideration into fewer principal variables.

Feature Extraction: Feature extraction is a procedure in dimensionality reduction of extracting principal variables (features) from some random variables under consideration, usually achieved by extracting one principal variable (feature) as mapping from multiple random variables.

Feature Selection: Feature selection is the process of selecting important principal variables (features) from some random variables under consideration, usually achieved by selecting a principal variable (feature) as one of the random variables.

Multifactor Model: Multifactor models in finance are models that use characteristics sorted portfolios or information extracted from such portfolios as risk factors that explain expected returns of financial assets.

Principal Component Analysis: Principal component analysis is a dimensionality reduction technique that reduces multiple (correlated) random variables into smaller number of (uncorrelated and orthogonal) random variables such the explained variance is maximized.

Chapter 14
Riesz Potential With Logarithmic Kernel in Generalized Hölder Spaces:
Theorems on Inversion and Isomorphisms

Boris Grigorievich Vakulov
Southern Federal University, Russia

Yuri Evgenievich Drobotov
https://orcid.org/0000-0003-1318-9204
Southern Federal University, Russia

ABSTRACT

The multidimensional Riesz potential type operators are of interest within mathematical modelling in economics, mathematical physics, and other, both theoretical and applied, disciplines as they play a significant role for analysis on fractal sets. Approaches of operator theory are relevant to researching various equations, which are widespread in financial analysis. In this chapter, integral equations with potential type operators are considered for functions from generalized Hölder spaces, which provide content terminology for formalizing the concept of smoothness, briefly described in the presented chapter. Results on potentials defined on the unit sphere are described for convenience of the analysis. An inverse operator for the Riesz potential with a logarithmic kernel is carried out, and the isomorphisms between generalized Hölder spaces are proven.

INTRODUCTION

Let a natural $n \geq 2$ stand for the dimension of R^n – the set of all vectors $x = (x_1, x_2, \ldots, x_n)$ with real coordinates, thus $x_i \in \mathrm{R}$, $i = \overline{1, n}$. Being supplied with the metric

DOI: 10.4018/978-1-7998-5083-0.ch014

$$|x-\sigma|=\sqrt{(x_1-\sigma_1)^2+...+(x_n-\sigma_n)^2},$$

R^n is a Euclidean space, and $|x|=|x-0|$, while an inner product in R^n could be defined as

$$x\cdot\sigma=x_1\sigma_1+...+x_n\sigma_n,$$

or, due to the parallelogram identity, $x\cdot\sigma=\frac{1}{2}\left(|x+\sigma|^2-|x|^2-|\sigma|^2\right)$. This allows to express the metric through the inner product:

$$|x-\sigma|=\sqrt{|x|^2+|\sigma|^2-2x\cdot\sigma}$$

A unit sphere S^{n-1} in R^n is considered as a set of points, equidistant from the origin by a distance of one, i.e.

$$S^{n-1}:=\left\{\sigma\in R^n:|\sigma|=1\right\}.$$

It is clear, that, for an arbitrary $x\in R^n$, $x/|x|\in S^{n-1}$. For $x,\sigma\in S^{n-1}$, the relation (1) becomes

$$|x-\sigma|=\sqrt{2}\sqrt{1-x\cdot\sigma}$$

The purpose of the paper is to investigate solutions of an integral equation with a spherical convolution operator

$$(Kf)(x)=\int_{S^{n-1}}k(x\cdot\sigma)f(\sigma)d\sigma,\ x\in S^{n-1},$$

which is to be achieved through applying the Fourier—Laplace multiplier theory. In a nutshell, the latter assume, that if the preimage *f* can be decomposed into a Fourier series, then the coefficients of such a decomposition for the image *Kf* are defined in the specific way, briefly described below.

Eventually, the approach allows to achieve theorems on reflections between various function spaces and outline the properties of integral equations. In the present paper, isomorphisms between generalized Hölder spaces are proved for a kind of *Kf* – the Riesz potential type operator with a logarithmic kernel

$$(K^\alpha f)(x)=\int_{S^{n-1}}\frac{f(\sigma)}{|x-\sigma|^{n-1-\alpha}}\ln\frac{r}{|x-\sigma|}d\sigma,\ x\in S^{n-1},$$

where $r\in R$ is a fixed constant. Due to the relation (2), K^α is indeed a particular instance of *K* with

$$k(x\cdot\sigma)=|x-\sigma|^{\alpha-n+1}\ln\frac{r}{|x-\sigma|}.$$

Let the common definition of a potential operator be reminded according to a monograph by N.S. Landkof (1973). Suppose G is a region in R^n, which is to be considered further coincident with R^n, $K(x,\sigma)$ is a real function, defined on $G\times G$, and μ is a signed measure with support in G. Then, for any μ-measurable domain $\Omega(\mu)$, the formal expression

$$U_K^{\mu}(x)=\int\limits_{\Omega(\mu)}K(x,\sigma)\,d\mu(\sigma)$$

is called "the K-potential of the signed measure μ" (p. 58). In this paper, the measure μ is fixed implicitly, and $d\sigma=d\mu(\sigma)$ for short. In fact, $d\sigma$ is the area element of the sphere.

An M. Riesz kernel is defined as a function of the point $x\in R^n$, $n\geq 2$,

$$k_{\alpha}(x)=A(n,\alpha)\,|x|^{\alpha-n},$$

where the positive constant $A(n,\alpha)$ is a normalization factor (Landkof, 1973, p. 43). Assuming

$$K(x,\sigma)=k_{\alpha}(x-\sigma)$$

and, which follows from applying the Fourier—Laplace multiplier theory,

$$A(n,\alpha)=-\left\{2^{\alpha}\,\pi^{\frac{n-3}{2}}\sin\left[\frac{\pi}{2}(\alpha-n+1)\right]\Gamma\left(\frac{\alpha}{2}\right)\Gamma\left(\frac{\alpha-n+3}{2}\right)\right\}^{-1},$$

provides the definition of the Riesz potential of order α:

$$(I^{\alpha}f)(x)=A(n,\alpha)\int\limits_{S^{n-1}}\frac{f(\sigma)}{|x-\sigma|^{n-1-\alpha}}d\sigma,\ x\in S^{n-1}.$$

Accepting $K(x,\sigma)=k(x\cdot\sigma)$ from (5) in the general representation provides K^{α} from (4), and the similarity of its kernel to the Riesz one clarifies the operator's naming. The function

$$f:x\in S^{n-1}\to f(x)\in R$$

is usually called the density of the potential.

$K^\alpha f$ is studied here for densities from the generalized Hölder space. The one supplies with a way of formalizing the smoothness properties of a mapping and is defined below. Proving the isomorphisms between function spaces means the inverse operator for K^α is calculated – in the terms of its Fourier—Laplace multiplier, as part of the study.

Background

Both I^α and K^α can be considered as particular cases of

$$\left(K^{\alpha,\nu} f\right)(x) = \int\limits_{S^{n-1}} \frac{f(\sigma)}{|x-\sigma|^{n-1-\alpha}} \ln^\nu \frac{r}{|x-\sigma|} d\sigma,\ \nu \in \mathrm{R}, x \in \mathrm{S}^{n-1},$$

namely, $I^\alpha = K^{\alpha,0}$ and $K^\alpha = K^{\alpha,1}$. Owing to the complicated nature of $K^{\alpha,\nu}$, considering the ones separately allows not only to facilitate the study, but also to highlight the special properties in each case. As we have started from the general theory, reflected in the monograph by Landkof (1973), it should be emphasized, that the Riesz potential is considered there for all dimensions $n \geq 3$. Landkof stated the results on the basic properties of the spatial potential and general theorems on Green functions and the Dirichlet problem.

The following result on the spherical Riesz potential is essential in the scope of the presented study. At first, let a spherical hypersingular integral be defined according to the monograph by Samko (2002, p. 159):

$$\left(D^\alpha f\right)(x) = \frac{1}{A(n,-\alpha)} \int\limits_{S^{n-1}} \frac{f(\sigma)-f(x)}{|x-\sigma|^{n-1+\alpha}} d\sigma,\ x \in \mathrm{S}^{n-1},$$

D^α converges absolutely for $0<\mathrm{Re}\,\alpha<1$ in the case of nice functions f and conventionally for $0<\mathrm{Re}\,\alpha<2$ in the case of $f \in C^N\left(\mathrm{S}^{n-1}\right)$, $N \leq \infty$, as the limit of the truncated hypersingular operator:

$$\left(D^\alpha f\right)(x) = \frac{1}{A(n,-\alpha)} \lim_{\varepsilon \to \infty} \int\limits_{S_\varepsilon^{n-1}(x)} \frac{f(\sigma)-f(x)}{|x-\sigma|^{n-1+\alpha}} d\sigma,\ x \in \mathrm{S}^{n-1},$$

where $S_\varepsilon^{n-1}(x) = \left\{\sigma \in S^{n-1} : |\sigma - x| > \varepsilon\right\}$. Herewith, for the spherical harmonics Y_m, $m = \overline{0,\infty}$, $D^\alpha Y_m = \lambda_m Y_m$ with

$$\lambda_m = \Gamma\left(m + \frac{n-1+\alpha}{2}\right) \Big/ \Gamma\left(m + \frac{n-1-\alpha}{2}\right) - \Gamma\left(\frac{n-1+\alpha}{2}\right) \Big/ \Gamma\left(\frac{n-1-\alpha}{2}\right), m=0,1,2,\ldots.$$

For I^α and D^α, the following inversion theorem holds (Samko, 2002, p. 160):

Theorem 1. *The operator* $\left(I^{\alpha}\right)^{-1}$ *inverse to the spherical potential* I^{α} *is expected to be*

$$\left(I^{\alpha}\right)^{-1}=c_{\alpha}E+D^{\alpha},\ c_{\alpha}=\Gamma\left(\frac{n-1+\alpha}{2}\right)\Big/\Gamma\left(\frac{n-1-\alpha}{2}\right),$$

where E is the identity operator:

$Ef = f.$

Theorem 1 was first applied to investigate the hölderian properties of I^{α} in (Valulov, 1986) – in the terms of the generalized Hölder spaces $H_k^{\omega}\left(S^{n-1}\right)$, $k\geq 0$, and with regard to a relatively weak restriction on the real α to be positive. The following definition of the function spaces $H_k^{\omega}\left(S^{n-1}\right)$ was used.

Let $W_{k,N}$ stand for a class of multipliers $\left\{k_m\right\}_{m=0}^{\infty}$ through the spherical harmonics, $|k_m|<\infty$, which allow the following asymptotic:

$$k_m=\sum_{j=0}^{N}c_j m^{\lambda-j}+O\left(m^{\lambda-N-\varepsilon}\right),\ m\to\infty,$$

where $c_0\neq 0$, $0<\varepsilon<1$, $\lambda\in R$ and $N=0,1,\ldots$, $C\left(S^{n-1}\right)$ denote the space of all continuous, and $C^{\infty}\left(S^{n-1}\right)$ – of all infinitely differentiable on S^{n-1} functions. The closure of $C^{\infty}\left(S^{n-1}\right)$ with respect to the norm

$$\|\cdot\|_{C^{\alpha}}=\|\cdot\|_{C}+\left\|D^{\alpha}\cdot\right\|_{C},$$

where D^{α} is a spherical convolution operator with a multiplier from $W_{\alpha,[(n+1)/2]}$, is to be considered as a space $C^{\alpha}\left(S^{n-1}\right)$. Here, [•] means the integer part of the argument.

For an integer $k\geq 0$, the generalized Hölder space on a unit sphere is

$$H_k^{\omega}\left(S^{n-1}\right)=\left\{f\in C\left(S^{n-1}\right):M_d\left(D^k f,t\right)\leq c\omega(t)\right\},$$

where M_d is the local continuity modulus, coincident with the Euclidean metric on S^{n-1}:

$$M_d\left(f,x,t\right)=\sup_{x,\sigma\in S^{n-1}:|x-\sigma|\leq t}\left|f(x)-f(\sigma)\right|.$$

The general definition of M_d and the one of the Zygmund—Bary—Stechkin function class Φ_{β}^{δ} are provided in the main results section.

Specific Hölder spaces on a sphere were considered in (Werens, 1981; Nikolsky & Lizorkin, 1984) as special cases of more generalized functional spaces. Equivalent normalizations in the Hölderian spaces on a sphere were studied in (Vakulov & Samko, 1987; Samko & Vakulov, 2000).

The generalized Hölder spaces are defined in the terms of an arbitrary continuity modulus. Such spaces on a sphere are considered in (Dzhafarov, 1966, 1985).

In the presented terms, the following properties are true for the reflections by I^α and D^α (Vakulov, 1986):

Theorem 2. *The spherical Riesz potential* I^α, $0<\alpha<1$, *is bounded from* $H_0^\omega\left(S^{n-1}\right)$, $\omega\in\Phi_{1-\alpha}^0$, *to* $H^{\omega_\alpha}\left(S^{n-1}\right)$, $\omega_\alpha(\tau)=\tau^\alpha\,\omega(\tau)$.

Theorem 3. *The spherical hypersingular integral* D^α, $0<\alpha<1$, *is bounded from* $H_0^\omega\left(S^{n-1}\right)$, $\omega\in\Phi_1^\alpha$, *to* $H^{\omega_{-\alpha}}\left(S^{n-1}\right)$, $\omega_{-\alpha}(\tau)=\tau^{-\alpha}\,\omega(\tau)$.

These two theorems are proved via the so-called Zygmund type estimates:

$$M_d\left(I^\alpha f,x,h\right)\le c_1\,h\int_h^2\frac{M_d\left(f,x,t\right)}{t^{2-\alpha}}dt,\ c_1>0,$$

$$M_d\left(D^\alpha f,x,h\right)\le c_2\int_h^2\frac{M_d\left(f,x,t\right)}{t^{2-\alpha}}dt,\ c_2>0,$$

which hold for any $f\in C\left(S^{n-1}\right)$. At the same time, the results are used to prove

Theorem 4. *The spherical Riesz potential* I^α, $\alpha>0$, *is isomoprhic between* $H_k^\omega\left(S^{n-1}\right)$ *and* $H_{k+[\alpha]}^{\omega_\alpha}\left(S^{n-1}\right)$*:*

$$I^\alpha\left(H_k^\omega\left(S^{n-1}\right)\right)=H_{k+[\alpha]}^{\omega_\alpha}\left(S^{n-1}\right),\ \textit{if}\ \omega\in\Phi_{1-\alpha+[\alpha]}^0,\ \omega_\alpha(\tau)=\tau^{\alpha-[\alpha]}\,\omega(\tau).$$

Theorem 5. *Let* $w(x)=\left|x-e_{n+1}\right|^\mu$, $0<\mu<n+1$, *and f satisfies the following conditions:*

$$wf\in C\left(S^{n-1}\right),\ \left(wf\right)\left(e_{n+1}\right)=0.$$

Then, the following estimate holds:

$$M_d\left(I_{S^{n-1}}^\alpha f,x,h\right)\le c\,h^\gamma\int_h^2\frac{M_d\left(wf,x,t\right)}{t^{1-\alpha+\gamma}}dt,\ \gamma=\min\{1,\mu\}.$$

A similar result holds for the weighted generalized Hölder spaces:

Theorem 6. *Let* $\varphi_\alpha(t)=t^{\alpha-[\alpha]}\varphi(t)$, $\varphi\in\Phi^{\max\{0,\mu-n\}}_{\min\{1-\alpha+[\alpha],\mu-\alpha+[\alpha]\}}$, $w(x)=|x-\sigma|^{\mu}$, $x,\sigma\in S^{n-1}$, $\alpha-[\alpha]<\mu<n-\alpha+[\alpha]+1$, *then*

$$I^{\alpha}_{S^{n-1}}\left(H_k^{\varphi}\left(S^{n-1},w\right)\right)=H^{\varphi_\alpha}_{k+[\alpha]}\left(S^{n-1},w\right),\ \alpha>0,\ \alpha\neq 1,2,\ldots.$$

For $\alpha=1,2,\ldots$, $\varphi\in\Phi_1^{\max\{0,\mu-n\}}$, $0<\mu<n+1$, $\mu\neq n$, *the following holds:*

$$I^{\alpha}_{S^{n-1}}\left(\overset{\circ}{H}{}_k^{\varphi}\left(S^{n-1},w\right)\right)=\overset{\circ}{H}{}^{\varphi}_{k+\alpha}\left(S^{n-1},w\right),$$

where

$$\overset{\circ}{H}{}_k^{\omega}\left(S^{n-1},w\right)=\left\{f\in C\left(S^{n-1}\right):wD^kf\in H_k^{\omega}\left(S^{n-1}\right),\ \lim_{x\to a_m}wD^kf=0\right\},$$

$$w(x)=\prod_{m=0}^{l}|x-a_m|^{\beta_m},\ x,a_m\in S^{n-1},$$

D^k *is a spherical convolution operator with the Fourier-Laplace multiplier* $\{\lambda_m\}\in W_{k,N}$, $N>n+2$, $d_m\neq 0$, $m=0,1,2,\ldots$.

The result on inversion was extended on the complex α and weighted generalized Hölder spaces in (Vakulov, 2001), which is discussed below.

$K^{\alpha,\nu}$ in its general definition was explored for $0<\mathrm{Re}\alpha<1$ and $r>3$ in (Vakulov et. al., 2003). The study outlined the conditions for $K^{\alpha,\nu}$ to be bounded in $H_0^{\omega}\left(S^{n-1}\right)$ and its special weighted analogue, i.e. their dependency on α and ν. We shall provide the corresponding theorems in the main results' section in order to relate them to the new results.

ISOMORPHISMS BETWEEN THE GENERALIZED HöLDER SPACES

General terms of the Fourier—Laplace multiplier theory

A spherical harmonic $Y_m(\sigma)$, $\sigma\in S^{n-1}$, of order m is, in fact, the restriction to the unit sphere S^{n-1} of a harmonic polynomial Y_m, which is a homogeneous of degree m polynomial, satisfying the equation $\Delta Y_m=0$, where

$$\Delta f=\frac{\partial^2 f}{\partial x_1^2}+\ldots+\frac{\partial^2 f}{\partial x_n^2}$$

is the Laplace operator (Samko, 2002, p. 10). The explicit representation is

$$Y_m(x) = \sum_{|j|=m} p_j x^j ,$$

where $p_j = p_{j_1,\dots,j_n}$ are constants, $|j|=j_1+\dots+j_n$, and $x^j = x_1^{j_1} \dots x_n^{j_n}$.

The special value of Y_m are that they are the eigenfunctions of every spherical convolutional operator (3), i.e.

$$K\,Y_m = k_m\,Y_m ,$$

and this fact is known as the Funk—Hecke formula (Samko, 2002, p. 13). The sequence $\{k_m\}_{m=0}^{\infty}$ is called the Fourier—Laplace multiplier of *K*, and can be calculated as

$$k_m = \frac{2\pi^{\frac{n-1}{2}}}{\Gamma((n-1)/2)} \int_{-1}^{1} k(t) P_m(t) \left(1-t^2\right)^{\frac{n-3}{2}} dt .$$

Here, $P_m(t)$ are the generalized Legendre polynomials, which are defined as

$$P_m(t) = \begin{cases} T_m(t), & n=2; \\ \left(C_{m+n-3}^m\right)^{-1} C_m^{\frac{n-2}{2}}(t), & n \geq 3, \end{cases}$$

where $T_m(t)$ are the Chebyshev polynomials, C_m^λ are the Gegenbauer ones, and C_{m+n-3}^m is the binomial coefficient. Due to the relations between $T_m(t)$, C_m^λ and the Jacobi polynomials $P_m^{(\rho,\sigma)}(x)$

$$T_m(t) = \frac{m!}{(1/2)_m} P_n^{(-1/2,-1/2)}(t),$$

$$C_m^\lambda(t) = \frac{(2\lambda)_m}{(\lambda+1/2)_m} P_m^{(\lambda-1/2,\,\lambda-1/2)}(t),\ \lambda \neq 0,$$

$P_m(t)$ can be redefined as

$$P_m(t) = K_m(n) P_m^{\left(\frac{n-3}{2},\frac{n-3}{2}\right)},$$

$$K_m(n) = \begin{cases} m!/(1/2)_m, & n=2; \\ \left(C_{m+n-3}^m\right)^{-1} \dfrac{(n-2)_m}{((n-1)/2)_m}, & n \geq 3, \end{cases}$$

so (4) can be represented as

$$k_m = \frac{2\pi^{\frac{n-1}{2}} K_m(n)}{\Gamma((n-1)/2)} \int_{-1}^{1} k(t)\left(1-t^2\right)^{\frac{n-3}{2}} P_m^{\left(\frac{n-3}{2},\frac{n-3}{2}\right)} dt .$$

Thus, after several obvious transformations and accepting $t=x\bullet\sigma$, the latter can be written as

$$k_m = -\frac{2\pi^{\frac{n-1}{2}} K_m(n)}{\Gamma((n-1)/2)} \int_{-1}^{1} (1-t)^{\frac{\alpha}{2}-1} (1+t)^{\frac{n-3}{2}} \ln\frac{1-t}{m} P_m^{\left(\frac{n-3}{2},\frac{n-3}{2}\right)} dt .$$

This allows to formulate (3) as

$$Kf = \sum_{m,\mu} k_m f_{m\mu} Y_{m\mu}(x),\ f(x) = \sum_{m,\mu} f_{m\mu} Y_{m\mu}(x),\ x \in S^{n-1},$$

where $Y_{m,\mu}(x)$ are the orthonormal spherical harmonics, $\mu=1,2,\ldots,d(m)$,

$$d(m) = (n+2m-2)\frac{(n+m-3)!}{m!(n-2)!},\ m=0,1,2,\ldots,$$

$$f_{m\mu} = \int_{S^{n-1}} f(\sigma) Y_{m\mu}(\sigma) d\sigma .$$

The spherical Riesz potential (7) is generated by the Fourier—Laplace multiplier

$$k_m^4 = \frac{\Gamma(m+(n-1)/2-\alpha/2)}{\Gamma(m+(n-1)/2+\alpha/2)},$$

and the normalizing factor $A(n,\alpha)$ is essential to satisfy (6).

Inversion of the Riesz Potential Type Operator

We shall use the following results on integral calculus of the Jacobi polynomials $P_m^{(\rho,\sigma)}(x)$, which are presented, for instance, in the book by Prudnikov, Brychkov & Marichev (1992): the first formula on p. 583 and the second – on p. 596. Here, the ones are merged into

Lemma 1. *Let a,* Reγ>0, Reρ> -1, *then*

$$\int_{-a}^{a}(t+a)^{\gamma-1}(a-t)^{\rho}P_m^{(\rho,\sigma)}\left(\frac{t}{a}\right)dt=\frac{(-1)^m}{m!}(\sigma-\gamma+1)_m\mathrm{B}(\gamma,\rho+m+1)(2a)^{\gamma+\rho};$$

$$\int_{-a}^{a}(t+a)^{\gamma-1}(a-t)^{\rho}\ln\frac{t+a}{2a}P_m^{(\rho,\sigma)}\left(\frac{t}{a}\right)dt=\frac{(-1)^m}{m!}(\sigma-\gamma+1)_m\mathrm{B}(\gamma,\rho+m+1)(2a)^{\gamma+\rho}$$
$$\times\left[\psi(\gamma-\sigma)+\psi(\gamma)-\psi(\gamma-\sigma-m)-\psi(\gamma+\rho+m+1)\right]$$

Thus, the following result on the multiplier k_m holds:

Lemma 2. *The Fourier—Laplace multiplier of K^α is represented as*

$$k_m=-\frac{2^{\frac{n+\alpha-1}{2}}\pi^{\frac{n-1}{2}}}{m!}\frac{K_m(n)}{\Gamma((n-1)/2)}\left(\frac{n-\alpha+1}{2}\right)_m\mathrm{B}\left(\frac{\alpha}{2},\frac{n-1}{2}+m\right)$$
$$\times\left\{1+\ln\frac{2}{r}\left[\psi\left(\frac{\alpha-n+3}{2}\right)+\psi\left(\frac{\alpha}{2}\right)-\psi\left(\frac{\alpha-n+3}{2}-m\right)-\psi\left(\frac{\alpha+n-1}{2}+m\right)\right]\right\}.$$

Proof. Let the integral in (14) be considered:

$$I=\int_{-1}^{1}(1-t)^{\frac{\alpha}{2}-1}(1+t)^{\frac{n-3}{2}}\ln\frac{1-t}{m}P_m^{\left(\frac{n-3}{2},\frac{n-3}{2}\right)}dt.$$

Perform variable change τ= -*t* and represent the logarithm as a sum of two logarithms:

$$\ln\frac{\tau+1}{r}=\ln\left(\frac{\tau+1}{2}\cdot\frac{2}{r}\right)=\ln\frac{\tau+1}{2}+\ln\frac{2}{r}.$$

Then, the following holds:

$$I=(-1)^m\left\{\int_{-1}^{1}(1+\tau)^{\frac{\alpha}{2}-1}(1-\tau)^{\frac{n-3}{2}}P_m^{\left(\frac{n-3}{2},\frac{n-3}{2}\right)}(\tau)d\tau\right.$$

$$\left.+\ln\frac{2}{r}\int_{-1}^{1}(1+\tau)^{\frac{\alpha}{2}-1}(1-\tau)^{\frac{n-3}{2}}\ln\frac{\tau+1}{2}P_m^{\left(\frac{n-3}{2},\frac{n-3}{2}\right)}(\tau)d\tau\right\}.$$

These two integrals can be calculated with using formulae 1 and 2 from Lemma 1, respectively:

$$\int_{-1}^{1}(1+t)^{\frac{\alpha}{2}-1}(1-t)^{\frac{n-3}{2}}P_m^{\left(\frac{n-3}{2},\frac{n-3}{2}\right)}(t)dt=2^{\frac{n+\alpha-3}{2}}\frac{(-1)^m}{m!}\left(\frac{n-\alpha+1}{2}\right)_m\mathrm{B}\left(\frac{\alpha}{2},\frac{n-1}{2}+m\right),$$

$$\int_{-1}^{1}(1+\tau)^{\frac{\alpha}{2}-1}(1-\tau)^{\frac{n-3}{2}}\ln\frac{\tau+1}{2}P_m^{\left(\frac{n-3}{2},\frac{n-3}{2}\right)}(t)d\tau=2^{\frac{n+\alpha-3}{2}}\frac{(-1)^m}{m!}\left(\frac{n-\alpha+1}{2}\right)_m\mathrm{B}\left(\frac{\alpha}{2},\frac{n-1}{2}+m\right)$$

$$\times\left[\psi\left(\frac{\alpha-n+3}{2}\right)+\psi\left(\frac{\alpha}{2}\right)-\psi\left(\frac{\alpha-n+3}{2}-m\right)-\psi\left(\frac{\alpha+n-1}{2}+m\right)\right].$$

Bringing the results together provides the statement of the lemma.

Lemma 2 allows to prove the following theorem on the representation of K^α through the Riesz potential $I^{\alpha}_{S^{n-1}}$ with the normalizing factor $A(n,\alpha)$ and an operator with a specific multiplier:

Theorem 7. *K^α is a composition of the Riesz potential I^α, defined in (7) and corresponding to the multiplier k_m^4, defined in (15), and a spherical convolution operator R, generated by the following multiplier:*

$$l_m=-2^{\frac{n+\alpha-1}{2}}\pi^{\frac{n-1}{2}}K_m(n)\left(m+\frac{n-1}{2}-\frac{\alpha}{2}\right)\Gamma\left(\frac{\alpha}{2}\right)\left[m\,\mathrm{B}\left(\frac{n-1}{2},m\right)\Gamma\left(\frac{n-\alpha+1}{2}\right)\right]^{-1}$$

$$\times\left\{1+\ln\frac{2}{r}\left[\psi\left(\frac{\alpha-n+3}{2}\right)+\psi\left(\frac{\alpha}{2}\right)-\psi\left(\frac{\alpha-n+3}{2}-m\right)-\psi\left(\frac{\alpha+n-1}{2}+m\right)\right]\right\}.$$

Proof. We shall use the following properties of the Pochhammer symbol and the Gamma function:

$$(a)_k=\frac{\Gamma(a+k)}{\Gamma(a)},\ \Gamma(z+1)=z\Gamma(z).$$

The ones provide the following:

$$\left(\frac{n-\alpha+1}{2}\right)_m \mathrm{B}\left(\frac{\alpha}{2},\frac{n-1}{2}+m\right)=\frac{\Gamma\left(\frac{n-\alpha+1}{2}+m\right)}{\Gamma\left(\frac{n-\alpha+1}{2}\right)}\frac{\Gamma\left(\frac{\alpha}{2}\right)\Gamma\left(\frac{n-1}{2}+m\right)}{\Gamma\left(\frac{n+\alpha-1}{2}+m\right)}$$

$$=k_m^4\left(m+\frac{n-1}{2}-\frac{\alpha}{2}\right)\frac{\Gamma\left(\frac{\alpha}{2}\right)\Gamma\left(\frac{n-1}{2}+m\right)}{\Gamma\left(\frac{n-\alpha+1}{2}\right)}$$

Thus, the multiplier k_m^4 can be extracted from k_m as a cofactor.

In addition, it can be noticed, that as m is a non-negative integer, the following relation holds:

$$m! = \Gamma(m+1).$$

Together with the previously used properties, the one provides

$$\frac{\Gamma\left(\frac{\alpha}{2}\right)\Gamma\left(\frac{n-1}{2}+m\right)}{m!\,\Gamma\left(\frac{n-\alpha+1}{2}\right)}\frac{\Gamma(m)}{\Gamma(m)}=\frac{\Gamma\left(\frac{\alpha}{2}\right)}{m\,\mathrm{B}\left(\frac{n-1}{2},m\right)\Gamma\left(\frac{n-\alpha+1}{2}\right)},$$

from which the statement of the theorem follows immediately:

$$K^\alpha = I^\alpha R.$$

Theorem 8. *The inverse operator for K^α is expected to be a composition of the spherical hypersingular integral D^α, defined by (8), and a spherical convolution operator A with the specific multiplier, i.e.*

$$\left(K^\alpha\right)^{-1}=\left(c_\alpha E+D^\alpha\right)A^{-1},$$

where

$$c_\alpha=\Gamma\left(\frac{n-1+\alpha}{2}\right)\Big/\Gamma\left(\frac{n-1-\alpha}{2}\right),$$

and

$$(Af)(x)=\int_{S^{n-1}} a(x\cdot\sigma)f(\sigma)d\sigma,\ x\in S^{n-1},$$

$$a(x\cdot\sigma)=\begin{cases}\dfrac{1}{\pi}\sum\limits_{m=0}^{\infty} l_m^{-1}T_m(x\cdot\sigma), & n=2;\\ \Gamma\left(\dfrac{n-2}{2}\right)\Big/\left(4\pi^{\frac{n}{2}}\right)\sum\limits_{m=0}^{\infty}(2m+n-2)\,l_m^{-1}C_m^{\frac{n-2}{2}}(x\cdot\sigma), & n\geq 3,\end{cases}$$

is a spherical convolution operator, generated by the Fourier—Laplace multiplier $\{l_m^{-1}\}_{m=0}^{\infty}$ *with* l_m *given in (16).*

Proof. The statement of the theorem follows from Theorem 7, as the inverse operator's multiplier is defined by $k_m^{-1}=\left(k_m^4 l_m\right)^{-1}$.

Theorems on Isomorphisms

There are two principal problems to be considered in studying the smoothness property of the reflection by an operator: in what terms the concept can be defined and what methods are to be used for investigating the existence of the property. For the first problem, the terms of the Hölder spaces are proposed, while the second one can be solved by applying the Zygmund type estimates, in which the local continuity modulus of the image is to be majorized by some integral operator of the modulus of its preimage – the density function, for the potential type operators.

The theory of the generalized Hölder spaces provides sufficiently convenient terms for defining and studying the concept of smoothness. Thus, even if the “usual” smoothness (i.e. integer order differentiability) on a sphere is considered, it is essential to clarify this concept. It can be defined through two fundamentally different approaches (Vakulov & Samko, 1987): in the terms, basing on the Laplace—Beltrami operator, and in the ones, related to differentiation in the Cartesian coordinates. Both ways lead to, in general, equivalent Hölderian classes $H^{\lambda}(S^n)$ with non-integer λ, and to certainly different ones with integer $\lambda\geq 1$.

The generalized Hölder spaces are based on the concept of the local continuity modulus. In its general form, the one can be defined as follows: let d be a metric on a subset $\Omega\subseteq R^n$, f be a bounded function on Ω. Then the functional

$$M_d(f,x,t)=\sup_{y\in\Omega:d(x,y)\leq t}\left|f(x)-f(y)\right|,$$

defined for all $t\in T\subseteq R_+$ and $x\in\Omega$, is the local continuity modulus of f. Here, R_+ is the set of all positive real values.

To define the generalized Hölder space on a unit sphere, we shall use the class W, which contains all such functions ω, defined on an interval $[0;l]$, that

- $\omega \in C[0;l]$, i.e. ω is continuous on $[0;l]$;
- $\omega(0)=0$, $\omega(t)>0$ with $t>0$;
- $\omega(t)$ is almost increasing.

Thus, the set

$$H^{\omega}\left(S^{n-1}\right)=\left\{f\in C\left(S^{n-1}\right): M_r\left(f,x,t\right)\leq c\,\omega\left(t\right)\right\},\ c>0,$$

supplied with a norm

$$\|f\|_{H^{\omega}\left(S^{n-1}\right)}=\|f\|_{C\left(S^{n-1}\right)}+\sup_{t>0}\frac{M_d\left(f,t,x\right)}{\omega\left(t\right)}$$

is called the generalized Hölder space. The one is, in fact, a particular case of the H_k^{ω} spaces, considered in the background section: $H_0^{\omega}=H^{\omega}$. The general problem is on $K^{\alpha,\nu}$, and the following results, firstly provided in (Vakulov et. al., 2003), are of interest. Let

$$\omega_{\alpha,\nu}\left(t\right)=\omega\left(t\right)t^{\mathrm{Re}\,\alpha}\ln^{\nu}\frac{r}{t},$$

and Φ_{β}^{δ}, $\beta>\delta\geq 0$, denote the class of all functions $\omega\in W$, which satisfy the following conditions:

$$\int_0^{\tau}\left(\frac{\tau}{t}\right)^{\delta}\frac{\omega\left(t\right)}{t}\,dt\leq c_1\,\omega\left(\tau\right);$$

$$\int_{\tau}^{l}\left(\frac{\tau}{t}\right)^{\beta}\frac{\omega\left(t\right)}{t}\,dt\leq c_2\,\omega\left(\tau\right),$$

where c_1 and c_2 are constants, independent on τ, $0<\tau<l/2$. We shall use Φ^{δ} to denote Φ_{β}^{δ} without the second condition and Φ_{β} will mean Φ_{β}^{δ} without the first one.

In these terms, the following properties are revealed:

Theorem 9. *Let* $0<\mathrm{Re}\,\alpha<1$, $\nu\in\mathbb{R}$. *If* $\omega\in\Phi_{1-\mathrm{Re}\,\alpha}$, *then* $K^{\alpha,\nu}$ *is bounded from* $H^{\omega}\left(S^{n-1}\right)$ *to* $H^{\omega_{\alpha,\nu}}\left(S^{n-1}\right)$.

The space $\overset{\circ}{H}{}^{\omega}\left(S^{n-1},w\right)$ consists of all functions $f\in H^{\omega}\left(S^{n-1}\right)$, for which additionally holds

$$\lim_{x \to a}(w f)(x) = 0.$$

Theorem 10. *Let* $0<\mathrm{Re}\alpha<1$, $v \in \mathrm{R}$, $w(x)=|x-a|^{\mu}$, $a \in \mathrm{S}^{n-1}$, *and* $\omega \in \Phi_{\min\{1,\mu\}-\mathrm{Re}\alpha}$, *if* $\mathrm{Re}\alpha<\mu<n-1$, *or* $\omega \in \Phi^{\mu+1-n}_{1-\mathrm{Re}\,\alpha}$, *if* $n-1\leq\mu<n-\mathrm{Re}\alpha$. *Then* $K^{\alpha,v}$ *is bounded from* $H_0^{\omega}(\mathrm{S}^{n-1}, w)$ *to* $H_0^{\omega_{\alpha,v}}(\mathrm{S}^{n-1}, w)$.

Now, let $v=1$ and

$$\omega_{\alpha}(t) = t^{\mathrm{Re}\alpha}\omega(t).$$

The following result on the weighted generalized Hölder space $\overset{\circ}{H}{}^{\omega}(\mathrm{S}^{n-1}, w)$ with

$$w(x) = \prod_{j=1}^{m} |x - a_j|^{\mu_j}, \; x, a_j \in \mathrm{S}^{n-1}, j=1,\ldots,m,$$

is known from (Vakulov, 2001):

Theorem 11. *Let* $0<\mathrm{Re}\alpha<1$. *For all* $\omega \in \Phi^{0}_{\min\{1,\mu_j\}-\mathrm{Re}\alpha}$, $\mathrm{Re}\alpha<\mu_j<n-1$, *as well as for all* $\omega \in \Phi^{\max \mu_j - n+1}_{1-\mathrm{Re}\alpha}$, $n-1\leq\mu_j<n-\mathrm{Re}\alpha$, $j=1,\ldots,m$, *the spherical Riesz potential* I^{α}, *defined in (7), is isomorphic between* $\overset{\circ}{H}{}^{\omega}(\mathrm{S}^{n-1}, w)$ *and* $\overset{\circ}{H}{}^{\omega_{\alpha}}(\mathrm{S}^{n-1}, w)$:

$$I^{\alpha}\left(\overset{\circ}{H}{}^{\omega}(\mathrm{S}^{n-1}, w)\right) = \overset{\circ}{H}{}^{\omega_{\alpha}}(\mathrm{S}^{n-1}, w).$$

Thus, for K^{α} the following result, analogous to Theorem 10, holds:

Theorem 12. *Let all the conditions on* α, ω *and* μ_j, $j=1,\ldots,m$, *from Theorem 11 be satisfied. Then* K^{α} *is an isomorphism from* $H_0^{\omega}(\mathrm{S}^{n-1}, w)$ *to* $H_0^{\omega_{\alpha}}(\mathrm{S}^{n-1}, w)$:

$$K^{\alpha}\left(\overset{\circ}{H}{}^{\omega}(\mathrm{S}^{n-1}, w)\right) = \overset{\circ}{H}{}^{\omega_{\alpha}}(\mathrm{S}^{n-1}, w).$$

Due to Theorem 8, the representation $(K^{\alpha})^{-1}=(I^{\alpha})^{-1}R^{-1}$ holds, and the statement of the theorem follows immediately from Theorem 11.

SOLUTIONS AND RECOMMENDATIONS

Fractal sets significantly widen the scope of functional analysis and its applications in financial modelling as they generalize the classical approaches, based on the concept of a smooth manifold. Fractional calculus appears to provide a convenient theory of integration over fractal sets and non-integer-dimensional spaces, as well as to define key methods for studying specific problems. Let the definitions of functions and integrals on fractals be provided here following (Tarasov, 2010) in order to outline briefly the motivation for fractional calculus operators to be considered while studying fractal models in financial mathematics.

Let Ω be a non-empty subset of the n-dimensional Euclidean space R^n, and let $\{E_i\}$ be a countable family of disjoint subsets of diameter at most ε, covering Ω:

$$\Omega \subset \bigcup_{i=1}^{\infty} E_i \text{ , diam}(E_i) \le \varepsilon \text{ for all } i,$$

where diam(E_i)= sup$\{r(x,y)$: $x,y \in E_i\}$, $r(\bullet)$ denotes a metric. A characteristic function of a subset E_i is defined as follows:

$$\chi_{E_i}(x) = \begin{cases} 1, & x \in E_i; \\ 0, & x \notin E_i. \end{cases}$$

A function $f(x)$, defined on Ω, is called a simple one, if

$$f(x) = \begin{cases} f_k, & x \in E_k; \\ 0, & x \notin \bigcup_{k=1}^{\infty} E_k, \end{cases} \quad f_i \in R \text{, and } f(x) = \sum_{i=1}^{\infty} f_i \chi_{E_i}(x).$$

Let the simple function $f(x)$ be integrable on Ω, i.e. $\forall i$: $f_i \neq 0$ $\mu_H(E_i) < \infty$, where

$$\mu_H(\Omega, D) = \lim_{\varepsilon \to 0} \mu_H^{(\varepsilon)}(\Omega, D),$$

$$\mu_H^{(\varepsilon)}(\Omega, D) = \inf \left\{ \sum_{i=1}^{\infty} \omega(D) \left[\text{diam}(E_i) \right]^D : \Omega \subset \bigcup_{i=1}^{\infty} E_i, \text{diam}(E_i) \le \varepsilon \right\},$$

$$\omega(D) = \frac{\pi^{D/2}}{2^n \Gamma(D/2+1)}.$$

Then the Lebesgue–Stieltjes integral can be defined by

$$\int_{\Omega} f(x)d\mu_H(x)=\sum_{i=1}^{\infty} f_i\mu_H(E_i,D)=\omega(D)\lim_{\mathrm{diam}(E_i)\to 0}\sum_{E_i} f(x_i)\left[\mathrm{diam}(E_i)\right]^D .$$

As it is always possible to divide the subset $\Omega\subset\mathrm{R}^n$ into the collection of ε-cubes, defined as

$$E_{i_1\ldots i_n}=\left\{(x_1,\ldots,x_n)\in\Omega : i_k\varepsilon\le x_k\le(i_k+1)\varepsilon,\ i_k\in\mathrm{N}\right\},$$

then

$$d\mu_B(x)=\lim_{\mathrm{diam}\left(E_{i_1\ldots i_n}\right)\to 0}\omega(D)\left[\mathrm{diam}(E_i)\right]^D,$$

where

$$\mu_B(\Omega,D)=\omega(D)\zeta^D(\Omega),\ \zeta^D(\Omega)=\lim_{\varepsilon\to 0}\zeta_\varepsilon^D(\Omega),$$

$$\zeta_\varepsilon^D(\Omega)=\inf\left\{\sum_{i=1}^{\infty}\left[\mathrm{diam}\left(E_{i_1\ldots i_n}\right)\right]^D:\Omega\subset\bigcup_{i_1\ldots i_n}^{\infty}E_{i_1\ldots i_n},\mathrm{diam}\left(E_{i_1\ldots i_n}\right)\le\varepsilon\sqrt{n}\right\}.$$

Considering the Euclidean metric $|x-y|=\left(\sum_{i=1}^{n}|x_i-y_i|^2\right)^{\frac{1}{2}}$, $x,y\in\mathrm{R}^n$, Ω can be parameterized using polar coordinates: $\rho=r(x,0)=|x|$ and the angle φ. Within this parametrization, a spherically symmetric covering by the $E_{\rho,\Omega}$ sets around the centre at the origin can be considered, thus

$$d_{\mu_B}(\rho,\varphi)=\lim_{\mathrm{diam}\left(E_{r,\varphi}\right)\to 0}\omega(D)\left[\mathrm{diam}\left(E_{\rho,\varphi}\right)\right]^D=d\varphi^{D-1}\rho^{D-1}dr .$$

If $f(x)$ is assumed to be symmetric with respect to some centre $x_0\in\Omega$, i.e. $f(x)$=const for $\forall x\in\Omega$: $|x-x_0|=\rho$ and arbitrary ρ, then the centre of symmetry can be shifted with the transformation

$$\Omega\to\Omega' : x\to x'=x-x_0 ,$$

and the integral over Ω can be represented as

$$\int_{\Omega} f\,d\mu_B=\frac{2\pi^{D/2}}{\Gamma(D/2)}\int_0^{\infty} f(\rho)\rho^{D-1}dr=\frac{2\pi^{D/2}\Gamma(D)}{\Gamma(D/2)}\left(I_-^D f\right)(0),$$

where

$$\left(I_-^\alpha f\right)(x) := \frac{1}{\Gamma(D)} \int_x^\infty \frac{f(t)}{(t-x)^{1-\alpha}} dt, \ -\infty<x<\infty,$$

is the right-sided Riemann–Liouville integral, studied in fractional calculus (Samko et. al., 1993).

Along with I_-^α, the left-sided fractional integral is considered as (Samko et al., 1993, p. 33)

$$\left(I_+^\alpha f\right)(x) := \frac{1}{\Gamma(D)} \int_{-\infty}^x \frac{f(t)}{(x-t)^{1-\alpha}} dt, \ -\infty<x<\infty.$$

Fractional integration operators with constant limits occur in many fields of mathematics, and due to analogies in mathematical physics, such operators came to be called potential type operators. Thus, the Riesz potential over the real axis is considered as the following operator (Samko et al., 1993, p. 214):

$$\left(I^\alpha f\right)(x) = \frac{1}{2\Gamma(\alpha)\cos(\alpha\pi/2)} \int_{-\infty}^\infty \frac{f(t)}{|t-x|^{1-\alpha}} dt, \ \mathrm{Re}\alpha>0, \ \alpha\neq 1,3,5,\ldots,$$

and its useful modification is

$$\left(H^\alpha f\right)(x) = \frac{1}{2\Gamma(\alpha)\sin(\alpha\pi/2)} \int_{-\infty}^\infty \frac{\mathrm{sgn}(x-t)}{|x-t|^{1-\alpha}} f(t)\, dt, \ \mathrm{Re}\alpha>0, \ \alpha\neq 2,4,6,\ldots,$$

with I^α and H^α being defined on functions $f \in L_p(\mathrm{R})$, $1 \leq p < 1/\mathrm{Re}\alpha$, while $0<\mathrm{Re}\alpha<1$.

The connection between these operators and the fractional integrals, defined above, is evident:

$$I^\alpha = \left[2\cos\left(\frac{\alpha\pi}{2}\right)\right]^{-1}\left(I_+^\alpha + I_-^\alpha\right), \ H^\alpha = \left[2\sin\left(\frac{\alpha\pi}{2}\right)\right]^{-1}\left(I_+^\alpha - I_-^\alpha\right).$$

In the multidimensional case, the Riesz potentials appear to be negative fractional powers of the Laplace operator (Samko et al., 1993, p. 483):

$$(-\Delta)^{\alpha/2} f = \mathsf{F}^{-1}|x|^{-\alpha}\mathsf{F} f = \begin{cases} I^\alpha f, & \mathrm{Re}\alpha > 0; \\ D^{-\alpha} f, & \mathrm{Re}\alpha < 0, \end{cases}$$

where F denotes the multidimensional Fourier transform:

$$\mathsf{F} f = \hat{f}(x) = \int_{\mathbf{R}^n} e^{ix\cdot t} f(t)\, dt, \ x \in \mathrm{R}^n.$$

Theorems on isomorphisms describe the classes of correctness for the integral equations with corresponding operators. This is of great interest also because the connections between the hypersingular integral and classical partial derivatives allows to transform formally a problem of financial mathematics to the one of integral equations' theory. This gives a reason to assume the results, presented in this paper, to be useful in computing complicated financial mathematics models of a new kind.

FUTURE RESEARCH DIRECTIONS

In the framework of the multiplier theory, $K^{\alpha,\nu}$ is to be studied in its general definition. Integrability, smoothness and other properties are to be revealed for ranges of ν's values and various function spaces. The results on these topics are expected to widen the scope of analysis on fractal sets and its applications in financial modelling.

At the same time, the variable order fractional calculus operators in functional spaces with also variable (dependent on coordinates) defining characteristics are studied intensively now. For one-dimensional case, such problems have been considered in (Ginsburg & Karapetyants, 1994; Karapetyants & Ginsburg, 1995; Samko, 1998). The variable order fractional calculus operators have been considered in papers (Samko & Ross, 1993; Ross & Samko, 1995; Samko, 1995; Vakulov & Kochurov, 2010, 2011; Samko & Vakulov, 2011; Vakulov et. al., 2011; Odzijewicz et. al., 2013). Considering α, ν or even both of them as variables is promising for operator theory and its applications.

ACKNOWLEDGMENT

This research was supported by Southern Federal University [grant number VnGr-07/2020-04-IM].

REFERENCES

Dzhafarov, A. S. (1966). Nailuchshee priblizhenie konechnymi sfericheskimi summami i nekotorye differencial'nye svojstva garmonicheskih v share funkcij. In L. Kudryavcev (Ed.), *Teoremy vlozhenija i ih prilozhenija. Trudy simpoziuma po teoremam vlozheniya. Baku, 1966 god* (pp. 75–81). Nauka.

Dzhafarov, A. S. (1985). Konstruktivnoe opisanie obobshhennyh klassov Besova na mnogomernoj sfere. *DAN SSSR*, *285*(3), 542–546.

Ginsburg, A. I., & Karapetyants, N. K. (1994). Drobnoe integrodifferencirovanie v gel'derovskih klassah peremennogo porjadka. *Доклады российской академии наук*, *339*(4), 439–441.

Karapetyants, N. K., & Ginsburg, A. I. (1995). Fractional integrodifferentiation in Hölder classes of arbitrary order. *Georgian Mathematical Journal*, *2*(2), 141–150. doi:10.1007/BF02257475

Kurosh, A. G., Markushevich, A. I., & Rashevskij, P. K. (Eds.). (1948). *Matematika v SSSR za 30 let (1917-1947)*. OGIZ.

Landkof, N. S. (1973). *Foundations of Modern Potential Theory*. Springer.

Nikolsky, S. M., & Lizorkin, P. I. (1984). Priblizhenie spericheskimi polinomami. *Tr. MIAN SSSR, 166*, 186–200.

Odzijewicz, T., Malinowska, A. B., & Torres, D. F. M. (2013). Fractional variational calculus of variable order. In A. Almeida, L. Castro, & F.-O. Speck (Eds.), *Advances in Harmonic Analysis and Operator Theory: The Stefan Samko Anniversary Volume* (pp. 291–301). Birkhäuser. doi:10.1007/978-3-0348-0516-2_16

Prudnikov, A. P., Brychkov, Yu. A., & Marichev, O. I. (1992). Integrals and Series. Volume 2. Special Functions. Gordon and Breach Science Publishers.

Ross, B., & Samko, S. G. (1995). Fractional integration operator of a variable order in the Holder spaces $H^{\lambda}(S_{n-1})$. *International Journal of Mathematics and Mathematical Sciences, 18*(4), 777–788. doi:10.1155/S0161171295001001

Samko, N., & Vakulov, B. (2011). Spherical fractional and hypersingular integrals of variable order in generalized Holder spaces with variable characteristic. *Mathematische Nachrichten, 2-3*(284), 355–369. doi:10.1002/mana.200810113

Samko, S. G. (1995). Fractional integration and differentiation of variable order. *Analysis Mathematica, 21*(3), 213–236. doi:10.1007/BF01911126

Samko, S. G. (1998). Differentiation and integration of variable order and the spaces $L^{p(x)}$. *Contemporary Mathematics, 212*, 203–219. doi:10.1090/conm/212/02884

Samko, S. G. (2002). *Hypersingular integrals and their applications*. Taylor & Francis.

Samko, S. G., Kilbas, A. A., & Marichev, O. I. (1993). *Fractional integrals and derivatives: theory and applications*. Gordon and Breach Science Publishers.

Samko, S. G., & Ross, B. (1993). Integration and differentiation to a variable fractional order. *Integral Transforms and Special Functions, 1*(4), 277–300. doi:10.1080/10652469308819027

Samko, S. G., & Vakulov, B. G. (2000). On equivalent norms in fractional order function spaces of continuous functions on the unit sphere. *Fractional Calculus & Applied Analysis, 3*(4), 401–433.

Tarasov, V. E. (2010). *Fractional Dynamics: Applications of Fractional Calculus to Dynamics of Particles, Fields and Media*. Springer. doi:10.1007/978-3-642-14003-7

Vakulov, B. G. (1986). Operator tipa potenciala na sfere v obobshhennyh klassah Gjol'dera. *Izv.vuzov. Matem., 11*, 66–69.

Vakulov, B. G. (2001). O dejstvii operatora rissova potenciala kompleksnogo porjadka po Rn v vesovyh prostranstvah Gjol'dera. *Izvestija vuzov. Severo-Kavkazskij region. Estestvennye nauki, 4*, 47-49.

Vakulov, B. G. (2005). Sfericheskie operatory tipa potenciala v vesovyh prostranstvah Gjol'dera peremennogo porjadka. *Vladikavkazskij matematicheskij zhurnal, 7*(2), 26-40.

Vakulov, B. G., & Drobotov, Yu. E. (2017). Variable order Riesz potential over Ŕn on weighted generalized variable Hölder spaces [Russian, English abstract]. *Siberian Electronic Mathematical Reports, 14*, 647–656.

Vakulov, B. G., & Karapetjanc, N. K. (2003). Operatory tipa potenciala na sfere s osobennostjami na poljusah. *Doklady Akademii Nauk*, *392*(2), 151–154.

Vakulov, B. G., Karapetjanc, N. K., & Shankishvili, L. D. (2003). Operatory sfericheskoj svertki so stepenno-logarifmicheskim jadrom v obobshhennyh prostranstvah Gjol'dera. *Izv. vuzov. Matem*, *2*, 3–14.

Vakulov, B. G., & Kochurov, E. S. (2010). Operatory drobnogo integrirovanija i differencirovanija peremennogo porjadka v prostranstvah Gjol'dera $H^{\omega(x,t)}$. *Vladikavkazskij matematicheskij zhurnal*, *12*(4), 3-11.

Vakulov, B. G., & Kochurov, E. S. (2011). Ocenki tipa Zigmunda dlja operatorov drobnogo integrirovanija i di_erencirovanija peremennogo porjadka. *Izv. vuzov. Sev. Kavk. region. Estestv. nauki. Specvypusk*, 15-17.

Vakulov, B. G., Kochurov, E. S., & Samko, N. G. (2011). Ocenki tipa Zigmunda dlja operatorov drobnogo integrirovanija i differencirovanija peremennogo porjadka. *Izv. vuzov. Matematika*, *6*, 25–34.

Vakulov, B. G., & Samko, S. G. (1987). Ob jekvivalentnyh normirovkah v prostranstvah funkcij drobnoj gladkosti na sfere tipa $!^{\lambda}(S_{n-1})$, . Izv. vuzov. *Matem*, *12*, 68–71.

Werens, M. (1981). Best approximation on the unit sphere in Rk. In P. Butzer, E. Gärlich, & B. Szökefalvi-Nagy (Eds.), *Proceedings of the Conference held at the Mathematical Research Institute at Oberwolfach Black Forest*, (pp. 233-245). Basel, Switzerland: Birkhäuser.

KEY TERMS AND DEFINITIONS

Bounded Operator: Let *U* and *V* be two vector spaces over the same ordered field, and they are equipped with norms. A linear operator *K* from *U* to *V* is called bounded, it there exists a constant *C*>0 such that $\|K x\|_V \le C\|x\|_U$, *x*∈*U*.

Euler Beta-Function: The Euler integral of the first kind $B(z,w)=\int_0^1 x^{z-1}(1-x)^{w-1}\,dx$, Re *z*>0, Re *w*>0, is known as the beta function. It relates to the gamma-function as $B(z,w)=\frac{\Gamma(z)\Gamma(w)}{\Gamma(z+w)}$.

Euler Gamma-Function: The Euler integral of the second kind $\Gamma(z)=\int_0^\infty x^{z-1}e^{-x}\,dx$, Re *z*>0, with $x^{z-1}=e^{(z-1)\ln x}$ is known as the gamma-function. It is well defined for all complex *z* with Re *z*>0 and can be extended to the half-plane Re *z*≤0, *z*≠0, -1, -2,..., by analytic continuation via the reduction formula Γ(*z*+1)=*z*Γ(*x*), Re *z*>0.

Isomorphism: An isomorphism is a homomorphism that is a bijection, i.e. it is a mapping, that preserves sets and relations among elements and can be reversed by an inverse mapping.

Jacobi Polynomials: The Jacobi polynomials are defined as

$$P_n^{(\rho,\sigma)}(z)=\frac{1}{n!}\Gamma\begin{bmatrix}\rho+n+1\\ \rho+\sigma+n+1\end{bmatrix}\sum_{k=0}^{n}2^{-k}\binom{n}{k}\Gamma\begin{bmatrix}\rho+\sigma+n+k+1\\ \rho+k+1\end{bmatrix}(z-1)^k$$, Re ρ, Re σ> -1, where

$$\binom{n}{k}=\frac{n(n-1)...(n-k+1)}{k!}$$, k=1,2,3,….

Pochhammer Symbol: The Pochhammer symbol is $(z)_n= z(z+1)\ \ldots\ (z+n-1)$, n- 1,2,3,… .

Psi-Function: The psi-function is defined as $\psi(z)=\frac{\Gamma'(z)}{\Gamma(z)}=\frac{d}{dz}\ln\Gamma(z)$. It is an analytical in the whole z plane function, except at the points z=0, -1, -2,…, at which it has simple poles.

Chapter 15
Momentum Investing Across Different Asset Classes

Zrinka Orlović
Faculty of Economics and Business, University of Zagreb, Croatia

Zrinka Lovretin Golubić
https://orcid.org/0000-0002-6446-8505
Faculty of Economics and Business, University of Zagreb, Croatia

Davor Zoričić
https://orcid.org/0000-0002-0206-3422
Faculty of Economics and Business, University of Zagreb, Croatia

ABSTRACT

Instead of traditionally looking at investing in different types of asset classes in order to exploit diversification effects, investors are turning to the underlying performance drivers built-in in many asset classes – factors. The intuition is that assets earn risk premiums because they are exposed to underlying risk factors. Factor models were developed as a simplification and continuation of diversification principle and mean-variance efficiency introduced by Harry Markowitz. This chapter will focus on one of the standard investment and cross section factors called momentum. It became very popular since 1993 when Jegadeesh and Titman documented that strategies that buying stocks that have performed well in the past and selling stocks that have performed poorly generate significant positive returns. This chapter aims to provide an introduction to factor models development and momentum effects on stock and bond markets – description of methodology and detailed literature overview.

KEY CONCEPTS OF MODERN PORTFOLIO THEORY

Publishing a paper "Portfolio selection" back in 1952, Harry Markowitz opened a new chapter in finance – modern portfolio theory. Based on risk-return optimization, he developed efficient frontier of investment portfolios such that each of them had the greatest possible expected rate of return given their

DOI: 10.4018/978-1-7998-5083-0.ch015

level of risk and such that each of them had the lowest level of risk given their expected return. Based on expected return – risk rule, investors will (or should) choose portfolios that are on the efficient frontier and which are in most cases diversified. Investor's utility is described with two measures: expected return and variance of the expected return, which is also a measure of the total risk of an investment. Markowitz emphasized that adequate diversification will be achieved if securities with high covariance between them will be avoided. He recommended investing in securities of different industries given the lower covariance compared to securities from the same industry (Markowitz, 1952, p. 89). Being aware of the problem of covariance estimation, in his first book from 1959 Markowitz suggested the development of a model for covariance estimation which opened the door for development of factor models (Markowitz, 1999, p. 8). The work of Markowitz was supplemented with Tobin's separation theorem and the inclusion of risk-free assets in portfolio analysis.

As mentioned previously, factor models were developed as an answer how to simplify the process of Markowitz's portfolio in a way that requirements for the number of inputs needed for the analysis and choice of the portfolio were decreased (Orsag, 2015, p. 325). Factor models were developed together by Markowitz and Sharpe, but Sharpe drew more attention to factor models in his doctoral thesis in 1963. He described how factor models can simplify portfolio analysis. With further work of Sharpe (1964), the most known single-factor model was formulated – the Capital Asset Pricing Model (hereinafter CAPM). Further development of the model was contributed by John Lintner (1965) and Jan Mossin (1966). The CAPM is a special formulation of the single-factor model which states that there is only one factor that matters, the market portfolio. This means that the model depends only on one factor which is considered as one of the shortcomings of the model. Also, it is based on many strong, more theoretically grounded assumptions. One of the assumptions states that investors have mean-variance utility. However, research on developed markets has shown that given the fact that investors are more concerned about losses than contended with gains, utility function often has an asymmetric treatment of risk. Kraus and Litzenberger (1976), Friend and Westerfield (1980) and Harvey and Siddique (2000) are some of the researchers who examined and showed that higher order moments (skewness and kurtosis) carry risk premiums. Ang et al. (2006) showed that stock with greater downside risk has higher returns. In his initial phase of research, Markowitz also favored semivariance of returns as more appropriate measure of risk since investors are more concerned about losses and poor performance of the portfolio (Markowitz et al., 1993, p. 307).

Another CAPM assumption states that investors have homogeneous expectations. Also, that all investors are focused on one holding period in which they are trying to maximize the utility of their wealth selecting portfolios based on expected returns and standard deviations. Then perfect liquidity and divisibility of investments, investors as price takers and the assumption that there are no taxes or transaction costs. With reference to the latter, Ang (2014) explained that taxes affect expected returns and can be regarded as a systematic factor. Mentioned assumptions are valid only in the perfect market, which in reality doesn't exist so CAPM was demolished by many researchers. However, basic intuition is still valid: the underlying factors of assets determine risk premiums and these risk premiums are compensation for investors' losses during bad times (Ang, 2014). Given such intuition and to prevail shortcomings of the CAPM, multifactor models were introduced according to which the returns on security are affected by several factors. The most famous multifactor model which includes the traditional CAPM market portfolio and the additional two factors which explain the stock returns is Fama–French model (1993). Two factors they simply called size (small minus big) and value (high minus low). Given the fact that investors attribute to small-capitalization companies better profitability results, the higher return was expected which could be also explained with the higher risk profile of such companies compared to companies with higher capitalization. Therefore, the higher return which is required for such smaller companies is called size premium (Orsag, 2015, p. 399). Similarly, the value factor is elaborated. Investors usually give better prospects to companies which are underestimated, compared to overestimated ones. Mentioned three factors are the most commonly used factors tested when the three-factor model is in question. However, it is important to mention that in their work Fama and French included two additional factors related to the bond market and those are maturity and default risk factors. Carhart (1997) expanded the Fama-French three-factor model factor for stocks by adding fourth-factor "winners minus losers" called momentum. Before Carhart (1997), Jegadeesh and Titman (1993) showed profitability of momentum strategy, but it was not explained through the Fama-French model until Carhart. Since then allocating assets based on factors became very popular among researchers and portfolio managers. Momentum became very popular since 1993 when Jegadeesh and Titman documented that strategies that buy stocks that have performed well in the past and sell stocks that have performed poorly generate significant positive returns.

Factor Investing As A New Type Of Investing

Ang (2014) considers CAPM as the first theory of factor risk which states that assets that crash when the market loses money are risky and because of that have to reward their holders with high risk premiums. Different types of assets have different exposures to market factors. Examples of market factors are interest rates, value-growth investing, low-volatility investing and momentum portfolios, latter being separately defined and explained in this chapter. Besides market factors, it is possible to identify macro factors, like inflation and economic growth. Ang (2014) stated that when thinking about making a profit, factors become relevant for investors, not assets. Investing in different types of assets requires a detailed analysis of the factor content of a particular asset. Further, he states that assets are bundles of factors. Some types of assets are considered as factors themselves, like equities, but there are also other types of assets that contain different types of factors – volatility risk, interest rate risk and default risk. The risk premium which is earned by holders of such investments is reflecting underlying risk factors of that investment. Additionally, in line with behavioral finance – different investors prefer different risk factors. This is derived from different investor behavior, since some investors are more and some are less risk averse (Ang, 2014, p. 195-196).

When creating an investing strategy, it would be wise to imitate the market since the market is the best allocator and no investment strategy would ensure superior results compared to the market. Imitation of the market comes down to passive strategy and investing in the market portfolio which consists of all assets and investments from the market. The weight of each investment in the market portfolio is determined based on the value of its market capitalization in total market capitalization (Orsag, 2015, p. 296). In other words, the market portfolio contains all tangible and non-tangible assets (like human capital) so the construction of it becomes impossible. Due to that, in practice, the market portfolio is related to the investment portfolio of securities, most commonly to a stock portfolio on the market. However, the measure of such a portfolio doesn't exist as well since the stock market is usually approximated with some market index. Such an index consists of several chosen stocks which are the most active and liquid on the market and it is assumed to represent the movement and changes in the whole capital asset market. Also, it is assumed to represent an efficient portfolio of risky assets traded in the market. For the approximation of market portfolio stock indices which are based on market capitalization (cap-weighted indices) are usually used. One of the reasons why cap-weighted indices are used is that such indices are easy to construct and easily traded. Additionally, such an index was used in CAPM. As elaborated before, since CAPM is based on many presumptions that are not valid in the real world, there is a good theoretical background to believe that stock indices based on market capitalization are not efficient investments. Research on the developed markets (Haugen and Baker, 1991; Grinold, 1992) has shown that cap-weighted indices are not mean-variance efficient i.e. they are below the efficient frontier of their constituents. If they were positioned on the efficient frontier of their constituents, the investor would be properly rewarded for exposure to systematic risk and there would be no exposure to unrewarded risk factors. Since research showed the opposite, for such indices diversification effect is not exploited to the maximum extent possible, therefore investors are exposed to unrewarded risk factors. Research of Amenc et al. (2006) on the developed market showed that even naïve method of construction of portfolio in a way that each constituent has the same weight (equally-weighted portfolio) results with superior outcome in comparison with cap-weighted indices. Considering all the above mentioned, in the last few years new approaches have been developed to offer more efficient indices (or portfolios) to investors as opposed to cap-weighted ones. Such strategies are called "Smart beta" strategies and based on definition, they blur the difference between active and passive investment management. "Smart beta" strategies are not uniquely defined but the intuition of using such strategies is the same. It may be possible to achieve higher returns than the market using different relatively passive investment strategies (low turnover) that involve no more risk than would be assumed by investing in a low-cost total stock market index fund which has a beta of one (Malkiel, 2014, p. 127). "Smart beta" strategies define different techniques of creating portfolios as alternatives to cap-weighted indices. Some of them are global minimum variance portfolio, maximum decorrelation, maximum diversification, diversified minimum variance, risk parity and factor risk parity (Amenc et al., 2013). In such a strategy, the investor doesn't have to be a stock picker to be able to beat the market, as most active managers are, and the fees are well below those charged by the active managers. The key is to tilt the portfolio in a certain direction, toward various characteristics that have historically generated returns larger than market returns (Malkiel, 2014, p. 127). Tilts could be an investment in smaller versus larger companies, value versus growth, winners versus losers and low- volatility stocks versus high-volatility stocks. Such tilts essentially are risk factors. In case some "Smart beta" strategy generated higher than the market return, excess return should be interpreted as a reward for assuming extra risk and investors should be aware of that (Malkiel, 2014, p. 133).

Research has shown that tilting a portfolio towards stocks that were "winners" in the previous period carries a higher premium for investors. In comparison to other strategies, it has been documented that momentum factor often has low correlations with other factors (such as value and size) which enables the increase of diversification potential. In addition, the momentum factor tends to have a relatively high risk premium. There are two possible explanations why momentum exists: the first is based on behavioral considerations and the second on slow response to new information (Malkiel, 2014, p. 129). For the first reason for the appearance of momentum Shiller (2000) claims that a psychological feedback mechanism exists among investors transmitting a certain degree of momentum into stock prices, especially during periods of enthusiasm. Stock prices are rising and individuals are somehow intuitively drawn into the market. The second reason for the momentum presence has an explanation in the existence of lag in the reaction of investors to news and lack of adjustment in their expectations. Investors do not adjust their expectations immediately when news arises, especially news of company earnings that exceeded the anticipation. Some research has shown that abnormally high returns follow positive earnings surprises as market prices appear to respond to earnings information only gradually (Rendleman et al., 1982, p. 269). Studies of Hong and Stein (1999) and Kahneman and Riepe (1998) have documented return reversals over longer holding periods. They argue that investors are reacting to waves of optimism and pessimism that cause prices to deviate systematically from their fundamental values. Justification of such behavior has the roots in behavioral finance – an overreaction to past events is consistent with behavioral factors, where investors are systematically overconfident of their ability to forecast either future stock prices or future corporate earnings. Also, it is worth mentioning a few more authors who have different arguments for momentum profits to exist. Liu and Zhang (2008) suggested that risk is an important driver of momentum and in addition, they stated that many previous studies have failed to document direct evidence of risk on momentum portfolios. Liu and Zhang (2011) argued that irrationality is not necessary to explain momentum profits. Their results suggested that momentum is consistent with the value maximization of firms.

Momentum has been studied in many academic papers focusing primarily on stock markets. In recent times momentum was also observed in bond and other markets. Most of the research related to the examination of momentum existence, no matter on which market, according to Jegadeesh and Titman (1993) used the same methodology, but with some adjustments. The remaining part of this chapter is related to the description of the methodology used when identifying momentum or reversal effect with the following detailed literature overview to enhance the theoretical background of momentum investing.

METHODOLOGY DESCRIPTION

This section describes the most frequent and the current widely-used methodology which tests the existence of momentum effect. It is introduced by Jegadeesh and Titman in 1993 and used for stocks on the U.S. market.

The methodology is used to test profitability for a large number of trading strategies. These strategies were formed based on stock's past performance over the previous three to 12 months (formation period). The holding period considered in the study also changes from three to 12 months. More precisely, the formation period and holding period were three, six, nine and 12 months. A total number of strategies with no gap between formation and holding period was 16. Those were primarily examined strategies which included portfolios with the overlapping holding period. Besides these strategies, they tested an additional 16 strategies that skip a week between formation and holding period. The aim of this step is to avoid or at least reduce the potential impact of price pressure, bid-ask spread and lagged reaction effects. Each stock was classified according to its past performance by cumulative returns over the formation period (three to 12 months):

$$\textit{Cumulative Return} = \sum_{t=1}^{J} R_{it} \tag{1}$$

where R_{it} is the return for stock i in month t and J represent the months in formation period.

For each month entire series of stocks are grouped into decile portfolios in ascending order based on cumulative returns. Each decile portfolio was an equally weighted portfolio. Stocks that performed poorly are placed in the bottom decile portfolio and are assigned as loser portfolio. Those are stocks that achieved the lowest past returns and placed them into portfolio 1. The group with the second lowest returns are selected into portfolio 2 and so on. The most attractive stocks, which performed well in the past, are placed in the top decile portfolio designated as the winner portfolio. On the other hand, those stocks achieved the highest returns and are placed into portfolio 10. This position is held for the next three, six, nine and 12 months. In each month the long position is taken on the winner portfolio and short position on loser portfolio. In other words, the momentum strategy buys the winner and sells the loser portfolio. Strategies are replicated for each subsequent period, where the new winner and new loser portfolio were constructed. For each holding period, the average return is calculated for the winner and loser portfolio. Lastly, to determine momentum profitability it is needed to deduct the average loser portfolio return from average winner portfolio return:

$$\overline{R}_{winner-loser} = \overline{R}_{winner} - \overline{R}_{loser} \tag{2}$$

A momentum strategy is profitable if past winners outperform past losers, in other words, the difference between average winner portfolio return and average loser portfolio return should be positive:

$$\overline{R}_{winner} - \overline{R}_{loser} > 0 \tag{3}$$

The following hypotheses are tested with a significance of 5%:

$$H_0 : \overline{R}_{winner-loser} = 0 \quad H_1 : \overline{R}_{winner-loser} \neq 0 \tag{4}$$

If there is evidence for the momentum effect, the winner-loser portfolio should generate significant abnormal returns. To determine the significance of before mentioned hypotheses following test is used:

$$t = \frac{\mu_{winner} - \mu_{loser}}{\sqrt{\frac{\sigma^2_{winner}}{N_{winner}} + \frac{\sigma^2_{loser}}{N_{loser}}}} \tag{5}$$

LITERATURE REVIEW FOR MOMENTUM IN STOCK MARKET

Since 1993 when Fama and French introduced factors that explain stock and bond returns, academics continued investigating the area of factors even more. Factor investing became much more popular and in the last 20 years, researches revealed new factors that can reward investors for taking risks. A factor that is in the focus in this chapter is momentum.

The same year Jegadeesh and Titman found evidence of momentum profitability among stocks. Since then factor momentum burst onto the academic scene and has been studied in many academic papers. There are a couple of common attributes in most of the empirical research. Firstly, the majority of work is focused on most developed countries. There are fewer papers concerning emerging and less developed countries. Secondly, momentum is mostly observed in stock markets. Some researches expanded their work to other markets such as bond markets, currencies, real estate, and commodities but the number of these studies is much smaller than studies concerning stock markets. And thirdly, papers focusing on momentum no matter on which market usually used methodology presented in work by Jegadeesh and Titman. The methodology presented by Jegadeesh and Titman (1993) was primarily created to be used on stocks, but when using in other markets methodology was adjusted to specifics of a certain market. The rest of this section focuses on recent findings about factor momentum in the stock market. The following sections include bond and other markets.

First published research about momentum investing is offered by Cowles and Jones in 1937. They collected stock data over the period from 1920 to 1935. In the article, they stated: "taking one year as the unit of measurement for the period from 1920 to 1935, the tendency is very pronounced for stocks which have exceeded the median in one year to exceed it also in the year following". It can be seen, that is exactly what we call today momentum. Another early research concerning momentum in stocks was published by Robert A. Levy in 1967. His sample included weekly closing prices of 200 stocks listed on the New York Stock Exchange from October 1960 to October 1965. He considered 26 weeks in the past and ranked stocks based on their past performance. According to results from his analysis, it was concluded that investors should buy stock with a significantly higher current price than the average price of the last 27 weeks to achieve abnormal returns in the future. In the finance literature, this was accepted as Levy's trading rule. His article was under some methodology criticism, but there was little attention given to his work in academic literature. After Jegadeesh and Titman's publication in 1993 momentum in stocks became important topic among researches. Since then there is a wide range of academic papers about the profitability of momentum strategies among stocks but also with extension to a different class of assets.

The most important article for stock momentum in the United States, as mentioned a couple of times before is work by Jegadeesh and Titman (1993). Taking the horizon of three to 12 months from 1965 to 1989, trading strategies that buy past winners and sell past losers on average earn about one percent per month. A strategy that selected stocks based on their past 12 month performance and held the portfolio for three months is shown to be the most profitable. Chan et al. (1996) examined the period from January 1977 to January 1993 and found similar results like Jegadeesh and Titman (1993). A trading strategy that selects stocks based on their past six month returns and holds them for six months earned on average 15.4% per year while the same strategy constructed by Jegadeesh and Titman earned on average 12.01% per year. Rouwerhoust (1998) covered the period from 1978 to 1995 for 12 developed European countries (Austria, Belgium, Denmark, France, Germany, Italy, The Netherlands, Norway, Spain, Sweden, Switzerland, and the United Kingdom). He used monthly data for stock returns to test the profitability of momentum strategies. Momentum portfolio construction was the same as used by Jegadeesh and Titman (1993). From the results, it can be seen that the momentum effect is present in all 12 countries. This conclusion is in line with Jegadeesh and Titman (1993) and Chan et al. (1996). Additionally, he showed that international European and U.S. momentum strategies are affected by similar factors that drive the profitability of momentum strategies. Lui et al. (1999) used monthly returns for UK stocks and showed the presence of momentum effects during the period from January 1976 to December 1996. Like Jegadeesh and Titman (1993) the most profitable is strategy based on 12 month formation period and three month holding period. Contrary to Jegadeesh and Titman (1993) they did not examine portfolios with overlapping holding periods. For the same developed market Hon and Tonks (2003) confirmed Lui et al. (1999) conclusion. The estimation period was longer and included monthly returns from January 1955 to December 1996. The formation and holding periods were also extended. Buying better performing stocks and selling worst performing stocks in the previous three to 24 months generates significant profits for holding a position from three to 24 months. Same year August et al. (2000) found momentum for German stocks from 1974 to 1997. Their findings for the German market were confirmed by Schiereck et al. (1999). Glaser and Weber (2003) proved the existence of a momentum effect on the German stock market. Based on past performance over the three to 12 months stocks were divided into 5 equally-weighted monthly-rebalanced portfolios. Momentum was discovered by Mengoli (2004) on the Italian stock market from January 1950 to June 1995 using monthly total returns for stocks listed on the Milan Stock Exchange. Stocks are ranked in ascending order based on the previous three to 12 months. These stocks were ranked into quintiles and holding period varied from three to 36 months which was different from Jegadeesh and Titman (1993). A return from the winner minus loser portfolio for each holding period was significant and positive. Hammami (2013) tested momentum profitability among two sub periods: 1927–1963 and 1964–2009. The sample included monthly returns for the New York Stock Exchange (NYSE), American Stock Exchange (AMEX) and National Association of Securities Dealers Automated Quotation (NASDAQ) stocks. The focus of the paper is to determine the behavior of momentum during good and bad times. To distinguish bad and good economic conditions the expected market risk premium is estimated using the regression analysis. Overall results indicated that momentum is only significant during good economic conditions. Bird et al. (2017) used daily and monthly returns for 24 developed stock markets from 1990 to 2012. The emphasis was on testing both time-series and cross sectional-momentum strategies. They examined the same length of formation and holding period of three, six, nine and 12 months. The main conclusion stated that both momentum strategies are profitable across the majority of 24 developed markets. Following the methodology by Jegadeesh and Titman (1993), Bergsten (2019) tested momentum profitability for the Swedish stock market for the period from 1999 to 2018. All winner looser tested portfolios were positive and statistically significant with only two exceptions (formation 12/holding nine and formation 12/holding 12 months). When observing newer data this conclusion for the Swedish stock market is in line with Gong et al. (2015).

Rouwerhoust (1999) collected data for 20 emerging markets (Argentina, Brazil, Chile, Colombia, Greece, Indonesia, India, Jordan, Korea, Malaysia, Mexico, Nigeria, Pakistan, Philippines, Portugal, Taiwan, Thailand, Turkey, Venezuela, Zimbabwe) and found positive and significant momentum effect in 17 of 20 countries. Equally weighted momentum portfolio constructed of all twenty countries was also profitable with an average excess return of 0.39% per month. When comparing with an internationally diversified portfolio for developed markets, the magnitude of momentum profits in an internationally diversified portfolio for emerging markets is less intense. Van der Hart et al. (2003) made the same comparison and affirm his conclusion. They took in observation 32 worldwide emerging markets from January 1982 to May 1999. Stocks were ranked based on one to 36 previous monthly returns and 15% of the best performing was taken into the winner portfolio. This procedure was made for each country. In line with Rouwerhoust (1999), there are countries in which momentum strategies generate positive and significant returns. The authors also made an internationally diversified portfolio and concluded that momentum returns in emerging markets are smaller than returns in developed markets. Van der Hart et al. (2005) included 31 emerging countries from Latin America, Europe, Africa, and the Middle East from 1988 to 2004. First, equally weighted winner and loser portfolios were formed for each country and then combined into an internationally diversified portfolio. These portfolios were held for the next six months. They showed that the average return for an international momentum portfolio is 0.74% per month, meaning that momentum effects exist in these emerging markets. Muga and Santamaria (2007) investigated momentum strategies for Latin American emerging markets (Argentina, Brazil, Chile, and Mexico). Countries are tested separately and together for the whole region. Because of a limited number of securities in emerging markets, they divided stocks into quintiles instead of deciles used by Jegadeesh and Titman (1993). In some parts of the observed period, these countries were affected by financial and other economic crises so authors took a period from 1996 to 2001 to analyze momentum strategies. The results showed that momentum exists in every emerging market and in the observed Latin America region. On the average region, momentum portfolio return is 1.17% per month which is the same and even higher momentum profit in emerging than in developed markets. Comparing to previous literature, like Rouwerhoust (1999), Van der Hart et al. (2005) and Griffin et al. (2003) this conclusion is very different from theirs. Groot et al. (2010) made research from January 1997 to November 2008 to determine if there is a momentum effect in 24 frontier emerging markets from Africa, Asia, Europe, and South America. The methodology used in research is similar to Jegadeesh and Titman (1993). Based on past one to 36 month returns stocks were sorted in ascending order and divided into quintiles for each country. Portfolios were constructed for each country separately and then combined into an internationally diversified portfolio. They found momentum effect at the country level in frontier emerging countries which is in line with Rouwerhoust (1999) and Chan et al. (2000) and also the existence of momentum effect in an internationally diversified portfolio. Cakici et al. (2013) using data for 18 emerging markets examined value and momentum effects on their stock markets. They grouped emerging markets as follows: Asia, Latin America, and Eastern Europe emerging markets. Asia included China, India, Indonesia, South Korea, Malaysia, Philippines, Taiwan and Thailand, Latin America refers to Argentina, Brazil, Chile, Colombia, and Mexico while Eastern Europe includes Czech Republic, Hungary, Russia, Poland, and Turkey. First, every region was tested separately and then they considered all 18 countries together. They used monthly stock data from January 1990 to December 2011. Momentum was measured as the difference between winner and loser portfolio also used by Jegadeesh and Titman (1993). Momentum was found for Asia and Latin America region and also for all 18 emerging markets together, but there is no momentum effect in the Eastern Europe region when studied small and big stocks together. Zaremba and Konieczka (2015) observed 11 Central and Eastern European emerging stock markets to see are there value, size and momentum premiums. Stocks listed on Bulgaria, Croatia, Czech Republic, Estonia, Hungary, Latvia, Lithuania, Poland, Romania, Slovakia, and Slovenia stock markets from December 2000 to December 2013 were taken into observation. Just like Cakici et al. (2013), Zaremba and Konieczka (2015) revealed no evidence of momentum effect across the Central and Eastern European region. During the period from 1990 to 2013 Cakici et al. (2016) examined the momentum profitability individually among 18 emerging stock markets: China, India, Indonesia, South Korea, Malaysia, Philippines, Taiwan, and Thailand in Asia, Argentina, Brazil, Chile, Colombia, and Mexico in Latin America and the Czech Republic, Hungary, Russia, Poland, and Turkey in Eastern Europe. Data used for analysis were on a monthly basis. Generally looking, the momentum effect is weak and only positive and statistically significant in Chile and India. In opposition to Cakici et al. (2016) for a newer period, Vuong and Vu (2018) found momentum in Brazil, Chile, and Mexico from 2006 to 2015. They formed momentum portfolios based on cumulative stock returns from t-12 to t-2. Peru was included as a fourth emerging market but positive and significant momentum premiums were not found.

To sum up, when using the single country approach, the momentum effect in emerging markets is mostly positive but not always statistically significant. Also, it can be seen that diversified international portfolios produce positive and significant returns but the magnitude of momentum profit is less intense than in developed economies. Due to the inability of establishing statistically significant momentum returns in some emerging markets, some researchers tested the reversal effect in emerging stock markets. The reversal phenomenon is inverse from momentum, meaning that past losers outperform past winners.

One group of papers observed emerging and developed markets in the same article to be able to compare these markets for the same period. An example of this kind of article is paper by Ejaz and Polak (2014) in which they tested the momentum effect in stock markets of the Middle East. The sample included monthly stock returns from January 2009 to December 2013 for the United Arab Emirates, Egypt, Marocco, Oman, Jordan, and Saudi Arabia. They tested strategy based on six month formation period and six month holding period. The results showed the presence of momentum in all countries included in the sample. The same year, Hanauer and Linhart (2015) collected stock returns data and accounting data from July 1996 to June 2012 for 21 emerging and 24 developed countries. The sample was divided into four emerging regions: Latin America region (Brazil, Chile, Colombia, Mexico, and Peru), Europe, Middle East and Africa region (Czech Republic, Hungary, Russia, Poland, Turkey, Egypt, Morocco, and South Africa), Asia region (China, India, Indonesia, South Korea, Malaysia, Philippines, Taiwan, and Thailand) and Brasil, Russia, India, and China region. They constructed a global sample that includes 21 emerging and 24 developed countries and an emerging market sample which contains stocks from four previously mentioned regions. The main conclusion states that in all regions there is a momentum positive premium. In contrast with Cakici et al. (2013), they find a positive and statistically significant momentum effect in Emerging Eastern Europe. Chui et al. (2000) observed eight different emerging and developed economies to see if there is any evidence for momentum positive returns. Momentum was tested for portfolio based on past six month returns and for six month holding period. In contrary to Jegadeesh and Titman (1993) they value weighted winner and loser portfolios. From the results, it can be seen that there is only a positive and statistically significant momentum effect in Hong Kong, while in Taiwan, Singapore, Malaysia, Japan, and Thailand obtained results for momentum effects are insignificant. In Korea and Indonesia, momentum strategies do not generate any profits. Hong et al. (2003) investigated the profitability of momentum strategies among international developed and emerging countries (Australia, Canada, France, Germany, Hong Kong, United Kingdom, Malaysia, South Korea, Japan, Singapore, Taiwan). The estimation period started in January 1987 and ended in December 2001. The methodology applied by Jegadeesh and Titman (1993) showed significant profits of momentum strategies in Australia, Canada, France, Germany, Hong Kong, and the United Kingdom while there is no momentum effects in Malaysia, South Korea, Japan, Singapore, and Taiwan. Findings are similar to Hameed and Kusnadi (2002) who also find no momentum profits in the following emerging economies: Hong Kong, Malaysia, Singapore, South Korea, Taiwan, and Thailand. As stated before, Chui et al. (2000) only found momentum profits for Hong Kong. Griffin et al. (2003) also included in a sample a large range of emerging and developed countries (40 countries) to test momentum profitability for each country and regions. Statistically, significant momentum profit is only found in a few emerging markets. Overall, it is shown that momentum in Asia is weaker if compering with other continents, especially Europe. Momentum portfolio for Europe generated 0.77% per month which is similar to Rouwenhorst (1998) whose momentum portfolio earned 0.93% per month. A momentum profit in emerging markets is weaker than in a developed market which is in line with previous literature.

Literature Review For Momentum In Bond Market

Previous work for momentum on bond markets is scarce. There are a couple of common attributes concerning the literature review for the bond market. Mostly, momentum is tested for corporate bonds and there is much less work concerning momentum in government bonds. Also, the majority of existing work focuses on the American bond market. There is one group of papers that examined only factor momentum and these papers are going to be summarized below.

Khang and King (2004) collected monthly data for the prices of investment-grade bonds covering the period from 1978 to 1998. While examining the profitability of bond momentum portfolios based on past bonds returns they did not found momentum, instead there was significant evidence of return reversal for investment-grade corporate bonds. Momentum portfolios were formed with the formation and holding period from one to six months. They concluded that there is a strong effect of return reversal in short to the intermediate horizon. Also, this kind of behavior is mostly noticed in the first half of the period from 1978 to 1987. Gebhardt et al. (2005) covered the period from January 1973 to December 1996 containing data for corporate bond prices and equities prices. They establish that a reversal effect exists from three to 12 months horizons and that there is no evidence of momentum among investment-grade corporate bonds. Also analyzing equities they found evidence of momentum spillover from equities to investment corporate bonds of the same firm. This means that stock returns predict bond returns but not vice versa. Furthermore, stock returns and stock prices adjust more quickly than bond returns and bond prices to common firm information. Pospisil and Zhang (2010) analyzed momentum and reversal effects in the corporate bond market for a large sample of high-yield and investment-grade bonds. Merrill Lynch U.S. High Yield Index and Merrill Lynch U.S. Broad Corporate Index contain bonds used in their article. Using Bloomberg they collected monthly data from December 1996 to August 2009 for bond price and credit spread. They utilized a similar method used by Jegadeesh and Titman (1993) but with some adjustments because they analyzed the bond market. The observed period was divided into two parts which included two credit cycles. A first credit cycle covered the recession of the early 2000s and second was associated with the financial crisis in 2007. The results showed that there is a momentum effect in high-yield bonds and a reversal effect in investment-grade bonds. Similar results for investment-grade bonds are found in Khang and King (2004) and Gebhardt et al. (2005). Jostova et al. (2013) observed momentum effects using a sample of around 81 thousand U.S. corporate bonds from January 1973 to June 2011. This paper contributes to the existing literature in many ways. They included the largest cross-section and longest time-series of U.S. corporate bonds used as a sample for empirical analysis. They found evidence of momentum among noninvestment grade corporate bonds but there is no momentum effect in investment-grade corporate bonds. The results of the empirical study of Jostova et al. (2013) also showed that there is higher momentum profitability among noninvestment grade bonds of private than public firms. Similar to Gebhardt et al. (2005) they found momentum spillover from equities to investment grade and noninvestment grade corporate bonds. Using daily prices for U.S. Treasury coupon bonds from 1973 to 2018 Maeso et al. (2019) proved the profitability of momentum strategies among these securities for holding period from nine to 12 months.

Another group of papers is observing the profitability of several factors where one of them is factor momentum. Since other factors are not in focus in this chapter, by the end of this section most significant conclusions concerning factor momentum are going to be presented.

Paper by Asness et al. (2013) is very popular when talking about momentum. They examined momentum in different asset classes: government bonds, currencies, stocks, and commodities. When observing bond markets they obtained government bond data for the period from January 1982 to July 2011 for 10 countries: Australia, Canada, Denmark, Germany, Japan, Norway, Sweden, Switzerland, the United Kingdom, and the United States. Based on bonds past performance the sample was divided into three equal groups and labeled as winner and loser portfolio. They concluded that momentum portfolios generate positive returns. Houweling and Zundert (2017) using data for corporate bonds from January

1994 to June 2015 examined the performance of a couple of factors, but in this chapter focus is factor momentum. Following Jostova et al. (2013) they defined momentum as the past six month return using one month implementation lag. Overall, they showed that momentum in the corporate bond market generates economically meaningful and statistically significant alphas. When observing investment-grade corporate bonds there is no momentum effect which is consistent with Jostova et al. (2013). Also, they concluded that a momentum factor portfolio constructed using equity definition and then applied to corporate bonds work very well. Israel et al. (2018) studied the performance of four risk factors using Fama-MacBeth regression. They used monthly data for U.S. corporate bonds over the period from January 1997 to April 2015. To make a comparable sample of bonds they selected representative bonds for each issuer for every month by their seniority, maturity, age, and size. For factor momentum, they used two momentum measures. Those are credit momentum and equity momentum. Credit momentum is defined as six month bond excess return while equity momentum as six month equity return of the bond issuer. Results showed that momentum can predict corporate bond excess return which means that past winners outperform past losers. They also showed that momentum has a greater impact among less liquid bonds issued by less transparent firms.

Literature Review For Momentum In Other Asset Classes

As seen before, momentum is a very popular return generating factor across stocks and bonds. Except being tested for stocks and bonds some academic researchers wanted to determine the benefits of momentum investing in other asset classes such as currencies, commodities, industries and real estate. Concerning foreign exchange markets, momentum strategy is a relatively new topic and there is little documented literature that examined the existence of momentum profitability. The same situation is concerning commodities, industries, sectors and real estate. In the following section is presented just a brief overview of before mentioned asset classes.

White and Okunev (2001) tested momentum strategies from January 1975 to June 2000 for eight currencies used in Australia, Canada, France, Germany, Japan, Switzerland, the United Kingdom, and the United States. Using Jegadeesh and Titman methodology for each month and for each country they ranked currencies in ascending order from one to seven based on the difference between the short-run and long-run moving average of prior currencies returns. They established the existence of momentum effect in currencies which implies the effectiveness of the Jegadeesh and Titman technique in other markets. Momentum in currencies is also found in an article by Menkhoff et al. (2012). The sample consisted of 48 countries and covered the period from January 1976 to January 2010. For the mentioned period they collected data for spot exchange rates and one month forward exchange rates for 48 currencies. Portfolios were formed based on past returns achieved in the previous one to 12 months and were held in a period between one to 12 months. Ahmed et al. (2018) increased the sample of observed currencies considering previous researches. The sample included 66 currency exchange rates from December 1984 to December 2015. Based on currencies' past performance they were divided into five portfolios each month. Throughout holding period winner minus loser portfolios generate significant and positive returns. Covering a period from January 1979 to July 2011 Asness et al. (2013) examined momentum in ten currencies. For the same period, except currencies, they tested momentum in stocks, government bonds and commodities. As mentioned before, when constructing a momentum portfolio the sample was sorted into three equal groups. For 27 different commodity futures and for ten currencies they formed winner and loser portfolios and proved the existence of momentum. The intensity of momentum profitability is greater for commodities when comparing to currencies. Erb and Harvey (2006) pointed out that the momentum strategy with a formation period of 12 months and a holding period of one month is profitable in commodities. Taking into sample 31 U.S. commodity futures Miffre and Rallis (2007) tested momentum strategies for the period from January 1979 to September 2004. They analyzed momentum strategy for formation period of one, three, six and 12 months where holding period included the same months. When a combination of all months is made the total number of momentum strategies is 16. The difference between winner and loser portfolios returns for 13 strategies is positive and statistically significant. For only 6-12, 12-6 and 12-12 momentum strategies momentum effect is not found. Momentum in commodities is also found by Gorton et al. (2013) who used 31 commodity futures for a period between 1969 and 2006. To have a better view of momentum across industries it is proposed to read the article by Moskowitz and Grinblatt (1999) and Asness et al. (2000) which found positive returns when deducting loser from winner portfolios. Momentum in private real estate is examined by Marcato and Key (2005) and found for a period from six to 12 months.

CONCLUSION

Ever since 1952 when Harry Markowitz introduced Modern portfolio theory, investors are combining securities into investment portfolio in order to exploit diversification opportunities. Reducing market risk while achieving optimal return, in the long run, is in the utmost interest of each investor. Instead of traditionally looking at investing in different asset classes to harvest diversification benefits, nowadays investors are turning to the underlying performance drivers built-in in many asset classes – factors. Factor models were developed as a continuation and simplification of Markowitz's portfolio optimization. In essence, factor models are explaining returns of securities with one or more factors that have the most significant impact on the securities' returns. To harvest the benefits when creating a strategy investor should follow the market trend. However, the market includes all assets, tangible and intangible so its construction becomes impossible. Therefore, in practice, the market portfolio is approximated with investment in the index which will present the market movements and changes – capitalization-weighted stock index. Research has shown that such indices are not efficient, meaning that the diversification effect is not exploited to the maximum extent possible. Therefore, investors are exposed to unrewarded risk factors.

In the last few years, a new approach of investing has been developed with characteristics between active and passive investment management. "Smart beta" strategies include the wide specter of creating a portfolio as an alternative to cap-weighted indices. The key is to tilt the portfolio in a certain direction, toward various characteristics that have historically generated returns larger than market returns. Tilts could be an investment in smaller versus larger companies, value versus growth, winners versus losers and low-volatility stocks versus high-volatility stocks. Such tilts essentially are risk factors.

Research has shown that tilting a portfolio towards stocks that were "winners" in the previous period carries a higher premium for investors. In comparison to other strategies, it has been documented that momentum factor often has low correlations with other factors (such as value and size) which enables the increase of diversification potential. In addition, the momentum factor tends to have a relatively high risk premium. Momentum became very popular since 1993 when Jegadeesh and Titman documented that strategies that buy stocks that have performed well in the past and sell stocks that have performed poorly generate significant positive returns.

The popularity of momentum as return generating factor continued for the next 30 years and even today is often used as an investing factor. Except being identified for stock markets evidence of momentum profitability was found in other asset classes like bonds, currencies, commodities, industries and real estates. Overall when looking at research that refers to momentum strategy it can be seen that there are some similarities within these papers. Firstly, momentum strategies are mostly tested for stock markets and separately tested for emerging and developed markets. Results prove the existence of momentum effect in developed and emerging markets, but the magnitude of generated return for emerging is smaller than in developed markets. Given the fact that in most researches for emerging markets statistically significant momentum returns was not present, some researcher turned to reversal effect testing. Secondly, the majority of work is tested for developed countries while there are fewer papers that tested a momentum effect in emerging markets. And thirdly, the methodology used is the one established by Jegadeesh and Titman. A methodology was primarily created to be used for stocks, but when using in other asset classes methodology was adjusted to specifics of a certain market. Also, the adjustments are made when tested for stocks depending on the economic development and liquidity of the specific market.

Based on literature about momentum in bond markets it can be concluded that vast of research is made for corporate bonds and just a few papers are referring to government bonds. Momentum is found in some corporate bond but the reversal effect prevails. Momentum investing is a new topic for currencies, commodities, sectors and real estates but the existing literature showed benefits of momentum in these asset classes. Momentum turned to be a very profitable factor of systematic risk so it is not odd why it is often used by portfolio managers.

This chapter provided an extensive literature review about momentum investing. But, there is considerable scope for research on this issue, such as investigating the momentum profitability across different major events that affect the global economy. For example, the financial economic crisis that began in 2007. In line with this, it is possible to observe the impact of major events concerning economies individually.

REFERENCES

Ahmed, H., Naka, A., Wuthisatian, P., & Lakefront, N. O. L. (n.d.). *Behavior of Momentum in the Foreign Exchange Market: Evidence from Portfolio Approach*. Academic Press.

Amenc, N., Goltz, F., & Le Sourd, V. (2006). *Assessing the Quality of Stock Market Indices: Requirements for Asset Allocation and Performance Measurement*. Nice: An EDHEC Risk & Asset Management Research Centre Publication.

Amenc, N., Goltz, F., & Martellini, L. (2013). *Smart Beta 2.0*. EDHEC-Risk Institute. doi:10.3905/jii.2013.4.3.015

Ang, A. (2014). *Asset Management: A Systematic Approach to Factor Investing*. Oxford University Press. doi:10.1093/acprof:oso/9780199959327.001.0001

Ang, A., Chen, J., & Xing, Y. (2006). Downside risk. *Review of Financial Studies*, *19*(4), 1191–1239. doi:10.1093/rfs/hhj035

Asness, C. S., Moskowitz, T. J., & Pedersen, L. H. (2013). Value and momentum everywhere. *The Journal of Finance*, *68*(3), 929–985. doi:10.1111/jofi.12021

August, R., Schiereck, D., & Weber, M. (2000). Momentumstrategien am deutschen Aktienmarkt: neue empirische Evidenz zur Erklärung des Erfolgs (No. 35294). Darmstadt Technical University, Department of Business Administration, Economics and Law, Institute for Business Studies (BWL).

Bergsten, S. (2019). *Momentum strategies on the Swedish market*. Academic Press.

Bird, R., Gao, X., & Yeung, D. (2017). Time-series and cross-sectional momentum strategies under alternative implementation strategies. *Australian Journal of Management*, *42*(2), 230–251. doi:10.1177/0312896215619965

Cakici, N., Fabozzi, F. J., & Tan, S. (2013). Size, value, and momentum in emerging market stock returns. *Emerging Markets Review*, *16*, 46–65. doi:10.1016/j.ememar.2013.03.001

Cakici, N., Tang, Y., & Yan, A. (2016). Do the size, value, and momentum factors drive stock returns in emerging markets? *Journal of International Money and Finance*, *69*, 179–204. doi:10.1016/j.jimonfin.2016.06.001

Carhart, M. M. (1997). On persistence in mutual fund performance. *The Journal of Finance*, *52*(1), 57–82. doi:10.1111/j.1540-6261.1997.tb03808.x

Chan, K., Hameed, A., & Tong, W. (2000). Profitability of momentum strategies in the international equity markets. *Journal of Financial and Quantitative Analysis*, *35*(2), 153–172. doi:10.2307/2676188

Chan, L. K., Jegadeesh, N., & Lakonishok, J. (1996). Momentum strategies. *The Journal of Finance*, *51*(5), 1681–1713. doi:10.1111/j.1540-6261.1996.tb05222.x

Chui, A. C., Wei, K. C., & Titman, S. (2000). Momentum, legal systems and ownership structure: An analysis of Asian stock markets. *Sheridan, Momentum, Legal Systems and Ownership Structure: An Analysis of Asian Stock Markets*.

Cowles, A. III, & Jones, H. E. (1937). Some a posteriori probabilities in stock market action. *Econometrica*, *5*(3), 280–294. doi:10.2307/1905515

De Groot, W., Pang, J., & Swinkels, L. (2010). *Value and Momentum in frontier emerging markets.* Working Paper. Available at http://ssrn. com/abstract=1600023

Ejaz, A., & Polak, P. (2014). Short term momentum effect: a case of Middle East stock markets. *Ejaz, A*, 104-112.

Erb, C. B., & Harvey, C. R. (2006). The strategic and tactical value of commodity futures. *Financial Analysts Journal*, *62*(2), 69–97. doi:10.2469/faj.v62.n2.4084

Fama, E. F., & French, K. R. (1993). Common risk factors in the returns on stocks and bonds. *Journal of Financial Economics*, *33*(1), 3–56. doi:10.1016/0304-405X(93)90023-5

Friend, I., & Westerfield, R. (1980). Co-skewness and capital asset pricing. *The Journal of Finance*, *35*(4), 897–913. doi:10.1111/j.1540-6261.1980.tb03508.x

Gebhardt, W. R., Hvidkjaer, S., & Swaminathan, B. (2005). Stock and bond market interaction: Does momentum spill over? *Journal of Financial Economics*, *75*(3), 651–690. doi:10.1016/j.jfineco.2004.03.005

Glaser, M., & Weber, M. (2003). Momentum and turnover: Evidence from the German stock market. *Schmalenbach Business Review, 55*(2), 108–135. doi:10.1007/BF03396669

Gong, Q., Liu, M., & Liu, Q. (2015). Momentum is really short-term momentum. *Journal of Banking & Finance, 50*, 169–182. doi:10.1016/j.jbankfin.2014.10.002

Gorton, G. B., Hayashi, F., & Rouwenhorst, K. G. (2013). The fundamentals of commodity futures returns. *Review of Finance, 17*(1), 35–105. doi:10.1093/rof/rfs019

Griffin, J. M., Ji, X., & Martin, J. S. (2003). Momentum investing and business cycle risk: Evidence from pole to pole. *The Journal of Finance, 58*(6), 2515–2547. doi:10.1046/j.1540-6261.2003.00614.x

Grinold, R. C. (1992). Are Benchmark Portfolios Efficient? *Journal of Portfolio Management, 19*(1), 34–40. doi:10.3905/jpm.1992.34

Hameed, A., & Kusnadi, Y. (2002). Momentum strategies: Evidence from Pacific Basin stock markets. *Journal of Financial Research, 25*(3), 383–397. doi:10.1111/1475-6803.00025

Hammami, Y. (2013). Momentum investing across economic states: Evidence of market inefficiency in good times. *Applied Financial Economics, 23*(1), 51–56. doi:10.1080/09603107.2012.705426

Hanauer, M. X., & Linhart, M. (2015). Size, value, and momentum in emerging market stock returns: Integrated or segmented pricing? *Asia-Pacific Journal of Financial Studies, 44*(2), 175–214. doi:10.1111/ajfs.12086

Harvey, C., & Siddique, A. (2000). Conditional skewness in asset pricing tests. *The Journal of Finance, 55*(3), 1263–1295. doi:10.1111/0022-1082.00247

Haugen, R. A., & Baker, N. L. (1991). The Efficient Market Inefficiency of Capitalization-Weighted Stock Portfolios. *Journal of Portfolio Management, 17*(1), 35–40. doi:10.3905/jpm.1991.409335

Hon, M. T., & Tonks, I. (2003). Momentum in the UK stock market. *Journal of Multinational Financial Management, 13*(1), 43–70. doi:10.1016/S1042-444X(02)00022-1

Hong, D., Lee, C., & Swaminathan, B. (2003). *Earnings momentum in international markets.* Available at SSRN 390107

Hong, H., & Stein, J. C. (1999). A Unified Theory of Underreaction, Momentum Trading and Overreaction in Asset Markets. *The Journal of Finance, 54*(6), 2143–2184. doi:10.1111/0022-1082.00184

Houweling, P., & Van Zundert, J. (2017). Factor investing in the corporate bond market. *Financial Analysts Journal, 73*(2), 100–115. doi:10.2469/faj.v73.n2.1

Israel, R., Palhares, D., & Richardson, S. (2018). Common factors in corporate bond returns. *Journal of Investment Management, 16*(2), 17–46.

Jegadeesh, N., & Titman, S. (1993). Returns to Buying Winners and Selling Losers: Implications for Stock Market Efficiency. *The Journal of Finance, 48*(1), 65–91. doi:10.1111/j.1540-6261.1993.tb04702.x

Jostova, G., Nikolova, S., Philipov, A., & Stahel, C. W. (2013). Momentum in corporate bond returns. *Review of Financial Studies, 26*(7), 1649–1693. doi:10.1093/rfs/hht022

Kahneman, D., & Riepe, M. W. (1998). Aspects of Investor Psychology. *Journal of Portfolio Management, 24*(4), 52–65. doi:10.3905/jpm.1998.409643

Khang, K., & King, T. H. D. (2004). Return reversals in the bond market: Evidence and causes. *Journal of Banking & Finance, 28*(3), 569–593. doi:10.1016/S0378-4266(03)00035-9

Kraus, A., & Litzenberger, R. H. (1976). Skewness preference and the valuation of risk assets. *The Journal of Finance, 31*(4), 1085–1100.

Levy, R. A. (1967). Relative strength as a criterion for investment selection. *The Journal of Finance, 22*(4), 595–610. doi:10.1111/j.1540-6261.1967.tb00295.x

Lintner, J. (1965). The valuation of risk assets and the selection of risky investments in stock portfolios and capital budgets. *The Review of Economics and Statistics, 47*(1), 13–37. doi:10.2307/1924119

Liu, L. X., & Zhang, L. (2008). Momentum profits, factor pricing, and macroeconomic risk. *Review of Financial Studies, 21*(6), 2417–2448. doi:10.1093/rfs/hhn090

Liu, L. X., & Zhang, L. (2011). *Investment-based momentum profits*. National Bureau of Economic Research.

Lui, W., Strong, N., & Xu, X. (1999). The profitability of momentum investing. *Journal of Business Finance & Accounting, 26*(9-10), 1043–1091. doi:10.1111/1468-5957.00286

Maeso, J. M., Martellini, L., & Rebonato, R. (2019). *Factor Investing in Fixed-Income – Cross-Sectional andTime-Series Momentum in Sovereign Bond Markets*. EDHEC-Risk Institute.

Malkiel, B. G. (2014). Is Smart Beta Really Smart? *The Journal of Portfolio Management, 40*(5), 127-134.

Marcato, G., & Key, T. (2005). Direct investment in real estate. *Journal of Portfolio Management, 31*(5), 55–69. doi:10.3905/jpm.2005.593888

Markowitz, H. (1959). *Portfolio selection: Efficient diversification of investments* (Vol. 16). John Wiley.

Markowitz, H. M. (1952). Portfolio Selection. *The Journal of Finance, 7*(1), 77–91.

Markowitz, H. M. (1999). The Early History of Portfolio Theory: 1600-1960. *Financial Analysts Journal, 55*(4), 5–16. doi:10.2469/faj.v55.n4.2281

Markowitz, H. M., Todd, P., Xu, G., & Yamane, Y. (1993). Computation of mean-Semivariance efficient sets by the Critical Line Algorithm. *Annals of Operations Research, 45*(1), 307–317. doi:10.1007/BF02282055

Mengoli, S. (2004). On the source of contrarian and momentum strategies in the Italian equity market. *International Review of Financial Analysis, 13*(3), 301–331. doi:10.1016/j.irfa.2004.02.012

Menkhoff, L., Sarno, L., Schmeling, M., & Schrimpf, A. (2012). Currency momentum strategies. *Journal of Financial Economics, 106*(3), 660–684. doi:10.1016/j.jfineco.2012.06.009

Miffre, J., & Rallis, G. (2007). Momentum strategies in commodity futures markets. *Journal of Banking & Finance, 31*(6), 1863–1886. doi:10.1016/j.jbankfin.2006.12.005

Moskowitz, T. J., & Grinblatt, M. (1999). Do industries explain momentum? *The Journal of Finance*, *54*(4), 1249–1290. doi:10.1111/0022-1082.00146

Mossin, J. (1966). Equilibrium in a Capital Asset Market. *Econometrica*, *34*(4), 768–783. doi:10.2307/1910098

Muga, L., & Santamaria, R. (2007). The momentum effect in Latin American emerging markets. *Emerging Markets Finance & Trade*, *43*(4), 24–45. doi:10.2753/REE1540-496X430402

Orsag, S. (2015). *Investicijska analiza*. Zagreb, Hrvatska: Avantis, HUFA.

Pospisil, L., & Zhang, J. (2010). Momentum and reversal effects in corporate bond prices and credit cycles. *Journal of Fixed Income*, *20*(2), 101–115. doi:10.3905/jfi.2010.20.2.101

Rendleman, R. J. Jr, Jones, C. P., & Latane, H. A. (1982). Empirical anomalies based on unexpected earnings and the importance of risk adjustments. *Journal of Financial Economics*, *10*(3), 269–287. doi:10.1016/0304-405X(82)90003-4

Rouwenhorst, K. G. (1998). International momentum strategies. *The Journal of Finance*, *53*(1), 267–284. doi:10.1111/0022-1082.95722

Rouwenhorst, K. G. (1999). Local return factors and turnover in emerging stock markets. *The Journal of Finance*, *54*(4), 1439–1464. doi:10.1111/0022-1082.00151

Schiereck, D., De Bondt, W., & Weber, M. (1999). Contrarian and momentum strategies in Germany. *Financial Analysts Journal*, *55*(6), 104–116. doi:10.2469/faj.v55.n6.2317

Sharpe, W. F. (1964). Capital Asset Prices: A Theory of Market Equilibrium under Conditions of Risk. *The Journal of Finance*, *19*(3), 425–442.

Shiller, R. J. (2000). *Irrational Exuberance*. Princeton University Press.

Tobin, J. (1958). Liquidity Preference as Behavior Towards Risk. *The Review of Economic Studies*, *25*(2), 65–86. doi:10.2307/2296205

Van der Hart, J., de Zwart, G., & van Dijk, D. (2005). The success of stock selection strategies in emerging markets: Is it risk or behavioral bias? *Emerging Markets Review*, *6*(3), 238–262. doi:10.1016/j.ememar.2005.05.002

Van der Hart, J., Slagter, E., & Van Dijk, D. (2003). Stock selection strategies in emerging markets. *Journal of Empirical Finance*, *10*(1-2), 105–132. doi:10.1016/S0927-5398(02)00022-1

Vuong, N. B., & Vu, T. T. (2018). Size, value and momentum in stock returns: The case of Latin American emerging markets. *Aestimatio: The IEB International. The Journal of Finance*, (17), 82–103.

White, D. R., & Okunev, J. (2001). *Do Momentum Based Strategies Still Work in Foreign Currency Markets?* Available at SSRN 264574

Zaremba, A., & Konieczka, P. (2015). Are value, size and momentum premiums in CEE emerging markets only illusionary? *Finance a úvěr-Czech. Journal of Economics and Finance*, *65*(1), 84–104.

KEY TERMS AND DEFINITIONS

Factor Investing: Type of investing that aims to identify specific drivers (factors) of return across different assets classes.

Factor Models: Models in which returns on security are affected by several factors which are approximated by some comprehensive index or variable which has the most significant effect.

Formation Period: The time period in which the past performance of assets classes is observed and based on past performance, divided into groups. From technical point of view, it refers to "in-sample" analysis.

Holding Period: The time period in which the investor holds investment (different asset classes). From technical point of view, it refers to "out-of-sample" analysis.

Loser Portfolio: Portfolio which contains stocks or other asset class that have performed poorly in the previous observed period.

Momentum Strategy: Type of investing that buys asset that have performed well in the previous period (winner asset) and sells asset that have performed poorly in the previous period (looser asset), meaning that past winners are outperform past losers.

Reversal Effect: Phenomenon that is opposite to momentum strategy, more precisely strategy that buys asset that have performed poorly in the previous period and sells asset that have performed well in the previous period.

Winner Portfolio: Portfolio which contains stocks or other asset class that have performed the best in the previous observed period.

Chapter 16
Coupon Bond Duration and Convexity Analysis:
A Non-Calculus Approach

Vedran Kojić
https://orcid.org/0000-0002-6802-1719
Faculty of Economics and Business, University of Zagreb, Croatia

Margareta Gardijan Kedžo
https://orcid.org/0000-0001-5390-057X
Faculty of Economics and Business, University of Zagreb, Croatia

Zrinka Lukač
https://orcid.org/0000-0003-2986-6345
Faculty of Economics and Business, University of Zagreb, Croatia

ABSTRACT

Coupon bond duration and convexity are the primary risk measures for bonds. Given their importance, there is abundant literature covering their analysis, with calculus being used as the dominant approach. On the other hand, some authors have treated coupon bond duration and convexity without the use of differential calculus. However, none of them provided a complete analysis of bond duration and convexity properties. Therefore, this chapter fills in the gap. Since the application of calculus may be complicated or even inappropriate if the functions in question are not differentiable (as indeed is the case with the bond duration and convexity functions), in this chapter the properties of bond duration and convexity functions by using elementary algebra only are proved. This provides an easier way of approaching this problem, thus making it accessible to a wider audience not necessarily familiar with tools of mathematical analysis. Finally, the properties of these functions are illustrated by using empirical data on coupon bonds.

DOI: 10.4018/978-1-7998-5083-0.ch016

INTRODUCTION

Macaulay's duration and convexity are the most widely used measures of risk both in financial theory and practice. Hence, it is not surprising that the literature is abundant with various titles describing the principals and properties of these two measures. In literature, the common approach to analyzing the properties of Macaulay's coupon bond duration and bond convexity is to use differential calculus of real functions with several real variables (see for example (Aljinović, Marasović & Šego, 2011), (Choudhry, 2001), (Fabozzi, 2006), (Fabozzi, 2007), (Fabozzi & Manu, 2010), (Fabozzi & Manu, 2012), (La Grandville, 2000), (La Grandville, 2001), (Hawawini, 1982), (Hawawini, 1984), (Orsag, 2011) (Pianca, 2005), (Smith, 1998), (Zipf, 2003)). On the other hand, there are also papers which approach the problem of the bond's price properties by using a student-friendly approach via non-calculus (for example (Lawrence & Shankar, 2007) and (Malkiel, 1962)). The main obstacle to using calculus in the analysis of the Macaulay's coupon bond duration and bond convexity is the fact that duration and convexity with respect to coupon-rate (ceteris paribus), yield to maturity (ceteris paribus) or maturity (ceteris paribus) are not continuous functions, not to mention differentiable. In practice, coupon rate, yield to maturity and maturity are discrete variables, so the duration and convexity have to be seen as sequences of real numbers rather then continuous functions. For that reason, Gardijan, Kojić & Šego (2012), Kojić & Lukač (2015), and Kojić & Lukač (2017) have presented the analysis of the Macaulay's coupon bond duration properties by using a non calculus approach. Šego & Škrinjarić (2014) analysed bond convexity properties without using calculus, however in their analysis they didn't take into account the fact that whenever there is a change in any variable of convexity, the corresponding bond price is changing too. This resulted in an incomplete non-calculus analysis of bond convexity properties. To the best of our knowledge, the complete rigorous non-calculus analysis of coupon bond convexity properties is missing in the relevant literature on finance. Therefore, this chapter aims to fill in the missing gap by presenting the complete analysis here. The structure of this chapter is as follows. After the introduction, the second section presents notation used in this study. The third section presents the properties and proofs of bond's price. The non-calculus analysis of Macauly's coupon bond duration and bond convexity is given in the fourth and the fifth section, respectively. The chapter ends with final conclusions in the sixth section.

Notation

In this chapter, the following coupon bond notation is used:

- N: face value, bond's par value
- I: contractual interest rate, bond's coupon-rate
- i: annual coupon payment, a year interest payment
- n: bond maturity, number of payments, n years
- k: annual yield to maturity of the bond
- $r=1+k$: annual period discount factor at rate k
- P: (market) bond's price
- $P(k)$: market price bond as a function of k ceteris paribus
- $P(i)$: market price bond as a function of i ceteris paribus
- $P(n)$: market price bond as a function of n ceteris paribus
- D: Macaulay's bond duration

- $D(k)$: Macaulay's bond duration as a function of k ceteris paribus
- $D(i)$: Macaulay's bond duration as a function of i ceteris paribus
- $D(n)$: Macaulay's bond duration as a function of n ceteris paribus
- C: bond convexity
- $C(k)$: bond convexity as a function of k ceteris paribus
- $C(i)$: bond convexity as a function of i ceteris paribus
- $C(n)$: bond convexity as a function of n ceteris paribus

COUPON BOND PRICE PROPERTIES

For the sake of clarity and thoroughness, the results about coupon bond price and Macaulay's coupon bond duration properties presented in the third and the fourth section of this chapter follow authors' previous research and results (Gardijan, Kojić & Šego (2012), Kojić & Lukač (2015) and Kojić & Lukač (2017)).

In this chapter we consider only the case when coupon bond has equal annual coupon payments, which are equal to $I=iN$, where i is the bond's coupon-rate and N is the bond's par value. The bond's price is then given by

$$P=\sum_{t=1}^{n}\frac{iN}{(1+k)^{t}}+\frac{N}{(1+k)^{n}}=\sum_{t=1}^{n}\frac{iN}{r^{t}}+\frac{N}{r^{n}} \tag{1}$$

Formula (1) is called the open form formula for bond's price P.

Proposition 1. If $i=k$, then $P=N$ (that is, if bond's coupon-rate is equal to yield to maturity, then the bond's price is equal to its par value). If $i>k$, then $P>N$, and if $i<k$, then $P<N$.

Proof of Proposition 1. By applying the formula for the sum of the first n terms of a geometric sequence to (1), we obtain the closed form of (1) which is given by (2):

$$P=\sum_{t=1}^{n}\frac{iN}{r^{n}}+\frac{N}{r^{n}}=\frac{iN}{r}\frac{r\left(r^{n}-1\right)}{r^{n}\left(r-1\right)}+\frac{N}{r^{n}}=\frac{N}{r^{n}}\left(\frac{\left(r^{n}-1\right)i}{r-1}+1\right)=\frac{N}{\left(1+k\right)^{n}}\left[\left(\left(1+k\right)^{n}-1\right)\frac{i}{k}+1\right]. \tag{2}$$

By using (2), it is easy to see that from $i=k$ it follows that $P=N$. If $i>k>0$, then $i/k>1$which implies that $P>N$. Similarly, from $0<i<k$ it follows that $i/k<1$ and $P<N$. Therefore, if bond's coupon-rate i is greater (less) than yield to maturity k, then the bond's price is greater (less) than its par value **Q.E.D.**

As we can see from relation (2), the coupon bond's price P is a function of bond's coupon-rate i, yield to maturity k and maturity n. Thus, $P=P(i, k, n)$. It is therefore useful to analyse the coupon bond's price P with respect to change of its variables i, k and n under assumption ceteris paribus. For simplicity reasons, although P is the function of three variables, we will use the notation $P=P(i)$, $P=P(k)$ and $P=P(n)$ whenever we analyse P with respect to change of one variable only. For example, in this context $P(i)$ means that we consider the bond's price P as a function of bond's coupon-rate i, while the variables k and n are kept constant.

In order to illustrate the properties of P, let us look at the following examples.

Example 1. Let us consider a bond with nominal value $N = 100$ which pays out annual coupons at a coupon rate $i = 0.05$ with remaining 10 years to maturity. We analyse the bond's price as a function of annual discount rate k. Figure 1 shows a graph of $P(k)$. It is obvious that $P(k)$ is a monotonically decreasing function. Bond price decreases at an increasing rate as discount rate increases, *ceteris paribus*.

Figure 1. The shape of the bond's price as a function of discount rate (Example 1) Source: Authors.

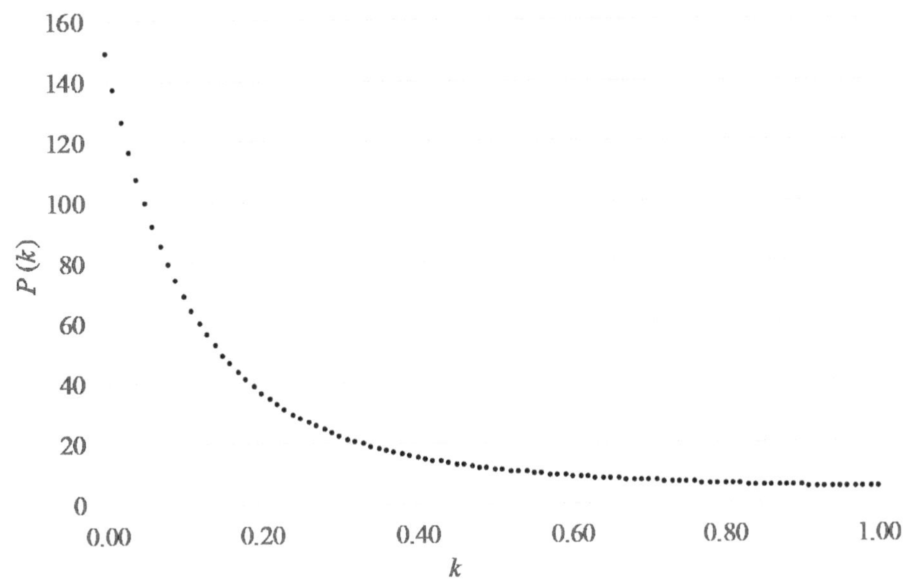

Example 2. Let us consider a bond with nominal value $N = 100$ which pays out annual coupons at a coupon rate i with remaining 10 years to maturity. Suppose that annual discount rate is $k = 0.05$. We analyse the bond's price as a function of coupon rate i. Figure 2 shows a graph of $P(i)$. It is obvious that $P(i)$ is monotonically increasing, i.e. price increases as coupon rate increases, *ceteris paribus*.

Example 3. Let us consider a bond with nominal value $N = 100$ which pays out annual coupons at a coupon rate i. Suppose that annual discount rate is $k = 0.05$ and that coupon rates can be $i_1 = 0.06$

Figure 2. The shape of the bond's price as a function of discount rate (Example 2) Source: Authors.

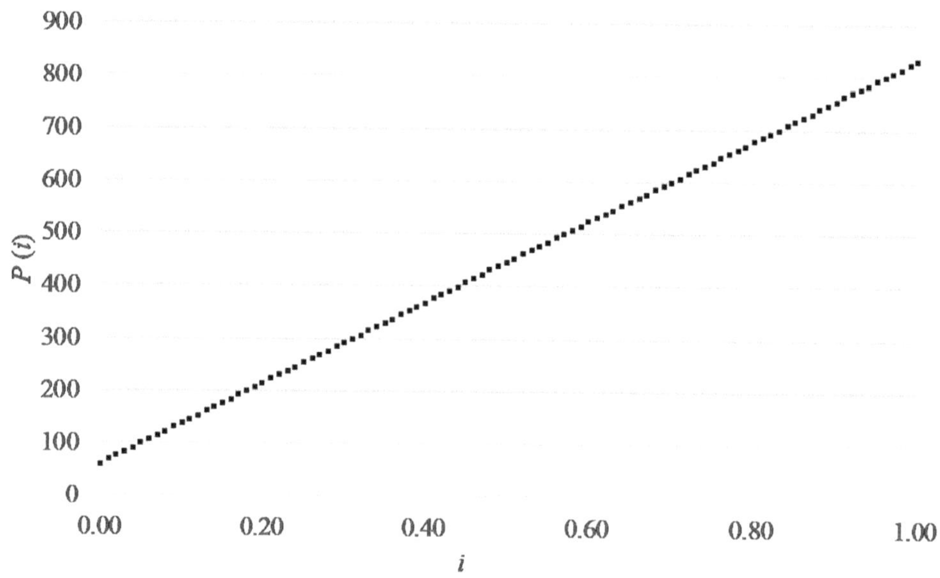

> k, $i_2 = 0.05 = k$ and $i_3 = 0.04 < k$. It follows that $L_P(i_1) = 120$, $L_P(i_2) = 100$ and $L_P(i_3) = 80$. We analyse the bond's price as a function of time to maturity at chosen coupon rates i_s, $s = \{1, 2, 3\}$. Figure 3 shows a graph of $P(n,\ i=i_s)$. It is obvious that function $P(n,\ i=0.06)$ is decreasing with maximal asymptotical value 120, function $P\ (n,\ i=0.05)$ is a constant and function $P(n,\ i=0.04)$ is decreasing with minimal asymptotical value 80.

Figure 3. The shape of the bond's price as a function of discount rate (Example 3) Source: Authors.

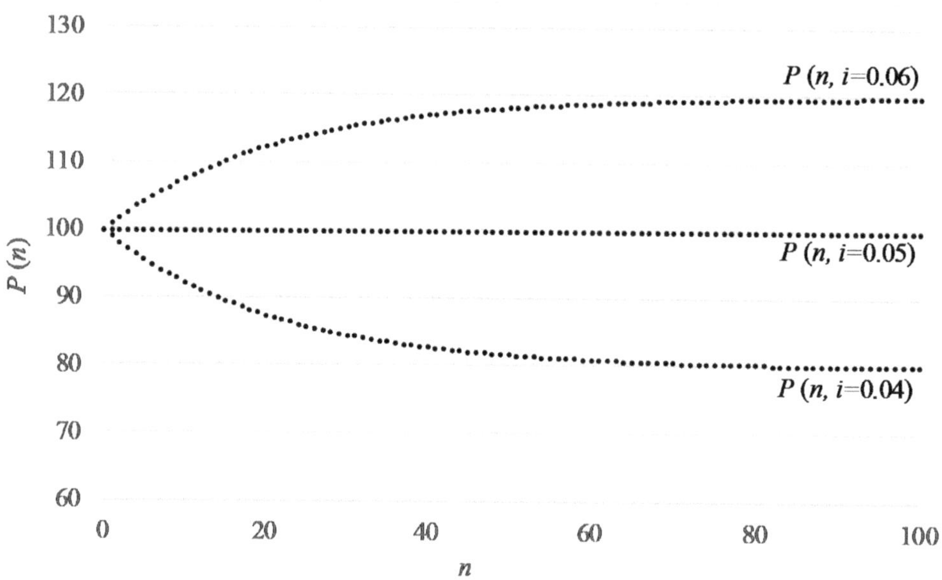

The next theorem states the general properties of P (see Gardijan, Kojić & Šego (2012)).

Theorem 1. Properties of P with respect to change of its variables are as follows:

(a) Function $P = P(k)$ is monotonically decreasing ceteris paribus, i.e. for any two annual yields to maturity such that $k_1 \leq k_2$ inequality $P(k_1) \geq P(k_2)$ holds.
(b) Function $P = P(i)$ is monotonically increasing ceteris paribus, i.e. for any two coupon-rates such that $i_1 \leq i_2$ inequality $P(i_1) \leq P(i_2)$ holds.
(c) The limit of $P = P(n)$ when n approaches infinity is equal to $L_P = \lim_{n\to+\infty} P(n) = \frac{iN}{k}$.

Furthermore, if $i = k$, then function $P(n)$ is a constant ceteris paribus, i.e. $P(n) = N$. If $i > k$ then $P(n)$ is an increasing function ceteris paribus, and if $i < k$ then $P(n)$ is a decreasing function ceteris paribus.

Proof of Theorem 1.

(a) The claim is trivial because $P=P(k)$ is the sum of $n+1$ monotonically decreasing functions in variable k (see (1)).
(b) Let $i_1 \leq i_2$, that is $i_2 - i_2 \geq 0$. In order to prove the claim, we have find the sign of the expression $P(i_2)-P(i_1)$:

$$P(i_2)-P(i_1)=\sum_{t=1}^{n}\frac{i_2N}{r^t}+\frac{N}{r^n}-\left(\sum_{t=1}^{n}\frac{i_1N}{r^t}+\frac{N}{r^n}\right)=\sum_{t=1}^{n}\frac{(i_2-i_1)N}{r^t}\geq 0 \tag{3}$$

Since $P(i_2)-P(i_1)\geq 0$ for all $i_1 \leq i_2$, function $P=P(i)$ is monotonically increasing. This proves the claim (b).
(c) From (2) it follows

$$L_P=\lim_{n\to\infty}\frac{N}{(1+k)^n}\left[\left((1+k)^n-1\right)\frac{i}{k}+1\right]=\lim_{n\to\infty}\left[\frac{Ni}{k}-\frac{Ni}{(1+k)^n k}+\frac{N}{(1+k)^n}\right]=\frac{Ni}{k}$$

Furthermore,

$$P(n+1)-P(n)=\sum_{t=1}^{n+1}\frac{iN}{r^t}+\frac{N}{r^{n+1}}-\left(\sum_{t=1}^{n}\frac{iN}{r^t}+\frac{N}{r^n}\right)=\frac{N}{r^{n+1}}(i+1-r)=\frac{N}{r^{n+1}}(i-k) \tag{4}$$

Thus, from (4) it follows that if $i=k$, function $P(n)$ is a constant ceteris paribus. Furthermore, if $i>k$ then $P(n)$ is an increasing function ceteris paribus, and if $i<k$ then $P(n)$ is a decreasing function ceteris paribus. **Q.E.D.**

MACAULAY'S COUPON BOND DURATION PROPERTIES

In this section we analyse the properties of the Macaulay's bond duration (see Aljinović, Marasović & Šego (2011)).

Macaulay's bond duration D is defined by the following formula:

$$D = \frac{1}{P}\left(\sum_{t=1}^{n} t \cdot \frac{iN}{(1+k)^t} + n \cdot \frac{N}{(1+k)^n}\right) = \frac{1}{P}\left(\sum_{t=1}^{n} t \cdot \frac{iN}{r^t} + n \cdot \frac{N}{r^n}\right) \tag{5}$$

Here, the bond's price P is given by (1) or (2). By taking the derivative of (1) with respect to the discount factor r (as in Aljinović, Marasović & Šego, 2011), we get

$$\frac{dP}{dr} = \sum_{t=1}^{n} \frac{-tiN}{r^{t+1}} + \frac{-nN}{r^{n+1}} = \left(\sum_{t=1}^{n} \frac{tiN}{Pr^t} + \frac{nN}{Pr^n}\right) \cdot \frac{-P}{r} = D \cdot \frac{-P}{r} \tag{6}$$

or equivalently

$$E_{P,r} = \frac{\frac{dP}{P}}{\frac{dr}{r}} = \frac{r}{P} \cdot \frac{dP}{dr} = -D \tag{7}$$

Thus, we have the following interpretations of Macaulay's coupon bond duration (taken from Aljinović, Marasović & Šego (2011)):

1. Macaulay's coupon bond duration represents the value of elasticity of bond's price with respect to change of the discount factor r. In other words, if the discount factor (on the given level) increases by 1%, the bond's price decreases approximately by D%.
2. Macaulay's coupon bond duration is the volatility measure. If duration is long, the corresponding bond's price is more sensitive to change of yield to maturity.

The relation (7) can be reformulated as

$$\frac{dP}{P} = -D\frac{dr}{r} \tag{8}$$

If Δr is small enough, differential dr can be approximated by the difference Δr. Therefore, from (8) it follows

$$\Delta P \approx -DP\frac{\Delta r}{r} \tag{9}$$

Therefore, for small changes in yield to maturity, $\Delta k = \Delta r$, the bond's price can be approximated by (9). The closed form of formula (5) is given by (see Aljinović, Marasović & Šego, 2011):

$$D = \frac{iN}{P} \frac{r\left(r^n - 1\right) - n\left(r - 1\right)}{r^n \left(r - 1\right)^2} + \frac{nN}{Pr^n} \qquad (10)$$

Duration can be seen as a function of three variables: yield to maturity k, coupon-rate i and maturity n. In the same manner as in the previous section, we will use the notation $D=D(k)$, $D=D(i)$ and $D=D(n)$ whenever we analyse D with respect to change of one variable only, keeping all the other variables fixed. In order to analyse the Macaulay's bond duration properties without using calculus, first we need the following lemma.

Lemma 1. For all real numbers a and b such that $a>0$ and $b>0$, there exists the positive integer n such that $na > b$.

Proof of Lemma 1. In literature, this lemma is called The Principle of Archimedes. For proof, see for example (Zorich, 2004). **Q.E.D.**

In the rest of this section, the analysis of the properties of the coupon bond duration follows the one given in (Gardijan, Kojić & Šego, 2012) and (Kojić & Lukač, 2015).

In order to illustrate the properties of D, let us look at the following examples.

Example 4. Let us consider a bond with nominal value $N = 100$ which pays out annual coupons at a coupon rate $i = 0.05$. We assume that annual discount rate is $k = 0.06$. We analyse the duration as a function of time to maturity n which varies from 0 to 50 years. Figure 4 shows a graph of $D(n)$. It is obvious that $D(n)$ is a monotonically increasing function, i.e. duration increases as time to maturity increases, *ceteris paribus*, but at a decreasing rate.

Figure 4. The shape of the duration as a function of maturity (Example 4) Source: Authors.

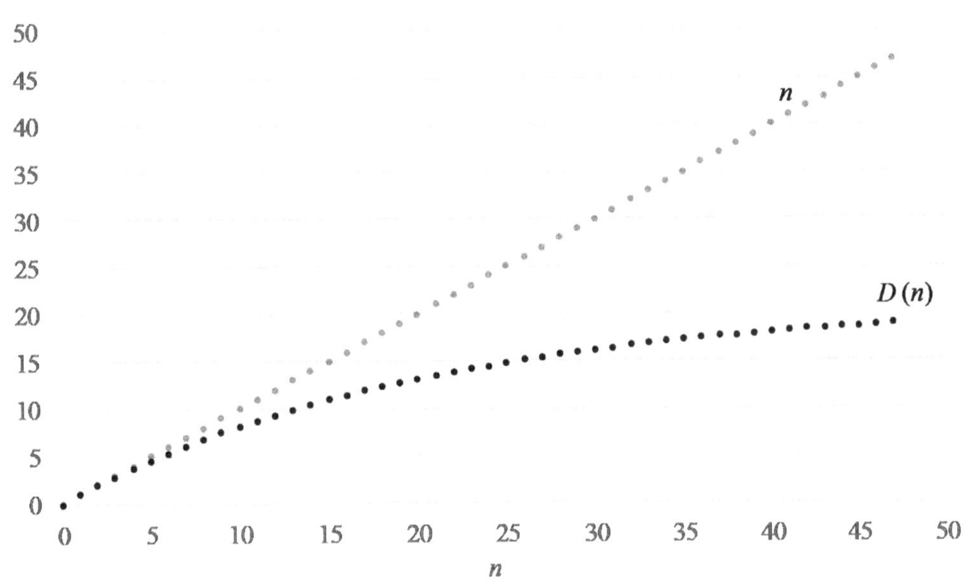

Example 5. Let us consider a bond with nominal value $N = 100$ which pays out annual coupons at a coupon rate i with 10 years to maturity. Suppose that the annual discount rate is $k = 0.05$. We analyse duration as a function of a coupon rate i which varies from 0 to 100%. Figure 5 shows a graph of $D(i)$. It is obvious that $D(i)$ is monotonically decreasing function, i.e. duration decreases as coupon rate increases, *ceteris paribus*.

Figure 5. The shape of the duration as a function of maturity (Example 5) Source: Authors.

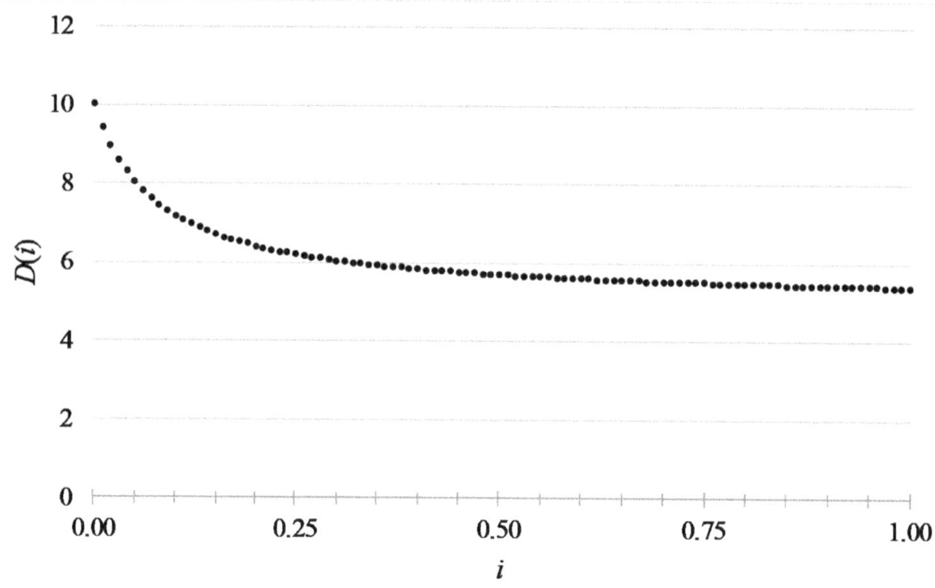

Example 6. Let us consider a bond with nominal value $N = 100$ which pays out annual coupons at a coupon rate i with 10 years to maturity. We assume that annual discount rate is k. We analyse the duration as a function of annual discount rate k which varies from 0 to 100%. Figure 6 shows a graph of $D(k)$. It is obvious that $D(k)$ is a monotonically decreasing function, i.e. duration decreases as the annual discount rate increases, *ceteris paribus*.

Example 7. Let us consider a bond with nominal value $N = 100$ which pays out annual coupons at a coupon rate i. Suppose that annual discount rate is $k = 0.05$. By equation (21), $L_D = 21$. We want to analyse duration as a function of time to maturity $D(n)$ at different values of coupon rates. Suppose that coupon rates are $i_1 = 0.02$, $i_2 = 0.10$, and $i_3 = 0.20$ and time to maturity n varies from 0 to 160. We analyse the duration as a function of time to maturity n at different coupon rates. Graphs of L_D, $D(n, i_1)$, $D(n, i_2)$, $D(n, i_3)$ are shown Figure 7. It is obvious that $D(n, 0.02)$ first increases and then decreases and asymptotically approaches to the limit value $L_D = 21$ because $i_1 = 0.02 < k = 0.05$. On the other hand, $i_2 = 0.10$ and $i_3 = 0.20$ are greater than $k = 0.05$, therefore we observe that functions $D(n, 0.10)$ and $D(n, 0.20)$ are increasing with maximal asymptotical value $L_D = 21$.

Figure 6. The shape of the duration as a function of maturity (Example 6) Source: Authors.

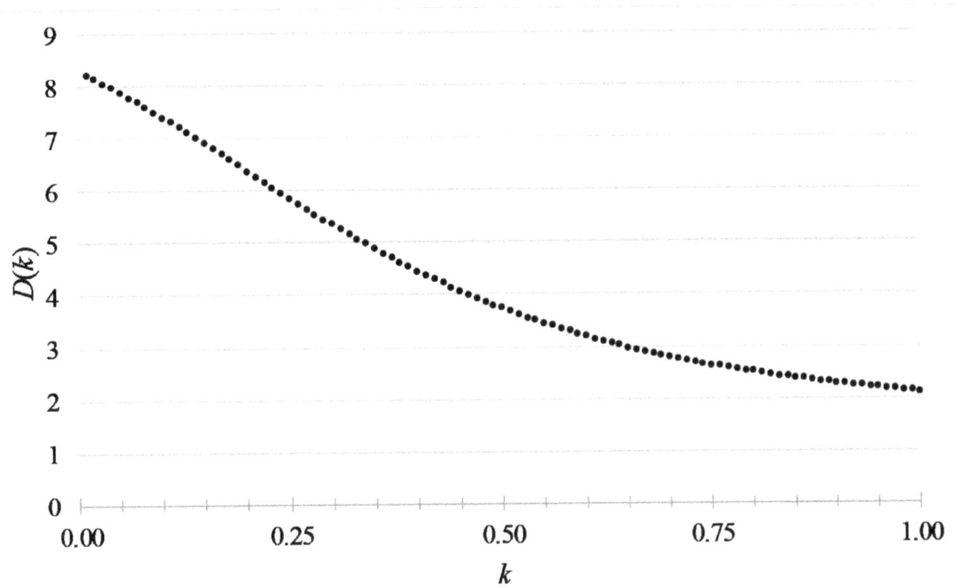

Figure 7. The shape of the duration as a function of time to maturity for chosen coupon rates $i_1 = 0.02 < k$, $i_2 = 0.10 > k$ and $i_3 = 0.20 > k$ Source: Authors.

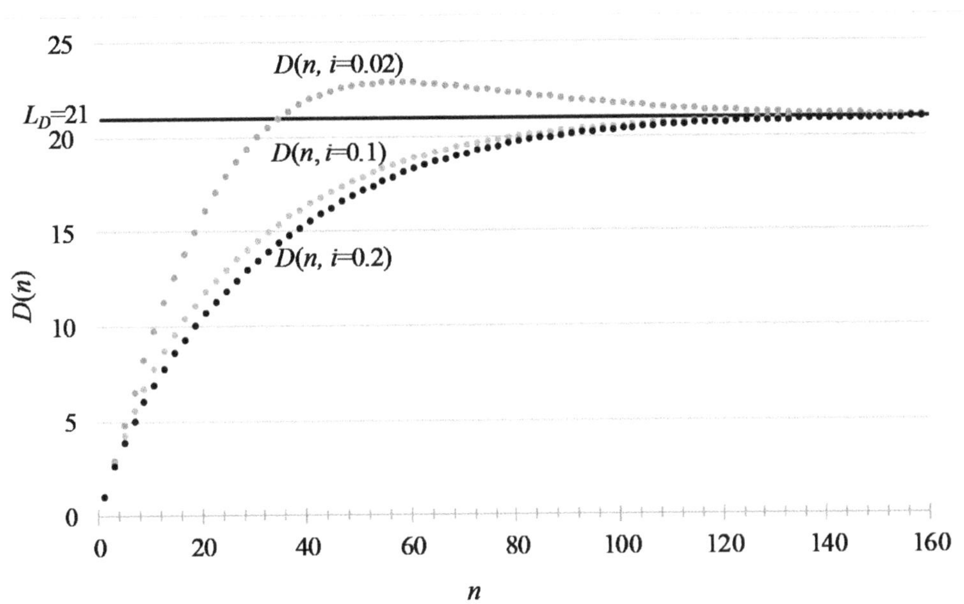

The next theorem states the general properties of D.

Theorem 2. Properties of D with respect to change of its variables are as follows:

(a) Value of duration is always positive.
(b) Value of duration is always less or equal to bond's maturity, i.e. $D(n) \leq n$.
(c) Function $D=D(i)$ is monotonically decreasing ceteris paribus, i.e. for any two coupon-rates such that $i_1 \leq i_2$ inequality $D(i_1) \geq D(i_2)$ holds.
(d) Function $D=D(k)$ is monotonically decreasing ceteris paribus, i.e. for any two yields to maturity such that $k_1 \leq k_2$ inequality $D(k_1) \geq D(k_2)$ holds.
(e) The limit of function $D = D(n)$ when n approaches infinity is equal to the value $L_D = \lim_{n \to +\infty} D(n) = 1 + \frac{1}{k}$.

Furthermore, if $i \geq k$, then function $D(n)$ is increasing with maximal asymptotical value L_D. However, if $0 < i < k$, the shape of the duration as the function of maturity $D(n)$ is as follows: at first the duration function increases until it reaches its maximum and after that it decreases and asymptotically approaches the limit value L_D.

Proof of Theorem 2.

(a) The claim is trivial since all terms in (5) are positive.
(b) From (5) we get

$$D = \sum_{t=1}^{n} t \cdot \left(\frac{\frac{iN}{(1+k)^t}}{P} \right) + n \left(\frac{\frac{N}{(1+k)^t}}{P} \right) \leq \sum_{t=1}^{n} n \cdot \left(\frac{\frac{iN}{(1+k)^t}}{P} \right) + n \left(\frac{\frac{N}{(1+k)^t}}{P} \right)$$
$$= n \cdot \frac{\sum_{t=1}^{n} \left(\frac{iN}{(1+k)^t} \right) + \frac{N}{(1+k)^t}}{P} = n \cdot \frac{P}{P} = n. \tag{11}$$

Thus, $D(n) \leq n$.

(c) Let i be a given coupon-rate and let $\delta > 0$ be a positive real number. Let $D(i)$ and $P(i)$ denote the duration and the bond's price as functions of coupon-rate i, respectively, *ceteris paribus*. Then

$$P(i+\delta) = \sum_{t=1}^{n} \frac{(i+\delta)N}{(1+k)^t} + \frac{N}{(1+k)^n} \tag{12}$$

and

$$D(i+\delta)=\frac{1}{P(i+\delta)}\left[\sum_{t=1}^{n}t\frac{(i+\delta)N}{(1+k)^{t}}+\frac{nN}{(1+k)^{n}}\right] \tag{13}$$

We consider the difference $D(i+\delta)-D(i)$:

$$\begin{aligned}D(i+\delta)-D(i)&=\frac{1}{P(i+\delta)}\left[\sum_{t=1}^{n}t\frac{(i+\delta)N}{(1+k)^{t}}+\frac{nN}{(1+k)^{n}}\right]-\frac{1}{P(i)}\left[\sum_{t=1}^{n}t\frac{iN}{(1+k)^{t}}+\frac{nN}{(1+k)^{n}}\right]\\&=\frac{1}{P(i+\delta)P(i)}\left\{\left[\sum_{t=1}^{n}t\frac{(i+\delta)N}{(1+k)^{t}}+\frac{nN}{(1+k)^{n}}\right]P(i)-\left[\sum_{t=1}^{n}t\frac{iN}{(1+k)^{t}}+\frac{nN}{(1+k)^{n}}\right]P(i+\delta)\right\}.\end{aligned} \tag{14}$$

By putting the expressions for bond's prices $P(i)$ i $P(i+\delta)$ into the braces of the term in the right hand side of (14), we get

$$\begin{aligned}&D(i+\delta)-D(i)\\&=\frac{1}{P(i+\delta)P(i)}\left\{\left[i-(i+\delta)\right]\frac{nN}{(1+k)^{n}}\sum_{t=1}^{n}\frac{N}{(1+k)^{t}}+\left[(i+\delta)-\delta\right]\frac{N}{(1+k)^{n}}\sum_{t=1}^{n}\frac{tN}{(1+k)^{t}}\right\}\\&=\frac{1}{P(i+\delta)P(i)}\cdot\frac{\delta N}{(1+k)^{n}}\sum_{t=1}^{n}\frac{(t-n)N}{(1+k)^{t}}.\end{aligned} \tag{15}$$

Note that in relation (15) the summation terms $(t-n)$ are negative for all $t<n$, i.e. for all $t=1, 2, \ldots, n-1$. On the other hand, terms δ, N, $(1+k)^n$ and $P(i+\delta)P(i)$ have positive values and therefore $D(i+\delta)-D(i)<0$, i.e. $D(i+\delta)<D(i)$. Thus, whenever coupon-rate increases, duration decreases, ceteris paribus.

(d) Let $r>0$. It suffices to show that if yield to maturity k increases to the level $k+r$, then inequality $D(k+r)<D(k)$ holds.

Let $\alpha=\frac{1+k}{1+k+r}$, $K_t=\frac{iN}{(1+k)^{t}}$, $M=\frac{N}{(1+k)^{n}}$. Note that $0<\alpha<1$. Now we want to show that inequality

$$D(k+r)<D(k) \tag{16}$$

holds. By putting α, K_t i M into (10), from (16) we get the sequence of equivalent inequalities (17)-(19):

$$\frac{\sum_{t=1}^{n} tK_t\alpha^t + nM\alpha^n}{\sum_{t=1}^{n} K_t\alpha^t + M\alpha^n} \le \frac{\sum_{t=1}^{n} tK_t + nM}{\sum_{t=1}^{n} K_t + M}, \tag{17}$$

$$\begin{aligned}&\left(\sum_{t=1}^{n} tK_t\alpha^t\right)\left(\sum_{t=1}^{n} K_t\right) + nM\alpha^n\left(\sum_{t=1}^{n} K_t\right) + M\left(\sum_{t=1}^{n} tK_t\alpha^t\right) + M^2 n\alpha^n \\ &\le \left(\sum_{t=1}^{n} tK_t\right)\left(\sum_{t=1}^{n} K_t\alpha^t\right) + nM\left(\sum_{t=1}^{n} K_t\alpha^t\right) + M\alpha^n\left(\sum_{t=1}^{n} tK_t\right) + M^2 n\alpha^n,\end{aligned} \tag{18}$$

$$\begin{aligned}&\sum_{t=1}^{n} t\alpha^t K_t^2 + \left[\sum_{t=1}^{n} t\alpha^t K_t^2 + \sum_{j=1}^{n-1}\sum_{k=j+1}^{n}\left(j\alpha^j + k\alpha^k\right)K_jK_k\right] + nM\alpha^n\left(\sum_{t=1}^{n} K_t\right) + M\left(\sum_{t=1}^{n} tK_t\alpha^t\right) \\ &\le \left[\sum_{t=1}^{n} t\alpha^t K_t^2 + \sum_{l=1}^{n-1}\sum_{m=l+1}^{n}\left(l\alpha^m + m\alpha^l\right)K_lK_m\right] + \sum_{t=1}^{n} t\alpha^t K_t^2 + nM\left(\sum_{t=1}^{n} K_t\alpha^t\right) + M\alpha^n\left(\sum_{t=1}^{n} tK_t\right).\end{aligned} \tag{19}$$

Since $0<\alpha<1$, from $j<k$ it follows that $\alpha^j-\alpha^k>0$. By rearranging the terms in (19), we obtain the following equivalent inequality:

$$\sum_{j=1}^{n-1}\sum_{k=j+1}^{n} \underbrace{\underbrace{(j-k)}_{\le 0}\underbrace{(\alpha^j-\alpha^k)}_{\ge 0}K_jK_k}_{\le 0} + \sum_{t=1}^{n} \underbrace{\underbrace{(\alpha^t-\alpha^n)}_{\ge 0}\underbrace{(t-n)}_{\le 0}}_{\le 0} MK_t \le 0. \tag{20}$$

The inequality (20) obviously holds because all the terms under the both sum operators are non-positive, so the whole term on the left hand side of the inequality (20) is non positive. Given the fact that inequality (20) holds and it is equivalent to (16), we conclude that (16) is also true.

(e) (e) Let us first calculate the limit of the function $D(n)$. In order to do so, we will use relation (10), value L_p from Theorem 1 (c) and the well-known limit $\lim_{n\to+\infty}\frac{n^p}{a^n}=0$, with n and p being positive integers and a a real number such that $a>1$. Now we have

$$L_D = \lim_{n\to\infty} D(n) = \lim_{n\to\infty} \frac{N}{P(n)}\left(i\frac{r\left(r^n - 1\right) - n\left(r-1\right)}{r^n\left(r-1\right)^2} + \frac{n}{r^n} \right)$$
$$= \lim_{n\to\infty}\frac{N}{P(n)}\cdot \lim_{n\to\infty}\left[\left(i\cdot\frac{r^{n+1} - r - nr + n}{r^n\left(r-1\right)^2}\right) + \frac{n}{r^n}\right] = \frac{N}{\frac{Ni}{k}}\cdot i\cdot\frac{r}{\left(r-1\right)^2} = 1 + \frac{1}{k}. \tag{21}$$

Next, we want to determine the sign of the term $D(n+1)–D(n)$. We have

$$P(n)D(n) = \sum_{t=1}^{n} t\frac{iN}{(1+k)^t} + \frac{nN}{(1+k)^n} \tag{22}$$

$$P(n+1)D(n+1) = \sum_{t=1}^{n+1} t\frac{iN}{(1+k)^t} + \frac{(n+1)N}{(1+k)^{n+1}} \tag{23}$$

From (22) and (23) we get

$$P(n+1)D(n+1) - P(n)D(n) = \frac{(n+1)iN}{(1+k)^{n+1}} + \frac{N}{(1+k)^n}\left(\frac{n+1}{1+k} - n\right). \tag{24}$$

On the other hand,

$$P(n+1)D(n+1) - P(n)D(n) = \left(P(n) + \frac{iN}{(1+k)^{n+1}} - \frac{N}{(1+k)^n} + \frac{N}{(1+k)^{n+1}}\right)D(n+1) - P(n)D(n)$$
$$= P(n)\left[D(n+1) - D(n)\right] + \left(\frac{iN}{(1+k)^{n+1}} - \frac{N}{(1+k)^n} + \frac{N}{(1+k)^{n+1}}\right)D(n+1). \tag{25}$$

From (24) and (25) we get

$$P(n)\left[D(n+1) - D(n)\right] = -\left(\frac{iN}{(1+k)^{n+1}} - \frac{N}{(1+k)^n} + \frac{N}{(1+k)^{n+1}}\right)D(n+1)$$
$$+\frac{(n+1)iN}{(1+k)^{n+1}} + \frac{N}{(1+k)^n}\left(\frac{n+1}{1+k} - n\right) = \frac{N}{(1+k)^{n+1}}\left[-(i-k)D(n+1) + (ni + i + 1 - nk)\right]. \tag{26}$$

Since $P(n)>0$, from (26) it follows that the sign of the term $D(n+1)-D(n)$ is positive if and only if the right hand side in (26) is positive. In the same manner, the sign of the term $D(n+1)-D(n)$ is negative if and only if the right hand side in (26) is negative.

In order to determine the shape of the function $D(n)$, we have to consider two cases: $i\geq k$ and $i<k$.

Let us first consider the case $i\geq k$. Since $D(n+1)\leq n+1$ (see (11)), from (26) it follows

$$P(n)\left[D(n+1)-D(n)\right]=\frac{N}{(1+k)^{n+1}}\left[(i-k)\left(-D(n+1)+n\right)+i+1\right]$$
$$\geq\frac{N}{(1+k)^{n+1}}\left[(i-k)(-n-1+n)+i+1\right]=\frac{N}{(1+k)^{n}}\geq 0. \tag{27}$$

Thus, in this case, function $D(n)$ is increasing with maximal asymptotic value L_D.

Let us now consider the second case, that is $i<k$, or $k-i>0$. First we will show that in this case there exists a positive integer n_0 such that for all positive integers $n>n_0$ the last term in (26) is less than or equal to 0. By using (26), it is trivial to see that inequality

$$P(n)\left[D(n+1)-D(n)\right]\leq 0 \tag{28}$$

is equivalent to

$$(k-i)\cdot\left(D(n+1)-n\right)+i+1\leq 0 \tag{29}$$

that is

$$(k-i)\cdot D(n+1)+i+1\leq(k-i)\cdot n \tag{30}$$

Since $D(n+1)$ approaches the limit L_D as n approaches infinity, we know that for a given $\varepsilon>0$ there exists a positive integer n_0 with the property that the inequalities $-\varepsilon+L_D<D(n+1)<L_D+\varepsilon$ hold for all positive integers n such that $n>n_0$. In order to prove inequality (30), let us first prove the following equivalent but stronger inequality:

$$(k-i)\cdot\left(L_D+\varepsilon\right)+i+1<(k-i)n \tag{31}$$

Let $a=k-i$ and let $b=(k-i)\cdot\left(L_D+\varepsilon\right)+i+1$. Since $k-i>0$, we have a, $b>0$. By applying Lemma 1, we know that there exists a positive integer n' such that (31) holds for all $n>n'$. Thus, for all integers $n>max\{n_0,n'\}$ the inequality (28) holds, which means that after the nth term the function $D(n)$ becomes a decreasing function. Furthermore, as n approaches infinity, $D(n)$ approaches the limit L_D. Note that in the case of $i<k$ function $D(n)$ reaches its maximum which is greater than L_D and then decreases and asymptotically approaches its limit L_D. By using formulas (2) and (10) it is easy to show that

Figure 8. The shape of the duration as the function of maturity Source: Authors.

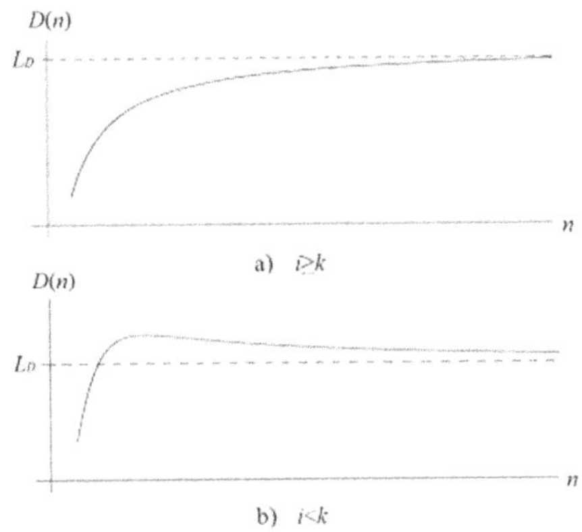

$$D(1)=1<D(2) \tag{32}$$

and $D(1)=1<1+\frac{1}{k}=L_D$. Therefore, first the function $D(n)$ increases until it reaches its maximum (which is necessarily greater than L_D) and then begins to decrease and asymptotically approaches its limit L_D. Figure 8 shows the shape of the function $D=D(n)$, where n is a continuous variable.

Kojić & Lukač (2017) noticed that this proof of the Theorem 2 (e) is not complete. They stated that this proof proves only the case shown in Figure 8 a), but that there is still an open question waiting to be answered as why the cases shown in Figure 10 b) and Figure 10 c) are not possible. Therefore, we will present the final part of the proof of the Theorem 2 (e) as in (Kojić & Lukač, 2017).

To illustrate that the hypothetical shapes of $D(n)$, presented in Figure 10 are not possible, let us consider a bond with nominal value $N = 100$ which pays out annual coupons at a coupon rate i. Suppose that

Figure 9. The shape of the duration as a function of time to maturity for chosen values of coupon rates $\bar{i}$={0.002, 0.004, …, 0.104) Source: Authors.

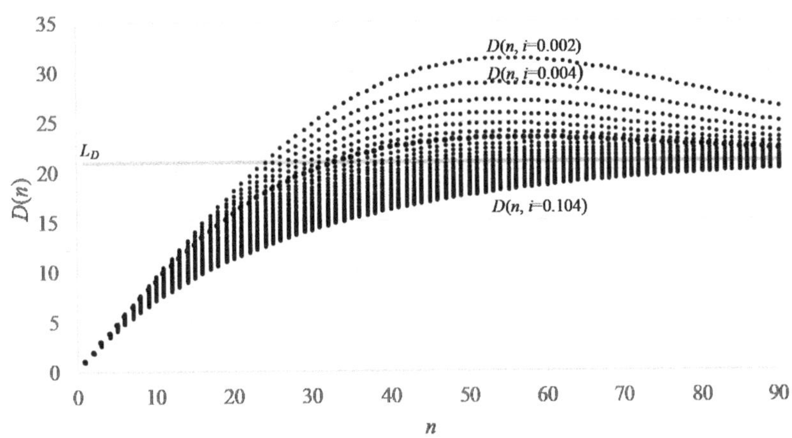

annual discount rate is $k = 0.05$. Following (21), $L_D = 21$. We want to analyse duration as a function of time to maturity $D(n)$ at different values of discount rates assuming that coupon rates could take values from 0.2% to 10.4% in steps of 0.002. In other words, all coupon rates are a member of a discrete set of values $\bar{i}=\{0.002, 0.004, \ldots, 0.104\}$. Time to maturity n varies from 0 to 90 in our example. We analyse the duration as a function of time to maturity n at different coupon rates. Graphs $D\ (n,\ i=\bar{i})$ are shown Figure 9. It is obvious that for all $\bar{i} < k$ shown in the graph, functions $D\ (n,\ i=\bar{i})$ have a unique maximum.

By using the principle of Archimedes, we have already shown that there exists a number n^* such that sequence $D(n^*)$, $D(n^*+1)$, $D(n^*+2)$, $D(n^*+3)$, … is decreasing (see Figure 4.7. a)). Let $n_{\min}$ be the smallest positive integer number such that $D(n)$ after the $n_{\min}{}^{th}$ element is a decreasing sequence. Then, it is obvious that inequalities

$$D(n_{\min} - 1) \le D(n_{\min}) \ge D(n_{\min}+1) \tag{33}$$

hold (otherwise we would have the contradiction with the definition of the number $n_{\min}$). Thus, $(n_{\min}, D(n_{\min}))$ is a local maximum of the function $D(n)$.

It remains to prove that $(n_{\min}, D(n_{\min}))$ is the unique (global) maximum. Let us consider the following equation:

$$D(n+1) - D(n) = 0 \tag{34}$$

Furthermore, let $l(n)= k(k-i)n-k^2-2k+i$ and let $d\left(n\right)=\dfrac{\left(i-k\right)^2}{\left(1+k\right)^n}$. It is easy to see that equation (34) is equivalent to the equation

$$l(n) = d(n) \tag{35}$$

Figure 10. Hypothetical possibilities for the shape of Macaulay's duration as the function of maturity Source: Authors.

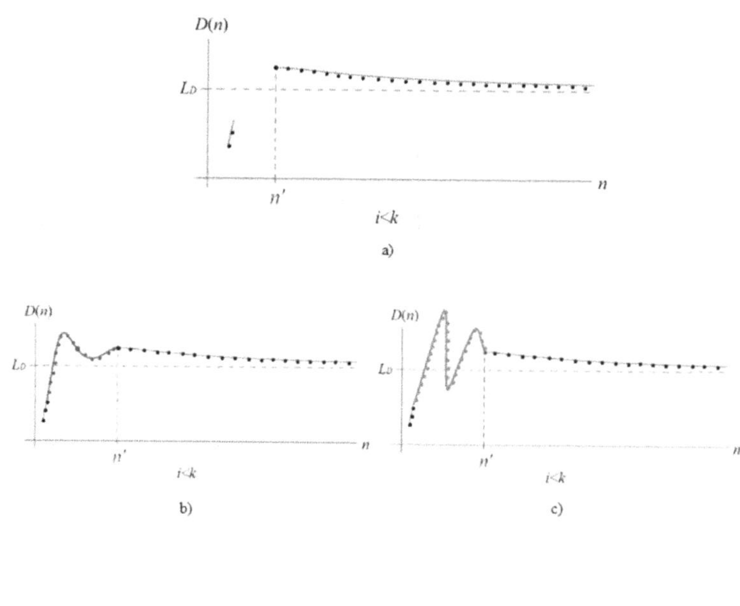

It is easy to see that $l(0)= -k^2 - 2k+i= -k^2-k-(k-i)<0$ and $d(0)= (i-k)^2>0$. Since $l(n)$ is a strictly increasing line and $d(n)$ is a strictly decreasing exponential function, it is obvious that equations (35) and (34) have at most one positive integer-valued solution, but exactly one real-valued solution (see Figure 11).

Figure 11. Intersection of the functions l(n) and d(n) Source: Authors.

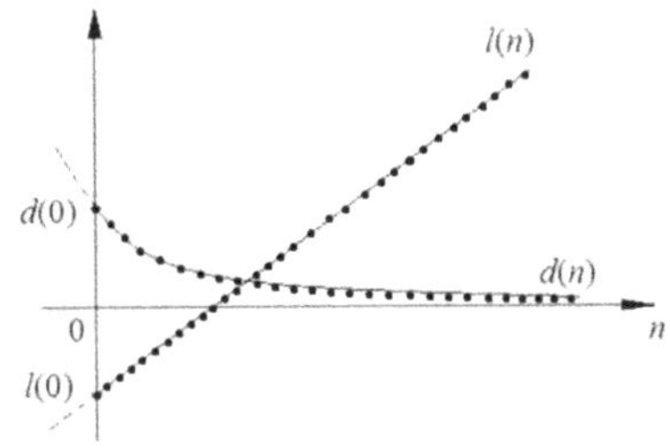

Thus, this completes the proof of the statement (e) of Theorem 2. **Q.E.D.**

COUPON BOND CONVEXITY PROPERTIES

In addition to duration, convexity is another important measure in the risk analysis of the bonds. Recall that a change in the price of a bond can be approximated by an expression that is related to the duration and the convexity of the bond (Šego & Škrinjarić, 2014). Therefore, it is important to know the properties of convexity. In this section, we provide an analysis of the properties of convexity as a function of coupon-rate i, yield to maturity k, and the maturity n of a given coupon bond. We perform the analysis of convexity without using differential calculus. We use simple algebraic manipulations instead, just as we did when we analyzed properties of duration in the previous section. As for the non-calculus approach in the existing literature, Šego & Škrinjarić (2014) did analyse the properties of convexity without the use of differential calculus. However, they neglected the fact that whenever there is a change in any of the variables of the convexity function, the corresponding price of the bond also changes, which by definition must be calculated in order to calculate the convexity itself.

As in the previous section, here we will also use the notation $C=C(k)$, $C=C(i)$ and $C=C(n)$ whenever we analyse C with respect to change of one variable only, keeping all the other variables fixed.

The convexity of the coupon bond, C, is defined by the formula

$$C=\frac{1}{P\cdot(1+k)^2}\left(\sum_{t=1}^{n}t(t+1)\cdot\frac{iN}{(1+k)^t}+n(n+1)\cdot\frac{N}{(1+k)^n}\right)=\frac{1}{P\cdot r^2}\left(\sum_{t=1}^{n}t(t+1)\cdot\frac{iN}{r^t}+n(n+1)\cdot\frac{N}{r^n}\right) \quad (36)$$

where the price of the coupon bond is calculated by (1).

Proposition 2. The closed form of the formula (36) is given by the following expression:

$$C = \frac{2i(1+k)^{n+2} - 2i(1+k)(1+k+kn) + n(n+1)k^2(k-i)}{k^2(1+k)^2\left[i\left((1+k)^n - 1\right) + k\right]} \tag{37}$$

The proof of the Proposition 2 can be found in (Smith, 1998).

In order to illustrate the properties of C, let us look at the following examples.

Example 8. Let us consider a bond with nominal value $N = 100$ which pays out annual coupons at a coupon rate $i= 0.06$ with 10 years to maturity. Suppose that annual discount rate is $k = 0.05$. We analyse the convexity as a function of time to maturity n which varies from 0 to 50 years. Figure 12 shows the graph of $C(n)r^2$ and $n(n+1)$ as a functions of n. It is obvious that $C(n)r^2$ increases as time to maturity increases, *ceteris paribus*, and at an increasing rate, but is never greater than $n(n+1)$.

Figure 12. The relationship of $C(n)\cdot r^2$ and $n(n+1)$ as functions of time to maturity (Example 8) Source: Authors.

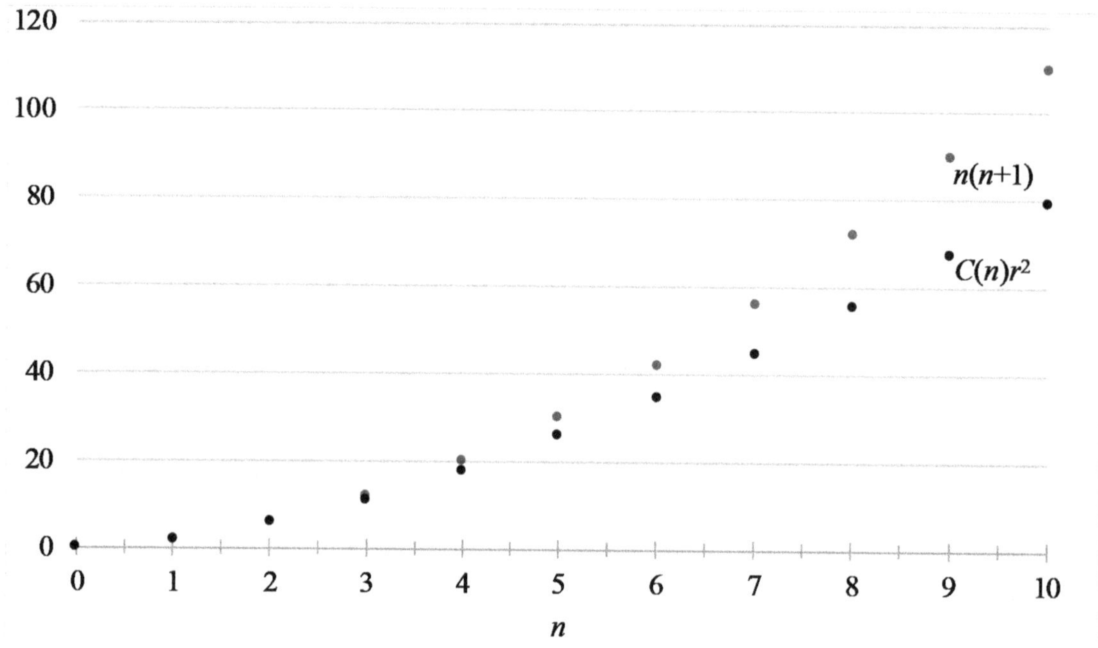

Example 9. Let us consider a bond with nominal value $N = 100$ which pays out annual coupons at a coupon rate i with remaining 10 years to maturity. Suppose that annual discount rate is $k = 0.05$. We analyse the convexity as a function of coupon rate i which varies from 0 to 100%. Figure 13 shows a graph of $C(i)$. It is obvious that $C(i)$ is a monotonically decreasing function, i.e. convexity decreases as coupon rate increases, *ceteris paribus*, and at an increasing rate.

Figure 13. The shape of the convexity as a function of coupon rate (Example 9) Source: Authors.

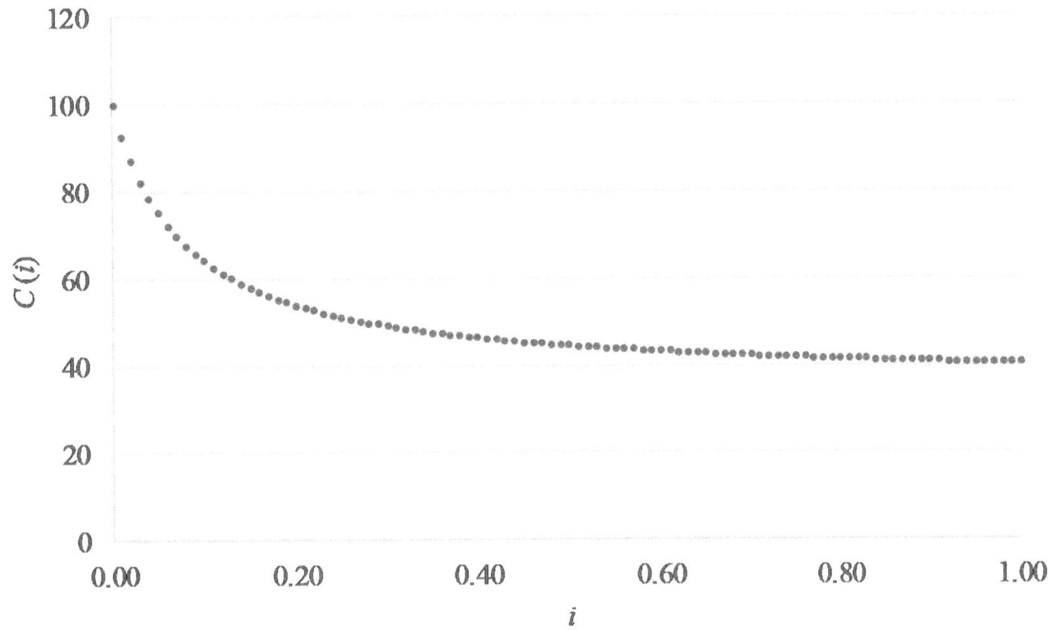

Example 10. Let us consider a bond with nominal value $N = 100$ which pays out annual coupons at a coupon rate $i = 0.05$ with remaining 10 years to maturity. Suppose that annual discount rate is k. We analyse the convexity as a function of discount rate k which varies from 0 to 100%. Figure 14 shows a graph of $C(k)$. It is obvious that $C(k)$ is a monotonically decreasing function, therefore convexity decreases as discount rate increases, *ceteris paribus*. and at an increasing rate.

Figure 14. The shape of convexity as a function of a discount rate (Example 10) Source: Authors.

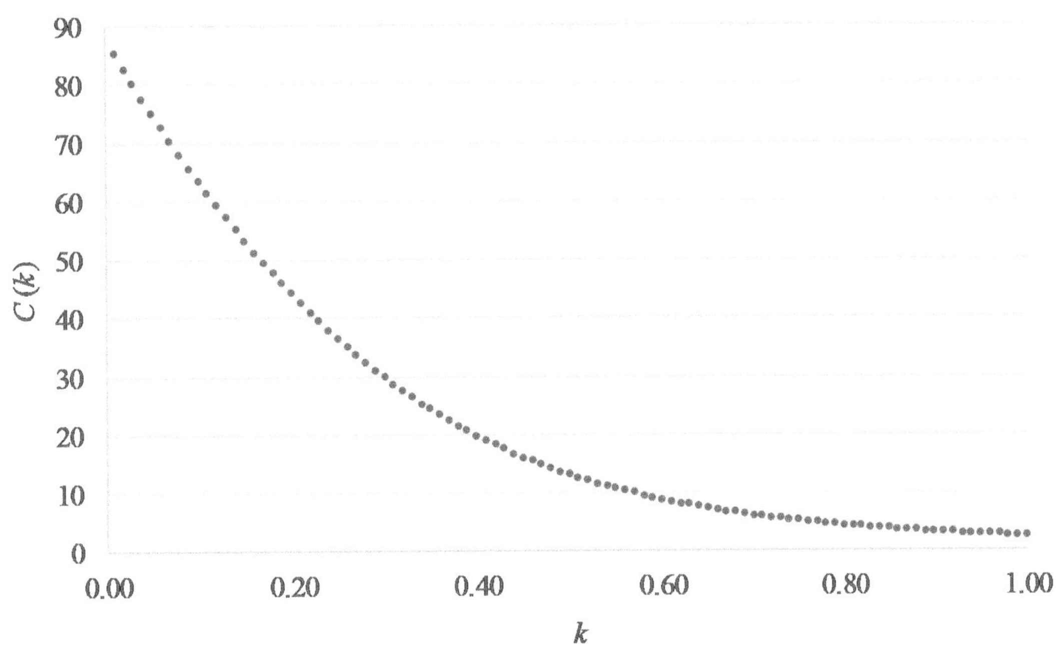

Example 11. Let us consider a bond with nominal value $N = 100$ which pays out annual coupons at a coupon rate i and the annual discount rate is $k = 0.05$. Following (21), $L_C = 800$. We want to analyse the convexity as a function of time to maturity $D(n)$ at different values of coupon rates. Suppose that coupon rates could be $i_1 = 0.02$, $i_2 = 0.10$, and $i_3 = 0.20$ and time to maturity n varies from 0 to 100. We analyse the convexity as a function of time to maturity n at different coupon rates. Graphs of L_c, $C(n, i_1)$, $C(n, i_2)$, and $C(n, i_3)$ are shown in Figure 15. It is obvious that $C(n, i_1 = 0.02)$ first increases and after that decreases and asymptotically approaches to the limit value $L_c = 800$ because $i_1 = 0.02 < k = 0.05$. On the other hand, $i_2 = 0.10$ and $i_3 = 0.20$ are greater than $k = 0.05$, therefore we observe that functions $C(n, i_2 = 0.10)$ and $C(n, i_3 = 0.20)$ are increasing functions of n with maximal asymptotical value $L_C = 800$.

Figure 15. The shape of convexity as a function of time to maturity n for fixed coupon rates $i_1 = 0.02 < k$, $i_2 = 0.10 > k$, $i_3 = 0.20 > k$ (Example 11) Source: Authors.

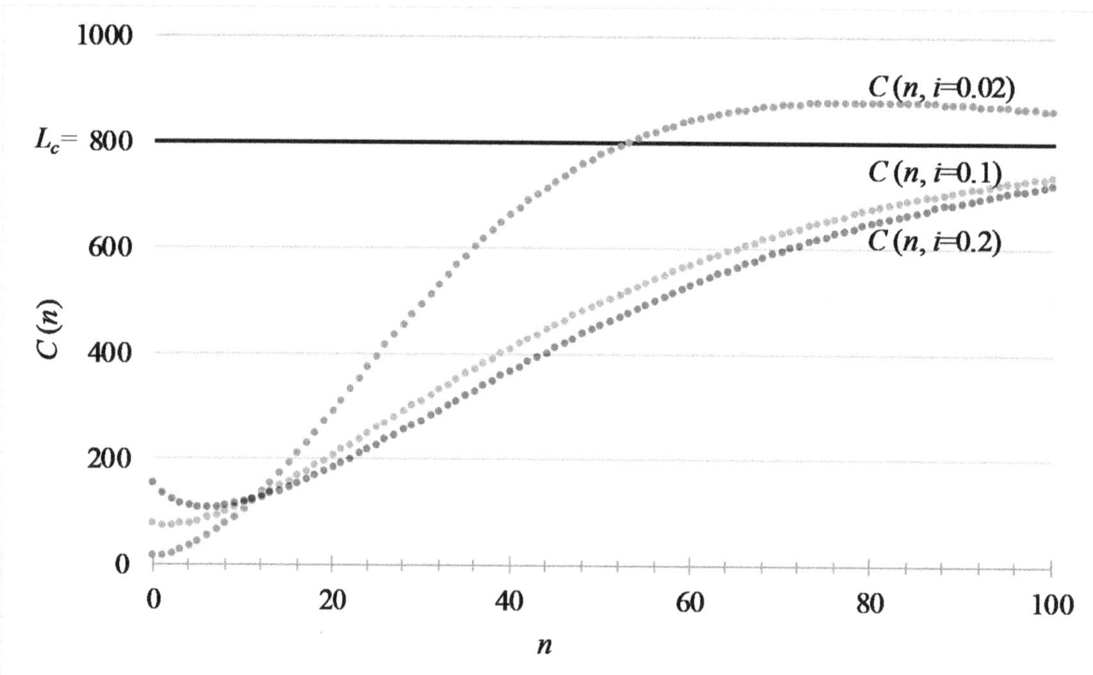

The next theorem states the general properties of C.

Theorem 3. Properties of C with respect to change of its variables are as follows:

(a) Value of convexity is always positive.
(b) If we consider convexity $C(n)$ as a function of maturity n, then the following inequality holds: $1 \leq (1+k)^2 C(n) \leq n(n+1)$.
(c) Function $C = C(i)$ is monotonically decreasing ceteris paribus, i.e. for any two coupon-rates such that $i_1 \leq i_2$ inequality $C(i_1) \geq C(i_2)$ holds.

(d) Function $C = C(k)$ is monotonically decreasing ceteris paribus, i.e. for any two yields to maturity such that $k_1 \le k_2$ inequality $C(k_1) \ge C(k_2)$ holds.

(e) The limit of function $C = C(n)$ when n approaches infinity is equal to the value $L_C = \lim_{n \to +\infty} C(n) = \frac{2}{k^2}$.

Furthermore, if $i \ge k$, then function $C(n)$ is increasing with maximal asymptotical value L_C. However, if $0 < i < k$, the shape of the convexity function $C(n)$ is similar to the shape of the duration function $D(n)$: at first the convexity function increases until it reaches its maximum and after that it decreases and asymptotically approaches the limit value L_C.

Proof of Theorem 3.

(a) The positivity of convexity for any (positive) value of k, i and n follows directly from the definition of convexity (36).

(b) Using relations (36) and (1), we obtain the following inequality:

$$\begin{aligned} C(n) &= \frac{1}{P(n)r^2}\left(\sum_{t=1}^{n} \underbrace{t(t+1)}_{\le n(n+1)} \cdot \frac{iN}{r^t} + n(n+1) \cdot \frac{N}{r^n}\right) \\ &\le \frac{1}{P(n)r^2}\left(\sum_{t=1}^{n} n(n+1) \cdot \frac{iN}{r^t} + n(n+1) \cdot \frac{N}{r^n}\right) = \frac{n(n+1)}{P(n)r^2}\underbrace{\left(\sum_{t=1}^{n}\frac{iN}{r^t} + \frac{N}{r^n}\right)}_{=P(n)} = \frac{n(n+1)}{r^2}. \end{aligned} \tag{38}$$

From (38) we have $r^2C(n) \le n(n+1)$. On the other hand,

$$C(n) = \frac{1}{P(n)r^2}\left(\sum_{t=1}^{n} \underbrace{t(t+1)}_{\ge 1} \cdot \frac{iN}{r^t} + \underbrace{n(n+1)}_{\ge 1} \cdot \frac{N}{r^n}\right) \ge \frac{1}{P(n)r^2} P(n) \tag{39}$$

and therefore the inequality $r^2C(n) \ge 1$ follows.

(c) Let i be a given coupon-rate expressed as a percentage and let $\delta > 0$ be a positive real number. Let $C(i)$ denote convexity and let $P(i)$ denote the bond's price as functions of coupon-rate i, ceteris paribus. Then

$$P(i+\delta) = \sum_{t=1}^{n} \frac{(i+\delta)N}{r^t} + \frac{N}{r^n} \tag{40}$$

and

$$C(i+\delta)=\frac{1}{r^2P(i+\delta)}\left[\sum_{t=1}^{n}t(t+1)\frac{(i+\delta)N}{r^t}+\frac{n(n+1)N}{r^n}\right] \tag{41}$$

Next we consider the difference $C(i+\delta)-C(i)$:

$$C(i+\delta)-C(i)=\frac{1}{r^2P(i+\delta)}\left[\sum_{t=1}^{n}t(t+1)\frac{(i+\delta)N}{r^t}+\frac{n(n+1)N}{r^n}\right]-\frac{1}{r^2P(i)}\left[\sum_{t=1}^{n}t(t+1)\frac{iN}{r^t}+\frac{n(n+1)N}{r^n}\right]$$
$$=\frac{1}{r^2P(i+\delta)P(i)}\left\{\left[\sum_{t=1}^{n}t(t+1)\frac{(i+\delta)N}{r^t}+\frac{n(n+1)N}{r^n}\right]P(i)-\left[\sum_{t=1}^{n}t(t+1)\frac{iN}{r^t}+\frac{n(n+1)N}{r^n}\right]P(i+\delta)\right\}.$$

By putting the expressions for bond's prices $P(i)$ and $P(i+\delta)$ into the braces of the previous expression and after some rearranging, we obtain

$$C(i+\delta)-C(i)=\frac{1}{r^2P(i+\delta)P(i)}\cdot\frac{\delta N}{r^n}\left(\sum_{t=1}^{n}\left[t(t+1)-n(n+1)\right]\frac{N}{r^t}\right).$$

Since δ, N, r^n and $P(i+\delta)P(i)$ are always positive, and since $t(t+1)-n(n+1)\leq 0$ for all $t = 1, 2, \ldots, n$, it follows that $C(i+\delta) \leq C(i)$, which proves claim (c).

(d) Let $\delta > 0$. In order to prove the claim, it suffices to show that if yield to maturity k increases to the level $k+r$, then inequality $C(k+r)<C(k)$ holds.

Let us first show that inequality

$$C(k+\delta) < C(k) \tag{42}$$

holds. By using (37), from (42) we obtain the equivalent inequality

$$\frac{r^2}{(r+\delta)^2}P(k)\left(\sum_{t=1}^{n}t(t+1)\frac{iN}{(r+\delta)^t}+n(n+1)\frac{N}{(r+\delta)^n}\right)\leq P(k+\delta)\left(\sum_{t=1}^{n}t(t+1)\frac{iN}{r^t}+n(n+1)\frac{N}{r^n}\right)$$

Since $\frac{r^2}{(r+\delta)^2}<1$, we have

$$\frac{r^2}{(r+\delta)^2}P(k)\left(\sum_{t=1}^{n}t(t+1)\frac{iN}{(r+\delta)^t}+n(n+1)\frac{N}{(r+\delta)^n}\right)<P(k)\left(\sum_{t=1}^{n}t(t+1)\frac{iN}{(r+\delta)^t}+n(n+1)\frac{N}{(r+\delta)^n}\right). \tag{43}$$

Therefore, in order to prove (42), it is enough to show that inequality (44) holds:

$$P(k)\left(\sum_{t=1}^{n} t(t+1)\frac{iN}{(r+\delta)^t}+n(n+1)\frac{N}{(r+\delta)^n}\right)\le P(k+\delta)\left(\sum_{t=1}^{n} t(t+1)\frac{iN}{r^t}+n(n+1)\frac{N}{r^n}\right) \quad (44)$$

Let $\alpha=\frac{r}{r+\delta}$, $K_t=\frac{iN}{r^t}$, $M=\frac{N}{r^n}$. Note that $0<\alpha<1$. The inequality (44) is equivalent to the sequence of the following inequalities:

$$\left(\sum_{t=1}^{n}K_t+M\right)\left(\sum_{t=1}^{n}t(t+1)K_t\alpha^t+n(n+1)M\alpha^n\right)\le\left(\sum_{t=1}^{n}K_t\alpha^t+M\alpha^n\right)\left(\sum_{t=1}^{n}t(t+1)K_t+n(n+1)M\right),$$

$$\left(\sum_{t=1}^{n}K_t\right)\left(\sum_{t=1}^{n}t(t+1)K_t\alpha^t\right)+M\left(\sum_{t=1}^{n}t(t+1)K_t\alpha^t\right)+n(n+1)M\alpha^n\left(\sum_{t=1}^{n}K_t\right)$$
$$\le\left(\sum_{t=1}^{n}K_t\alpha^t\right)\left(\sum_{t=1}^{n}t(t+1)K_t\right)+M\alpha^n\left(\sum_{t=1}^{n}t(t+1)K_t\right)+n(n+1)M\left(\sum_{t=1}^{n}K_t\alpha^t\right),$$

$$\sum_{t=1}^{n}t(t+1)K_t^2\alpha^t+\sum_{j=1}^{n-1}\sum_{k=j+1}^{n}\left(j(j+1)\alpha^j+k(k+1)\alpha^k\right)K_jK_k+M\sum_{t=1}^{n}t(t+1)K_t\alpha^t+n(n+1)M\alpha^n\sum_{t=1}^{n}K_t$$
$$\le\sum_{t=1}^{n}t(t+1)K_t^2\alpha^t+\sum_{j=1}^{n-1}\sum_{k=j+1}^{n}\left(k(k+1)\alpha^j+j(j+1)\alpha^k\right)K_jK_k+M\alpha^n\sum_{t=1}^{n}t(t+1)K_t+n(n+1)M\sum_{t=1}^{n}K_t\alpha^t.$$

If we put all the terms in the last inequality to the left hand side, we obtain the equivalent inequality (45):

$$\sum_{j=1}^{n-1}\sum_{k=j+1}^{n}\left(j^2+j-k^2-k\right)\left(\alpha^j-\alpha^k\right)K_jK_k+M\sum_{t=1}^{n}\left[t(t+1)-n(n+1)\right]\left(\alpha^t-\alpha^n\right)K_t\le 0 \quad (45)$$

Since $0<\alpha<1$ and $j<k$, we have $\alpha^j-\alpha^k>0$. Furthermore, $t\le n$ implies $\alpha^t-\alpha^n\ge 0$, so we have $(j^2+j-k^2-k)(\alpha^j-\alpha^k)\le 0$ and $[t(t+1)-n(n+1)](\alpha^t-\alpha^n)\le 0$. Thus, as inequality (45) is true, so is inequality (42). This proves claim (d) of the theorem.

(e) (e) In the process of computing limit L_C we will use the well-known expression for the limit $\lim_{n\to+\infty}\frac{n^p}{a^n}=0$ (see Zorich, 2004), where n and p are natural numbers and a is the real number such that $a>1$. From (37) it follows that

$$\lim_{n\to+\infty} C(n) = \lim_{n\to+\infty} \frac{2i(1+k)^2\left(1-\frac{1+k+kn}{(1+k)^{n+1}}\right)+\frac{n(n+1)k^2(k-i)}{(1+k)^n}}{k^2(1+k)^2\left[i\left(1-\frac{1}{(1+k)^n}\right)+\frac{k}{(1+k)^n}\right]} = \frac{2}{k^2}.$$

Furthermore, we want to determine the sign of the difference $C(n+1)-C(n)$. On one hand we have

$$P(n+1)C(n+1)-P(n)C(n)=\frac{1}{(1+k)^2}\left(\frac{(n+1)(n+2)iN}{(1+k)^{n+1}}+\frac{(n+1)(n+2)N}{(1+k)^{n+1}}-\frac{n(n+1)N}{(1+k)^n}\right). \tag{46}$$

On the other hand,

$$\begin{aligned}&P(n+1)C(n+1)-P(n)C(n)\\&=\left[C(n+1)-C(n)\right]P(n)+\left(-\frac{N}{(1+k)^n}+\frac{iN}{(1+k)^{n+1}}+\frac{N}{(1+k)^{n+1}}\right)C(n+1).\end{aligned} \tag{47}$$

By equating (46) and (47), and after some rearranging, we obtain the relation

$$\begin{aligned}P(n)\left[C(n+1)-C(n)\right]&=\frac{2N\left[n+1+(1+k)C(n+1)\right]}{(1+k)^{n+2}}\\&+\frac{N}{(1+k)^{n+3}}\left((n+1)(n+2)-(1+k)^2C(n+1)\right)(i-k).\end{aligned} \tag{48}$$

Since $P(n) > 0$, from (48) it follows that the sign of the difference $C(n+1)-C(n)$ is positive if and only if the right hand side of the equality (48) is positive. In the same manner, the sign of the difference $C(n+1)-C(n)$ is negative if and only if the right hand side of the equality (48) is negative.

We have to consider two cases: $i \geq k$ and $i < k$. Let us first consider the case $i \geq k$. Since claim (b) of this theorem implies that $(1+k)^2C(n+1) \leq (n+1)(n+2)$, we have

$$P(n)\left[C(n+1)-C(n)\right] \geq \frac{2N\left[n+1+(1+k)C(n+1)\right]}{(1+k)^{n+2}} > 0 \tag{49}$$

Thus in this case $C(n)$ is an increasing function with maximal asymptotic value L_C.

Let us now consider the second case, that is $i < k$, or $k–i > 0$. First we will show that in this case there exists a positive integer n_0 such that for all positive integers $n>n_0$ the right hand side of the equality (48) is less than 0. Note that inequality (50):

$$\frac{2N\left[n+1+(1+k)C(n+1)\right]}{(1+k)^{n+2}}+\frac{N}{(1+k)^{n+3}}\left((n+1)(n+2)-(1+k)^2C(n+1)\right)(i-k)<0 \tag{50}$$

is equivalent to inequality (51):

$$(2+2k+k-i)(1+k)C(n+1)<(n+1)\left[n(k-i)-2i-2\right] \tag{51}$$

Since $C(n+1)$ approaches the limit L_C as n approaches infinity, we know that for a given $\varepsilon>0$ there exists a positive integer n_0 with the property that the inequalities $-\varepsilon-L_C<C(n+1)<L_C+\varepsilon$ hold for all positive integers n such that $n>n_0$. In order to prove inequality (51), let us first prove the following equivalent but stronger inequality (52):

$$\left(2+2k+\underbrace{k-i}_{>0}\right)(1+k)(\varepsilon+L_C)<(n+1)\left[n\underbrace{(k-i)}_{>0}-2i-2\right] \tag{52}$$

According to the Archimedes' Axiom, there exists a natural number n_1 such that for all natural numbers $n > n_1$ the inequality $n(k–i)\geq2(i+1)$ holds. Also, according to the Archimedes' Axiom, there exists a natural number $n_2 > n_1$ such that inequality (52) holds for all natural numbers $n \geq n_2$. Therefore, (52) holds for all $n \geq n_2$, which means that also the inequality (51) holds for all $n \geq n_2$. In other words, the expression on the right hand side of the relation (48) is negative for all $n \geq n_2$, which means that after the n_2^{th} term $C(n)$ becomes a decreasing function. Furthermore, as n approaches infinity, $C(n)$ approaches the limit L_C. Let n_{min} be the smallest natural number for which the inequality $C(n+1)<C(n)$ holds. Since n_{min} is the smallest number with such property, it means that the inequality $C(n_{min}-1)\leq C(n_{min})$ should hold as well. Otherwise we would have a contradiction with the definition of the number n_{min}. Therefore, inequalities (53) should hold:

$$C(n_{min}-1)\leq C(n_{min})\geq C(n_{min}+1) \tag{53}$$

In other words, from (53) we conclude that function $C(n)$ reaches a local maximum in point n_{min} and the value of that local maximum is $C(n_{min})$. Let us now show that this is the only extreme of function $C(n)$. In order to do so, we consider the following equation in n:

$$C(n+1) - C(n) = 0. \tag{54}$$

Let

$$l_C(n) = \underbrace{-ik^3(k-i)n^2}_{<0}$$
$$+\left(2i^2(1+k)k^2 + ik^2(k-i)(2-k)\right)n + 2i^2(1+k)k^2 + 2ik^2(k-i) + 2i(1+k)^2(k-i)k\ ,$$

and let $d_C(n) = \frac{(i-k)^2}{(1+k)^n}$. Using the closed form (37), it is easy to show that the equation (54) is equivalent to the equation (55):

$$l_C(n) = d_C(n). \tag{55}$$

Note that $d_C(0) = 2i(k-i)(1+k)k > 0$ and

$$l_C(0) = 2i^2(1+k)k^2 + 2ik^2\underbrace{(k-i)}_{>0} + \underbrace{2i(1+k)^2(k-i)k}_{>d(0)} > d(0)$$

Given the fact that $n \geq 0$, that the graph of the function $l_C(n)$ is a parabola which opens down and that $d_C(n)$ is a strictly decreasing exponential function, the graphs of the functions $l_C(n)$ and $d_C(n)$ intersect at most in one point (see Figure 16).

Figure 16. Graphs of functions $l_C(n)$ and $d_C(n)$ Source: Authors.

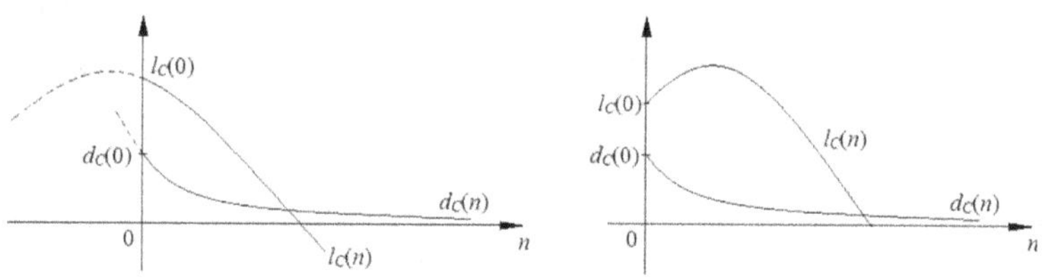

This shows that $n_{\min}$ is the only extreme of the function $C(n)$. From the formula (37) we have

$$C(1) = \frac{2}{(1+k)^2} < \frac{2}{(1+k)^2}\left(1 + \frac{3i+2}{ik+i+1}\right) = C(2) \tag{56}$$

and $C(1) < \frac{2}{k^2} = L_C$, which means that indeed the function $C(n)$ first increases, then reaches its maximum which is necessarily greater than L_C, and after that begins do decrease and asymptotically approaches the limit value L_C. Figure 17 depicts the shape of the convexity function $C=C(n)$ as a function of maturity n, where n is considered as a continuous variable **Q.E.D.**

Figure 17. The shape of the convexity function C=C(n) as a function of maturity n Source: Authors.

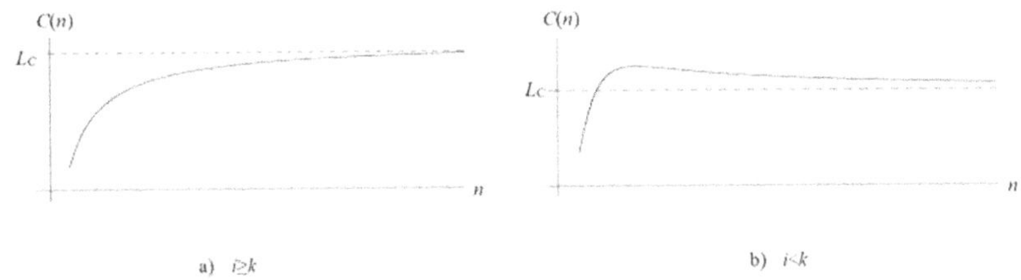

CONCLUSION

In this chapter we have analyzed the properties of coupon bond price, duration and convexity without using calculus. These results are already well-known in the literature, however here we have proved the properties by using only elementary algebra and finite sums. This is important because in real life these functions are not even continuous, not to mention differentiable. As a matter of fact, whenever in practice we deal with coupon bond price, duration and convexity, we deal with sequences, meaning that in a strict sense calculus does not apply. However, the proofs we have presented here do not require functions to be continuous, not to mention differentiable. Given the simplicity of the tools we have used to analyse the coupon bond price, duration and convexity, it is enough to consider these functions as sequences of real numbers. This makes elementary algebra manipulations and finite sums appropriate tools for analysing properties in question. Therefore, the contribution of this chapter is reflected in the presentation of the new non-calculus proofs of coupon bond convexity properties. In this way we have not only treated the problem in a way appropriate for treating non-differentiable functions, but we have also avoided non trivial terms which might appear in the process of applying techniques of calculus. Furthermore, this non-calculus analysis has also provided some additional insight into the nature of the problem. We hope that this non calculus approach might help many of those who are not necessary familiar with tools of mathematical analysis.

REFERENCES

Aljinović, Z., Marasović, B., & Šego, B. (2011). *Financial Modelling*. Faculty of Economics, Business and Tourism.

Choudhry, M. (2001). *Bond and Money Markets: Strategy, Trading, Analysis*. Butterworth-Heinemann.

Fabozzi, F. J. (2006). *Bond Markets, Analysis and Strategies*. Prentice Hall Inc.

Fabozzi, F. J. (2007). *Fixed income analysis*. John Wiley & Sons Inc.

Fabozzi, F. J., & Mann, S. V. (2010). *Introduction to Fixed Income Analytics Relative Value Analysis, Risk Measures and Valuation*. John Wiley & Sons, Inc. doi:10.1002/9781118266649

Fabozzi, F. J., & Mann, S. V. (2012). *The Handbook of Fixed Income Securities*. McGraw-Hill.

Gardijan, M., Kojić, V., & Šego, B. (2012). Bond Duration: Propositions and Applications. In Z. Aljinović & B. Marasović (Eds.), *Mathematical models in analysis of the Croatian financial market* (pp. 5–26). University of Split: Faculty of Economics.

Hawawini, G. (1984). On the relationship between Macaulay's Bond Duration and the Term to Maturity. *Economics Letters*, *16*(3-4), 331–337. doi:10.1016/0165-1765(84)90185-X

Hawawini, G. A. (1982). On the Mathematics of Macaulay's Duration. In G. A. Hawawini (Ed.), *Bond Duration and Immunization: Early Developments and Recent Contributions*. Retrieved from https://flora.insead.edu/fichiersti_wp/inseadwp1982/82-03.pdf

Kojić, V., & Lukač, Z. (2015). A non-calculus Analysis of Macaulay's Coupon Bond Duration Properties. In *Proceedings of the 3rd International Symposium on Economics and Social Sciences* (pp. 156-168). Tokyo, Japan: International Business Academics Consortium (iBAC).

Kojić, V., & Lukač, Z. (2017). Technical Note: The Shape of the Macaulay's Duration as the Function of Coupon Bond Maturity Derived Without Derivatives. In *Proceedings of the 14th International Symposium on Operational Research SOR'17* (pp. 332-337). Ljubljana: Slovenian Society Informatika - Section for Operational Research.

La Grandville, O. (2000). *Bond pricing and portfolio analysis*. MIT Press.

La Grandville, O. (2001). *Bond pricing and portfolio analysis: protecting investors in the long run*. Massachusetts Institute of Technology.

Lawrence, E. R., & Shankar, S. (2007). A Simple and Student-friendly Approach to the mathematics of bond prices. *Quarterly Journal of Business & Economics*, *46*(4), 91–99. https://datapro.fiu.edu/campusedge/files/articles/lawrencee1115123823 20.pdf

Malkiel, B. (1962). Expectations, Bond Prices and the Term Structure of Interest Rates. *The Quarterly Journal of Economics*, *76*(2), 197–218. doi:10.2307/1880816

Orsag, S. (2011). *Securities, Investments and Financing Instruments*. Revicon.

Pianca, P. (2005). *Maximum Duration of Below Par Bonds: A Closed–form Formula*. doi:10.2139srn.738445

Šego, B., & Škrinjarić, T. (2014). Bond Convexity Properties. *Proceedings of the Faculty of Economics and Business in Zagreb*, *12*(2), 65–73.

Smith, D. J. (1998). A Note on the Derivation of Closed-Form Formulas for Duration and Convexity Statistics On and Between Coupon Dates. *Journal of Financial Engineering*, *7*(2).

Zipf, R. (2003). *Fixed Income Mathematics*. Academic Press.

Zorich, V. A. (2004). *Mathematical Analysis I*. Springer-Verlag.

KEY TERMS AND DEFINITIONS

Archimedes: Archimedes of Syracuse (287-221 BC) is considered as the greatest mathematician of antiquity and one of the greatest of all time. He was not Greek mathematician only, but also physicist, inventor and astronomer. Archimedes anticipated modern calculus and analysis by applying concepts of infinitesimals and the method of exhaustion to derive and prove a range of geometrical theorems, including the area of a circle, the surface area and volume of a sphere, and the area under a parabola. Famous mathematician Leibniz, one of the founders of differential calculus, said "When you study the works of Archimedes, you cease to be amazed by the achievements of modern mathematicians."

Bond: Any interest-bearing or discounted government or corporate security that obligates the issuer to pay the bondholder a specified sum of money, usually at specific intervals, and to repay the principal amount of the loan at maturity.

Calculus: Originally called "infinitesimal calculus" or "the calculus of infinitesimals", is the mathematical study of continuous change. Calculus is invented by mathematicians Newton and Leibnitz. It has two major branches: differential calculus which concerns instantaneous rates of change, and integral calculus which concerns accumulation of quantities.

Convexity: Mathematical concept that measures sensitivity of the market price of an interest-bearing bond to changes in interest rate levels. It is a measure of the curvature, or the degree of the curve, in the relationship between bond prices and bond yields.

Coupon Bond: Bond issued with detachable coupons that must be presented to a paying agent or the issuer for (semi)annual interest payment. These are bearer bonds, so whoever presents the coupon is entitled to the interest.

Duration: Concept first developed by Frederick Macaulay in 1938 that measures bond price volatility by measuring the "length" of a bond. It is a weighted-average term-to-maturity of the bond's cash flows, the weights being the present value of each cash flow as a percentage of the bond's full price.

Elementary Algebra: A part of algebra, one of the main branches of mathematics. Unlike abstract algebra which deals with general algebraic structures, elementary algebra operates with quantities without fixed values known as real variables.

Finite Sums: Unlike infinite sums (series) which can converge or diverge, the finite sum is the sum of finite number of terms or numbers (the result of the finite sum of numbers is always a number).

Geometric Sequence: Also known as geometric progression, is a sequence of numbers where each term after the first is found by multiplying the previous one by a fixed non-zero number called the common ration.

Chapter 17
Selected Applications of Grey Models in Stock Price Prediction

Tihana Škrinjarić
https://orcid.org/0000-0002-9310-6853
Faculty of Economics and Business, University of Zagreb, Croatia

Mirjana Čižmešija
https://orcid.org/0000-0002-9873-7291
Faculty of Economics and Business, University of Zagreb, Croatia

ABSTRACT

This chapter examines the possibilities of utilizing the results of Grey Models (GM) in the portfolio selection. Namely, stock price prediction represents one of the most important steps in the portfolio management. Many different models and methods have been developed for this purpose over the decades. The GM models could be utilized for such purpose. However, this approach is still relatively unknown today although research in the Far East has shown that applications of GM approach have good forecasting capabilities. That is why this chapter aims to popularize the GM approach of modeling stock prices and to combine the estimation results with the portfolio performance measurement. The benefits of using GM models within the portfolio management are empirically confirmed using daily data on the stock market index CROBEX from Zagreb Stock Exchange during the period from September 2, 2019, until February 7, 2020. The GM(2,1) model is the best performing one with respect to out of sample forecasts and based on portfolio performance measures important to the investor.

INTRODUCTION

Portfolio management represents a process of managing money (Fabozzi and Pachamanova, 2016), in which several issues and steps need to be defined. These include defining the investor's preferences, goals and limitations; knowing to evaluate financial products and market conditions; constructing the investment portfolio and a trading strategy which will ensure the achievement of the mentioned goals; and finally, evaluation of the performance of such investment strategies (Fabozzi and Markowitz, 2011).

DOI: 10.4018/978-1-7998-5083-0.ch017

It is obvious that knowledge in many different fields is needed so that successful portfolio management can be conducted over time. This is especially true when it comes to quantitative modeling. Many different mathematical and statistical models and methods have been developed over the decades in order to answer specific questions in the area of portfolio management. Since the area of quantitative finance which consists of different models, techniques and approaches has been expanding rapidly, several attempts have been made to classify and categorize them (Granger, 1989; Taylor and Allen, 1992; Ho et al. 2002; Wallis, 2011): econometric approach such as autoregressive integrated moving average, generalized autoregressive conditional heteroskedasticity (AR(I)MA-GARCH), extreme value theory (EVT), non-parametric approaches such as data envelopment analysis (DEA), multiple criteria decision model (MCDM) and other related areas within the operations research (OR), neural networks, etc. All of the approaches have their advantages and shortfalls (for discussion, please see Jo, 2003; Liu et al., 2012; Khuman et al., 2014). The majority of the methodologies are used for forecasting purposes. In order to do so, a mathematical model is needed which is used to try to make accurate predictions (Kayacan et al., 2010).

Since the interest of quantitative modeling within the portfolio management is growing, it is not surprising that the methodological approaches are evolving, combining ideas and concepts from other approaches and that relatively unknown methodologies are emerging in the literature as well. One approach which is relatively unknown compared to some usual econometric approaches of modeling stock price, return and risk is the Grey Systems Theory (GST). This theory has been in development since the 1980s in the Far East (Lin et al., 2005; Liu et al., 2016; Yin, 2013). GST consists of different models and methods which can be used in the area of decision-making under uncertainties, i.e. when the data is "grey". The term "grey" data means that not all information is available for the decision-maker, due to ambiguity, information distortion, etc. This methodology is very appropriate for portfolio management, as many problems arise here due to data uncertainty. Investors often have to make certain decisions without full data available. Although much data and information on the stock markets are available on a daily basis, there is a lot of "grey" data that needs to be modeled adequately. It is not surprising that the research interest in GST applications on stock markets has grown in the last decade. There exist both theoretical and practical papers which deal with GST models and their usefulness on the stock market (Rathnayaka et al., 2016).

Thus, the main objectives of this chapter are to give an overview of the existing research which focuses on forecasting stock prices via the GST approach and to empirically evaluate the usefulness of this approach within the portfolio management. Although the amount of literature on this topic has been growing in the last couple of years (see Delcea, 2015; Camelia, 2015a,b for a bibliometric analysis), there exist several gaps in terms of interpreting the results from the investor's point of view. Namely, in order to determine the usefulness of a model as a tool for stock price prediction, the investor has to define certain criteria. One group of criteria includes the goodness of fit measures which usually compare the forecasts from the model to the real out of sample values of the time series which is being forecasted. However, when the time series has certain economic meaning and interpretation, other aspects have to be taken into consideration. This includes the characteristics of the predicted values. If the time series is the stock price, the investor is interested if the value is going to rise or fall, compared to the current value, as this is important for the value of the portfolio and the whole trading process. This chapter is going to include such aspects of the analysis as well. That is why the contribution of this research is found in a critical overview of the previous related research, as well as in the detailed empirical research which will provide guidance for future (potential) investors on how to fully implement the GST approach within the portfolio management. The main focus of this research within the GST methodology will be the Grey Model (GM) and its extensions, which are commonly used for the purpose of prediction. Since one of the most important things within the portfolio management includes the forecasting of time series, the GM model is appropriate to consider as a tool for those purposes.

The rest of the chapter is structured as follows. The second section gives an overview of the previous related research. The third section describes the methodology used in the fourth, empirical part of the chapter. The discussion and conclusion are given in the final, fifth section.

RELATED LITERATURE REVIEW

The amount of literature within this area of research has been growing in the last decade. This section focuses on the empirical work which has applied the GM model or some variations in forecasting the movements on the stock markets. There are many technical papers that extend the basic models or combine them with other methodological approaches. Such research is focused on increasing the forecasting accuracy of the GM methodology. This is, of course, very interesting and useful. However, there is a lack of research that interprets the results from the investor's standpoint. Namely, the GM models can be applied as a tool in a dynamic portfolio rebalancing over time. Such research is lacking in the existing literature. An increasing trend is found in the number of papers that combine different methodologies with the GST models. Thus, the interest is obviously rising within this area of research.

Hsu et al. (2009) is a technical paper that combines several approaches for the purpose of increasing forecasting accuracy of stock price prediction. Authors combine GM, Fourier series, and Markov state transition into a Markov–Fourier grey model (MFGM). The resulting model has a better forecasting accuracy compared to some basic models (for the period October 1996 to August 2007 and Taiwanese stock market index). Chen et al. (2010) have applied a Nash nonlinear grey Bernoulli model (NNGBM) on the Taiwanese stock market indices for the third quarter of 2008. The authors were motivated by the fact that many stock market movements are nonlinear, which linear models cannot capture adequately. Several linear GM models have been compared to the proposed NNGBM, where the results indicated that the newer approach improved forecasting precision of stock indices' values. On the other hand, the model is more complicated and the complexity is greater compared to basic GM models. This research is also more technical in the sense that several measures of forecasting accuracy are calculated and commented on. However, there are no simulated trading strategies and their descriptions which can help the investors to apply this approach to the stock market. Other technical papers include those which solely make numerical comparisons: Ji et al. (2011) compare unbiased GM(1,1) to the modified unbiased GM(1,1) model; Liu et al. (2015) compare four GM(1,1) type models in order to comment on time series which are most suitable for each model. Other work is focused on the optimization of the model parameters (e.g. Xiao, 2000; He et al., 2005; Jie and Bo, 2012). An overview of the selected models is also found in the literature. These papers concisely describe several GM models with their basic characteristics and then empirically evaluate their forecasting accuracy. Rathnayaka et al. (2015) compare the GM(1,1), GM(2,1), Grey Verhulst and non-linear Grey Bernoulli models on the Colombo Stock Exchange, for the period October 2014 – March 2015. The first part of the paper gives an overview of each model, whereas the rest of the paper evaluates the accuracy of forecasts. No investment trading is simulated in this research.

Some research deals with GM models for risk prediction as well. Such papers incorporate the GM in the GARCH (generalized autoregressive conditional heteroskedasticity) models. Lin et al. (2005) introduced the GM approach in the GARCH models. The basic motivation was found in the error term within the GARCH model, where it represents the unexpected change due to different information available on the market, with uncertainties. The several step process was described on how to model and estimate the GM-GARCH model, with an empirical exercise at the end of the paper. The results of the analysis (period: January 3 1995 - April 18 2005, Nikei, Dow Jones, CAC 40 and FTSE indices) shown that the predictive accuracy of the variance was enhanced by including the GM modeling in the first step. Geng and Zhang (2015) extend the GARCH model by firstly modeling the error term via GM(1,1) model and the genetic algorithm. Several GARCH family models have been estimated with the inclusion of the GM approach in the first step for 3 years on the Chinese market (July 2011 – July 2014). Again, as in previous literature, authors find that the predictions from the GM based models are better compared to the traditional models. However, as previously mentioned for other sub-groups of papers, this research also focuses solely on the predictability of the models, i.e. the statistical measures, but not other relevant information which investors seek when forecasting future movements on the stock market. Duan et al. (2018) combined the Elliot Wave Theory (EWT) with GM modeling, as the EWT is popular within the technical analysis of the stock market. Authors proposed a novel approach to combining the properties of Fibonacci sequences and the background value of the GM model (please see details in the methodology description). An application was made on the Chinese market, where the results showed that such approach can be applied on the stock market for the purpose of better forecasting.

A combination of other popular methodologies with GM modeling is found in the following papers. Huang and Jane (2008) combine the Grey Relational Analysis, the ARX (autoregressive exogenous), GM and Rough Set (RS) theory to simulate trading strategies on the Taiwanese stock market (period: first quarter 2003 – first quarter 2007). What is peculiar here is that simulated strategies obtained extraordinary returns: almost 35% in one year. Thus, it is questionable why such an analysis and approach is not popular today in trading on the stock markets. The authors observed only the return characteristics of the simulated strategies. An almost identical analysis was made in Huang et al. (2008), where authors used the same data. The methodological change was the introduction of cluster analysis as well. A comparison of two models was given in Yongzhong and Hongjuan (2005), namely, the GM(1,1) and Verhlust GM models. The authors analyzed the Shanghai Composite index for the period of February 2000 – March 2004. The result of the analysis showed that the GM(1,1) model forecasts stock prices more accurately in the short run, whilst the other model was better for long-term forecasts. The accuracy of the prediction was compared in Doryab and Salehi (2017). The GM, nonlinear GM, Bernoulli GM, and Nash nonlinear GM were compared on the Teheran Stock Exchange. The authors concluded that the nonlinear GM and Bernoulli models were the most accurate in the observed period (2005-2015). Again, as in many other papers, no strategies were found in the research. Thus, potential investors did not obtain information on how to utilize the results. Škrinjarić and Šego (2019) have compared the GM(1,1) and GM(2,1) model on the Zagreb Stock Exchange not only via the forecast accuracy but also based on simulating the trading strategies as well. Several measures within financial modeling have been calculated and compared as well. In that way, investors could obtain information on how to utilize the results of the estimation procedure within portfolio management. The observed period was January – June 2019, and the GM(1,1) was found to be the best concerning out of sample forecasts and portfolio performance measurement. However, authors have simulated strategies based on the estimated parameters for the first five months of 2019 (static estimation).

As can be seen from the literature overview, although the research within this area is growing, there are still some gaps in the literature. It is not sufficient to examine only the statistical properties of the estimated models. Investors are also interested (not only in statistical point of view) in portfolio performance measurement and how to successfully implement the results of the estimated models in practice. That is why the rest of this chapter will compare several models not only by the criteria of forecasting accuracy, but also based on portfolio performance measures of simulated strategies out of sample.

METHODOLOGY DESCRIPTION

Grey Model (GM)

The description of GM models will be concisely described in this section. Interested readers can refer to Liu et al. (2006); Liu and Lin (2010) or Liu et al. (2016) for greater details. In essence, the differential calculus and differential equations are the basics within this approach. A first order differential equation with constant parameters is given in the following form:

$$\frac{dy}{dt} + ay = b, \tag{1}$$

where $\frac{dy}{dt}$ represents the derivative of function $y(t)$, which is unknown. In the literature, this function is called the background value. a and b are real numbers. If the background value is positive and consists of grey numbers, its information density is infinite (if when $\Delta t \rightarrow 0$, it is always true that $y(t+\Delta t) \neq y(t)$), and the derivative $\frac{dy}{dt}$ satisfies the horizontal mapping, a Grey differential equation can be formed as follows. The data

$$Y^{(0)} = \{y^{(0)}(1), y^{(0)}, \ldots, y^{(0)}(n)\} \text{ (2)} \tag{2}$$

represents a sequence of non-negative numbers, where it holds that $n \geq 4$. The first order accumulated generating operation (AGO) of this sequence is defined as

$$Y^{(1)} = \{y^{(1)}(1), y^{(1)}(2), \ldots, y^{(1)}(n)\}, \tag{3}$$

where it holds that:

$$y^{(1)}(k)= \sum_{i=1}^{k} y^{(0)}(i), \tag{4}$$

and $k \in \{1,2,..., n\}$. The idea of defining the AGO sequence in (3) and (4) is to reduce the randomness of the original series, i.e. to smooth it out. Furthermore, from (4) it can be concluded that the AGO sequence is monotonically increasing, which means that $y^{(1)}(k)>0$ holds, which ensures the condition of the positive value of the background value $y(t)$, as previously mentioned.

In the next step, the mean sequence $X^{(1)}$ is defined as follows:

$$X^{(1)} = \{x^{(1)}(2), x^{(1)}(3), \ldots, x^{(1)}(n)\}, \tag{5}$$

in which every element is defined as

$$x^{(1)}(k) = \frac{y^{(1)}(k) + y^{(0)}(k-1)}{2}. \tag{6}$$

Values in (5), i.e. (6) are defined so that the horizontal mapping condition can hold for the formation of Grey Model, as follows:

$$y^{(0)}(k) + ax^{(0)}(k) = b, \tag{7}$$

which is called the GM(1,1) model. The first unit value refers to the order of the differential equation in (7), and the second unit to the number of observed variables. Thus, (7) is the first order differential Grey equation in one variable. It is solved in the usual fashion of solving differential equations, with the solution given in the form:

$$y^{(0)}(k) = \left(y^{(0)}(1) - \frac{b}{a}\right)e^{-a(k-1)}(1-e^{a}). \tag{8}$$

The solution in (8) is then used to forecast values out of sample: $y^{(0)}(l)$, with $l \in \{n+1, n+2, \ldots\}$.

Another simple GM model is the GM(2,1) model which is useful for wavelike sequences behaviour. For this model, the 1-AGO sequence needs to be defined:

$$\alpha^{(1)}Y^{(0)} = \{\alpha^{(1)}y^{(0)}(1), \alpha^{(1)}y^{(0)}(2), \ldots, \alpha^{(1)}y^{(0)}(n)\}, \tag{9}$$

where every element is defined as:

$$\alpha^{(1)}y^{(0)}(k) = y^{(0)}(k) - y^{(0)}(k-1). \tag{10}$$

Now, the GM(2,1) Grey differential equation can be formed:

$$\alpha^{(1)}Y^{(0)} + a_1Y^{(0)} + a_2X^{(1)} = b. \tag{11}$$

Since this is a second order differential equation, the solution depends on the roots of the characteristic equation $r^2 + a_1r + a_2 = 0$. The solution to (11) is used for forecasting out of sample, as the solution in (8) for the GM(1,1) model.

ARIMA Models

Most commonly used models of forecasting on the stock markets are the ARIMA (autoregressive integrated moving average) and GARCH models. Since the focus of this chapter are the stock prices, the

ARIMA models will be described, which will be the benchmark for comparison purposes in the empirical section. Details can be found in Francq and Zakoian (2019), Wei (2005) and Mills (2019). If a time series y_t is stationary, the ARMA(p,q) model for describing its pattern can be defined as:

$$y_t = \mu + \sum_{i=1}^{p} \phi_i y_{t-i} + \sum_{j=1}^{q} \theta_j \varepsilon_{t-j} + \varepsilon_t , \tag{12}$$

where μ is a constant, p is the lag length of the series y, q is the lag length of the moving average process and ε_t is the error term. If the original series is integrated (i.e. non-stationary) of order 1, then the first differences are modeled in (12) instead of the original values. When the model in (12) satisfies the conditions of invertibility and stationarity, this form is used for forecasting purposes. In order to select lags p and q the usual Box-Jenkins procedure is used.

EMPIRICAL RESULTS

Data Description

In order to empirically evaluate the usefulness of GM models within the portfolio management, daily data on the stock market index CROBEX has been collected from ZSE (2020). The observed period includes 107 observations in total, ranging from September 2, 2019, until February 7, 2020. Since the GM models are useful when not much data is available, the relatively short time span does not represent

Figure 1. Stock market index CROBEX in the whole sample
Source: ZSE (2020)

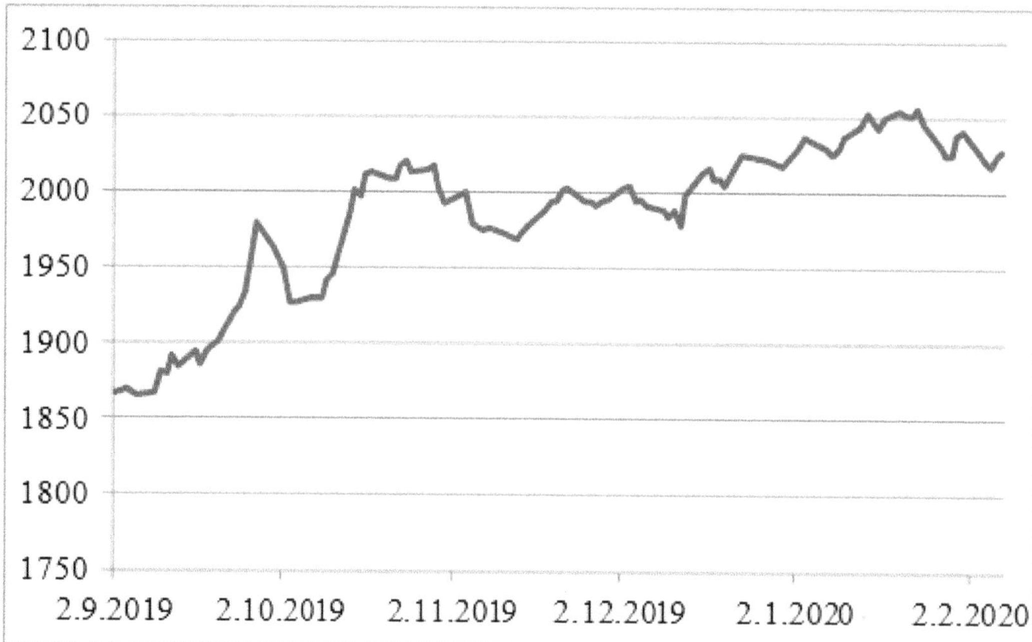

a problem. Indeed, the literature advises to use GM models for small samples, as it works better when not much data is available (please see Liu et al., 2016). Although the ARMA models perform better when the sample is greater, the time span should be the same for comparability purposes. The values of the index CROBEX are depicted in Figure 1. The whole sample will be split into two sub-samples: the first one will be used for the estimation purposes, from September 2, 2019, to January 14, 2020; and the rest of the sample will be used for out of sample forecasts and evaluation (ranging from January 15 – February 7, 2020).

The GM models ask for the positive values of the background value (as shown in the theoretical section), which means that values of the original series CROBEX will be used for purpose of estimating GM(1,1) and GM(2,1) models. However, ARMA models ask for stationary time series, thus the original series was tested for the presence of unit root. The results are given in Table 1, where it is obvious that the series CROBEX is nonstationary in levels (based on Augmented Dickey-Fuller test). Thus, the series was differenced once and the unit root test was performed once again, with results given in Table 2. Thus, an ARIMA model will be estimated in the next subsection.

Table 1. Unit root test results, CROBEX in levels

Value:	Constant and linear trend included	Constant included
Test value	-2.298 (0.4309)	-2.140 (0.2295)
Critical values	At 1%: -4.048 ; at 5%: -3.454; at 10%: -3.152	At 1%: -3.493 ; at 5%: -2.889; at 10%: -2.581

Source: Authors
Note: *p*-values are given in brackets

Table 2. Unit root test results, CROBEX in first difference

Value:	Constant and linear trend included	Constant included
Test value	-8.827 (0.000)	-8.743 (0.000)
Critical values	At 1%: -4.048 ; at 5%: -3.454; at 10%: -3.152	At 1%: -3.493 ; at 5%: -2.889; at 10%: -2.581

Source: Authors
Note: *p*-values are given in brackets

Estimation Results

Firstly, several benchmark models have been estimated for comparison purposes in the first subsample. The Box-Jenkins procedure was utilized in order to compare several ARIMA(p,d,q) models and the results are given in Table 3, where the Akaike information criterion is shown for several model specifications, where $d = 1$ (the original series was differenced once). The values in Table 3 indicate that the optimal model is the ARIMA(2,1,2). Thus, this model was the first one chosen for the benchmark.

Another model that was chosen for comparison purposes to the GM models is the sample average, as a naive approach, often used in the comparison of forecasting capabilities.

Finally, the GM(1,1) and GM(2,1) models have been estimated as well. All of the estimation results are shown in Table 4. The first part of the table refers to the estimated parameters for each model, whereas

Table 3. Values of Akaike information criteria for different values of p and q of the ARMA(p,q) model

AR / MA	0	1	2	3
0	7.422455	7.430653	7.451966	7.441800
1	7.429185	7.446927	7.468056	7.462823
2	7.461185	7.480732	**7.364559**	7.421129

Source: Authors

the last three rows compare the goodness of fit (Log L denotes the log-likelihood of the model, and AIC and SIC denote the Akaike and Schwartz information criteria respectively). It is not surprising that the average value model is the worst performing one, as it assumes that the in-sample average value will continue to hold out of sample as well. However, the best performing model is the ARIMA one, as it has the best values of Log L and the information criteria. This holds for in-sample estimation.

Table 4. Comparison of estimation results of ARIMA(2,1,2), sample average, GM(1,1) and GM(2,1) models, estimation in sample

Parameters / diagnostics	Benchmark models		Grey models	
	Sample average	ARIMA(2,1,2)	GM(1,1)	GM(2,1)
$\overline{CROBEX}$	1972.257 (5.317)***	-	-	-
$\hat{\mu}$	-	2.303 (1.426)	-	-
$\hat{\phi}_1$	-	1.354 (0.071)***	-	-
$\hat{\phi}_2$	-	-0.818 (0.085)***	-	-
$\hat{\theta}_1$	-	-1.314 (0.028)***	-	-
$\hat{\theta}_2$	-	0.968 (0.020)***	-	-
$\hat{a}$	-	-	0.0008 ($5.8\cdot10^{-5}$)***	-
$\hat{a}_1$	-	-	-	0.0008 ($5.8\cdot10^{-5}$)***
$\hat{a}_2$	-	-	-	0.427 (0.294)
$\hat{b}$	-	-	1903.999 (5.909)***	1902.690 (5.940)***
Log L	-474.2450	**-311.6760**	-409.1085	-408.0310
AIC	10.67966	**7.364559**	9.450770	9.448988
SIC	10.70762	**7.507254**	9.507458	9.534019

Source: Authors

Note: standard errors are given in brackets. *, ** and *** denote statistical significance on 10%, 5% and 1%. Bold values indicate best performance by row.

The literature emphasizes the out of sample forecasting performance as the most important criteria which should be observed. That is why in Table 5 we compare out of sample forecasting errors which are usually used in the related research. Three basic forecasting errors are calculated, as follows:

RMSE – root mean squared error, calculated as

$$RMSE = \sqrt{\frac{\sum_{t=T+1}^{T+h}\left(\hat{y}_t - y_t\right)^2}{h}},$$

where the h denotes the number of periods which are being forecasted out of sample, y_t are the true value of the time series and $\hat{y}_t$ are the forecasted values based on a model;

MAE – mean absolute error, calculated as

$$MAE = \frac{\sum_{t=T+1}^{T+h}\left|\hat{y}_t - y_t\right|}{h};$$

and

MAPE - calculated as

$$MAPE = \frac{\sum_{t=T+1}^{T+h}\frac{\left|\hat{y}_t - y_t\right|}{y_t}}{h}100\%.$$

As is seen in Table 5, the best performing model out of sample is the GM(2,1), as it has the lowest values of every error. It is followed by the GM(1,1) model. This is in accordance with previously mentioned literature which compares the GM models to standard econometric ones such as the ARMA models. This indicates that the investor can use such models in order to forecast future stock price movements in order to determine when to buy or sell stock so that the portfolio value can be obtained on a certain level over time, or even increased. However, the majority of literature stops here with the analysis, but investors seek to implement such results in practice. That is why the next subsection describes how to implement such results and compares the portfolio strategies.

Table 5. Comparison of out of sample forecasts of ARIMA(2,1,2), sample average, GM(1,1) and GM(2,1) models

Forecast accuracy measures	Benchmark models		Grey models	
	Sample average	ARIMA(2,1,2)	GM(1,1)	GM(2,1)
RMSE	53.02734	38.60732	28.89052	**27.31318**
MAE	44.92095	30.23953	22.27815	**20.46657**
MAPE	2.277996	1.506843	1.098697	**1.009190**

Source: Authors
Note: bold values indicate best performance by row

Comparison Of Simulated Strategies

This subsection deals with a comparison of the simulated trading strategies based on the forecasts of every model from the previous subsection, except for the sample average. The sample average is a too naïve strategy, which would result in no buying or selling. That is why the simulation excludes this from further analysis. The other three strategies which were included in the simulation are those based on the ARIMA model and the GM models. It is assumed that the investor invests one monetary unit in CROBEX on day T (i.e. it is assumed that the investor buys the stocks which constitute index CROBEX on day T). In the first step, the first forecasted value in the out of sample period is collected for every model. This means that in time T (last observed day in the in-sample period), investors have the first out of sample forecasted values in all three models. Then, the investor compares the true value of the CROBEX on day T to the forecasted values for T+1. If a model forecasts price increase, the investor is going to hold on to the portfolio, as he anticipates that its value will increase. If a forecasted value is lower compared to the true value of CROBEX on day T, the investor sells the entire portfolio on day T so that he has more money to buy the entire portfolio on day T+1 as he anticipates the lower value tomorrow. Such a procedure is repeated in the entire out of sample period, i.e. until the $T+h$ day (last day in the analysis, February 7, 2020). The value of every portfolio is constructed based on the true return, i.e. CROBEX value on that day. This means, that the investor is deciding on buying or selling based on the forecasted values in every model. However, true portfolio values have to be calculated based on the true values of the CROBEX index every day. In that way, the values of the simulated portfolios are comparable. After this procedure has been done for the entire out of sample period, the values of simulated portfolios have been depicted in Figure 2. Since the best out of sample forecasting abilities were found for the GM(2,1) model, it is not surprising that this portfolio obtained the best values over time. It is followed by the GM(1,1) portfolio value. Both portfolios obtained a value that was greater than the unit value at the end of the period. This means that investors could have obtained an increase in the portfolio value in the end. This is not true for the ARIMA model. Due to the decline of the CROBEX value in the observed period (see Figure 1), better values could not be obtained. Although, it could be said that in bad times (when the market is falling), GM models could provide forecasts which will enable the investor to at least save his portfolio value..

Furthermore, investors are interested in several portfolio performance measures. These were calculated for all three portfolios and are given in Table 6. All of the performance measures have been calculated for the out of sample period: average and total return as return measures, the standard deviation and Value

Figure 2. Simulated values of strategies, out of sample
Source: Authors

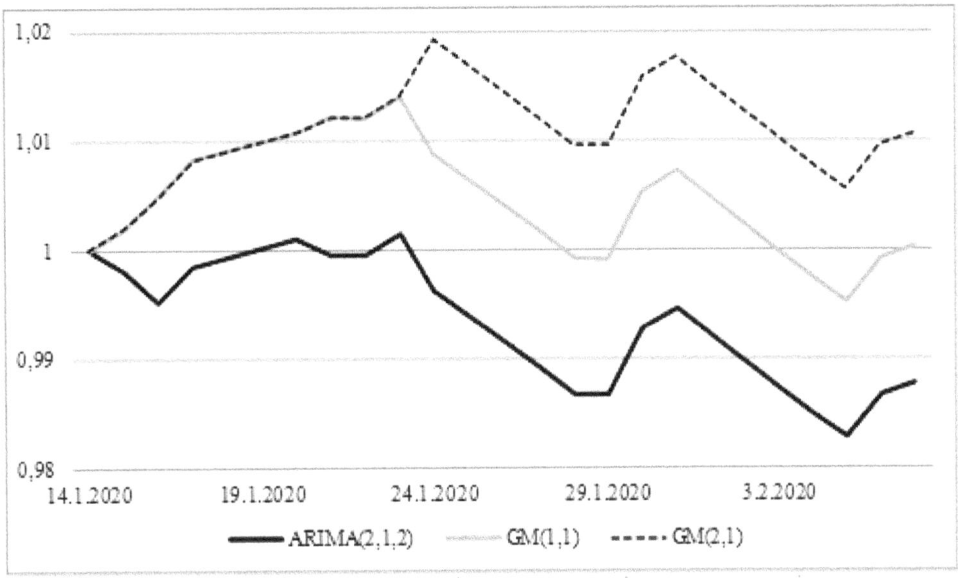

at Risk (VaR) as risk measures; and finally, the return over risk and the Certainty Equivalents (CE) as measures which take into consideration both measures at once. The VaR measure is calculated based on the assumption of the normality of the return distribution, as all return series for all three portfolios were tested via the Jarque-Bera test and were found to be normally distributed on usual levels of statistical significance (test values with respective p-values are given as follows: 0.31 and 0.86 (ARIMA); 1.19 and 0.55 GM(1,1) and 1.77 with 0.41 for GM(2,1) model). The values of CE are the values that indicate an investor's utility which is equal to the expected utility he would obtain if he accepted an uncertain gamble. The calculation of CE values depends on the portfolio expected (average) return and risk, and the risk aversion. Thus, several values of CE have been calculated, due to different risk aversion investor can be characterized with. CE is estimated as follows: CE $\approx E(\mu)-0.5\gamma\sigma^2$, where the portfolio expected return is denoted with $E(\mu)$ and the portfolio risk is the variance denoted with σ^2. The parameter γ denotes the coefficient of absolute risk aversion. Greater values of this parameter indicate that the investor is more risk averse. Details can be found in Cvitanić and Zapatero (2004); Guidolin and Timmermann (2008) and Varian (1992). Based on the majority of measures, the GM(2,1) portfolio has the best performance. Exceptions are the risk measures (standard deviation and VaR). However, if the investor considers both risk and return simultaneously, the greater risk he has to bear due to greater expected return is really compensated by return which leads to greater utility from such strategy. This shows that GM models can be very useful in the portfolio management, both in terms of risk and return.

CONCLUSION

The main aim of this chapter included familiarizing the readers with an alternative approach within the portfolio management, found in the GST approach of forecasting stock prices. The main conclusions

Table 6. Comparison of portfolio characteristics of simulated strategies

Portfolio characteristics / Portfolio	ARIMA(2,1,2)	GM(1,1)	GM(2,1)
Average return	-0.00068	0.00002	**0.00059**
Standard deviation	**0.00370**	0.00377	0.00371
Total return	-0.01221	0.00024	**0.01063**
Return/Risk	-0.18258	0.00531	**0.16003**
CE (γ =1)	-0.00253	-0.00186	**-0.00126**
CE (γ =2)	-0.00438	-0.00375	**-0.00312**
CE (γ =5)	-0.00993	-0.00940	**-0.00868**
CE (γ =10)	-0.01919	-0.01881	**-0.01796**
Value at Risk, 95%	-0.02592	**-0.02637**	-0.02598

Source: Authors
Note: bold values indicate best performance by row. CE denotes certainty equivalent.

which arise from observing such methodology are as follows. Firstly, it is a relatively simple approach compared to some more complicated econometric models which ask for specific data characteristics and are much parameterized. Secondly, the forecasts from GM models can be easily implemented in portfolio management. This was shown in the latter part of the empirical analysis. The investor needs to define his goals in order to fully exploit such results. Although more papers are found in the last couple of years that deal with similar topics as does this chapter, the majority of the research focuses either on numerical examples or solely on the goodness of fit measures that give only partial information to the investors.

This research extended the existing papers by including the portfolio performance measures which are important to the investor. These include both risk and return measures. Based on the obtained results, investors are advised to consider the GM models in forecasting future price movement on the stock market. When the investor decides on his goals, he can utilize the forecasted values from GM models in order to make decisions on when to buy or sell a stock. If the model predicts that the buying signal is greater than the selling one, the investor could obtain positive returns, i.e. profits. A similar conclusion could arise if the model predicts that the future price is going to be such that it is better to sell today. In that way, the investor could do short selling and make profits in such cases as well. This study shows that different approaches of modeling can be utilized in the portfolio selection procedure. Since a dynamic analysis is a must due to turbulent changes on the stock markets, the GM models could enhance the whole process of stock selection. Furthermore, since this methodology can be applied on daily and weekly frequencies, GM models could be more useful for speculative behavior. However, trading costs should be taken into consideration. For a longer time horizons, the fundamental based investors could use such models in order to forecast price and financial ratio movements in the long run. This could be helpful to obtain a fundamental analysis of financial ratios *apriori* and make investment decisions in that way.

The shortfalls of the study are as follows. Two simple models have been examined: the GM(1,1) and GM(2,1). Other models have been developed over time, with studies combining other methodological approaches from other areas of mathematics and statistics with the GM models. Thus, future work should examine the portfolio management possibilities for such new approaches. Some of them could include the Grey-Fuzzy models (Wang, 2002); Grey-Fourier (Hsu, 2003); Grey-Taguchi (Yao and Chi, 2004), etc. Furthermore, this study was an exercise on the stock market portfolio as a whole (the stock market index). Investors need to balance out their portfolios based on many different stocks over time. Thus, future work needs to consider strategies and how to construct them based on evaluating many GM models and their characteristics. This will bring such analysis closer to the real-life investment problems. There are many interesting questions that are still unanswered within this methodology and applications in portfolio management. That is why future work will tackle some of these problems as well.

REFERENCES

Camelia, D. (2015a). Grey systems theory in economics – bibliometric analysis and applications' overview. *Grey Systems Theory and Application*, *5*(2), 244–262.

Camelia, D. (2015b). Grey systems theory in economics – a historical applications review. Grey Systems Theory and Application, 5(2), 263–276. doi:10.1108/GS-05-2015-0018

Chen, C. I., Hsin, P. H., & Wu, C. S. (2010). Forecasting Taiwan's major stock indices by the Nash nonlinear grey Bernoulli model. *Expert Systems with Applications*, *37*(12), 7557–7562. doi:10.1016/j.eswa.2010.04.088

Cvitanić, J., & Zapatero, F. (2004). *Introduction to the Economics and Mathematics of Financial Markets*. MIT Press.

Delcea, C. (2015). Grey systems theory in economics – a historical applications review. *Grey Systems: Theory and Application*, *5*(2), 263–276. doi:10.1108/GS-05-2015-0018

Doryab, B., & Salehi, M. (2017). Modeling and forecasting abnormal stock returns using the nonlinear Grey Bernoulli model. *Journal of Economics, Finance and Administrative Science*, *23*(4), 95–112.

Duan, H., Xiao, X., Yang, J., & Zeng, B. (2018). Elliott wave theory and the Fibonacci sequence-gray model and their application in Chinese stock market. *Journal of Intelligent & Fuzzy Systems*, *34*(3), 1813–1825. doi:10.3233/JIFS-17108

Fabozzi, F. J., & Markowitz, H. M. (2011). *The Theory and Practice of Investment Management, Asset Allocation, Valuation, Portfolio Construction and Strategies*. John Wiley & Sons, Inc. doi:10.1002/9781118267028

Fabozzi, F. J., & Pachamanova, D. A. (2016). *Portfolio Construction and Analytics*. John Wiley & Sons, Inc.

Francq, C., & Zakoian, J. M. (2019). *GARCH Models. Structure, Statistical Inference and Financial Applications* (2nd ed.). John Wiley & Sons. doi:10.1002/9781119313472

Geng, L.-Y., & Zhang, Z. F. (2015). Forecast of Stock Index Volatility Using Grey GARCH Type Models. *The Open Cybernetics & Systemics Journal*, *9*(1), 93–98. doi:10.2174/1874110X01509010093

Granger, C. J. (1989). Combining forecasts – twenty years later. *Journal of Forecasting*, *8*(1), 167–173. doi:10.1002/for.3980080303

Guidolin, M., & Timmermann, A. (2008). International Asset allocation under Regime Switching, Skew, and Kurtosis Preferences. *Review of Financial Studies, 21*(2), 889–935. doi:10.1093/rfs/hhn006

He, W., Song, G., & Wu, A. (2005). On a gens arithmetic for parameters estimating of model GM(1, 1). *Systems Engineering Theory & Practice, 25*(1), 69–75.

Ho, S., Xie, M., & Goh, T. (2002). A comparative study of neural network and box-jenkins ARIMA modeling in the time series prediction. *Computers & Industrial Engineering, 42*(2), 371–375. doi:10.1016/S0360-8352(02)00036-0

Hsu, L. C. (2003). Applying the Grey prediction model to the global integrated circuit industry. *Technological Forecasting and Social Change, 70*(6), 563–574. doi:10.1016/S0040-1625(02)00195-6

Huang, K. Y., & Jane, C. J. (2008). A Novel Model for Stock Portfolio Based on ARX, RS and a New Grey Relational Grade Theories. In *Proceedings 2008 IEEE Conference on Cybernetics and Intelligent Systems*. (pp.417-422). Chengdu, China: IEEE. 10.1109/ICCIS.2008.4670874

Huang, K. Y., Jane, C. J., & Chang, T. C. (2008). A RS Model for Stock Market Forecasting and Portfolio Selection Allied with Weight Clustering and Grey System Theories. In *Proceedings 2008 IEEE Congress on Evolutionary Computation*. (pp. 1240-1246). Chengdu, China: IEEE. 10.1109/CEC.2008.4630955

Ji, P., Zhang, J., Zou, H., & Zheng, W. (2011). A modified Unbiased GM(1,1) model. *Proceedings of 2011 IEEE International Conference on Grey Systems and Intelligent Services*.

Jie, C., & Bo, Z. (2012). Study on parameters characteristics of NGM (1,1,k) prediction model with multiplication transformation. *Grey Systems: Theory and Application, 2*(1), 24-35. doi:10.1109/GSIS.2011.6044076

Jo, T. C. (2003). The effect of virtual term generation on the neural based approaches to time series prediction. In *Proceedings of the IEEE fourth conference on control and automation* (vol. 3, pp. 516-520). Montreal, Canada: IEEE. 10.1109/ICCA.2003.1595075

Kayacan, E., Ulutas, B., & Kaynak, O. (2010). Grey system theory-based models in time series prediction. *Expert Systems with Applications, 37*(2), 1784–1789.

Khuman, A. S., Yang, Y., & John, R. (2014). A commentary on some of the intrinsic differences between grey systems and fuzzy systems. In *2014 IEEE International Conference on Systems, Man, and Cybernetics (SMC)*. San Diego, CA: IEEE.

Lin, C. T., Hung, J. C., & Wang, Y. H. (2005). Forecasting the One-period-ahead Volatility of the International Stock Indices: GARCH Model vs. GM(1,1)-GARCH model. *Journal of Grey System, 8*(1), 1–12.

Liu, S., Forrest, J., & Yang, Y. (2012). A brief introduction to grey systems theory. *Grey Systems: Theory and Application, 2*(2), 89–104. doi:10.1108/20439371211260081

Liu, S., & Lin, Y. (2006). *Grey Information Theory and Practical Applications*. Springer.

Liu, S., & Lin, Y. (2010). *Grey systems, Theory and Applications*. Springer.

Liu, S., Yang, Y., & Forrest, J. (2016). Grey Data Analysis: Methods, Models and Applications. Singapore: Springer Science + Business Media.

Liu, S., Zeng, B., Liu, J., Xie, N., & Yang, Y. (2015). Four basic models of GM(1, 1) and their suitable sequences. *Grey Systems: Theory and Application*, *5*(2), 141–156. doi:10.1108/GS-04-2015-0016

Mills, T. C. (2019). *Applied Time Series Analysis - A Practical Guide to Modeling and Forecasting*. Academic Press.

Rathnayaka, R. M. K. T., Seneviratna, D. M. K. N., & Jianguo, W. (2015). Grey system based novel approach for stock market forecasting. Grey Systems. *Theory and Application*, *5*(2), 178–193.

Rathnayaka, R. M. K. T., Seneviratna, D. M. K. N., Jianguo, W., & Arumawadu, H. I. (2016). An unbiased GM(1,1)-based new hybrid approach for time series forecasting. Grey Systems. *Theory and Application*, *6*(3), 322–340.

Škrinjarić, T., & Šego, B. (2019). Grey Systems Modeling as a Tool for Stock Price Prediction. In *Proceedings of the The 15th International Symposium on Operational Research* (pp. 429-434). Bled, Slovenia: Slovenian Society Informatika.

Taylor, M., & Allen, H. (1992). The use of technical analysis in the foreign exchange market. *Journal of International Money and Finance*, *11*(3), 304–314. doi:10.1016/0261-5606(92)90048-3

Varian, H. R. (1992). *Microeconomic Analysis* (3rd ed.). W. W. Norton & Co.

Wallis, K. F. (2011). Combining forecasts – forty years later. *Applied Financial Economics*, *21*(1-2), 33–41. doi:10.1080/09603107.2011.523179

Wang, Y. F. (2002). Predicting stock price using fuzzy Grey prediction system. *Expert Systems with Applications*, *22*(1), 33–39. doi:10.1016/S0957-4174(01)00047-1

Wei, W. W. S. (2005). *Time Series Analysis: Univariate and Multivariate Methods* (2nd ed.). Pearson.

Xiao, X. (2000). On parameters in grey models. *Journal of Grey System*, *11*(4), 73–78.

Yao, A. W. L., & Chi, S. C. (2004). Analysis and design of a Taguchi–Grey based electricity demand predictor for energy management systems. *Energy Conversion and Management*, *45*(7), 1205–1217. doi:10.1016/j.enconman.2003.08.008

Yin, M. S. (2013). Fifteen years of grey system theory research: A historical review and bibliometric analysis. *Expert Systems with Applications*, *40*(7), 2767–2775. doi:10.1016/j.eswa.2012.11.002

Yongzhong, C., & Hongjuan, L. (2005). A Comparison of Two Grey Models in Predicting Stock Index. *Journal of Grey System*, *1*, 73–76.

ZSE. (2020). *Zagreb Stock Exchange data on CROBEX*. Retrieved from: https://zse.hr/default.aspx?id=44101&index=CROBEX

KEY TERMS AND DEFINITIONS

Financial Decision-Making: Analyzing the financial issues an investor, investment company or institutional investor is facing in order to determine the problems and possibilities so that good decisions can be made which will result in the best interest for the decision maker.

Financial Forecasting: Processing the financial data and predicting future values based on historical characteristics of the data.

Forecasting Capability: The ability to accurately forecast future values, based on the information which is available at the time of making the forecasts.

Grey Data: Data full of uncertainties, with a lot of ambiguities, without complete information.

Portfolio Management: Set of activities that need to be made so that the investor can form a portfolio of financial investments and manage them over time.

Quantitative Finance: Mathematical, statistical, and econometric models and methods which represent a tool in order to facilitate the financial decision making.

Uncertain Data: Data that contains noise which distorts the original true values which are as a result unknown.

Chapter 18
A Review of Standard Spectral Risk Measures

Mohammed Berkhouch
https://orcid.org/0000-0001-7207-4517
LISAD Laboratory, ENSA, Ibn Zohr University, Agadir, Morocco

Ghizlane Lakhnati
LISAD Laboratory, ENSA, Ibn Zohr University, Agadir, Morocco

ABSTRACT

Spectral risk measures are defined as the most attractive subclass of coherent quantile-based risk measures, with a remarkable aptitude for concretizing the decision-maker's subjective attitude toward risk. This chapter raises the problem of underrepresentation of the subclass of spectral risk measures by reviewing the standard spectral risk measures proposed in the literature. In parallel, a discussion about the approaches behind the conception of these risk measures is held. Through this discussion, the authors spot a number of problems with each of these proposals that stand against the reliable applicability of these risk measures in practice.

INTRODUCTION

In quantitative risk management, measuring risk is of crucial importance. For such purpose, a variety of *risk measures* have been proposed in the financial literature. Risk measures are quantitative tools that map financial positions, modelled by random variables, to capital amounts which serve as a hedging against the underlying potential risks. The authors refer the reader to (Pflug & Römisch, 2007; Delbaen, 2012; McNeil et al., 2005; Föllmer & Schied, 2016) for a comprehensive review of the use of risk measures in modern risk management. In this sense, the development of risk measurement theory has been sustained with the proposition of axiomatic approaches for risk measures. Especially, after the pioneering work of (Artzner et al., 1999), who defined the class of coherent risk measures as risk measures that satisfy desirable properties that have been conceded by the modern risk theory, namely: Monotonicity, Translation Invariance, Sub-additivity and Positive Homogeneity.

DOI: 10.4018/978-1-7998-5083-0.ch018

Among coherent risk measures an attractive subclass, called *spectral risk measures*, has emerged. Spectral risk measures were primarily introduced, by (Acerbi, 2002), as an extension for *Expected Shortfall* (Acerbi & Tasche, 2002). Beside coherence, spectral risk measures are law-invariant and co-monotonically additive (Kusuoka, 2001). Yet, the substantial contribution brought by this subclass consists in considering the psychological behavior of the decision-maker in the risk measurement process. In fact, a spectral risk measure is characterized with a *weighting function* that attributes subjective weights to the potential outcomes of a financial position, according to the decision-maker's attitude toward risk.

Due to its distinctive features, the subclass of spectral risk measures has been the subject of a wide scope of surveys and works, since its introduction. For instance, spectral risk measures have been studied in the framework of modern portfolio theory (e.g., (Acerbi & Tasche, 2002; Adam et al., 2008; Brandtner, 2013)), for futures cleaning house margin requirements (e.g., (Cotter & Dowd, 2006)), in the framework of Extreme Value Theory (e.g., (Fałdziński et al., 2012)) and on the problem of comparative risk-aversion (e.g., (Brandtner & Kürsten, 2015)), to name a few.

By virtue of the theoretical attractiveness of spectral risk measures, various representative spectral measures have been proposed in the literature, despite the lack of sufficient guidance on how to construct a weighting function that reflects the subjective risk-aversion of decision-makers in a decent way. Mainly, the attempts that have been suggested, in this sense, are from (Acerbi, 2002; Wang, 1995; Wang, 2000; Cherny & Madan, 2008; Dowd et al., 2008; Furman et al., 2017; Berkhouch et al., 2018). In this paper, the authors review, examine and discuss these different proposed approaches. Throughout this discussion, the researchers identify a number of problems within each of these proposals. In other words, through this study the authors spot the problem of underrepresentation of the class of spectral risk measures and conclude that the set of spectral risk measures (or weighting functions) that have been proposed in the financial literature to date does not incorporate the comprehensive theoretical properties of an actual spectral risk measure. Therefrom, the authors argue that more researches shall be conducted in this direction, with the aim of proposing consistent approaches for constructing representative risk measures that appropriately reflect the theoretical appeal of the concept of spectral risk measures.

The rest of the present paper is structured as follows: In the second section, the researchers provide a theoretical background about risk measures, in general, and spectral risk measures, in particular. In the third section, the authors examine different spectral risk measures introduced in the literature and discuss different approaches behind the emergence of these measures. Through this section, a number of issues are spotted for each approach. The last section concludes.

BACKGROUND

Let (Ω,F,P) be an atomless probability space. Consistently with the literature on risk measures, the authors consider the space $L^\infty := L^\infty(\Omega,F,P)$ of equivalent classes of essentially bounded random variables on (Ω,F,P). Throughout this paper, $X \in L^\infty$ is a random variable modelling the random future outcomes of a financial position. The authors identify constant random variables with real numbers. The authors denote $E[X] = \int_\Omega X dP$, $F_X(x) = P(X \leq x)$ and $F_X^{-1}(\alpha) = \inf\{x: F_X(x) \geq \alpha\}$ the expected value, the probability function (c.d.f.) and its generalized inverse for X, respectively. The authors say that a pair of random variables $X, Y \in L^\infty$ is co-monotone when $(X(\omega) - X(\omega'))(Y(\omega) - Y(\omega')) \geq 0$ for all $(\omega,\omega') \in \Omega \times \Omega$.

A risk measure is understood as a tool providing assessment of a capital amount that serves as a buffer against potential future losses. The researchers state the following definition of a risk measure:

***Definition 2.1* (Risk measure).** *A risk measure is a functional ρ, mapping a financial position X to a real scalar $\rho(X)$, that represents the extra cash which has to be risk-freely invested and added to X to make it acceptable.*

$\rho: L^\infty \longrightarrow R$

$X \longmapsto \rho(X)$

Each class of risk measures proposed in the literature is based on a specific set of theoretical axioms. In what follows, the authors provide some of them:

- *Monotonicity*: if $X \leq Y$, then $\rho(X) \geq \rho(Y)$ for all $X, Y \in L^\infty$.
- *Translation Invariance:* $\rho(X + C) = \rho(X) - C$ for all $C \in R$ and $X \in L^\infty$.
- *Convexity:* $\rho(\lambda X+(1-\lambda)Y) \leq \lambda\rho(X)+(1-\lambda)\rho(Y)$ for all $X,Y \in L^\infty$ and $\lambda \in [0,1]$.
- *Sub-additivity:* $\rho(X + Y) \leq \rho(X) + \rho(Y)$ for every pair $X, Y \in L^\infty$.
- *Positive Homogeneity:* $\rho(\lambda X) = \lambda\rho(X)$ for all $\lambda \geq 0$ and $X \in L^\infty$.
- *Law Invariance*: If $X, Y \in L^\infty$ have the same distribution under P, succinctly $X =_p Y$, then $\rho(X) = \rho(Y)$.
- *Co-monotone Additivity:* $\rho(X + Y) = \rho(X) + \rho(Y)$ for every co-monotonic pair $X, Y \in L^\infty$.

One can interpret these properties as follows: *Monotonicity* ensures that if a financial position, compared to another position, generates worse results then its inherent risk will be greater. *Translation Invariance* requires that if a certain risk-free capital is added to a given risky financial position, then its risk shall decrease by the same amount. *Subadditivity* translates the pivotal principle of *diversification*, which states that the risk associated with the combination of two financial positions is always less than the sum of individual risks. *Positive Homogeneity* implies the proportionality between risk and the financial position's size. *Law Invariance* means that the value of the risk measure depends on the probability distribution, which entails that the risk measure at hand is estimable from empirical data. *Co-monotone Additivity* describes a situation of perfect association between two financial positions, which entails no diversification contingency. For more on the financial interpretations of the above listed properties and others, the researchers refer the reader to (McNeil et al., 2005; Delbaen, 2012; Föllmer & Schied, 2016).

Remark 2.2. *A risk measure that fulfills Law invariance is labeled law invariant. If it satisfies Monotonicity and Translation Invariance, it is called monetary. If it is a monetary risk measure that attends Convexity, it is entitled convex. If it is a convex risk measure that respects Positive Homogeneity, it is called coherent. If it possesses Co-monotone Additivity, it is labeled co-monotone.*

Following (Artzner et al., 1999), a decent risk measure that meets the financial intuition is a measure that satisfies the coherence axioms. In particular, *Value-at-Risk* (*VaR*) is not a coherent risk measure since it fails to hold the Sub-additivity property, in general. Besides, *VaR* has been heavily criticized from both theoretical and practical perspectives, see e.g., (Krause, 2003; Jorion, 2006). To overcome the limitations of *VaR*, (Acerbi & Tasche, 2002) proposed the Expected Shortfall (*ES*) as a coherent risk measure that considers the diversification benefit (Sub-additivity), see (Yamai & Yoshiba, 2005) for a comparative study between *VaR* and *ES*. Based on the concept of *ES*, (Acerbi, 2002) introduced a more general class of coherent risk measures, called *spectral risk measures*.

Typically, decision-makers differ on how they perceive risk due to their subjective preferences and psychological considerations. The aim behind the conception of spectral risk measures consists in taking account of this discrepancy in the course of the risk measurement process. Hence, instead of considering the average of financial losses beyond the *VaR*, as it is the case for *ES*, spectral risk measures consider a weighted average of different levels of ES_{α}:

$$\rho^{\mu}(X) = \int_{[0,1]} ES_{\alpha}(X)\, d\mu(\alpha),\ \forall\, X \in L^{\infty} \tag{2.1}$$

where, $d\mu$ is a measure on [0,1] that provides weights which characterize risk-aversion. Otherwise, the expression (2.1) can be reformulated as a weighted combination of the quantiles (*VaR*) of the random variable X using a *weighting function* ϕ, see definition (2.3) below. For more technical details on this reformulation, the reader is referred to (Acerbi, 2002).

***Definition* 2.3. (*Spectral risk measure*)** *A spectral risk measure* $\rho_{\phi}: L^{\infty} \rightarrow \mathrm{R}$ *might be formally defined by:*

$$\rho_{\phi}(X) = -\int_{[0,1]} F_X^{-1}(p)\, \phi(p)\, dp,\ \forall\, X \in L^{\infty} \tag{2.2}$$

where, ϕ is a weighting function supposed to reflect the risk-aversion attitude toward risk.

The weights are defined over $p \in [0,1]$, a range of cumulative probabilities. Thus, ϕ is a right-continuous integrable function defined on [0,1], that assigns different weights to different p-quantiles of X, as a way for the user to manifest his attitude toward risk.

Each spectral risk measure ρ_{ϕ} is generated by a weighting function ϕ, also called *spectrum*. In order for ϕ to be an admissible spectrum, it shall be defined such that ρ_{ϕ} be coherent and give a realistic description of the subjective risk-aversion. Therefore, some theoretical properties are required for an admissible spectrum:

i) *Positivity:* $\phi(p) \geq 0, \forall p \in [0,1]$. Naturally, ϕ shall attribute positive weights to different p-quantiles.
ii) *Normalisation*: $\int_0^1 \phi(p)\, dp = 1$. Meaning that the weights should sum up to 1.
iii) *Non-decreasiness w.r.t. p*: $\frac{\partial \phi}{\partial p} \geq 0$..

This property ensures that the weights associated with worst financial losses are never less than the weights attributed to better outcomes. Otherwise, more weights should be attached to higher financial losses.

***Remark* 2.4.** *The above mentioned properties are shown, in (Acerbi, 2002), to be necessary and sufficient conditions for the coherence of spectral risk measures.*

Despite guaranteeing the coherence of a spectral risk measure ρ_ϕ, the properties *i)–iii)* are not sufficient to ensure the well-behavior of ρ_ϕ. In order to further capture the discrepancy between different users in terms of risk-aversion, the authors include the following fourth condition:

iv) *Non-decreasiness w.r.t. r (a risk-aversion parameter)*: $\partial\phi / \partial r \geq 0$..

This property implies that, all other things being equal, more the decision-maker is risk averse more weights he puts on the p-quantiles of a risky financial position *X*.

The last property entails that the weighting function φ shall be parameterized with an explicit risk-aversion degree. Thus, the higher the risk aversion degree is more the decision-maker overestimates risks. In this regard, the case when $\partial\phi / \partial r = 0$ *.is irrelevant and condition iv) could even be restated in a strict form.*

Beyond coherence spectral risk measures are law-invariant and co-monotone additive, both desirable properties with major relevance in practice, see e.g., (Dhaene et al., 2002; Adam et al., 2008). Further, (Kusuoka, 2001) showed that any law-invariant, comonotone and coherent risk measure can be expressed through a spectral risk measure. Moreover, this class of risk measures is compatible with the concepts of first and second stochastic order which state dominance between random variables in terms of preferences, for more on this see (Föllmer & Schied, 2016). What is more, another significant attraction is that spectral risk measures can be easily estimated in practice, since they are weighted averages of the distribution quantile *VaR* and we have good estimation methodologies for *VaR*, see for instance (Acerbi, 2002; Biswas & Sen, 2019).

Meeting all these features together with taking into consideration the risk-aversion dimension, make spectral risk measures a particularly interesting subclass of quantile-based risk measures.

Spectral risk measures were earlier introduced, in the actuarial theory, under a different label: *concave distortion risk measures*. Distortion risk measures are rooted in the dual theory of choice under risk, developed by (Yaari, 1987; Wang, 2000). This class of risk measures consists in applying a *distortion function g* on the original cumulative distribution function F_X, in order to reflect the decision-maker's attitude toward risk. Formally, a distortion function g: $[0,1] \rightarrow [0,1]$ is an increasing function satisfying $g(0) = 0$ and $g(1) = 1$.

***Definition* 2.6 (Distortion risk measures).** *Let g be a distortion function, the associated distortion risk measure is defined by:*

$$\rho_g(X) := \int_\Omega X \, d(goP) \tag{2.3}$$

$$= \int_{[0,\infty[} g(P(X > x))dx + \int_{]-\infty,0]} (g(P(X > x)) - 1)dx. \tag{2.4}$$

Then, a distortion risk measure of a risky position *X*, $\rho_g(X)$, corresponds to the expectation of *X* calculated under the distorted probability measure *goP*.

Generally, distortion and spectral risk measures share the following properties: Monotonicity, Translation Invariance, Positive Homogeneity, Law Invariance and co-monotone Additivity. It is shown that a distortion risk measure ρ_g is sub-additive (then coherent) if and only if the distortion function g is concave. Further, the distortion function g is related to the weighting function φ with: $\partial g / \partial p = \phi(p)$ .for p∈ [0,1]. For more details, the authors refer to (Denneberg, 1994; Wang et al., 1997; Wang & Dhaene, 1998; Wirch & Hardy, 2001; Henryk & Silvia, 2006; Sereda et al., 2010; Nguyen & Sriboonchitta, 2010).

Standard Spectral Risk Measures Revisited and Discussion

From a theoretical point of view, spectral risk measures are attractive. Nevertheless, to date there has been no clear consensus on how to construct a weighting function φ and various attempts have been proposed in the literature. In this section, the authors are going to examine and discuss these proposals.

- ***Value-at-Risk:***

Value-at-Risk (VaR_α) at a confidence level $\alpha \in [0,1]$ represents the α-quantile of a financial position X, defined as:

$$VaR_\alpha(X) = -\inf\{x \in \mathrm{R}: P(X \leq x) \geq \alpha\} = -F_X^{-1}(\alpha), \forall X \in L^\infty. \tag{3.1}$$

Hence, VaR_α at a confidence level α can be expressed through a degenerate spectral form by making use of the Dirac function, namely:

$$\phi_{VaR\alpha}(p) = Dirac_\alpha(p), \text{ for } p \in [0,1]. \tag{3.2}$$

This means that VaR_α puts an infinite weight on the α-quantile of X and no weight elsewhere. Thus, a decision-maker who uses VaR_α is extremely concerned about the minimum potential loss that could occur with the probability α but, at the same time, is totally indifferent with regard to any other extreme financial loss, which is inconsistent with a rational risk-aversion attitude. Moreover, such weighting function violates the coherence conditions *ii*) and *iii*), which is supported by the fact that VaR_α fails to hold the Sub-additivity property in general. Regarding condition *iv*), $\phi_{VaR\alpha}$ does not depend on an explicit risk-aversion parameter. Thus, VaR_α is engendered by a degenerate weighting function $\phi_{VaR\alpha}$, that violates the conditions of an admissible spectrum and reflects an extreme psychological profile. Therefore, by no means VaR_α can be used as a spectral risk measure.

- ***Expected Loss:***

Expected Loss (E) is a parsimonious measure of risk that gives the mean among the entire set of potential outcomes of a financial position X. In terms of p-quantiles, E is given by:

$$E(X) = -\int_0^1 F_X^{-1}(p)\,dp, \forall X \in L^\infty. \tag{3.3}$$

Then, E is characterized with the unit indicator function as a weighting function:

$$\phi_E(p) = 1_{[0,1]}(p), \text{ for } p \in [0,1]. \tag{3.4}$$

This implies that Expected Loss places equal weights on all p-quantiles of X. Hence, E represents the profile of a decision-maker who is absolutely risk-neuter and does not seem concerned about the degree of severity of financial losses. Furthermore, the spectrum ϕ_E satisfies the coherence conditions $i) - iii)$ but, according to condition $iv)$, it misses an explicit risk-aversion parameter. Therefore, E is a law-invariant, co-monotone and coherent risk measure characterized with a spectrum ϕ_E that is apt only for expressing the behavior of a risk-neuter user and, therefore, does not account for the discrepancy of psychological profiles in the real world.

- ***Expected Shortfall:***

Expected Shortfall (ES_α) at a confidence level $\alpha \in [0,1]$, (Acerbi & Tasche, 2002), is the most common representative of spectral risk measure that corresponds to the average of the $(1 - \alpha)$ % worst financial losses beyond VaR_α, formally:

$$ES_\alpha(X) = -\frac{1}{1-\alpha}\int_0^1 F_X^{-1}(p)\,dp, \forall X \in L^\infty . \tag{3.5}$$

Thereby, ES_α is generated by the following weighting function:

$$\phi_{ES_\alpha}(p) = \frac{1}{1-\alpha} 1_{[\alpha,1]}(p), \forall p \in [0,1]. \tag{3.6}$$

Thus, $\phi_{ES\alpha}$ fulfills the coherence conditions $i) - iii)$. However, it does not depend on an explicit risk-aversion parameter but rather on a confidence level α, which is mainly defined by the regulations. Also, $\phi_{ES\alpha}$ attributes equal weights to tail quantiles (beyond the α-quantile) and zero weights to non-tail quantiles, which is again an atypical attitude of a user who does not care about the severity of financial losses once VaR_α is exceeded. Then, ES_α is a law-invariant, co-monotone and coherent measure of risk of which the associated spectrum only incorporates the behavior of a decision-maker who is tail risk-neuter.

Comment 3.1. *The researchers report Value-at-Risk, despite the fact that it is not coherent in general, because it is the most used measure of risk in practice and does admit a degenerate spectral formulation. Expected Loss and Expected Shortfall can be regarded as singular spectral risk measures, since ϕ_E and $\phi_{ES\alpha}$ do not depend on an explicit risk-aversion parameter (then, according to condition iv):* $\partial\phi_E / \partial r = \partial\phi_{ES_\alpha} / \partial r = 0$, *which makes them inappropriate for a risk-averse decision-maker.*

- ***Wang transform:***

This is a distortion risk measure introduced, in (Wang, 2000), in response to the limitations regarding Expected Shortfall. Namely, the fact that Expected Shortfall ignores valuable information in the non-tail part of the distribution and does not account for the severity of extreme losses. The Wang's transform is based on the following weighting function:

$$\phi_{Wang}(p)=\frac{\eta\left[\mathcal{N}^{-1}(p)+\lambda\right]}{\eta\left[\mathcal{N}^{-1}(p)\right]}, for\ p\in[0,1] \tag{3.7}$$

$$=e^{-\lambda\left[\mathcal{N}^{-1}(p)+\frac{\lambda}{2}\right]} \tag{3.8}$$

Where, η and $\mathcal{N}$ are the density and cumulative distribution functions of the standard normal distribution, respectively. (Wang, 2000) showed that, for $\lambda \geq 0$, the Wang transform is a concave distortion risk measure, therefore ϕW_{ang} fulfills the coherence conditions i)–iii). Thus, the Wang transform is a law-invariant, co-monotone and coherent measure of risk. However, the Wang transform is based on an underlying assumption of normality and does not depend on an explicit risk-version parameter. The parameter λ is a market price of risk term defined such that the normality of the random variable X is preserved throughout the transformation.

- ***Beta transform:***

The Beta transform is a subclass of distortion risk measures proposed by (Wirch & Hardy, 1999). The associated weighting function is expressed in the following form:

$$\phi_{Beta}(p)=\frac{1}{\beta(m,n)}p^{m-1}(1-p)^{n-1}, for\ p\in[0,1]. \tag{3.9}$$

where, $\beta(m,n)$ is the beta function with the parameters $m > 0$ and $n > 0$. It is shown in (Wirch & Hardy, 1999) that the Beta transform is a concave distortion risk measure for $m \leq 1$ and $n \geq 1$. Thus, for $0 < m \leq 1$ and $n \geq 1$ the spectrum ϕ_{Beta} satisfies the coherence conditions *i*) – *iii*) and, therefore, the Beta transform is a law-invariant, comonotone and coherent measure of risk. The parameters m and n, respectively, control the effect of the right and left tails of the underlying distribution. However, it does not depend on an explicit risk-aversion parameter.

- ***Proportional hazard transform:***

This is a distortion risk measure proposed and discussed in (Wang, 1995; Wang, 1996; Wang et al., 1997). In fact, the PH transform is a special case of the Beta transform for $m = \frac{1}{\gamma}$.and $n = 1$ with $\gamma \geq 1$. Thus, the PH transform is generated by the following weighting function:

$$\phi_{PH}(p) = \frac{1}{\gamma} p^{\frac{1}{\gamma}-1}, \textit{for } p \in [0,1]. \tag{3.10}$$

where, $\gamma \geq 1$. Hence, the PH transform is a law-invariant, co-monotone and coherent risk measure. The parameter γ can be regarded as a risk-aversion degree; then, the spectrum ϕ_{PH} fulfills condition *iv*) if and only if $p \leq e^{-\gamma}$. Therefrom and as stated by (Hardy, 2006) there is no easy way to interpret the parameter γ.

- ***MinMaxVaR transform:***

The MinMaxVaR risk measure was introduced, by (Cherny & Madan, 2008), as an acceptability index for assessing the performance of trading strategies used in the context of conic finance theory. MinMaxVaR is a concave distortion measure of risk, corresponding to the following weighting function:

$$\phi_\delta(p) = \left(p^{-\frac{1}{\delta-1}} - 1 \right)^{\delta}, \text{for } p \in [0,1]. \tag{3.11}$$

where, the parameter $\delta \geq 0$ is a stress level. Meaning, the higher the value of δ the more severe the distortion of the underlying distribution function. In fact, three other concave distortion risk measures were defined in the same logic in (Cherny & Madan, 2008). Thus, ϕ_δ fulfills the coherence conditions *i*)–*iii*). Moreover, the partial derivative of ϕ_δ with respect to δ is given by:

$$\frac{\partial \phi_\delta}{\partial \delta} = \left(p^{\frac{-1}{\delta+1}} - 1 \right)^{\delta} \left[\ln\left(p^{\frac{-1}{\delta+1}} - 1 \right) + \frac{\delta \ln(p)}{(\delta+1)^2 \left(1 - p^{\frac{1}{\delta+1}} \right)} \right].$$

Hence, the spectrum ϕ_δ meets condition *iv*) if and only if

$$\left(p^{\frac{-1}{\delta+1}} - 1 \right) p^{\delta/(\delta+1)^2 \left(1 - p^{\frac{-1}{\delta+1}} \right)} \geq 1..$$

The complexity of the latter expression makes the interpretation of the parameter δ not obvious, and then condition *iv*) does not hold in general.

Comment 3.2. *Contrary to the Expected Shortfall, the above introduced distortion risk measures (Wang, Beta, PH and MinMaxVaR transformations) have the advantage of using the whole loss distribution which means a better use of the available information and that these measures can be more reliable for comparing different risky distributions. These distortion risk measures are parameterized in terms of one or two parameters that control the amount of distortion. Once these parameters are considered as* *risk-aversion degrees for the corresponding spectral risk measures, it makes it difficult to give a clear interpretation for these parameters according to condition iv). Therefrom, one can claim that a distortion parameter is not necessarily a sound risk-aversion degree.*

- ***Exponential spectral risk measure:***

This is a popular spectral risk measure introduced by (Dowd et al., 2008) based on an exponential utility function, parameterized by the absolute Arrow-Pratt risk-aversion coefficient $a > 0$, namely: $U_a(x) = -e^{-ax}$. Thus, exponential spectral risk measures are generated from the following weighting function:

$$\phi_{Exp_a}(p) = \frac{ae^{-a(1-p)}}{1-e^{-a}}, \text{for } p \in [0,1].. \tag{3.12}$$

Such weighting function respects the coherence conditions *i)–iii)* and explicitly depends on a risk-aversion parameter $a > 0$. However, it is not clear under which assumptions condition *iv)* is satisfied since the calculation of the partial derivative leads to:

$$\frac{\partial \phi_{Exp_a}}{\partial a} = \frac{e^{-a(1-p)\left[e^{-a}\left[(a-1)^2+a(1+p)\right]+a(1-p)-1\right]}}{\left(1-e^{a}\right)^2}.$$

Hence, Exponential spectral risk measure is law-invariant, co-monotone and coherent. Yet, the authors in (Dowd et al., 2008) declare the exponential spectral risk measure to be well-behaved with respect to the absolute Arrow-Pratt coefficient and illustrate that for specific values of a (a=5 and a=25) and for a particular standard normal distribution, but this cannot be generalized by virtue of the just risen remark regarding condition *iv)*. Since the latter condition is not fulfilled in general, then once violated one can expect an aberrant behavior regarding risk-aversion from ϕ_{Expa}.

- ***Power spectral risk measure:***

This spectral risk measure was also introduced in (Cotter & Dowd, 2006), based on a power utility function $U_c(x) = \frac{x^{1-c}}{1-c}$. with $c \in (0,1)$ is the relative Arrow-Pratt risk-aversion coefficient. From this utility function emerges the following weighting function:

$$\phi_{Powc}(p) = c(1-p)^{c-1}, \text{for } p \in [0,1]. \tag{3.13}$$

This spectrum attends the conditions of coherence *i)–iii)* and is explicitly parameterized with a risk-aversion coefficient $c \in (0,1)$. Nevertheless, ϕ_{Powc} does not comply with condition *iv)*, in general, since:

$$\frac{\partial \phi_{Pow_c}}{\partial c} = (1-p)^{c-1}\left[1 + c\ln(1-p)\right].$$

Moreover, the power spectral risk measure exhibits an abnormal behavior as illustrated by (Dowd et al., 2008): for a high degree of risk-aversion c, compared to a lower value of c, ϕ_{Powc} attributes more weights to lower financial losses and relatively less weights to higher financial losses, which is inconsistent with the risk-aversion intuition.

Comment 3.3. *In (Dowd et al., 2008), the authors concluded from their results that considering a utility-based approach in order to construct an admissible spectrum could lead to worrying inconsistencies, that run counter the spirit of spectral risk measures, and must be restricted and done carefully. Thus, one cannot pick up any utility function and expect to get an appropriate admissible spectrum. Therefore, this calls into question the efficiency of the entire approach. Moreover, the inconsistent results in (Dowd et al., 2008) are further discussed in (Wächter & Mazzoni, 2013). In addition to that, even though it seems quite natural to think of making use of the utility theory for defining a weighting function for spectral risk measures, the authors argue that the approach on which (Dowd et al., 2008) based their work gives rise to the following objection: while spectral risk measures are, in principle, supposed to reflect the decision-maker's attitude toward risk via a weighting function by implementing a deformation upon the cumulative probabilities p ∈ [0,1]; the notion of utility function (Samuelson, 1937), in the other hand, was originally introduced as an instrument that incorporates a modification upon the p-quantiles or the realizations of the concerned financial position X. Based on this, the researchers claim that the utility-based approach in (Dowd et al., 2008) is not appropriately useable for tackling the problem at hand and the inconsistencies stated by (Dowd et al., 2008) confirm this. In this sense, (Sriboonchitta et al., 2010) claim that the latter approach is purely heuristic, is not theoretically justified and fails to consistently connect spectral risk measures with the utility theory. Therefrom, (Sriboonchitta et al., 2010) propose an alternative approach that provides a justified relation between spectral risk measures and utilities.*

- ***Gini Shortfall:***

Gini Shortfall (*GS*) was recently introduced, by (Furman et al., 2017), as a linear combination of Expected Shortfall (ES_α) and a tail-Gini function ($TGini_\alpha$). Expressly:

$$GS_\alpha^\lambda(X) = ES_\alpha(X) + \lambda TGini_\alpha(X), \forall X \in L^\infty \tag{3.14}$$

with, $\alpha \in [0,1]$ is a confidence level and $\lambda \geq 0$ is a loading parameter. Tail-Gini is a *variability measure* (Rockafellar et al., 2006) that considers risk on tails, and was built upon the famous *Gini coefficient* (Gini, 1921), namely:

$$Gini(X) = 4\,Cov[F_X^{-1}(U), U],\ \forall X \in L^\infty \tag{3.15}$$

where, U is a uniformly distributed random variable, i.e., $U \sim U_{[0,1]}$. For more on the Gini coefficient, the authors refer to (Giorgi, 1993, 2005; Yitzhaki, 1998; Yitzhaki & Schechtman, 2012). From the above linear combination, came out a new spectral risk measure characterized with the following spectrum:

$$\phi_{GS_\alpha^\lambda}(p) = \frac{1}{(1-\alpha)^2}\left(1-\alpha+4\lambda\left(p-\frac{1+\alpha}{2}\right)\right)1_{[\alpha,1]}(p), \textit{for } p \in [0,1]. \tag{3.16}$$

The authors (Furman et al., 2017) showed, via the Choquet integral framework (Choquet, 1954), that GS_α^λ is a law-invariant, co-monotone and coherent risk measure for $\lambda \in \left[0, \frac{1}{2}\right]$.

This means that GS_α^λ is a spectral risk measure and the conditions *i*) – *iii*) are satisfied. However, GS_α^λ depends on a loading parameter λ and a confidence level α, which are often required by regulators, but not on an explicit risk-aversion parameter. Therefrom, GS_α^λ fails to take into account the variety in terms of attitude toward risk between decisionmakers, which is the ultimate task expected from a spectral risk measure.

- ***Extended Gini Shortfall:***

Extended Gini Shortfall (*EGS*) was freshly introduced, in (Berkhouch et al., 2018), as a generalization of Gini Shortfall (*GS*). The Extended Gini Shortfall measure of risk emerged from a linear combination of Expected Shortfall (ES_α) and a new measure of variability, called tail Extended Gini ($TEGini_{r,\alpha}$), expressly:

$$EGS_{r,\alpha}^\lambda(X) = ES_\alpha(X) + \lambda TEGini_{r,\alpha}(X), \forall X \in L^\infty \tag{3.17}$$

where, α is a confidence level, $\lambda \geq 0$ is a loading parameter and $r > 1$ is a degree of risk-aversion. The variability measure $TEGini_{r,\alpha}$ is defined based on the well-known Extended Gini coefficient (Yitzhaki, 1983):

$$EGini_r(X) = -2r\, Cov[X,(1-F_X(X))^{r-1}], \forall X \in L^\infty. \tag{3.18}$$

For more on this coefficient, see e.g., (Chakravarty, 1988; Yitzhaki & Schechtman, 2005, 2012). Similarly to Gini Shortfall (GS), (Berkhouch et al., 2018) proved through the Choquet integral framework that *EGS* is a spectral risk measure characterized by the following weighting function:

$$\phi_{EGS_{r,\alpha}^\lambda}(X) = \frac{1-\alpha+2\lambda\left[(1-\alpha)^{r-1}-r(1-p)^{r-1}\right]}{(1-\alpha)^2}1_{[\alpha,1]}(p), \textit{for } p \in [0,1]. \tag{3.19}$$

Hence, the spectrum $\phi_{EGS^{\lambda}_{r,\alpha}}$ fulfills the coherence conditions *i)–iii)* for $\lambda \in [0,1/(2(r-1)(1-p)^{r-2})]$, and it is parameterized with an explicit risk-aversion degree $r > 1$. Further, $\phi_{EGS^{\lambda}_{r,\alpha}}$ attends condition *iv)* under a necessary and sufficient condition as stated in ((Berkhouch et al., 2018), Proposition 3.9).

Therefrom, *EGS* is law-invariant, co-monotone and coherent under the condition $\lambda \in [0,1/(2(r-1)(1-p)^{r-2})]$; further, it has the potential to exhibit the discrepancy in terms of risk-aversion, while *GS* is a specific case that arises for a particular type of psychological profile represented by $r = 2$.

Comment 3.4. *The approach behind the introduction of EGS (and GS as a special case) presents some additional upsides. First, EGS captures variability, a crucial concept in risk management (Rockafellar et al., 2006), that measures the magnitude of dispersion of the random outcomes of a financial position. Second, EGS is defined in terms of tail risks (extreme risks) by combining both a classic tail risk measure and a tail variability measure. Further, the spectrum* $\phi_{EGSr,\alpha}\lambda$ *manifests dependence on three different parameters: a loading parameter, a confidence level and a risk-aversion degree which makes it more precise from a regulatory perspective. Moreover, this approach takes advantage of the prominent Gini and Extended Gini coefficients which have been widely studied and applied in a plenty of disciplines beyond economics and finance, for a non-exhaustive list of works on this sense the authors refer the reader to (Greselin & Zitikis, 2018).*

FUTURE RESEARCH DIRECTIONS

As a sequel for the present chapter, the authors are determined to further develop the studied topic and are working on a separate project aiming for a proposal of a new family of risk measure that, at once, fulfill the required theoretical properties of a decent risk measure and count for the appropriate incorporation of the psychological attitude toward risk.

CONCLUSION

Among the class of coherent measures of risk (Artzner et al., 1999), spectral risk measures are of particular relevance. Especially, as this subclass coincides with law-invariant, comonotone and coherent risk measures. Moreover, spectral risk measures were primarily designed with the intention of taking into account the decision-maker's attitude toward risk through the notion of weighting functions. Thus, each spectral risk measure is generated by an underlying weighting function or spectrum. Therefore, defining a decent spectral risk measure goes back to defining an appropriate and well-behaved weighting function.

Various tentatives for defining a spectral risk measure have been proposed in the literature. Starting by Value-at-Risk which admits a degenerate spectral form, but cannot be considered as an actual spectral risk measure, essentially on the basis of lack of coherence. Other side, Expected loss and Expected Shortfall are classic spectral risk measures, yet each one of their underlying spectra is suitable only for a specific and extreme type of psychological profile and does not account for the discrepancy between decision-makers in terms of attitude toward risk.

Other proposals originated from the insurance theory under the terminology of concave distortion risk measures, (Wang, 1995; Wang, 2000; Cherny & Madan, 2008) for instance. These measures are characterized with some parameters that reflect the level of distortion applied to the original distribution function. However, they exhibit some nuances regarding the interpretability of these parameters once adapted to the spectral risk measures context.

A legitimate attempt for constructing the spectrum of spectral risk measures was proposed in (Dowd et al., 2008), by having recourse to the notion of utility function. Although this proposal may seem a natural approach for considering the risk-aversion dimension, the researchers claim that this is in discordance with the primitive definition of spectral risk measures. Since a spectral risk measure is originally designed as a tool for applying a distortion on the cumulative probabilities $p \in [0,1]$, while a utility function is, by definition, supposed to place modifications on the realizations of the underlying random variable X. Moreover, this claim is emphasized by the inconsistencies spotted by the authors (Dowd et al., 2008) through their results. For more on this, the authors refer to (Sriboonchitta et al., 2010; Wächter & Mazzoni, 2013).

From another perspective, Extended Gini Shortfall introduced in (Berkhouch et al., 2018) (Gini Shortfall as a special case by (Furman et al., 2017)) constitutes another proposal with an attractive spectrum. This spectral risk measure allows for seizing both concepts of expectation and variability of tail risks and does depend on an explicit parameter for describing risk-aversion. However, the well-behavior of this spectral risk measure, notably regarding condition *iv*), is restricted by a necessary and sufficient condition as stated in ((Berkhouch et al., 2018), Proposition 3.9) and for which we do not have a clear financial interpretation.

To sum up, a spectral risk measure is attractive from a theoretical point of view and this concept has been illustrated in the literature with various proposals. However, to each of these proposals we can attribute some flaws in terms of representativity and/or well-behavior. Therefrom, one can tell that we do not yet have a substantial and consistent representative for the subclass of spectral risk measures. This entails that more investigations shall be conducted in this direction in future researches, so that these measures of risk can be reliably operative in practice. Nonetheless, suggestions such as the prospect theory (Kahneman & Tversky, 2013) could be used to first identify an asymptotic behavior for the decision-maker and then choose the most adequate spectral risk measure to quantify their exposition to risk.

REFERENCES

Acerbi, C. (2002). Spectral measures of risk: A coherent representation of subjective risk aversion. *Journal of Banking & Finance*, *26*(7), 1505–1518. doi:10.1016/S0378-4266(02)00281-9

Acerbi, C., & Tasche, D. (2002). Expected shortfall: A natural coherent alternative to value at risk. *Economic Notes*, *31*(2), 379–388. doi:10.1111/1468-0300.00091

Adam, A., Houkari, M., & Laurent, J.-P. (2008). Spectral risk measures and portfolio selection. *Journal of Banking & Finance*, *32*(9), 1870–1882. doi:10.1016/j.jbankfin.2007.12.032

Artzner, P., Delbaen, F., Eber, J.-M., & Heath, D. (1999). Coherent measures of risk. *Mathematical Finance*, *9*(3), 203–228. doi:10.1111/1467-9965.00068

Berkhouch, M., Lakhnati, G., & Righi, M. B. (2018). Extended gini-type measures of risk and variability. *Applied Mathematical Finance*, *25*(3), 295–314. doi:10.1080/1350486X.2018.1538806

Biswas, S., & Sen, R. (2019). *Kernel based estimation of spectral risk measures*. arXiv preprint arXiv:1903.03304

Brandtner, M. (2013). Conditional value-at-risk, spectral risk measures and (non-) diversification in portfolio selection problems–a comparison with mean–variance analysis. *Journal of Banking & Finance*, *37*(12), 5526–5537. doi:10.1016/j.jbankfin.2013.02.009

Brandtner, M., & Kürsten, W. (2015). Decision making with expected shortfall and spectral risk measures: The problem of comparative risk aversion. *Journal of Banking & Finance*, *58*, 268–280. doi:10.1016/j.jbankfin.2015.03.012

Chakravarty, S. R. (1988). Extended gini indices of inequality. *International Economic Review*, *29*(1), 147–156. doi:10.2307/2526814

Cherny, A., & Madan, D. (2008). New measures for performance evaluation. *Review of Financial Studies*, *22*(7), 2571–2606. doi:10.1093/rfs/hhn081

Choquet, G. (1954). Theory of capacities. *Annales de l'Institut Fourier*, *5*, 131–295. doi:10.5802/aif.53

Cotter, J., & Dowd, K. (2006). Extreme spectral risk measures: An application to futures clearinghouse margin requirements. *Journal of Banking & Finance*, *30*(12), 3469–3485. doi:10.1016/j.jbankfin.2006.01.008

Delbaen, F. (2012). *Monetary Utility Functions*. Osaka University CSFI Lecture Notes Series.

Denneberg, D. (1994). Conditioning (updating) non-additive measures. *Annals of Operations Research*, *52*(1), 21–42. doi:10.1007/BF02032159

Dhaene, J., Denuit, M., Goovaerts, M. J., Kaas, R., & Vyncke, D. (2002). The concept of comonotonicity in actuarial science and finance: Theory. *Insurance, Mathematics & Economics*, *31*(1), 3–33. doi:10.1016/S0167-6687(02)00134-8

Dowd, K., Cotter, J., & Sorwar, G. (2008). Spectral risk measures: Properties and limitations. *Journal of Financial Services Research*, *34*(1), 61–75. doi:10.100710693-008-0035-6

Föllmer, H., & Schied, A. (2016). *Stochastic Finance: An Introduction in Discrete Time*. De Gruyter Textbook. De Gruyter. doi:10.1515/9783110463453

Fałdziński, M., Osińska, M., & Zdanowicz, T. (2012). Detecting risk transfer in financial markets using different risk measures. *Central European Journal of Economic Modelling and Econometrics*, *4*(1), 45–64. doi:10.24425/cejeme.2012.119275

Furman, E., Wang, R., & Zitikis, R. (2017). Gini-type measures of risk and variability: Gini shortfall, capital allocations, and heavy-tailed risks. *Journal of Banking & Finance*, *83*, 70–84. doi:10.1016/j.jbankfin.2017.06.013

Gini, C. (1921). Measurement of inequality of incomes. *Economic Journal (London)*, *31*(121), 124–126. doi:10.2307/2223319

Giorgi, G. M. (1993). A fresh look at the topical interest. *Metron*, *51*(1-2), 83–98.

Giorgi, G. M. (2005). *Bibliographic portrait of the gini concentration ratio. Technical report.* University Library of Munich.

Greselin, F., & Zitikis, R. (2018). From the classical gini index of income inequality to a new Zenga-type relative measure of risk: A modellers perspective. *Econometrics, 6*(1), 4. doi:10.3390/econometrics6010004

Hardy, M. R. (2006). An introduction to risk measures for actuarial applications. *SOA Syllabus Study Note,* 19.

Henryk, G., & Silvia, M. (2006). *On a relationship between distorted and spectral risk measures.* Faculty Working Papers 15/06, School of Economics and Business Administration, University of Navarra.

Jorion, P. (2006). *Value at Risk* (3rd ed.). The New Benchmark for Managing Financial Risk. McGraw-Hill Education.

Kahneman, D., & Tversky, A. (2013). Prospect theory: An analysis of decision under risk. In Handbook of the fundamentals of financial decision making (Part I, pp. 99-127). DOI: doi:10.1142/9789814417358_0006

Krause, A. (2003). Exploring the limitations of value at risk: How good is it in practice? *The Journal of Risk Finance, 4*(2), 19–28. doi:10.1108/eb022958

Kusuoka, S. (2001). On law invariant coherent risk measures. In *Advances in mathematical economics* (pp. 83–95). Springer. doi:10.1007/978-4-431-67891-5_4

McNeil, A., Frey, R., & Embrechts, P. (2005). *Quantitative Risk Management: Concepts, Techniques, and Tools. Business Pro collection.* Princeton University Press.

Nguyen, H. T., & Sriboonchitta, S. (2010). On Choquet integral risk measures. In *Integrated Uncertainty Management and Applications* (pp. 15–22). Springer. doi:10.1007/978-3-642-11960-6_2

Pflug, G., & Römisch, W. (2007). *Modeling, Measuring and Managing Risk.* World Scientific., doi:10.1142/6478

Rockafellar, R. T., Uryasev, S., & Zabarankin, M. (2006). Generalized deviations in risk analysis. *Finance and Stochastics, 10*(1), 51–74. doi:10.100700780-005-0165-8

Samuelson, P. A. (1937). A note on measurement of utility. *The Review of Economic Studies, 4*(2), 155–161. doi:10.2307/2967612

Sereda, E. N., Bronshtein, E. M., Rachev, S. T., Fabozzi, F. J., Sun, W., & Stoyanov, S. V. (2010). Distortion risk measures in portfolio optimization. In *Handbook of portfolio construction* (pp. 649–673). Springer. doi:10.1007/978-0-387-77439-8_25

Sriboonchitta, S., Nguyen, H. T., & Kreinovich, V. (2010). How to relate spectral risk measures and utilities. *International Journal of Intelligent Technologies and Applied Statistics, 3*(2), 141–158.

Wächter, H. P., & Mazzoni, T. (2013). Consistent modeling of risk-averse behavior with spectral risk measures. *European Journal of Operational Research, 229*(2), 487–495. doi:10.1016/j.ejor.2013.03.001

Wang, S. (1995). Insurance pricing and increased limits ratemaking by proportional hazards transforms. *Insurance, Mathematics & Economics, 17*(1), 43–54. doi:10.1016/0167-6687(95)00010-P

Wang, S. (1996). Ordering of risks under ph-transforms. *Insurance, Mathematics & Economics*, *18*(2), 109–114. doi:10.1016/0167-6687(95)00031-3

Wang, S., & Dhaene, J. (1998). Comonotonicity, correlation order and premium principles. *Insurance, Mathematics & Economics*, *22*(3), 235–242. doi:10.1016/S0167-6687(97)00040-1

Wang, S. S. (2000). A class of distortion operators for pricing financial and insurance risks. *The Journal of Risk and Insurance*, *67*(1), 15–36. doi:10.2307/253675

Wang, S. S., Young, V. R., & Panjer, H. H. (1997). Axiomatic characterization of insurance prices. *Insurance, Mathematics & Economics*, *21*(2), 173–183. doi:10.1016/S0167-6687(97)00031-0

Wirch, J. L., & Hardy, M. R. (1999). A synthesis of risk measures for capital adequacy. *Insurance, Mathematics & Economics*, *25*(3), 337–347. doi:10.1016/S0167-6687(99)00036-0

Wirch, J. L., & Hardy, M. R. (2001). *Distortion risk measures: Coherence and stochastic dominance*. Paper presented in International Congress on Insurance: Mathematics and Economics.

Yaari, M. E. (1987). The dual theory of choice under risk. *Econometrica*, *55*(1), 95–115. doi:10.2307/1911158

Yamai, Y., & Yoshiba, T. (2005). Value-at-risk versus expected shortfall: A practical perspective. *Journal of Banking & Finance*, *29*(4), 997–1015. doi:10.1016/j.jbankfin.2004.08.010

Yitzhaki, S. (1983). On an extension of the gini inequality index. *International Economic Review*, *24*(3), 617–628. doi:10.2307/2648789

Yitzhaki, S. (1998). More than a dozen alternative ways of spelling gini. In *Research in economic inequality*. Citeseer.

Yitzhaki, S., & Schechtman, E. (2005). The properties of the extended gini measures of variability and inequality. *SSRN*, *815564*. Advance online publication. doi:10.2139srn.815564

Yitzhaki, S., & Schechtman, E. (2012). *The Gini Methodology: A Primer on a Statistical Methodology*. Springer Series in Statistics. Springer New York.

ADDITIONAL READING

Acerbi, C. (2002). Spectral measures of risk: A coherent representation of subjective risk aversion. *Journal of Banking & Finance*, *26*(7), 1505–1518. doi:10.1016/S0378-4266(02)00281-9

Arıkan, E., & Fichtinger, J. (2017). The risk-averse newsvendor problem under spectral risk measures: A classification with extensions. *European Journal of Operational Research*, *256*(1), 116–125. doi:10.1016/j.ejor.2016.06.002

Berkhouch, M., Lakhnati, G., & Righi, M. B. (2018, April). A new class of spectral risk measures. [Paper presentation]. In 2018 4th International Conference on Optimization and Applications (ICOA) (pp. 1-5). IEEE.

Brandtner, M. (2013). Conditional Value-at-Risk, spectral risk measures and (non-) diversification in portfolio selection problems–A comparison with mean–variance analysis. *Journal of Banking & Finance*, *37*(12), 5526–5537. doi:10.1016/j.jbankfin.2013.02.009

Brandtner, M., & Kürsten, W. (2015). Decision making with Expected Shortfall and spectral risk measures: The problem of comparative risk aversion. *Journal of Banking & Finance*, *58*, 268–280. doi:10.1016/j.jbankfin.2015.03.012

Dowd, K., & Blake, D. (2006). After VaR: The theory, estimation, and insurance applications of quantile-based risk measures. *The Journal of Risk and Insurance*, *73*(2), 193–229. doi:10.1111/j.1539-6975.2006.00171.x

Fichtinger, J. (2011). *The single-period inventory model with spectral risk measures*. Peter Lang International Academic Publishers.

Kahneman, D., & Tversky, A. (2013). Prospect theory: An analysis of decision under risk. In Handbook of the fundamentals of financial decision making: Part I (pp. 99-127). DOI: doi:10.1142/9789814417358_0006

Sereda, E. N., Bronshtein, E. M., Rachev, S. T., Fabozzi, F. J., Sun, W., & Stoyanov, S. V. (2010). Distortion risk measures in portfolio optimization. In *Handbook of portfolio construction* (pp. 649–673). Springer., doi:10.1007/978-0-387-77439-8_25

Sriboonchitta, S., Nguyen, H. T., & Kreinovich, V. (2010). How to relate spectral risk measures and utilities.

Szegö, G. (2002). Measures of risk. *Journal of Banking & Finance*, *26*(7), 1253–1272. doi:10.1016/S0378-4266(02)00262-5

KEY TERMS AND DEFINITIONS

Admissible Spectrum: A weighting function that satisfies the three first conditions i)-iii) detailed above in the present chapter.

Expected Shortfall: The expected shortfall, at a given level of confidence α in the unit interval, is a measure of risk that represents the mean loss beyond the corresponding value-at-risk.

Risk Measure: A mapping that associates a real value to a given financial position, which represents the risk value.

Risk-Aversion: A quantitative variable that reflects the psychological behavior or attitude toward risk of a given investor.

Utility Function: A mapping that evaluates the satisfaction brought by a specific realization for a given investor.

Value-at-Risk: The value-at-risk, at a given level of confidence α in the unit interval, is a risk measure that coincides with the α-quantile of the underlying financial position.

Variability Measure: A function that allows the quantification of the variability or dispersion of the realizations of a given random variable (modeling a financial position).

Weighting Function: For a given risky financial position, a weighting function associates to each realization a given weight which, in the context of the present chapter, reflects the investor's psychological aspect regarding risk.

ENDNOTES

1 Corresponding author. Https://orcid.org/ 0000-0001-7207-4517.

2 This research received no specific grant from any funding agency in the public, commercial, or not-for-profit sectors.

Compilation of References

Abid, F., Mroua, M., & Wong, W.-K. (2007). *The Impact of Option Strategies in Financial Portfolios Performance: Mean-Variance and Stochastic Dominance Approaches*. Retrieved from http://ssrn.com/abstract=982332

Abid, F., Mroua, M., & Wong, W.-K. (2014). International Diversification Versus Domestic Diversification: Mean-Variance Portfolio Optimization and Stochastic Dominance Approaches. *Journal of Risk and Financial Management, 2014*(2), 45–66. doi:10.3390/jrfm7020045

Acerbi, C. (2002). Spectral measures of risk: A coherent representation of subjective risk aversion. *Journal of Banking & Finance, 26*(7), 1505–1518. doi:10.1016/S0378-4266(02)00281-9

Acerbi, C., & Tasche, D. (2002). Expected shortfall: A natural coherent alternative to value at risk. *Economic Notes, 31*(2), 379–388. doi:10.1111/1468-0300.00091

Acharya, V. V., & Richardson, M. P. (2009). *Restoring financial stability: how to repair a failed system* (Vol. 542). John Wiley & Sons. doi:10.1002/9781118258163

Adam, A., Houkari, M., & Laurent, J.-P. (2008). Spectral risk measures and portfolio selection. *Journal of Banking & Finance, 32*(9), 1870–1882. doi:10.1016/j.jbankfin.2007.12.032

Adinya, I., Oke, T., & Edeki, S. O. (2019). Analysis of Month-of-the-year Effect in an Emerging Market via Stochastic Dominance Approach. *Academy of Entrepreneurship Journal, 25*(2), 1–6.

Agenor, P. R., & Pereira da Silva, L. (2018). Financial Spillovers, Spillbacks, and the Scope for International Macroprudential Policy Coordination. Policy Paper N° 97, Bank of International Settlements.

Aggarwal, R., Prabhal, N. R., & Puri, M. (2002). Institutional allocation in initial public offerings: Empirical evidence. *The Journal of Finance, 57*(3). https://www.nber.org/papers/w9070.pdf

Aggarwal, R., Akhigbe, A., & McNulty, J. E. (2006). Are differences between acquiring bank profit efficiency priced in financial markets? *Journal of Financial Services Research, 30*(3), 265–286. doi:10.100710693-006-0419-4

Aharoni, G., Grundy, B., & Zeng, Q. (2013). Stock returns and the Miller Modigliani valuation formula: Revisiting the Fama French analysis. *Journal of Financial Economics, 110*(2), 347–357. doi:10.1016/j.jfineco.2013.08.003

Aharony, J., & Loeb, M. (1977). Mean-Variance Vs Stochastic Dominance: Some Empirical Findings On Efficient Sets. *Journal of Banking & Finance, 1*(1), 95–102. doi:10.1016/0378-4266(77)90020-6

Ahmed, H., Naka, A., Wuthisatian, P., & Lakefront, N. O. L. (n.d.). *Behavior of Momentum in the Foreign Exchange Market: Evidence from Portfolio Approach*. Academic Press.

Akins, W. M., Abell, M. P., & Diggins, E. M. (2005, January 1). Enhancing Drilling Risk & Performance Management Through the Use of Probabilistic Time & Cost Estimating. *Society of Petroleum Engineers, SPE/IADC Drilling Conference*. 10.2118/92340-MS

Alberto Alesina & Roberto Perotti. (1995). *The Political Economy of Budget Deficits* (Vol. 42). Staff Papers - International Monetary Fund.

Aljinović, Z., Marasović, B., & Šego, B. (2011) Financial Modeling (2nd ed.). Split: Faculty of Economics Split.

Aljinović, Z., Marasović, B., & Šego, B. (2011). *Financial Modelling*. Faculty of Economics, Business and Tourism.

Al-Khazali, O. M., Koumanakos, E. P., & Pyun, C. S. (2008). Calendar anomaly in the Greek stock market: Stochastic dominance analysis. *International Review of Financial Analysis*, *17*(3), 461–474. doi:10.1016/j.irfa.2007.02.001

Allen, D. E., Powell, R. J., & Golab, A. (2010). *Volatility and correlations for stock markets in the emerging economies of Central and Eastern Europe: Implications for European investors*. Available at SSRN 1611472.

Allen, F., & Gale, D. (2004). Competition and financial stability. *Journal of Money, Credit and Banking*, *36*(3), 453–480. doi:10.1353/mcb.2004.0038

Allen, L., & Saunders, A. (2004). Incorporating systemic influences into risk measurements: A survey of the literature. *Journal of Financial Services Research*, *26*(2), 161–191. doi:10.1023/B:FINA.0000037545.38154.8a

Almazari, A. A. (2013). Capital Adequacy, Cost Income Ratio and the Performance of Saudi Banks. *International Journal of Academic Research in Accounting. Finance and Management Sciences*, *3*(4), 284–293.

Al-Obaidan, A. M., & Scully, G. W. (1991). Efficiency differences between private and state-owned enterprises in the international petroleum industry. *Applied Economics*, *23*(2), 237–246. doi:10.1080/00036849200000122

Al-Thani, F. F. J., & Merna, T. (2005, January 1). *Risk and Uncertainty Modeling in the Oil and Gas Industry*. Society of Petroleum Engineers, SPE Middle East Oil and Gas Show and Conference. doi:10.2118/93129-MS

Amadeo, K. (2019). *Public debt with its pros and cons, How to tell when it's too high. An online publication of the balance*. Retrieved from the balance online on October 20th, 2019. https://www.thebalance.com/what-is-the-public-debt-3306294

Amel, D., Barnes, C., Panetta, F., & Salleo, C. (2004). Consolidation and efficiency in the financial sector: A review of the international evidence. *Journal of Banking & Finance*, *28*(10), 2493–2519. doi:10.1016/j.jbankfin.2003.10.013

Amenc, N., Goltz, F., & Le Sourd, V. (2006). *Assessing the Quality of Stock Market Indices: Requirements for Asset Allocation and Performance Measurement*. Nice: An EDHEC Risk & Asset Management Research Centre Publication.

Amenc, N., Goltz, F., & Martellini, L. (2013). *Smart Beta 2.0*. EDHEC-Risk Institute. doi:10.3905/jii.2013.4.3.015

Amihud, Y. (2002). Illiquidity and stock returns: Cross-section and time series effects. *Journal of Financial Markets*, *5*(1), 31–56. doi:10.1016/S1386-4181(01)00024-6

Amihud, Y., Hameed, A., Kang, W., & Zhang, H. (2015). The illiquidity premium: International evidence. *Journal of Financial Economics*, *117*(2), 350–368. doi:10.1016/j.jfineco.2015.04.005

Anagnostopoulos, K., & Mamanis, G. (2010). A portfolio optimization model with three objectives and discrete variables. *Computers & Operations Research*, *37*(7), 1285–1297. doi:10.1016/j.cor.2009.09.009

Ang, A. (2014). *Asset Management: A Systematic Approach to Factor Investing*. Oxford University Press. doi:10.1093/acprof:oso/9780199959327.001.0001

Ang, A., Chen, J., & Xing, Y. (2006). Downside risk. *Review of Financial Studies*, *19*(4), 1191–1239. doi:10.1093/rfs/hhj035

Ang, A., Hodrick, R. J., Xing, Y., & Zhang, X. (2006). The cross-section of volatility and expected returns. *The Journal of Finance*, *61*(1), 259–299. doi:10.1111/j.1540-6261.2006.00836.x

Ang, A., Hodrick, R. J., Xing, Y., & Zhang, X. (2009). High idiosyncratic volatility and low returns: International and further U.S. evidence. *Journal of Financial Economics*, *91*(1), 1–23. doi:10.1016/j.jfineco.2007.12.005

Annaert, J., Van Osselaer, S., & Verstraete, B. (2008). Performance Evaluation of Portfolio Insurance Strategies Using Stochastic Dominance Criteria. *Journal of Banking & Finance*, *33*(2), 272–280. doi:10.1016/j.jbankfin.2008.08.002

Aouni, B., Doumpos, M., Pérez Gladish, B., & Steuer, R. E. (2018). On the increasing importance of multiple criteria decision aid methods for portfolio selection. *The Journal of the Operational Research Society*, *69*(5), 1–18. doi:10.1080/01605682.2018.1475118

Arrawatia, R., Mishra, A., & Dawar, A. (2015). Bank Competition and Efficiency: Empirical Evidence from Indian Market. *International Journal on Law and Management*, *57*(3), 217–231. doi:10.1108/IJLMA-03-2014-0029

Artzner, P., Delbaen, F., Eber, J., & Heath, D. (1999). Coherent measures of risk. *Mathematical Finance*, *9*(3), 203–228. doi:10.1111/1467-9965.00068

Ashraf, D., Rizwan, M. S., & L'Huillier, B. (2016). A net stable funding ratio for Islamic banks and its impact on financial stability: An international investigation. *Journal of Financial Stability*, *25*, 47–57. doi:10.1016/j.jfs.2016.06.010

Asness, C. S., & Frazzini, A. (2013). The devil in HML's details. *Journal of Portfolio Management*, *39*(4), 49–68. doi:10.3905/jpm.2013.39.4.049

Asness, C. S., Moskowitz, T. J., & Pedersen, L. H. (2013). Value and Momentum Everywhere. *The Journal of Finance*, *68*(3), 929–985. doi:10.1111/jofi.12021

Assibong, P. A., Wogu, I. A. P., Sholarin, M. A., Misra, S., Damasevičius, R., & Sharma, N. (2020). The politics of artificial intelligence behavior and human rights violation issues in the 2016 US Presidential Elections: An appraisal. In Data Management, Analytics, and Innovation. Advances in Intelligent Systems and Computing, (vol 1016). Springer. DOI doi:10.1007/978-981-13-9364-8_22

Atilgan, Y., Bali, T. G., Demirtas, K. O., & Gunaydin, A. D. (2018). Downside Beta and Equity Returns around the World. *Journal of Portfolio Management*, *135*(3), 725–753.

Atilgan, Y., Bali, T. G., Demirtas, K. O., & Gunaydin, A. D. (2020). Left-tail momentum: Underreaction to bad news, costly arbitrage and equity returns. *Journal of Financial Economics*, *135*(3), 725–753. doi:10.1016/j.jfineco.2019.07.006

Atilgan, Y., Demirtas, K. O., & Gunaydin, A. D. (2020). Downside beta and the cross section of equity returns: A decade later. *European Financial Management*, *26*(2), 316–347. doi:10.1111/eufm.12258

August, R., Schiereck, D., & Weber, M. (2000). Momentumstrategien am deutschen Aktienmarkt: neue empirische Evidenz zur Erklärung des Erfolgs (No. 35294). Darmstadt Technical University, Department of Business Administration, Economics and Law, Institute for Business Studies (BWL).

Avgouleas, E., & Cullen, J. (2014). Excessive Leverage and Bankers' Pay: Governance and Financial Stability Costs of a Symbiotic Relationship. *The Columbia Journal of European Law*, *21*(1), 7–46.

Bachmann, C., Tegtmeier, L., Gebhardt, J., & Steinborn, M. (2019). The "sell in May" effect: An empirical investigation of globally listed private equity markets. *Managerial Finance*, *45*(6), 793–808. doi:10.1108/MF-07-2018-0322

Baker, M., & Wurgler, J. (2007). Investor sentiment in the stock market. *Journal of Economic Perspectives, 21*(2). https://pubs.aeaweb.org/doi/pdfplus/10.1257/jep.21.2.129

Bali, T. G., Cakici, N., & Whitelaw, R. F. (2011). Maxing out: Stocks as lotteries and the cross-section of expected returns. *Journal of Financial Economics, 99*(2), 427–446. doi:10.1016/j.jfineco.2010.08.014

Bali, T. G., Cakici, N., & Whitelaw, R. F. (2014). Hybrid tail risk and expected stock returns: When does the tail wag the dog? *Review of Asset Pricing Studies, 4*(2), 206–246. doi:10.1093/rapstu/rau006

Ball, R. (1978). Anomalies in relationships between securities' yields and yield-surrogates. *Journal of Financial Economics, 6*(2-3), 103–126. doi:10.1016/0304-405X(78)90026-0

Banz, R. W. (1981). The relationship between return and market value of common stocks. *Journal of Financial Economics, 9*(1), 3–18. doi:10.1016/0304-405X(81)90018-0

Barakat, A., & Hussainey, K. (2013). Bank governance, regulation, supervision, and risk reporting: Evidence from operational risk disclosures in European banks. *International Review of Financial Analysis, 30*, 254–273. doi:10.1016/j.irfa.2013.07.002

Barbić, T., & Čondić-Jurkić, I. (2011). Relationship between macroeconomic fundamentals and stock market indices in selected CEE countries. *Economic Review (Kansas City, Mo.), 62*(3-4), 113–133.

Barbić, T., & Čondić-Jurkić, I. (2017). Do fiscal variables affect stock market returns in EU countries? *Economic Review (Kansas City, Mo.), 68*(3), 253–266.

Baron, D. (1982). A Model of the Demand for Investment Banking Advising and Distribution Services for New Issues. *The Journal of Finance, 37*(4), 955–976. doi:10.1111/j.1540-6261.1982.tb03591.x

Barr, D. J., Levy, R., Scheepers, C., & Tily, H. J. (2013). Random effects structure for confirmatory hypothesis testing: Keep it maximal. *Journal of Memory and Language, 68*(3), 255–278. doi:10.1016/j.jml.2012.11.001 PMID:24403724

Basdas, Ü. (2011). The day-of-the-week effect for Istanbul stock exchange: A stochastic dominance approach. *Journal of Applied Finance & Banking, 1*(4), 223–238.

Basher, S. A., & Sadorsky, P. (2006). Day-of-the-week effects in emerging stock markets. *Applied Economics Letters, 13*(10), 621–628. doi:10.1080/13504850600825238

Battaglini, M., Nunnari, S., & Palfrey, T. R. (2018). *The Political Economy of Public Debt: A Laboratory Study. CEPR Discussion Papers 13097*. C.E.P.R. Discussion Papers.

Battese, G. E., & Coelli, T. J. (1995). A Model for technical inefficiency effects in a stochastic frontier production function for panel data. *Empirical Economics, 20*(2), 325–332. doi:10.1007/BF01205442

Bawa, V. S. (1975). Optimal Rules for Ordering Uncertain Prospects. *Journal of Financial Economics, 2*(1), 95–121. doi:10.1016/0304-405X(75)90025-2

Bawa, V. S. (1982). Stochastic Dominance: A Research Bibliography. *Management Science, 28*(6), 698–712. doi:10.1287/mnsc.28.6.698

Bawa, V. S., & Lindenberg, E. B. (1977). Capital market equilibrium in a mean-lower partial moment framework. *Journal of Financial Economics, 5*(2), 189–200. doi:10.1016/0304-405X(77)90017-4

Beccalli, E., & Frantz, P. (2009). M&A Operations and performance in banking. *Journal of Financial Services Research, 36*(2-3), 203–226. doi:10.100710693-008-0051-6

Beck, T., De Jonghe, O., & Schepens, G. (2013). Bank competition and stability: Cross-country heterogeneity. *Journal of Financial Intermediation, 22*(2), 218–244. doi:10.1016/j.jfi.2012.07.001

Beck, T., Demirgüç-Kunt, A., & Levine, R. (2000). A New Database on Financial Development and Structure. *The World Bank Economic Review, 14*(3), 597–605. doi:10.1093/wber/14.3.597

Beck, T., Demirgüç-Kunt, A., & Merrouche, O. (2010). Islamic vs. conventional banking: Business model, efficiency and stability. *Journal of Banking & Finance, 37*(2), 433–447. doi:10.1016/j.jbankfin.2012.09.016

Beitel, P., Schiereck, D., & Wahrenburg, M. (2004). Explaining M&As Success in European Banks. *European Financial Management, 10*(1), 109–139. doi:10.1111/j.1468-036X.2004.00242.x

Bekaert, G., Harvey, C. R., & Lundblad, C. (2007). Liquidity and expected returns: Lessons from emerging markets. *Review of Financial Studies, 20*(6), 1783–1831. doi:10.1093/rfs/hhm030

Belloumi, M. (2010). The relationship between tourism receipts, real effective exchange rate and economic growth in Tunisia. *International Journal of Tourism Research, 12*(5), 550–560.

Benveniste, L. M., & Paul, A. S. (1989). How investment bankers determine the offer price and allocation of new issues. *Journal of Financial Economics, 24*(2), 343–361. doi:10.1016/0304-405X(89)90051-2

Berger, A. N., Demsetz, R. S., & Strahan, P. E. (1999). The consolidation of the financial services industry: Causes, consequences, and implications for the future. *Journal of Banking & Finance, 23*(2–4), 135–194. doi:10.1016/S0378-4266(98)00125-3

Berger, A. N., & Mester, L. J. (1997). Inside the Black Box: What explains the differences in the efficiencies of financial institutions? *Journal of Banking & Finance, 21*(7), 895–947. doi:10.1016/S0378-4266(97)00010-1

Bergsten, S. (2019). *Momentum strategies on the Swedish market*. Academic Press.

Berkhouch, M., Lakhnati, G., & Righi, M. B. (2018). Extended gini-type measures of risk and variability. *Applied Mathematical Finance, 25*(3), 295–314. doi:10.1080/1350486X.2018.1538806

Bhandari, L. C. (1988). Debt/equity ratio and expected common stock returns: Empirical evidence. *The Journal of Finance, 43*(2), 507–528. doi:10.1111/j.1540-6261.1988.tb03952.x

Bildik, R. (2004). *Are calendar anomalies still alive? Evidence from Istanbul Stock Exchange. Evidence from Istanbul Stock Exchange (May 27, 2004)*. Academic Press.

Bin, D. (2020). The politics of public debt: Financialization, class, and democracy in neoliberal brazil. Studies in Critical Social Science. Brill. doi:10.1163/9789004408722

Bird, R., Gao, X., & Yeung, D. (2017). Time-series and cross-sectional momentum strategies under alternative implementation strategies. *Australian Journal of Management, 42*(2), 230–251. doi:10.1177/0312896215619965

Bishop, C. M. (1995). *Neural Networks for Pattern Recognition*. Oxford University Press.

Bishop, J. A., Formby, J. P., & Thistle, P. D. (1969). Convergence of the South and Non-South Income Distributions, 1969-1979. *The American Economic Review, 82*(1), 262–272.

Biswas, S., & Sen, R. (2019). *Kernel based estimation of spectral risk measures*. arXiv preprint arXiv:1903.03304

Black, F. (1972). Capital market equilibrium with restricted borrowing. *The Journal of Business, 45*(3), 444–455. doi:10.1086/295472

Blahous, C. P. (2013). *Why we have federal deficits: The policy decisions that created them*. Research paper, Mercatus Center, George Mason University. https://www.mercatus.org/ publication/why-we-have-federal-deficits-policydecisions-created-them

Bloomberg L.P. (2020). *Stock prices of various indexes from 01/04/1988 to 31/12/2019*. Retrieved Jan. 8, 2020 from Bloomberg database.

Bollen, N. P. B. (1999). *Measuring the Benefits of Option Strategies for Portfolio Management, report prepared for Catalyst Institute*. Retrieved from http://www2.owen.vanderbilt.edu/nick.bollen/themes/asx1.pdf

Bookstaber, R., & Clarke, R. (1984, October). Option Portfolio Strategies: Measurement and Evaluation. *The Journal of Business*, *57*(4), 469–492. doi:10.1086/296275

Booth, J. R., Tehranian, A., & Trennepohl, G. L. (1985). Efficiency analysis and option portfolio selection. *Journal of Financial and Quantitative Analysis*, *4*(4), 435–450. doi:10.2307/2330760

Borges, M. R. (2009). *Calendar effects in stock markets: critique of previous methodologies and recent evidence in European countries*. Academic Press.

Borosak, B., Bykova, A., Heger, N., Muck, B., Schwarzhappel, M., Vasaros, G., & Zenz, D. (2019). wiiw Handbook of Statistics 2019: Central, East and Southeast Europe. The Vienna Institute for International Economic Studies, wiiw.

Borse Frankfurt - historical data of stock trading. (n.d.). Retrieved February 17, 2019, from www.boerse-frankfurt.de

Branda, M. (2016). Mean-value at risk portfolio efficiency: approaches based on data envelopment analysis models with negative data and their empirical behaviour. *A Quarterly Journal of Operations Research, 14*(1), 77-99.

Branda, M., & Kopa, M. (2013). *From stochastic dominance to DEA-risk models: portfolio efficiency analysis*. International Workshop "Stochastic Programming for Implementation and Advanced Applications" (STOPROG–2012), Neringa, Lithuania.

Branda, M. (2013). Diversification-consistent data envelopment analysis with general deviation measures. *European Journal of Operational Research*, *226*(3), 626–635. doi:10.1016/j.ejor.2012.11.007

Branda, M., & Kopa, M. (2012). DEA-Risk Efficiency and Stochastic Dominance Efficiency of Stock Indices. *Czech Journal of Economics and Finance*, *62*(2), 106–126.

Branda, M., & Kopa, M. (2012). DEA-Risk Efficiency and Stochastic Dominance Efficiency of Stock Indices. *Finance a Uver. Czech Journal of Economics & Finance*, *62*(2).

Branda, M., & Kopa, M. (2014). On relation between DEA-risk models and stochastic dominance efficiency tests. *Central European Journal of Operations Research*, *22*(1), 13–35. doi:10.100710100-012-0283-2

Brandimarte, P. (2014). *Handbook in Monte Carlo Simulation. Applications in Financial Engineering, Risk Management and Economics*. John Wiley & Sons, Inc.

Brandtner, M. (2013). Conditional value-at-risk, spectral risk measures and (non-) diversification in portfolio selection problems–a comparison with mean–variance analysis. *Journal of Banking & Finance*, *37*(12), 5526–5537. doi:10.1016/j.jbankfin.2013.02.009

Brandtner, M., & Kürsten, W. (2015). Decision making with expected shortfall and spectral risk measures: The problem of comparative risk aversion. *Journal of Banking & Finance*, *58*, 268–280. doi:10.1016/j.jbankfin.2015.03.012

Brealey, R., Myers, S., & Allen, F. (2006). *Corporate Finance* (8th ed.). McGraw-Hill Irwin.

Breiman, L. (2001). Random Forests. *Machine Learning, 45*(1), 5–32. doi:10.1023/A:1010933404324

Brooks, C., & Persand, G. (2001). Seasonality in Southeast Asian stock markets: Some new evidence on day-of-the-week effects. *Applied Economics Letters, 8*(3), 155–158. doi:10.1080/13504850150504504

Brooks, R., Levy, H., & Yoder, J. (1987). Using stochastic dominance to evaluate the performance of portfolios with options. *Financial Analysts Journal, 43*(March/April), 79–82. doi:10.2469/faj.v43.n2.79

Brown, S. J., & Warner, J. B. (1980). Measuring security price performance. *Journal of Financial Economics, 8*(3), 205–258. doi:10.1016/0304-405X(80)90002-1

Bruni, R. (2017). Stock Market Index Data and indicators for Day Trading as a Binary Classification problem. *Data in Brief, 10*, 569–575. doi:10.1016/j.dib.2016.12.044 PMID:28070548

Bruni, R., & Bianchi, G. (2015). Effective Classification using Binarization and Statistical Analysis. *IEEE Transactions on Knowledge and Data Engineering, 27*, 2349–2361. doi:10.1109/TKDE.2015.2416727

Bryant, M. (2014). 'Artificial intelligence could kill us all'. Meet the man who takes that risk seriously. *The Next Web (TNW)*. https://thenextweb.com/insider/2014/03/08/ai-could-kill-all-meet-mantakes-risk- seriously/#.tnw_hVchaHqU

Budapest Stock Exchange - historical data of stock trading. (n.d.). Retrieved February 17, 2019, from www.bse.hu

Burr Porter, R., & Gaumnitz, J. E. (1972). Stochastic Dominance vs. Mean-Variance Portfolio Analysis: An Empirical Evaluation. *The American Economic Review, 62*(3), 438–446.

Bussière, M., Chudik, A., & Sestieri, G. (2012). *Modelling global trade flows: results from a GVAR model*. Globalization and Monetary Policy Institute Working Paper 119, Federal Reserve Bank of Dallas.

Bussière, M., Fidrmuc, J., & Schnatz, B. (2005). *Trade Integration of Central and Eastern European Countries: Lessons from a Gravity Model*. ECB Working Paper No. 545.

Bybel, N., Rutledge, G. P., & Worley, M. (2009). *Capital Raising Strategies*. Bybel Rutledge LLP.

Cakici, N., Fabozzi, F. J., & Tan, S. (2013). Size, value, and momentum in emerging market stock returns. *Emerging Markets Review, 16*, 46–65. doi:10.1016/j.ememar.2013.03.001

Cakici, N., Tang, Y., & Yan, A. (2016). Do the size, value, and momentum factors drive stock returns in emerging markets? *Journal of International Money and Finance, 69*, 179–204. doi:10.1016/j.jimonfin.2016.06.001

Camelia, D. (2015b). Grey systems theory in economics – a historical applications review. Grey Systems Theory and Application, 5(2), 263–276. doi:10.1108/GS-05-2015-0018

Camelia, D. (2015a). Grey systems theory in economics – bibliometric analysis and applications' overview. *Grey Systems Theory and Application, 5*(2), 244–262.

Campa, J. M., & Hernando, I. (2004). Shareholder value creation in European M&As. *European Financial Management, 10*(1), 47–81. doi:10.1111/j.1468-036X.2004.00240.x

Campa, J. M., & Hernando, I. (2006). M&A performance in the European financial industry. *Journal of Banking & Finance, 30*(12), 3367–3392. doi:10.1016/j.jbankfin.2006.06.006

Carhart, M. M. (1997). On persistence in mutual fund performance. *The Journal of Finance, 52*(1), 57–82. doi:10.1111/j.1540-6261.1997.tb03808.x

Carp, L. (2012). Can Stock Market Development Boost Economic Growth? Empirical Evidence from Emerging Markets in Central and Eastern Europe. *Procedia Economics and Finance, 3*, 438–444. doi:10.1016/S2212-5671(12)00177-3

Castellano, R., & Giacometti, R. (2001). Performance of a Hedged Stochastic Portfolio Model in the Presence of Extreme Events. *Computational Economics*, *17*(2/3), 239–252. doi:10.1023/A:1011632311173

Cecchetti, S. G., Mohanty, M. S., & Zampolli, F. (2010). *The future of public debt: Prospects and implications* (BIS Working Papers No. 300). Basel: Bank for International Settlements.

Chakravarty, S. R. (1988). Extended gini indices of inequality. *International Economic Review*, *29*(1), 147–156. doi:10.2307/2526814

Chang, E. C., Pinegar, J. M., & Ravichandran, R. (1993). International Evidence on the Robustness of the Day-of-the-Week Effect. *Journal of Financial and Quantitative Analysis*, *28*(4), 497–513. doi:10.2307/2331162

Chan, K., Hameed, A., & Tong, W. (2000). Profitability of momentum strategies in the international equity markets. *Journal of Financial and Quantitative Analysis*, *35*(2), 153–172. doi:10.2307/2676188

Chan, L. K., Jegadeesh, N., & Lakonishok, J. (1996). Momentum strategies. *The Journal of Finance*, *51*(5), 1681–1713. doi:10.1111/j.1540-6261.1996.tb05222.x

Charnes, J. (2012). *Financial Modeling with Crystal Ball and Excel*. John Wiley & Sons, Inc. doi:10.1002/9781119203216

Chen, L., Pelger, M., & Zhu, J. (2019). *Deep learning in asset pricing*. Available at SSRN 3350138

Chen, C. I., Hsin, P. H., & Wu, C. S. (2010). Forecasting Taiwan's major stock indices by the Nash nonlinear grey Bernoulli model. *Expert Systems with Applications*, *37*(12), 7557–7562. doi:10.1016/j.eswa.2010.04.088

Cheng, C., Wang, Z., Liu, M., & Ren, X.-H. (2019). Risk measurement of international oil and gas projects based on the Value at Risk method. *Petroleum Science*, *16*(1), 199–216. doi:10.100712182-018-0279-1

Cheng, Y., Wang, Y., McVay, D., & Lee, W. J. (2010, April 1). Practical Application of a Probabilistic Approach to Estimate Reserves Using Production Decline Data. *Society of Petroleum Engineers. SPE Economics & Management*, *2*(01), 2010. doi:10.2118/95974-PA

Chen, N., Roll, R., & Ross, S. (1986). Economic Forces and the Stock Market. *The Journal of Business*, *59*(3), 383–403. doi:10.1086/296344

Cherny, A., & Madan, D. (2008). New measures for performance evaluation. *Review of Financial Studies*, *22*(7), 2571–2606. doi:10.1093/rfs/hhn081

Cheung, Y., & Lai, K. S. (1993). Finite-sample sizes of Johansen's likelihood ratio tests for cointegration. *Oxford Bulletin of Economics and Statistics*, *55*(3), 315–328. doi:10.1111/j.1468-0084.1993.mp55003003.x

Chia, R. C. J., Liew, V. K. S., & Syed Khalid Wafa, S. A. W. (2006). *Calendar anomalies in the Malaysian stock market (No. 516)*. University Library of Munich.

Choquet, G. (1954). Theory of capacities. *Annales de l'Institut Fourier*, *5*, 131–295. doi:10.5802/aif.53

Choudhry, M. (2001). *Bond and Money Markets: Strategy, Trading, Analysis*. Butterworth-Heinemann.

Chow, G. C., & Lin, A. L. (1971). Best linear unbiased interpolation, distribution, and extrapolation of time series by related series. *The Review of Economics and Statistics*, *53*(4), 372–375. doi:10.2307/1928739

Chronopoulos, D. K., Girardone, C., & Nankervis, J. C. (2010). Post-merger bank efficiency and stock market reaction: the case of the US versus Europe. In F. Fiordelisi, P. Molyneux, & D. Previati (Eds.), *New Issues in Financial Institutions Management* (pp. 122–138). Palgrave Macmillan. doi:10.1057/9780230299153_8

Chronopoulos, D. K., Girardone, C., & Nankervis, J. C. (2013). How do stock markets in the US and Europe price efficiency gains from bank M&As? *Journal of Financial Services Research, 43*(3), 243–263. doi:10.100710693-012-0132-4

Chudik, A., & Pesaran, M. H. (2011). Infinite-dimensional VARs and factor models. *Journal of Econometrics, 163*(1), 4–22. doi:10.1016/j.jeconom.2010.11.002

Chudik, A., & Pesaran, M. H. (2016). Theory and Practice of GVAR Modelling. *Journal of Economic Surveys, 30*(1), 165–197. doi:10.1111/joes.12095

Chui, A. C., Wei, K. C., & Titman, S. (2000). Momentum, legal systems and ownership structure: An analysis of Asian stock markets. *Sheridan, Momentum, Legal Systems and Ownership Structure: An Analysis of Asian Stock Markets.*

Cinko, M., & Avci, E. (2009). Examining the day of the week effect in Istanbul Stock Exchange (ISE). *International Business & Economics Research Journal, 8*(11).

Clarke, R. G. (1987). Stochastic dominance properties of option strategies. In F. J. Fabozzi (Ed.), *Advances in Futures and Options Research* (Vol. 2). JAI Press.

Clausius, R. (1870). On a mechanical theorem applicable to heat. *The London, Edinburgh and Dublin Philosophical Magazine and Journal of Science, 40*(265), 122–127. doi:10.1080/14786447008640370

Cliff, T. M., & Denis, J. D. (2004). Do Initial Public Offering Firms Purchase Analyst Coverage with Underpricing? *The Journal of Finance, LIX*(6), 2871–2901. doi:10.1111/j.1540-6261.2004.00719.x

Cochrane, J. H. (2011). Presidential address: Discount rates. *The Journal of Finance, 66*(4), 1047–1108. doi:10.1111/j.1540-6261.2011.01671.x

Cohen, J. (1960). A coefficient of agreement for nominal scales. *Educational and Psychological Measurement, 20*(1), 37–46. doi:10.1177/001316446002000104

Colwell, R., & Davis, E. (1992). Output and Productivity in Banking. *The Scandinavian Journal of Economics, 94*, S111–S129. doi:10.2307/3440252

Competition Commission of India. (2018a). *Suo Motu Case No. 01 of 2015.* Retrieved from https://www.cci.gov.in/sites/default/files/Suo-%20Moto%2001-2015.pdf

Cont, R. (Ed.). (2010). *Encyclopedia of Quantitative Finance.* Wiley. doi:10.1002/9780470061602

Cooper, W. W., Seiford, L. M., & Tone, K. (2006). *Introduction to Data Envelopment Analysis and Its Uses.* Springer.

Cota, B., Erjavec, N., & Arnerić, J. (2008). The Impact of Macroeconomic Variables on Croatian Stock Market. In *An Enterprise Odyssey. International Conference Proceedings* (pp. 70). University of Zagreb, Faculty of Economics and Business.

Cotter, J., & Dowd, K. (2006). Extreme spectral risk measures: An application to futures clearinghouse margin requirements. *Journal of Banking & Finance, 30*(12), 3469–3485. doi:10.1016/j.jbankfin.2006.01.008

Cowles, A. III, & Jones, H. E. (1937). Some a posteriori probabilities in stock market action. *Econometrica, 5*(3), 280–294. doi:10.2307/1905515

Cox, J. C., & Ross, S. A. (1976). The valuation of options for alternative stochastic processes. *Journal of Financial Economics, 3*(1-2), 145–166. doi:10.1016/0304-405X(76)90023-4

Creswell, J. W. (2003). *Research design: Qualitative and quantitative approaches.* SAGE.

Cross, F. (1973). The behavior of stock prices on Fridays and Mondays. *Financial Analysts Journal*, *29*(6), 67–69. doi:10.2469/faj.v29.n6.67

Cvitanić, J., & Zapatero, F. (2004). *Introduction to the Economics and Mathematics of Financial Markets*. MIT Press.

Cybo-Ottone, A., & Murgia, M. (2000). Mergers and shareholder wealth in European banking. *Journal of Banking & Finance*, *24*(6), 831–859. doi:10.1016/S0378-4266(99)00109-0

Dalen, D.M., Hoel, M., & Strøm, S. (2008). Kalkulasjonsrenten på lang sikt i en usikker verden. *Samfunnsøkonomen*, 8.

Damodar, N. (2004). *Basic econometrics*: The Mc-Graw Hill. Retrieved from: http://eprints.stiperdharmawacana.ac.id/180/1/Basic%20Econometrics%20-%20Gujarati.pdf

Daniel, K., Grinblatt, M., Titman, S., & Wermers, R. (1997). Measuring mutual fund performance with characteristic-based benchmarks. *The Journal of Finance*, *52*(3), 1035–1058. doi:10.1111/j.1540-6261.1997.tb02724.x

Daniel, K., & Titman, S. (1998). Characteristics or covariances. *Journal of Portfolio Management*, *24*(4), 24–33. doi:10.3905/jpm.1998.24

Daryakin, A., & Andriashina, S. (2015). Problems of Evaluation and Management of Operational Risks in Banks. *Procedia Economics and Finance*, *24*, 156–165. doi:10.1016/S2212-5671(15)00637-1

Dash, M., & Goel, A. (2014). A Comparison of ITM and OTM Protective-Puts and Covered-Calls. *Asian Journal of Finance & Accounting*, *6*(1), 126–137. doi:10.5296/ajfa.v6i1.3945

De Giorgi, E. (2005). Reward-risk portfolio selection and stochastic dominance. *Journal of Banking & Finance*, *29*(4), 895–926. doi:10.1016/j.jbankfin.2004.05.027

De Groot, W., Pang, J., & Swinkels, L. (2010). *Value and Momentum in frontier emerging markets*. Working Paper. Available at http://ssrn. com/abstract=1600023

Dees, S., di Mauro, F., Pesaran, M. H., & Smith, L. V. (2007). Exploring the International Linkages of the Euro Area: A Global VAR Analysis. *Journal of Applied Econometrics*, *22*(1), 1–38. doi:10.1002/jae.932

Deeva, G. (2017). Comparing entropy and beta as measures of risk in asset pricing. *Acta Universitatis Agriculturae et Silviculturae Mendelianae Brunensis*, *65*(6), 1889–1894. doi:10.11118/actaun201765061889

Delbaen, F. (2012). *Monetary Utility Functions*. Osaka University CSFI Lecture Notes Series.

Delcea, C. (2015). Grey systems theory in economics – a historical applications review. *Grey Systems: Theory and Application*, *5*(2), 263–276. doi:10.1108/GS-05-2015-0018

DeLong, G. L., & DeYoung, R. (2007). Learning by observing: Information spillovers in the execution and valuation of commercial bank M&As. *The Journal of Finance*, *62*(1), 181–216. doi:10.1111/j.1540-6261.2007.01205.x

DeMiguel, V., Martin Utrera, A., Nogales, F. J., & Uppal, R. (2017). *A portfolio perspective on the multitude of firm characteristics*. Academic Press.

Denneberg, D. (1994). Conditioning (updating) non-additive measures. *Annals of Operations Research*, *52*(1), 21–42. doi:10.1007/BF02032159

DeYoung, R., Evanoff, D. D., & Molyneux, P. (2009). Mergers and Acquisitions of Financial Institutions: A Review of the Post-2000 Literature. *Journal of Financial Services Research*, *36*(2-3), 87–110. doi:10.100710693-009-0066-7

Dhaene, J., Denuit, M., Goovaerts, M. J., Kaas, R., & Vyncke, D. (2002). The concept of comonotonicity in actuarial science and finance: Theory. *Insurance, Mathematics & Economics*, *31*(1), 3–33. doi:10.1016/S0167-6687(02)00134-8

Di Giorgio, G., & Rotondi, Z. (2008). *Monetary Policy*. Financial Stability and Interest Rate Rules.

Diamond, D. W., & Kashyap, A. K. (2016). *Liquidity requirements, liquidity choice, and financial stability* (Vol. 2). Handbook of macroeconomics. Elsevier. doi:10.3386/w22053

Dickey, D., & Fuller, W. (1981). Likelihood Ratio Statistics for Autoregressive Time Series with a Unit Root. *Econometrica*, *49*(4), 1057–1072. doi:10.2307/1912517

Dickson, D., Slaughter, A. & Mittal, A. (2019, Apr. 23). Succeeding amid uncertainty: A preview of the years ahead. *Deloitte Insights, Collection Decoding the O&G downturn*, 1-6.

Discussion, E. (2016). *Public debt: Meaning, objectives, and problems. Question and answer forum. An online publication of economic discussion.* https://www.economicsdiscussion.net/debt-2/public-debt-meaning-objectives-and-problems/12812

Dixit, A. K., & Pindyck, R. S. (1994). Investment under uncertainty. Princeton University Press. doi:10.1515/9781400830176

Doryab, B., & Salehi, M. (2017). Modeling and forecasting abnormal stock returns using the nonlinear Grey Bernoulli model. *Journal of Economics, Finance and Administrative Science*, *23*(4), 95–112.

Dowd, K., Cotter, J., & Sorwar, G. (2008). Spectral risk measures: Properties and limitations. *Journal of Financial Services Research*, *34*(1), 61–75. doi:10.100710693-008-0035-6

Duan, H., Xiao, X., Yang, J., & Zeng, B. (2018). Elliott wave theory and the Fibonacci sequence-gray model and their application in Chinese stock market. *Journal of Intelligent & Fuzzy Systems*, *34*(3), 1813–1825. doi:10.3233/JIFS-17108

Dumitrescu, S., & Horobet, A. (2009). *On the Causal Relationship between Stock Prices and Exchange Rates: Evidence from Romania*. Available at SSRN 1341703.

Dzhafarov, A. S. (1966). Nailuchshee priblizhenie konechnymi sfericheskimi summami i nekotorye differencial'nye svojstva garmonicheskih v share funkcij. In L. Kudryavcev (Ed.), *Teoremy vlozhenija i ih prilozhenija. Trudy simpoziuma po teoremam vlozheniya. Baku, 1966 god* (pp. 75–81). Nauka.

Dzhafarov, A. S. (1985). Konstruktivnoe opisanie obobshhennyh klassov Besova na mnogomernoj sfere. *DAN SSSR*, *285*(3), 542–546.

Eckert, C., & Gatzert, N. (2017). Modeling operational risk incorporating reputation risk: An integrated analysis for financial firms. *Insurance, Mathematics & Economics*, *72*, 122–137. doi:10.1016/j.insmatheco.2016.11.005

Edirisinghe, N. C. P., & Zhang, X. (2007). Generalized DEA model of fundamental analysis and its application to portfolio optimization. *Journal of Banking & Finance*, *31*(11), 3311–3335. doi:10.1016/j.jbankfin.2007.04.008

Edirisinghe, N. C. P., & Zhang, X. (2010). Input/output selection in DEA under expert information, with application to financial markets. *European Journal of Operational Research*, *207*(3), 1669–1678. doi:10.1016/j.ejor.2010.06.027

Eichengreen, B. (1998). Exchange rate stability and financial stability. *Open Economies Review*, *9*(1), 569–608. doi:10.1023/A:1008373022226

Ejaz, A., & Polak, P. (2014). Short term momentum effect: a case of Middle East stock markets. *Ejaz, A*, 104-112.

Erb, C. B., & Harvey, C. R. (2006). The strategic and tactical value of commodity futures. *Financial Analysts Journal*, *62*(2), 69–97. doi:10.2469/faj.v62.n2.4084

European Commission. (2018). *European Financial Stability and Integration Review 2018*. Directorate-General for Financial Stability.

Fabozzi, F. J., Markowitz, H. M., Kolm, P. N., & Gupta, F. (2012). Mean-Variance Model for Portfolio Selection. In *Encyclopedia of Financial Models*. Retrieved from https://onlinelibrary.wiley.com/doi/full/10.1002/9781118182635.efm0003

Fabozzi, F. J. (2006). *Bond Markets, Analysis and Strategies*. Prentice Hall Inc.

Fabozzi, F. J. (2007). *Fixed income analysis*. John Wiley & Sons Inc.

Fabozzi, F. J., & Mann, S. V. (2010). *Introduction to Fixed Income Analytics Relative Value Analysis, Risk Measures and Valuation*. John Wiley & Sons, Inc. doi:10.1002/9781118266649

Fabozzi, F. J., & Mann, S. V. (2012). *The Handbook of Fixed Income Securities*. McGraw-Hill.

Fabozzi, F. J., & Markowitz, H. M. (2011). *The Theory and Practice of Investment Management, Asset Allocation, Valuation, Portfolio Construction and Strategies*. John Wiley & Sons, Inc. doi:10.1002/9781118267028

Fabozzi, F. J., & Pachamanova, D. A. (2016). *Portfolio Construction and Analytics*. John Wiley & Sons, Inc.

Faisal, N., & Majid, M. S. A. (2016). Re-examination of calendar anomalies in the Indonesian stock market. *Journal of Applied Economic Sciences, 11*(8/46), 1714-1723.

Fałdziński, M., Osińska, M., & Zdanowicz, T. (2012). Detecting risk transfer in financial markets using different risk measures. *Central European Journal of Economic Modelling and Econometrics, 4*(1), 45–64. doi:10.24425/cejeme.2012.119275

Fama, E. F., & French, K. R. (1992). The cross-section of expected stock returns. *The Journal of Finance, 47*(2), 427-465.

Fama, E. F., & French, K. R. (1993). *Common risk factors in the returns on stocks and bonds*. Academic Press.

Fama, E. F. (1970). Efficient capital markets: A review of theory and empirical work. *The Journal of Finance, 25*(2), 383–417. doi:10.2307/2325486

Fama, E. F., & French, K. R. (1992). The cross-section of expected stock returns. *The Journal of Finance, 47*(2), 427–465. doi:10.1111/j.1540-6261.1992.tb04398.x

Fama, E. F., & French, K. R. (1993). Common risk factors in the returns on stocks and bonds. *Journal of Financial Economics, 33*(1), 3–56. doi:10.1016/0304-405X(93)90023-5

Fama, E. F., & French, K. R. (2015). A five-factor asset pricing model. *Journal of Financial Economics, 116*(1), 1–22. doi:10.1016/j.jfineco.2014.10.010

Fama, E. F., & French, K. R. (2017). International tests of a five-factor asset pricing model. *Journal of Financial Economics, 123*(3), 441–463. doi:10.1016/j.jfineco.2016.11.004

Fama, E. F., & MacBeth, J. D. (1973). Risk, return and equilibrium: Empirical tests. *Journal of Political Economy, 81*(3), 607–636. doi:10.1086/260061

Federal Law of 22 April 1996 No. 39-FZ "On the securities market". (n.d.). Available at https://www.cbr.ru/Content/Document/File/36165/39-FZ.pdf

Feldkircher, M., & Huber, F. (2016). The international transmission of US shocks-Evidence from Bayesian global vector autoregressions. *European Economic Review, 81*, 167–188. doi:10.1016/j.euroecorev.2015.01.009

Feldkircher, M., Huber, F., & Pfarrhofer, M. (2020). Factor Augmented Vector Autoregressions, Panel VARs, and Global VARs. In P. Fuleky (Ed.), *Macroeconomic Forecasting in the Era of Big Data. Advanced Studies in Theoretical and Applied Econometrics* (Vol. 52). Springer. doi:10.1007/978-3-030-31150-6_3

Feng, G., Giglio, S., & Xiu, D. (2017). *Taming the factor zoo*. Chicago Booth research paper, (17-04).

Fishman, G. (2013). Monte Carlo: Concepts, Algorithms and Applications. Springer Science & Business Media.

Francq, C., & Zakoian, J. M. (2019). *GARCH Models. Structure, Statistical Inference and Financial Applications* (2nd ed.). John Wiley & Sons. doi:10.1002/9781119313472

Frazzini, A., & Pedersen, L. H. (2014). Betting against beta. *Journal of Financial Economics*, *111*(1), 1–25. doi:10.1016/j.jfineco.2013.10.005

Fredriksson, A., & Moro, A. (2014). Bank–SMEs relationships and banks' risk-adjusted profitability. *Journal of Banking & Finance*, *41*, 67–77. doi:10.1016/j.jbankfin.2013.12.026

French, K. R. (1980). Stock Returns and the Weekend Effect. *Journal of Financial Economics*, *8*(1), 55–69. doi:10.1016/0304-405X(80)90021-5

Freyberger, J., Neuhierl, A., & Weber, M. (2017). Dissecting characteristics nonparametrically (No. w23227). National Bureau of Economic Research.

Friend, I., & Westerfield, R. (1980). Co-skewness and capital asset pricing. *The Journal of Finance*, *35*(4), 897–913. doi:10.1111/j.1540-6261.1980.tb03508.x

FSDH. (2017). *Nigerian public debt – A comparative analysis. A publication of Proshare Intelligent Investing online.* Retrieved on the 21st of October, 2019. From: https://www.proshareng.com/news/NIGERIA%20ECONOMY/Nigerian-Public-Debt-%E2%80%93-A-Comparative-Analysis-/35222

Furman, E., Wang, R., & Zitikis, R. (2017). Gini-type measures of risk and variability: Gini shortfall, capital allocations, and heavy-tailed risks. *Journal of Banking & Finance*, *83*, 70–84. doi:10.1016/j.jbankfin.2017.06.013

Gandenberger, O. (1980). Öffentliche Verschuldung II. Theoretische Grundlagen. In W. Albers & ... (Eds.), *Handwörterbuch der Wirtschaftswissenschaft* (pp. 480–504). G. Fischer.

Gandhi, D. K., & Saunders, A. (1981). The superiority of stochastic dominance over mean variance efficiency criteria: Some clarifications. *Journal of Business Finance & Accounting*, *8*(1), 51–59. doi:10.1111/j.1468-5957.1981.tb00803.x

Gardijan, M. (2016). *Assessing the relative efficiency of portfolio hedging strategies with options* (Unpublished doctoral dissertation). University of Zagreb, Faculty of Economics and Business.

Gardijan, M., & Kojić, V. (2012). DEA-based investment strategy and its application in the Croatian stock market. *Croatian Operational Research Review*, *3*(1), 203–212.

Gardijan, M., Kojić, V., & Šego, B. (2012). Bond Duration: Propositions and Applications. In Z. Aljinović & B. Marasović (Eds.), *Mathematical models in analysis of the Croatian financial market* (pp. 5–26). University of Split: Faculty of Economics.

Gardijan, M., & Škrinjarić, T. (2015). Equity portfolio optimization: A DEA based methodology applied to the Zagreb Stock Exchange. *Croatian Operational Research Review*, *6*(2), 405–417. doi:10.17535/crorr.2015.0031

Gebhardt, W. R., Hvidkjaer, S., & Swaminathan, B. (2005). Stock and bond market interaction: Does momentum spill over? *Journal of Financial Economics*, *75*(3), 651–690. doi:10.1016/j.jfineco.2004.03.005

Geddes, R. (2008). *IPO and subsequent placement of shares.* Olympus - Business.

Geng, L.-Y., & Zhang, Z. F. (2015). Forecast of Stock Index Volatility Using Grey GARCH Type Models. *The Open Cybernetics & Systemics Journal*, *9*(1), 93–98. doi:10.2174/1874110X01509010093

Georgantopoulos, A. G. G., & Tsamis, A. D. (2008, December). The Istanbul Stock Exchange: Testing the significance of calendar anomalies. In *7th Annual Conference of the Hellenic Finance and Accounting Association* (pp. 12-13). Academic Press.

Ghenimi, A., Chaibi, H., & Omri, M. A. B. (2017). The effects of liquidity risk and credit risk on bank stability: Evidence from the MENA region. *Borsa Istanbul Review*, *17*(4), 238–248. doi:10.1016/j.bir.2017.05.002

Gheorghiu, S., Popescu, C., & Gheorghiu, V. M. (2008). The utilization of Monte Carlo Simulation Method in the oil industry. *Bulletin of the Petroleum-Gas University from Ploiesti, Economics Science Series*, *40*(5C), 1-9.

Gini, C. (1921). Measurement of inequality of incomes. *Economic Journal (London)*, *31*(121), 124–126. doi:10.2307/2223319

Ginsburg, A. I., & Karapetyants, N. K. (1994). Drobnoe integrodifferencirovanie v gel'derovskih klassah peremennogo porjadka. *Доклады российской академии наук*, *339*(4), 439–441.

Giorgi, G. M. (1993). A fresh look at the topical interest. *Metron*, *51*(1-2), 83–98.

Giorgi, G. M. (2005). *Bibliographic portrait of the gini concentration ratio. Technical report*. University Library of Munich.

Glaser, M., & Weber, M. (2003). Momentum and turnover: Evidence from the German stock market. *Schmalenbach Business Review*, *55*(2), 108–135. doi:10.1007/BF03396669

Glomsrød, S., & Osmundsen, P. P. (Eds.). (2005). *Petroleum industry regulation within stable states. Recent economic analysis of incentives in petroleum production and wealth management. Ashgate Studies in Environmental and Natural Resource Economics 2005*. Ashgate Publishers.

Gnezdilov, I., Levin, M., & Tolmacheva, O. (2018). Problems and prospects for the placement of shares of Russian enterprises through IPO. In *Russian regions in the focus of change: Collection of reports from special events*. http://elar.urfu.ru/bitstream/10995/68202/1/978-5-8295-0582-0_2018-88.pdf

Godfrey, L. G. (1978a). Testing Against General Autoregressive and Moving Average Error Models When the Regressors Include Lagged Dependent Variables. *Econometrica*, *46*(6), 1293–1302. doi:10.2307/1913829

Godfrey, L. G. (1978b). Testing for Higher Order Serial Correlation in Regression Equations When the Regressors Include Lagged Dependent Variables. *Econometrica*, *46*, 1303–1310.

Gong, Q., Liu, M., & Liu, Q. (2015). Momentum is really short-term momentum. *Journal of Banking & Finance*, *50*, 169–182. doi:10.1016/j.jbankfin.2014.10.002

Gorton, G. B., Hayashi, F., & Rouwenhorst, K. G. (2013). The fundamentals of commodity futures returns. *Review of Finance*, *17*(1), 35–105. doi:10.1093/rof/rfs019

Granger, C. J. (1989). Combining forecasts – twenty years later. *Journal of Forecasting*, *8*(1), 167–173. doi:10.1002/for.3980080303

Green, J., Hand, J. R., & Zhang, X. F. (2017). The characteristics that provide independent information about average us monthly stock returns. *Review of Financial Studies*, *30*(12), 4389–4436. doi:10.1093/rfs/hhx019

Greselin, F., & Zitikis, R. (2018). From the classical gini index of income inequality to a new Zenga-type relative measure of risk: A modellers perspective. *Econometrics*, *6*(1), 4. doi:10.3390/econometrics6010004

Griffen, J. M., Kelly, P. J., & Nardari, F. (2010). Do Market Efficiency Measures Yield Correct Inferences? A Comparison of Developed and Emerging Markets. *Review of Financial Studies*, *23*(8), 3225–3277. doi:10.1093/rfs/hhq044

Griffin, J. M., Ji, X., & Martin, J. S. (2003). Momentum investing and business cycle risk: Evidence from pole to pole. *The Journal of Finance*, *58*(6), 2515–2547. doi:10.1046/j.1540-6261.2003.00614.x

Grinold, R. C. (1992). Are Benchmark Portfolios Efficient? *Journal of Portfolio Management*, *19*(1), 34–40. doi:10.3905/jpm.1992.34

Gu, S., Kelly, B., & Xiu, D. (2018). Empirical asset pricing via machine learning (No. w25398). National Bureau of Economic Research.

Gu, A. Y. (2003). The Declining January Effect: Evidence from the U.S. Equity Market. *The Quarterly Review of Economics and Finance*, *43*(2), 395–404. doi:10.1016/S1062-9769(02)00160-6

Guidolin, M., & Timmermann, A. (2008). International Asset allocation under Regime Switching, Skew, and Kurtosis Preferences. *Review of Financial Studies*, *21*(2), 889–935. doi:10.1093/rfs/hhn006

Gujarati, D. N. (2009). *Basic econometrics*. Tata McGraw-Hill Education. Retrieved from: http://eprints.stiperdharmawacana.ac.id/180/1/Basic%20Econometrics%20-%20Gujarati.pdf

Guo, Z. (2012). *Two Essays on Stochastic Dominance and One Essay on Correlation Stress Tests* (Doctoral dissertation). University of Konstanz, Faculty of Politics, Law and Economics. Retrieved from http://kops.uni-konstanz.de/handle/123456789/24222

Guran, C. B., Ugurlu, U., & Tas, O. (2019). Mean-Variance Portfolio Optimization of Energy Stocks Supported with Second Order Stochastic Dominance Efficiency. *Finance a Uver*, *69*(4), 366–383.

Gu, S., Kelly, B. T., & Xiu, D. (2019). *Autoencoder asset pricing models*. Available at SSRN. doi:10.2139srn.3335536

Hadar, J., & Russell, W. (1969). Rules for Ordering Uncertain Prospects. *The American Economic Review*, *59*(1), 25–34.

Hagendorff, J., & Keasey, K. (2009). Post-merger strategy and performance: Evidence from the US and European banking industries. *Accounting and Finance*, *49*(4), 725–751. doi:10.1111/j.1467-629X.2009.00306.x

Haggard, K. S., & Witte, H. D. (2010). The Halloween effect: Trick or treat? *International Review of Financial Analysis*, *19*(5), 379–387. doi:10.1016/j.irfa.2010.10.001

Hall, P., Park, B. U., & Samworth, R. J. (2008). Choice of neighbor order in nearest-neighbor classification. *Annals of Statistics*, *36*(5), 2135–2152. doi:10.1214/07-AOS537

Hameed, A., & Kusnadi, Y. (2002). Momentum strategies: Evidence from Pacific Basin stock markets. *Journal of Financial Research*, *25*(3), 383–397. doi:10.1111/1475-6803.00025

Hammami, Y. (2013). Momentum investing across economic states: Evidence of market inefficiency in good times. *Applied Financial Economics*, *23*(1), 51–56. doi:10.1080/09603107.2012.705426

Hanauer, M. X., & Linhart, M. (2015). Size, value, and momentum in emerging market stock returns: Integrated or segmented pricing? *Asia-Pacific Journal of Financial Studies*, *44*(2), 175–214. doi:10.1111/ajfs.12086

Hanley, K. (1993). Underpricing of Initial Public Offerings and the Partial Adjustment Phenomenon. *Journal of Financial Economics*, *34*(2), 231–250. doi:10.1016/0304-405X(93)90019-8

Hanley, K., & Wilhelm, W. (1994). Evidence on the Strategic Allocation of Initial Public Offerings. *Journal of Financial Economics*, 37.

Hanoch, G., & Levy, H. (1969). The Efficiency Analysis of Choices Involving Risk. *The Review of Economic Studies*, *36*(3), 335–346. doi:10.2307/2296431

Hanoch, G., & Levy, H. (1970). Relative Efficiency of Efficiency Criteria for Portfolio Selection. *Journal of Financial and Quantitative Analysis*, *5*(1), 63–76. doi:10.2307/2979007

Harbo, I., Johansen, S., Nielsen, B., & Rahbek, A. (1998). Asymptotic inference on cointegrating rank in partial systems. *Journal of Business & Economic Statistics*, *16*(4), 388–399.

Hardy, M. R. (2006). An introduction to risk measures for actuarial applications. *SOA Syllabus Study Note,* 19.

Harrison, W. R. (1988). Stochastic dominance analysis of futures and option strategies for hedging feeder cattle. *Agricultural and Resource Economics Review*, *27*(2), 270–280. doi:10.1017/S1068280500006596

Harvey, C. R., Liu, Y., & Zhu, H. (2016). … and the Cross-Section of Expected Returns. *Review of Financial Studies*, *29*(1), 5–68. doi:10.1093/rfs/hhv059

Harvey, C. R., & Siddique, A. (2000). Conditional skewness in asset pricing tests. *The Journal of Finance*, *55*(3), 1263–1295. doi:10.1111/0022-1082.00247

Hassan, M. K., Khan, A., & Paltrinieri, A. (2019). Liquidity risk, credit risk and stability in Islamic and conventional banks. *Research in International Business and Finance*, *48*, 17–31. doi:10.1016/j.ribaf.2018.10.006

Hastie, T., Tibshirani, R., & Friedman, J. (2001). *The Elements of Statistical Learning: Data Mining, Inference, and Prediction*. Springer. doi:10.1007/978-0-387-21606-5

Hatefi, M. A. (2018). Assessment of Risk Factors of a Completed Oil and Gas Project, with the Use of a Hybrid EVM-SAW Method. *Journal of Energy Management and Technology*, *2*(1), 42–53.

Haugen, R. A., & Baker, N. L. (1991). The Efficient Market Inefficiency of Capitalization-Weighted Stock Portfolios. *Journal of Portfolio Management*, *17*(1), 35–40. doi:10.3905/jpm.1991.409335

Hawawini, G. A. (1982). On the Mathematics of Macaulay's Duration. In G. A. Hawawini (Ed.), *Bond Duration and Immunization: Early Developments and Recent Contributions*. Retrieved from https://flora.insead.edu/fichiersti_wp/inseadwp1982/82-03.pdf

Hawawini, G. (1984). On the relationship between Macaulay's Bond Duration and the Term to Maturity. *Economics Letters*, *16*(3-4), 331–337. doi:10.1016/0165-1765(84)90185-X

Hawking, S., Tegmark, M., Russell, S., & Wilczek, F. (2014). Transcending complacency on super-intelligent machines. *Hoffpost*.

Haykin, S. (1999). *Neural Networks: A Comprehensive Foundation*. Prentice Hall.

Hemler, M. L., & Miller, T. W. (2015). *The Performance of Options-Based Investment Strategies: Evidence for Individual Stocks During 2003–2013*. Mendoza College of Business, University of Notre Dame. Retrieved from https://www.optionseducation.org/referencelibrary/research-articles/page-assets/perf-options-strategies.aspx

Henryk, G., & Silvia, M. (2006). *On a relationship between distorted and spectral risk measures*. Faculty Working Papers 15/06, School of Economics and Business Administration, University of Navarra.

Hesse, H., & Cihak, M. (2007). *Cooperative banks and financial stability*. International Monetary Fund. IMF working paper: WP/07/2.

He, W., Song, G., & Wu, A. (2005). On a gens arithmetic for parameters estimating of model GM(1, 1). *Systems Engineering Theory & Practice*, *25*(1), 69–75.

Higgins, J. G. (1993). Planning for risk and uncertainty in oil exploration. *Long Range Planning*, *26*(1), 111–122. doi:10.1016/0024-6301(93)90239-C

Holtfrerich, C., Feld, L. P., Heun, H., Illing, G., Kirchgässner, G., Kocka, J., Schularick, M., Streeck, W., Wagschal, U., Walter, S., & Von Weizsäcker, C. C. (2016). Government Debt: Causes, effects and limits. German National Academy of Sciences Leopoldina. Union der deutschen Akademien der Wissenschaften e. V.

Hong, D., Lee, C., & Swaminathan, B. (2003). *Earnings momentum in international markets.* Available at SSRN 390107

Hong, H., & Stein, J. C. (1999). A Unified Theory of Underreaction, Momentum Trading and Overreaction in Asset Markets. *The Journal of Finance*, *54*(6), 2143–2184. doi:10.1111/0022-1082.00184

Hon, M. T., & Tonks, I. (2003). Momentum in the UK stock market. *Journal of Multinational Financial Management*, *13*(1), 43–70. doi:10.1016/S1042-444X(02)00022-1

Ho, P.-H., Lin, C.-Y., & Tsai, W.-C. (2016). Effect of country governance on bank privatization performance. *International Review of Economics & Finance*, *43*, 3–18. doi:10.1016/j.iref.2015.10.028

Horobet, A., & Dumitrescu, S. (2009). On the causal relationships between monetary, financial and real macroeconomic variables: Evidence from Central and Eastern Europe. *Economic Computation and Economic Cybernetics Studies and Research*, *43*(3), 1–17.

Ho, S., Xie, M., & Goh, T. (2002). A comparative study of neural network and box-jenkins ARIMA modeling in the time series prediction. *Computers & Industrial Engineering*, *42*(2), 371–375. doi:10.1016/S0360-8352(02)00036-0

Ho, T. K. (1998). The Random Subspace Method for Constructing Decision Forests. *IEEE Transactions on Pattern Analysis and Machine Intelligence*, *20*(8), 832–844. doi:10.1109/34.709601

Hou, K., Xue, C., & Zhang, L. (2020). Replicating Anomalies. *Review of Financial Studies*, *33*(5), 2019–2133. doi:10.1093/rfs/hhy131

Houweling, P., & Van Zundert, J. (2017). Factor investing in the corporate bond market. *Financial Analysts Journal*, *73*(2), 100–115. doi:10.2469/faj.v73.n2.1

Hsiao, C. (1985). Benefits and limitations of panel data. *Econometric Reviews*, *4*(1), 121–174. doi:10.1080/07474938508800078

Hsing, Y. (2011). Macroeconomic Variables and the Stock Market: The Case of Croatia. *Economic Research Journal*, *24*(4), 41–50. doi:10.1080/1331677X.2011.11517479

Hsu, L. C. (2003). Applying the Grey prediction model to the global integrated circuit industry. *Technological Forecasting and Social Change*, *70*(6), 563–574. doi:10.1016/S0040-1625(02)00195-6

Huang, K. Y., & Jane, C. J. (2008). A Novel Model for Stock Portfolio Based on ARX, RS and a New Grey Relational Grade Theories. In *Proceedings 2008 IEEE Conference on Cybernetics and Intelligent Systems.* (pp.417-422). Chengdu, China: IEEE. 10.1109/ICCIS.2008.4670874

Huang, K. Y., Jane, C. J., & Chang, T. C. (2008). A RS Model for Stock Market Forecasting and Portfolio Selection Allied with Weight Clustering and Grey System Theories. In *Proceedings 2008 IEEE Congress on Evolutionary Computation.* (pp. 1240-1246). Chengdu, China: IEEE. 10.1109/CEC.2008.4630955

Huizinga, H. P., Nelissen, J. H. M., & Vander Vennet, R. (2001). *Efficiency effects of bank mergers and acquisitions in Europe.* Working Paper No. 106, Ghent University, Belgium.

Hyndman, R. J., & Athanasopoulos, G. (2018). Forecasting: principles and practice (2nd ed.). OTexts.

IMF. (2001). *Guidelines for public debt management. An online publication of The International Monetary Fund (IMF).* Retrieved on the 25th of October, 2019 from: https://www.imf.org/external/np/mae/pdebt/2000/eng/index.htm

Ince, H., & Trafalis, T. B. (2007). Kernel principal component analysis and support vector machines for stock price prediction. *IIE Transactions, 39*(6), 629–637. doi:10.1080/07408170600897486

Indrakanti, N., & Sridevi, V. (2019). Non performing Loans in BRICS Countries. *International Journal of Recent Technology and Engineering, 8*(3S3), 625-630.

Information Age. (2018). *How digital technology is helping consumers tackle rising debt. An online publication of information age online*. Retrieved from https://www.information-age.com/digital-technology-rising-consumer-debt-123472498/

Institute of International Finance (IIF). (2018). *Global debt monitor database, July 2018. IFF estimates of global debt stock are based on household, nonfinancial sector, corporate financial, and public sector debt for 72 countries.* IIF.

International Monetary Fund. (2017). Regional Economic Outlook, Europe: Europe Hitting Its Stride. World Economic and Financial Surveys. Washington, DC: International Monetary Fund.

Isakov, D., & Morard, B. (2001). Improving Portfolio Performance with Option Strategies: Evidence from Switzerland. *European Financial Management, 7*(1), 73–91. doi:10.1111/1468-036X.00145

Israel, R., Palhares, D., & Richardson, S. (2018). Common factors in corporate bond returns. *Journal of Investment Management, 16*(2), 17–46.

Ivashkovskaya, I. V. (2008). Pricing Efficiency Of Russian IPO. *The Journal Corporate Finance.*

Ivashkovskaya, I., & Kharlamov, L. (2007). Pricing efficiency of Russian IPOs. *Corporate Finance, 3*(3). Available at URL: https://cyberleninka.ru/article/v/effektivnost-tsenoobrazovaniya-rossiyskih-ipo

Izenman, A. J. (2008). *Modern multivariate statistical techniques: Regression, classification, and manifold learning.* Springer. doi:10.1007/978-0-387-78189-1

Jaffe, J., & Westerfield, R. (1985). The Week-End Effect in Common Stock Returns: The International Evidence. *The Journal of Finance, 40*(2), 433–454. doi:10.1111/j.1540-6261.1985.tb04966.x

Jakšić, S. (2009). *Analysis of Influence of Selected Macroeconomic Variables on CROBEX* (Unpublished master's thesis). Faculty of Economics and Business, University of Zagreb.

Jakšić, S. (2008). Impact of Monetary Aggregate M4 and Interest Rates on CROBEX Index. *Proceedings of the Faculty of Economics and Business in Zagreb, 6*(1), 131–139.

James, G., Witten, D., Hastie, T., & Tibshirani, R. (2013). *An Introduction to Statistical Learning: with Applications in R*. Springer. doi:10.1007/978-1-4614-7138-7

Javanmardi, L. (2013). *Portfolio Selection by Second Order Stochastic Dominance based on the Risk Aversion Degree of Investors* (Doctoral dissertation). University of Toronto, Graduate Department of Chemical Engineering and Applied Chemistry.

Jegadeesh, N. (1990). Evidence of predictable behavior of security returns. *The Journal of Finance, 45*(3), 881–898. doi:10.1111/j.1540-6261.1990.tb05110.x

Jegadeesh, N., & Titman, S. (1993). Returns to buying winners and selling losers: Implications for stock market efficiency. *The Journal of Finance, 48*(1), 65–91. doi:10.1111/j.1540-6261.1993.tb04702.x

Jehle, G. A., & Reny, P. J. (2011). *Advanced Microeconomic Theory* (3rd ed.). Pearson Education Limited.

Jenkinson, T., & Ljungqvist, A. (2001). *Going public – The theory and evidence on how companies raise equity finance* (2nd ed.). Oxford University Press.

Jianu, I., & Jianu, I. (2018). The Share Price and Investment: Current Footprints for Future Oil and Gas Industry Performance. *Energies, 11*(2), 448. doi:10.3390/en11020448

Jie, C., & Bo, Z. (2012). Study on parameters characteristics of NGM (1,1,k) prediction model with multiplication transformation. *Grey Systems: Theory and Application, 2*(1), 24-35. doi:10.1109/GSIS.2011.6044076

Ji, P., Zhang, J., Zou, H., & Zheng, W. (2011). A modified Unbiased GM(1,1) model. *Proceedings of 2011 IEEE International Conference on Grey Systems and Intelligent Services.*

Johansen, S. (1992). Cointegration in partial systems and the efficiency of single-equation analysis. *Journal of Econometrics, 52*(3), 231–254. doi:10.1016/0304-4076(92)90019-N

Johnson, P. (2011). The financial stability of sustainable organisations. *Journal of Business & Economics Research, 9*(10), 1–65.

Jorion, P. (2000). *Value at risk.* Retrieved from: http://bear.warrington.ufl.edu/aitsahlia/Financial_Risk_Management.pdf

Jorion, P. (2006). *Value at Risk* (3rd ed.). The New Benchmark for Managing Financial Risk. McGraw-Hill Education.

Joro, T., & Na, P. (2006). Portfolio performance evaluation in a mean–variance–skewness framework. *European Journal of Operational Research, 175*(1), 446–461. doi:10.1016/j.ejor.2005.05.006

Jostova, G., Nikolova, S., Philipov, A., & Stahel, C. W. (2013). Momentum in corporate bond returns. *Review of Financial Studies, 26*(7), 1649–1693. doi:10.1093/rfs/hht022

Jo, T. C. (2003). The effect of virtual term generation on the neural based approaches to time series prediction. In *Proceedings of the IEEE fourth conference on control and automation* (vol. 3, pp. 516-520). Montreal, Canada: IEEE. 10.1109/ICCA.2003.1595075

Jurczenko, E., & Maillet, B. (2006). *Multi-moment Asset Allocation and Pricing Models.* John Wiley & Sons, Ltd.

Kahneman, D., & Tversky, A. (2013). Prospect theory: An analysis of decision under risk. In Handbook of the fundamentals of financial decision making (Part I, pp. 99-127). Doi:10.1142/9789814417358_0006

Kahneman, D., & Riepe, M. W. (1998). Aspects of Investor Psychology. *Journal of Portfolio Management, 24*(4), 52–65. doi:10.3905/jpm.1998.409643

Kahneman, D., & Tversky, A. (1979). Prospect Theory: An Analysis of Decision under Risk. *Econometrica, 47*(2), 263–291. doi:10.2307/1914185

Karapetyants, N. K., & Ginsburg, A. I. (1995). Fractional integrodifferentiation in Hölder classes of arbitrary order. *Georgian Mathematical Journal, 2*(2), 141–150. doi:10.1007/BF02257475

Karatzoglou, A., Smola, A., Hornik, K., & Zeileis, A. (2004). kernlab - An S4 Package for Kernel Methods in R. *Journal of Statistical Software, 11*(9), 1–20. doi:10.18637/jss.v011.i09

Kara, Y., Boyacioglu, M. A., & Baykan, O. K. (2011). Predicting direction of stock Price index movement using artificial neural networks and support vector machines: The sample of the Istanbul stock exchange. *Expert Systems with Applications, 38*(5), 5311–5319. doi:10.1016/j.eswa.2010.10.027

Karolyi, G. A., Lee, K., & van Dijk, M. A. (2012). Understanding commonality in liquidity around the world. *Journal of Financial Economics, 105*(1), 82–112. doi:10.1016/j.jfineco.2011.12.008

Kato, K., & Schallheim, J. S. (1985). Seasonal and size anomalies in the Japanese stock market. *Journal of Financial and Quantitative Analysis*, *20*(2), 243–260. doi:10.2307/2330958

Kayacan, E., Ulutas, B., & Kaynak, O. (2010). Grey system theory-based models in time series prediction. *Expert Systems with Applications*, *37*(2), 1784–1789.

Kelly, F. C. (1930). *Why You Win or Lose: The Pshycology of Speculation*. Academic Press.

Kelly, B. T., Pruitt, S., & Su, Y. (2019). Characteristics are covariances: A unified model of risk and return. *Journal of Financial Economics*, *134*(3), 501–524. doi:10.1016/j.jfineco.2019.05.001

Keong, L. B., Yat, D. N. C., & Ling, C. H. (2010). Month-of-the-year effects in Asian countries: A 20-year study (1990-2009). *African Journal of Business Management*, *4*(7), 1351–1362.

Khadem, M. M. R. K., Piya, S., & Shamsuzzoha, A. (2018). Quantitative risk management in gas injection project: A case study from Oman oil and gas industry. *Journal of Industrial Engineering International*, *14*(3), 637–654. doi:10.100740092-017-0237-3

Khagram, S., Fung, A., & De Renzio, P. (Eds.). (2013). *Open Budgets: The Political Economy ofTransparency, Participation.* https://www.brookings.edu/book/open-budgets-the-political-economy-of-transparency-participation-and-accountability/

Khang, K., & King, T. H. D. (2004). Return reversals in the bond market: Evidence and causes. *Journal of Banking & Finance*, *28*(3), 569–593. doi:10.1016/S0378-4266(03)00035-9

Khuman, A. S., Yang, Y., & John, R. (2014). A commentary on some of the intrinsic differences between grey systems and fuzzy systems. In *2014 IEEE International Conference on Systems, Man, and Cybernetics (SMC)*. San Diego, CA: IEEE.

Kiefer, N. M., Vogelsang, T. J., & Bunzel, H. (2000). Simple robust testing of regression hypotheses. *Econometrica*, *68*(3), 695–714. doi:10.1111/1468-0262.00128

Kimoto, K., Asakawa, K., Yoda, M., & Takeoka, M. (1990). Stock market prediction system with modular neural network. *Proceedings of the International Joint Conference on Neural Networks*. 10.1109/IJCNN.1990.137535

Knight, F. (1921). *Risk, Uncertainty, and Profit*. Houghton Mifflin Company.

Kogan, L., & Tian, M. H. (2015). *Firm characteristics and empirical factor models: A model-mining experiment*. FRB International Finance Discussion Paper.

Kohers, G., Kohers, N., Pandey, V., & Kohers, T. (2004). The Disappearing Day-of-the-Week Effect in the World's Largest Equity Markets. *Applied Economics Letters*, *11*(3), 167–171. doi:10.1080/1350485042000203797

Kohers, T., Huang, M., & Kohers, N. (2000). Market perceptions of efficiency in bank holding company mergers: The roles of the DEA and SFA models in capturing merger potential. *Review of Financial Economics*, *9*(2), 101–120. doi:10.1016/S1058-3300(00)00019-7

Kojić, V., & Lukač, Z. (2017). Technical Note: The Shape of the Macaulay's Duration as the Function of Coupon Bond Maturity Derived Without Derivatives. In *Proceedings of the 14th International Symposium on Operational Research SOR'17* (pp. 332-337). Ljubljana: Slovenian Society Informatika - Section for Operational Research.

Kojić, V., & Lukač, Z. (2015). A non-calculus Analysis of Macaulay's Coupon Bond Duration Properties. In *Proceedings of the 3rd International Symposium on Economics and Social Sciences* (pp. 156-168). Tokyo, Japan: International Business Academics Consortium (iBAC).

Kosarenko, N. (2011). The securities market in Russia: a training manual. Flint.

Kozak, S., Nagel, S., & Santosh, S. (2018). Interpreting factor models. *The Journal of Finance, 73*(3), 1183–1223. doi:10.1111/jofi.12612

Kozak, S., Nagel, S., & Santosh, S. (2020). Shrinking the cross-section. *Journal of Financial Economics, 135*(2), 271–292. doi:10.1016/j.jfineco.2019.06.008

Králik, L. I. (2012). *Macroeconomic Variables and Stock Market Evolution*. Romanian Statistical Review.

Kraus, A., & Litzenberger, R. H. (1976). Skewness preference and the valuation of risk assets. *The Journal of Finance, 31*(4), 1085–1100.

Krause, A. (2003). Exploring the limitations of value at risk: How good is it in practice? *The Journal of Risk Finance, 4*(2), 19–28. doi:10.1108/eb022958

Krish, P. (2018). *Indian banks have very low capital compared to other countries*. Retrieved from https://www.moneycontrol.com/news/business/indian-banks-have-very-low-capital-compared-to-other-countries-3150211.html

Kroll, Y., & Levy, H. (1980). Sampling Errors and Portfolio Efficient Analysis. *Journal of Financial and Quantitative Analysis, 15*(3), 655–688. doi:10.2307/2330403

Kuhn, M. (2020). *caret: Classification and Regression Training. R package version 6.0-85*. https://CRAN.R-project.org/package=caret

Kuhn, M., & Johnson, K. (2013). *Applied predictive modeling*. Springer. doi:10.1007/978-1-4614-6849-3

Kulhanek, L. (2012). The Relationship between stock markets and gross domestic product in the Central and Eastern Europe. In *Proceedings of the 7th International Conference On Currency, Banking And International Finance - How Does Central And Eastern Europe Cope Up With The Global Financial Crisis?* (vol. 1). University of Economics in Bratislava.

Kurosh, A. G., Markushevich, A. I., & Rashevskij, P. K. (Eds.). (1948). *Matematika v SSSR za 30 let (1917-1947)*. OGIZ.

Kusuoka, S. (2001). On law invariant coherent risk measures. In *Advances in mathematical economics* (pp. 83–95). Springer. doi:10.1007/978-4-431-67891-5_4

Kvalevåg, T. (2009, May). *How do discounted cash flow analysis and real options differ as basis for decision making about oil and gas field developments?* (Master thesis). Copenhagen Business School.

La Grandville, O. (2000). *Bond pricing and portfolio analysis*. MIT Press.

La Grandville, O. (2001). *Bond pricing and portfolio analysis: protecting investors in the long run*. Massachusetts Institute of Technology.

Lakonishok, J., & Smidt, S. (1988). Are Seaosonal Anomalies Real? A Ninety-year Perspective. *Review of Financial Studies, 1*(4), 403–425. doi:10.1093/rfs/1.4.403

Lakshan, A. I., & Wijekoon, W. (2017). The use of financial ratios in predicting corporate failure in Sri Lanka. *GSTF Journal on Business Review, 2*(4), 37–43.

Lambert, D. (1980). *Commodity Channel Index: Tool for Trading Cyclic Trends. Commodities Magazine*.

Landkof, N. S. (1973). *Foundations of Modern Potential Theory*. Springer.

Lawrence, E. R., & Shankar, S. (2007). A Simple and Student-friendly Approach to the mathematics of bond prices. *Quarterly Journal of Business & Economics, 46*(4), 91–99. https://datapro.fiu.edu/campusedge/files/articles/lawrencee111512382320.pdf

Lean, H. H., Smyth, R., & Wong, W. K. (2007). Revisiting calendar anomalies in Asian stock markets using a stochastic dominance. *Journal of Multinational Financial Management, 17*(2), 125–141. doi:10.1016/j.mulfin.2006.05.003

Lee, J., & Stewart, G. (2010). Asymmetric volatility and volatility spillovers in Baltic and Nordic stock markets. *European Journal of Economics Finance and Administrative Sciences*, 25.

Lee, C.-C., & Hsieh, M.-F. (2014). Bank reforms, foreign ownership, and financial stability. *Journal of International Money and Finance, 40*, 204–224. doi:10.1016/j.jimonfin.2013.09.001

Lee, K. (2011). The world price of liquidity risk. *Journal of Financial Economics, 99*(1), 136–161. doi:10.1016/j.jfineco.2010.08.003

Lehman, R., & McMillan, L. G. (2011). Options for volatile markets: managing volatility and protecting against catastrophic risk (2nd ed.). Hoboken, NJ: John Wiley & Sons, Inc. doi:10.1002/9781118531518

Léon, F. (2014). *Measuring competition in banking: A critical review of methods*. Clermont University Working Paper. Retrieved from https://ideas.repec.org/p/cdi/wpaper/1577.html

Levy, H. (1973). Stochastic Dominance, Efficiency Criteria, and Efficient Portfolios: The Multi-Period Case. *The American Economic Review, 63*(5), 986–994.

Levy, H. (2006). *Stochastic dominance: Investment Decision Making under Uncertainty* (2nd ed.). Springer.

Levy, H. (2015). *Stochastic dominance: Investment decision making under uncertainty*. Springer.

Levy, R. A. (1967). Relative strength as a criterion for investment selection. *The Journal of Finance, 22*(4), 595–610. doi:10.1111/j.1540-6261.1967.tb00295.x

Lewellen, J., Nagel, S., & Shanken, J. (2010). A skeptical appraisal of asset pricing tests. *Journal of Financial Economics, 96*(2), 175–194. doi:10.1016/j.jfineco.2009.09.001

Lhabitant, F.-S. (2000). *Derivatives in portfolio management: Why beating the market is easy*. EDHEC risk and asset management research centre working chapter. Retrieved from https://risk.edhec.edu/publications/derivatives-portfolio-management-why-beating-market-easy

Liaw, A., & Wiener, M. (2002). Classification and Regression by randomForest. *R News, 2*(3), 18–22.

Lim, S. Y., Mun Ho, C., & Dollery, B. (2010). An empirical analysis of calendar anomalies in the Malaysian stock market. *Applied Financial Economics, 20*(3), 255–264. doi:10.1080/09603100903282648

Lim, S., Oh, K. W., & Zhu, J. (2014). Use of DEA cross-efficiency evaluation in portfolio selection: An application to Korean stock market. *European Journal of Operational Research, 236*(1), 361–368. doi:10.1016/j.ejor.2013.12.002

Lin, C. T., Hung, J. C., & Wang, Y. H. (2005). Forecasting the One-period-ahead Volatility of the International Stock Indices: GARCH Model vs. GM(1,1)-GARCH model. *Journal of Grey System, 8*(1), 1–12.

Lindholm, R. W. (1950). *Public finance and fiscal policy: An analysis of government spending, revenue, and debt*. Pitman.

Linn, S. C., & Lockwood, L. J. (1988). Short-term Stock Price Patterns: NYSE, AMEX, OTC. *Journal of Portfolio Management, 14*(2), 30–34. doi:10.3905/jpm.1988.409139

Lintner, J. (1965). Security prices, risk, and maximal gains from diversification. *The Journal of Finance, 20*(4), 587–615.

Lintner, J. (1965). The valuation of risk assets and the selection of risky investments in stock portfolios and capital budgets. *The Review of Economics and Statistics, 47*(1), 13–37. doi:10.2307/1924119

Liu, S., Yang, Y., & Forrest, J. (2016). Grey Data Analysis: Methods, Models and Applications. Singapore: Springer Science + Business Media.

Liu, L. X., & Zhang, L. (2008). Momentum profits, factor pricing, and macroeconomic risk. *Review of Financial Studies, 21*(6), 2417–2448. doi:10.1093/rfs/hhn090

Liu, L. X., & Zhang, L. (2011). *Investment-based momentum profits*. National Bureau of Economic Research.

Liu, S., Forrest, J., & Yang, Y. (2012). A brief introduction to grey systems theory. *Grey Systems: Theory and Application*, *2*(2), 89–104. doi:10.1108/20439371211260081

Liu, S., & Lin, Y. (2006). *Grey Information Theory and Practical Applications*. Springer.

Liu, S., & Lin, Y. (2010). *Grey systems, Theory and Applications*. Springer.

Liu, S., Zeng, B., Liu, J., Xie, N., & Yang, Y. (2015). Four basic models of GM(1, 1) and their suitable sequences. *Grey Systems: Theory and Application*, *5*(2), 141–156. doi:10.1108/GS-04-2015-0016

Ljungqvist, A. (2006). IPO Underpricing. In Handbook of Corporate Finance: Empirical Corporate Finance. Academic Press.

Lo, A. W., & Hasanhodzic, J. (2010). *The Evolution of Technical Analysis: Financial Prediction from Babylonian Tablets to Bloomberg Terminals*. Bloomberg Press.

Lončar, S., & Tepavac, E. (2012). Primena algoritma za trećestepenu stohastičku dominaciju u rangiranju investicija. *Škola biznisa, 2012*(2), 119–127.

Lopes, A., Lanzer, E., Lima, M., & da Costa, N. (2008). DEA investment strategy in the Brazilian stock market. *Economic Bulletin*, *13*(2), 1–10.

Lucchetti, R.J. (2019). *Basic Econometrics*. Academic Press.

Lucey, B. M., & Zhao, S. (2008). Halloween or January? Yet another puzzle. *International Review of Financial Analysis*, *17*(5), 1055–1069. doi:10.1016/j.irfa.2006.03.003

Lui, W., Strong, N., & Xu, X. (1999). The profitability of momentum investing. *Journal of Business Finance & Accounting*, *26*(9-10), 1043–1091. doi:10.1111/1468-5957.00286

Lukač, Z., & Neralić, L. (2013). *Operational Research*. Element.

Lukashov, A., & Mogin, A. (2008). *IPO from I to O. A Handbook for CFOs and Investment Analysts*. Alpina Publisher.

Lvutin, P.P., & Fetzer, O. (2007) Initial public offerings: a review of studies. *Journal of Corporate Finance*, 1.

Maberly, E. D., & Pierce, R. M. (2003). The Halloween effect and Japanese equity prices: Myth or exploitable anomaly. *Asia-Pacific Financial Markets*, *10*(4), 319–334. doi:10.100710690-005-4240-0

Maeso, J. M., Martellini, L., & Rebonato, R. (2019). *Factor Investing in Fixed-Income – Cross-Sectional andTime-Series Momentum in Sovereign Bond Markets*. EDHEC-Risk Institute.

Majka, M. (2019). *_naivebayes: High Performance Implementation of the Naive Bayes Algorithm in R_. R package version 0.9.6*. https://CRAN.R-project.org/package=naivebayes

Makri, V., Tsagkanos, A., & Bellas, A. (2014). Determinants of non-performing loans: The case of Eurozone. *Panoeconomicus*, *61*(2), 193–206. doi:10.2298/PAN1402193M

Malkiel, B. G. (2014). Is Smart Beta Really Smart? *The Journal of Portfolio Management, 40*(5), 127-134.

Malkiel, B. (1962). Expectations, Bond Prices and the Term Structure of Interest Rates. *The Quarterly Journal of Economics, 76*(2), 197–218. doi:10.2307/1880816

Marasović, B. (2016). Model za rebalans portfelja s uključenim transakcijskim troškovima i donjom polu-apsolutnom devijacijom kao mjerom rizika. *Ekonomska Misao i Praksa, 2*, 515–534.

Marasović, B., & Babić, Z. (2011). Two-step multi-criteria model for selecting optimal portfolio. *International Journal of Production Economics, 134*(1), 58–66. doi:10.1016/j.ijpe.2011.04.026

Marasović, B., & Kalinić, T. (2019). Is the expected utility- entropy decision model for stock selection applicable on emerging capital markets? *Economic and Social Development: Book of Proceedings, 39*, 225–235.

Marcato, G., & Key, T. (2005). Direct investment in real estate. *Journal of Portfolio Management, 31*(5), 55–69. doi:10.3905/jpm.2005.593888

Marilyn, K. (2013). *Ex-post facto research: Dissertation and scholarly research, Recipes for success*. Dissertation Success LLC. http://www.dissertationrecipes.com/wp-content/uploads/2011/04/Ex-Post-Facto-research.pdf

Markowitz, H. (1952). Portfolio Selection. *Journal of Finance*, 77-91.

Markowitz, H. (1959). *Portfolio selection: Efficient diversification of investments* (Vol. 16). John Wiley.

Markowitz, H. M. (1952). Portfolio Selection. *The Journal of Finance, 7*(1), 77–91.

Markowitz, H. M. (1952). Portfolio selection. *The Journal of Finance, 7*, 77–91.

Markowitz, H. M. (1999). The Early History of Portfolio Theory: 1600-1960. *Financial Analysts Journal, 55*(4), 5–16. doi:10.2469/faj.v55.n4.2281

Markowitz, H. M., Todd, P., Xu, G., & Yamane, Y. (1993). Computation of mean-Semivariance efficient sets by the Critical Line Algorithm. *Annals of Operations Research, 45*(1), 307–317. doi:10.1007/BF02282055

Mashayekhi, M., & Gras, R. (2015). Rule Extraction from Random Forest: the RF+HC Methods. In Advances in Artificial Intelligence. Canadian AI 2015. Lecture Notes in Computer Science, (vol. 9091). Springer.

Mateev, M., & Videv, A. (2008). Multifactor asset pricing model and stock market in transition: New empirical tests. *Eastern Economic Journal, 34*(2), 223–237. doi:10.1057/palgrave.eej.9050031

Mathuva, D. (2009). Capital adequacy, cost income ratio and the performance of commercial banks: The Kenyan scenario. *The International Journal of Applied Economics and Finance, 3*(2), 35–47. doi:10.3923/ijaef.2009.35.47

Mba, P. N., Yuni, D. N., & Oburota, C. S. (2013). Analysis of domestic debt: Implication for economic growth in Nigeria. *Global Journal of Social Sciences, 12*, 1-9. https://researchcyber.com/major-causes-nigerian-debt-burden-crisis/

McNeil, A., Frey, R., & Embrechts, P. (2005). *Quantitative Risk Management: Concepts, Techniques, and Tools. Business Pro collection*. Princeton University Press.

McNulty, J. E., & Akhigbe, A. (2017). What do a bank's legal expenses reveal about its internal controls and operational risk? *Journal of Financial Stability, 30*, 181–191. doi:10.1016/j.jfs.2016.10.001

Mejean, A., & Hope, C. (2013). Supplying synthetic crude oil from Canadian oil sands: A comparative study of the costs and CO_2 emissions of mining and in situ recovery. *Energy Policy, 60*, 27–40. doi:10.1016/j.enpol.2013.05.003

Mengoli, S. (2004). On the source of contrarian and momentum strategies in the Italian equity market. *International Review of Financial Analysis*, *13*(3), 301–331. doi:10.1016/j.irfa.2004.02.012

Menkhoff, L., Sarno, L., Schmeling, M., & Schrimpf, A. (2012). Currency momentum strategies. *Journal of Financial Economics*, *106*(3), 660–684. doi:10.1016/j.jfineco.2012.06.009

Merton, R. C., Scholes, M. S., & Gladstein, M. L. (1982). The Returns and Risks of Alternative Put-Option Portfolio Investment Strategies. *The Journal of Business*, *55*(1), 1–55. doi:10.1086/296153

Merton, R. C., Scholes, M., & Gladstein, M. L. (1978). The returns and risks of alternative call option portfolio investment strategies. *The Journal of Business*, *51*(2), 183–242. doi:10.1086/295995

Miffre, J., & Rallis, G. (2007). Momentum strategies in commodity futures markets. *Journal of Banking & Finance*, *31*(6), 1863–1886. doi:10.1016/j.jbankfin.2006.12.005

Mikheeva, N. (2017). Advantages and disadvantages of some methods of increasing capital of commercial banks. *Bulletin of OSU*, *13*(119).

Mills, T. C. (2019). *Applied Time Series Analysis - A Practical Guide to Modeling and Forecasting*. Academic Press.

Mizuno, H., Kosaka, M., Yajima, H., & Komoda, N. (1998). Application of Neural Network to Technical Analysis of Stock Market Prediction. *Studies in Informatics and Control*, *7*(3), 111–120.

Moller, N., & Zilca, S. (2008). The evolution of the January Effect. *Journal of Banking & Finance*, *32*(3), 447–457. doi:10.1016/j.jbankfin.2007.06.009

Moreira, J. M., Jorge, A. M., Soares, C., & Sousa, D. J. F. (2006). Improving SVM-Linear predictions using CART for example selection. In *Proceedings of the 16th International Conference on Foundations of Intelligent Systems*. Springer-Verlag. 10.1007/11875604_70

Moskowitz, T. J., & Grinblatt, M. (1999). Do industries explain momentum? *The Journal of Finance*, *54*(4), 1249–1290. doi:10.1111/0022-1082.00146

Mossin, J. (1966). Equilibrium in a capital asset market. *Econometrica*, *34*(4), 768–783. doi:10.2307/1910098

Mozgaleva, T. (2007). IPO process of Russian banks. *Finance and Credit*.

Muga, L., & Santamaria, R. (2007). The momentum effect in Latin American emerging markets. *Emerging Markets Finance & Trade*, *43*(4), 24–45. doi:10.2753/REE1540-496X430402

Murty, M. N., & Devi, V. S. (2011). *Pattern Recognition: An Algorithmic Approach*. Springer-Verlag. doi:10.1007/978-0-85729-495-1

Newey, W. K., & West, K. D. (1987). A simple, positive semi-definite, heteroskedasticity and autocorrelation consistent covariance matrix. *Econometrica*, *55*(3), 703–708. doi:10.2307/1913610

Nguyen, H. T., & Sriboonchitta, S. (2010). On Choquet integral risk measures. In *Integrated Uncertainty Management and Applications* (pp. 15–22). Springer. doi:10.1007/978-3-642-11960-6_2

Nikolsky, S. M., & Lizorkin, P. I. (1984). Priblizhenie spericheskimi polinomami. *Tr. MIAN SSSR*, *166*, 186–200.

Nnadi, M. A., & Tanna, S. (2013). Analysis of Cross-border and Domestic Mega-M&As of European Commercial Banks. *Managerial Finance*, *39*(9), 848–862. doi:10.1108/MF-01-2010-0006

Nnadi, M. A., & Tanna, S. (2014). Post Acquisitions Profitability of Banks: A Comparison of Domestic and Cross Border Acquisitions in the European Union, *Global. Business and Economic Review*, *16*(3), 310–331.

Novy-Marx, R. (2013). The other side of value: The gross profitability premium. *Journal of Financial Economics*, *108*(1), 1–28. doi:10.1016/j.jfineco.2013.01.003

Odzijewicz, T., Malinowska, A. B., & Torres, D. F. M. (2013). Fractional variational calculus of variable order. In A. Almeida, L. Castro, & F.-O. Speck (Eds.), *Advances in Harmonic Analysis and Operator Theory: The Stefan Samko Anniversary Volume* (pp. 291–301). Birkhäuser. doi:10.1007/978-3-0348-0516-2_16

Ogryczak, W., & Ruszczynski, A. (1999). From stochastic dominance to mean-risk models: Semideviations as risk measures. *European Journal of Operational Research*, *116*(1), 33–50. doi:10.1016/S0377-2217(98)00167-2

Okoye, E. I. (2000). The Nigerian debt problem: Causes consequences and policy options. African Banking and Finance Review, 1.

Olson, D., & Zoubi, T. (2017). Convergence in bank performance for commercial and Islamic banks during and after the Global Financial Crisis. *The Quarterly Review of Economics and Finance*, *65*, 71–87. doi:10.1016/j.qref.2016.06.013

Ormos, M., & Zibriczky, D. (2014). Entropy-Based Financial Asset Pricing. *PLoS One*, *9*(12), 1–21. doi:10.1371/journal.pone.0115742 PMID:25545668

Orsag, S. (2015). *Investicijska analiza.* Zagreb, Hrvatska: Avantis, HUFA.

Orsag, S. (2011). *Securities, Investments and Financing Instruments.* Revicon.

Paridha, T., & Padhi, D. (2018). Does Bank Competition Affect Financial Stability in Banking Sector: Some Empirical Evidence from India. Competition Commission of India Working Paper. Retrieved from https://www.cci.gov.in/sites/default/files/whats_newdocument/3.%20Does%20Bank%20Competition%20Affect%20Financial%20Stability%20in%20Banking%20Sector.pdf

Park, H. J., & Fuller, W. A. (1995). Alternative Estimators and Unit Root Tests for the Autoregressive Process. *Journal of Time Series Analysis*, *16*(4), 415–429. doi:10.1111/j.1467-9892.1995.tb00243.x

Pasiouras, F., Tanna, S., & Zopounidis, C. (2009). The impact of regulations on banks' cost and profit efficiency: Cross-country evidence. *International Review of Financial Analysis*, *18*(5), 294–302. doi:10.1016/j.irfa.2009.07.003

Pastor, J. T., & Ruiz, J. L. (2007). Variables with negative values in DEA. In J. Zhu & W. D. Cook (Eds.), *Modeling Data Irregularities and Structural Complexities in Data Envelopment Analysis.* Springer. doi:10.1007/978-0-387-71607-7_4

Patari, E., Leivo, T., & Honkapuro, S. (2012). Enhancement of equity portfolio performance using data envelopment analysis. *European Journal of Operational Research*, *220*(3), 786–797. doi:10.1016/j.ejor.2012.02.006

Patel, J. B., & Evans, D. A. (2003). Seasonal Stock Return Patterns in the Seven Industrialized Nations. *Journal of Applied Business Research*, *19*(3). Advance online publication. doi:10.19030/jabr.v19i3.2177

Pereverzev, N. (2016). Methodology for assessing the effectiveness of IPO. *Financial Director*, 2.

Pesaran, M. H., Schuermann, T., & Treutler, B. J. (2007). Global Business Cycles and Credit Risk. In M. Carey & R. StultzUniversity of Chicago Press (Eds.), *The risks of financial institutions*. doi:10.7208/chicago/9780226092980.003.0010

Pesaran, M. H., Schuermann, T., Treutler, B. J., & Weiner, S. M. (2006). Macroeconomic Dynamics and Credit Risk: A Global Perspective. *Journal of Money, Credit and Banking*, *38*(5), 1211–1262. doi:10.1353/mcb.2006.0074

Pesaran, M. H., Schuermann, T., & Weiner, S. M. (2004). Modeling regional interdependencies using a global error-correcting macroeconometric model. *Journal of Business & Economic Statistics*, *22*(2), 129–162. doi:10.1198/073500104000000019

Pesaran, M., Shin, Y., & Smith, R. (2000). Structural analysis of vector error correction models with exogenous I(1) variables. *Journal of Econometrics*, *97*(2), 293–343. doi:10.1016/S0304-4076(99)00073-1

Pettengil, G. N. (2003). A Survey of the Monday Effect Literature. *Quarterly Journal of Business and Economics*, *42*(3/4), 3–27.

Philippatos, G. C., & Gressis, N. (1975). Conditions of Equivalence Among E-V, SSD and E-H Portfolio Selection Criteria: The Case for Uniform, Normal and Lognormal Distributions. *Management Science*, *21*(6), 617–625. doi:10.1287/mnsc.21.6.617

Philippatos, G. C., & Wilson, C. J. (1972). Entropy, market risk, and the selection of efficient portfolios. *Applied Economics*, *4*(3), 209–220. doi:10.1080/00036847200000017

Philpot, J., & Peterson, C. A. (2011). A brief history and recent developments in the day-of-the-week effect literature. *Managerial Finance*, *37*(9), 808–816. doi:10.1108/03074351111153203

Pianca, P. (2005). *Maximum Duration of Below Par Bonds: A Closed -form Formula.* doi:10.2139srn.738445

Pilinkus, D. (2009). Stock market and macroeconomic variables: evidences from Lithuania. *Ekonomika ir vadyba*, *14*, 884-891.

Pilinkus, D., & Boguslauskas, V. (2009). The Short-Run Relationship between Stock Market Prices and Macroeconomic Variables in Lithuania: An Application of the Impulse Response Function. *Economics of Engineering Decisions*, *65*(5).

Pilinkus, D. (2010). Macroeconomic indicators and their impact on stock market performance in the short and long run: The case of the baltic states. *Technological and Economic Development of Economy*, *16*(2), 291–304. doi:10.3846/tede.2010.19

Pinho, C., & Melo, A. (2018). Composition of an Optimal Portfolio in the Capital market – Elton & Gruber Model in Portugal's Capital Market. *Account and Financial Management Journal*, *3*(8), 1678–1685. doi:10.31142/afmj/v3i8.03

Plastun, A., Sibande, X., Gupta, R., & Wohar, M. E. (2020). Historical evolution of monthly anomalies in international stock markets. *Research in International Business and Finance*, *52*, 101127. doi:10.1016/j.ribaf.2019.101127

Pop, I. (2006). An approach of the Naive Bayes classifier for the document classification. *General Mathematics*, *14*(4), 135–138.

Pospisil, L., & Zhang, J. (2010). Momentum and reversal effects in corporate bond prices and credit cycles. *Journal of Fixed Income*, *20*(2), 101–115. doi:10.3905/jfi.2010.20.2.101

Powers, J., & McMullen, P. R. (2002). Using data envelopment analysis to select efficient large cap securities. *Journal of Business and Management*, *7*(2), 31–42.

Practice, P. D. M. (2019). *Cloud technology for effective public debt management: Are we there yet? A publication of PDM Practice.* Retrieved from http://pdmpractice.org/ict-technologies-for-effective-public-debt-management-are-we-there-yet/

Prats, M. A., & Sandoval, B. (2016). *Stock Market and Economic Growth in Eastern Europe. Economics Discussion Papers, No 2016-35.* Kiel Institute for the World Economy.

Prudnikov, A. P., Brychkov, Yu. A., & Marichev, O. I. (1992). Integrals and Series. Volume 2. Special Functions. Gordon and Breach Science Publishers.

Qian, B., & Rasheed, K. (2007). Stock market prediction with multiple classifiers. *Applied Intelligence*, *26*(1), 25–33. doi:10.100710489-006-0001-7

Qian, J., & Philip, S. (2007). How do laws and institutions shape financial Contracts? The case of bank loans. *The Journal of Finance*, 62.

Qi, M., & Zhang, G. P. (2008). Trend time series modeling and forecasting with neural networks. *IEEE Transactions on Neural Networks*, *19*(5), 808–816. doi:10.1109/TNN.2007.912308 PMID:18467210

R Core Team. (2019). *R: A language and environment for statistical computing*. R Foundation for Statistical Computing. URL https://www.R-project.org/

Rack, V. (2017, June). *Business model innovation in the oil and gas supply industry* (Master thesis). Nord University.

Radman Peša, A., & Festić, M. (2014). Panel regression of stock market indices dynamics in south-eastern European economies. *Economic Research Journal*, *27*(1), 673–688.

Ramos, S. B., & Veiga, H. (2011). Risk factors in oil and gas industry returns: International evidence. *Energy Economics*, *33*(3), 525–542. doi:10.1016/j.eneco.2010.10.005

Rashid, A., & Kausar, S. (2019). Testing the Monthly Calendar Anomaly of Stock Returns in Pakistan: A Stochastic Dominance Approach. *Pakistan Development Review*, *58*(1), 83–104. doi:10.30541/v58i1pp.83-104

Rathnayaka, R. M. K. T., Seneviratna, D. M. K. N., & Jianguo, W. (2015). Grey system based novel approach for stock market forecasting. Grey Systems. *Theory and Application*, *5*(2), 178–193.

Rathnayaka, R. M. K. T., Seneviratna, D. M. K. N., Jianguo, W., & Arumawadu, H. I. (2016). An unbiased GM(1,1)-based new hybrid approach for time series forecasting. Grey Systems. *Theory and Application*, *6*(3), 322–340.

Reinhart, C. M., Reinhart, V. R., & Rogoff, K. S. (2012). Public debt overhangs: Advanced-economy episodes since 1800. *The Journal of Economic Perspectives*, *26*(3), 69–86. doi:10.1257/jep.26.3.69

Rendleman, R. J. Jr, Jones, C. P., & Latane, H. A. (1982). Empirical anomalies based on unexpected earnings and the importance of risk adjustments. *Journal of Financial Economics*, *10*(3), 269–287. doi:10.1016/0304-405X(82)90003-4

Resti, A. (1998). Can Mergers Foster Efficiency? The Italian Case. *Journal of Economics and Business*, *50*(2), 157–169. doi:10.1016/S0148-6195(97)00075-1

Richardson, J., & Yu, W. (2018). Calculation of estimated ultimate recovery and recovery factors of shale-gas wells using a probabilistic model of original gas in place, *Society of Petroleum Engineers. SPE Reservoir Evaluation & Engineering*, *21*(03), 638–653. Advance online publication. doi:10.2118/189461-PA

Richmond, J. (1982). A general method for constructing simultaneous confidence intervals. *Journal of the American Statistical Association*, *77*(378), 455–460. doi:10.1080/01621459.1982.10477832

Righi, M., & Borenstein, D. (2018). A simulation comparison of risk measures for portfolio optimization. *Finance Research Letters*, *24*, 105–112. doi:10.1016/j.frl.2017.07.013

Ripley, B. D. (2007). *Pattern Recognition and Neural Networks*. Cambridge University Press.

Rockafellar, R. T., Uryasev, S., & Zabarankin, M. (2006). Generalized deviations in risk analysis. *Finance and Stochastics*, *10*(1), 51–74. doi:10.100700780-005-0165-8

Rock, K. (1986). Why new issues are underpriced. *Journal of Financial Economics*, 15.

Rosenberg, B., Reid, K., & Lanstein, R. (1985). Efficient Capital Markets: II. *Persuasive Evidence of Market Inefficiency*, *11*(3), 9–16.

Ross, B., & Samko, S. G. (1995). Fractional integration operator of a variable order in the Holder spaces $H^{\lambda}(S_{n-1})$. *International Journal of Mathematics and Mathematical Sciences*, *18*(4), 777–788. doi:10.1155/S0161171295001001

Rossi, M. (2015). The efficient market hypothesis and calendar anomalies: A literature review. *International Journal of Managerial and Financial Accounting*, *7*(3-4), 285–296. doi:10.1504/IJMFA.2015.074905

Rossi, M., & Gunardi, A. (2018). Efficient market hypothesis and stock market anomalies: Empirical evidence in four European countries. *Journal of Applied Business Research*, *34*(1), 183–192. doi:10.19030/jabr.v34i1.10111

Rothschild, M., & Stiglitz, J. (1970). Increasing Risk I: A Definition. *Journal of Economic Theory*, *2*(3), 225–243. doi:10.1016/0022-0531(70)90038-4

Rouwenhorst, K. G. (1998). International momentum strategies. *The Journal of Finance*, *53*(1), 267–284. doi:10.1111/0022-1082.95722

Rouwenhorst, K. G. (1999). Local return factors and turnover in emerging stock markets. *The Journal of Finance*, *54*(4), 1439–1464. doi:10.1111/0022-1082.00151

Rozeff, M. S., & Kinney, W. R. Jr. (1976). Capital Market Seasonality: The Case of Stock Returns. *Journal of Financial Economics*, *3*(4), 379–402. doi:10.1016/0304-405X(76)90028-3

Rubinstein, R. Y., & Kroese, D. P. (2016). *Simulation and the Monte Carlo Method* (3rd ed.). John Wiley & Sons, Inc. doi:10.1002/9781118631980

Runde, J. (1998). Clarifying Frank Knight's discussion of the meaning of risk and uncertainty Cambridge. *Journal of Economics*, *22*(5), 539–546.

Russell, F. T. S. E. (2018, March). *FTSE Country Classification Process*. Retrieved February 17, 2019, from https://research.ftserussell.com/products/downloads/FTSE_Country_Classification_Paper.pdf

Russell, F. T. S. E. (2019, September). *FTSE Classification of Equity Markets*. Retrieved December 10, 2019, from https://research.ftserussell.com/products/downloads/FTSE-Country-Classification-Update-2019.pdf

Russell, S. J. (2010). *Artificial intelligence: a modern approach*. Prentice Hall.

Ryan, J. A., & Ulrich, J. M. (2019). *quantmod: Quantitative Financial Modelling Framework. R package version 0.4-15*. https://CRAN.R-project.org/package=quantmod

Sallehudin, H., Nurhizam Satar, M. S., Abu-Bakar, N. A., Baker, R., Yahya, F., & Md-Fadzil, A. F. (2019). Modeling the Enterprise Architecture Implementation in the Public Sector using HOT-Fit Framework. *International Journal of Advanced Computer Science and Applications*, *10*(8), 2019.

Sallehudin, H., Razak, R. C., Ismail, M., Md-Fadzil, A. F., & Baker, R. (2018). *Cloud Computing Implementation in the Public Sector: Factors and Impact*. Asia-Pacific Journal of Information Technology and Multimedia.

Samawi, H. M. (2017). Improving the Efficiency of the Monte-Carlo Methods Using Ranked Simulated Approach. In Monte-Carlo Simulation-Based Statistical Modeling. Springer Nature Singapore Pte Ltd.

Samitas, A., & Kenourgios, D. (2007). Macroeconomic factors' influence on'new'European countries' stock returns: The case of four transition economies. *International Journal of Financial Services Management*, *2*(1/2), 34–49. doi:10.1504/IJFSM.2007.011670

Samko, N., & Vakulov, B. (2011). Spherical fractional and hypersingular integrals of variable order in generalized Holder spaces with variable characteristic. *Mathematische Nachrichten*, *2-3*(284), 355–369. doi:10.1002/mana.200810113

Samko, S. G. (1995). Fractional integration and differentiation of variable order. *Analysis Mathematica, 21*(3), 213–236. doi:10.1007/BF01911126

Samko, S. G. (1998). Differentiation and integration of variable order and the spaces $L^{p(x)}$. *Contemporary Mathematics, 212*, 203–219. doi:10.1090/conm/212/02884

Samko, S. G. (2002). *Hypersingular integrals and their applications*. Taylor & Francis.

Samko, S. G., Kilbas, A. A., & Marichev, O. I. (1993). *Fractional integrals and derivatives: theory and applications*. Gordon and Breach Science Publishers.

Samko, S. G., & Ross, B. (1993). Integration and differentiation to a variable fractional order. *Integral Transforms and Special Functions, 1*(4), 277–300. doi:10.1080/10652469308819027

Samko, S. G., & Vakulov, B. G. (2000). On equivalent norms in fractional order function spaces of continuous functions on the unit sphere. *Fractional Calculus & Applied Analysis, 3*(4), 401–433.

Samuelson, P. A. (1937). A note on measurement of utility. *The Review of Economic Studies, 4*(2), 155–161. doi:10.2307/2967612

Sayyar, H., Basiruddin, R., Elhabib, M., & Abdul Rasid, S. (2015). The impact of audit quality on firm performance: Evidence from Malaysia. *Journal of Advanced Review on Scientific Research, 10*(1), 1–19.

Schiereck, D., De Bondt, W., & Weber, M. (1999). Contrarian and momentum strategies in Germany. *Financial Analysts Journal, 55*(6), 104–116. doi:10.2469/faj.v55.n6.2317

Scotland, P. (2019). *Blog: The world must not sleep-walk into another debt crisis. The Commonwealth. A presentation by the Commonwealth Secretary-General. An online publication of Commonwealth News Room*. Retrieved from https://thecommonwealth.org/blog/blog-world-must-not-sleep-walk-another-debt-crisis

Scott, R. C., & Horvath, P. A. (1980). On the Direction of Preference for Moments of Higher Order than the Variance. *The Journal of Finance, 35*(4), 915–919. doi:10.1111/j.1540-6261.1980.tb03509.x

Sealey, C. Jr, & Lindley, J. T. (1977). Inputs, outputs and a theory of production and cost at depository financial institutions. *The Journal of Finance, 32*(4), 1251–1266. doi:10.1111/j.1540-6261.1977.tb03324.x

Šego, B., & Škrinjarić, T. (2014). Bond Convexity Properties. *Proceedings of the Faculty of Economics and Business in Zagreb, 12*(2), 65–73.

Šego, B., & Škrinjarić, T. (2018). Kvantitativna istraživanja Zagrebačke burze - pregled istraživanja od osnutka do 2018. Godine. *Ekonomski Pregled, 69*(6), 655–743. doi:10.32910/ep.69.6.3

Sengupta, R., & Vardhan, H. (2019). *How Banking Crisis is impeding India's Economy*. Retrieved from https://www.ideasforindia.in/topics/money-finance/how-banking-crisis-is-impeding-india-s-economy.html

Seni, G., & Elder, J. (2010). Ensemble Methods in Data Mining: Improving Accuracy Through Combining Predictions. *Synthesis Lectures on Data Mining and Knowledge Discovery, 2*(1), 1–126. doi:10.2200/S00240ED1V01Y200912DMK002

Sereda, E. N., Bronshtein, E. M., Rachev, S. T., Fabozzi, F. J., Sun, W., & Stoyanov, S. V. (2010). Distortion risk measures in portfolio optimization. In *Handbook of portfolio construction* (pp. 649–673). Springer. doi:10.1007/978-0-387-77439-8_25

Seyhun, H. N. (1993, June). Can Omitted Risk Factors Explain the January Effect? A Stochastic Dominance Approach. *Journal of Financial and Quantitative Analysis, 28*(2), 195–213. doi:10.2307/2331286

Shannon, C. (1948). A Mathematical Theory of Communication. *The Bell System Technical Journal*, *27*(3), 379–423. doi:10.1002/j.1538-7305.1948.tb01338.x

Sharma, D. (2018). Stock Market Performance and Efficiency of Banks in a Developing Economy: Evidence from the Indian Banking Sector. *IIM Kozhikode Society & Management Review*, *7*(2), 1–16.

Sharpe, W. F. (1964). Capital asset prices: A theory of market equilibrium under conditions of risk. *The Journal of Finance*, *19*(3), 425–442.

Sharpe, W. F. (1964). Capital Asset Prices: A Theory of Market Equilibrium under Conditions of Risk. *The Journal of Finance*, *19*(3), 425–442.

Shen, C.-H., Chen, Y.-K., Kao, L.-F., & Yeh, C.-Y. (2009). *Bank liquidity risk and performance.* Paper presented at the 17th Conference on the theories and practices of securities and financial markets, Hsi-Tze Bay, Kaohsiung, Taiwan.

Shih, V. (2004). Dealing with Non-Performing Loans: Political Constraints and Financial Policies in China. *The China Quarterly*, *180*(180), 922–944. doi:10.1017/S0305741004000682

Shiller, R. J. (2000). *Irrational Exuberance*. Princeton University Press.

Shin, F. B., & Kil, D. H. (1998). Classification Cramer–Rao bounds on stock price prediction. *Journal of Forecasting*, *17*(5-6), 389–399. doi:10.1002/(SICI)1099-131X(1998090)17:5/6<389::AID-FOR703>3.0.CO;2-N

Sikavica, P., Hunjak, T., Begičević Ređep, N., & Hernaus, T. (2014). *Business decision-making*. Zagreb: Školska knjiga.

Sineviciene, L., & Vasiliauskaite, A. (2012). Fiscal policy interaction with private Investment: The case of the Baltic States. *The Engineering Economist*, *23*(2), 233–241.

Singh, P. (2007). *Global Competitiveness of Indian Banks: A study of select banking indicators, issues of concern and opportunities*. Retrieved from http://dspace.iimk.ac.in/handle/2259/48

Škrinjarić, T., & Šego, B. (2019). Grey Systems Modeling as a Tool for Stock Price Prediction. In *Proceedings of the The 15th International Symposium on Operational Research* (pp. 429-434). Bled, Slovenia: Slovenian Society Informatika.

Škrinjarić, T. (2014). Investment Strategy on the Zagreb Stock Exchange Based on Dynamic DEA. *Croatian Economic Survey*, *16*(1), 129–160. doi:10.15179/ces.16.1.5

Smith, L. V., & Galesi, A. (2014). *GVAR Toolbox 2.0*. Retrieved from https://sites.google.com/site/gvarmodelling/gvar-toolbox

Smith, D. J. (1998). A Note on the Derivation of Closed-Form Formulas for Duration and Convexity Statistics On and Between Coupon Dates. *Journal of Financial Engineering*, *7*(2).

Sriboonchitta, S., Nguyen, H. T., & Kreinovich, V. (2010). How to relate spectral risk measures and utilities. *International Journal of Intelligent Technologies and Applied Statistics*, *3*(2), 141–158.

Starmer, C. (2000). Developments in Non-Expected Utility Theory: The Hunt for a Descriptive Theory of Choice under Risk. *Journal of Economic Literature*, *38*(2), 32–382. doi:10.1257/jel.38.2.332

Stattman, D. (1980). Book values and stock returns. *The Chicago MBA: A Journal of Selected Papers*, *4*(1), 25-45.

Steeley, J. M. (2001). A Note on Information Seasonality and the Disappearence of the Weekend Effect in the UK Stock Market. *Journal of Banking & Finance*, *25*(10), 1941–1956. doi:10.1016/S0378-4266(00)00167-9

Stein, L. (1871). *Lehrbuch der Finanzwissen- schaft* (2nd ed.). Brockhaus. Von Stein.

Stevens, P. (2016, May). International Oil Companies: The Death of the Old Business Model. In *The Royal Institute of International Affairs*. London: Chatham House. Retrieved October 25, 2016 from https://www.chathamhouse.org/sites/files/chathamhouse/publications/research/2016- 05-05-international-oil-companies-stevens.pdf

Streeck, W. (2013). *The politics of public debt: Neoliberalism, capitalist development, and the restructuring of the state*. MPIfG Discussion Paper, No. 13/7, Max Planck Institute for the Study of Societies (MPIfG). Retrieved from http://www.publicseminar.org/2014/02/the-politics-of-public-debt/

Şükrüoğlu, D., & Nalin, H. T. (2014). The Macroeconomic Determinants of Stock Market Development in Selected European Countries: Dynamic Panel Data Analysis. *International Journal of Economics and Finance*, *6*(3), 64–71. doi:10.5539/ijef.v6n3p64

Suslick, S. B., Schiozer, D., & Rodriguez, M. R. (2009). Uncertainty and Risk Analysis in Petroleum Exploration and Production. *TERRÆ*, *6*(1), 30–41.

Syllignakis, M. N., & Kouretas, G. P. (2010). German, US and Central and Eastern European stock market integration. *Open Economies Review*, *21*(4), 607–628. doi:10.100711079-009-9109-9

Szado, E., & Schneeweis, T. (2012). *Option-Based Risk Management in a Multi-Asset World*. Options Education documents. Retrieved from https://www.optionseducation.org/ referencelibrary/research-articles/page-assets/options-based-risk-mgmt-summary.aspx

Taiwo, O., & Adesola, O. A. (2013). Exchange rate volatility and bank performance in Nigeria. *Asian Economic and Financial Review*, *3*(2), 178.

Tangjitprom, N. (2011). The calendar anomalies of stock return in Thailand. *Journal of Modern Accounting and Auditing*, *7*(6), 565.

Tanna, S., & Yousef, I. (2019). Mergers and acquisitions: Implications for Acquirers market risk. *Managerial Finance*, *45*(4), 545–562. doi:10.1108/MF-09-2018-0446

Tarasov, V. E. (2010). *Fractional Dynamics: Applications of Fractional Calculus to Dynamics of Particles, Fields and Media*. Springer. doi:10.1007/978-3-642-14003-7

Taylor, J. B., & Wieland, V. (2016). Finding the equilibrium real interest rate in a fog of policy deviations. *Business Economics (Cleveland, Ohio)*, *51*(3), 147–154. doi:10.105711369-016-0001-5

Taylor, M., & Allen, H. (1992). The use of technical analysis in the foreign exchange market. *Journal of International Money and Finance*, *11*(3), 304–314. doi:10.1016/0261-5606(92)90048-3

Thaler, R. (Ed.). (1993). *Advances in Behavioral Finance* (Vol. 2). Russell Sage Foundation, Princeton University Press.

The Guardian News Paper. (2020). *Uproar as Senate approves Buhari's $22.7b loan request*. The Guardian Online News: https://guardian.ng/news/uproar-as-senate-approves-buharis-22-7b-loan-request/

The Zagreb Stock Exchange Website. (n.d.). Available from: www.zse.hr

Thurber, M., Hults, D., & Heller, P. (2011). Exporting the "Norwegian Model": The effect of administrative design on oil sector performance. *Energy Policy*, *39*(9), 5366–5378. doi:10.1016/j.enpol.2011.05.027

Times of India. (2018). *No cartelisation among banks in fixing savings bank rates, says CCI*. Retrieved from https://timesofindia.indiatimes.com/business/india-business/no-cartelisation-among-banks-in-fixing-savings-bank-rates-says-cci/articleshow/63897976.cms

Tinic, S. (1988). Anatomy of initial public offerings of common stock. *The Journal of Finance, 43*(4), 789–822. doi:10.1111/j.1540-6261.1988.tb02606.x

Tobin, J. (1958). Liquidity Preference as Behavior Towards Risk. *The Review of Economic Studies, 25*(2), 65–86. doi:10.2307/2296205

Tolstel, M. S. (2008). *Factors influencing the development of IPO of commercial banks in Russia.* Academic Press.

Tolstel, M. S. (2011). *Commercial Bank readiness for IPO: A new approach to valuation.* Academic Press.

Tong, T., Singh, T., & Li, B. (2018). Country-level macro-corporate governance and the outward foreign direct investment: Evidence from China. *International Journal of Social Economics, 45*(1), 107–123. doi:10.1108/IJSE-09-2016-0243

Tong, W. (2000). Intenational Evindence on Weekend Anomalies. *Journal of Financial Research, 23*(4), 495–522. doi:10.1111/j.1475-6803.2000.tb00757.x

Trennepohl, G., & Dukes, W. (1981). An Empirical Test of Option Writing and Buying Strategies utilizing In-the-money and Out-of-the-money Contracts. *Journal of Business Finance & Accounting, 8*(2), 185–202. doi:10.1111/j.1468-5957.1981.tb00813.x

Tsaih, R., Hsu, Y., & Lai, C. C. (1998). Forecasting S&P 500 stock index futures with a hybrid AI system. *Decision Support Systems, 23*(2), 161–174. doi:10.1016/S0167-9236(98)00028-1

Tse, Y. K., & Zhang, X. (2004). *A Monte Carlo Investigation of Some Tests for Stochastic Dominance.* Institutional Knowledge at Singapore Management University. doi:10.1080/00949650310001593221

Tversky, A., & Kahnemann, D. (1974). Judgment under Uncertainty: Heuristics and Biases. *Science. New Series, 185*(4157), 1124–1131. doi:10.1126cience.185.4157.1124 PMID:17835457

Ulrich, J. (2019). *TTR: Technical Trading Rules. R package version 0.23-6.* https://CRAN.R-project.org/package=TTR

Umana, K. (2018). *Major causes of the Nigerian debt burden and crisis. Business and economics online.* Retrieved on the 21st of October, from https://researchcyber.com/major-causes-nigerian-debt-burden-crisis/

United Nations Inter-agency Task Force on Financing for Development (UNITFFD). (2018). *Financing For Sustainable Development Report 2018.* UNITFFD.

United Nations Inter-agency Task Force on Financing for Development (UNITFFD). (2019). *Financing for Sustainable Development Report 2019.* Available from https://developmentfinance.un.org/fsdr2019

Urio, H., & Tanna, S. (2012). Consolidation and Performance in the EU Banking Industry: A Survey. In M. Fethi, C. Gaganis, F. Pasiouras, & C. Zopounidis (Eds.), *Financial Services: Efficiency and Risk Management* (pp. 1–40). Nova Science Publishers.

Usta, I., & Kantar, Y. M. (2011). Mean-Variance-Skewness-Entropy Measures: A Multi-Objective Approach for Portfolio Selection. *Entropy (Basel, Switzerland), 13*(1), 117–133. doi:10.3390/e13010117

Vakulov, B. G. (2001). O dejstvii operatora rissova potenciala kompleksnogo porjadka po Rn v vesovyh prostranstvah Gjol'dera. *Izvestija vuzov. Severo-Kavkazskij region. Estestvennye nauki, 4*, 47-49.

Vakulov, B. G. (2005). Sfericheskie operatory tipa potenciala v vesovyh prostranstvah Gjol'dera peremennogo porjadka. *Vladikavkazskij matematicheskij zhurnal, 7*(2), 26-40.

Vakulov, B. G., & Kochurov, E. S. (2010). Operatory drobnogo integrirovanija i differencirovanija peremennogo porjadka v prostranstvah Gjol'dera $H^{\omega(x,t)}$. *Vladikavkazskij matematicheskij zhurnal, 12*(4), 3-11.

Vakulov, B. G., & Kochurov, E. S. (2011). Ocenki tipa Zigmunda dlja operatorov drobnogo integrirovanija i di_erencirovanija peremennogo porjadka. *Izv. vuzov. Sev. Kavk. region. Estestv. nauki. Specvypusk*, 15-17.

Vakulov, B. G. (1986). Operator tipa potenciala na sfere v obobshhennyh klassah Gjol'dera. *Izv.vuzov. Matem.*, *11*, 66–69.

Vakulov, B. G., & Drobotov, Yu. E. (2017). Variable order Riesz potential over Ŕn on weighted generalized variable Hölder spaces [Russian, English abstract]. *Siberian Electronic Mathematical Reports*, *14*, 647–656.

Vakulov, B. G., & Karapetjanc, N. K. (2003). Operatory tipa potenciala na sfere s osobennostjami na poljusah. *Doklady Akademii Nauk*, *392*(2), 151–154.

Vakulov, B. G., Karapetjanc, N. K., & Shankishvili, L. D. (2003). Operatory sfericheskoj svertki so stepenno-logarifmicheskim jadrom v obobshhennyh prostranstvah Gjol'dera. *Izv. vuzov. Matem*, *2*, 3–14.

Vakulov, B. G., Kochurov, E. S., & Samko, N. G. (2011). Ocenki tipa Zigmunda dlja operatorov drobnogo integrirovanija i differencirovanija peremennogo porjadka. *Izv. vuzov. Matematika*, *6*, 25–34.

Vakulov, B. G., & Samko, S. G. (1987). Ob jekvivalentnyh normirovkah v prostranstvah funkcij drobnoj gladkosti na sfere tipa $! ^{\lambda}(S_{n-1})$, . Izv. vuzov. *Matem*, *12*, 68–71.

Van der Hart, J., de Zwart, G., & van Dijk, D. (2005). The success of stock selection strategies in emerging markets: Is it risk or behavioral bias? *Emerging Markets Review*, *6*(3), 238–262. doi:10.1016/j.ememar.2005.05.002

Van der Hart, J., Slagter, E., & Van Dijk, D. (2003). Stock selection strategies in emerging markets. *Journal of Empirical Finance*, *10*(1-2), 105–132. doi:10.1016/S0927-5398(02)00022-1

Vander Vennet, R. (1996). The effect of mergers and acquisition on the efficiency and profitability of EC credit institutions. *Journal of Banking & Finance*, *20*(9), 1531–1558. doi:10.1016/S0378-4266(96)00014-3

Vander Vennet, R. (2002). Cost and profit efficiency of financial conglomerates and universal banks in Europe. *Journal of Money, Credit and Banking*, *34*(1), 254–282. doi:10.1353/mcb.2002.0036

Varian, H. R. (1992). *Microeconomic Analysis* (3rd ed.). W. W. Norton & Co.

Veit, D., Clemons, E., Benlian, A., Buxmann, P., Hess, T., Kundisch, D., & Spann, M. (2014). Business Models – An Information Systems Research Agenda. *Business & Information Systems Engineering*. Retrieved February 10, 2015 from http://www.wiwi.uniaugsburg.de/de/bwl/veit/lehre/downloads/bm_bise_paper.pdf

Venables, W. N., & Ripley, B. D. (2002). *Modern Applied Statistics with S* (4th ed.). Springer. doi:10.1007/978-0-387-21706-2

von–Neumann, J., & Morgenstern, O. (1953). *Theory of Games and Economic Behavior*. Princeton University Press.

Vuong, N. B., & Vu, T. T. (2018). Size, value and momentum in stock returns: The case of Latin American emerging markets. *Aestimatio: The IEB International. The Journal of Finance*, (17), 82–103.

Wächter, H. P., & Mazzoni, T. (2013). Consistent modeling of risk-averse behavior with spectral risk measures. *European Journal of Operational Research*, *229*(2), 487–495. doi:10.1016/j.ejor.2013.03.001

Wager, T. D., Keller, M. C., Lacey, S. C., & Jonides, J. (2005). Increased sensitivity in neuroimaging analyses using robust regression. *NeuroImage*, *26*(1), 99–113. doi:10.1016/j.neuroimage.2005.01.011 PMID:15862210

Wallis, K. F. (2011). Combining forecasts – forty years later. *Applied Financial Economics*, *21*(1-2), 33–41. doi:10.1080/09603107.2011.523179

Wang, S. (1995). Insurance pricing and increased limits ratemaking by proportional hazards transforms. *Insurance, Mathematics & Economics*, *17*(1), 43–54. doi:10.1016/0167-6687(95)00010-P

Wang, S. (1996). Ordering of risks under ph-transforms. *Insurance, Mathematics & Economics*, *18*(2), 109–114. doi:10.1016/0167-6687(95)00031-3

Wang, S. S. (2000). A class of distortion operators for pricing financial and insurance risks. *The Journal of Risk and Insurance*, *67*(1), 15–36. doi:10.2307/253675

Wang, S. S., Young, V. R., & Panjer, H. H. (1997). Axiomatic characterization of insurance prices. *Insurance, Mathematics & Economics*, *21*(2), 173–183. doi:10.1016/S0167-6687(97)00031-0

Wang, S., & Dhaene, J. (1998). Comonotonicity, correlation order and premium principles. *Insurance, Mathematics & Economics*, *22*(3), 235–242. doi:10.1016/S0167-6687(97)00040-1

Wang, Y. F. (2002). Predicting stock price using fuzzy Grey prediction system. *Expert Systems with Applications*, *22*(1), 33–39. doi:10.1016/S0957-4174(01)00047-1

Warren, G. (2019). Choosing and Using Utility Functions in Forming Portfolios. *Financial Analysts Journal*, *75*(3), 39–69. doi:10.1080/0015198X.2019.1618109

Wei, W. W. S. (2005). *Time Series Analysis: Univariate and Multivariate Methods* (2nd ed.). Pearson.

Welch, I. (1992). Sequential sales, learning, and cascades. *The Journal of Finance, 47*(2). Available at URL: http://citeseerx.ist.psu.edu/viewdoc/download?doi=10.1.1.24.340&rep=rep1&type=pdf

Welkenhuysen, K., Rupert, J., Compernolle, T., Ramirez, A., Swennen, R., & Piessens, K. (2017). Considering economic and geological uncertainty in the simulation of realistic investment decisions for CO2-EOR projects in the North Sea. *Applied Energy*, *185*(part 1), 745–761. doi:10.1016/j.apenergy.2016.10.105

Werding, M. (2014). *Demographischer Wandel und öffentliche Finanzen. Langfrist-Projektion 2014-2060 unter besonderer Berücksichtigung des Rentenreform-Pakets der Bundesregierung*. Arbeitspapier 01/2014. Wiesbaden: Sachverständigenrat zur Begutachtung der gesamtwirtschaftlichen Entwicklung.

Werens, M. (1981). Best approximation on the unit sphere in Rk. In P. Butzer, E. Gärlich, & B. Szökefalvi-Nagy (Eds.), *Proceedings of the Conference held at the Mathematical Research Institute at Oberwolfach Black Forest*, (pp. 233-245). Basel, Switzerland: Birkhäuser.

White, D. R., & Okunev, J. (2001). *Do Momentum Based Strategies Still Work in Foreign Currency Markets?* Available at SSRN 264574

Whitmore, G. A. (1970). Third-Degree Stochastic Dominance. *The American Economic Review*, *60*(3), 457–459.

Williams, B. (2012). *The Economics of Cloud Computing: An Overview For Decision Makers*. https://www.ciscopress.com/articles/printerfriendly/1925617

Wingender, J., & Groff, J. E. (1989). On Stochastic Dominance Analysis of Day-of-the-week Return Patterns. *Journal of Financial Research*, *12*(1), 51–55. doi:10.1111/j.1475-6803.1989.tb00100.x

Wirch, J. L., & Hardy, M. R. (2001). *Distortion risk measures: Coherence and stochastic dominance*. Paper presented in International Congress on Insurance: Mathematics and Economics.

Wirch, J. L., & Hardy, M. R. (1999). A synthesis of risk measures for capital adequacy. *Insurance, Mathematics & Economics*, *25*(3), 337–347. doi:10.1016/S0167-6687(99)00036-0

Wogu, I. A. P., Misra, S., Assibong, P. A., Ogiri, S. O., Maskeliunas, R., & Damasevicius, R. (2018). Super-intelligent machine operations in 21st-century manufacturing industries: A boost or doom to political and human development? In *Towards Extensible and Adaptable Methods in Computing*. Academic Press.

Wogu, I. A. P., Misra, S., Assibong, P. A., Olu-Owolabi, E. F., Maskeliunas, R., & Damasevicius, R. (2019). Artificial intelligence, smart classrooms, and online education in the 21st century: Implications for human development. *Journal of Case on Information Technology*, *21*(3). https://www.igi-global.com/article/artificial-intelligence-smart-classrooms-and-online-education-in-21st-century/227679?camid=4v1

Wogu, I. A. P., Sanjay Misra, J., Assibong, P. A., Adewumi, A., Maskeliunas, R., & Damasevicius, R. (2018). A critical review of the politics of artificial intelligent machines, alienation, and the existential risk threat to America's labor force. In *Computational Science and Its Applications*. Springer. https://rdcu.be/5XTm https://link.springer.com/chapter/10.1007/978-3-319-95171-3_18

Wogu, I. A., Elegbeleye, A., Uwaoma, K. U., Chukwuedo, C. N., Edogiawere, M., Aguziendu, C., & Misra, S. (2020). The politics of domestic violence laws against women and the dignity of womanhood: An appraisal of human factor issues in emerging polities. In S. Misra & A. Adewumi (Eds.), *Handbook of Research on the Role of Human Factors in IT Project Management* (pp. 221–242). IGI Global. doi:10.4018/978-1-7998-1279-1.ch015

Wogu, I. A., Katende, J. O., Elegbeleye, A., Roland-Otaru, C. O., Apeh, H. A., Ifeanyi-Reuben, N. J., & Misra, S. (2020). Artificial intelligence, other minds, and human factor development: The fate of man in the world of machines. In S. Misra & A. Adewumi (Eds.), *Handbook of Research on the Role of Human Factors in IT Project Management* (pp. 205–220). IGI Global. doi:10.4018/978-1-7998-1279-1.ch014

Wong, W. K., Phoon, K. F., & Lean, H. H. (2008). Stochastic dominance analysis of Asian hedge funds. *Pacific-Basin Finance Journal*, *16*(3), 204–223. doi:10.1016/j.pacfin.2007.07.001

Wu, D., & Olson, D. L. (2008). A comparison of stochastic dominance and stochastic DEA for vendor evaluation. *International Journal of Production Research*, *46*(8), 2313–2327. doi:10.1080/00207540601039775

Xiao, X. (2000). On parameters in grey models. *Journal of Grey System*, *11*(4), 73–78.

Yaari, M. E. (1987). The dual theory of choice under risk. *Econometrica*, *55*(1), 95–115. doi:10.2307/1911158

Yakob, N. A., Beal, D., & Delpachitra, S. (2005). Seasonality in the Asia Pacific stock markets. *Journal of Asset Management*, *6*(4), 298–318. doi:10.1057/palgrave.jam.2240183

Yalcin, Y., & Yucel, E. M. (2006). The day-of-the-week effect on stock-market volatility and return: Evidence from emerging markets. *Finance a Uver-Czech Journal of Economics and Finance*, *56*(5-6), 258–279.

Yamai, Y., & Yoshiba, T. (2005). Value-at-risk versus expected shortfall: A practical perspective. *Journal of Banking & Finance*, *29*(4), 997–1015. doi:10.1016/j.jbankfin.2004.08.010

Yang, J., Feng, Y., & Qiu, W. (2017). Stock Selection for Portfolios using Expected Utility-Entropy Decision Model. *Entropy (Basel, Switzerland)*, *19*(10), 508. doi:10.3390/e19100508

Yang, J., & Qiu, W. (2005). A measure of risk and a decision-making model based on expected utility and entropy. *European Journal of Operational Research*, *163*(3), 792–799. doi:10.1016/j.ejor.2004.01.031

Yang, J., & Qiu, W. (2014). Normalized expected utility-entropy measure of risk. *Entropy (Basel, Switzerland)*, *16*(7), 3590–3604. doi:10.3390/e16073590

Yang, J., Zhang, L., & Chen, X. (2010). Normalized expected utility-entropy investment decision model and its application in stock selection. In *Proceedings of the IEEE International Conference on Progress in Informatics and Computing*, (pp. 220–224). Shanghai, China: IEEE. 10.1109/PIC.2010.5687461

Yao, A. W. L., & Chi, S. C. (2004). Analysis and design of a Taguchi–Grey based electricity demand predictor for energy management systems. *Energy Conversion and Management*, *45*(7), 1205–1217. doi:10.1016/j.enconman.2003.08.008

Yared. P. (2019). Rising Government Debt: Causes and Solutions for a Decades-Old Trend. *Journal of Economic Perspectives, 33*(2), 115–140.

Yeyati, E. L., & Micco, A. (2007). Concentration and foreign penetration in Latin American banking sectors: Impact on competition and risk. *Journal of Banking & Finance*, *31*(6), 1633–1647. doi:10.1016/j.jbankfin.2006.11.003

Yin, M. S. (2013). Fifteen years of grey system theory research: A historical review and bibliometric analysis. *Expert Systems with Applications*, *40*(7), 2767–2775. doi:10.1016/j.eswa.2012.11.002

Yitzhaki, S. (1983). On an extension of the gini inequality index. *International Economic Review*, *24*(3), 617–628. doi:10.2307/2648789

Yitzhaki, S. (1998). More than a dozen alternative ways of spelling gini. In *Research in economic inequality*. Citeseer.

Yitzhaki, S., & Schechtman, E. (2005). The properties of the extended gini measures of variability and inequality. *SSRN, 815564*. Advance online publication. doi:10.2139srn.815564

Yitzhaki, S., & Schechtman, E. (2012). *The Gini Methodology: A Primer on a Statistical Methodology*. Springer Series in Statistics. Springer New York.

Yongzhong, C., & Hongjuan, L. (2005). A Comparison of Two Grey Models in Predicting Stock Index. *Journal of Grey System*, *1*, 73–76.

Yusuf, Y., Gunasekaran, Y., Musa, A., Dauda, A., Nagham, M., El-Berishy, M., & Cang, S. (2014). A relational study of supply chain agility, competitiveness and business performance in the oil and gas industry. *International Journal of Production Economics*, *147*, 531–543. doi:10.1016/j.ijpe.2012.10.009

Zagreb stock exchange - historical data of stock trading. (n.d.). Retrieved February 17, 2019, from https://www.zse.hr/

Zagst, R., & Kraus, J. (2011). Stochastic dominance of portfolio insurance strategies. *Annals of Operations Research*, *185*(1), 75–103. doi:10.100710479-009-0549-9

Zaremba, A., & Konieczka, P. (2015). Are value, size and momentum premiums in CEE emerging markets only illusionary? *Finance a úvěr-Czech. Journal of Economics and Finance*, *65*(1), 84–104.

Zemke, S. (1999). Nonlinear index prediction. *Physica A*, *269*(1), 177–183. doi:10.1016/S0378-4371(99)00091-6

Zhang, S. (2001). General N-th Degree Stochastic Dominance. *Tsinghua Science and Technology*, *6*(1), 93–96.

Zhang, Z., & Lis, M. (2020). Modeling Green Energy Development Based on Sustainable Economic Growth in China. *Sustainability*, *12*(4), 1368. doi:10.3390u12041368

Zhao, S., Moeira, F., & Wang, T. (2018). *The Relationship among Sovereign Ratings, Bank Ratings and Bank Performances, Evidence from European Commercial Banks*. University of Edinburgh Business School Working Paper. Retrieved from www.efmaefm.org/0EFMAMEETINGS/.../2018.../EFMA2018_0265_fullpaper.pdf

Zhikharev, K. (2011). Ways to increase the capitalization of the banking system of the country. *Economics of Megacities and Regions, 3*(43).

Zhu, J. (2019). *DEA Frontier Free Version*. http://www.deafrontier.net/deafree.html

Zhu, L., Zhang, Z., & Fan, Y. (2015). Overseas oil investment projects under uncertainty: How to make informed decisions? *Journal of Policy Modeling*, *37*(5), 742–762. doi:10.1016/j.jpolmod.2015.08.001

Zipf, R. (2003). *Fixed Income Mathematics*. Academic Press.

Zopounidis, C., & Doumpos, M. (2002). Multi-criteria decision aid in ðnancial decision making: Methodologies and literature review. *Journal of Multi-Criteria Decision Analysis*, *11*(4-5), 167–186. doi:10.1002/mcda.333

Zorich, V. A. (2004). *Mathematical Analysis I*. Springer-Verlag.

ZSE. (2020). *Zagreb Stock Exchange data on CROBEX*. Retrieved from: https://zse.hr/default.aspx?id=44101&index=CROBEX

About the Contributors

Tihana Škrinjarić, PhD, is employed as an assistant professor at the Department of Mathematics at the Faculty of Economics and Business of the University of Zagreb. Her research areas are risk management, econometrics and financial economics, with special focus on regime switching methodology and portfolio management. She has published more than 80 publications in the abovementioned research areas; she has participated at dozen of international conferences on econometrics and operational research. Tihana has been a member of the Croatian Operational Research Society and the Croatian Statistical Association.

Mirjana Čižmešija, PhD, is a full professor at the Department of Statistics, Faculty of Economics and Business Zagreb (FEB). Her doctoral thesis titled Statistical and methodological background of business tendency surveys was defended in 2001 at FEB. Her research interests include business and consumer surveys, statistical methods for management decision-making and business forecasting. She has been working on numerous research projects, out of which, founded by the Croatian Science Foundation, stand out: The role of economic sentiment in explaining macroeconomic trends: methodological improvements and new areas of application (as a project leader) and Economic sentiment: statistical, political, behavioural, and media aspects of its influence on economic activity (as a researcher). She has published more than 100 scientific articles and studies. She has been a reviewer for many respectable international journals, some of which are Quality & Quantity, Economic Research and The World Economy. She is a member of the review panels by Croatian Science Foundation and by the Swiss National Science Foundation and the member of the editorial board of several scientific journals and conferences. She was the Head of the Department of statistics and the president of the FEB Graduate studies committee.

Bryan Christiansen is the Chief Executive Officer of Global Training Group, Ltd., based in London, England. A former business lecturer at universities in Russia, Turkey, and the USA, he has traveled to 41 countries where he has conducted international business since 1985 in multiple languages and various industries with Global 500 firms and smaller. Christiansen received his Bachelor of Science degree in Marketing at the University of the State of New York in 1996 and his MBA degree at Capella University in 2003. He is now working on his PhD at the University of Sunderland in the United Kingdom. The author of 26 Scopus-indexed Reference books on business, cultural studies, economics, and psychology, he is fluent in Chinese, Japanese, Spanish, and Turkish. Christiansen is currently working with a Russian theoretical mathematician on a new economic model for developing nations.

* * *

Linus Eze Akujuobi conducts research and teaches at the Department of Financial Management Technology, Federal University of Technology, Owerri, Imo State, Nigeria.

Christian Amu is a lecturer and a postgraduate Ph.D research student at the Federal University of Technology, Owerri. His research interest is on public debt and economic development of sub-Saharan African economy: Evidence from Nigeria and Ghana. He holds a B.Sc degree in Accountancy and M.Sc degree in Financial Management Technology. He is an Associate member (ACA) of the Institute of Chartered Accountants of Nigeria (ICAN). He teaches Financial Management, Cost Accounting, Financial Accounting, Management Accounting, and Taxation. He has authored and co-authored very few journal articles which are published in some reputable national and international journals. He has attended a few national and international conferences.

Mohammed Berkhouch is currently a Ph.D student, at the National School of Applied Sciences, Ibn Zohr University Agadir - Morocco. He received a Specialized Master degree in Financial Engineering and a Bachelor degree in Applied Mathematics. His research interests mainly include: financial markets, financial risks measurement and management, portfolio selection, quantitative finance, behavioral finance, modeling in Insurance, evaluation of financial assets and derivatives instruments, data analysis, econometrics and time series, and extreme values theory. More information is available at https://orcid.org/0000-0001-7207-4517.

Rituparna Das teaches at Adamas University as Professor. Prior to this, he taught at the University of Petroleum and Energy Studies as Associate Professor, headed the Centre for Studies in Banking and Finance, established by the Reserve Bank of India corpus and also the Centre of Risk Management and Derivatives. His PhD on Econometrics is preceded by dual Masters in Economics and Management. Earlier he taught at National Law University, National Institute of Bank Management (established by the Reserve Bank of India), National University of Juridical Sciences and Indian Institute of Social Welfare and Business Management.. His areas of preference and international publications include Strategies, Bank Risk Management, Financial Economics and Policy Research. He is Life Member of the Ramakrishna Mission Institute of Culture, the Indian Statistical Institute, the Indian Economic Association and the Indian Econometric Society. He received the Honours of being 'Financial Economics and Risk Educator and Author' from Marquis Who's Who and 'One of the IBC's Leading Educators of the World' from International Biographical Centre.His profiles are available at https://www.linkedin.com/in/rpd and https://orcid.org/0000-0002-6877-9343,

Yuri Evgenievich Drobotov received his B.Math from Southern Federal University in 2014. He continues his studies at Institute of Mathematics, Mechanics and Computer Sciences named after I. I. Vorovich and works on the problems of operator theory in non-standard function spaces, integral equations, fractional calculus and contact mechanics.

Margareta Gardijan Kedžo, PhD, is an Assistant Professor University of Zagreb Faculty of Economics & Business where she teaches several courses on both undergraduate, graduate and integrated studies: Mathematics, Financial mathematics and Financial modelling. She obtained her PhD in quantitative economics at her home faculty in December 2016. She actively participated in several scientific conferences, projects, workshops and seminars and she is an author/co-author of 28 publications: scientific and professional papers, chapters, books, workbooks and other. Her field of scientific interest is financial modelling and data envelopment analysis with application in economics and finance.

Sorin Alexandru Gheorghiu graduated Petroleum and Gas Engineering Faculty within Petroleum-Gas University from Ploiesti, Romania. He has more than 20 years of experience in oil and gas industry, especially in reservoir engineering. Also he obtained two Master Diplomas, one in Drilling of Deviated Wells and the second one in Management in petroleum industry. At the same time, he holds a PhD in Reservoir Engineering obtained at the same university (i.e. Petroleum-Gas University from Ploiesti) in 2008. He has a wide experience in the oil field modeling and simulation, working in several important oil companies: Schlumberger, Kuwait Oil Company etc. In the first years of his career was acting as academic staff within Petroleum-Gas University from Ploiesti. He is currently working as Senior Specialist Reservoir Engineering at Kuwait Oil Company.

A. Doruk Günaydin received his MS in Mathematical Finance from Boston University in 2010 and his PhD in Finance from Sabanci University in 2016. In the same year, he was hired as Assistant Professor at the Sabanci University Business School. Professor Gunaydin specializes in empirical asset pricing, determinants of equity returns and international finance. His academic work has been published in prominent journals such as Journal of Financial Economics, Journal of Portfolio Management, Journal of International Money and Finance among others.

Murat Isiker graduated from Istanbul Bilgi University with B.A Economics. He completed MSc in Economics at Queen Mary, University of London. He currently continues on his Ph.D studies in the field of Finance at Istanbul Technical University. He works as a Research Assistant in the Management Department of Istanbul Sabahattin Zaim University.

Saša Jakšić is an Assistant Professor at the Department of Statistics of the Faculty of Economics and Business, University of Zagreb, where he obtained a PhD in quantitative economics in 2012. He published several scientific articles (3 book chapters, 14 articles, 8 conference proceedings) and attended 13 international conferences. He received Mijo Mirković award for the scientific work in 2012. His research interests include econometrics, time series analysis and macroeconometric modelling. His teaching activities include undergraduate courses (Statistics, Business Statistics, Financial Series Modelling) and graduate courses (Methods of Applied Mathematical and Statistical Analysis). He was a researcher on two scientific projects funded by the Ministry of Science, Education and Sport and a team member on two Croatian Science Foundation Projects. He acquired additional professional education and attended various seminars on applied econometrics.

Ivana Jerković graduated in 2019 from Faculty of Science at the University of Split with a master's degree in Mathematics and Computer Science. As a student, she was awarded Dean's award for academic excellence in undergraduate programme of Mathematics and Computer Science in which she got her bachelor's degree. She worked as a Software Developer at Ericsson Nikola Tesla d.d. for half a year in 2019 and is currently working as a Teaching Assistant at the Faculty of Economics, Business and Tourism at the University of Split. She is interested in researches related to the application of mathematical methods in the field of economics.

Tea Kalinić graduated in 2016 from Faculty of Science at University of Split with a degree in Mathematics and Computer Science and is currently working as a Teaching Assistant at University of Split, Faculty of Economics, Business and Tourism.

Hafiz Waqas Kamran holds PhD, majoring in Finance and Risk Management. He is working as an Assistant Professor at Iqra University (IU), Karachi, Pakistan. He has a teaching experience of more than 7 years with 25 research publications. He has a good command over R-Studio, STATA, SPSS-AMOS, and EViews.

Usama Ali Khan is a Ph.D. (Finance) Candidate at UMass Boston. His research interests include Empirical Asset Pricing, Machine Learning, and Deep Learning. His dissertation research is based on Deep Learning Applications in Asset Pricing.

Vedran Kojić, PhD, has been employed at the Faculty of Economics and Business (FEB), University of Zagreb since 2011. In 2016 he gained a doctoral degree and he currently holds the title of an Assistant Professor and works at the Department of Mathematics at FEB in Zagreb. He teaches several mathematics courses: Matematika and Gospodarska matematika (in Croatian), and Mathematics for Business, Dynamic Methods for Economics and Finance, and Game theory and Business (in English). His main research interests are applications of mathematical inequalities in economics, geometric programming, mathematical economics and game theory. He is an author of more than 30 publications (scientific and professional papers, books, chapters), and he participated at 12 international conferences.

Ghizlane Lakhnati is Professor, Ph.D, at the National School of applied Sciences, Ibn Zohr university Agadir - Morocco. She received her Ph.D degree from Paris 1 Panthéon-Sorbonne university. She is trained in disciplines such as: statistics, probability theory, applied mathematics, risk management and insurance, financial economics, and econometrics. Her research interest focuses in: finance, portfolio theory, quantitative finance, behavioral finance, financial mathematics, game theory and decision theory, risk modelling, and financial markets.

Zrinka Lovretin Golubić was born in 1986 in Zagreb, Croatia. She graduated in 2010 at the Faculty of Economics and Business, University of Zagreb. From September 2010 till April 2017 she worked in INA-INDUSTRIJA NAFTE, d.d. in Treasury Sector, Funding Department on different positions and last two years as a Funding Expert. She was preparing financial plan, managing the financial covenants, negotiating and signing of various loan facility agreements. She was included in analysis and control of subsidiaries from treasury point of view. Currently, she works as a teaching and research assistant at the Department of Managerial Economics, Faculty of Economics and Business, University of Zagreb and attending University Postgraduate (Doctoral) Study Programme. Her research interest is focused on investment analysis, portfolio management and corporate finance. She is a member of Croatian Statistical Association.

Zrinka Lukač, PhD, is a full professor at the Department of Mathematics, Faculty of Economics and Business Zagreb (FEB), where she teaches at the undergraduate and doctoral program, as well as at the English-taught undergraduate program. She obtained the BSc degree in Pure Mathematics from Faculty of Science, Department of Mathematics, University of Zagreb, and MSc degree in Operational

Research as well as PhD degree in Economics from Faculty of Economics and Business Zagreb (FEB). She was a Fulbright Scholar at Leeds School of Business, University of Colorado. From 2012-18 she was the Head of the Department of Mathematics at FEB. Currently she is the president of the Croatian Operational Research Society. Her research interests lie primarily in the area of the Operational Research and Optimization. She is member of the editorial board of several scientific journals and conferences and Editor in Chief of the Croatian Operational Research Review journal.

Branka Marasović, PhD., employed in the Department of Quantitative methods, Faculty of Economics, Business and Tourism at the University of Split and is currently employed as the Head of the Department. Her fields of interest are mathematics for business, quantitative methods in management, financial modeling, actuarial mathematics. Even though she is employed as an associate professor, since June 2014 she has received the title of scientific adviser, due to her hard work connected to these scientific areas. Branka Marasović PhD. has published: over thirty scientific papers, three professional papers, University textbook "Financijsko modeliranje" (the first edition and the second, amended edition), scientific books "Matematički modeli u financijskom upravljanju" and "Matematički modeli u analizi razvoja hrvatskog financijskog tržišta". Branka Marasović is a member of the editorial board of the scientific journal Management: Journal of Contemporary Management Issues published by Faculty of Economics Business and Tourism Split.

Sanjay Misra is full Professor of Computer Engineering at Covenant University (400-500 ranked University by THE) Ota, Nigeria. He has 25 years of wide experience in academic administration and research in various universities in Asia, Europe, and Africa. He is Ph.d. in Information and Know. Engg (Software Engineering) from the University of Alcala, Spain and M.Tech.(Software Engineering) from Motilal Nehru National Institute of Technology, India. As per SciVal(SCOPUS- Elsevier) analysis- He is the most productive researcher (no. 1-) in whole Nigeria during 2012-2017, 2013-2018 and 2014-2019(in all subjects), in computer science no 1 in whole country and no 4 in whole continent. Total around 400 articles(SCOPUS/Web of Science) with more than 200 coauthors around the world (-90 in JCR/SCIE Journals) in the core & application area of Software Engg (SQA, SPI, SPM), Web engg, Health Informatics, Intelligent systems etc. He has delivered more than 80 keynote speeches/invited talks/ public lectures in reputed conferences and institutes around the world (traveled around 60 countries). He got several awards for outstanding publications (2014 IET Software Premium Award(UK)), and from TUBITAK-Turkish Higher Education, and Atilim University). He edited (with colleagues) 42 LNCS & 6 IEEE proceedings, several books, editor in chief of book series IT Personnel and Project Management, International Journal of Human Capital and Information Technology Professionals (IJHCITP)-IGI Global, and of 3 journals(IJ) and editor in various SCIE journals. He is a software engineer and previously held academic positions at FUT Minna - Nigeria (as Head Department of Computer Engineering and Head-Department of Cyber Security), Atilim University - Turkey, Subharati University and UP Technical University - India. He is also visiting/Collaborative professor at the University of Alcala – Spain(since 2011-), UCV- Valparaiso – Chile(since 2013-), UNICEN, Tandil – Argentina(since 2011-), and Atilim University – Turkey(since 2011-). His current research covers the areas of software quality assurance, software process improvement, software project management, object-oriented technologies, XML, SOA, Web services, cognitive informatics, artificial intelligence, neural network, health Informatics, e-learning, cloud computing, and cybersecurity. Prof Sanjay is coordinating/working/collaborating with several research groups (as visiting/adjunct professor/collaborative researcher) in various universities and industry around the world (Spain, Argentina, Turkey, Singapore, Chile, Brazil, Mexico, Norway, France, South Africa, Malaysia, Nigeria, Myanmar, Vietnam, India).

Josephine Mazzi Namayanja is an Assistant Professor of Management Science and Information Systems in the College of Management at University of Massachusetts, Boston. She received her Ph.D in Information Systems at University of Maryland, Baltimore County in May 2015 and her M.S in Information Systems in May 2010. She has a broad interest in research primarily in data mining where her work poses potential benefits in various domains such as healthcare, cyber security, big data, project management and financial analytics.

Gargi Guha Niyogi specializes in Accounting, Banking and Finance. She is in academic profession for last one decade.rior to this she taught in Swami Vivekanada Group of Institutes, Distance MBA Education, Vidyasagar University. Her broader research interests lie in the areas of Financial Supermarket, Credit Rating, Social impact of Financial reforms, E-commerce and Financial literacy. She has published internationally in these areas and has presented papers at international conferences on Accounts and Finance. She has also published one book on E-commerce under the Cengage Publications. Her teaching and research area includes Accountancy, General Management, Indian Financial System, Taxation, Financial Reporting and Financial Statement Analysis.

Sharon Njie is currently a Doctoral Candidate of Public Policy and Administration with a concentration in International Development at the Nelson Mandela College of Government and Social Sciences program at Southern University and A & M College, Baton Rouge, Louisiana, USA. She is equally a Research Associate at the Nelson Mandela Institute for Research. Sharon is currently a Graduate Teaching Assistant at the Honor's College at Southern University and A &M College. She holds a Bachelor's Degree in Business Administration from the Bamenda University of Science and Technology Cameroon and a Master's Degree in Business Administration (MBA) from Covenant University Nigeria. Her Current research works have been accepted at several Conferences: Black Doctoral Network; National Institute of Science; West Texas A&M University; Louisiana Academy of Science. Sharon's Research interest is in Social Science and Policy related research. Recently, she has been involved in the Political Economy of Artificial Intelligence (AI).

Nathaniel Chinedum Nwezeaku teaches and conducts research in the Department of Financial Management Technology, Federal University of Technology, Owerri, Imo State, Nigeria.

Abdelnaser Omran is currently an academic scholar at Faculty of Engineering Sciences, Bright Star University in Libya. He is an avid writer, contributed many publications in field of environmental sciences and engineering, construction and project management, risk management and related issues. So far, he published more than 250 articles in international journals and proceeding papers at local and international conferences. Besides that, he had written 7 books and 15 chapters in different books.

Zrinka Orlović was born in 1994 in Zagreb, Croatia. She graduated in 2018 at the Faculty of Economics and Business, Analysis and Business Planning. Currently, she works as a Teaching and Research Assistant at the Department of Managerial Economics, Faculty of Economics and Business, University of Zagreb. She is also currently attending University Postgraduate (Doctoral) Study Programme. Her interest is focused on financial economics, particularly investment analysis, and portfolio management.

Benedict Anayochukwu Ozurumba is an Associate Professor at the Federal University of Technology, Owerri (FUTO). He holds a B.Sc (Hons) in Econs, M.Sc (Econs), M.Sc and Ph.D in Financial Management Technology. He has served the University as Head, Department of Financial Management Technology, (2018 to date), former Deputy Director, Public Procurement Research Center, former Deputy Director, Center for Entrepreneurial Studies, Central Bank of Nigeria (CBN) Certified Microfinance Trainer & Consultant. Ben is also a member of African Centre for Research & Policy Analysis, member and national Secretary of the Nigerian Economic Society. He is also a member of International Academy of Business and Behavioural Sciences (IABBS), USA, Chartered Institute of Finance & Control of Nigeria and International Society for Development & Sustainability, Japan. His research interest is in the area of Public Debt and Sustainable Growth.

Cătălin Popescu is Professor of Management at Petroleum-Gas University from Ploiesti, Romania. His research and consulting interest include general management, engineering management, project management, quantitative methods for business and management, human resource management, operations management, energy and environmental management, feasibility studies and petroleum economics. He received in 1991 a degree in Engineering, a degree in Management (2000) and a PhD (2001) in Automated Systems concern Modelling and simulation of production systems, from the University of Oil and Gas from Ploiesti, Romania. He became, in 2016, PhD Advisor for Engineering and Management domain with a habilitation thesis entitled: Researches and contributions to the development of managerial tools for the sustainable management of conventional and non-conventional resources of energy and for the innovation in education and research. Dr. Popescu has published over 220 articles and conference papers, 9 books, 3 books chapters and he was involved in more than 32 scientific research grants and international projects. His international experience includes participations and presentations with scientific papers in more than 27 countries and membership in more than 30 scientific committees of some prestigious international conferences or symposiums.

Sailesh Tanna is currently Associate Professor within the Business School at Coventry University, UK. In his academic career spanning over 30 years, he has made significant contributions in research, having published widely in reputable journals and scholarly works. His research deals with the application of quantitative techniques in economics and financial management, with specialisation in banking, corporate finance and economics of emerging markets. He has actively supervised doctoral students in these areas, many of whom now hold academic positions in higher education.

Oktay Taş is currently working as Professor at Istanbul Technical University in Management Engineering department. He obtained his PhD degree at Berlin Technical University. He published several papers in highly reputable indexed journals in the field of accounting and finance. He mainly focuses on the fields such as accounting standards of financial derivatives, financial risk management and portfolio management.

Umut Ugurlu obtained his PhD degree from the Management Engineering Department of Istanbul Technical University. He is currently assistant professor in the Management Department of Bahcesehir University, Turkey. His main research interests are electricity price forecasting and portfolio choice.

Hodian Urio, a former director of the Institute of Accountancy Arusha, studied for his PhD at Coventry University under the supervision of Dr Sailesh Tanna during the period 2006-2011. He then taught at Mount Meru University in Arusha, Tanzania, before retirement.

Boris Grigorievich Vakulov received his Ph.D. in Physical and Mathematical Sciences in Rostov State University in 1986. He is the author of about a hundred scientific papers on various problems of functional analysis, operator theory, and their applications in economics and mechanics. A renowned specialist in fractional calculus, he continues his research and educational work at Southern Federal University, acts as a scientific advisor and opponent in implementation of master's and doctoral theses.

Silvija Vlah Jerić is currently an assistant professor at Faculty of Economics and Business – Zagreb, University of Zagreb. She worked as project engineer/programmer at Pliva d.d. before joining Faculty of Economics and Business – Zagreb as teaching and research assistant. She gained her PhD in 2012 and MSc degree in 2008, both in the area of operational research at Faculty of Economics and Business – Zagreb, but her BSc degree has been gained at Department of Mathematics of Faculty of Science, University of Science in the area of Computer Science. Her main research interests are in the fields of quantitative methods in economics and operational research, especially machine learning and data mining, as well as optimization algorithms and models.

Ikedinachi Ayodele Power Wogu obtained his Doctoral Degree (PhD) from Covenant University Ota, Nigeria with a specialization in (Leadership and Political Philosophy) from the Department of Political Science & International Relations, College of Development Studies, Covenant University where his PhD Thesis was adjudged the best Postgraduate Thesis arising from the College of Leadership and Development Studies. Before this Doctoral degree, he had initially obtained two Masters' Degrees: one in Ethics and Social and Political Philosophy (M. Phil) and the other, a Masters' of Arts Degree in Epistemology and African Metaphysics (M.A), both from the Department of Philosophy, University of Ibadan (UI), Oyo State, Nigeria. His Bachelor's Degree; B.A (Hons.) was obtained in Philosophy (Contemporary Ethics) from the Department of Philosophy, University of Benin, Benin City, Edo State, Nigeria. Thus, he is what you may righty describe as a young Philosopher/Social Scientist and Leadership Consultant or simply, as an Existentialist Political Philosopher. Since the completion of his Doctoral research, he had extended his research focus to include studies in the multidisciplinary and interdisciplinary research areas of the social science and humanities disciplines. Thus, he and a team of multidisciplinary researchers he works with, conduct and extend research in the core areas of Philosophy, Leadership, International Politics, Contemporary Ethics, Moral and Political Philosophy, Epistemological, African Metaphysics, The History and Philosophy of Science, Ontology and Greek Philosophy. Hence, findings arising from research in these clusters have led to the presentation and publication of research papers in both local and core listed international conferences. To date, he has authored or co-authored over 93 publications comprising of Journal articles, Books, Book chapters, Book reviews, Editorial Reviews Keynote addresses, Monographs and Peer-reviewed conference proceeding/papers, with indexing in reputable indexing bodies like IEEE, Thomson Reuters, Scopus, ISI, Springer, Tailor and Francis, Web of Science and Google scholar, to mention but a few. He currently serves as an editor /ad Hoch editor of the International Journal of Human Capital and Information Technology Professionals (IJHCITP), Educational Research Journal MS: (ERJ); A Book of chapters: Handbook of Research on the Role of Human Factors in IT Project Management; Journal of International and Global Studies (JIGS); International Journal of Political Science and Development (IJPSD) and an IGI Global Book of Chapters: Recent Applications of Financial Risk Modelling and Portfolio Management. He currently teaches and conducts research in the Department of Political Science and Administration, Rhema University Nigeria, Aba, Abia State.

Ibrahim Yousef is a Principal Lecturer (Associate Professor) in the School of Administrative & Financial Sciences at the University of Petra, Jordan. He has taught various economics, business, and finance courses at undergraduate and postgraduate levels and published in areas involving applications of quantitative techniques in corporate finance, such as capital structure, dividend policy, corporate governance, mergers and acquisitions, risk management. His current research focusses on the area of banking and corporate finance seeking to evaluate the implication of mergers and acquisitions and the capital structure of firms.

Davor Zoričić currently holds Assistant professor position at the Department of Managerial Economics, Faculty of Economics and Business, University of Zagreb. He received his Ph.D. from the University of Zagreb for his research on yield curve modelling possibilities in the Croatian financial market. His research interests cover primarily topics in the field of financial economics, particularly in investments and corporate finance. In 2006 he passed the Investment advisor exam organized by Croatian Financial Services Supervisory Agency. In 2007 he spent 3 months as a Visiting Scholar at the University of California, Berkeley. He is a member of the Croatian Association of Financial Analysts, Croatian Statistical Association and Croatian Operational Reseach Society.

Index

F

G

H

I

J

K

L

M

N

O

P

Q

R

S

T

U

V

W

www.ingramcontent.com/pod-product-compliance
Lightning Source LLC
LaVergne TN
LVHW060357300926
849162LV00006B/1289